Lecture Notes in Computer Science 10293

Commenced Publication in 1973
Founding and Former Series Editors:
Gerhard Goos, Juris Hartmanis, and Jan van Leeuwen

More information about this series at http://www.springer.com/series/7409

Fiona Fui-Hoon Nah · Chuan-Hoo Tan (Eds.)

HCI in Business, Government and Organizations

Interacting with Information Systems

4th International Conference, HCIBGO 2017
Held as Part of HCI International 2017
Vancouver, BC, Canada, July 9–14, 2017
Proceedings, Part I

 Springer

Editors
Fiona Fui-Hoon Nah
Missouri University of Science
  and Technology
Rolla, MO
USA

Chuan-Hoo Tan
National University of Singapore
Singapore
Singapore

ISSN 0302-9743   ISSN 1611-3349 (electronic)
Lecture Notes in Computer Science
ISBN 978-3-319-58480-5   ISBN 978-3-319-58481-2 (eBook)
DOI 10.1007/978-3-319-58481-2

Library of Congress Control Number: 2017939341

LNCS Sublibrary: SL3 – Information Systems and Applications, incl. Internet/Web, and HCI

Printed on acid-free paper

This Springer imprint is published by Springer Nature
The registered company is Springer International Publishing AG
The registered company address is: Gewerbestrasse 11, 6330 Cham, Switzerland

Foreword

The 19th International Conference on Human–Computer Interaction, HCI International 2017, was held in Vancouver, Canada, during July 9–14, 2017. The event incorporated the 15 conferences/thematic areas listed on the following page.

A total of 4,340 individuals from academia, research institutes, industry, and governmental agencies from 70 countries submitted contributions, and 1,228 papers have been included in the proceedings. These papers address the latest research and development efforts and highlight the human aspects of design and use of computing systems. The papers thoroughly cover the entire field of human–computer interaction, addressing major advances in knowledge and effective use of computers in a variety of application areas. The volumes constituting the full set of the conference proceedings are listed on the following pages.

I would like to thank the program board chairs and the members of the program boards of all thematic areas and affiliated conferences for their contribution to the highest scientific quality and the overall success of the HCI International 2017 conference.

This conference would not have been possible without the continuous and unwavering support and advice of the founder, Conference General Chair Emeritus and Conference Scientific Advisor Prof. Gavriel Salvendy. For his outstanding efforts, I would like to express my appreciation to the communications chair and editor of *HCI International News*, Dr. Abbas Moallem.

April 2017   Constantine Stephanidis

HCI International 2017 Thematic Areas and Affiliated Conferences

Thematic areas:

- Human–Computer Interaction (HCI 2017)
- Human Interface and the Management of Information (HIMI 2017)

Affiliated conferences:

- 17th International Conference on Engineering Psychology and Cognitive Ergonomics (EPCE 2017)
- 11th International Conference on Universal Access in Human–Computer Interaction (UAHCI 2017)
- 9th International Conference on Virtual, Augmented and Mixed Reality (VAMR 2017)
- 9th International Conference on Cross-Cultural Design (CCD 2017)
- 9th International Conference on Social Computing and Social Media (SCSM 2017)
- 11th International Conference on Augmented Cognition (AC 2017)
- 8th International Conference on Digital Human Modeling and Applications in Health, Safety, Ergonomics and Risk Management (DHM 2017)
- 6th International Conference on Design, User Experience and Usability (DUXU 2017)
- 5th International Conference on Distributed, Ambient and Pervasive Interactions (DAPI 2017)
- 5th International Conference on Human Aspects of Information Security, Privacy and Trust (HAS 2017)
- 4th International Conference on HCI in Business, Government and Organizations (HCIBGO 2017)
- 4th International Conference on Learning and Collaboration Technologies (LCT 2017)
- Third International Conference on Human Aspects of IT for the Aged Population (ITAP 2017)

Conference Proceedings Volumes Full List

HCI in Business, Government and Organizations

Program Board Chair(s): **Fiona Fui-Hoon Nah,
USA and Chuan-Hoo Tan, Singapore**

The full list with the Program Board Chairs and the members of the Program Boards of all thematic areas and affiliated conferences is available online at:

http://www.hci.international/board-members-2017.php

HCI International 2018

The 20th International Conference on Human–Computer Interaction, HCI International 2018, will be held jointly with the affiliated conferences in Las Vegas, NV, USA, at Caesars Palace, July 15–20, 2018. It will cover a broad spectrum of themes related to human–computer interaction, including theoretical issues, methods, tools, processes, and case studies in HCI design, as well as novel interaction techniques, interfaces, and applications. The proceedings will be published by Springer. More information is available on the conference website: http://2018.hci.international/.

General Chair
Prof. Constantine Stephanidis
University of Crete and ICS-FORTH
Heraklion, Crete, Greece
E-mail: general_chair@hcii2018.org

http://2018.hci.international/

Contents – Part I

**Information Systems in Healthcare, Learning,
Cultural Heritage and Government**

Novel Interaction Devices and Techniques

Contents – Part II

Analytics, Visualization and Decision Support

Human-Centred Design in Information Systems

Advanced Nuclear Interface Modeling Environment (ANIME): A Tool for Developing Human-Computer Interfaces for Experimental Process Control Systems

Ronald Boring[1(✉)], Roger Lew[2], and Thomas Ulrich[1,2]

[1] Idaho National Laboratory, Idaho Falls, ID, USA
{ronald.boring,thomas.ulrich}@inl.gov
[2] University of Idaho, Moscow, ID, USA
{rogerlew,ulrich}@uidaho.edu

Abstract. In this paper, we review the development of the Advanced Nuclear Interface Modeling Environment (ANIME). ANIME was developed over the course of four years to support prototyping of distributed control system (DCS) interfaces for the Human System Simulation Laboratory (HSSL), a full-scale control room simulator at Idaho National Laboratory. Originally, ANIME consisted of software code developed to facilitate formative design of replacement control systems for legacy control rooms at nuclear power plants. ANIME was found to be an effective tool to test design concepts prior to formal system specification and deployment. ANIME, which is based on Microsoft Windows Presentation Foundation (WPF) libraries, allowed rapid application development that could be evaluated using operator-in-the-loop studies in the HSSL. These software tools for modernizing control room interfaces were also used to develop the novel Computerized Operator Support System (COSS) interface, which allows advanced prognostics and visualization. Over time, additional opportunities led to the development of a more extensive library of tools, including support for microworld simulation.

Keywords: Process control · Distributed control system · Control room · Microworld · Prototype

1 Introduction

In 2011, researchers at Idaho National Laboratory (INL) undertook a project to support commercial nuclear utilities on control room modernization. This work was sponsored by the U.S. Department of Energy's Light Water Reactor Sustainability (LWRS) Program. The then U.S. commercial fleet of nuclear power plants (NPPs), consisting of 105 reactors, was facing obsolescence issues in its main control rooms. NPPs are historically licensed by the U.S. Nuclear Regulatory Commission for 40 years of operation, after which the utility licensee must shut down if it has not applied for and received a plant life extension. A byproduct of these original 40-year licenses was that the plants had stockpiled suitable spare parts to allow the original control room design—with minor modifications—to be maintained over this period of time. In the ensuing years, however,

© Springer International Publishing AG 2017
F.F.-H. Nah and C.-H. Tan (Eds.): HCIBGO 2017, Part I, LNCS 10293, pp. 3–15, 2017.
DOI: 10.1007/978-3-319-58481-2_1

the dominant technology shifted from analog to digital. Other process control industries outside the nuclear industry began the process of digitizing control rooms, and few vendors now remain who build or service legacy analog technologies.[1] The prospect of life extensions brings the reality that the stockpiles of legacy instrumentation and control (I&C) devices cannot feasibly be prolonged into the next generation of operation. Moreover, despite the high reliability of analog I&C, the lack of vendors to maintain these devices—let alone to build new replacements—will prove a considerable challenge toward the long-term sustainability of legacy control rooms.

The LWRS Control Room Modernization project therefore sought to identify suitable replacement technologies for legacy I&C. This research led in 2012 to the building of the Human System Simulation Laboratory (HSSL; see Fig. 1), a full-scope and full-scale research simulator consisting of plant training simulators paired with touchscreen, glasstop mimics of analog control boards [1]. Since the HSSL provided a virtual representation of the main control room, it was not limited to a single plant, and it was possible to reconfigure the simulator to represent a wide variety of the main control rooms of NPPs in the U.S. At the time of the writing of this paper, the HSSL includes six plant models for boiling and pressurized water reactors by vendors such as General Electric, Westinghouse, and Combustion Engineering.

Fig. 1. The human system simulation laboratory at Idaho national laboratory.

A key element of the reconfigurability of the HSSL is the ability not only to switch between different plants but also to develop and evaluate replacement technologies for analog I&C on the control boards [2]. In some cases, the replacement technology is simply like-for-like technology—such as replacing an analog gauge with an equivalent digital meter. Such upgrades may be seen as extending the life of the control boards, but they do not represent significant modernization, which involves redesigning the layout and functionality of the boards to reflect the capabilities of digital control systems. The standard of modern control systems is the distributed control system (DCS), which

---

[1] *Analog* is a term used broadly here to denote a physical control or indicator that is directly wired to a physical system or sensor. In practice, the system may be electric, pneumatic, hydraulic, or mechanical. Many legacy plants now feature a data bus that intercepts analog signals and digitizes them for the plant computer and plant data historian. These digital piggy-backs do not affect the primary analog signal used to control or monitor the plant systems.

features one or more displays with embedded indicator values and soft controls. An emerging upgrade scenario for NPPs features the addition of DCS displays on the control boards. The upgrades are typically accomplished system by system, resulting in hybrid legacy-new, analog-digital control boards. DCS displays are mounted to the boards and surrounded by legacy analog I&C. Although the term *hybrid* might in some contexts be seen as pejorative or incomplete, it represents a realistic, systematic way to upgrade the plant systems during regular refueling outages without requiring extensive plant downtime simply to modify the main control room.

A DCS platform represents a complex software development environment. In many cases, the DCS foregoes ease of development and software industry-standard rapid application and agile development processes in order to meet stringent quality assurance requirements. Additionally, a DCS introduces added complexity to the training simulator. The DCS must either be emulated within or interfaced to the simulator as a standalone system. Certain functionality required in simulators, such as the ability to freeze the system for crew debriefs, is not necessarily present in a system designed for real-time plant operations in which a freeze function is not a possibility.

In order to address these two shortcomings common to many DCS platforms—the slow development cycle and the complexity of interfacing with the simulator—INL researchers teamed with researchers from University of Idaho in 2012 to develop a simplified prototyping environment for DCS design. This project, which has come to be called Advanced Nuclear Interface Modeling Environment (ANIME), began as a small piece of code written in the C# programming environment. ANIME began as a mimic of a DCS by serving as a human-computer interface (HCI) skin on the simulator [3]. By recasting existing I&C objects from the simulator glasstop displays as DCS elements in a picture-in-picture display on the HSSL bays, it was possible to imitate DCS functionality without actually implementing the DCS.

ANIME quickly became a prototyping tool for testing modernized hybrid control boards. Using the DCS-like functionality, it was possible to evaluate early design concepts for control boards using operator-in-the-loop studies. Licensed reactor operators from commercial NPPs in the U.S. traveled to the HSSL, where they benchmarked legacy board configurations with analog I&C against modernized design concepts [4]. In this manner, it was possible to test the HCI formatively—early in the design of a modernization—long before the DCS was finalized. It was possible to determine design issues prior to implementation—a good case study for user centered design principles. The basic prototypes of ANIME served to develop key usability evaluation concepts like As Low As Reasonable Assessment (ALARA) [5] and the overall usability method known as the Guideline for Operational Nuclear Usability and Knowledge Elicitation (GONUKE) [6]. From this initial implementation as DCS-like prototypes and operator-in-the-loop studies, additional features and functions have been added to the ANIME library of prototyping code. These features are described in the remainder of this paper.

2   Current ANIME Implementation

ANIME is based on Windows Presentation Foundation (WPF), a platform for creating user interfaces in Microsoft Windows [7]. WPF integrates disparate aspects of the interface, from multimedia to on-screen graphical objects. By allowing the development of user interface content as a type of skin or style sheet, it becomes possible to harmonize the interface. For example, it is possible to change common visual attributes of graphical objects, thus creating a customizable look and feel for the interface. WPF may be accessed from multiple means as part of the .NET library in Microsoft Windows. In the implementation of ANIME, it serves as a library of common and advanced indicators and controls featured in a DCS. ANIME currently consists of multiple parts, including:

- Prebuilt WPF libraries and C# sample code of common components that are featured in a DCS. For example, valve components come predefined with a look and feel suitable to the DCS and with functionality for interfacing with a software simulator. It is possible to change the parameters of the WPF library to change the look and feel of the DCS. For example, it is possible to change the appearance of the user interface from a Westinghouse Ovation to a Honeywell Experion DCS with minimal parameter adjustment. The components also feature predefined behaviors, e.g., a valve may draw its status from a value in the linked simulator database, and it may feature control action behavior such as `open` and `close` that map their state back to the simulator database and effectively change the state of that component.
- Prebuilt WPF libraries of advanced visualization and human factors design concepts. For example, there are advanced features for trending and alarms, including properties to highlight components in displays to represent alarm states.
- Prebuilt libraries for interfacing with full-scope simulators from GSE Systems, Western Services Corporation, and L3 MAPPS. These libraries are available as standard protocol libraries (e.g., OLE for Process Control) and as .NET custom advanced programming interfaces (APIs). These libraries also allow interfacing with additional DCS platforms.
- Prebuilt libraries to allow limited remote access via a custom virtual private network (VPN) interface. These libraries allow remote, secure access between simulator platforms and external systems. The VPN acts as a codec for communicating between two disparate systems, which may be locally or remotely linked. The codec ensures only predefined information may pass between systems.
- Prebuilt libraries of simplified process modules suitable for microworld implementation. An example is the COSSplay system described in Sect. 3.3 below, in which ANIME is put into a standalone program without connections to a larger simulator. COSSplay is, among other applications, used for evaluating first-of-a-kind control room interfaces using student operators.

3   Current ANIME Applications

3.1   Background

In the four years since its conception, ANIME has been applied to a number of applications, ranging from prototypes of conventional and advanced DCS prototypes to standalone process control systems for psychological research. Three of these applications are described below.

3.2   Prototypes for Commercial Distributed Control Systems

ANIME has been used to support control room modernization efforts at existing NPPs by mimicking the functionality of commercial DCS platforms [8]. To use a genericized example, an electric utility decided it would upgrade its NPP main control room in a stepwise fashion, focusing first on systems where it would see improvement in electricity production or decreased maintenance costs due to aging components. The utility reviewed plant systems and created a modernization plan by which it would gradually upgrade systems and their corresponding footprint on the control boards system by system. The utility decided that it would purchase a digital turbine control system (TCS) from a DCS vendor. The DCS vendor prepared a detailed product specification and provided an HCI style guide to indicate the look and feel of the interface. The TCS specification covered all essential control functions such as latch, speed control, and load control; operational overviews like general turbine overviews, valve and trip tests, and diagnostics; required bypass functions; and system maintenance.

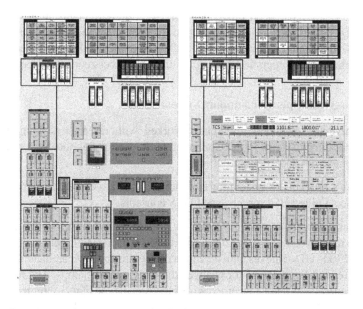

Fig. 2. An example of the legacy control boards (left) and an upgraded TCS (right).

Using the HCI style guide, previously developed TCS DCS screenshots, and the specification, the ANIME development team created DCS screen mockups that matched the TCS. These mockups were then overlaid on the existing glasstop control boards using the Microsoft Windows topmost picture-on-picture functionality, hiding the existing analog TCS. The net result was a mimic of an LCD touchscreen placed on the control boards (see Fig. 2).

The prototype indicators and controls in ANIME were paired to their equivalent components in the simulator, thus keeping the existing TCS model intact on the simulator. Where there was new functionality added, C# code was incorporated in ANIME to bridge the simulator TCS control logic with the proposed digital TCS. Thus, new code was developed only where essential to model new functionality, but the underlying simulator model was not modified. The focus on difference modeling ensured rapid development times and a high level of prototype functionality without the need for plant model redevelopment. In this manner, the prototype TCS could be developed substantially faster than the actual DCS, because the prototype TCS did not need to create new control logic nor meet stringent quality assurance requirements that would be required of the actual DCS.

The ANIME-based prototype was tested through a series of scenarios representative of TCS use. Licensed reactor operators were brought into the HSSL for operator-in-the-loop evaluation. The testing followed an early stage evaluation [9], thereby allowing operators to get hands-on experience with a close approximation of the proposed TCS and provide feedback to the design and functionality of the TCS early in the design stage. Initial skepticism by the TCS vendor of the value of a third-party prototype that mimicked the TCS was replaced by appreciation that issues in the design of the TCS were identified and corrected long before deployment, thereby preventing costly reworks of the TCS.

TCS prototypes have been developed for five different plants that mimic two commercial DCS platforms. Additional systems like chemical and volume control have also been developed into DCS prototypes [10]. The same method has been used for early digital to modern digital upgrades in the form of plant process computer displays.

3.3   Computerized Operator Support System

INL and University of Idaho researchers worked with researchers from Argonne National Laboratory to develop the Computerized Operator Support System (COSS) [11]. The premise of COSS is twofold:

- To provide a prognostics system for fault detection to assist operators, and
- To provide a unified HCI for advanced DCS concepts.

In this configuration, COSS consists of an ANIME-based multifunction DCS [12] coupled with the standalone PRO-AID (formerly PRODIAG) intelligent fault detection system [13]. PRO-AID achieves fault detection by monitoring key parameters like pressure, flow rate, and temperature for changes that may be anomalous. The monitoring approach is generalized—not concerned with the physical type of measurement. Rather, when detected, faults are mapped on a system or component specific basis. When faults are identified, e.g., there is a descending value corresponding to a slow leak, PRO-AID passes that fault to ANIME for operator notification. The power of PRO-AID is its ability to pick up a wide range of anomalies and to detect faults prior to them triggering setpoint alarms. Setpoint alarms typically occur when the fault impacts the ability of the system to function properly. In contrast, PRO-AID detected anomalies may serve as early warning, allowing operators to mitigate the fault without loss of critical systems or components.

In terms of the HCI of COSS, while the idea of software assistants for operators is not novel, the combination of multiple assistants within a single DCS represents a unique application. COSS features an interactive piping and instrumentation diagram (PID) view; a computer based procedure system; a fault highlighting method; trend and prioritized alarms; a notification engine; and the PRO-AID prognostics fault detection engine (see Fig. 3). A few of these features are worth noting, because they individually represent state-of-the-art practice in DCS development.

Fig. 3. COSS displaying fault highlight (green), computer based procedure system (light grey), and alarm system (red and yellow). (Color figure online)

The computer-based procedure system, for example, might be considered a Type 4 system. IEEE-1786, *IEEE Guide for Human Factors Applications of Computerized Operating Procedure Systems (COPS) at Nuclear Power Generating Stations and Other Nuclear Facilities* [14], distinguishes three types of computer-based procedures: Type 1 procedures feature digital views of the text of the procedures, Type 2 procedures additionally incorporate embedded indicators, and Type 3 procedures further allow soft controls directly from the procedure. The ANIME implementation of computer-based procedures in COSS includes Type 3 functionality. In addition, it allows the automation of procedure execution, minimizing the interactions required by the operator to control that system. We propose that this functionality represents a Type 4 computer-based procedure, an additional layer of functionality beyond the three categories in IEEE-1786.

The alarm display is also worth noting. There are three alarm cues represented on the displays. The primary alarm indicator is modeled dimensionally on the annunciator tiles found in conventional control rooms. Within the same footprint, the alarm provides not just a binary status but also a trend display, the boundary conditions for alarm entry, a color-coded prioritized alarm scheme, and information on sensor parity, in case there is a drift in one or more sensor values. A secondary cue is embedded in the PID, in which alarmed components are imbued with a shadowed outline. This outline—colloquially known as the *green aura*—highlights affected systems. Finally, when appropriate, the PRO-AID notification will appear in the faceplate area within COSS. This notification will direct the operator's attention to the fault, cause, and solution, along with a shot clock to count down until the required point of action, e.g., if there's a slow leak, this might indicate the point at which the leak causes a fault.

COSS has been developed with an eye toward optimizing the HCI elements. Using feedback and performance measures obtained from operator-in-the-loop studies, the ANIME graphical front end of COSS has evolved the presentation of information. Below, we present three cases where the design of the HCI has been improved through iterative evaluation using operators:

- Initial efforts at representing the PID centered on simplified views, but operator feedback revealed a distinct preference for greater detail, resulting in more complex views. While a preference for more complex graphics may seem counterintuitive to the philosophy of design simplicity, the ability of experts to use complex representations to achieve situational overviews is an important finding.
- Another example of the evolution of the COSS HCI involves the number of displays used to represent the information. COSS was initially designed to fit on a single display embedded on the control boards. This design philosophy represented a dashboard view, with all functions of the system integrated into a single viewing area. More recent implementations have seen the shift to multiple displays, with a wider dispersal of information across the control boards. This allows a harmonized system replacement while also allowing greater detail for each function. For example, a dedicated alarm display ensures that a greater number of systems can be included in the COSS alarm system.
- Finally, early versions of the COSS HCI relied heavily on the dullscreen design philosophy to minimize color as much as possible [15]. While dullscreen is maintained in newer versions of COSS, the allowable items that are deemed important enough to colorize have been increased. Original designs tended to use color only for alarm states. Recent iterations have also included color for a broader spectrum of meaningful information. Valve positions, e.g., open vs. closed, were previously depicted in monochrome. However, the salience of such indicators across the control room was small. By adding color to indicate the valve position, it is considerably easier for operators to determine this key status at a glance, even across the control room.

3.4 COSSplay

The previously described implementations of ANIME consist of WPF code as a front end paired with an underlying full-scope simulator. The same HCI approach can also be applied equally well without the underlying simulator. When a simplified process control model is used instead of the full-scope simulator, the resulting environment is knows as a microworld [16]. Because the microworld adaptation of ANIME was first used to evaluate new features of COSS, the microworlds within ANIME have broadly been called COSSplay [17]. COSSplay is word play on *cosplay*, the popular activity of dressing in costumes after popular anime, video game, and comic book characters. However, because microworlds are a form of simulation much like a video game, the idea of gamification also playfully permeates COSSplay.

A chief advantage of this microworld approach is that the process control can be simplified considerably. This approach allows testing of HCI concepts without the confounds of a highly complex and disparate control interface for multiple systems. The simplified nature of the COSSplay control system therefore allows evaluation of very specific aspects of the HCI.

Additionally, because the microworld represents a simplified interface, it is possible to train and test non-professional operators, thereby enabling studies with larger sample sizes than would be possible with actual control room operators. For many plants, for example, there are fewer than 30 total operators—a number that is unachievable in most studies and yet is a necessity in many experimental designs to achieve sufficient statistical power for significance testing. By using less experienced operators—even students —it becomes possible to draw strong inferences about study findings. Of course, there are limits to the external validity or generalizability of some studies using this approach. Reactor operators using conventional analog control systems may actually exhibit much of the functionality of the system as a mental model, since no operational model exists independent of manual control [18]. Still, many facets of the HCI are generalizable even with different test participants from the target population. For example, perceptual characteristics will remain largely invariant across levels of operator expertise, such that the microworld may prove an ideal place to test the visual salience of particular interface elements. The microworld may also be used as pilot testing or screening for features that are later evaluated with actual professional operators.

A final advantage of microworlds is that no high fidelity simulation is required. Many industries do not have the full-scope simulators commonly employed in nuclear power, or many novel systems have not yet been fully modeled and deployed as simulation codes. In the absence of such robust simulators, it is quite possible to use the microworld as a low fidelity prototyping engine to drive dynamic mockups of planned systems. The microworld is an ideal early stage prototyping tool for enlisting operator-in-the-loop feedback in interfacing with an emerging DCS.

A good example of the uses of COSSplay is the recent work to develop a microworld simulator (see Fig. 4) to evaluate a novel method of assessing situation awareness [19]. By embedding animated visual markers in a gamified NPP HCI, it is possible to compare visual attention to eye tracking. The disadvantage of eye tracking is that the analysis can be laborious, while some eye trackers may require frequent recalibration for accurate data collection. By testing student operators' ability to detect moving visual markers in areas of interest that feature key parameters, it is possible to duplicate functionally much of the data that are collected by eye tracking yet in a more robust and less laborious manner. ANIME libraries were used to create the simplified process control. Additionally, new basic elements including control logic models of particular systems were added to the ANIME library in the process. The graphical functions for displaying the visual markers were also built in WPF and have now become part of the ANIME library. The study illustrates that the ANIME library is extensible—adding new visual elements or underlying functions as required and thereby expanding the code library.

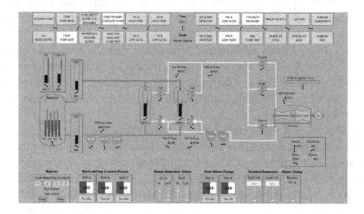

Fig. 4. A simplified nuclear power plant microworld interface developed in ANIME.

4 Planned ANIME Applications

Although ANIME already represents a mature product for DCS prototype development, there remain important research and deployment activities ahead. These include:

- Advanced HCI development. Currently, the features of ANIME are linked to common DCS functionality. While the transition from analog to digital control rooms is revolutionary within the nuclear industry, there remains opportunity to improve the state of the art for process control. RevealFlow [20], a design philosophy that centers not on current status but change in status—from trend data to predictive displays—remains a promising expansion of ANIME, both in terms of novel ways of graphically representing control information and incorporation of intelligent controls.
- Advanced control system platform. Currently, ANIME is being integrated into a suite of tools that can be used for prototype development and evaluation in process control, particularly as experimental control software. There exists a need for software between research tools like LabView and full-blown DCS applications. As national scientific user facilities such as experimental reactors increasingly become a reality at the U.S. national laboratories, it is crucial to have software that is capable of meeting experimental rigor, human factors standards, and extensive security requirements. ANIME is positioned as a tool to be made more widely available to support such user research communities.
- Risk monitoring and modeling. Features in COSS hint at new directions that are possible with ANIME to support risk. In particular, the PRO-AID prognostics system offers a template for how a DCS may be used to monitor critical parameters and detect faults. Additionally, the computer-based procedure system affords the opportunity to

model human actions in the face of a full plant model. Current efforts in computation-based human reliability analysis like the Human Unimodel for Nuclear Technology to Enhance Reliability (HUNTER) [21] create a virtual plant operator that interfaces with thermo-hydraulic (TH) models. These TH models are often simplified versions of plants and may not represent the full spectrum of plant behavior, especially the interactions of redundant safety systems. To allow a more realistic risk model of emergent plant performance, it is necessary to enlist high fidelity models such as full-scope simulators. ANIME can serve as a scheduling tool for Monte Carlo simulation of possible outcomes in response to a variety of operator performance. This interface may also be represented as a look-ahead real-time monitoring system to assist operator decision-making in the face of plant upsets [22].

Table 1 identifies current and future solutions in the ANIME toolset. This table is not exhaustive, but it positions ANIME as a tool that may be used immediately to prototype new HCI and DCS concepts for control rooms, to a point in the future when it may help realize and implement these concepts as a production DCS system. ANIME began out of necessity to prototype conventional DCS interfaces and has evolved to be a tool for advanced HCI. As ANIME continues to evolve, it is anticipated that it may very well find equally useful application outside the control room.

Table 1. Current and proposed applications of ANIME.

	Current applications	Potential applications
Low fidelity simulation	Microworld	Microworld design mockups
High fidelity simulation	DCS prototype	Intelligent and advanced HCI systems (e.g., Risk Monitors)
Deployment	Experimental prototyping environment	Distributed control system for process control

Acknowledgements. The lead author of this paper (Ronald Boring) is grateful to his co-authors (Roger Lew and Thomas Ulrich) for their creative development of ANIME. Credit for the current implementation of ANIME resides entirely with their programming prowess and creative HCI ideas. The authors mutually acknowledge Kirk Fitzgerald and Brandon King at INL, for their work in building and maintaining the simulator and infrastructure to make ANIME possible; Kenneth Thomas at INL, for his vision in championing the implementation of COSS; and Rick Vilim at Argonne National Laboratory, for his collaboration in bringing PRO-AID to the COSS platform. Finally, we acknowledge early discussions with simulator staff at NuScale Power, who provided invaluable initial brainstorming about using WPF for simulator applications.

References

1. Boring, R.L.: Overview of a reconfigurable simulator for main control room upgrades in nuclear power plants. In: Proceedings of the Human Factors and Ergonomics Society 56th Annual Meeting, pp. 2050–2054 (2012)
2. Boring, R.L., Joe, J.C.: Lessons learned using a full-scale glasstop simulator for control room modernization in nuclear power plants. In: Proceedings of the Human Factors and Ergonomics Society 57th Annual Meeting, pp. 1712–1716 (2013)

3. Lew, R., Boring, R.L., Joe, J.C.: A flexible visual process control development environment for microworld and distributed control system protoyping. In: Proceedings of the International Symposium on Resilient Control Systems (2014)
4. Ulrich, T.A., Boring, R.L.: Example user centered design process for a digital control system in a nuclear power plant. In: Proceedings of the Human Factors and Ergonomics Society 57th Annual Meeting, pp. 1727–1731 (2013)
5. Boring, R.L.: As low as reasonable assessment (ALARA): applying discount usability to control room verification and validation. Risk, reliability and safety: innovating theory and practice. In: Proceedings of the European Safety and Reliability Conference, pp. 950–955 (2016)
6. Boring, R.L., Ulrich, T.A., Joe, J.C., Lew, R.T.: Guideline for operational nuclear usability and knowledge elicitations (GONUKE). Procedia Manufact. 3, 1327–1334 (2015)
7. Chappell, D.: Introducing windows presentation foundation. Microsoft Developer Netw. Tech. Artic. (2016)
8. Boring, R.L., Joe, J.C.: Baseline evaluations to support control room modernization at nuclear power plants. In: Proceedings of ANS NPIC & HMIT, pp. 911–922 (2015)
9. Boring, R.L., Joe, J.C., Ulrich, T.A., Lew, R.T.: Early-stage design and evaluation for nuclear power plant control room upgrades. In: Proceedings of the Human Factors and Ergonomics Society 58th Annual Meeting, pp. 1909–1913 (2014)
10. Lew, R., Ulrich, T.A., Boring, R.L.: Nuclear reactor crew evaluation of a computerized operator support system HMI for chemical and volume control system. In: Proceedings of Human-Computer Interaction 2017 (2017, in press)
11. Boring, R.L., Lew, R., Thomas, K.D., Ulrich, T.: Computerized operator support system to aid decision making in nuclear power plants. Procedia Manufact. 3, 5261–5268 (2015)
12. Lew, R., Ulrich, T., Boring, R., Thomas, K.: A functional prototype for a computerized operator support system. In: Proceedings of the International Symposium on Resilient Control Systems (2014)
13. Vilim, R.B., Park, Y.S., Heifetz, A., Pu, W., Passerini, S., Grelle, A.: Monitoring and diagnosis of equipment faults. Nucl. Eng. Int. Mag. 24–27 (2013)
14. IEEE Guide for Human Factors Applications of Computerized Operating Procedure Systems (COPS) at Nuclear Power Generating Stations and Other Nuclear Facilities. IEEE-1786 (2011)
15. Braseth, A.: Information-rich design for large-screen displays. Nucl. Eng. Int. 59, 22–24 (2014)
16. Boring, R., Kelly, D., Smidts, C., Mosleh, A., Dyre, B.: Microworlds, simulators, and simulation: framework for a benchmark of human reliability data sources. In: Joint Probabilistic Safety Assessment and Management and European Safety and Reliability Conference, 16B-Tu5-5 (2012)
17. Ulrich, T.A., Werner, S., Lew, R., Boring, R.L.: COSSplay: validating a computerized operator support system using a microworld simulator. Commun. Comput. Inf. Sci. 617, 161–166 (2016)
18. Lew, R., Lau, N., Boring, R.L., Anderson, J.: The role of HCI in cross-sector research on grand challenges. In: Nah, F.H., Tan, C.-H. (eds.) HCIBGO 2016. LNCS, vol. 9751, pp. 519–530. Springer, Cham (2016). doi:10.1007/978-3-319-39396-4_48
19. Ulrich, T., Boring, R., Lew, R., Werner, S.: A comparison of an attention acknowledgement measure and eye tracking: application of the as low as reasonable assessment (ALARA) discount usability principle for control system studies. In: Proceedings of Human-Computer Interaction 2017 (2017, in press)

20. Boring, R., Ulrich, T., Lew, R.: RevealFlow: a process control visualization framework. In: Schmorrow, D.D.D., Fidopiastis, C.M.M. (eds.) AC 2016. LNCS (LNAI), vol. 9744, pp. 145–156. Springer, Cham (2016). doi:10.1007/978-3-319-39952-2_15
21. Boring, R., Mandelli, D., Rasmussen, M., Herberger, S., Ulrich, T., Groth, K., Smith, C.: Human unimodel for nuclear technology to enhance reliability (HUNTER): a framework for computational-based human reliability analysis. In: 13th International Conference on Probabilistic Safety Assessment and Management (PSAM 13), Paper A-531, pp. 1–7 (2016)
22. Boring, R.L., Ulrich, T.A., Lew, R.T.: Dynamic operations way finding system (DOWS) for nuclear power plants. Commun. Comput. Inf. Sci. **529**, 497–502 (2015)

How Can Emails from Different Types of Leaders Influence Employees?

Eric Brangier[✉] and Laura Dovero

Université de Lorraine, PErSEUs EA 7312, User-Lab,
Faculté des Sciences Humaines et Sociales, Île du Saulcy, 57006 Metz, France
eric.brangier@univ-lorraine.fr, laura@dovero.org

Abstract. How can different types of emails be perceived by readers as different leadership styles? Is email content understood as a part of leadership? How can emails develop or destroy the e-leadership? This research tries to answer these questions. It studies the influence on what work and their involvement in their job represents for employees through the different kinds of e-communications used by supervisors. Three scenarios that represent three different kinds of e-communications sent by email from a direct supervisor were designed to relate to Transformational, Transactional and Laissez-Faire leadership styles. A questionnaire measuring (a) motivation to succeed on a project, (b) emotional commitment to superior, (c) perceived performance and (d) perceived interpersonal justice were associated with the three scenarios. Scenarios and questionnaires were submitted to 51 employees. They had to put in the state of mind of the employee who receives the three kinds of e-communication, then they had to answer the questionnaire. The results show that there are real differences in the perception of leadership. Emails sketching characteristics of transactional and transformational leaderships had significantly higher scores than emails drawing on a "Laissez-faire" type leadership; i.e. (a) motivation to achieve and succeed in a project, (b) emotional commitment, (c) perceived performance of the employee, and (d) perceived interpersonal justice become higher when the emails seem to be more related to transactional and transformational e-leaderships. Hence, this paper underlines the important effect of leaders' e-communication on the subordinates' perceptions about their own work through the measurement of perceived performance and motivation, but also their hierarchical relationship through their perceived interpersonal justice and their emotional commitment.

Keywords: e-leadership · Organizational communication · Email work's perceptions · Hierarchical relationship

1 Introduction

More than one hundred billion business emails are sent each day! How are they perceived by employees, including those written by managers, asking them to work within the constraints of time, quality, money, market, and customers…? Several studies have highlighted the importance of electronic communications in managing emotions at work and the psychosocial risks attached [19]. They have sought to characterize such emails

© Springer International Publishing AG 2017
F.F.-H. Nah and C.-H. Tan (Eds.): HCIBGO 2017, Part I, LNCS 10293, pp. 16–26, 2017.
DOI: 10.1007/978-3-319-58481-2_2

[7], to define the effects of dispersion and confusion on users [8], to regulate the uses of emails [18] or to understand the intensive uses of emails by managers. But few studies have apprehended emails in the form of hierarchical communications to measure the effects of emails on the perception of leadership by employees.

Nowadays, some employees receive only emails from their managers, without having face-to-face contact with them. The aim of this paper is to sum up a research on the influence of emails written by supervisors on the representations that employees have for their work, their involvement and their leader: How and why emails develop or destroy e-leadership?

2 Theoretical Background

Professional communication plays a central role in leadership efficiency as well as promoting a good working environment when it is of good quality as it motivates and engages employee commitment. An essential aspect of the quality of the supervisor's communication is the information content conveyed [4, 5]. The language used by the supervisors when communicating with subordinates will guide their performance [15]. Bad communication from the supervisors will lead to employees misunderstanding the goals required by the organization. With time it will result in lower performance levels. However, when leaders give clearly indicated goals, in a motivating, enthusiastic language with an appropriate choice of words this could result in increased performance. This is what this article seeks to illustrate.

2.1 The Different Types of Leadership Styles

There are many different approaches to studying leadership. We will focus on three leadership styles which have been frequently studied over the last few years [15, 26].

Transformational Leadership. It encourages employees to become committed members of their work group and to devote themselves to the company's success. Four dimensions have been related to this leadership style [10]:

- Idealized influence which refers to the ability of the leader to motivate employees through his/her charisma, making him a role model;
- Inspirational motivation, the ability of the leader to inspire the employees with a sense of challenge.
- Intellectual stimulation which consists in the leader's ability to boost his/her employees to be innovative and creative in their projects and to challenge their routine work practices.
- Finally, individualized consideration which relates to the attention given to each employee by the leader enabling employees' self-fulfillment.

Transactional Leadership. Here the action to motivate is concentrated more on the individual's interest than on collective interest. Rewards or punishments will depend on the achievement or not of goals targeted. Three dimensions are often related to this type of leadership [10]:

- Contingent reward is the ability to set goals to be reached and then reward the employee according to goal achievement [17];
- Active management by exception where the manager supervises the employee's work and corrects it to keep it in line with the company's targeted aims.
- Passive management by exception, here the leader intervenes when standards are not met.

Laissez Faire Leadership. Here professional conduct has only one dimension, i.e. the absence of leadership behaviour. The leader abdicates responsibilities and avoids making decisions.

In short, leadership can be understood through 8 dimensions (4 for transformational, 3 for transactional and 1 for laissez-faire). The 8 leadership dimensions have been reduced to 6 in the "Full range leadership theory" [1]. Inspirational motivation and idealized influence are grouped under 'charisma' and passive management by exception and laissez-faire are grouped under 'passive avoidant' (Table 1).

Table 1. Dimensions of the "Full range leadership theory".

Leadership	Transformational	Transactional	Laissez-faire
Full range leadership theory (reduced from 8 to 6 dimensions)	– Charisma (idealized influence + inspirational motivation) – Intellectual stimulation – Individual consideration	– Contingent reward – Active management by exception	
		Passive avoidant (passive management by exception + not invested in relations)	

2.2 Leadership and Electronic Communication

Few studies have focused on leaders' electronic communication. Initial research studies have indicated a positive link between the transformational leader and communication skills, hence revealing the relationship between styles of leadership and communication. More recently, an important link has been shown between communication and certain types of leadership [24] highlighting the fact that the type of leadership style practiced would produce a particular style of communication.

2.3 The Effect of Different Leadership Styles on Work

Lots of effects of leadership are well known. Leadership styles influence employee performances and results, but also how employees perceive their work. Illustrating this, transformational leadership is a good predictor of job satisfaction whereas transactional leadership is a good predictor of job performance [10]. But what about the leadership which is expressed through emails? When receiving an email what does the employee perceive about the leadership of his/her supervisor? Is he/she motivated by it or not? Do they think that their leader's reaction is fair or unfair? Does the email encourage them to commit themselves to their company's goals or remain indifferent?

In order to understand these questions, we must broaden our understanding of the dimensions related to leadership, also taking into account: motivation, perceived performance, emotional commitment to superiors and perceived interactional justice.

- Motivation represents the energy of our behaviors. It describes the inner and outer forces which produce the spark, the direction, the intensity and persistence of behavior. There is an undeniably positive link between transformational leadership and motivation in the workplace [10]. Employees who work with a transformational leader have better job satisfaction and are more motivated to achieve better perform-ance in their work [3]. Transformational leadership is able to motivate its employees to achieve better performance [11]. Transactional leadership can bring about greater employee motivation. [25] Both transformational and transactional leaderships seem to increase motivation through interaction with their co-workers.
- Perceived performance is a good indicator of the effective performance of employees [14, 16]. For the company it relates to the total value of behaviors carried out by one person at a given period. Several meta-analyses [9, 10, 22] have found an important positive link between transformational and transactional leadership styles, and different indicators of objective and subjective performance, whereas the laissez-faire leadership style is negatively correlated with these indicators.
- Emotional commitment corresponds to a sort of emotional force which connects a person to a process of professional action [2, 13]. Emotional commitment reflects a person's attachment to his/her company. It is both a good indicator of job satisfaction, but also a predictor of an intention to leave a company [23].
- Organizational justice [12] renders the person's reaction to decisions made about them by the organization as well as the procedures used to make these decisions. Perceived justice has a positive effect on commitment and job satisfaction within the organization. Perceived justice is also a predictor of the quality of the relationship between the leader and his/her employee, particularly of interactional justice.

For these four variables, the laissez-faire leadership style has not been widely researched upon, namely because it is a style of leadership where the leader's role is avoided and is passive. Subsequently, communication means being poor, we expect a negative impact on the employee's representation of work.

3 Problem and Method

Many studies have investigated the impact of the amount of emails on work intensifi-cation and its effects. However, very few studies have focused on the impact of the content of supervisors' emails on the representations of employees. None has sought to experimentally measure the impact of e-leadership types on the perceptions that employees have of their work and their relationship to the supervisor. In this research, we aim to evaluate the effects of three e-leadership forms (Transformational, Transac-tional and Laissez-Faire leaderships).

3.1 Problem and Hypothesis

Our main problem is to understand, on the one hand, if the different types of leadership are identified in the emails and on the other if the four variables measured in this study, i.e. – motivation, perceived performance, emotional commitment, and perceived justice, vary significantly according to the type of email received.

Our main assumption is therefore: the difference in leader's emails leads to significantly different results in employees' perception of work. More specifically, we postulate that receiving a transformational style email will lead to scores for "Perceived interpersonal justice", "Perceived performance", "Perceived emotional commitment" and "Motivation to succeed in a project" being higher than scores for emails received with a transactional leadership type, the latter getting a higher score than an email with a "laissez-faire" leadership type.

As a consequence, we postulate that the "Laissez-faire" type leadership results in much lower scores than the transactional and transformational types of communication on the four variables studied.

3.2 Method

Building the Scenarios and Defining the Instructions. 51 employees were faced with three types of email using expressions extracted from professional emails of 5 employees over three months.

The instructions for the experiment were the following: 'You have to deal with Mr. Smith's case. Whatever the content of this file, put yourself in the situation in which you receive emails of type *"A, B and C from your superior in the firm's hierarchy asking you to carry out your work... Read these emails carefully, putting yourself in the state of mind of an employee who receives them"* (Table 2).

These three types of emails were divided into four parts: an informative part; a complaint by the customer reported by the superior; monitoring of the work carried out, an email at the end of the task and congratulations. However, there are also differences:

- Email A renders a weak leadership of the 'laisser-faire' type. The sentence "I am not concerned" is an example of avoidance of the role of leader.
- Email B includes sentences such as: "I'd like you to take up the challenge" in order to reflect the inspirational motivation dimension. Or the sentence "If ever you find a new angle, don't hesitate to submit it to me" reflects intellectual stimulation. Finally, the sentence "I'm always available in case of a problem" reflects both individual consideration and the personal sacrifice which a charismatic leader will always be prepared to make.
- Email C is based on the principles of transactional leadership. For example, the sentences "I'd like you to sort this out to avoid any repercussions on the company's image"; "We'll have to meet our deadline soon" reflects active management by exception, the sentences "You have achieved the goal expected for this file, I'll keep this in mind"; "I'll take your performance on this file into account" reflects contingent reward.

Table 2. Descriptions and contents of the emails.

Email A "Laisser-faire"	Email B 'transformational'	Email C "transactional"
Hello, Please find attached Mr. Smith's file which is a sensitive one. I have been instructed to give it to you to handle	Hello, Please find attached Mr. Smith's file which is a sensitive one. I know it's a tricky file and will be challenging for you, but I know that you are capable of dealing with it. You can work on it with John, try a new approach and don't hesitate to contact me if you have any problems, I'll be available	Hello, Please find attached Mr. Smith's file which is the sensitive one we talked about and which I think you can handle. Try to get it sorted rapidly, I'll take your performance on this file into account during assessment
Then the following day a new email, with usual polite forms, and the following elements:		
I have received a complaint from Mr. Smith about you. I am not concerned so I'm sending it to you to deal with	I have received a complaint from Mr. Smith. According to him the solutions offered are not satisfactory. I know he's a difficult customer but I'd like you to take up the challenge. I know you are capable of convincing him and sorting things out. Let me know how things go	I have received a complaint from Mr. Smith. According to him the solutions offered are not satisfactory. I'd like you to sort this out to avoid any repercussions on the company's image
The day after a new email with usual polite forms and the following elements:		
I have received your reminders on the Smith file, I'll send you my conclusions later	For the Smith file, if you find a new angle don't hesitate to submit it to me, I'd like to see your report soon	I'm expecting your report on the Smith file. Our deadlines will have to be met soon
Finally, a new email with usual polite forms and the following elements:		
Thank you for dealing with the Smith file. Good Day	I'd like to congratulate you on the Smith file, the customer is delighted you've done a great job with the team! Good Day	You have achieved the goal expected for the Smith file. Congratulations. I won't forget, I will keep it in mind. Good Day

Characteristics of the Sample. The final sample was made up of 51 people (27/51 men and 24/51 women) executives (21/51) employees (30/51). The average age was 33 years old and varied between 20 and 57 years old. The average time spent on messaging for their job is approximately four hours a day. The employees receive an average of 20.6 emails every day in their job, of which 4.6 emails come from their superior. 62.7% of the people in the sample live with partners and 37.3% are single. Finally, their professional experience averaged at around 9.8 years.

Procedure and Measures. In this study, four variables particularly interest us: emotional commitment to the supervisor, employee's perceived performance, motivation to succeed in the project entrusted and employee's perceived interpersonal justice.

These four measures were evaluated in the questionnaire with items taken from several scales.

- Emotional commitment to the supervisor: 6 items from Vandenberghe [23]. The items from the initial research were not changed. Here is an example of an item: "I admire my supervisor".
- Perceived performance: 3 items from Sanchez, Truxillo and Bauer [20]. The initial items were changed in order to adapt them to our questionnaire, for example: "I think I have passed the test I have just taken" was changed to "I think I have succeeded in the project assigned to me".
- Motivation to succeed in the project: 7 items from Sanchez, Truxillo and Bauer [20]. The initial items were changed in order to adapt them to our study for example, the item: "If I concentrate and work hard I can get a high score" was changed to "If I concentrate and work hard on this file I can successfully deal with it".
- Perceived interpersonal justice: 4 items, Colquitt [6]. The items from the initial study were not changed. Here's an example of an item: "My superior treats me with dignity".

4   Results

How did the 51 people respond to the scales – Emotional commitment to supervisor; Perceived performance; Motivation to succeed in the project; Perceived interpersonal justice – according to the emails they were reading? What do their answers teach us?

Our main assumption is that different emails generate a significant difference in the psychological impacts on the scores of the variables studied. To this end, a variance analysis with repeated measures was carried out between the different types of communication and each dimension of the questionnaire. Table 3 indicates the averages of the scores obtained for each type of communication according to the four variables.

Table 3. Score averages for each scale according to the type of communication.

Types of emails received	Perceived interpersonal justice	Perceived performance	Perceived emotional commitment	Motivation to succeed in the project
A-Laisser-faire	1,70	1,46	0,78	1,32
B-Transformational	5.20	5.22	4.86	4.80
C-Transactional	4.21	4.68	2.92	5.00

The results of the Student test validate most of the assumptions: the laissez–faire leadership communication obtained much lower scores than the two other forms of communication on the four variables studied (always $p < .05$).

Concerning the emails of the transactional and transformational type, the results merit a more detailed analysis:

- For the variable "perceived interpersonal justice", we note a higher average score for the transformational email (5.20), the transactional email has a score of 4.21 and finally the laissez-faire communication has a weaker score, of about 1.7. The variance analysis shows significant differences for each type of communication ($p < .02$).

- Perceived performance indicated different scores depending on the type of communication received: the transformational email obtained the highest average with about 5.22. This is followed by the communication inspired by a transactional leader which obtained an average score of about 4,68, finally the laissez-faire type of communication with a score of about 1.46. For each pair the differences are significant (using Bonferroni's method, $p < .02$).

- Emotional commitment is strongest in the transformational situation (4.86), weaker in the transactional situation (2.92), and very weak (0.78) in the laissez-faire type communication. The Student tests revealed significant differences for each pair ($p < .02$), i.e. between "transformational – transactional emails", "transactional - laissez-faire" and "transformational - laisser-faire".

- Motivation to succeed in the project introduced a slight difference. In fact, the average score for transactional communication is higher than for transformational communication. However, there isn't a significant difference between transactional and transformational communications for motivation to succeed in a project. ($p > .05$).

5   Discussion and Conclusion

The four variables measured in this study vary significantly depending on the type of communication received. Even if the electronic communications do not contain non-verbal pointers which could support leadership [21]; our study confirms that electronic communications generate similar results to oral communications.

But this research also highlights another major phenomenon: the important impact of the language used on the employees' perceptions of their relationship with the supervisor, their perception of justice, their performance and their motivation. Each type of communication has resulted in noticeably different scores. The employees receiving specific information concerning a project entrusted to them are extremely sensitive to the wording and the content. Our research confirms the fact that communication is a fundamental factor for the successful of organization and employees' performance [22]. The wording chosen in the emails impacts directly on employees' perceived performance and their perception in general, as suggested in Murphy and Clark's study [15].

Since the direct supervisors spend between a third and two thirds of their time interacting with their subordinates [27] it is important to take into account the way in which information is communicated in order to motivate co-workers, enabling them to increase their commitment to their organization and to their supervisor and consequently improve their overall performance to the benefit of their company. It is therefore an important issue, the wording in a sentence can completely change the vision that a person has of his/her project goals, performance and relationship with his/her contact person. This vision will directly affect results of the work done such as satisfaction and the employees objective performance.

The transformational leader possesses specific characteristics which enables him/her to establish a good working relationship with his/her employees. His/her way of communicating motivates employees to exceed the levels of performance initially planned [11].

As for transactional leadership, it obtained much higher scores than the laissez-faire leadership communication but lower than transformational, except for the variable-motivation to succeed in a project. Quite often this type of communication is more focused on economic or material exchange. It focuses its communication on rewards, which motivate employees and is consistent with several studies according to which transactional leadership can bring about high levels of employee motivation [25].

Finally, the "laissez-faire" leadership communication reveals an avoidance of the role of leader, there is very little communication as he/she withdraws from situations in which he/she could be involved. This lack of communication has a negative impact on the employees' representations. It obtains much lower scores than the two other types of communication, and for each of the variables tested. Thus illustrating that badly constructed communication weakens organizational performance.

This study reveals the importance of electronic communication in organization psychology and information systems management, and more precisely its effect on the employee representations concerning their work and their relationship to their direct supervisor. The content and quality of the information conveyed in an email from a direct supervisor affects motivation, perceived performance, perceived interpersonal justice and emotional commitment to the supervisor. The three types of emails based on the different leaderships styles were simulated through three scenarios. The results are unmistakable: minimal communication and avoidance behavior from the laissez-faire leadership will lead to much lower scores than richer communications from the trans-formational and transactional leaderships. However, a type of behavior and communi-cation based on the relationship that transformational leadership is likely to produce leads to much higher scores than communication based mainly on goal achievement likely to be produced by transactional leadership.

Even if the obvious limitation of this study is its experimental methodology (but also its strength!), it nevertheless raises the very topical question of electronic leadership, of the relational quality of emails, and the harmful repercussions for both the employees and the organizations. Our study proves that the emails received correlate to the employee's perceptions. It also draws a management line: writing emails using transformational leadership characteristics is profitable for the professional perceptions of the employees and no doubt for the employees themselves!

References

1. Avolio, B.: Full Leadership Development: Building the Vital Forces in Organization. Sage Publications, Thousand Oaks (1999)
2. Bakar, H.A., Dibleck, K.E., McCroskey, J.C.: Mediating role of supervisory communication practices on relations between leader-member exchange and perceived employee commitment to workgroup. Commun. Monogr. 77, 637–656 (2010). doi:10.1080/03637751.2010.499104
3. Bass, B.M., Bass, R.: The Bass Handbook of Leadership: Theory, Research, and Managerial Applications. Free Press, New York (2008)

4. Berson, Y., Avolio, B.J.: Transformational leadership and the dissemination of organizational goals: a case study of a telecommunication firm. Leadersh. Quart. **15**(5), 625–646 (2004)
5. Bycio, P., Hackett, R.D., Allen, J.S.: Further assessments of Bass's (1985) conceptualization of transactional and transformational leadership. J. Appl. Psychol. **80**(4), 468–478 (1995). http://dx.doi.org/10.1037/0021-9010.80.4.468
6. Colquitt, J.A.: On the dimensionality of organizational justice: a construct validation of a measure. J. Appl. Psychol. **86**, 386–400 (2001)
7. Créno, L., Cahour, B.: Les cadres surchargés par leurs emails: déploiement de l'activité et expérience vécue. *Activités* [En ligne], 13-1 ǀ 2016, mis en ligne le 15 avril 2016, consulté le 11 septembre 2016 (2016). http://activites.revues.org/2698
8. Datchary, C.: *La dispersion au travail,* Octarès Editions, coll. « Travail & activité humaine », 192 p., préf. Laurent Thévenot, EAN: 9782915346886 (2011)
9. Dumdum, U.R., Lowe, K.B., Avolio, B.J.: A meta-analysis of transformational and transactional leadership correlates of effectiveness and satisfaction: an update and extension. In: Avolio, B., Yammarino, F. (eds.) Transformational and Charismatic Leadership: The Road Ahead, pp. 35–66. JAI, Amsterdam (2002)
10. Judge, T.A., Piccolo, R.F.: Transformational and transactional leadership: a meta-analytic test of their relative validity. J. Appl. Psychol. **89**, 755–768 (2004)
11. Krishnan, V.R.: Transformational leadership and outcomes: Role of relationship duration. Leadersh. Organ. Dev. J. **26**(6), 442–457 (2005)
12. Lavelle, J.J., Rupp, D.E., Brockner, J.: Taking a multi-focus approach to the study of justice, social exchange, and citizenship behavior: the target similarity model. J. Manag. **33**(6), 841–866 (2007)
13. Meyer, J.P., Herscovitch, L.: Commitment in the workplace toward a general model. Hum. Resour. Manag. Rev. **11**, 299–326 (2001)
14. Motowidlo, S.J.: Job performance. In: Borman, W.C., Ilgen, D.R., Klimoski, R.J., at Weiner, I.B. (dir.) Handbook of Psychology. Industrial and Organizational Psychology, vol. 12. Wiley, Hoboken (2003)
15. Murphy, C., Clark, J.R.: Picture this: how the language of leaders drives performance. Organ. Dyn. **45**, 139–146 (2016)
16. Pillai, R., Schriesheim, C.A., Williams, E.S.: Fairness perceptions and trust for transformational and transactional leadership: a two-sample study. J. Manag. **25**(6), 897–933 (1999)
17. Podsakoff, P.M., Bommer, W., Podsakoff, N., Mackenzie, S.B.: Relationships between leader reward and punishment. behavior and subordinate attitudes, perceptions, and behaviors: a meta-analytic review of existing and new research. Organ. Behav. Hum. Decis. Process. **99**(2), 13–142 (2006)
18. Prost, M., Zouinar, M.: De l'hyper-connexion à la déconnexion: quand les entreprises tentent de réguler l'usage professionnel des e-mails. *Perspectives interdisciplinaires sur le travail et la santé* [En ligne], 17-1 ǀ 2015, mis en ligne le 01 novembre 2012, consulté le 29 août 2016 (2012). http://pistes.revues.org/4454
19. De la Rupelle, G., Fray, A.M., Kalika, M.: Messagerie électronique, facteur de stress dans le cadre de la relation managériale. Revue de gestion des ressources humaines **1**, 13–28 (2014)
20. Sanchez, R.J., Truxillo, D.M., Bauer, T.N.: Development and examination of an expectancy based measure of test-taking motivation. J. Appl. Psychol. **85**, 739–750 (2000)
21. Tidwell, L.C., Walther, J.B.: Computer-mediated communication effects on disclosure, impressions, and interpersonal evaluations: getting to know one another a bit at a time. Hum. Commun. Res. **28**, 317–348 (2002). doi:10.1111/j.1468-2958.2002.tb00811.x

22. Tourish, D., Hargie, O.: Communication and organizational success. In: Dans Hargie, O., et Tourish, D. (Dir.) Auditing Organizational Communication. A Handbook of Research, Theory and Practice, No. 2, pp. 3–26. Routledge, London (2009)

23. Vandenberghe, C., Bentein, K.: A closer look at the relationship between affective commitment to supervisors and organisations and turnover. J. Occup. Organ. Psychol. **82**, 331–348 (2009)

24. De Vries, R.E., Bakker-Pieper, A., Oostenveld, W.: Leadership = communication? The relations of leaders' communication styles with leadership styles, knowledge sharing and leadership outcomes. J. Bus. Psychol. **25**(3), 367–380 (2010). http://doi.org/10.1007/s10869-009-9140-2

25. Whittington, J.L., Coker, R.H., Goodwin, V.L., Ickes, W., Murray, B.: Transactional leadership revisited: Self-Other agreement and its consequences. J. Appl. Soc. Psychol. **39**(8), 1860–1886 (2009). doi:10.1111/j.1559-1816.2009.00507.x

26. Yammarino, F., Dionne, S., Chun, J., Dansereau, F.: Leadership and levels of analysis: a state-of-the science review. Leadersh. Quart. **16**(6), 879–919 (2005)

27. Zorn, T.E.: Bosses and buddies: constructing and performing simultaneously hierarchical and close friendship relationships. Underst. Relat. Process. **6**, 122–147 (1995)

Discuss Attractive Factor of E-Scooter with Miryoku Engineering and Fuzzy Kano Model

Jianxin Cheng[✉], Yixiang Wu[✉], and Le Xi[✉]

School of Art Design and Media, East China University of Science and Technology,
No. 130, Meilong Road, Xuhui District, Shanghai 200237, China
cjx.master@gmail.com, wuyixiang_15@163.com, 1955678@qq.com

Abstract. Along with the industrial progress and the improvement of life quality, the product functionality and usability have become the basic demands. The modern users lay more emphasis on pleasure, special use experience and memory empathy brought by the products. Miryoku engineering is a research which helps designers better understand customers' specific perceptual cognition and then catch a relatively accurate preference of customers. Miryoku engineering advocators suggested a new perspective on human emotions, i.e. the use of adjectives to represent various emotions. In this study, firstly using the Evaluation Grid Chart of Miryoku Engineering, the author interviewed participants who were over 30 years old and had studied industrial design for more than five years, to catch the personal cognition of attractiveness of E-scooter. In order to make the attractive factors more representative, the author used the KJ Method to simplify the items. These evaluation items were selected to form the questionnaire in the next step. Attractive factors of E-scooter appearance were led into "Fuzzy Kano Model"(FKM) and entitled with particular "quality attributes" to explore the relationship between attractive factors and customer satisfaction. 10 attractive factors were selected as evaluation index items, participant feelings were investigated with bidirectional questionnaire, influences of attractive factors on consumer satisfaction were verified through calculating.

Keywords: Fuzzy Kano Model · Attractiveness · Miryoku engineering · Appearance design · E-scooter

1 Introduction

Along with the industrial progress and the improvement of life quality, the product functionality and usability have become the basic demands. The modern users lay more emphasis on pleasure, special use experience and memory empathy brought by the products. social values gradually become open and diverse, people transit from material to spiritual enjoyments, pursuing fashion and beautifying oneself have become a significant aesthetic tendency in modern time. Under such circumstances, consumer emotions are stronger, consumer demand level and contents are various. Particularly, consumer demand level rises from low to high, consumers pay attention not only on qualities and functions, but also on art, culture, symbol, individual satisfaction and joyful spirit of products. Emotional shopping tendency of consumers determines that emotional

© Springer International Publishing AG 2017
F.F.-H. Nah and C.-H. Tan (Eds.): HCIBGO 2017, Part I, LNCS 10293, pp. 27–36, 2017.
DOI: 10.1007/978-3-319-58481-2_3

elements will be emphasized by more and more designers in future. Design directed by emotional content can be regarded as the heart of current design practices, research, and education (Demirbilek and Sener 2003). In another word, emotions are "felt" and can play significant roles during product interactions, such as impacting the decision of whether or not to buy (Jordan 2000; Norman 2004). Khalid (2001) pointed out, "the decision to buy can be momentary, so consumer demands can then be created very quickly, while other demands are long established." Relying on individual judgment and preference, consumers buy products which can fulfill their subjective consciousness. Products which not only have cool appearances, satisfying functions and high qualities, but also can bring consumers psychological satisfaction are demanded in market. What consumers actually want are high-quality products which symbolize individual character, taste, identity and position. Under such situation, exploring consumer demands, expectations and preferences is necessary and significant. However, it can be challenging to measure consumer preferences and emotions on products and risky to develop new products. It has been estimated that up to one third of new products fail at the launch stage (Cooper and Kleinschmidt 1987). So it can be told that it is crucial to capture their emotional feedback on the products, because consumers tend to make buying decisions increasingly emotionally, avoiding the rational processing of large quantities of information (Katicic et al. 2006). Thus, more and more companies are willing to invest on researching the relationship between consumer emotions, references and new products; in order to design more attractive products and satisfy consumer expectations, consumer preferences and emotions on new products shall be learned. Moreover, it is important that product designers are sufficient for designing attractive new products, because attractiveness of new products themselves plays a key element impacting consumers' purchasing decisions (Masato 2000). However, it is absolutely not easy to scale consumer references and emotions on products.

2   Related Work

Kansei Engineering and relevant researches have been largely promoted and consumers' subjective emotional demands are valued in product design. As a customer-emotion-oriented new product developing technology, Kansei Engineering is defined as "a technology which materializes consumer emotions and images on products into design elements" (Nagamachi 1995), it is successfully applied in actual product design and has already been widely used in product design to explore the relationship between consumer emotions and product design elements. Owing to the fact that human emotions are extremely subjective, circumstance-related and individual, an accurate measurement of consumer emotions is generally impractical. In this regard, to consolidate consumer's emotional requirements, Kansei engineering advocators suggested a new perspective on human emotions, i.e. the use of Kansei words or adjectives to represent various emotions (Ota and Aoyama 2001). Relation between product design elements and product kansei images are explored in Kansei Engineering. The general idea is: firstly, define consumer emotional demand space and product design space; secondly, select proper adjectives for products among numerous adjectives and match them with test samples; thirdly, inquire consumer emotions through Semantic Differential Method and establish the relationship between consumer demand space and product design elements. But after all, only consumer emotions rather than preferences on products can be found with such evaluating method, so the products designed in such process may only have limited power to impact consumer satisfaction.

Researching consumer satisfaction plays an important role in early stage of product development, consumer subjective feelings about product are key affecting elements to consumer satisfaction, therefore, it is significant to find out affecting elements to consumer satisfaction and categorize consumer demands. Kano et al. (1984a, b) made a two-dimensional diagram to present the relationship between consumer satisfaction and fulfilling demand degree as shown in Fig. 1. On basis of consumer reactions, indexes are categorized with Kano Model as: must-be quality, one-dimensional quality and attractive quality. According to this theory, products with attractive qualities can make consumers satisfied while products without attractive quality can not (Kano et al. 1984a, b). Generally, attractive qualities are not expected and not expressed by consumers. They can bring "surprise" to consumers sometimes. If one-dimensional qualities are realized, consumer will feel satisfied, otherwise, customers will not (Lee and Newcomb 1997). Investigating consumer demands with Kano Model is an important part in new product development and innovation process. consumer comments are meaningful for new product development because consumer demands evaluation affects the success of new product development for target consumers. Rashid et al. (2010), Hwang et al. (2014) used Kano Model and Kano Regression Method, verified consumer preferences, satisfaction and emotional experiences inspired by social and cultural products. The results of their researches offered designers with a better cognitive approach about how to design better products to meet consumer demands.

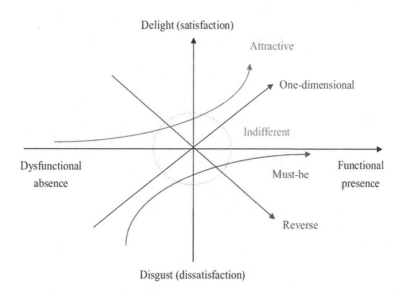

Fig. 1. An illustration of the Kano model

Same like material demands, emotional demands on style design are also human demands in essence, it is not difficult to understand that Kano Model can be applied in emotional area of style design. Yao Xiang et al. based on Kano Model Categorization Method and categorized emotional demands of style design as must-be quality, one-dimensional quality and attractive quality. Design emotion is represented and expressed with adjectives. Design emotional qualities correlate closely with design characteristics, about product style design, through investigating the relationship between style design characteristics and emotional demands, it can be judged that which design characteristic leads to what emotion and which emotion belong to which quality level. Yao and Hu (2014) evaluated beauty elements of vehicle appearance in their researches, during evaluation process, participants were asked to evaluate 12 beauty elements of vehicle appearance in Kano Bidirectional Questionnaire. According to evaluation results, it was found that consumer demands could be captured more accurately with Fuzzy Kano Model (FKM), and that importing FKM in dealing with consumer emotions was more objective and fairer than importing Kano Model. Their researches were beneficial for designers in recognizing these beauty elements of vehicle appearance and putting their efforts in improving attractive qualities and increasing consumer satisfaction, influential for customers in accepting vehicle appearance.

Markus Hartono and Tan Kay Chuan (2011) described how Kano Model was helpful to Kansei Engineering in services, they also introduced a comprehensive framework consisted of Kano Model and Kansei Engineering. Kano Model was applied and inserted in Kansei Engineering to reveal the relationship between service qualities and consumer reactions. In case studying, Kansei Engineering is applied to capture and transfer consumer emotional demands, Kano Model is used to assist Kansei Engineering and deeply explore the relationship between service elements and consumer emotions. Kansei Engineering promotes emotion elements to merge with product design elements, but it can not tell influences of different emotion elements on purchasing decisions. Tama et al. (2015) combined Kansei Engineering and Kano Model in their study to improve design of ceramic souvenirs and better meet consumer expectations. During study, they categorized or sorted emotion adjectives in accordance with Kano Model, then they calculated and analyzed the emotion adjectives which affected consumer satisfaction the most and developed such adjectives as key for further design.

Miryoku engineering was a research developed by Masao Inui and Japanese scholar Junichiro Sanui in referring to the book The Psychology of Personal Constructs written by clinical psychologist Kelly, which provides the designers a method to make the customers' fuzzy perceptual cognition become specific when executing product development. It was understood that some ways to choose products by customers and the experience of successful product design can catch the products' charm essence, thus a design full of charm would be created. The method clearly discussed the similarity or difference relationship in the comparison between object A and B mainly by individual interviews, thus the individual qualities of target objects were sorted out. The charm factors will be the key points to successful products if they can be obtained in the products design and development as well as applied and transformed to actual product aspects, so the extraction of charm has been worked on finding by many designers in the design process. The product evaluation construction method provides an analytic approach to product charm factors with theory basis among the related researches in miryoku engineering, providing stimulation according to the category of the theme and in the form of depth interviews to know the customers' feeling about the products' charm, making the participants have obvious feeling difference after the comparison of preference degree among participants, so the participants' original concept to the subject will be known, thus leading to the participants' more definite analyzing the original evaluation concept and connecting its upper abstract concept with lower specific description, and then a network diagram of participants' evaluation structure of products will be sorted out.

3   Research Method and Process

"Miryoku" is a Japanese word, means "strong attraction". So-called miryoku is a kind of power which appeals public feeling and make people puzzling, i.e. power which causes people confused, it can induce people to take certain actions, for example, consumer decision-making behavior. It is the subjective preference of consumers and has direct and close relationship with consumers' values. From a design perspective, the extraction of miryoku is the element which a lot of designers are committed to look for in design process. Miryoku, can be regarded as a generic term of power to conquer public feeling such as allure, attraction, induced force, appeal and inspiring power, etc. Miryoku engineering is a research which helps designers better understand customers' specific perceptual cognition and then catch a relatively accurate preference of customers. Miryoku engineering advocators suggested a new perspective on human emotions, i.e. the use of adjectives to represent various emotions. In this study, "kansei images" of E-scooter's Front Face were led into Fuzzy Kano Model and entitled with particular "quality attributes" to explore the relationship between kansei images and customer satisfaction. In this study, using the Evaluation Grid Chart of Miryoku Engineering, the author interviewed participants who were over 30 years old and had studied industrial design for more than five years, to catch the personal cognition of attractiveness of E-scooter's Front Face.

Now people is paying more and more attention to living environment quality and physical health. Green travel is one of social hot topics. E-scooter is naturally the first choice, especially a equipment suitable for mid-short distance traffic, according to the survey, the main reason which citizens select light electric vehicle as transportation means instead of walk is: car is expensive, bicycle requires human power to drive, bus system is not perfect enough, the driving of motorcycle is relatively dangerous and meanwhile prohibited in many cities, however, E-scooter avoids training, cumbersome registration procedure and expensive insurance cost. As a personal traffic carrier, with the characteristics of low carbon and environmental protection, electric vehicles will become one of mainstream traffic tools in the future. researchers and designers engaged in this field need to study user's preferences based on miryoku engineering.

In order to analyze the attractive factors of E-scooter's front face, an interview is conducted by using EMG method. Interview time is 1 h and interview place is in a separate room which has no external interruption. The number of people who

Table 1. Preference of a participant to E - scooter's Front Face

Upper level		Original evaluation item (middle level)	Lower level (specific description)	
	Headlight, its overall shape has edges and corners, is very sharp	Headlight shape is prismatic, just like two eyes Wild (upper level attractive factor)		Headlight is located in front panel, its shape is prismatic have edges and corners, just like eagle's eyes
	The profile of front panel is smooth and sleek	The profile of front panel is sleek and graceful Sleek (upper level attractive factor)		The profile of front panel is smooth and sleek
	The shape of wind deflector bottom is inverted U, contracts outside-in, line is sleek and graceful	The shape of wind deflector bottom is inverted U Sleek (upper level attractive factor)		The shape of wind deflector bottom is inverted U, contracts outside-in, line is smooth
	The profile of wind deflector bottom is lower convex, line is smooth and graceful	The profile of wind deflector bottom is lower convex Soft (upper level charm factor)		The profile of wind deflector bottom is lower convex
	The intake grille of decoration is in shape of V	Intake grille of V shape Tangible (upper level charm factor)		The intake grille of decoration is in shape of V, and composed of multi-V

participated in investigation and survey is 30. They are made up of 18–38 years' old men and women, some of them have 2 years' experience of driving E–scooter, some are designers who study E-scooter. These experts and scholars as well as experienced E-scooter drivers will be asked the attractive factors they think with regard to E-scooter's front face, thus explore the key factors E-scooter's front face design generates attraction. Specific method is as follows: 1. Prepare 20 sample drawing cards, card size is half of A4 paper size and every sample card size has the same specification, each sample card is selected from a variety of E-scooter's front face, among which are made by several major manufacturers in market, interview will be conducted based on the classification of 20 sample cards. 2. The cards which are partial to E-scooter's front face are grouped by their preferences. 3. The original evaluation item, which is established by different preferences and reasons, original evaluation item will be asked by comparing groups. 4. Each original evaluation item is processed into "upper" and "lower" levels. The upper level is asked the reason of original evaluation item and the lower level is asked the specific features of evaluation item. According to above said process, the structure of evaluation item of each participant can be displayed. Table 1 shows the preference of a participant to E-scooter's Front Face.

In order to make the attractive factors more representative, the author used the KJ Method to simplify the items. These evaluation items were selected to form the questionnaire in the next step. KJ Method to simplify the headlight of E-scooter's front face is shown in Table 2.

Table 2. KJ Method to simplify the headlight of E-scooter's Front Face

1. Polygon diamond shape (14)	←	Diamond shape appearance 10, jewel type 2, hexagon 2
2. Like diamond and like eyes (17)	←	Eagle eye shape 10, like eyes 1, rhombus 3, like a pair of big wings 3
3. Smiling face of V shape (13)	←	Headlight of V shape 10, smiling face type 3
4. Roundness (11)	←	Round headlight 9, ring shape 2
5. Outer convex big eye lamp (5)	←	Like big eye 1, big elliptic headlight 1, outer convex round headlight 3
6. Combination form of two circles (13)	←	Calabash shape headlight 4, curve eight shape 5, two round lights 3
7. Nearly square (10)	←	Square headlight 2, square 7, rectangle 1
8. Nearly trapezoidal (12)	←	Inverted trapezoidal 5, trapezoidal 3, nearly inverted trapezoidal 4
9. Goose egg shape (15)	←	Goose egg shape 3, egg shape 4, elliptic 3, semi-elliptic shape 3, like water drop 2

Attractive factors of E-scooter's front face were led into "Fuzzy Kano Model" and entitled with particular "quality attributes" to explore the relationship between attractive factors and customer satisfaction. In traditional Kano model survey, participants give only one answer to positive and negative questions, this ignores the uncertainty of participant's thought. When the answer which a customer gives to a product attribute is uncertain, the survey data to this part of the customer by traditional Kano model is not accurate. Considering the uncertainty of customer satisfaction, a demand classification method of fuzzy Kano model is put forward.

Both fuzzy Kano model and traditional Kano model conduct survey of customer satisfaction in the form of positive and negative questionnaire, the biggest difference lies in the design of the questionnaire. Traditional Kano questionnaire only allows you to select a most satisfied answer for positive and negative questions, however, fuzzy Kano questionnaire allows clients to give fuzzy satisfaction values to multiple survey items (in the form of percentage, their values are between [0, 1], the sum of row elements is equal to 1). The questionnaires of traditional Kano model and fuzzy Kano model are shown in Tables 3 and 4 respectively.

Table 3. Traditional Kano questionnaire

Function of product	Like	So shall is be	Not to matter	Can tolerate	Dislike
Realizable		✓			
Irrealizable				✓	

Table 4. Fuzzy Kano questionnaire

Function of product	Like	So shall is be	Not to matter	Can tolerate	Dislike
Realizable		0.6	0.2	0.2	
Realizable			0.6	0.3	0.1

4　Discussion and Analysis of Results

First of all, take the above simplified 10 upper level attractive factors as evaluation items, and ask participants' ideas respectively with a group of bidirectional questionnaires (sufficient and unsufficient quality). The influence of every perceptual image vocabulary on satisfaction degree of customers can be known by calculation, thus, we deduce which words belong to attractive quality from the 10 perceptual image words. Table 5 shows the result analysis of FKM analysis.

Table 5. Attribute priorities of upper level attractive factor

Attractive factor	FKM					
	M	A	O	I	R	Category
Lovely	0	14	2	12	0	A
Wild	0	6	0	22	2	I
Retro	0	4	0	26	0	I
Glaring	1	4	0	24	1	I
Rounded	0	10	0	20	0	I
Rational	0	8	0	18	2	I
Delicate	7	9	8	4	0	A
Rational	0	0	0	26	0	I
Minimalistic	0	16	1	14	0	A
Flexible	1	6	2	18	0	I

Note: M: Must-be O: One-dimensional A: Attractive I: Indifferent R: Reverse

Take the fuzzy Kano questionnaire of a participant as example, assume that the function matrix X = [0.7 0.3 0 0 0] can realize, the function matrix Y = [0 0 0.5 0.5 0] cannot realize, they generate fuzzy interactive matrix. The generated fuzzy interactive matrix is made positional correspondence of Kano quality attributes decision matrix, the membership degree vector of A, M, O, I can be known, $t_a = 0.7$, $t_m = 0$, $t_o = 0$, $t_i = 0.3$. Because the same evaluation factor generally belongs to multiple Kano attribute category at the same time, in order to obtain more accurate and reliable data, threshold α is introduced for filtering. For the choice of α values, it is found by Meng and He (2013), (through setting different values of α), that α = 0.4 is the optimal value, it can guarantee information not only distortionless, but also less cross. If the membership degree vector t of Kano attribute category is greater than α, it is set that the attribute vector of this attribute category is expressed by 1, otherwise expressed by 0. Above steps are repeated, tendency categories of demand for products of each participant are statistically analyzed, the highest frequency tendency of demand for the product of participants is the attribute category of demand.

According to FKM classification results, there are 10 charm quality attributes, among which minimalistic, delicate and lovely are three types of charismatic quality, other 7 types are indifferent quality, then designers can firstly integrate charismatic quality attributes with the design of E-scooter's Front Face.

For example, emotional vocabulary minimalistic, at present, in the fierce competition and fast pace modern city life, the mental and psychological pressure of people increase gradually, they hope they can relax their tense nerve, make body and mind get stretch. The concise and straightforward style can provide real psychological support. Specifically, minimalistic style is characterized by rejecting delicate and intricate decoration form, seeking a combination of simple geometric shape and fluent lively line/plane. When consumers find E-scooter's Front Face has minimalistic characteristic, they psychologically feel fresh and clear, thus are attracted by the appearance of E-scooter's front face. That is to say, it takes a key role in the design form of E-scooter's front face to strengthen the research of minimalistic style. The author thinks that its style design can be summarized into abstract geometrical body, and carry on combination permutation arrangement by making full use of three forming rules-dot, line, face, can increase modelling change in local place, thus design minimalistic modelling so as to make E-scooter's front face attractive.

From the point of delicate view, delicate refers to product modelling is relatively fine, the design of main structure style is more reasonable, the treatment of a length of circular arc, a raised modeling as well as local modelling scale, quantity relationship in product shape is more harmonious, lead to the exquisite overall visual effect of products. With the development of social economy, people begin to pursue the high level of life quality, reflected in pursuit of quality and class when purchase E-scooter. In the choice of E-scooter, when consumers find E-scooter's front face with fine quality, will psychologically feel delicate and elegant, can produce a kind of slap-up feeling, thus are attracted by E-scooter's front face.

Once more, from the point of lovely view, lovely is a psychological natural reaction to some characteristics of product modeling, such as cartoon, novel and fun. Lovely products are usually designed by using bionic technique, realistically reproduce the form of natural things, let people have a unique taste after observation, as a result, the psychological distance between people and products becomes short. As the life rhythm of modern people speeds up, the life pressure of people increases, people expect to pursue the happy relaxed way of life, therefore, tend to pursuit a product with fun and friendly feeling to entertain their life. Based on this, when consumers find E-scooter's front face has lovely feature, will psychologically feel affinity, be associated with a kind of fun and joy, and have a unique taste experience, thus be attracted by E-scooter's front face.

References

Demirbilek, O., Sener, B.: Product design, semantics and emotional response. Ergonomics **46**(13–14), 1346–1360 (2003)

Jordan, R.: Designing Pleasurable Products. Taylor & Francis, London (2000)

Norman, D.: Emotional Design: Why We Love (or hate) Everyday Things. Basic Books, New York (2004)

Khalid, H.M.: Can customer needs express affective design? In: Helander, M.G., Khalid, H.M., Tham, M.P. (eds.) Proceedings of the International Conference on Affective Human Factors Design, pp. 190–199. ASEAN Academic Press, London (2001)

Cooper, R.G., Kleinschmidt, E.J.: New product: What separates winners from losers? J. Prod. Innov. Manage **4**(3), 169–184 (1987)

Kreutzer, R.T., Merkle, W.: Die Notwendigkeit zur Neuausrichtung des Marketing. In: Die neue Macht des Marketing, pp. 13–17 (2008)

Masato, U.: The evolution of preference-based design. Research and Development Institute, Takenaka Corporation, Chiba, Japan (2000)

Nagamachi, M.: Kansei engineering: a new ergonomics consumer-oriented technology for product development. Int. J. Indus. Ergon. **15**(1), 3–11 (1995)

Ota, M., Aoyama, H.: Aesthetic design based on 'Kansei language'. In: 10th International Conference on Precision Engineering (ICPE), Yokohama, Japan, pp. 917–921 (2001)

Kano, K.H., et al.: How to delight your customers. J. Prod. Brand Manage. **5**(2), 6–17 (1984a)

Kano, N., et al.: Attractive quality and must-be quality. J. Japan. Soc. Qual. Control **14**(2), 39–48 (1984b)

Lee, M.C., Newcomb, J.F.: Applying the Kano methodology to meet customer requirements: NASA's microgravity science program. Qualify Manag. J. **4**(3), 95–110 (1997)

Rashid, et al.: A proposed computer system on Kano model for new product development and innovation aspect: a case study is conducted by an attractive attribute of automobile. Int. J. Eng. Sci. Technol. **2**(9), 1–12 (2010)

Hwang, S.-H., Tsai, I.-C., Mitsuhashi, T., Miyazaki, K.: The application of Kano model on exploring the attractive attributes of community culture products. Bull. Japan. Soc. Sci. Des. (JSSD) **61**(1), 27–36 (2014)

Yao, X., Hu, H.: Emotional level research of product modeling design based on Kano model. J. Wuhan Univ. Technol. (Information & Management Engineering) **2014**(5), 673–676 (2014)

Yadav, H.C., Jain, R., Shukla, S., et al.: Prioritization of aesthetic attributes of car profile. Int. J. Indus. Ergon. **43**(4), 296–303 (2013)

Hartono, M., Tan, K.C., Peacock, J.B.: Incorporating Kano's model and Markov chain into Kansei engineering in services. Crc Press (2012)

Tama, I.P., Azlia, W., Hardiningtyas, D.: Development of customer oriented product design using Kansei engineering and Kano model: case study of ceramic souvenir. Procedia Manuf. **4**, 328–335 (2015)

Meng, Q., He, L.: Fuzzy Kano based classification method and its application to quality attributes. Indus. Eng. J. **16**(3), 121–125 (2013)

The Relevance of Failure to Ensure Safety in Human-Robot Cooperation in Work Environments

Diego Compagna[✉]

Technische Universität Berlin, Berlin, Germany
diego.compagna@tu-berlin.de

Abstract. The paper is focusing on human–robot cooperation in work environments from the perspective of genuine sociological insights regarding human–robot interaction. Due to the typical range of application of robots, aspects of work safety were so far mainly emphasized as an issue of avoiding somatic harm. However, when it comes to social robots and to the design of settings of straight human-robot cooperation cognitive aspects should be taken into consideration. A crucial aspect for human-robot interaction (HRI) in work environments is avoiding strong routinization and a strong reduction in the human's attention. Especially if the robot is assuming a large workload the stated problem could arise and pose danger to safety. Systematically induced crisis in terms of confronting the humans with credible contingency in the form of small amounts of unexpected behavior could be a very effective solution. The humans cooperating with robots are not involved in a behavioral crisis in an everyday sense; the term "crisis" is used in a ethnomethodological meaning to describe a robot behavior that slightly surprises the human user. To achieve this goal and the intended benefit, the robot simply must act in such a way that is somewhat different from the human's expectations. When expectations do not meet with such surprise after a fair amount of interaction experience, humans automatically tend toward routinization.

Keywords: Social robotics · Human-robot interaction · Work safety · Sociology · Breaching experiments · Ethnomethodology

1 Introduction

The paper is focusing on human–robot cooperation in work environments from the perspective of human–robot interaction, and the sociological insights that were gathered so far in experiments conducted in the Fabrication Laboratory "MTI-engAge" at the Technical University of Berlin [1]. Due to the typical range of application of robots, aspects of work safety were so far mainly emphasized as an issue of avoiding somatic harm. However, when it comes to social robots and to the design of settings of straight human-robot cooperation cognitive aspects should be taken into consideration. Until now, the issues discussed in this paper were not relevant since most of the robots used in work environments are industrial robots that are used in production processes. In these typical industrial settings safety is ensured by separating the robots from the workers through security spaces or even fences. A new application area for robots is becoming

© Springer International Publishing AG 2017
F.F.-H. Nah and C.-H. Tan (Eds.): HCIBGO 2017, Part I, LNCS 10293, pp. 37–46, 2017.
DOI: 10.1007/978-3-319-58481-2_4

increasingly important as the development of service robots are gaining relevance in terms of reliability and versatility. However, to take part in collaborative actions with human workers clearly raises completely new challenges and demands new approaches for addressing safety issues.

This paper is emphasizing the fact that even if the interaction with the robot is intuitive and therefore unproblematic, it will pose a danger to safety due to an increased reduction of cognitive tasks as the robots assume the workload for the involved humans. If the robot fulfills the collaboration task with the human in a routinized way (unlike humans would), the human will adapt to the robot's predictable behavior very quickly and in doing so reduce his or her attention to a quite dangerous level. To address these new challenges and develop strategies to avoid them, I argue that the construction of interactive working robots can benefit from a sociological insights and basic assumptions about interaction among humans. From a sociological point of view interaction among humans is always endangered of failing. The probability of failing is usually assumed higher than succeeding. Therefore, one intriguing question is to ask how humans ensure a smoothly course of interaction. Sociological insights may help through the evaluation of human–human interaction to deduce relevant issues regarding human-robot interactions how to ensure safety in upcoming human-robot collaboration settings. A main aspect lies in the use of a conceptual instrument in the form of what we coined in our research group as a "behavioral crisis pattern". The term "crisis" is a conceptual term taken from a very circumscribed approach within sociological theories mainly known as "Ethnomethodology." Especially the approach of Ethnomethodology is highlighting the constant state of failure within interaction and the permanent repair strategies that are adopted by the interacting humans to coop with potentially unexpected behavior respectively with the slight overall contingency of the situation.

A crucial aspect for HRI in work environments is avoiding strong routinization and a strong reduction in the human's attention. Especially if the robot is assuming a large workload the stated problem could arise and pose danger to safety. Systematically induced crisis in terms of confronting the humans with credible contingency in the form of small amounts of unexpected behavior could be a very effective solution. The humans cooperating with robots are not involved in a behavioral crisis in an everyday sense; the term "crisis" is used in a ethnomethodological meaning to describe a robot behavior that slightly surprises the human user. To achieve this goal and the intended benefit, the robot simply must act in such a way that is somewhat different from the human's expectations. When expectations do not meet with such surprise after a fair amount of interaction experience, humans automatically tend toward routinization.

2 The Peculiar Relationship of Failure and Safety in Human-Robot Cooperation

Designing a safe human-robot interaction for collaborative work settings is a comparatively new challenge. From a sociological point of view, it is crucial to analyze basic elements and patterns of human-human interaction (HHI). A common theory regarding HHI on the micro level is to emphasize the use of symbols and the performative use of them in a constructivist way. Especially in collaborative work environments the interaction between a human and a robot is basically carried out through actions and gestures, less through communication in a strict sense, e.g. using words, talking with each other etc. The interaction is therefore based upon the understanding of gestures and actions as social cues and the ability to read them right, but also to anticipate the expectations of the collaborating partner. The situation is becoming increasingly social when it is built upon expected expectations, or at least when the human could describe it that way. Even if the robot is following a deterministic path, we can assume that if the human is ascribing expectations towards the robot and acting towards them (either way: fulfilling or willfully disappointing them) the situation can count as social. The described "as if" situation is typical for artificial intelligent research and can be followed back to one of the most influential and paradigmatic approaches within the field, the so called "Turing Test" by Alain Turing [2, 3].

Intriguing is the notion of Turing to design a test based on genuinely sociological assumptions [34]. The main underlying assumption of the so-called Turing Test is the ascription of intentionality and contingency undertaken by the human towards the artificial intelligence (A.I.). This concept is very familiar with most of the major sociological theories concerning the micro level of society, i.e. an interaction system. Alter and ego are relating to each other assuming that they are interested in exchanging whatever could be of interest. Furthermore, both are ascribing the other capabilities without having any proof of their existence. Especially the capability of being intentional and acting on the basis of expected expectations and even more on the presupposition to know that the other is also acting on this basis and is therefore expecting that Ego is acting orientated by expected expectations. It is of course quite hard to believe that a human can really assume a robot or a A.I. is consciously, intentionally expecting expectations and furthermore also assuming that the human is expecting that. However, the ingenious concept of Turing was to change the game by pointing out that the only thing that matters is not what is really going on in the mind (respectively the operations and input to output relations of the machine) but the mere assumptions that one – the human – will have or will develop towards the machine, i.e. the robot or the A.I. and that will be used as guidelines for the own future acting as well as thinking. This way of putting the challenge was – and for many reasons still is – a completely new and different approach to the riddle how to put the interaction between a human and a machine. Most of the approaches in HRI are still operating upon the implicitly acknowledged assumption that the relation between a human and a robot has to be modeled by taking into consideration the way how the human mind is functioning and processing information. By doing so the solipsistic mind is the cornerstone of the (most probably unmanageable) solution. In opposition to this viewpoint the Turing Test is putting the emphasis on the sole ascription of qualities, even if they do not really exist, if the human is acting toward the machine assuming that it is capable of expecting expectations, intentionality, taking always contingency as the outcome of the interaction into consideration, etc. the human's action will define the machine as assumed. According to the theorem of Thomas "If men define situations as real, they are real in their consequences" [35–37]: If the human is assuming that the robot is acting towards him or her in a very similar or even the precise same way how a human would do it, he or she will act towards the robot in a way that will establish the robot as human-like as possible – at least within the situational context of the interaction they are involved.

Accordingly, to an orientation towards expected expectations a basic assumption is that humans engaged in typical HHI situations also expect that the interaction could fail and they also are familiar with slightly breaches of their expected expectations respectively their assumed course of the interaction. These general theoretical propositions regarding HHI are put in the foreground by the approach developed by Harold Garfinkel, first coined as "Ethnomethodology" in the 1950's. Ethnomethodology follows the basic assumption that social reality is not predetermined by fix structures but created in situ between the interacting actors who act on behalf of methods. It is "the investigation of the rational properties of indexical expressions and other practical actions as contingent ongoing accomplishments of organized artful practices of everyday life" [4]. In other words: Each action needs an interpretation to be understandable and suitable for follow-up actions between two individuals (interaction). Therefore, ethnomethodology assumes that the meaning of an action as a symbol cannot be deduced from the symbol itself, as it is always vague and preliminary and pervaded by *indexical* expressions (e.g. 'this', 'here'), but emerges in the social context between the humans interacting with each other. To be accountable the involved humans use "methods" to understand how the action should be understood. These "ethnomethods" are *reflexive by nature*: "the activities, whereby members produce and manage settings of organized everyday affairs are identical with members' procedures for making those settings 'accountable'" [5].

Another important concept in Ethnomethodology and for the here presented approach to design HRI in collaborative work environments is sequentiality. Sequentiality is describing the fact that it is anything but random *when*, i.e. at what point in the interaction something happens. The sequential order is to be taken seriously and actions can be interpreted by formulating hypotheses and taking the following action as a verification or falsification (sequential interpretation).

As we already stated in recent published paper [6–8], a useful instrument to work out the quality of HRI is the ethnomethodological instrument of "Breaching Experiments" which was developed by Harold Garfinkel [9, 27, 28] to estimate the strategies (ethnomethods) that are adopted by humans to achieve a successful interaction between humans. We adopted this approach to work out new insights related to several studies in the field of HRI that were already leading to the assumption that the gaze of the robot is crucial for the assessment of the interaction. Especially for the successful and safe execution of cooperative tasks the gaze of the robot has a significant impact [10–12]. Even if a "point of interaction" – however embodied: as a face with eyes or just a light or a very simple emoticon like a smiley – is completely irrelevant for the mere functionality of a robot within work environments, it could be nonetheless vital for a healthy, cognitive exonerative HRI design. The general framework of this kind of research is referred to in typical HRI settings mostly quite vague as "point of interaction" [19, 33]. The so-called point of interaction can be very different things, the range goes from a specific interface or a specific action and therefore shows a strong affinity to HCI research in general. In the here presented research, the point of interaction is assumed to be crucial, due to the assumption that every interaction between a social robot and a human is focused and oriented towards it.

To understand the key factors, that are defining the HRI as sound and superior to developments focusing on mere functionality, it is insightful to take the HHI as a reference. Even if the implementation of HRI deviates from the standards of HHI, the orientation towards HHI is the key for the design of a proper and human-centered configuration of HRI. To achieve these goals, a conceptual framework based on some basic sociological assumptions in regard to the main factors that are characterizing interaction among humans is becoming increasingly important the more interactive the relationship between the robots and the humans will be. The framework should be able to identify the crucial features for a successful interaction and by doing so also increase the acceptance of the workers to willingly engage themselves in HRI.

From a sociological point of view, it is fruitful to consider HHI as a foil for the design of a safe HRI in work environments. Therefore, it is of paramount importance to consider the social addressability involved in the above mentioned general model of HHI. Addressability is an abstract prerequisite for interaction amongst humans in general, which has to be manifested and materialized for embodied forms of face-to-face communication. A point of interaction within a HRI setting becomes a social address mainly qua ascription of the entity that is dealing with it within the process of interaction. The reasons leading to the ascription of addressability is culturally shaped. The point of interaction serves as a mediator for the communicative act. A so-called point of interaction within HRI research should be defined as social address to be able to work with more elaborated concepts for the further understanding of gazes.

When it comes to the relevance of the point of interaction in the past decade as well as up-to-date studies in the field of HRI are focusing on the gaze and the gazing of the robot. The dominant aspect regarding social cues in HRI research was primarily and is still in most of the cases concerned with the use of the so-called social gaze and its importance in typical HRI settings. The research that was conducted so far is mostly concluding that social gaze has a favorable impact on nearly all the major aspects that are influencing the assessment of the interaction as a positive experience by the human. Fischer et al. [32] for instance summarized their research as follows:

> "Our qualitative and quantitative analyses show that people in the social gaze condition are significantly more quick to engage the robot, smile significantly more often, and can better account for where the robot is looking. In addition, we find people in the social gaze condition to feel more responsible for the task performance. We conclude that social gaze in assembly scenarios fulfills floor management functions and provides an indicator for the robot's affordance, yet that it does not influence likability, mutual interest and suspected competence of the robot." [32, p. 204]

In a quite typical setting for HRI research design, the gaze of the robot was tested in a tutoring situation. In this case the human had to teach the robot how to perform a cooperative task together with him or her. Both Moon et al. [10] and Zheng et al. [11, 12] presented similar results using a HRI test setting that was likewise the one of Fischer, however putting the focus not on the cooperative task in general but addressing a more concrete and haptic task regarding handover situations. They were able to "provide empirical evidence that using humanlike gaze cues during human-robot handovers [...] the timing and perceived quality of the handover event" [10, p. 2] can be improved. In most of the social gaze studies that were carried out in the recent past in HRI, the underlying models were orientated towards similar human-human interaction situations. The setting that were chosen to carry out the tests are a blueprint of the analogous human-human interaction situation. Not just situations that are typical for work cooperation and hand-over situations, but also the possibility of using the gaze as an acknowledging feedback of content-based exchange was also tested [31]. The overall results are similarly positive: "We argue that a robot – when using adequate online feedback strategies – has at its disposal an important resource with which it could pro-actively shape the tutor's presen-tation and help generate the input from which it would benefit most." [31, p. 268]

The above stated quotes and presented overall assessments related to the relevance and the function of social gaze within HRI in most of the recently conducted research dedicated to this topic, came so far to the mostly shared conclusion that the consideration and the proper implementation of social gaze is of paramount importance for a successful outcome in terms of a satisfying as well as both effective and efficient interaction between humans and robots.

Basic elements of typical HRI situation could manifest a wide range of complexity. However, the interaction between a human and a robot could be characterized as social regardless of the rate of complexity. Even human interactions involve a great range of degrees of sociality. HHI can range from routine and rule-governed settings to contin-gent forms and complex behaviors. The latter can best be described with a vocabulary of intentionality [13].

HHI are mainly structured by expectations. The expectations are mostly build upon the anticipation of the other's expectations (expected-expectations). Even if in everyday contexts quite seldom expectations are disappointed, a certain amount of deviation from the expected behavior is a phenomenon humans are familiar with in social interactions. This characteristic of HHI was framed by Luhmann as a situation of double contingency [14]. This description emphasizes the fact that among humans the possibility to act differently is always possible and quite common. For this reason, uncertain expectations are more stable than certain ones [15].

Also interesting is the fact that humans have the strong tendency to behave socially towards robots – due to the representations in mass media as embodied and socially embedded [16] – but also towards all sorts of technological objects, media and nature [17, 18]. Anthropomorphizing is an evolutionary asset of humans' behavior, since most of the competence to understand the environment is rooted in social interactions. This strategy is simply transferred to other areas and eventually enriched with specific knowl-edge regarding an artifact or the objects of nature [17]. Anthropomorphization is a cornerstone for intentionality, that is strictly linked to the ascription of agency towards the robot [19].

As already stated a sociologically inspired view ("breaching experiments" (Garfinkel), combined with a "frame analysis" (Goffman)) to evaluate HRI can work out the specifi-cally social aspects [20]. The breaching experiments developed by Garfinkel to demon-strate the fragility of social order, are used to make visible the latent mechanisms humans use to coordinate themselves within their social environment [5, 29, 30]. A breach in this regard is used to reveal the strategies adopted to navigate through social contexts creating a certain state of "normality". Conducting reaching experiments in HRI experiments can show if humans transfer these basic social-interaction strategies (ethnomethods) in the interaction setting with the robot. Especially if the robot is inducing flaws in the interaction experience and the human is adopting repair strategies to keep the interaction going. In these case the HRI setting is becoming comparable to a HHI situation and is framed by the human as social [6]. To be able to see the benefit of this approach it is helpful to underline a few basic assumptions about how in ethnomethodology interactions between humans (HHI) are understood. From the viewpoint of ethnomethodology in each HHI the humans must reestablish the meaning of the symbols (words, actions, etc.) they are using to be able to exchange information and/or cooperate with each other anew. For this reason, this approach is assuming that in most of the interactions slight adjustments to clarify the meaning of an action, a word etc. are inevitable. The meaning of a word, an object, etc., is never 100% clear and is always established ex post as an effect of the interacting partner's reaction. Therefore, HHI demands and automatically leads to a certain degree of awareness on the part of the interacting persons. A HRI design trying to replicate this very typical behavioral patterns for HHI is in this regard a very gentle way of increasing safety, since it involves a very common feature of HHI and proposes to transfer it to the design of HRI.

These thoughts in mind, even in non-humanoid robots in work environments, the implementation of basic social features can result in a superior and safer interaction experience. This goals are becoming increasingly important as the cooperation between worker and robots is becoming interactive. For this new direction in the field of human-robot cooperation in work environments it is crucial to highlight the difference between interacting with a machine and a human: A machine becomes predictable after a certain amount of time. On the one hand have humans the capability to surprise one another, on the other hand the meaning of every interaction must be deduced from a new definition of the world which is established anew with each interaction. Therefore, robots should of course not manifest a crisis behavior, rather implementing a sort of behavior leading to a very common experience in HHI. Just small perturbations that of course should not disturb the perceptions of reliability and trustworthiness toward the robot by the humans cooperating with it.

Findings of studies conducted with feedback systems that were designed to decrease the human's workload, concluded that the higher the degree of reduction is, the higher is also the risk of reduced attention [21]. Following the above stated assumptions related to deviation and expectation flaws that are typical in HHI, and that are leading to the breaching experiments as an instrument, a behavioral pattern could be designed [Societies]. The aim of such a behavioral pattern is to trigger a crisis in regard to the human's expectations toward the specific HRI sequence. The goal of this procedure is to create the illusion of a interaction situation that seems to be social in nature. Presumably the anthropomorphization of the robot is an important precondition for the realization of a crisis that is ascribed by the human as social. However, in most cases robots provoke these basic intentional ascriptions per se, which easily result in the human interaction partner assuming a certain agency [17, 19].

Considering different aspects of behavioral crisis patterns in working environments characterized by a cooperation between humans and robots, it is very important to take into consideration the complexity of the setting. Following the description of Kahn et al. [29] of the term interaction pattern, the robot's behavior should just slightly vary the action as expected by the human to achieve a breach. The robot doesn't have to deviate from the expected behavior in total or in part at all. It is crucial to distinguish the different framings involved in working environments characterized by human–robot cooperation. Depending from the different level of complexity, the realization of the breach can differ quite a lot. The same effect depending on the different levels of complexity can be implemented following the insights of social theories focusing on interaction: ethnomethodology [5], symbolic interactionism [22], role theory [23, 24] and (in part) structural functionalism [25, 26].

3   Conclusion

The presented suggestion to prevent reduced awareness in human–robot cooperation tasks by implementing a behavioral crisis pattern with the goal to induce a crisis could be easily misunderstood. The proposed approach is aiming at creating a certain amount of awareness and not – or just in rare cases a soft, low-level – alertness. It is very important to keep in mind the way how ethnomethodology is describing everyday HHI situations by emphasizing the strategies that are used to avoid failure in interaction (which is from this point of view much more probable that the other way around). It is also very important to remember that this means also, that interactions between humans are successful not because they are following solid structures but because of the capabilities of humans to constantly rearrange the meaning of an action, a word, etc. and to coop with a constantly different definition of a symbol respectively of the course of interaction – compared to how it was beforehand planned and/or anticipated. Ethnomethodology tends to highlight the management of micro-crisis that are usual for HHI regarding the rules and solid patterns that one is attempted to see in HHI. The parallels between the description of HHI provided by ethnomethodology and the above presented approach for the design of a safe HRI lies in realizing just very small perturbations rather than actual crises (in a strict sense). By doing so the perceptions of reliability and trustworthiness of the robot(s) will not be destabilized. Just the awareness is kept up to a very familiar rate, similar to the awareness that is in place when humans are engaging in HHI.

Acknowledgments. The Research presented in this paper was primarily supported by the German Ministry of Education and Research.

References

1. The Fabrication Laboratory "MTI-engAge" is financially supported by the German Ministry of Education and Research. http://www.mti-engage.tu-berlin.de/
2. Turing, A.M.: Computing machinery and intelligence. Mind **LIX**(236), 433–460 (1950). doi: 10.1093/mind/LIX.236.433. ISSN 0026-4423
3. Turing, A.M.: Computing machinery and intelligence. In: Epstein, R., Roberts, G., Beber, G. (eds.) Parsing the Turing Test. Philosophical and Methodological Issues in the Quest for the Thinking Computer, pp. 23–65. Springer, Netherlands (2008). doi:10.1007/978-1-4020-6710-5_3. ISBN 978-1-4020-6710-5
4. Lemert, C.: Reflexive properties of practical sociology. In: Social Theory: The Multicultural and Classic Readings, vol. 4, pp. 439–443. Westview Press, Philadelphia (2010)

5. Garfinkel, H.: Studies in Ethnomethodology, 11th edn. Polity Press, Cambridge (2007)
6. Compagna, D., Boblan, I.: Case-sensitive methods for evaluating HRI from a sociological point of view. In: Tapus, A., André, E., Martin, J.C., Ferland, F., Ammi, M. (eds.) Social Robotics. LNCS (LNAI), vol. 9388, pp. 155–163. Springer, Cham (2015). doi: 10.1007/978-3-319-25554-5_16
7. Compagna, D., Marquardt, M., Boblan, I.: Introducing a methodological approach to evaluate HRI from a genuine sociological point of view. In: Koh, J.T.K.V., Dunstan, B.J., Silvera-Tawil, D., Velonaki, M. (eds.) CR 2015. LNCS (LNAI), vol. 9549, pp. 55–64. Springer, Cham (2016). doi:10.1007/978-3-319-42945-8_5
8. Compagna, D., Weidemann, A., Marquardt, M., Graf, P.: Sociological and biological insights on how to prevent the reduction in cognitive activity that stems from robots assuming workloads in human-robot cooperation. Societies **6**, 1–11 (2016)
9. Garfinkel, H.: Studies in Ethnomethodology. Polity Press, Cambridge (1967)
10. Ajung, M., Troniak, D.M., Gleeson, B., Pan, M.K.X.J., Zheng, M., Blumer, B.A., MacLean, K., Croft. E.A.: Meet me where i'm gazing: how shared attention gaze affects human-robot handover timing. In: Proceedings of the 2014 ACM/IEEE International Conference on Human-Robot Interaction, pp. 334–341. ACM (2014)
11. Minhua, Z., Moon, A., Gleeson, B., Troniak, D.M., Pan, M.K.X.J., Blumer, B.A., Meng, M.Q.H., Croft, E.A.: Human behavioural responses to robot head gaze during robot-to-human handovers. In: Proceedings of the 2014 IEEE International Conference on Robotics and Biomimetics. IEEE, Bali (2014)
12. Zheng, M., Moon, A., Croft, E.A., et al.: Impacts of robot head gaze on robot-to-human handovers. Int. J. Soc. Robot. **7**(5), 783–798 (2015)
13. Rammert, W.: Where the action is: distributed agency between humans, machines, and programs. http://www.ssoar.info/ssoar/handle/document/1233 (2016). Accessed 21 Sept 2016
14. Luhmann, N.: Social Systems. Stanford University Press, Stanford (1995)
15. Luhmann, N.: Trust and Power: Two Works. Wiley, New York (1979)
16. Dautenhahn, K., Ogden, B., Quick, T.: From embodied to socially embedded agents—implications for interaction-aware robots. Cogn. Syst. Res. **3**, 397–428 (2002)
17. Dautenhahn, K.: Methodology and themes of human-robot interaction: a growing research field. Int. J. Adv. Robot. Syst. **4**, 103–108 (2007)
18. Reeves, B., Nass, C.: The Media Equation: How People Treat Computers, Television, and New Media Like Real People and Places, 1st edn. CSLI Publications, Stanford (1998)
19. Young, J.E., Sung, J., Voida, A., Sharlin, E., Igarashi, T., Christensen, H.I., Grinter, R.E.: Evaluating human-robot interaction. Int. J. Social Robot. **3**(1), 53–67 (2011)
20. Goffman, E.: Frame Analysis: An Essay on the Organization of Experience. Harvard University Press, Cambridge (1974)
21. Zühlke, D.: Nutzergerechte Entwicklung von Mensch-Maschine-Systemen_ Useware-Engineering fur technische Systeme. Springer, Heidelberg (2012)
22. Blumer, H.: Symbolic Interactionism—Perspective and Method, 10th edn. University of California Press, Berkeley (2007)
23. Goffman, E.: Embarrassment and social organization. In: Interaction Ritual—Essays on Face-to-Face Behavior. pp. 97–112. Aldine Transaction, Piscataway (1967)
24. Goffman, E.: The Presentation of Self in Everyday Life. Doubleday, New York City (1959)
25. Parsons, T.: The Social System, 2nd edn. Routledge, London (1991)
26. Parsons, T.: The Structure of Social Action: A Study in Social Theory with Special Reference to a Group of Recent European Writers. McGraw-Hill, New York (1937)

27. Garfinkel, H., Sacks, H.: On formal structures of practical actions. In: McKinney, J.C., Tiryakian, E. (eds.) Theoretical Sociology: Perspectives and Developments, vol. 345, pp. 337–366. Appleton-Century-Crofts, New York (1970)
28. Garfinkel, H.: Studies of the routine grounds of everyday activities. In: Farganis, J. (ed.) Readings in Social Theory: The Classic Tradition to Post-Modernism, 6th edn, pp. 287–295. McGraw-Hill, New York (2011)
29. Garfinkel, H.: Toward a Sociological Theory of Information. Paradigm Books, Boulder (2008)
30. Garfinkel, H. (ed.): Ethnomethodological Studies of Work. Routledge and Kegan Paul, London (1986)
31. Pitsch, K., Vollmer, A.-L., Mühlig, M.: Robot feedback shapes the tutor's presentation: how a robot's online gaze strategies lead to micro-adaptation of the human's conduct. Interact. Stud. **14**(2), 268–296 (2013)
32. Fischer, K., Jensen, L.C., Kirstein, F., Stabinger, S., Erkent, Ö., Shukla, D., Piater, J.: The effects of social gaze in human-robot collaborative assembly. In: Tapus, A., Tapus, A., André, E., Martin, J.C., Ferland, F., Ammi, M. (eds.) Social Robotics. LNCS, vol. 9388, pp. 204–213. Springer, Cham (2015). doi:10.1007/978-3-319-25554-5_21
33. Rakotonirainy, A.: Human-computer interactions: research challenges for in-vehicle technology. In: Proceedings of Road Safety Research Policing and Education Conference September (2003)
34. Heintz, B.: Die Herrschaft der Regel - Zur Grundlagengeschichte des Computers, 1st edn. Campus, Frankfurt (1993)
35. Thomas, W.I., Thomas, D.S.: The Child in America: Behavior Problems and Programs, pp. 571–572. Knopf, New York (1928)
36. Thomas, W.I.: The Unadjusted Girl. With Cases and Standpoint for Behavioral Analysis. Harper & Row, Evanston (1967). 42
37. Volkart, E.H. (ed.): Social Behavior and Personality. Contribution of Thomas to Theory and Social Research. Social Research Council, New York (1951). 14

Enhancing IS User Empowerment and Problem-Solving Behavior Through Training and Prompting

Brenda Eschenbrenner[✉]

University of Nebraska at Kearney, Kearney, NE, USA
eschenbrenbl@unk.edu

Abstract. Information systems (IS) users may learn to use IS through training, but may not be able to solve IS problems that arise. This may be because of limited skills and knowledge of IS problem-solving strategies to resolve these issues. Although previous IS research has studied various aspects of training and trainers as well as the influence on performance outcomes, research has not specifically focused on training problem-solving techniques or behaviors. Considering the potentially negative outcomes from being unable to resolve IS problems, such as inaccuracies or inefficiencies in performance outcomes, this research proposes to address this gap. Research studies have demonstrated that behavioral interventions, such as prompting and transfer of stimulus control, have influenced the use of desired behaviors in specific as well as novel situations. Prompting encourages the desired behavior to be utilized, the desired behavior can then be reinforced for continuous use, and prompting is eventually removed and stimulus control is transferred to a natural stimulus (e.g., IS problem). This research intends to evaluate the effectiveness of prompting and transfer of stimulus control to enhance users' sense of empowerment, efforts to solve IS problems, and performance outcomes. Therefore, this study intends to provide insights on methods of improving IS users abilities to solve IS problems by increasing users' sense of empowerment and problem-solving behaviors when utilizing software applications with the use of specific behavioral interventions (i.e., prompting and transfer of stimulus control).

Keywords: Information systems training · Information systems user · Information systems user empowerment · Problem-solving behavior · Prompting and transfer of stimulus control · Psychological Empowerment Theory · Theory of Trying · Social Cognitive Theory

1 Introduction

Information systems (IS) training is essential for users to learn and apply IS in an effective manner [1]. A conventional IS training entails initial delivery of information regarding the IS as well as demonstrations of its functions. Following this, opportunities for IS users to apply the learned knowledge to develop their own skills are provided. Also, guidance is provided in the form of feedback to help users further refine their newly acquired skills.

© Springer International Publishing AG 2017
F.F.-H. Nah and C.-H. Tan (Eds.): HCIBGO 2017, Part I, LNCS 10293, pp. 47–57, 2017.
DOI: 10.1007/978-3-319-58481-2_5

IS training does not typically focus on addressing problems that may arise when using IS. IS training may identify resources that can be utilized, but resource application training to resolve problems may be limited. Hence, individual users learn to use software applications, but do not specifically learn to address or resolve problems that arise when using the application. Their training may identify resources that can be utilized, but they are not specifically taught how to apply them when a problem is encountered. Therefore, utilization of these resources is limited or unproductive.

In addition, the ability to address these problems varies among many users. Some are able to effectively address almost any problem that they encounter, while others struggle. The struggles may result in the individual performing the task without the application (e.g., manually), avoiding the task altogether, or soliciting others to perform the task for them. The impact that these results can have include inefficiencies or inaccuracies in completing tasks, incompletion of tasks, or encumbering individuals who are capable of performing the task because of increased work load. Therefore, problem-solving behavior training is needed to assist IS users in addressing IS problems that they encounter. The research objective for this study is to assess improvements in individual's efforts and abilities to solve problems, as well as individual's sense of empowerment, through problem-solving behavior training interventions.

2   Literature Review

Organizations typically rely on training to develop or improve IS users' proficiency with information systems or software applications [1, 2]. Training has been addressed by several IS researchers [e.g., 1, 3]. For example, Webster and Martocchio [4] assessed the relationship of microcomputer playfulness, or one's unplanned and innovative usage of microcomputers, with training outcomes. Microcomputer playfulness was found to have positive relationships with outcomes such as satisfaction with the instructor and learning outcomes. No measurements, however, were taken of subjects' abilities to resolve subsequent problems encountered with IS usage.

Also, Compeau [5] identified behaviors of effective trainers such as subject-matter knowledge, instructional strategies such as demonstrations of skills being taught and providing opportunities to practice, as well as clear and adaptable explanations. Of the 53 effective training behaviors identified, none involved demonstrating or assisting in problem-solving methods. Compeau and Higgins [2] studied the effects of computer training using a lecture versus behavior-modeling style; Yi and Davis [3] studied observational learning processes effect on self-efficacy, knowledge acquisition, and performance outcomes; and Sharma and Yetton [1] studied the role of technical complexity and task interdependence in the context of training's influence on IS implementation outcomes of user satisfaction. None of these studies, however, focused specifically on problem-solving behavior training.

Therefore, research is lacking in assessing training interventions that specifically target problem-solving abilities of individuals when utilizing software applications. Although trainers may make users aware of various mechanisms that can be employed when a problem occurs, the focus of most training is on utilization of the various functions of an application or system and not how to deploy various problem-solving techniques when a problem occurs. Therefore, this research looks at behavioral education to develop a training program that will condition users to employ a set of problem-solving behaviors when a problem is encountered. Problem-solving behaviors, in this context, include a variety of alternative actions that can be taken when a problem is encountered to resolve the issue and continue completing the task. The behaviors can include attempting to utilize alternative functions, identifying existing examples and applying similar procedures to the task-at-hand, or conducting effective information searches.

Chase [6] indicates that "Examples of behavioral education have shown repeatedly that when one can identify the target behavior needed by a population and arrange for the population to contact direct training on the behavior, behavioral strategies and tactics will succeed in reliably producing the target behavior" (p. 350). Using behavioral interventions, training can be successful in generating a desired behavior. Training programs such as these have been previously developed and utilized in organizations for managers and employees. One training program utilized to increase the use of desired behaviors at appropriate times, with the behavior eventually occurring without prompts or additional stimuli, is prompting and transfer of stimulus control [7, 8]. The prompts, or stimuli, encourage the desired behaviors to be executed. Upon execution, the behavior can then receive reinforcement so the behavior will be utilized again in the future. Prompts can be, for example, verbal instructions, modeling desired behaviors, providing gestures, or physical guidance.

Eventually, the desired behavior must be executed by the occurrence of a discriminative or natural stimuli versus the prompt [7]. For instance, in the context of problem-solving, the problem itself would be the natural stimuli. Hence, prompts must eventually be removed so that the desired behavior occurs at the appropriate time and because of the presence of the natural stimuli, or transfer of stimulus control. Prompts can be removed by a number of techniques or modified techniques such as delaying successive prompts or gradually reducing the presence of the prompts (e.g., reducing the amount of guidance or instruction).

Prompting and transfer of stimulus control has been demonstrated to positively influence the application of desired behaviors [7]. For example, even though training to implement a positive reinforcement program in a classroom setting had previously occurred in separate instances (i.e., initially and after implementation when it was discovered that the program was not functioning as desired) to encourage usage of the program, desired performance outcomes were not achieved [9]. To improve the usage of the positive reinforcement program, prompts (along with feedback and self-assessment) were utilized to increase the accuracy of the program's techniques usage. Positive outcomes were achieved both with the prompts and after the removal of the prompts.

As another example, prompting and transfer of stimulus control have been successfully utilized to help individuals with mild disabilities acquire functional skill sets [10]. Through the use of prompts and performance feedback, individuals were able to acquire skills and transfer the use of the skills to naturally occurring stimuli (versus the prompts). In addition, some of the acquired skill sets were also applied in novel settings. In summary, these research studies show support for generating desired behaviors with prompts, and subsequently transferring stimulus control to natural stimuli. Also, textual prompts have been shown to be effective in promoting skill acquisition. Therefore, this research study looks to extend previous research to a software application context in which problem-solving behaviors are occasioned by prompts, with transfer of stimulus control being eventually transferred to the occurrence of a problem situation.

In the context for this research study, the target behavior desired is a set of problem-solving behaviors. Although one may argue that these behaviors may be applied to only a limited set of problems (i.e., those specific problems addressed during training), other researchers indicate that the generalization of these problem-solving behaviors is achievable. Previous suggestions have been made that acquiring a desired skill does not require comprehending all possible variations of the behavior and associated responses [11]. Previous research has also demonstrated that behavior training which focuses on explicit desired behaviors is not necessary to acquire the desired behavior [6]. Instead, some behavior training techniques can result in adaptive behaviors and only categories of these stimulants may be necessary.

In the context of problem solving, previous studies have demonstrated that direct reinforcement of the relationship between desired behaviors and naturally occurring stimuli is not always necessary [6]. Utilizing both stimulus control and response variations, resurgence can facilitate the production of novel behaviors through recognition of an array of contingencies. Resurgence can be created through increased practice. If practice integrates variation in stimuli associated with desired skills, transference as well as extensions of the skills can be facilitated as well.

When a behavior is discontinued due to novel situations, resurgence of previously learned behaviors associated with the stimulus of the novel situation is more likely to occur [6]. After solutions being derived from variations in behaviors has been established, novel situations are more likely to cause future variations in behavior. In essence, this will facilitate efforts to learn. Therefore, training users of software applications sets of problem-solving behaviors can be generalized to various problems that arise (increasing efforts to learn). Also, practice can increase the probability that the behaviors can be extended to problem variations.

In summary, the research proposed for this study looks to extend previous research by utilizing prompts to occasion the use of problem-solving behaviors when a problem occurs, and then transfer stimulus control to the problem itself. This research will employ prompts, similar to previous research studies [e.g., 10], so subjects have a list of problem-solving behaviors that they can refer back to when problems occur. Based on previous researchers' suggestions [e.g., 6], these problem-solving behaviors are expected to generalize to novel problems that are presented to research subjects, and then generalize to novel software applications.

Therefore, this study intends to evaluate the use of prompts and transfer of stimulus control to improve problem-solving with software applications. Applying the principles of prompts and transfer of stimulus control is expected to help increase the probability that an individual will address problems with a set of problem-solving behaviors (with the use of a prompt and after its removal), which should reduce the time needed to complete a task and increase the number of tasks that can be accomplished accurately in a given time period. Also, this research proposes to assess the generalizability of these problem-solving behaviors and efforts to novel software applications.

3 Theoretical Foundation and Hypotheses Development

3.1 Psychological Empowerment Theory

Empowerment has been defined "as increased intrinsic task motivation manifested in a set of four cognitions reflecting an individual's orientation to his or her work role: meaning, competence, ...self-determination, and impact" [12, p. 1443]. Meaning is the relative importance assigned. Competence is conceptualized as self-efficacy or one's belief in their ability to achieve a goal or outcome. Self-determination is one's ability to act with discretion or autonomy. Impact is the level of effect on resulting outcomes. Psychological empowerment has also been conceptualized as "a task motivation reflecting a sense of control in relation to one's work and an active orientation to one's work role... enables people to have a sense of ownership of their work and motivates them to complete their work and improve their performance" [13, p. 657].

Individuals who have empowerment are able to address challenges that arise and find novel methods of addressing these challenges [13]. Empowerment is viewed as a domain-specific variable and one that varies along a continuum [12]. The theory proposes that environmental factors (e.g., work-related) can influence empowerment which influences performance outcomes [13]. Antecedents to empowerment include information availability and access, with information being needed for empowerment in order for individuals to take initiative or comprehend [12]. Consequences of empowerment include proficiency and innovation.

In an IS context, user empowerment has been defined "as an active motivational orientation toward using an information technology (IT) application at work" [13, p. 658]. The dimensions of user empowerment include "competence of user, meaning of system usage, self-determination of user, and impact of system usage" [13, p. 658]. Competence refers to one's belief in their ability to use a system. Meaning of system usage encompasses the value an individual assesses system usage. Self-determination of user is an individual's perception of the discretion and autonomy regarding system usage. Impact of system usage is the level of effect on performance through system usage.

User empowerment has been demonstrated to influence IS usage, including developing connectedness or integration between tasks, using greater or more extended system functions, and identifying novel uses of a system [13]. Although perceived fit, job autonomy, and climate for achievement have been found to influence user empowerment, what has not been explored is the acquisition of information (i.e., problem-solving techniques and prompts) influence on user empowerment and the subsequent influence on trying to solve IS problems. Considering Empowerment Theory proposes, and previous research supports, information being an influential factor on empowerment and an outcome being proficiency, the hypothesis proposed for this study is information obtained from learning-to-try training and prompting will influence user empowerment, which will subsequently influence task performance with IS as well as system usage (i.e., problem-solving behaviors).

H1:   IS users who receive learning-to-try training will have greater user empowerment.

H2:   IS users who receive problem-solving prompts will have greater user empowerment.

   H2a: IS users who receive prompts during initial IS usage and subsequently have prompts removed will have greater user empowerment than those who do not receive the prompts.

   H2b: IS users who receive prompts during usage of an initial IS application will have greater user empowerment when utilizing a novel IS application than IS users who do not receive prompts.

H3:   IS users with greater user empowerment will utilize more problem-solving behaviors (i.e., trying to solve IS problems, discussed further below).

H4:   IS users with greater user empowerment will have better task performance.

3.2   Theory of Trying and Social Cognitive Theory

The Theory of Trying proposes that obstacles encountered when attempting to perform certain actions "influence expectations and attitudes that shape the formation of the intent to try or actual trying" [14, p. 431]. Also, "intention reflects a state of mind that drives one to take action as opposed to trying, which reflects action and even some parts of actual behavior" [14, p. 434]. The Theory of Reasoned Action proposes that an individual's goals, or attempts to carry out an action which may be hindered by impediments, are most likely to predict behaviors if obstacles are present. Trying has been proposed to be "defined as doing all the necessary pre-behaviors and otherwise satisfying all necessary conditions that are within volitional control for the performance of the subjective behavior" [14, p. 435].

Other IS-related constructs acknowledging attempts to use IS have emerged. For instance, the construct trying to innovate with IT has previously been referred to "as an individual's goal of finding novel uses of information technologies" [14, p. 435]. However, this research study proposes to study an individual's attempt *to solve IS-related problems*. Therefore, a new concept of trying to solve IS problems is proposed and conceptualized as an individual's attempt to solve an IS-related problem.

Social Cognitive Theory proposes that individuals learn through three primary learning components – personal/cognitive factors, the environment, and individual behaviors – and the interaction or "reciprocal determinism" of these factors [15, p. 23]. Personal/cognitive factors include individual cognitive abilities, characteristics, and traits. For example, individuals are able to utilize forethought to predict outcomes from their actions. The environment also influences learning through such mechanisms as modeled behaviors. Learning can occur by observing and evaluating the outcomes associated with observed actions. In addition, an individual learns by their own behaviors and evaluating the outcomes of these actions. The knowledge gained from these experiences can be stored as sets of rules in one's memory to be called on to direct future behaviors and refined in the future. These could be acquired from mechanisms such as training or stimulants such as prompts.

Developing proficiency at a task requires knowledge and cognitive skills, but can also require the actual application of the knowledge and cognitive skills in order to generate proficiency [15]. When individuals enact a given set of behaviors, they are able to obtain feedback which guides future actions. Individuals have pre-existing conceptions that are called upon when deciding upon actions to take. When the actions are enacted, feedback is obtained to inform and modify existing conceptions.

As has been previously noted, skill sets must be applied in a multifarious fashion to address evolving circumstances [15]. Also, "a fixed internal generator of behavior would be more of a hindrance than an aid. Skilled performance requires a generic conception, rather than a specific representation. Situational requirements help to specify how conception is best implemented into specific courses of actions... Subrules specify the enactment adjustments needed in each of these situations" [15, p. 110]. Individuals can selectively process information and learn not only from their own actions, but by observing the behavior of others through mechanisms such as instructional cues, behavioral modeling, and feedback. These observations allow individuals to identify patterns and comprehend underlying behavioral frameworks.

Social cognitive theory proposes that individuals create conceptions through use of symbolizing. Behaviors are derived from these conceptions. "Learning must be generative in nature, because skilled activities are seldom performed in exactly the same way; they must be varied to fit different circumstances... It is because people learn generative conceptions, rather than specific acts, that human skills have remarkable flexibility and utility" [15, p. 111]. Individuals learn by utilizing models, rule sets, and courses of actions that can be applied in varied circumstances.

Social Cognitive Theory suggests that individuals learn through training and instructions which can then influence behavior [15]. In this context, the instructions would be delivered in the form of training and prompts, and the influenced behaviors are trying to solve IS problems. Therefore, the hypotheses propose that information obtained from learning-to-try training (i.e., problem-solving training) and prompts will influence trying to solve IS problems, which will subsequently influence task performance (see the research model in Fig. 1).

H5: IS users who receive learning-to-try training will engage in more problem-solving behaviors (i.e., trying to solve IS problems).

H6: IS users who receive problem-solving prompts will utilize more problem-solving behaviors (i.e., trying to solve IS problems).

    H6a: IS users who receive prompts during initial IS usage and subsequently have prompts removed will utilize more problem-solving behaviors (i.e., trying to solve IS problems) than IS users who do not receive prompts.

    H6b: IS users who receive prompts during usage of an initial IS application will utilize more problem-solving behaviors (i.e., trying to solve IS problems) when utilizing a novel IS application than IS users who do not receive prompts.

H7: IS users who utilize more problem-solving behaviors (i.e., trying to solve IS problems) will have better task performance.

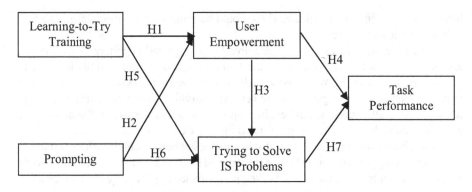

Fig. 1. Research model

4   Research Method

4.1   Overview

To test the research hypotheses, an experiment is proposed that will consist of four conditions in which subjects will/(won't) receive learning to try training (i.e., problem-solving strategies) and will/(won't) receive prompts (i.e., messages regarding strategies). Individuals will receive training for one IS application followed by training for a different IS application (to assess the generalizability of user empowerment and problem-solving behaviors). Transfer of stimulus control will be assessed by removing the prompts after the first IS application's initial use.

More specifically, to apply prompting and transfer of stimulus control, recommendations previously provided will be implemented as follows [7]:

1. Prompting strategy will be selected – prompts will include instructions and strategies for solving IS problems.
2. The learner's attention will be solicited by invoking a pop-up mechanism that the IS exercises are about to begin.
3. The IS exercise will be presented to the research participant.
4. If the research participant has not completed the exercise in a pre-established period of time, then a prompt with the instructions and strategies for solving IS problems will be provided.
5. When the research participant successfully completes the exercise, they will receive reinforcement in the form of a message that says congratulations on completing this exercise.
6. After subsequent exercises have been completed, transfer of stimulus control will occur by delaying the prompts.
7. As exercises are completed correctly, even without the presence of the prompt, congratulatory messages will continue to be displayed after correct completion of an exercise.

Learning-to-try training will consist of demonstrations of various problem-solving strategies that can be utilized when challenges arise using an IS application. The prompts will be messages displayed on the subjects computer screen reminding them of the various problem-solving strategies that they can utilize. The prompts will be provided to the assigned condition during the initial stages of the first IS application's use, but then subsequently removed as additional tasks are assigned to be completed. The proxy for trying to solve IS problems will be use of problem-solving behaviors. The software applications to be explored are Microsoft Excel and Access.

After receiving a series of problem-solving prompts, improvements will be determined by the use of problem-solving behaviors when a problem is encountered, less time to complete a particular task, and a greater number of tasks being accomplished accurately when using Excel before and after the prompts. After training for the second IS application (i.e., Microsoft Access), no additional learning to try training or prompts will be provided to assess the generalizability of problem-solving behaviors. Improvements in generalizability will be also be determined by the use of problem-solving behaviors when a problem is encountered, less time to complete a particular task, and a greater number of tasks being accomplished accurately when using Access.

4.2   Subjects

Undergraduate students will be recruited to participate who have minimal to no Microsoft Excel experience and no Microsoft Access experience. Hence, subjects will be more likely to encounter problems while completing Excel and Access exercises and need to engage in problem-solving behaviors to complete the exercises.

4.3   Procedures and Measures

Subjects will first complete a pre-study questionnaire to capture demographic information, sense of user empowerment, and need for cognition. Subsequently, subjects will receive Microsoft Excel training followed by problem-solving training or learning-to-try training for those in the training condition. Those not in the learning-to-try training condition will be provided information to review regarding the uses of Excel so that time will be equivalent in both conditions.

The subjects will then be asked to complete a set of Excel exercises. For those in the prompting condition, a prompt of various instructions and problem-solving strategies will be displayed for the subjects to use after a set period of time has passed. For subjects not in the prompting condition, no prompts or other messages during exercise completion will be provided. In all conditions, if an exercise is completed correctly, then the subject will receive a congratulatory message.

After a series of Excel exercises have been completed, subjects in the prompting condition will have a greater delay in receiving the prompt. The delayed timing of receiving the prompts will continue until the prompts are no longer displayed for the subjects to use.

Subsequently, all subjects will receive Microsoft Access training. Neither learning-to-try training nor prompts will be provided to any of the subjects to assess the generalizability of the problem-solving behaviors learned with the previous Excel training. Measurements will be taken of the number of problem-solving behaviors utilized, time to complete each exercise, number of exercises completed accurately before and after the prompts are provided during the Excel session and during the Access session. Subjects will be requested to complete a post-study survey to measure their sense of user empowerment, ability to solve Excel/Access problems, perceptions of the learning-to-try training, effectiveness of the prompts, ability to use problem-solving strategies with future uses of Excel/Access, and ability to use problem-solving strategies with novel applications.

5   Expected Contributions and Conclusion

The research proposed for this study intends to evaluate the use of behavioral training interventions (i.e., prompting and transfer of stimulus control) to improve perceptions of user empowerment and problem solving with software applications. Because abilities to conduct problem solving can vary among individuals, it's important to provide the appropriate resources and training to individuals to address IS problems. Also, considering the negative outcomes that can occur for those individuals who are unable to resolve or address a problem, this study can provide guidance in regards to the appropriate training and mechanisms that can be utilized to improve problem-solving and task performance.

Drawing upon Psychological Empowerment Theory, Theory of Trying, and Social Cognitive Theory, it's hypothesized that training and prompts will enhance users' sense of empowerment and problem-solving efforts, which will contribute to more positive task performance outcomes. This study will provide insight into the probability of increasing problem-solving behaviors when utilizing a software application with the use of specific behavioral training interventions and improvements in performance outcomes. Also, this research can shed light on the effects that specific problem-solving training can have on performance for existing IS and when using novel IS if problem-solving behaviors are generalized to new contexts. This study proposes to improve problem-solving behaviors by using a behavioral template in the form of a prompt, training users to perform problem-solving behaviors, and transfer stimulus control to the problem itself upon removal of the prompt.

Considering the increasing desire for self-directed training and greater proficiency in IS use, the need for IS users to independently solve IS problems continues to grow. This research proposes to evaluate the use of prompting and transfer of stimulus control to improve IS problem solving and task performance. The results may be taken into consideration when designing future IS training. Also, the results may be taken into consideration when designing help functions or learning aids, and the process of providing assistance when IS users encounter problems.

References

1. Sharma, R., Yetton, P.: The contingent effects of training, technical complexity, and task interdependence on successful information systems implementation. MIS Q. **31**(2), 219–238 (2007)
2. Compeau, D., Higgins, C.A.: Application of social cognitive theory to training for computer skills. Inf. Syst. Res. **6**(2), 118–143 (1995)
3. Yi, M.Y., Davis, F.D.: Developing and validating an observational learning model of computer software training and skill acquisition. Inf. Syst. Res. **14**(2), 146–169 (2003)
4. Webster, J., Martocchio, J.J.: Microcomputer playfulness: development of a measure with workplace implications **16**(2), 201–226 (1992)
5. Compeau, D.: The role of trainer behavior in end user software training. J. End User Comput. **14**(1), 23–32 (2002)
6. Chase, P.N.: Behavioral education: pragmatic answers to questions about novelty and efficiency. In: Lattal, K.A., Chase, P.N. (eds.) Behavior Theory & Philosophy, pp. 347–367. Kluwer Academic/Plenum Publishers, New York (2003)
7. Miltenberger, R.G.: Behavior Modification: Principles and Procedures, 4th edn. Thomson Wadsworth, Belmont (2008)
8. Billingsley, F.F., Romer, L.T.: Response prompting and the transfer of stimulus control: methods, research, and a conceptual framework. J. Assoc. Pers. Severe Handicap. **8**(2), 3–12 (1983)
9. Petscher, E.S., Bailey, J.S.: Effects of training, prompting, and self-monitoring on staff behavior in a classroom for students with disabilities. J. Appl. Bchav. Anal. **39**(2), 215–226 (2006)
10. Cuvo, A.J., Davis, P.K., O'Reilly, M.F., Mooney, B.M., Crowley, R.: Promoting stimulus control with textual prompts and performance feedback for persons with mild disabilities. J. Appl. Behav. Anal. **25**(2), 477–489 (1992)
11. Balsam, P.D., Deich, J.D., Ohyama, T., Stokes, P.D.: Origins of new behavior. In: O'Donahue, W.W. (ed.) Learning and Behavior Therapy, pp. 403–420. Allyn & Bacon, Boston (1998)
12. Spreitzer, G.M.: Psychological empowerment in the workplace: dimensions, measurement, and validation. Acad. Manag. J. **38**(5), 1442–1465 (1995)
13. Kim, H.W., Gupta, S.: A user empowerment approach to information systems infusion. IEEE Trans. Eng. Manag. **61**(4), 656–668 (2014)
14. Ahuja, M.K., Thatcher, J.B.: Moving beyond intentions and toward the theory of trying: effects of work environment and gender on post-adoption information technology use. MIS Q. **29**(3), 427–459 (2005)
15. Bandura, A.: Social Foundations of Thought and Action. Prentice Hall, Englewood Cliffs (1986)

Virtual World Versus Real World: An Economic Study of the Cyber Games Participation

Qingliang Fan[1], Xin Fu[2(✉)], and Shun Cai[2]

[1] Wang Yanan Institute of Studies in Economics, Xiamen University,
D312 Economics Building, Xiamen 361005, China
[2] School of Management, Xiamen University, Xiamen 361005, China
xfu@xmu.edu.cn

Abstract. In this paper, we examine the link between the virtual world attributes and real world economic variables. Specifically, we employ three cyber game attributes: playtime, in-game level and achievement (in terms of accomplished 'missions') as the measurements of cyber games participation. We explore the spatial variation of cyber game participation with respect to real world variables including gross regional product per capita, household dispensable income, unemployment rate, number of movie theaters per capita, etc. Moreover, we also study the effects of environmental variables such as precipitation, air pollution etc. on cyber games participation. Using the game data from a very popular cyber game in China and prefecture-level data in 2011, our empirical results show that the income and the availability of other leisure activities are negatively associated with cyber game participation.

Keywords: Cyber games · Consumption behavior · Economic impact · Human capital

1 Introduction

With the growing popularity of cyber games, relatively little attention has been paid to the economic analysis of cyber game participation. This paper aims to study how income level and other economic factors affect the cyber game participation. Different from other goods, such as [9] on coffee consumption and prices in the US, cyber game participation has its unique features. On one hand, playing too much games can deteriorate the player's health and human capital in the long run. On the other hand, cyber games, not different from other leisure activities, could help increase one's productivity. In the seminal paper on the theory of allocation of time, [3] laid the foundation of economic analysis of an economic agent's choice between leisure and production activities.

One of the key features of a virtual world is that the true identify of the players are usually concealed in the network. In this paper, we explore the relationship between cyber game participation and observable economic variables. E.g., how does cyber game participation rate affect local economic development?

F.F.-H. Nah and C.-H. Tan (Eds.): HCIBGO 2017, Part I, LNCS 10293, pp. 58–77, 2017.
DOI: 10.1007/978-3-319-58481-2_6

There might be two different motivations for the game players. First, like other games, cyber game is among the choices of leisure activities such as movies, concerts, etc. This is the relaxing and fun part of the game. Second, they try to 'escape reality'. The latter case raises a severe issue for human capital accumulation and could affect the economic growth in the long run. Cyber games could provide a shelter for some individuals to enjoy the virtual success (as measured by the game performance in our study) as the Chinese labor market is getting increasingly more competitive. We provide empirical evidence that people who have higher income would spend less time in playing cyber games, ceteris paribus. Also, we explore the relationship between cyber game participation with respect to the availability of substitutes such as movie theater, live music concert, performing art, professional sports games, etc., for cities with higher gross regional product per capita (GRPPC) are likely to have more options of after-work social activities. In addition, we explore whether unemployment or bad weather would affect the cyber game participation.

We here discuss briefly the representative features of cyber games that are distinct from other games. Cyber game (also called online games, online PC games, etc.) is a technology which connects players from the world wide web and enables them to play both competitively and cooperatively. Cyber games have the typical features of a virtual world: a synchronous, persistent network of people represented as avatars play different roles and interact with each other in the game. With the advancement of computer technology, cyber games are also becoming increasingly complex (in the perspective of characters design, balance of powers, strategic plays, etc.) and more visually enticing. The popularity of cyber games is accompanied by the rapid development of high speed Internet infrastructure and the increasing number of Internet users. For the consumer base, China has a big population of 'Netizens'. According to a recent report by China Internet Network Information Center, [6], China has approximately 649 million Internet users by 2014, which increases 2.1% than that of 2013, the Internet population rate reaches 47.9%. A big proportion of the Internet user population, especially young generation, play cyber games regularly. Cyber games have a big impact on Chinese youth, especially for male youth, which composed the majority of players population. It is reported in [5] that 65.4% of the players are male, and 66.8% of the players are young people who aged 10–29. They often play cyber games either at home, in Internet café or on smart phones. About 28.5% of these young players have college or higher degrees. Low-income or unwaged players play an important role in the gaming market, it accounts for 27.7% of the player population in 2013.

Gaming industry has developed significantly in China in recent years. The number of players and the market values of gaming industry are growing rapidly. According to the 2014 China Gaming Industry Report (an official report that is released by the Chinese Audio and Digital Game Community (GPC) annually), the number of players in the Chinese gaming market has reached 570 million by 2014, which increases 4.6% than that of 2013. Being the most popular and important game type, online PC game attained its advantages and has received a sales income of 60.89 billion RMB in 2014, which contributes to 53.19% of the total market incomes. Due to the device convenience, players are more likely to play mobile games to fill confetti time (e.g. waiting for a bus and queuing). Conversely, the players of PC games often have higher royalty of the game. The royal players are more willing to spend both time and money to get involved in PC games, purchasing additional virtual equipments and weapons which help players to increase their in-game competency, achieve higher in-game levels, or accomplish more interesting and challenging tasks.

Many researches focus on consumption behavior of conventional goods. In the empirical study of aggregated demand for cigarettes, [4] used a panel data of per capital consumption of cigarettes in state level. [8] studied demand for alcohol using survey data from the National Health Interview Study and find considerable heterogeneity in the price and income elasticities over the full range of the conditional distribution. [2] studied the rational consumption of tobacco using GMM method. [1] empirically studied the consumption of milk. Our study is the first to study how real world economic variables affect cyber game attributes using a novel dataset.

There would be potential endogenous problems with the income variable, since players of low income level would play more cyber games which in turn would affect future income. We employ the instrumental variable (IV) model to address this issue. We choose the freight volume per capita as the instrumental variable for income. Freight volume reflects the economic development of the region, we find a very strong positive correlation between the freight volume and average income of the region in our sample. On the other hand, the freight volume can only affect the behavior of playing cyber games indirectly and through the channel of income. Besides, the gaming data we have is gameplay telemetry in a month, while most of the real world economic variables are reported monthly and even annually. By taking the average of the daily cyber game data, we assume implicitly that the current level of game attributes are comparable among different prefectures. We also use quantile model to study the impact of control variable on different quantiles of cyber game participation.

The paper is organized as follows. In Sect. 2 we introduce the theoretical rational addiction model of the cyber game and the empirical model. Section 3 describes in details the data sources and variables. In Sect. 4 we provide and discuss the empirical results. Section 5 concludes this work and points out future work directions.

2   Model and Preliminaries

2.1   A Basic Economic Model

We here consider a very basic economic model. Assume the utility of an individual depends on two types of goods, the leisure activity goods A, here specifically the cyber games, and the non-leisure goods N. For simplicity, we assume the consumption set is composed of two goods, A and N, and N can be think of as a basket of goods other than A. We also assume the homogeneity of cyber games even though each game is not a perfect substitute of another game and continuity of the excess demand function. Moreover, the current utility also depends on the past consumption level of A, but not for N. The rational consumer's problem is to maximize the sum of lifetime utility discounted at a constant rate r, and denote $\beta = \frac{1}{1+r}$:

$$\sum_{t=1}^{\infty} \beta^{t-1} u(A_t, N_t, S_t) \tag{1}$$

where S is the stock of consumption capital of the individual, $u(\cdot)$ is a strongly concave function of A, N and S, and the past consumption of A affects current utility through the channel of 'learning by doing':

$$\Delta S = A_t - \delta S_t - h(D_t) \tag{2}$$

where $\Delta S = S_{t+1} - S_t$, δ is the instantaneous depreciation rate which measures the exogenous rate of disappearance of the physical and mental effects of past consumption of A, and D_t represents expenditures on endogenous depreciation or appreciation and $h(\cdot)$ is a real valued function. $C_t = N_t + P_t A_t$. Suppose I_0 is the initial value of wealth, C_0 is the initial condition indicating the level of goods A's consumption level at time 0. The utility maximization problem is subject to the following constraints

$$\sum_{t=1}^{\infty} \beta^{t-1} (N_t + P_t A_t) = I_0 \tag{3}$$

The first order conditions satisfy that the marginal utility of wealth is equal to the marginal utility of consumption of N_t in each period, denote $u(t) = u(A_t, N_t, S_t)$:

$$\frac{\partial u(t)}{\partial N_t} = I_t \tag{4}$$

And the marginal utility of current consumption of A, u_1 plus the next period's utility of today's consumption, u_2, equals $I_t P_t$, which is the marginal utility of wealth multiplies the current price of A:

$$\frac{\partial u(t)}{\partial A_t} + \beta \frac{\partial u(t+1)}{\partial A_t} = I_t \tag{5}$$

Assume that for a heterogeneous population H in each area (prefecture, in our case, and for simplicity of the notations we ignore the subscript i) there exists a finite partition $\{\chi_k\}_{k \in K}$ of the set $\mathbb{R}_+^H$ of all conceivable income assignments and for every $k \in K$ there is an aggregate demand function $F^k(P, G)$, where G denotes an income distribution function, such that

$$\frac{1}{|H|} \sum_{h \in H} f^h(P, x^h) = F^k(P, G_{x^h}) \tag{6}$$

for every nonnegative income assignment $x_{h \in H}^h$ in the set χ_k and for every $P \in \mathbb{P}$ which is any strictly positive price vector, and where $|H|$ is the number of population, $f^h(P, x^h)$ is the demand function for each individual $h \in H$ which is derived from the individual utility maximization problem.

2.2 The Empirical Model

The basic empirical model we consider in this section is

$$y_i = \alpha_i + \beta inc_i + \gamma X_i + \epsilon_i \tag{7}$$

where y_i is the variable of cyber game participation. We use three different variables to study the participation of cyber games in different dimensions. The playing time which is considered as the proxy for cyber game participation, the in-game level variable and achievement which is measured by the number of missions accomplished are the proxy for participation and performance of playing, respectively. The inc_i is dispensable income level of prefecture i, we also use GRPPC as income level proxy, X_i is a vector of other exogenous variables which are considered as the determinant of the cyber game variables, these variables include substitute goods, Internet penetration rate, unemployment rate, environmental variables such as rainfall, air pollution, etc.

Since the income variable could potentially affect other unobserved factors that also affect the average cyber games variable, we use the freight volume as an instrumental variable for income. From the economic model of cyber game participation, the income and other control variables would have different effects on different quantile of participation level. For example, for the higher quantile of playtime regions, there would be different preferences or habits and that would result in different impact of income. It is very plausible that the different quantile of playtime would response differently to the economic welfare and environmental variables. We therefore estimate a quantile regression model to identify the heterogeneous effects of income and other control variables across regions. The variables we consider in the quantile regression model is the same as in the aforementioned linear model [7].

3 Data Description

3.1 Dragon Nest

We use a realistic cyber game dataset from Dragon Nest[1] to investigate the proposed model. Dragon Nest is a free-to-play action Massive Multiplayer Online Role Playing Game (MMORPG) developed by *Eyedentity Games*[2]. The game incorporates a non-targeting combat system which provides players a fast paced action filled experience. Players have complete control over every single movement of their chosen character. The players are allowed to choose from a range of playable characters (e.g. Warrior, Archer, Cleric and Academic, etc.) to defeat

---

[1] http://dn.sdo.com/web9/home/index.asp.
[2] http://www.eyedentitygames.com/main.asp.

diverse monsters and other players. One player can have one or many characters in the game. Dragon Nest allows the players to initially play for free, but the players are encouraged to speed money in the game to explore and enjoy more game features, such as customized gear for the characters, mainly to increase the visual attractiveness for the characters.

Throughout the game, a number of designed tasks are provided in dungeons. In most MMORPGs, dungeon (often interchanges with the term *instance*) is defined as a private area where allows characters to team up and complete tasks without interference from other characters[3]. In dungeons, characters fight against groups of monsters using their skills and weapons. Dragon Nest also provides some more difficult and challenging tasks (known as missions in this game) for advanced players. Once the player accomplishes the mission, special honors or achievements will be given. Such honers/achievements would help to differentiate the player from other regular players and would be beneficial to enhance the player's reputation and influence in the virtual world. Accomplishing missions not only would help players to gain playing skills, but also to upgrade their in-game levels. Note that, Dragon Nest has an independent skill system, which indicates that a high level player is not necessarily a skillful player. A more experienced player that with a lower level can also overcome a less experienced player but with a higher level using his skills.

The Chinese version of Dragon Nest is published and operated by *Shengda Games*[4], one of the biggest and most successful game operators in China, since July 2010. In a few years, Dragon Nest has become one of the leading games of Shengda. Within 3 days of the official release, the number of Peak Concurrent Users (PCU) reaches 700,000[5]. In gaming industry, to attract and retain more players, game operators often employ some marketing strategies for product advertisements and promotions. The common promotion strategies include advertise the product in popular and authorized online game media (e.g. 17173[6] is renowned as the top game website in China), build player forum in the product official website and organize competitions regularly. Besides these online promotions, some offline marketing promotions are often employed by operators, especially at the beginning of the product launch. Practically, such regional promotions are often started from where the game operators geographically based. In the case of Dragon Nest, since *Shengda Games* is based in Shanghai, several promotions were held in Shanghai and the nearby cities.

3.2   The Cyber Game Data Set

The collected dataset contain one-month gameplay telemetry, from 1st March 2011 to 31st March 2011. In total, the game participation (including login details, playtime, social activities, achieved levels, coins, etc.) of 4,811,925 unique characters are collected. To reveal the relationship between the virtual world success

---

[3] http://www.wowwiki.com.

[4] http://www.shandagames.com/us-en/index.html.

[5] http://dn.178.com/201101/89835568248.html.

[6] http://www.17173.com/.

and real-world economic well beings, this study extracts the related information from two perspectives: (1) data from the virtual world - attributes that are associated with players' engagement and their in-game performances; (2) data from the real-world - for the given dataset, the unique attribute that relates to the real-world is the log-in IP. In this work, the virtual world success is measured by three representative gameplay attributes, namely the playtime, in-game level and achievement.

The raw dataset records every single login details, including character ID, login IP address, login timestamp and logout timestamp. Using this game log, the in-game playtime for a given character can be derived. As aforementioned, by accomplishing missions, players can upgrade their in-game level, the game server will automatically capture the every piece of game level update information (e.g. character ID, current level, new level, upgrade timestamp and map ID). The collected dataset includes the information of the completed missions, and the obtained achievements are also recorded. The three chosen gameplay attributes are defined as:

- playtime: this attribute refers to the aggregated game playtime for a given character during the observed time period (i.e. March 2011). Given a character, this attribute is derived from the login log by calculating each login time length and then aggregating them. The derived result is represented in Hour unit.
- in-game level: this attribute represents the achieved in-game level (i.e. the maximum recorded level) of a given character by the end of the observed time period (i.e. 31st March 2011). Note that, this attribute just indicates the current in-game level, but does not mean that the in-game levels are all achieved within the observed time period, as the level may be carried from previous months. In the released version of March 2011, the maximum in-game level of is 40. However, since Dragon Nest is a dungeon-driven game, reaching the maximum in-game level is not the end of the game. The main purpose of the game level-up is more like a tutorial to train the players using different skills and weapons, help them to get familiar with the game story and settings, and provide relative simple tasks for them to gain experiences and increase competency. In so doing, some players can quickly reach the maximum level, and then apply the obtained experiences and skills to accomplish more challenging missions in different dungeons.
- achievement: this attribute refers to the achievements that a given character obtained during the observed time period. The achievement is represented by the sum of the missions that a character accomplished in March 2011. It is important to note that the missions in Dragon Nest are with different difficulty levels. Obviously, the difficult mission would consume more time and resources to complete. However, due to the availability of the collected dataset, there is no associated information to distinguish the easy missions and difficult missions. In this work, the difficulty levels of completed missions are treated equally, only the number of accomplished missions are taken into account. This is a weakness of this work, and further investigations are required when the information of difficulty level become available.

Besides the attributes from the virtual world, we also use the Chinese IP library to convert the raw IP addresses captured in the login log to geo locations. This enables us to build the linkage between a virtual character and the location of real-life player, and the identified geo locations provide the basis for the further analysis of the related economic data.

3.3   Cyber Game Data Preprocessing

The raw data set contains $4,811,925$ unique characters and $11,552,998$ login records. Compared to other application domains, MMORPGs often result in relatively low player retention rate. For the vast majority of games, a significant proportion of players who signed up but never play the game at all. It has been reported that approximately 85% of players do not return after the first day, and game company should expect to lose 96% of their user base within 12 months [7]. This indicates that the raw data set includes loads of 'never-play' gamers information, but such information is beyond our research interests. For data preprocessing, first, this work employs a two-level filtering mechanism to filter out these players and select the ones who have spent sufficient amount of time to play the game. After the following filtering step, the number of characters reduces from $4,811,925$ to $64,448$. Specifically, we process the data as following:

- login level filtering: only the login duration that is longer than 10 min is regarded as a valid game-play login. This is because MMOPGs often require heavy user involvements than other types of games (e.g. mobile games). A simple task at least requires 5–10 min to complete and a dungeon would require longer. The raw login log may also capture some non-sense login details (e.g. the player suddenly loses the Internet connection, and the login duration is only a few seconds), and this step greatly reduces the volume of login log and would speed up the further computations and analysis.
- character level filtering: the login information will be aggregated according to the character IDs. Within the observed time period, the characters who either reach 60 login times or 30 h accumulative login time length will be retained for further analysis.

Second, for a given character, in principle, he/she may use different IP address to login the game. This may cause that the behavior of a single character being multiple counted when analyzing the collective behaviors for a given geo location. To address this, for each character, we initially list all identified geo locations that he/she has used for login, and then count the number of their login times. In this work, it is assumed that the most frequently used geo location is the place where a player actually based in the real-world. Hence, a one-to-one mapping table is derived to store the character ID and his/her the most frequent login geo location. In so doing, a character only contributes to the collective user behavior for a single geo location. In our data set we also have players from foreign countries outside China. Since the main focus of this paper is to study the relationship between playing game behaviors and Chinese prefecture variables, we deleted those players whose IP address is not from China. To reveal the relationship between virtual world success and real world economic well beings, all the in-game behaviors will be accumulated according to different geo locations. Given a geo location, the total number of based characters and their aggregated in-game performance will be calculated. Such data will then be used to derive the average playtime, in-game levels and achievement for a geo location. A summary of the pre-processed attributes is shown in Table 1. Figures 1 and 2 plot the geographic distributions of average play time and regional economic development in China, March, 2011.

Table 1. Summary of attributes

Dimensions	Attributes	Description
Data from the virtual world	Playtime	The accumulative game playing time for a given character
	Level	Achieved in-game level for a given character (min = 0, max = 40)
	Achievement	# of mission accomplished for a given character (min = 1, max = 675)
Data from the real-world	IP address	The originally recorded login IP address
	Geo location	The converted geo location for a given IP address
Aggregated data	Sum_character	# of included distinct characters in a given geo location
	Average_playtime	Given a geo location, the average playtime, it is derived from total_playtime/Sum_character (min = 0.17 h, max = 235.81 h)
	Average_level	Given a geo location, the average achieved in-game level, it is derived from total_level/Sum_character (min = 3, max = 40)
	Average_achievement	Given a geo location, the average number of accomplished missions, it is derived from total_mission/Sum_character (min = 1, max = 328)

At last, we sort the data according to prefectures and take the average of attributes as total quantity divided by the number of players in the prefecture.

3.4 Economic Data

Economic variables are from China Statistical Yearbook for Regional Economy (2012) and China City Statistical Yearbook (2012). The National Bureau of Statistics of China (NBSC) collects data from each prefecture and publishes them altogether each year. These two yearbooks have collected major social and economic indicators of China in 2011. We use GRPPC (gross regional product per capita) and per capita disposable income of urban households (Income) as proxy for income. The two variables are measured in the unit of 1000 RMB. We also control unemployment rate, Internet penetration rate, and the number of cinema per hundred people in the studied area. We use freight volume per capita as instrumental variable for income.

Meteorological data are from China Meteorological Data Sharing Service System of China Meteorological Administration. Data are reported by meteorological stations. We choose the data of each station to represent the level of its located prefecture. Data are collected on monthly precipitation and the number of days when daily precipitation is larger than 0.1 mm in March, 2011 (Days > 0.1 mm). Environmental variables are from China City Statistical Yearbook (2012). Data are collected on average API (air pollution index) which is measured as the arithmetic average of daily reported API of each city in March, 2011.

3.5   Summary statistics

Table 2 contains means, standard deviations and other statistics of the primary variables in the data set. The definitions of variables are given in the previous subsection.

Table 2. Summary Statistics

	Mean	Std. dev.	Median	Min	Max	Sample size
Login time	26.38	7.88	25.37	14.05	51.24	108
Mission	78.15	8.10	77.96	61.00	98.00	113
Level	26.41	2.91	26.12	20.68	32.25	112
Income	22.54	5.52	20.47	14.10	36.51	113
GRPPC	51.73	25.83	45.48	16.39	133.30	113
Cinema	3.77	3.31	2.75	0.43	17.65	113
Internet	37.21	17.12	34.88	10.18	74.95	113
Unemployment	3.18	0.81	3.30	0.70	5.40	113
Precipitation	26.21	30.04	15.90	0.00	135.50	113
Days > 0.1 mm	6.35	5.63	5	0	23	113
API	69.15	11.97	69.00	26.61	117.00	113

Notes: Income and GRPPC are measured in 1000 RMB, Internet and Unemployment are in %, and API is measured in $\mu g/m^3$

4   Empirical Results

In Table 3, we report the OLS results of login time on income and other control variables. We find that income level is negatively associated with cyber game participation. As the average income level increases by 1%, the average play time reduces by about 0.34 h (about 20 min) as shown in column (1). This result is robust to both income proxy variables, dispensable income and GRPPC. It shows that the unbalanced regional economic development level has significant impact on the cyber games participation. For high income regions, the opportunity cost

Ave_Login

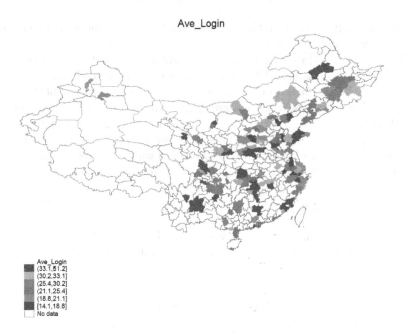

Fig. 1. Spatial distribution of average login time across 108 prefectures in China.

of playing cyber games are higher compared to low income area. In addition, metropolitans have more options for leisure activities such as concerts, shows, etc. It can be seen from column (5), which is our main model, that the higher numbers of movie theaters per person is correlated with less game time. The marginal effect of alternative leisure activities is very robust, with the coefficient being very close in magnitude and significantly negative as shown in columns (3)–(7). This shows the substitution effect of other leisure activities is strong for the average playing time. Notice that the income level is highly correlated with the number of movie theaters in our data, as shown in column (3) and (4), such that the coefficient of income variable is not significant if we only use movie as control. Unemployment rate is positively related to the playing time after controlling other variables. As the unemployment rate increase by 1%, the average play time increase by 0.06 h. This again supports the theory of time allocation: in aggregate level, the time spent on online games is negatively correlated with regular work. The environmental variables are not significant in the regression whether we use rainfall or air pollution variables. This environmental variable result shows that on the average level playing behavior is not affected by the outside environment.

Next, we turn attention to the achievement variable. Table 4 shows the regression results. Most importantly, the number of missions accomplished in the game is also negatively correlated with income level. An increase of 1% in income level, which is about 220 RMB for the sample average, is associated with the decrease of

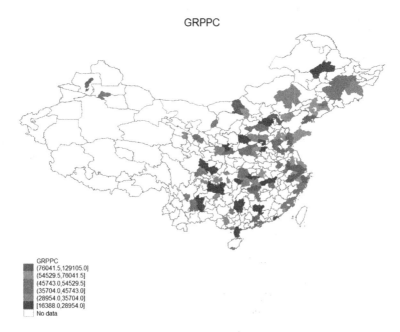

Fig. 2. Map of GRPPC of 108 prefectures in China. *Notes*: Figure shows a negative relationship between average playing time and GRPPC, this observation is formally studies in the following regression analysis.

Table 3. OLS estimation of login time

	Dependent variable: log average login time						
	(1)	(2)	(3)	(4)	(5)	(6)	(7)
Log income	−0.3436***		−0.2263*		−0.4848***		−0.3707**
	(0.1005)		(0.1294)		(0.1793)		(0.1671)
Log GRPPC		−0.1676***		−0.1116*		−0.2806**	
		(0.0507)		(0.0636)		(0.1079)	
Movie			−0.0644*	−0.0664*	−0.068*	−0.0732**	−0.0695*
			(0.0359)	(0.0348)	(0.0354)	(0.0339)	(0.0364)
Int. penetration rate					0.5586**	0.7357**	0.4464*
					(0.2564)	(0.2974)	(0.2504)
Unemployment					0.0612*	0.068**	0.0672*
					(0.0329)	(0.0335)	(0.0344)
Precipitation					0.0013		
					(0.0009)		
Days > 0.1 mm						0.0037	
						(0.0043)	
Log API							−0.061
							(0.125)
Observations	108	108	108	108	108	108	108
R-squared	0.0747	0.0728	0.0994	0.1003	0.1657	0.1795	0.1501
p-value of F test	0.0009	0.0013	0.0002	0.0004	0.0001	0.0001	0.0001

Notes: Standard errors are reported in parentheses. Significance levels 0.1, 0.05 and 0.01 are noted by *, ** and *** respectively. Intercept are included but not reported.

Table 4. OLS estimation of mission

	Dependent variable: log average mission						
	(1)	(2)	(3)	(4)	(5)	(6)	(7)
Log income	−0.0981*** (0.0349)		−0.0558 (0.0402)		−0.1612** (0.0670)		−0.1336** (0.0661)
Log GRPPC		−0.0406*** (0.0149)		−0.0197 (0.0186)		−0.0943*** (0.0331)	
Movie			−0.0230** (0.0116)	−0.0253** (0.0123)	−0.0261** (0.0116)	−0.0284** (0.0122)	−0.0268** (0.0118)
Int. penetration rate					0.2574*** (0.0881)	0.3260*** (0.0970)	0.2302*** (0.0870)
Unemployment					0.0334*** (0.0103)	0.0364*** (0.0109)	0.0344*** (0.0103)
Precipitation					0.0003 (0.0003)		
Days > 0.1 mm						0.0004 v	
Log API							−0.0112 (0.0719)
Observations	113	113	113	113	113	113	113
R-squared	0.0489	0.0367	0.0758	0.0707	0.1950	0.2070	0.1870
p-value of F test	0.0058	0.0075	0.0023	0.0012	0.0001	0.0000	0.0001

Notes: Standard errors are reported in parentheses. Significance levels 0.1, 0.05 and 0.01 are noted by *, ** and *** respectively. Intercept are included but not reported.

0.10 of accomplished missions. As it shows in column (5), the coefficient increase in magnitude to 0.16 after we control for more variables. It suggests that the average performance, or game-playing 'productivity' is higher in lower income regions. Performance in cyber games is related to human capital, as the game-playing requires many skills that reflect human capital. However, the higher performance in cyber games does not translate to higher local economic development level. On the contrary, it shows the opposite association. This might infer the negative effect of playing cyber games in China, though we need to investigate more in the link between playing cyber games and income level. Internet penetration rate and unemployment are positively related to missions. Similar to the study of playing time, environmental variables are not significant here.

For level data, the OLS regression results are not very significant except for that of income and substitute effects. The underlying issue with the level data is that level does not reflect the quality of players in respect to playing skills. Also, some players who already achieved level 40 in our sample which is the maximum level one can get from playing this game. But the player can keep accomplishing new missions after achieving level 40. And even for players whose level is not yet 40, the level variables are accumulative and current level depend heavily on when the players starts to play the game. The starting time is unfortunately not recorded in our data. All relationships between the three LHS variable and RHS control variables are shown in Figs. 3, 4 and 5.

In summary of the OLS results, there are substantial evidence that after controlling for other determinant of cyber game participation, the coefficient of income is negative, which suggests that on prefecture-level, the effect of income

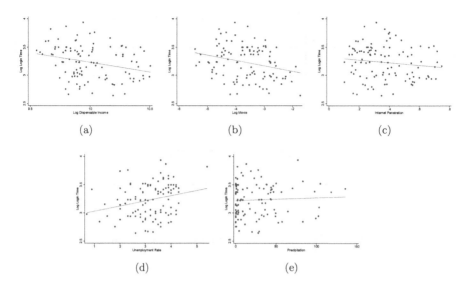

Fig. 3. Scatter plot of login time and control variables

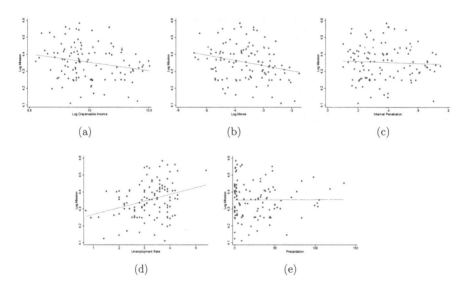

Fig. 4. Scatter plot of achievements and control variables

on cyber game participation is negative. It could imply that cyber game participation significantly decreases with the increase in income level (Table 5).

The estimation on the effect of income on cyber game participation might be biased by the problem of reverse causality and omitted variables. To address the endogeneity concerns, we employ the instrumental variable freight volume which is exogenous to cyber game participation but is correlated with regional income

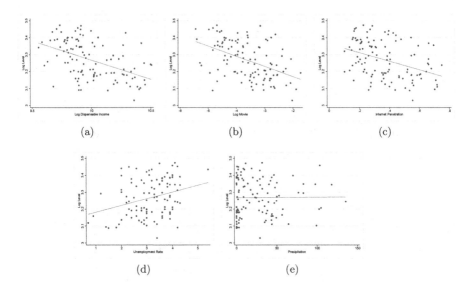

Fig. 5. Scatter plot of level and control variables

Table 5. OLS estimation of level

	Dependent variable: log average level						
	(1)	(2)	(3)	(4)	(5)	(6)	(7)
Log income	−0.2275***		−0.1552***		−0.1677***		−0.1309**
	(0.0372)		(0.0460)		(0.0637)		(0.0632)
Log GRPPC		−0.0981***		−0.0613***		−0.0567*	
		(0.0161)		(0.0193)		(0.0326)	
Movie			−0.0392***	−0.0439***	−0.0380***	−0.0419***	−0.0385***
			(0.0135)	(0.0131)	(0.0134)	(0.0134)	(0.0136)
Int. penetration rate					0.0411	0.0174	0.0130
					(0.0789)	(0.0966)	(0.0765)
Unemployment					0.0152	0.0194	0.0183
					(0.0123)	(0.0117)	(0.0129)
Precipitation					0.0003		
					(0.0003)		
Days > 0.1 mm						0.0004	
						(0.0004)	
Log API							−0.0545
							(0.0442)
Observations	112	112	112	112	112	112	112
R-squared	0.2334	0.1884	0.3027	0.2784	0.3195	0.2963	0.3216
p-value of F test	0.0000	0.0000	0.0000	0.0000	0.0000	0.0000	0.0000

Notes: Standard errors are reported in parentheses. Significance levels 0.1, 0.05 and 0.01 are noted by *, ** and *** respectively. Intercept are included but not reported.

level. Our findings are mostly robust as shown in Table 6 using instrumental variable method. Specifically, income is significantly negatively associated with playing time. Substitutes, Internet access and unemployment all have significant and the signs agree with previous OLS findings. Similar results are also for game

Table 6. 2SLS estimation on impact of cyber game attributes

	Login time		Mission		Level	
	(1)	(2)	(3)	(4)	(5)	(6)
Log income	−0.2142**		−0.3956*		−0.2408	
	(0.1060)		(0.2235)		(0.1733)	
Log GRPPC		−0.5299***		−0.1225		−0.0701
		(0.2040)		(0.0822)		(0.0811)
Movie	0.0015	−0.0029**	−0.0011*	−0.0010**	−0.0003	−0.0008**
	(0.0024)	(0.0012)	(0.0006)	(0.0004)	(0.0006)	(0.0004)
Int. penetration rate	0.2033**	0.1299**	0.3786*	0.3786*	0.0452	−0.0027
	(0.1013)	(0.0517)	(0.2648)	(0.2081)	(0.1555)	(0.0254)
Unemployment	0.0137	0.0580*	0.0274*	0.0360***	0.0156	0.0210
	(0.0547)	(0.0351)	(0.0151)	(0.0117)	(0.0145)	(0.0121)
Precipitation	0.0041*	0.0006	0.0001	0.0004	0.0001	0.0001
	(0.0021)	(0.0008)	(0.0005)	(0.0001)	(0.0001)	(0.0001)
Observations	108	108	113	113	112	112
R-squared	0.0807	0.1585	0.0894	0.2016	0.2595	0.2428

Notes: Standard errors are reported in parentheses. Significance levels 0.1, 0.05 and 0.01 are noted by *, ** and *** respectively. Intercept are included but not reported.

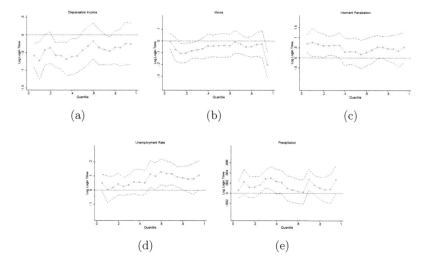

(a)   (b)   (c)

(d)   (e)

Fig. 6. Quantile regression estimates: login time. *Notes*: Figure graphs the estimated effect of income, substitute goods, etc., on the log of average login time at each quantile of the conditional distribution of the log of average login time and the associated 95% confidence interval.

performance measured by missions. The results are not significant for levels partly due to the aforementioned reasoning.

For the quantile regression results, Table 7 shows that the income is negative and significant in lower quantiles of cyber game participation after controlling for other variables. The result is not significant for higher quantiles as seen in Fig. 6. This means that the effect of income is not very significant for the higher quantile of participation in the perspective of login time. And also that for lower

Table 7. Quantile regression results for login time

	Quantiles				
	5th	25th	50th	75th	95th
Log income	−0.5801***	−0.5705***	−0.4353	−0.453*	−0.2526
	(0.2056)	(0.2124)	(0.3199)	(0.2425)	(0.3522)
Movie	−0.0023	−0.082**	−0.0399	−0.0501	−0.2039***
	(0.039)	(0.0403)	(0.0606)	(0.046)	(0.0668)
Int. penetration rate	0.7156***	0.6129**	0.3158	0.5397*	0.5343
	(0.2721)	(0.2811)	(0.4234)	(0.3209)	(0.4662)
Unemployment	0.0499	0.026	0.1138**	0.093**	0.1052*
	(0.0367)	(0.0379)	(0.057)	(0.0432)	(0.0628)
Precipitation	0.0006	0.0017*	0.001	0.0016	0.0027
	(0.001)	(0.001)	(0.0015)	(0.0011)	(0.0017)
Observations	108	108	108	108	108
Pseudo R^2	0.1331	0.1086	0.0965	0.0684	0.1415

Notes: Standard errors are reported in parentheses. Significance levels 0.1, 0.05 and 0.01 are noted by *, ** and *** respectively. Intercept are included but not reported.

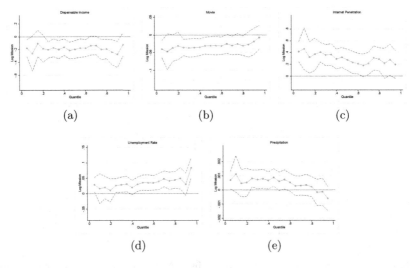

(a)   (b)   (c)

(d)   (e)

Fig. 7. Quantile regression estimates: mission. *Notes*: Figure graphs the estimated effect of income, substitute goods, etc., on the log of average login time at each quantile of the conditional distribution of the log of average login time and the associated 95% confidence interval.

quantiles, the absolute value coefficient of income is significantly higher than the higher quantiles. Therefore players in the lower quantiles of playing cyber games is more responsive to income level. We find it interesting that substitute activities such as movies are significant in lower quantile, but not so in higher quantile. Furthermore, for the highest quantile, it is significant again. Given the small sample size in the highest quantile, this result could be affect by a

Table 8. Quantile regression results for mission

	Quantiles				
	5th	25th	50th	75th	95th
Log income	−0.1772**	−0.2058***	−0.2002**	−0.2018**	−0.1252
	(0.0808)	(0.0770)	(0.0841)	(0.0967)	(0.1098)
Movie	−0.0404***	−0.0355**	−0.0302*	−0.0255	−0.0070
	(0.0149)	(0.0142)	(0.0155)	(0.0178)	(0.0203)
Int. penetration rate	0.4154***	0.4054***	0.2743**	0.3063**	0.1938
	(0.1052)	(0.1001)	(0.1095)	(0.1257)	(0.1428)
Unemployment	0.0291**	0.0263*	0.0362**	0.0419**	0.0839***
	(0.0144)	(0.0137)	(0.0150)	(0.0173)	(0.0196)
Precipitation	0.0007*	0.0008**	0.0006	0.0004	−0.0006
	(0.0004)	(0.0004)	(0.0004)	(0.0005)	(0.0005)
Observations	113	113	113	113	113
Pseudo R^2	0.1496	0.1222	0.1346	0.1359	0.1527

Notes: Standard errors are reported in parentheses. Significance levels 0.1, 0.05 and 0.01 are noted by *, ** and *** respectively. Intercept are included but not reported.

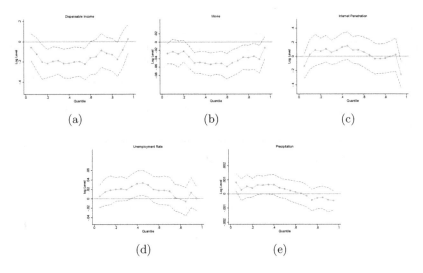

(a)   (b)   (c)

(d)   (e)

Fig. 8. Quantile regression estimates: level *Notes*: Figure graphs the estimated effect of income, substitute goods, etc., on the log of average login time at each quantile of the conditional distribution of the log of average login time and the associated 95% confidence interval.

few dominant regions. Or it could imply that for the very high quantile, movie or other substitute goods are becoming relevant again due to the fact that the game eventually lose its attractiveness to its top players which is very common in most cyber games. The cyber game company usually promote new games every two or three years to accommodate the decline of interests of its players. For lower quantile of cyber game participation, the Internet penetration rate is also

Table 9. Quantile regression results for level

	Quantiles				
	5th	25th	50th	75th	95th
Log income	−0.0560	−0.1942**	−0.19772**	−0.1176	0.0266
	(0.0813)	(0.0882)	(0.0868)	(0.0970)	(0.0873)
Movie	−0.0277*	−0.0355**	−0.05112***	−0.0365**	−0.0137
	(0.0150)	(0.0163)	(0.0160)	(0.0179)	(0.0161)
Int. penetration rate	−0.1373	0.1080	0.0894	−0.0329	−0.2555**
	(0.1060)	(0.1150)	(0.1132)	(0.1265)	(0.1139)
Unemployment	0.0054	0.0213	0.02932*	0.0021	0.0006
	(0.0145)	(0.0157)	(0.0155)	(0.0173)	(0.0156)
Precipitation	0.0008**	0.0006	0.0004	−0.0004	−0.0005
	(0.0004)	(0.0004)	(0.0004)	(0.0005)	(0.0004)
Observations	112	112	112	112	112
Pseudo R2	0.1731	0.1819	0.2404	0.1842	0.1152

Notes: Standard errors are reported in parentheses. Significance levels 0.1, 0.05 and 0.01 are noted by *, ** and *** respectively. Intercept are included but not reported.

significant. Unemployment rate has significant influence on the higher quantiles. Weather variable is in general not significant except for some lower quantiles. This means the rainfall e.g., would have some impact on the infrequent players.

The quantile results of achievement is similar to the finding of login time as shown in Table 8. All control variables have significant impact on the lower quantile and most are insignificant for the very high quantiles. We find that income is mostly negative and significant as shown in Fig. 8(a). Substitute goods is significantly negatively correlated to achievements in lower quantiles but not in higher quantiles. Weather variable is showing some significantly positive correlation in the lower quantiles also.

As the reasons stated in OLS regression results, level variable has some problems in being a good proxy for game performance. We could still observe the income and substitute has significant impact for lower quantiles. Other control variables are not significant for most quantiles with few exceptions (Table 9).

5   Conclusion

This paper uses the gaming data and economic data to empirically analyze the participation of cyber games. Using a prefecture-level Chinese data in 2011, our empirical results show that the income level is negatively associated with game participation, while other economic variables and environmental variables have more impact on the lower quantiles. The substitution effect of other leisure activities are strongly negative to the participation of cyber games. We check the robustness of the results using different regression models and measurements of participation including playing time, level and achievements. The study of individual level data and the weather's impact on the individual player's performance would be an interesting future research topic.

Acknowledgments. This work is supported by the National Natural Science Foundation of China (No. 71671149, 71631004 (Key Project), 71301133, 71572166, and 71202059), Natural Science Foundation of Fujian Province of China (No. 2016J01340) and the Fundamental Research Funds for the Central Universities (Project No. 20720161044).

References

1. Auld, M.C., Grootendorst, P.: An empirical analysis of milk addiction. J. Health Econ. **23**, 1117–1133 (2004)
2. Baltagi, B.H., Griffin, J.M.: The econometrics of rational addiction. J. Bus. Econ. Stat. **19**(4), 449–454 (2001)
3. Becker, G.S.: A theory of the allocation of time. Econ. J. **75**(299), 493–517 (1965)
4. Becker, G.S., Grossman, M., Murphy, K.M.: An empirical analysis of cigarette addiction. Am. Econ. Rev. **84**(3), 396–418 (1994)
5. CNNIC: 2013 Chinese online gamer behaviour analysis report (2013). http://www.cnnic.cn/hlwfzyj/hlwxzbg/wybg/201402/P020140228346868241995.pdf
6. CNNIC: The 35th china internet development statistical report (by Jan 2015) (2014). http://www.cnnic.cn/hlwfzyj/hlwxzbg/hlwtjbg/201502/P020150203548852631921.pdf
7. Debeauvais, T., Nardi, B., Schiano, D.J., Ducheneaut, N., Yee, N.: If you build it they might stay: retention mechanisms in world ofwarcraft. In: Proceeding of the 6th International Conference on the Foundations of Digital Games (FDG 2011), pp. 1–8 (2011)
8. Manning, W.G., Blumberg, L., Moulton, L.H.: The demand for alcohol: the dierential response to price. J. Health Econ. **14**, 123–148 (1995)
9. Olekalns, N., Bardsley, P.: Rational addiction to caffeine: an analysis of coffee consumption. J. Polit. Econ. **104**(5), 1100–1104 (1996)

Challenges in Research Generalizability: The Need for Standardization of Performance Metrics and Methodology

Kathryn A. Feltman[1,2(✉)], Kyle A. Bernhardt[1,2], and Amanda M. Kelley[1]

[1] U.S. Army Aeromedical Research Laboratory, Fort Rucker, AL, USA
{kathryn.a.salomon2.ctr,kyle.a.bernhardt2.ctr,
amanda.m.kelley.civ}@mail.mil
[2] Oak Ridge Institute for Science and Education, Oak Ridge, TN, USA

Abstract. The proliferation of psychological and psychophysiological metrics, data collection techniques, and data analysis strategies used throughout psychological research of operator performance presents cross-study synthesis complications. Currently, the lack of defined and established standardizations in psychological and psychophysiological research continues to present challenges to researchers studying an array of interrelated constructs. Without standardizations, differences in measurement implementation, data reduction techniques, and the interpretation of results make it difficult to directly compare studies and reach unequivocal conclusions while synthesizing literature and transfer laboratory findings to field-ready applications.

Keywords: Psychophysiological · Subjective · Standardization · Generalizability

1 Introduction

Scientists and researchers in all fields require, to some degree, standardization of the methodologies and measurements used in order to generalize and compare findings. The field of psychology, including psychophysiology and cognitive science, is challenged by the often times unobservable, latent constructs studied. While psychophysiological measurements and methods have been well established, their integration into research on emerging technologies, particularly those studied in applied environments, is ongoing. Of particular interest to the military aviation research community are measurements that may be integrated into the vehicle to provide real-time monitoring of the operator's state (e.g., fatigued, cognitive overload). In order to make advancements in this area, standardization of cognitive and subjective measures for purposes of determining construct validity as well as standardization of methodology for psychophysiological measures (e.g., data reduction) is needed. This will allow the community of researchers to more easily interpret findings relative to their own work and ultimately drive towards solutions to the shared mission.

Presently, several researchers and journals have begun examining the issues surrounding a lack of standardized methods, to include problems in replicability, the need for adequately powered studies, and increased openness and transparency in research (e.g., [1–3]) within the fields of psychology, neuroscience, and

© Springer International Publishing AG 2017
F.F.-H. Nah and C.-H. Tan (Eds.): HCIBGO 2017, Part I, LNCS 10293, pp. 78–89, 2017.
DOI: 10.1007/978-3-319-58481-2_7

psychophysiology. These, and other articles are a great reference for researchers looking to follow research best practices. The present paper will focus more closely on the problems of standardization and generalizability in regards to applied research. Researchers working in applied settings, such as military and government funded laboratories, rely highly on the ability to integrate other researchers' findings into research that can be used to solve specific and applied problems. However, the ability to do so with accuracy requires that the literature drawn upon follows some degree of standardization and has generalizable results. This paper examines this issue in the specific context of incorporation of cognitive and psychophysiological measures into operator monitoring in military settings.

2 Need for Similarity of Subjective and Cognitive Measures

The volume of valid and reliable cognitive tests and measures available for researchers is substantive. Often, the decision of which instruments to employ is determined by a number of factors in addition to psychometric properties: setting of data collection/experiment, limitations on time, equipment required, limitations on physical space, availability of trained test administrators, and cost. While there are certainly benefits to an expansive library of assessments to choose from, the degree of comparability across studies can be compromised thus resulting in misleading conclusions or seemingly contradictory results between studies. An example of this is the focal point of a recent publication on the operational definition of mild cognitive impairment following transient ischaemic attack and stroke [4]. The authors illustrate how different valid and accepted methodologies for determining mild cognitive impairment (i.e., three different cut-off scores from a neuropsychological test battery) led to varied results and conclusions including a diverse set of resultant incidence rates and relative risk ratios. Similarly, the International Collaboration on Mild Traumatic Brain Injury (mTBI) Prognosis published its recommendations with respect to methodological challenges in research [5]. Their comprehensive and critical review of the literature from 2001–2012 found 66 different operational definitions of mTBI in 101 articles regarding mTBI prognosis. The interchangeable use of the parallel terminology given to this vast expanse of definitions ultimately impedes effective communication among researchers as well as overall knowledge advancement.

Inconsistencies in subjective and cognitive measures across the literature produce difficulties in creating a standardized approach to studying phenomenon of interest to the military community. For example, the different branches of the military often face similar research questions, such as how to counteract fatigue in sustained operations. While different laboratories may utilize different approaches in studying the topic (e.g., one laboratory looking into medications to promote sleep, another laboratory looking into medications to promote wakefulness) inconsistency of measures used to determine fatigue levels will create difficulties in applying and comparing results between laboratories. By using a standardized set of subjective or cognitive measures when assessing a construct such as fatigue or cognitive workload, comparisons between laboratories become possible. Standardized approaches to research regarding physiological monitoring are also lacking, particularly in regards to applied settings such as military research. For example, a number of different researchers utilize different procedures in physiological data collection, which can also result in inconsistencies in findings and an inability to generalize results.

3 Methodological Differences in Psychophysiological Research

While several articles related to best practices of psychophysiological measurement exist (e.g., see: [6, heart rate variability; 7, electroencephalography; 8, respiration]), different methods for collecting psychophysiological data continue to persist throughout the literature. While there are often several practical reasons for using different methodology, such as different electrode placement to reduce the likelihood of movement artifacts in a study where participants are ambulatory or in a vehicle (e.g., [9]), the different methods used create inconsistency in research practices, particularly when examining the same underlying concept. For example, three separate articles each examined cognitive workload through cardiovascular activity to assess physiological changes in response to changes in task demands [10–12]. The three articles each reported either a different electrode lead placement, or did not report electrode placement at all. The most commonly recommended lead placement for psychophysiological research is a three-lead placement, based on Eintho-ven's triangle theory [13]. However, different lead placements are frequently observed in research articles, such as leads applied to the sternum or leads applied to the clavicles and lower left or right rib.

Furthermore, lead placement should be determined with consideration of the type of data analyses planned, such as a researcher planning to examine heart rate variability (HRV) data, which is frequently seen within the literature for a means of assessing operator cognitive state. The ability to obtain meaningful data for HRV analyses is dependent on the integrity of cardiac signal collected [6]. The quality of signal that is detected is influenced by where the leads are placed [14]. When considering the transition of laboratory monitoring into field-deployable monitoring, standardized methods of data collection, including lead placement, will assist in the interpretability and proper analyses of the data that is collected from any given location and thus increase the generalizability of the results. Improper meas-urement techniques may result in the adequate collection of meaningful data, which can then obscure the results and reduce the generalizability of the findings to other settings [15]. This is a point that researchers who are looking to move physiological monitoring from within the laboratory to field settings should keep in mind. For example, one study compared three mobile ECG recording devices for measuring R-R intervals and HRV, and found that the HRV analyses obtained by the devices were inconsistent and not recommended for use within research applications [16]. Thus, care should be taken in determining methods to be used for ECG data collection, including determination of electrode placement and recording devices, and standardized methods should be used as the science of identifying operator state through physiological monitoring is still in its infancy.

Similarly, several studies of workload and engagement using electroencephalography (EEG) have reported the use of different electrode sites for data analyzed. Some examples of different electrode sites used included the following: F3, F4, C3, and C4 [17]; Cz, Pz, P3, and P4 [18]; and Fz, Pz, O1, and O2 [9]. Each of these studies provide valuable information and insight into brain activity in response to various tasks; however, with a goal of moving towards psychophysiological measures that can be used to monitor an operator's state in real-time, examining the same EEG sites is paramount to progress. For example, in a recent article Cohen [19] discusses that researchers should strive to find a balance between replicating previous findings and producing new ones. The reproduction of existing findings will provide further support for the use of real-time monitoring of operators, when researchers can demonstrate that specific electrode sites reliably result in changes in response to certain cognitive activity, which can then be transitioned into practice.

The effects that can result when different methods are used in psychophysiological research were highlighted in an article by Caccioppo and Tassinary [20]. In this classic article discussing the use of physiological measures in psychological research, the authors highlight a study where the psychophysiological measurement was electrodermal response. Here it was shown that the conclusions drawn from the data differed depending on how the electrodermal response was expressed. Specifically, "when the electrodermal response was expressed in terms of the change in skin resistance, one individual (Subject A), appeared to show a response equal to that of another (Subject B). When the electrodermal response was expressed in terms of the change in skin conductance, however, Subject B appeared to show the stronger response to the stimulus. Thus, conclusions about the physiological effects of the stimulus were completely dependent on the measurement procedure used" (p. 17). This is similarly seen within EEG research, where the placement of the reference electrode can impact the quality and subsequently the interpretations and waveform analyses of the data recorded [21].

In addition to consistent electrode placement, researchers must also be careful to ensure that they are indeed manipulating the psychological construct they wish to assess. This was noted early by Ekman [22] in an article discussing that reliable differentiation of emotions through physiological measurements has been difficult to obtain given that a variety of additional emotions were likely elicited in the attempt to assess physiological response of the target emotion. Indeed, this problem persists today if researchers are not careful in their manipulations. For example, in a study examining the physiological response of the vigilance decrement, Pattyn and colleagues [23] discuss the different findings in vigilance research where some studies demonstrate a physiological response similar to "cognitive overload" (e.g., a decrease in heart rate variability) whereas others, including themselves, find a physiological response similar to that of "underload." These differences have been attributed to differences in event rates of the vigilance task, such that studies with higher event rates show a more characteristic overload response. Determining and properly manipulating the construct that researchers wish to address through physiological monitoring becomes a key concern with the continued research interest of real-time monitoring of operator state. That is, various laboratories studying this topic need to be certain they are identifying the same operator state in order for developed countermeasure technologies to be effectively implemented in operational settings outside of the laboratory. The issue of proper manipulation is critical not only for the validity and reliability of the data collected during the testing period, but also for the data that is collected during the baseline period as well.

4   Baseline Data Collection

The nature of collecting psychophysiological measurements to determine the state of an operator requires a comparison from the time period of interest to some baseline state. For example, in order to determine via physiological sensors if an operator is exhibiting signs of overload, a comparison must be made between the condition in which the operator is said to be overloaded and one in which he/she is in a normal, non-overload state. This baseline measurement allows researchers to observe physiological changes in response to specified stimuli, conditions in a flight simulator, or field mission phases [24]. Classically, baseline measurements have been implemented in two forms: *resting* (e.g., [25]) and *vanilla* [26]. A resting baseline entails that the participant remains in a wakeful, but relaxed, state and not exposed to the stimuli of interest for a predetermined duration. Logically, a resting baseline seeks to measure the lowest physiological activity; that is, to record a "basal" or "tonic" state to which experimental condition data are compared [24]. A vanilla baseline refers to measurements that are made while participants are performing a low demand version of the task [26]. Some researchers utilize a practice session of the task as a vanilla baseline. Other baselining methods have been proposed on the principle of regression to the mean. The logic implies that over repeated sampling from an individual's "population" of potential physiological responses, a stable mean estimate of that individual's normative state can be obtained [27]. For example, a *comprehensive* baseline refers to a baseline period consisting of a resting period, task instruction period, and a task practice period. Moreover, an *against-self* baseline has also been proposed. The against-self method utilizes the entire set of data for a participant (baseline, practice, and experimental task) and calibrates the experimental data section of interest against these data [27].

Researchers must critically examine several issues when selecting an appropriate baseline technique. For example, participants may experience anxiety in anticipation of performing the experimental task, resulting in an elevated physiological state. Gramer and Sprintschnik [28] evaluated the cardiovascular activity of participants before having to give a 5-min public speech. For participants that were informed of the task, the anticipation of waiting to perform the speech increased blood pressure. Similarly, Davidson, Marshall, Tomarken, and Henriques [29] found elevated heart rate when individuals were in the anticipation stage of having to give a speech, with those possessing characteristics of social phobia exhibiting a larger increase in heart rate. Thus, depending on the individual, some may experience elevated physiological baseline activation prior to performing a task. This situation may very well extend into military laboratories using aviators as subjects. Flight simulations are often manipulated to induce stressful flight conditions. For instance, simulator weather modifications, such as high winds and reduced visibility, produce higher workload flights for pilots [30]. Consequently, if an aviator becomes aware of a potentially difficult flight, he/she may exhibit increased pre-flight physiological arousal and skew baseline measurements.

Moreover, studies have reported the tendency of resting baseline measures to fluctuate over time. In their study, Gramer and Sprintschnik [28] reported slight increases in participant cardiac measures over time, even before the anticipation manipulation. It has also been shown that measures of resting baseline activity in the cardiovascular system can vary from day to day as well [31, 32]. Wet electrode electrodermal activity recordings may also display a drift during baseline acquisition and may require an adaption period before any data recording begins [33]. With these fluctuations, there is significant variation as to how long a baseline period should last. Recommendations of at least 10 min [26], but upwards of 15 min [36], for a resting baseline have been reported. Vanilla baselines of 10 min have also shown relatively good stability [26]. Stern and colleagues [24] give the recommendation that the resting baseline period should be, "long enough to provide a stable pre-stimulus level and long enough to provide sufficient data for appropriate analysis" (p. 50). Moreover, Keil et al. [34] stated, "The choice of baseline period is up to the investigators and should be appropriate to the experimental design" (p. 5). Thus, when examining the literature, one may find an extensive range of baseline recording lengths making results somewhat difficult to interpret between studies.

Other than length of the baseline period, the choice of baseline procedure can influence conclusions researchers draw from their data. In research that is attempting to classify operator states accurately, the baseline procedure used will likely, to some degree, influence the outcome of augmented cognition systems (e.g., adaptive automation) to accurately detect changes in the operator state relative to baseline. More specifically, the selection of a certain baseline technique can overemphasize changes particular operator state and underemphasize others [27]. This point was communicated by Fishel and colleagues [27] in an examination of baseline techniques in relation to real-time physiological monitoring of operators. Take, for example, two operator states considered to be anchored at two different physiological poles: overload and fatigue. High workload situations are typically accompanied by physiological arousal, while fatigue is accompanied by physiological depression [35]. Baselines of the opposite physiological pole may exaggerate operator states that lie in the other direction. That is, a resting baseline would be more sensitive to detecting physiological changes associated with an overload state and a vanilla/practice baseline would be more sensitive to detecting physiological changes associated with a fatigued state. On the other hand, baselines that are of a similar polarity would tend to underemphasize a response. For instance, a resting baseline would tend to be relatively insensitive to detecting a fatigue state accompanied by physiological deactivation because of the already low physiological arousal of the resting baseline.

Indeed, Fishel et al. [27] empirically explored whether resting and practice (vanilla) baselines overemphasized high workload and low workload states compared to the against-self method. In their study, participants underwent several physiological baseline procedures before performing a shooting task (high demand) and a surveillance task (low demand). Results indicated that, compared to the against-self method, the resting baseline technique showed a significant bias for detecting cardiac arousal on the shooting task. In contrast, the practice baseline demonstrated a significant bias to detecting lower cardiac arousal during the surveillance task compared to the against-self method. Thus, this study demonstrates how the methodological selection of a baseline can bias data to detect certain operator states.

From the above discussion, it can be inferred that the selection of physiological baselining procedures can severely hamper the comparison of results across studies and laboratories. Assume that two hypothetical military laboratories are each using measures of the cardiovascular system to support detecting changes in workload during simulated flights. Further assume Laboratory A decides to use a resting baseline to calibrate their data and

Laboratory B decides to use a task-practice baseline procedure. In general, Laboratory A is more likely to detect positive changes in workload than Laboratory B. That is, Laboratory B may fail to detect cardiac changes associated with increased cognitive workload more so than Laboratory A. Even though each laboratory may be testing under similar flight parameters and independent variable manipulations, the outcome results may not be comparable across laboratories and appear to be fairly inconsistent. In an applied setting, this inferred inconsistency has the potential to misinform decision makers and policy writers.

5   Data Analyses and Data Reduction

How the data itself is examined can play a crucial role in the replicability and generalizability of the research. The differences in data analyses become most apparent when examining the use of baseline data. Keil et al. [34] stressed that the removal baseline activity may result in distortions of electrophysiological data especially if experimental groups show differential activation patterns. Many psychophysiological researchers agree that baseline data is necessary to collect in order to determine changes in physiological response; however, a brief review of psychophysiological research quickly yields differences in how the baseline data collected was actually used in analyses. For example, some studies report baseline data being used to normalize the physiological measures collected throughout the study, by calculating the ratio of the average processed recording data and the baseline data (e.g., [9, 12]), whereas others report the use of baseline data as a comparison point for the remainder of data collected (e.g., report a change in baseline [36]).

Differences in methods used for data reduction and signal processing can also impede the generalizability of psychophysiological data relates to methods of data collection and data reduction. The sampling rate of psychophysiological signals can be found to vary from study to study within the literature. In an article examining different sampling rates when using respiratory sinus arrhythmia as a measure of heart rate variability, Riniolo and Porges [37] highlight that the importance of using the proper sampling rate, as the sampling rate chosen significantly affects "the ability to quantify accurately the amplitude of RSA because a slow sampling rate would be insensitive to small gradations when the amplitude of RSA is low" (p. 619). Thus, different sample rates can result in differences in the quality of data collected. Based on the Nyquist theorem [38] a sample should be taken at twice the maximum frequency expected to be encountered. Sample rates for different measures will naturally vary, such that changes in electrodermal or respiration activity are slow and can be sampled at lower rates, whereas changes in electrocortical or heart activity occur quicker and must be sampled at higher rates. Although it is not considered improper practice to sample physiological data at different rates (e.g., one researcher sampling HRV data at 256 Hz, with another sampling at 500 Hz), these differences will present alterations in the resolution and quality of the data [39], such that sampling HRV at 500 Hz would result in a greater resolution and more accuracy than a lower sampling rate. Weiergräber and colleagues [41] discuss some of the implications of differences in EEG sampling rates, and provide recommendations for best practices to follow. Additionally, they discuss that changes to sample rates can result in faulty frequency data and invalid results. Specifically, if sampling rates do not adhere to the Nyquist theorem, the frequency reconstruction becomes invalid and interpretations of the data may become false. Weiergräber and colleagues [41] identify that a review of the literature of EEG studies revealed that EEG recordings were being done outside of the technical range of the equipment used, thus resulting in invalid analyses. Thus, it is crucial for researchers to understand the importance of sampling rates in regards to the variables of interest (e.g., examining gamma waveforms vs. alpha waveforms).

Filtering and data reduction practices are also integral not only to the replicability of research, but the quality of the findings reported. The methods that researchers use to preprocess data and remove artifacts can vary from study to study, thus changing the possible quality of data analyzed and presented. In Cohen's [19] recent article on replication and rigor in electrophysiology research, he discusses some of the problems surrounding artifact removal. Specifically, he highlights cautions to be considered when using algorithms for artifact removal, and recommends manual cleaning of the data over algorithms. However, the practicality of such manual methods may not be feasible in applied research where the goal is to develop field-ready devices that process data in real time. It may be the case that more research on the validity of electrophysiological artifact decontamination algorithm development needs to become available to the general research community.

6   Conclusions and Recommendations

While technology continues to advance at a rapid pace, with increased capabilities to monitor the physiological changes of an individual in a variety of settings, the need to maintain scientific integrity through standardized measurement techniques is paramount. Increased interest in continuous, real time monitoring of operators to either inform adaptive automation [41], monitor performance to assist in system design [42, 43], or to be used in training evaluation [44], requires first the ability to reliably identify the operator state through the desired metrics. This, of course, relies on the use of standardized measures and methods that can be applied across studies, scenarios, and laboratories. Through the use of standardized research practices, we will be able to advance from the laboratory to the field. Several other articles are available that provide thorough reviews and recommendations of how researchers can work towards conducting research that is rigorous and replicable, for which the reader is highly encouraged to peruse (e.g., [1–3]). However, in regards to conducting applicable and scientifically useful research that can be used for future implementation of real-time operator monitoring, a few suggestions are outlined below.

Researchers are encouraged to conduct thorough literature reviews, as well as engage in discussions with fellow researchers in the field to determine the best cognitive and subjective measures to use when assessing a specific cognitive construct. Researchers should do the same for determining how to properly design tasks that assess the cognitive construct they want to examine through physiological measurement. Indeed, both of these are encouragements for researchers to engage in some replicability of previous findings. In order for research to transition from strictly laboratory-based findings to technology that can be used in an operationally relevant manner (i.e., operator state monitoring through physiological assessment to determine pilot cognitive overload) there needs to be a consistency in the literature that reliably identifies that subjective measurement A, as well as psychophysiological measurement devices B and C, always produce X change in data when the individual is placed in Y situation. Without such reproducible data, difficulties in transitioning research findings to applied settings will persist.

With respect to physiological baseline techniques, researchers should be cognizant of the underlying construct's essential nature. That is, some constructs are associated with physiological activation and some are associated with physiological deactivation. Researchers should carefully evaluate and justify their decision to utilize a certain baseline technique as opposed to using a technique out of convention. More importantly, in applied field research, the choice of baseline technique should reflect the operator's normal operating state. This prevents an introduction of positive or negative bias in operator state detection observed when polarized baseline techniques (e.g., resting) are used [27]. In general, applied researchers are less interested in changes from a resting state, but rather departures from a state in which the operator is under a normal operating progression. The former provides a basis for developing theory and generating research hypotheses, while the latter has direct implications for augmented system development and countermeasure deployment. Researchers should be explicit in their choice of baseline technique and provide a sound justification for employing the technique. Additionally, researchers should report and justify how experimental data were adjusted for baseline values (e.g., simple subtraction, change scores). Keil et al. [34] provides a thorough publication checklist for researchers using EEG methods, which includes baseline technique reporting.

Similar recommendations hold true for decisions in regards to sampling rates, data preprocessing, and data reduction. However, researchers are also encouraged to be open and detailed in their methodology used (see [19] for examples). Additionally, while researchers are sometimes constrained by either equipment or environment for the sampling rates they use in data collection, an explanation of why the decision was made to accept a lower sampling rate is encouraged, as well as a discussion on impacts that it may have had on the data quality, so that readers are fully aware of the reasoning behind such a decision.

The current state of the literature oftentimes shows divergent findings (e.g., variability in physiological response in measuring cognitive workload based on differences such as task length [45] or event rates [23]) on physiological measures of a cognitive construct, such as cognitive workload, which only further points to the need to follow similar research designs and protocols. This is also commonly seen in medical literature when an agreed-upon definition of a condition does not yet exist. This becomes essential as the field begins to transition into using devices that leave less of a "footprint" (e.g., reducing EEG measurements to just four electrodes). In order to be able to make the determination that only certain electrode sites are needed for detecting a change in cognitive workload, or that one psychophysiological measurement is enough to reliably detect a change in operator state, further work that demonstrates the reproducibility of this research is needed, and not only within laboratory settings, but also in operational settings.

References

1. Open Science Collaboration: estimating the reproducibility of psychological science. Science **349** (2015) http://dx.doi.org/10.1126/science.aac4716
2. Button, K.S., Ioannidis, J.P.A., Mokrysz, C., Nosek, B.A., Flint, J., Robinson, E.S.J., Munafò, M.R.: Power failure: why small sample size undermines the reliability of neuroscience. Nat. Rev. Neurosci. **14**, 365–376 (2013)
3. Larson, M.J.: Commitment to cutting-edge research with rigor and replication in psychophysiological science. Int. J. Psychophysiol. **102**, ix–x (2016)
4. Pendlebury, S.T., Mariz, J., Bull, L., Mehta, Z., Rothwell, P.M.: Impact of different operational definitions on mild cognitive impairment rate and MMSE and MoCA performance in transient ischaemic attack and stroke. Cerebrovasc. Dis. **36**(5–6), 355–362 (2013)
5. Kristman, V.L., Borg, J., Godbolt, A.K., Salmi, L.R., Cancelliere, C., Carroll, L.J., Holm, L.W., Nygren-de Boussard, C., Hartvigsen, J., Abara, U., Donovan, J., Cassidy, J.D. Methodological issues and research recommendations for prognosis after mild traumatic brain injury: results of the international collaboration on mild traumatic brain injury prognosis. Arch. Phys. Med. Rehab. **95**(3), S265–S277 (2014)
6. Berntson, G.G., Bigger, J.T., Eckberg, D.L., Grossman, P., Kaufmann, P.G., Malik, M., Nagaraja, H.N., Porges, S.W., Saul, J.P., Stone, P.H., van der Molen, M.W.: Heart rate variability: origins, methods, and interpretive caveats. Psychophysiology **34**, 623–648 (1997)
7. Pivik, R.T., Broughton, R.J., Coppola, R., Davidson, R.J., Fox, N., Nuwer, M.R.: Guidelines for the recording and quantitative analysis of electroencephalographic activity in research contexts. Psychophysiology **30**, 547–558 (1993)
8. Ritz, T., Dahme, B., Dubois, A.B., Folgering, H., Fritz, G.K., Harver, A., Kotses, H., Lehrer, P.M., Ring, C., Steptoe, A., Van de Woestijne, K.P.: Guidelines for mechanical lung function measures in psychophysiology. Psychophysiology **39**, 546–567 (2002)
9. Ryu, K., Myung, R.: Evaluation of mental workload with a combined measure based on physiological indices during a dual task of tracking and mental arithmetic. Int. J. Ind. Ergon. **35**, 991–1009 (2005)
10. Bonner, M.A., Wilson, G.F.: Heart rate measures of flight test and evaluation. Int. J. Aviat. Psychol. **12**(1), 63–77 (2002)
11. Durantin, G., Gagnon, J.F., Tremblay, S., Dehais, F.: Using near infrared spectroscopy and heart rate variability to detect mental overload. Behav. Brain Res. **259**, 16–23 (2014)
12. Hsu, B.W., Wang, M.J.J., Chen, C.Y.: Effective indices for monitoring mental workload while performing multiple tasks. Percept. Mot. Skills **121**(1), 94–117 (2015)
13. Berntson, G.G., Quigley, K.S., Lozano, D.: Cardiovascular psychophysiology. In: Cacioppo, J.T., Tassinary, L.G., Berntson, G.G. (eds.) Handbook of Psychophysiology, pp. 182–210. Cambridge University Press, New York (2007)
14. Kligfield, P., Gettes, L.S., Bailey, J.J., Childers, R., Deal, B.J., Hancock, W., van Herpen, G., Kors, J., Macfarlane, P., Mirvis, D., Pahlm, O., Rautaharju, P., Wagner, G.S.: Recommendations for the standardization and interpretation of the electrocardiogram. Circulation **115**, 1306–1324 (2007)
15. Strube, M.J., Newman, L.C.: Psychometrics. In: Cacioppo, J.T., Tassinary, L.G., Berntson, G.G. (eds.) Handbook of Psychophysiology, pp. 789–811. Cambridge University Press, New York (2007)
16. Weippert, M., Kumar, M., Kreuzfeld, S., Arndt, D., Rieger, A., Stoll, R.: Comparison of three mobile devices for measuring R-R intervals and heart rate variability: Polar S810i, Suunto t6 and an ambulatory ECG system. Eur. J. Appl. Physiol. **109**(4), 779–786 (2010)

17. Di Stasi, L.L., Diaz-Piedra, C., Suárez, J., McCamy, M.B., Martinez-Conde, S., Roca-Dorda, J., Catena, A.: Task complexity modulates pilot electroencephalographic activity during real flights. Psychophysiology 52(7), 951–956 (2015)

18. Fairclough, S.H., Venables, L., Tattersall, A.: The influence of task demand and learning on the psychophysiological response. Int. J. Psychophysiol. 56, 171–184 (2005)

19. Cohen, M.X.: Rigor and replication in time-frequency analyses of cognitive electrophysiology data. Int. J. Psychophysiol. 111, 80–87 (2017)

20. Cacioppo, J.T., Tassinary, L.G.: Inferring psychological significance from physiological signals. Am. Psychol. 45(1), 16–28 (1990)

21. Pizzagalli, D.A.: Electroencephalography and high-density electrophysiological source localization. In: Cacioppo, J.T., Tassinary, L.G., Berntson, G.G. (eds.) Handbook of Psychophysiology, pp. 56–84. Cambridge University Press, New York (2007)

22. Ekman, P., Levenson, R.W., Friesen, W.V.: Autonomic nervous system activity distinguishes among emotions. Science 221, 1208–1210 (1983)

23. Pattyn, N., Neyt, X., Henderickx, D., Soetens, E.: Psychophysiological investigation of vigilance decrement: Boredom or cognitive fatigue? Physiol. Behav. 93, 369–378 (2008)

24. Stern, R.M., Ray, W.J., Quigley, K.S.: Psychophysiological Recording. University Press Inc., New York (2001)

25. Pollak, M.H.: Heart rate reactivity to laboratory tasks and ambulatory heart rate in daily life. Psychosom. Med. 53, 25–35 (1991)

26. Jennings, J.R., Kamarck, T., Steward, C., Eddy, M., Johnson, P.: Alternate cardiovascular baseline assessment techniques: vanilla or resting baseline. Psychophysiology 29(6), 742–750 (1992)

27. Fishel, S.R., Muth, E.R., Hoover, A.W.: Establishing appropriate physiological baseline procedures for real-time physiological measurement. J. Cogn. Eng. Decis. Making 1, 286–308 (2007). doi:10.1518/15553407X255636

28. Gramer, M., Sprintschnik, E.: Social anxiety and cardiovascular responses to an evaluative speaking task: The role of stressor anticipation. Personality Individ. Differ. 44, 371–381 (2008). doi:10.1016/j.paid.2007.08.016

29. Davidson, R.J., Marshall, J.R., Tomarken, A.J., Henriques, J.B.: While a phobic waits: regional brain electrical and autonomic activity in social phobics during anticipation of public speaking. Biol. Psychol. 47(2), 85–95 (2000). doi:10.1016/S0006-3223(99)00222-X

30. Hart, S.G., Bortolussi, M.R.: Pilot errors as a source of workload. Hum. Factors 26(5), 545–556 (1984)

31. Miller, S.B., Ditto, B.: Cardiovascular responses to an extended aversive video game task. Psychophysiology 25(2), 200–208 (1988). doi:10.1111/j.1469-8986.1988.tb00988.x

32. Miller, S.B., Ditto, B.: Individual differences in heart rate response during behavioral challenge. Psychophysiology 26(5), 506–513 (1989). doi:10.1111/j.1469-8986.1989.tb00701.x

33. Boucsein, W., Fowles, D.C., Grings, W.W., Ben-Shakhar, G., Roth, W.T., Dawson, M.E., Filion, D.L.: Publication recommendations for electrodermal measurements. Psychophysiology 49(8), 1017–1034 (2012). doi:10.1111/j.1469-8986.2012.01384.x

34. Keil, A., Debener, S., Gratton, G., Junghofer, M., Kappenman, E.S., Luck, S.J., Luu, P., Miller, G.A., Yee, C.M.: Committee report: publication guidelines and recommendations for studies using electroencephalography and magnetoencephalograph. Psychophysiology 51(1), 1–21 (2014)

35. Borghini, G., Astolfi, L., Vecchiato, G., Mattia, D., Bablioni, F.: Measuring neurophysiological signals in aircraft pilots and car drivers for the assessment of mental workload, fatigue, and drowsiness. Neurosci. Biobehav. Rev. 44, 58–75 (2014). doi:10.1016/jneubiorev.2012.10.003

36. Mehler, B., Reimer, B., Coughlin, J.F., Dusek, J.A.: Impact of incremental increases in cognitive workload on physiological arousal and performance in young adult drivers. Transp. Res. Rec. **2138**, 6–12 (2009)

37. Riniolo, T., Porges, S.W.: Inferential and descriptive influences on measures of respiratory sinus arrthymia: sampling rate, R-wave trigger accuracy, and variance estimates. Psychophysiology **34**, 613–621 (1997)

38. Nyquist, H.: Certain topics in telegraph transmission theory. IEEE Trans. Commun. **47**, 617–644 (1928)

39. Bolek, J.E.: Digital sampling, bits, and psychophysiological data: A primer, with cautions. Appl. Psychophys. Biofeedback **38**(4), 303–308 (2013)

40. Weiergräber, M., Papazoglou, A., Broich, K., Muller, R.: Sampling rate, signal bandwidth and related pitfalls in EEG analysis. J. Neurosci. Methods **268**, 53–55 (2016)

41. Parasuraman, R.: Neuroergonomic perspectives on human systems integration: mental workload, vigilance, adaptive automation, and training. In: Boehm-Davis, D.A., Durso, F.T., Lee, J.D. (eds.) APA Handbook of Human Systems Integration, pp. 163–176. American Psychological Association, Washington, DC (2015)

42. Warm, J.S., Parasuraman, R., Matthews, G.: Vigilance requires hard mental work and is stressful. Hum. Factors **50**(3), 433–441 (2008)

43. RTO human factors, medicine panel task group: operator functional state assessment. Technical report, Research and Technology Organization (2004)

44. Borghini, G., Aricò, P., Graziani, I., Salinari, S., Sun, Y., Taya, F., Bezerianos, A., Thakor, N.V., Babiloni, F.: Quantitative assessment of the training improvement in a motor-cognitive task by using EEG, ECG, and EOG signals. Brain Topogr. **29**, 149–161 (2016)

45. Stuiver, A., Brookhuis, K.A., de Waard, D., Mulder, B.: Short-term cardiovascular measures for driver support: increasing sensitivity for detecting changes in mental workload. Int. J. Psychophysiol. **92**, 35–41 (2014)

The Adoption of Physiological Measures as an Evaluation Tool in UX

Vanessa Georges[1(✉)], François Courtemanche[1], Sylvain Sénécal[1],
Pierre-Majorique Léger[1], Lennart Nacke[2], and Romain Pourchon[1]

[1] HEC Montréal, Montréal, Canada
vanessa.georges@hec.ca
[2] University of Waterloo, Waterloo, Canada

Abstract. One of the challenges associated with the use of physiological signals as an evaluation tool in measuring user experience (UX) is their reduced usefulness when they are not specifically associated with user behavior. To address this challenge, we have developed a new evaluation tool which contextualizes users' physiological and behavioral signals while interacting with a system. We have conducted interviews with 11 UX practitioners, from various industries, to evaluate the usefulness of our tool. Through these interviews we gained a better understanding of the challenges facing industry practitioners when using physiological measures and assessed the functionalities provided by our tool.

Keywords: User experience · Interface design · Heatmaps · Eyetracking · Physiological computing · Cognitive load · Affective computing

1 Introduction

User experience (UX) has recently become of strategic importance in the information technology industry [14]. The Tech3Lab is an applied research lab in human-computer interaction at the HEC Montréal business school, specializing in user experience using eyetracking and neurophysiological and behavioral measures. Our research pertains to the development of new evaluation methods, ones that investigate the why instead of the how as information on how users feel about a system, game, or web interface is now a common requirement for all UX evaluation methods [5].

Our recent work with our industry partners has lead us to question a major discrepancy between industry and academic practices: while physiological measures are increasingly used in academia, the adoption of these methods as UX evaluation tools remains uncommon in industry. We have observed a growing demand for more quantitative user research to provide data-driven recommendations for change, which we implement using eyetracking and neurophysiological and behavioral measures. We therefore wanted to understand what can be done to facilitate their adoption in industry. In tackling this issue, we have sought to create a visualization tool that contextualizes physiological and behavioral signals to facilitate their use [4]. The visualization method that we created is UX heatmaps, an integrated visualization tool which contextualizes

© Springer International Publishing AG 2017
F.F.-H. Nah and C.-H. Tan (Eds.): HCIBGO 2017, Part I, LNCS 10293, pp. 90–98, 2017.
DOI: 10.1007/978-3-319-58481-2_8

physiological and behavioral signals to facilitate the interpretation of these measures [12].

2   Physiological Measures in UX

Traditional evaluation methods other than direct observation, for example questionnaires or interviews, mostly rely on self-reported data to assess the affective and cognitive states of users either during or after the interaction [6]. For example, Hassenzahl et al. have developed a questionnaire to evaluate users' feelings about a system [11]. The results assess the user's reflection on the interaction, but not the interaction itself [13]. Users' emotional and cognitive states can also be inferred using physiological signals, such as electrodermal activity, heart rate, eyetracking and facial expressions (see [2, 3] for reviews). As an evaluation method, electrodermal activity (EDA), which measures the electrical conductance of the skin, can provide practitioners with real-time information as to what the user is experiencing throughout the interaction. EDA is used as an indication of physiological arousal [8], as well as emotions. FaceReader [7], which analyzes facial expressions and infers the probability of seven discrete emotions (happy, sad, angry, surprised, scared, disgusted and neutral) and emotional valence (negative vs. positive) based on facial movements, can provide important temporal information without retrospective or social desirability bias. Furthermore, data is collected without interrupting the user in their authentic interaction.

However, these measures are still difficult to contextualize and interpret, as they are not specifically associated with user behavior or interaction states. Let's take the example of a user asked to browse the product offerings of an e-commerce website and purchase an item. With physiological data, we can infer that the user was frustrated at some point during the interaction, for example during the checkout process, but not the element that caused the negative emotion. We are therefore left wondering what was the button, task or area of the interface which caused the user to feel frustrated or angry. Physiological signals also require a certain degree of interpretation, as the output needs to be processed to transition from raw data to useful actionable insights. To meet these challenges, Kivikangas et al. [15] have developed a triangulation system to interpret physiological data from video game events. Other researchers have also developed tools that allow users' to manually assign subjective emotional ratings on visual interfaces [9] or to visualize emotional reactions using biometric storyboards [10].

While these research streams have produced interesting results, they are not easily transferable to new contexts of use, as they are based on internal information from the interactive system (e.g., video game logs, application events, or areas of interest). To address these issues, we developed a new visualization method, in the form of heatmaps, which highlights the areas where users were looking when they experienced specific cognitive and emotional states with a higher frequency, called UX heatmaps [12].

2.1   Physiological Heatmaps

To produce physiological heatmaps, different emotional (sadness, happiness, surprise, etc.) and cognitive (cognitive load, stress, etc.) states are first inferred from continuous physiological or behavioral signals. These states are then triangulated with eyetracking data and mapped onto an interface to create heatmaps. In other words, physiological data, for example electrodermal activity and heart rate (HR) are synchronized together, along with eyetracking data. A machine learning model is then used to infer an emotional or cognitive state for each gaze. These are then mapped out onto the interface in the form of heatmaps, which in turn highlight the areas where users tend to emotionally or cognitively react more strongly. Figure 1 illustrates heatmaps generated by participant 01 during our session. On the top interface, a negative valence (red) and positive valence (yellow) heatmaps are shown. The web page below, a cognitive load heatmap is presented.

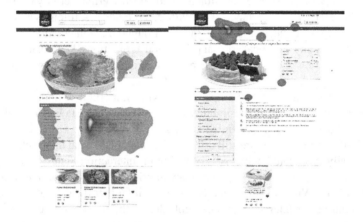

Fig. 1.   On the left-hand side, negative valence (red) and positive valence (yellow) heatmaps. On the right, a cognitive load heatmap (blue) is illustrated. (Color figure online)

3   Research Method

For this study, a total of 11 UX practitioners and consultants were recruited over a period of 4 weeks. None of the practitioners interviewed had seen our tool prior to the test. Each interview lasted about 1 h and a half, during which participants were asked to complete a UX evaluation report using the tool following a variation on the think aloud protocol, cooperative evaluation [16]. During the sessions, participants were asked to talk through what they were doing. The interviewer also took on a more active role, by asking questions along the way (e.g. 'why?' 'what do you think would happen?'). Participants were encouraged to ask for explanations along the way.

3.1 Pre-task Interview

We started each session with a preliminary interview to get background information on each participant (see Fig. 2), such as their number of years of experience in UX as well as their title and main functions within their company, to break the ice and assess their level of qualification. We then gathered their thoughts on physiological measures as a UX evaluation method and assessed their level of familiarity with such methods. Participants had between 2.5 and 24 years of experience in UX, for an average age of 8 years. We interviewed UX directors, consultants, ergonomists and strategists, all of which had heard of physiological measures as an evaluation method in user testing before being approached for this experiment; 7 out of the 11 participants had heard about it while in school, validating the predominance of these methods in academia. Out of all the UX practitioners recruited for this experiment, 8 had previously used physiological measures prior to the study. Eyetracking, being the most popular method overall, was mentioned by all; followed by FaceReader with 3 mentions.

Fig. 2. Experimental procedure.

3.2 Physiological Measure Introduction and Tutorial

After the introductory discussion, all participants were given a short PowerPoint presentation to introduce them to physiological measures, and were given a tutorial on the tool itself. To do so, we presented each participant with the tool, and went through all the functionalities, buttons and features available to them. We wanted the users to have the same basic knowledge and comprehension of the tool and measures before using it in the completion of a UX evaluation report. The interviewer assisted the participant throughout the experiment, as the goal of the session was not to assess the usability of the tool's interface, but the usefulness of its features and functionalities.

3.3 Evaluation Task

During the session, practitioners were asked to complete a user testing evaluation report using our UX heatmaps tool. We therefore provided them with a partially completed Power-Point report and a 15 participant data set from a previous study. The PowerPoint report included a study summary, a research scenario and qualitative data. We believed this would help UX experts integrate the information on physiological measures quickly and effectively, and also give them a concrete opportunity to use the tool to envision themselves using it in their own practice. First off, participants were briefed on the task at hand, before going through the partially completed report with the interviewer, to put them into context and get a sense of what was required of them. Participants had to complete a total of 2 PowerPoint slides. They were asked to: (1) generate and select data visualizations to include in their report using our tool, (2) interpret the results and (3) provide recommendations to the client.

The remainder of the time was used to discuss the advantages and disadvantages of physiological measures as an evaluation method, as well as the tool itself.

4   Results

Participants made interesting comments regarding physiological measures and our tool, which we will address in the following section. We are only reporting comments made by 3 or more participants. Interviewees mentioned the following as the ways in which they would use our tool in their own practice:

- Provide new avenues for research
- Form and confirm research hypotheses
- Guide discussions during interviews
- Confirm and validate findings
- Elaborate evaluation tests

The main contribution of our tool, as stated by 5 participants, is the comparison and the juxtaposition of different emotional and cognitive states. As participant 07 explained, "there are simply no other tools available that make this essential data accessible to us". Participants also mentioned the collaborative potential of our tool. The visualizations generated could be used communicate information to the various members of the design team, as well as with clients and management. For example, participant 10 suggested that the visualization generated could be shared with designers for them "to better understand the impact of their creative freedoms on the user".

4.1   Data Contextualization and Interpretation

Our goal in creating our tool was to address one of the main concerns associated with the use of physiological measures, the interpretation of physiological and behavioral signals. We set out to do these interviews with industry practitioners to find out how we fared at the task. Overall, participants found physiological heatmaps easy to interpret. As six participants mentioned, the visualizations were clear, intuitive and wielded powerful results that facilitated the interpretation of physiological signals.

Users stated that our tool was also easy to understand from a client's perspective. For example, participant 08 felt that customers would appreciate seeing the emotions generated by problematic areas directly onto the interface, adding "it goes beyond qualitative insight". Two participants found the interpretation of the data to be difficult without prior knowledge of physiological measures, one practitioner adding "the learning curve is relatively mild; the analysis should become more natural with time".

As illustrated in Fig. 3, participants were able to make insightful and actionable recommendations based on the visualizations generated with our tool; on the left, a gaze (green), a positive (yellow) and negative valence (red) heatmaps generated by P04. Although the focal element of the page was the text area below, the image clearly elicited positive emotions, while negative emotions or displeasure was experienced by users in correlation to the instructions of the recipe. By comparing regions of negative and positive valence, the

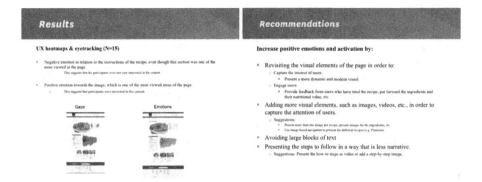

Fig. 3. An example of a completed report by a participant, translated from French to English (Color figure online)

practitioner identified problematic areas of the interface and was able to highlight the graphical elements behind them. Based on these results, the practitioner recommended to increase positive emotions and arousal experienced on the page by adding visual elements, such as videos and pictures, and revising the presentation of the recipe's instructions to avoid superfluous text areas.

When asked about their intent to reuse the tool, 10 out of the 11 practitioners interviewed stated that they would use the tool in their practice. However, when inquired further, 6 of them declared that their use of the tool would depend on the projects, using it only in the assignments where emotions are an important component or if clients specifically requested them to use physiological signals.

5   Discussion

When developing new UX evaluation tools using physiological measures, the ability to locate issues, the ease of use and interpretation and the reduction of analysis time represent important factors. Overall, participants found that physiological signals would be integrated more easily into their practice using our tool. Participants suggested the following improvements to UX heatmaps to further facilitate the adoption of physiological measures their current practice:

- The addition of an event timeline, or replay feature, to better understand overlapping UX heatmaps, to see the order in which the different emotional and cognitive states occurred. This would help with the interpretation of the visualizations.
- The inclusion of supplementary information, collected from traditional UX methods, such as participants' profiles and usability metrics. This would help them to integrate physiological methodologies more easily to the methods they currently use in their practice.
- The automatization of certain functions, such as groups and layer creation, to accelerate the interpretation of the visualizations generated with our tool. This would help them fit this analysis within their short development cycles.

Although our tool makes physiological measures more accessible to UX practitioners by addressing the interpretation of signals, there remains a lot of work to be done regarding some of the more technical aspects of physiological measurements. Participants expressed concerns regarding the time constraints pertaining to the actual experimental setup of such user testing, for example the selection of signals and the placement of sensors, as well as the resources needed to run the experiment. Knowledge of physiological measures is still needed, as the signals used for physiological heatmaps should be selected according to the psychological variables of interest (e.g. emotion, cognitive load, etc.). Physiological measurements still represent important time and financial constraints, as data collection, experimental setup and data extraction still have to be overseen by the UX professional.

As mentioned above, practitioners who use physiological measures are doing so in particular projects only, i.e. projects that require the evaluation of emotions or if these measures are requested by the client. This translates into a steep and ever present learning curve, as practitioners must re-learn how to use the tools and materials associated with the data collection of physiological signals at each use. Therefore, the practitioners are never able to develop an expertise. Unable to justify the financial investment due to sparse usage of such tools, practitioners often end up renting the equipment, which is very costly.

Having practitioners use our UX heatmaps tool in the completion of an actual user testing evaluation report following a cooperative evaluation protocol yielded great results. We would recommend using this method for the evaluation of new tools and methodologies as:

- Participants felt comfortable to criticize physiological methodologies and our tool
- Provided a more relaxed atmosphere where participants could see themselves as collaborators rather than as experimental subjects
- Helped them take ownership of the tool and explore the functionalities it offered
- Helped us get insights as to how this tool would be received in the community.

We had hoped that the interview process would generate new ideas and avenues of research, in addition to potential improvements to our tool. However, this did not occur. We may have had more in-depth insights as to new functionalities had we:

- Interviewed practitioners who were more familiar with or used physiological measures in their current practice
- Had practitioners used the tool over longer periods of time. In the sessions, interviewees had only between 25 to 35 min to use the tool and complete their task

6   Conclusion

The use of physiological measures, in combination with traditional methods, could help practitioners to better measure UX, as they each provide complementary information on how users feel about a system, game, or web interface. [12] While traditional evaluation methods can offer episodic data, i.e. before or after the interaction, physiological measures can provide moment-to-moment information [9]. The addition of physiological measures can help us identify the cognitive and emotional reactions users experienced using an interface, while a post-task interview can help us delve further, after we have identified these emotions.

The main research and development activities we undertake at the Tech3Lab aim at facilitating and fostering the adoption of new methodologies, such as eyetracking and physiological measures, in the fields of UX design and research. A first step towards this direction was the development of a physiological heatmaps tool to allow simpler and richer interpretation of physiological signals for UI evaluation. The interviews we conducted with UX practitioners were very helpful, in that they provided guidelines and user requirements insights for us to use in the development of future iterations to facilitate furthermore the adoption of physiological methodologies. Our next step will be to continue to develop our functionalities as well as find ways to simplify the data processing sequence associated with physiological signals, working closely with ergonomists and consultants of the industry to do so.

Acknowledgments. Authors want to thank Brendan Scully for manuscript revision and the UX practitioners who participated to this study This research was supported by NSERC (National Sciences and Engineering Research Council of Canada).

References

1. Smith, T.F., Waterman, M.S.: Identification of common molecular subsequences. J. Mol. Biol. **147**, 195–197 (1981). doi:10.1016/0022-2836(81)90087-5
2. Zhihong, Z., Pantic, M., Roisman, G.I., Huang, T.S.: A Survey of Affect Recognition Methods: Audio, Visual, and Spontaneous Expressions. IEEE Trans. Pattern Anal. Mach. Intell. **31**(1), 39–58 (2009)
3. Calvo, R.A., D'Mello, S.: Affect detection: an interdisciplinary review of models, methods, and their applications. IEEE Trans. Affect. Comput. **1**(1), 18–37 (2010)
4. Georges, V., Courtemanche, F., Sénécal, S., Baccino, T., Fredette, M., Léger, P.M.: (Forthcoming). UX heatmaps: mapping user experience on visual interfaces. In: 34rd Annual ACM Conference on Human Factors in Computing Systems
5. Hassenzahl, M., Tractinsky, N.: User experience-a research agenda. Behav. Inf. Technol. **25**(2), 91–97 (2006)
6. Roto, V., Vermeeren, A.P.O.S., Väänänen-Vainio-Mattila, K., Law, E., Obrist, M.: Course notes: user experience evaluation methods - which method to choose? In: Proceedings of the SIGCHI Conference on Human Factors in Computing Systems, (Paris, France). ACM (2013)
7. Zaman, B., Shrimpton-Smith, T.: The FaceReader: measuring instant fun of use. In: Proceedings of the 4th Nordic Conference on Human-Computer Interaction: Changing Roles, pp. 457–460. ACM, Oslo (2006)
8. Boucsein, W.: Electrodermal Activity. Springer, Berlin (2012)
9. Huisman, G., van Hout, M., van Dijk, E., van der Geest, T., Heylen, D.: LEMtool: measuring emotions in visual interfaces. In: Proceedings of the SIGCHI Conference on Human Factors in Computing Systems, pp. 351–360. ACM, Paris (2013)
10. Mirza-Babaei, P., Nacke, L.E., Gregory, J., Collins, N., Fitzpatrick, G.: How does it play better?: exploring user testing and biometric storyboards in games user research. Proceedings of the SIGCHI Conference on Human Factors in Computing Systems (CHI 2013), pp. 1499–1508. ACM, New York (2013)

11. Hassenzahl, M., Burmester, M., Koller, F.: AttrakDiff: Ein Fragebogen zur Messung wahrgenommener hedonischer und pragmatischer Qualitat (AttracDiff: A questionnaire to measure perceived hedonic and pragmatic quality). In: Ziegler, J., Szwillus, G. (eds.), Mensch & Computer 2003. Interaktion in Bewegung, pp. 187–196. B.G. Teubner, Stuttgart, Leipzig (2003)

12. Courtemanche, F., Léger, P.-M., Frédette, M., Sénécal, S., Georges, V., Dufresne, A.: Method and Product for Visualizing the Emotions of a User, Provisional patent application. US 62/121,552, p. 14 (2015)

13. Virpi, R., et al.: All about UX (2012). http://www.allaboutux.org/

14. Riedl, R., Léger, P.-M.: Fundamentals of NeuroIS. Springer, Berlin (2016)

15. Kivikangas, M., Nacke, L., Ravaja, N.: Developing a triangulation system for digital game events, observational video, and psychophysiological data to study emotional responses to a virtual character. Entertainment Comput. **2**(1), 11–16 (2011)

16. Dix, A., et al.: Human-computer interaction. Pearson Education (2004)

Project Management Implications and Implementation Roadmap of Human Readiness Levels

Victoria Newton[1,2(✉)], Alexander Greenberg[2], and Judi See[1]

[1] Sandia National Laboratories, Albuquerque, NM, USA
{vnewton,jesee}@sandia.gov
[2] The University of New Mexico, Albuquerque, USA
agreenbe@unm.edu

> "Human rather than technical failures now represent the greatest threat to complex and potentially hazardous systems."
> - James Reason

Abstract. A human readiness levels (HRL) scale provides a framework to factor in the human dimension during technology development. This framework promotes careful consideration of the human as a part of the system throughout the product lifecycle. Insufficient attention to the human component of the system can lead to added costs, delayed deliverables, system failure, and even the loss of human life in high-consequence systems. We make the economic and technical justification for using an HRL scale by evaluating a reactive case study within a national laboratory. We create a historical technology readiness level (TRL) adoption roadmap to forecast a potential HRL adoption roadmap. We identify characteristics of organizations that are most likely to adopt the scale and conclude by recommending several project management tactics to ensure successful implementation.

Keywords: Human readiness level · Technology readiness level · Adoption forecast · Roadmap · Project management

1 Introduction

Human factors and ergonomics is "the scientific discipline concerned with the understanding of interactions among human and other elements of the system, and the profession that applies theory, principles, data and methods to design in order to optimize human well-being and overall system performance" (IEA 2000). The Federal Aviation Administration defines human factors as a "multidisciplinary effort to generate and compile information

Sandia National Laboratories is a multi-mission laboratory managed and operated by Sandia Corporation, a wholly owned subsidiary of Lockheed Martin Corporation, for the U.S. Department of Energy's National Nuclear Security Administration under contract DE-AC04-94AL85000. SAND2017-2192 C.

© Springer International Publishing AG 2017
F.F.-H. Nah and C.-H. Tan (Eds.): HCIBGO 2017, Part I, LNCS 10293, pp. 99–111, 2017.
DOI: 10.1007/978-3-319-58481-2_9

about human capabilities and limitations and apply that information to equipment, systems, facilities, procedures, jobs, environments, training, staffing, and personnel management for safe, comfortable, and effective human performance" (FAA 2016). Human factors (HF) analysis is utilized in several fields, but is most prominent within the healthcare and aviation industries where a single human error can lead to potentially catastrophic consequences. HF is ideally applied proactively throughout system development. In many cases, however, it is applied retrospectively, examining the consequences of human errors after a costly or damaging incident.

Human factors and ergonomics assumes that humans are inevitability fallible. Therefore, an effort needs to be made to design products, systems, and processes to reduce human error and optimize human efficiency. Research spanning behavioral economics to organizational behavior reveals that people have a limited bandwidth for processing information. Furthermore, research by Kahneman (2013) showed that people attempt to reduce cognitive load by creating heuristics and are beholden to subconscious biases. This generally results in suboptimal decision making. Consequently, there is no way to completely eliminate human fallibility, only to decrease opportunities for error and mitigate their effects.

One attempt at managing human factors analysis and human errors throughout all stages of development and production is the concept of Human Readiness Levels (HRL). This scale was initially developed by Phillips at the Naval Postgraduate School (2010) and was designed to complement the previously existing Technology Readiness Levels (TRL) scale. HRLs are meant to integrate the human into the system and create a reliable and unbiased measure of the readiness of the technology for human operators/users (Endsley 2015).

The HRL scale is still currently in development and alternatives to the scale have been discussed, but have not been well-established. A draft HRL scale was developed by Endsley (2015) and can be viewed in Fig. 1. This specific HRL scale has not been established as the most optimal tool for incorporating the human component throughout the entire development and design processes. Since no particular HRL scale has been officially adopted, we consider HRLs as a general concept to consistently measure and define the human aspect in development, production, and related processes. Therefore, we advocate HRLs in terms of the implementation of a management process that incorporates the human component. HF is often used as a retrospective analysis- the HRL scale advocates that the human component is considered proactively throughout the entire product lifecycle. We refer to HRLs as a tool or measure that allows project teams to analyze, understand, and develop their components, processes, and systems from a human factors approach. This allows projects and programs to incorporate the human element from initial design through the end-user, rather than as a form of post-analysis.

While HRLs have been researched, the government sector has not implemented HRLs as a proponent of technology or system development. HRLs have not received sufficient justification to prove their impact to the success of a project. Thus, our research aims to answer:

1. Can we justify using human readiness levels by their economic benefits and technical needs?
2. Can we create implementation strategies for human readiness levels based on the forecasted adoption roadmap?

HRL	Description
9	Post deployment and sustainment of human performance capability
8	Human performance using system fully tested, validated, and approved in mission operations
7	HSI requirements verified through development test and evaluation in representative environment
6	System design fully matured by human performance analyses, metrics, and prototyping
5	HSI demonstration and early user evaluation of initial prototypes to inform design
4	Modeling and analysis of human performance conducted and applied within system concept
3	Mapping of human interactions and application of standards to proof of concept
2	Human capabilities & limitations and system affordances & constraints applied to preliminary designs
1	Human focused concept of operations defined

Fig. 1. HRLs scale as suggested by Endsley (2015)

To answer these questions, we examine a reactive case study wherein a human factors team was asked to analyze and discover errors within production that led to significant cost and schedule overruns as well as lot failures. The team found significant errors related to the human component and made several suggestions. The economic impact of these HF issues is analyzed in terms of the triple constraints: scope, cost, and schedule. We also evaluate some indirect benefits of incorporating HRLs. This provides rationale for implementing the HF approach earlier in the development process justifying the need for HRLs from an economic standpoint. Additionally, the negative project scope impact demonstrates the technical need for HRLs. We then use the historical TRL adoption model to create a roadmap of HRLs adoption within the government sector. Finally, our paper concludes with potential implementation strategies to increase the likelihood of successful HRL adoption within the government.

1.1 A Reactive Case Study

We provide a case study to demonstrate one instance of the specific human factors issues that arose from not incorporating the human component in the initial design phase or throughout development. This example comes from Sandia National Laboratories during development of a critical component on a large-scale weapons system. The case demonstrates a reactive approach to human factors wherein the human component was not considered until several issues were prominent and resulted in negative financial, schedule, and scope impacts. In our example, three lots of the component had failed and had to be discarded, which resulted in a halt in production. A human factors team was then consulted to review processes and evaluate the most common errors. They designed user-centered controls and processes to combat those errors as well as reduce the possibility of human errors further affecting the product. While this case refers to only one component, several issues were found, spanning across the various sectors of HF.

The HF team identified two plant and equipment issues within the component development. The first pertained to the tools provided to support visual inspection. The inspectors struggled to adequately detect contamination, which led to scrapping of 1.2% of the components. In essence, the contamination was not visible to the human eye under normal lighting conditions. Inspectors were being asked to perform a task they were not physically capable of completing. The HF team experimented with different types of supplemental lights and determined that the contamination fluoresced under one particular color of lighting. Following the change in lighting, inspectors were able to successfully detect contamination, and no components were scrapped. The second plant and equipment issue stemmed from several fixtures and accessories that resulted in damage to the component. The HF team recommended design changes to incorporate keyed features within the fixtures that facilitated proper alignment of the component and prevented damage.

Additionally, the HF team identified several issues in the processes of the component's production that were due to human errors. First, there was an issue pertaining to the assembly order of the component—13% of components had to be reworked and 4% of the reworked units had to be scrapped. The HF team analyzed the complete assembly process and identified a more effective and reliable ordering of the steps involved. After the assembly process was revised, only 3% of components needed to be reworked, and no components had to be scrapped, saving significant time and resources. Second, a process was implemented to enhance inspector's ability to read serial numbers, which reduced handling mishaps as well as human error when reading or recording the serial number.

Finally, the HF team identified issues within the people component via two more inspection processes. No prior process had been established to determine the coordination among four different vendors responsible for inspection and certification of piece parts used in this particular component. This resulted in a lack of communication among vendors as well as the inability to trace the life of production. Because of the poor traceability, a lot of 1,300 piece parts had to be scrapped, with a loss of $18,000 and a significant schedule delay. The HF team mapped the process among vendors to promote traceability of piece parts. Further, job aides were created to facilitate inspection of the piece parts and enhance consistency in inspection. Another phase of the production process required manual transcription of data, which resulted in high probabilities of human error while transcribing or reading the data. The HF team redesigned forms to remove unnecessary information and pre-populated them with static information such as serial numbers. The team also converted some paper information to electronic form. These changes resulted in 16 fewer days for completion and reduced the number of human error opportunities from 8000 to 400. Modifications also allowed operators to focus solely on the task, without the distractions associated with reading or transcribing data.

This case study provides a unique opportunity to not only examine the HF interventions, but also view the economic and business impact before and after implementing a HF analysis. With economic implications in mind, we take a project management approach while examining the benefits that resulted from incorporating the HF recommendations. Traditionally, the project management perspective allows an analyst to consider the triple constraints of a project: schedule, cost, and scope/quality.

Instead of analyzing the independent HF interventions, we consider the impact to production of component lots before and after the recommended suggestions (Fig. 2). We are able to quantify the impacts of the various HF recommendations through several metrics. The HF interventions resulted in a cost savings of 67% per lot, a 36% reduction in manufacturing time per lot, and a doubling in the number of components delivered. It is evident that implementing the HF recommendations resulted in significant cost savings, reduced delays, and increased quality and quantity. The technical and production teams were better able to meet their deliverables, saving both time and money.

Metric	Percent Improvements
Lot Cost	67%
Elapsed Time	36%
Components Delivered	98%
Yield	100%
Cost per Component Delivered	83%
Time per Component Delivered	67%

Fig. 2. The scope, cost, and schedule percent improvements from human factors interventions that were implemented on a defense project within the U.S. government.

1.2   A Proactive Approach

Frequently, human factors experts are brought in to assess situations once a failure has occurred. The Three Mile Island Nuclear Reactor Accident in 1979 was caused by an operator's failure to adequately assess a situation due to their lack of training as well as poor human usability and design of controls (GPU Nuclear Corp 1999). The fire in the King's Cross station of the London Underground in 1987 can be attributed to the same human errors (Fennell 1988). The Challenger Explosion in 1986 provides another example of a catastrophe wherein poor communication and arduous work schedules have been cited as partial contributors (Forrest 1996). These examples are used to show the breadth of human errors and accidents that led to the loss of human life. Each of these cases used post hoc analysis to determine the cause of system failures which was primarily human error.

We propose that investing in the human component throughout all stages of the product's lifecycle increases an organization's flexibility and enhances their capabilities. Furthermore, it provides the organization a competitive advantage. Most government organizations consider the human dimension only when there is system failure and significant negative consequences. Rather than the reactive approach, we suggest that taking a proactive approach would result in maximum benefits for an organization and the product development lifecycle. From a business perspective, the savings seen in our reactive case study could have been realized from the beginning of lot production had an HRL scale been considered since development. In addition to several quantifiable economic benefits that would results from adopting an HRL scale, we suggest several other latent benefits would also arise. We provide several potential examples to help gain an understanding of the types of advantages that may occur from a proactive use of HRLs, but suggest the added benefits be further researched.

If human factors are considered early in development, from a proactive approach, training would be significantly improved. The operator would be trained on the correct system initially and would not have to undergo retraining if reactive adjustments are made. This would also improve the operator's cognitive load and reduce the possibility of human error. It is prudent to implement the HF techniques from the beginning of development to reduce the negative impact to the users and decrease opportunities for human error.

Additionally, if a product is developed poorly, resulting in failures, the organization's reputation might be severely damaged and the customer's satisfaction may be adversely affected. The organization may appear as incompetent if a product was labelled as production-ready yet failed. In addition to the effects of reputation on customers, this would also impact the employee and end-user perspectives of the organization. The more incompetent an organization appears, the less trustworthy the organization is perceived by these essential stakeholders. For example, Japan lost their role as leader of the electronics industry when their competitors delivered better systems that led to more productive and efficient users. According to Panasonic's President Kazuhiro Tsuga, "Japanese firms were too confident about our technology and manufacturing prowess. We lost sight of the products from the customer's point of view" (Wakabayashi 2012).

2 Adoption Within the U.S. Government

We conducted an extensive literature review to capture the full picture of TRL adoption within the government sector. This helped us determine the key events leading to widespread adoption within the five stages of the Technology Adoption Lifecycle Rogers (2003). Based on the impact of an event, we determined the milestones that led to the completion of one stage and the beginning of the next. We used the historical adoption model of TRLs to create a forecasted HRL adoption model. The two scales' parallel nature allows us to make such predictions. This forecasted model was used to recommend project and organizational implementation strategies.

2.1 Historical TRL Adoption Model

We create a TRL adoption model to provide insight into the HRLs adoption roadmap. TRLs have largely become a requirement through most of the government and therefore have reached complete adoption within all relevant industries. Figure 3 reveals our historical TRL adoption roadmap as well as the most probable market share percentage

(S-curve) as TRL adoption increased over time. We also show the main government organization adopter through each stage of the lifecycle.

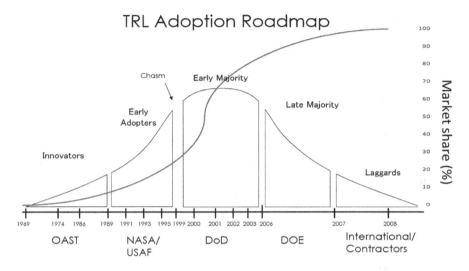

Fig. 3. Model of our TRL historical adoption roadmap and market share percent

The chasm, as described by Moore (2014), is the gap between early adopters and early majority. "Crossing the chasm" is often seen as the most difficult step in the technology adoption lifecycle. In the case of TRL adoption within the government, we suggest that the General Accounting Office (GAO) recommendation for DoD to begin implementing TRLs due to increased technological maturity and cost savings seen in private industry allowed TRLs to cross the chasm and reach the early majority stage. The specific events included in our historical TRL adoption roadmap are explained in further detail.

1969 – Report on advanced space station technology mentioned a new idea to assess maturity of new technologies called the "Technology Readiness Review" Mankins (2009)

1974 – Stan Sadin developed the first 7-level TRL scale with one line definitions as a tool for assessing technological maturity for NASA Mankins (2009)

1986 – Challenger Space Shuttle accident increased focus on rebuilding space agency's technological foundations through new programs Mankins (2009)

1989 – TRL use expanded due to the "Space Exploration Initiative". The TRL scale was extended to the 9-levels that are now the standard Mankins (2009)

1991 – TRLs became unilaterally used throughout the Civil Space Program Mankins (2009)

1990s – TRLs initial adoption within the U.S. Air Force (Whelan 2008)

1992-1994 – NASA's Office of Space Science used TRLs extensively to communicate with researchers, internal and external organizations, and its management chain Mankins (2009)

1995 – Mankins developed and explained the first complete set of TRL definitions Mankins (2009)

1999 –The U.S. General Accounting Office recommended the DoD "adopt a disciplined and knowledge-based approach of assessing technology maturity such as TRL" Mankins (2009)

2000 – First DoD adoption of NASA's TRL scales Mankins (2009)

2001 – Deputy under Secretary of Defense for Science and Technology issued a memorandum that endorsed the use of TRLs in new major programs (Whelan 2008)

2001 – Required use of TRLs in Department of Defense accelerates adoption (Olechowski 2015)

2003 – DoD developed their own formal guidelines and definitions for assessing technological maturity (Whelan 2008)

2006 – GAO Initiated review that resulted in the DoE producing their own Technology Readiness Assessment guidelines (Alexander 2007)

2007 – GAO recommended DOE adopt TRLs (Alexander 2008)

2008 – Language supporting the GAO recommendation was incorporated into the Congress budget allocation (Alexander 2008)

2.2   Forecasted HRL Adoption

HRLs development and implementation has been low since its inception in 2010. Based on market penetration, we estimate HRLs have only been adopted by the innovators (refer to Fig. 4). While the human element has previously been considered, the actual tool/framework of HRLs lineage and adoption growth can be seen below.

Phillips (2010) developed and tested a 9-levels Human Readiness Levels scale at the Naval Postgraduate School

Hale et al. (2011) created a 6-level Human Factors Readiness Level scale to assess human factors needs in human-machine interactions

2013 – Endsley examined the feasibility of the 9-level HRL scale as a parallel measure to TRLs

O'Neil et al. (2015) developed the Comprehensive Human Integration Evaluation Framework (CHIEF) Model- a 5 level scale to assess human system integration on total system performance which was implemented within the U.S. Coast Guard Office

2015 – Endsley presented on "Human System Integration: Challenges and Opportunities" at National Defense Industrial Association, which argues for the need to use an HRL framework

See and Morris (2016), researchers at Sandia National Laboratories, began examining the feasibility of integrating the HRL scale within the national laboratory

2017 – Newton, Greenberg, and See conduct research to justify the need for HRLs from an economic perspective and create a roadmap of HRL adoption

HRL Adoption Roadmap

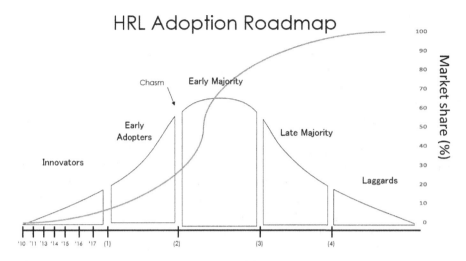

Fig. 4. Forecasted HRLs adoption roadmap and possible market share percent

Since we are currently in the innovators stage of HRL adoption, there must be four major catalysts that bridge each stage to the subsequent one. These catalysts are events that cross the gap separating each stage of the lifecycle and help to advance adoption. To determine the HRL adoption catalysts, we use the TRL adoption roadmap as a general guideline.

Prior to reaching the early adopter's stage, we believe that HRLs must have formal definitions and a finalized scale. The scale must be broad enough to cross disciplines, but specific enough that it can be implemented by an organization. We suggest that a feasibility study be conducted to determine how an HRL scale could actually be implemented. Current research within DoD is being performed to determine if HRLs could be adopted. Sandia National Laboratories is currently conducting research to determine if HRLs should be structured as a separate readiness scale or if they should be incorporated into the existing TRL scale (See and Morris 2016).

To cross the chasm, HRLs will need a strong champion that will encourage and convince government organizations to begin adopting HRLs. Due to the impact on TRLs, we suggest an organization like the GAO would be able to adequately provide proper justification by recommending HRLs be adopted within the government. Private organizations have an incentive to maximize profits which can be partially done by understanding the human element, although a formal HRL process may not be performed. GAO can examine the private industry and use these benefits to better understand and justify the need to use HRLs within the government. Formal policy from large government groups, like DoD and DOE, requiring the use of HRLs, will be needed to lead to the late majority stage of adoption. Finally, HRLs will reach the laggards when the requirements policy eventually extends to all contractors and suppliers, much like the TRL adoption.

3   Implementation Strategies

The TRL roadmap adoption model provides insight into a possible HRL roadmap adoption lifecycle and major implementation checkpoints. A TRL feasibility study conducted by the DoD provides added inferences into distinct implementation logistics and potential challenges in adopting HRLs into an organization. The first challenge is to evaluate potential organizations that would be most ideally suited for HRL adoption. We consider which processes need to be established within an organization to increase likelihood of a successful HRL implementation. HRL adoption is more likely to spread from one organization to another once the usefulness and triple constraint benefits can be empirically validated across government institutions. The first organization to unilaterally implement HRLs will likely need to demonstrate particular organizational characteristics. The second challenge is to examine implementation tactics within a specific organization, especially as it relates to project management.

Organizations that are most likely to adapt to significant changes are those that demonstrate organizational change management processes. Weiner (2009) treats organizational readiness as "a shared psychological state in which organizational members feel committed to implementing organizational change and confident in their collective abilities to do so." This indicates that everyone in the organization must act towards effectively implementing the changes and that each individual understands the justification for such modifications. These organizations tend to be much more adaptable and amenable to significant changes. Organizations that have a culture which fosters change and encourages individual responsibility will be more likely to successfully implement HRLs into their processes. Strong social capital is an aspect in organizations that lead to more flexible organizations and are also more likely to adapt to changes (Krebs 2008).

We suggest that organizations that previously demonstrate some level of human factors considerations are also more likely to successfully adopt HRLs. Organizations that already have HF experts incorporated into their projects is an indication that there is value in the human component of a system. Even if HF engineers are not necessarily incorporated into a project team, they are considered valued members. It is these organizations that clearly indicate the benefits of understanding and analyzing the human element. Furthermore, the foundational infrastructure will already be in place as the organization already has HF employees.

In addition to the organizational characteristics, we suggest several practical strategies that need to be in place for an organization to successfully adopt HRLs. DoD conducted a feasibility study to ensure successful implementation of TRLs and found that successful adoption is labor intensive (Graettinger et al. 2002). Additionally, DoD and DARPA Principal Investigators (PI) were already working under tight time constraints and exerted maximum cognitive efforts prior to implementing the TRLs. DoD found a third person objective observer to be effective for proper TRL utilization to help overcome the PI's constraints, but this method still required extensive interactions with each PI. We suggest that for successful HRL application, sub-groups of people or a super-user group is required to apply and utilize HRLs to reduce the cognitive load on the PIs. These super-users can consult with all necessary stakeholders (e.g. production workers, end-users of the product, and PIs) and work with the project manager to ensure all human component aspects have been accounted for in the project. The most appropriate option for a super-user is a human factors engineer or subject matter expert.

Successful implementation would also include directives from executives and upper-management to adequately permeate company culture. Policy requirements ensure HRLs would be used within all technology development initiatives. We suggest a project manager be assigned for implementation of HRLs within an organization. This would be beneficial to create a plan and control and monitor the scope, cost, and schedule of implementation. We do not provide a specific implementation plan in this paper, but the project manager needs to consider the variation of research topics, project sizes, and individual requirements within their organization. Furthermore, this manager should also develop a plan for handling projects in various stages.

In addition to implementing HRLs within an organization, the management team needs to consider how HRLs will affect their project processes and procedures. As a parallel, TRLs have often been used by DoD to act as a threshold to technological maturity prior to acquisition of a new project. Technologies must reach a TRL 6 before they are ready for insertion into acquisition programs. Similarly, HRLs need to be defined and optimized for the specific organization and project types. The product or process development stage that maximizes HRL utility must also be evaluated. Project managers need to ask questions based on potential HRL impact to the project. Will the system or component levels be evaluated? Have we considered the working and operational environments? Additionally, a contingency plan could be necessary. For example, if a project reaches completion but the HRL is too low for acquisition what are the countermeasures?

The benefits of adopting an HRL scale or its equivalent are evident in scope, cost, and schedule, as well as increases in user and customer trust, the reduction of cognitive load, and training efficacy. There are however a few added costs as a result of incorporating the human component. First, adding the HRL scale requires a human factors engineer to be a core team member on projects, or at least needs to review projects during every stage of development. This leads to an investment in human capital requiring additional budget allocation for the HF engineer's salary. Incorporating an HRL scale will entail additional requirements prior to advancing to further stages in development. For example, a product must reach an appropriate readiness level across all scales to meet its design standards and to pass reviews. Adopting an HRL scale would be an additional metric of maturity by which to gauge a project, process, or product. If a product does not have a high enough HRL measure, more efforts would need to be put towards development to increase the HRL. This may require additional costs up front, but would result in significant cost savings in the long run, as shown by our case study.

4 Conclusion

Our research provides the business and economic justification for implementing HRLs and provides a potential roadmap for HRL adoption within the government sector. Results from additional research that is currently being conducted are needed before HRLs will reach the early adopters stage. We mentioned several latent benefits of using an HRL scale, but further undertakings need to occur to realize these added benefits. As mentioned in our adoption roadmap, a feasibility study such as the current effort at Sandia National Laboratories (See and Morris 2016) would help define the HRL scale to ensure it meets the needs of the organization. Finally, it would be helpful to create guidelines for organizations to be able to easily implement HRLs within an organization or program. Creating a foundational procedure for incorporating HRLs into a project will lead to project managers who are able to include HRLs in their processes.

Additional research can be done that extends past the early adopter's stage of the adoption lifecycle. Further, industry adoption can help to understand the benefits of HRLs. For example, understanding how HRLs might impact specific fields, such as healthcare, can provide insight to how HRLs may be enforced within that industry. Creating technologies for all users, rather than the "average" user, can also propel human factors considerations. This would be especially important for individuals with disabilities and would increase a technology's market potential. Researchers need to understand how the human is a part of the system as research, production, and applications continue to grow in areas like TSensor systems (Walsh 2014), edge computing, robotics, artificial intelligence, and human augmentation (Sanwal 2017). Studies should be conducted to determine the best method for incorporating HRLs for each of these industry trends.

References

Alexander, D., Holton, L., Sutter, H.: Technology readiness assessment of a large DOE waste processing facility. Presented at Technology Maturation Conference, Virginia Beach, VA (2007)

Alexander, D.: Proceedings from Waste Management 2008 Conference: Technology Readiness Assessment of Department of Energy Waste Processing Facilities: Lessons Learned. Next Steps, Phoenix, AZ (2008)

Endsley, M.: Human system integration: challenges and opportunities. In: Plenary speaker at National Defense Industrial Association Human Systems Conference, Alexandria, VA, February 2015

Federal Aviation Administration Reauthorization Act of 2016. Retrieved from: s:\legcnsl\lexa\dor15\av\bill\tnfaara.3s.xml

Fennell, D.: Investigation into the King's Cross underground fire. Department of Transport, London, England (1988)

Forrest, J.: The Space Shuttle Challenger disaster: A failure in decision support system and human factors management (1996). http://www.dssresources.com/cases/spaceshuttlechallenger/index.html. Accessed

Graettinger, C., Garcia, S., Siviy, J., Schenk, R., Van Syckle, P.: Using the technology readiness levels scale to support technology management in the DoD's ATD/STO environments: A findings and recommendations report conducted for Army CECOM (Special Report CMU/SEI-2002-SR-027) (2002)

GPU Nuclear Corp. Ten briefing papers (1999). http://www.world-nuclear.org/information-library/safety-and-security/safety-of-plants/three-mile-island-accident.aspx. Accessed

Hale, K., Fuchs, S., Carpenter A., Stanney, K.: Proceedings of the Human Factors and Ergonomics Society 55th Annual Meeting: A Scale for Assessing Human Factors Readiness Levels. Las Vegas, Nevada (2011)

IEA. The discipline of ergonomics. International Ergonomics Association (2000). http://www.iea.cc/whats/. Accessed

Kahneman, D.: Thinking, Fast and Slow. Farrar, Straus and Giroux, New York (2013)

Krebs, V.: Social capital: the key to success for the 21st century organization. IHRIM J. **8**(5), 38–42 (2008)

Mankins, J.C.: Technology readiness assessments: a retrospective. Acta Astronaut. **65**(9–10), 1216–1223 (2009). doi:10.1016/j.actaastro.2009.03.058

Moore, G.A.: Crossing the chasm: Marketing and selling high-tech products to mainstream customers, 3rd edn. HarperBusiness, New York (2014)

Olechowski, A., Eppinger, E., Joglekar, N.: Proceedings of PICMET '15: Management of the Technology Age: Technology Readiness Levels at 40: A Study of State-of-the-Art Use, Challenges, and Opportunities, Portland, Oregon (2015)

O'Neil, M., Shattuck, L., Sciarini, L.: A framework for assessing and communicating human systems integration efficacy across the system lifecycle. Procedia Manufact. **3**, 3054–3061 (2015)

Phillips, E.: The development and initial evaluation of the human readiness level framework (Master's dissertation). Naval Postgraduate School, Monterey, CA (2010). http://calhoun.nps.edu/handle/10945/5255. Accessed

Reason, J.: Human error: Models and management. Br. Med. J. **320**(7237), 768–770 (2000)

Rogers, E.M.: Diffusion of innovations, 5th edn. Free Press, Glencoe (2003)

Sanwal, A.: CB Insights trends report. Keynote presentation at CB Insights Innovation Summit 2017, Santa Barbara, CA (2017)

See, J., Morris, J.: Incorporating human readiness levels at Sandia National Laboratories. Paper presented at Resilience Week, Chicago, IL August 2016. Abstract retrieved from https://secureweb.inl.gov/resweek2016/OnlineProceedings/IEEE_1Column/See_SNL_IEEE_1_080316.docx.pdf

Wakabayashi, D.: How Japan lost its electronics crown. Wall Street J. (2012). https://www.wsj.com/articles/SB10000872396390444840104577551972061864692. Accessed

Walsh, S.: Proceedings from the TSensors Summit for Trillion Sensor Roadmap: Current Status of the TSensor Systems Roadmap, La Jolla, CA (2014)

Weiner, B.: A theory of organizational readiness for change. Implementation Sci. **4**(67) (2009). doi:10.1186/1748-5908-4-67

Whelan, D.: Presentation to Department of Energy Fusion Energy Science Advisory Committee: Impact of Technology Readiness Levels on Aerospace R&D (2008)

Context-Awareness and Mobile HCI: Implications, Challenges and Opportunities

Xiangang Qin[1,2(✉)], Chee-Wee Tan[1], and Torkil Clemmensen[1]

[1] Copenhagen Business School, Frederiksberg, Denmark
{xq.itm,cwt.itm,tc.itm}@cbs.dk
[2] Beijing University of Posts and Telecommunications, Beijing, China
qinxiangang@bupt.edu.cn

Abstract. Context-awareness endows mobile devices and services with the capability of interacting with users in an efficient, intelligent, natural and smart fashion. Consequently, context-awareness makes a significant difference to mobile HCI. However, the challenges brought by context-awareness to users of mobile devices are rarely examined in depth. In this paper, previous conceptions of context and their contribution to context-awareness in mobile HCI is scrutinized and a preliminary context-computer interaction (CCI) model is advanced to illustrate the interaction characterized by mobile context-awareness. Furthermore, the paper examines the limitations of information processing models and review alternative models of context. We also address user experience challenges related to the enablement of mobile context-awareness and highlight avenues for future research issues. Specifically, we found that context-awareness has been employed broadly in developing applications and services on mobile platform, has had a huge impact on mobile user experience, and has altered the interaction between humans and computers by giving the latter a more active role to play. The significance of context-awareness in the usage of mobile systems calls for systematic and in-depth appreciation of its impact on mobile HCI.

Keywords: Context-awareness · Mobile HCI · User centric

1 Introduction

Since the term "context-aware" was first proposed to describe the computing ability "of a mobile user's applications to discover and react to changes in the environment to discover and react to changes in the environment they are situated in" [1], it has received extensive scholarly attention across the fields of ubiquitous (or distributed and pervasive) computing, ambient intelligence, artificial intelligence, internet of things and user interface [2–7]. More recently, due to advances in computing capabilities and sensor technologies, the concept of context-awareness has also found its way into a diversity of industrial applications like healthcare, mobile advertising, mobile learning, museum and tour guides, recommender system and virtual reality [8–10]. For this reason, Mobile Context-Awareness (MCA) and its implications for context-driven service innovations has been acknowledged as a promising future in Human Computer Interaction (HCI) [11].

© Springer International Publishing AG 2017
F.F.-H. Nah and C.-H. Tan (Eds.): HCIBGO 2017, Part I, LNCS 10293, pp. 112–127, 2017.
DOI: 10.1007/978-3-319-58481-2_10

1.1 General Challenges of Mobile Context-Awareness (MCA)

Despite the optimism surrounding context-awareness, developers are confronted with challenges on how to capture, interpret, fuse and present contextual information in order to realize context-aware applications and services. Because smart phones yield rich contextual information through the facilitation of interactions with humans, the definition and categorization of context is very much dependent on the research objective, application domain and use cases, differing substantially from one situation to another. The forms of context-awareness also vary because the interaction between humans and computers is not yet clear with regards to the role of the former (active/passive) [12], the way of display contextual information (implicit/explicit) [13] and the level of automation. Furthermore, mobile context-awareness (MCA) also bring about challenges to user experience. These challenges to user experience (e.g., absence of control, distracting interruption, inappropriate feedback and privacy) not only constitute theoretical conundrums, but they also affect the actual user experience in practice [14].

1.2 Challenges for User-Centric MCA

MCA is a rapidly growing topic of interest for both academics and practitioners due to the increasing dynamism and richness of contextual information afforded by smart devices. Although context-awareness is intended to address issues in user experience caused by small screen size and ever-shifting context in smart devices, it is accompanied by its own side effects such as distracting interruptions, loss of control and privacy risk [14]. Consequently, there are calls for an in-depth appreciation of how user experiences (UX) are shaped by mobile context-aware systems.

In classifying the architecture of context-aware systems into five layers, [15] discovered that the bulk of research (237 articles in total) published between 2000 and 2007 tends to concentrate on layers associated with concept and research, network, middleware and application. A mere 6.7% of the published articles touch on user infrastructure and only 1.5% (3) discussed usability issues. Even though the few studies, which have examined the issue of UX for MCA (device and application), have put forth general guidelines for designing mobile context-aware systems (i.e., avoiding unnecessary interruptions, ensuring user control, guaranteeing system visibility, incorporating contextual settings, preventing information overflow, securing user's privacy, selecting an appropriate level of automation and tailoring content to match individual needs) [12, 14], there is a dearth of research that has been devoted to a dedicated scrutiny of how such systems can be designed from a user-centered perspective [16].

We begin the paper with the application developers' perspective on context-awareness, and gradually move towards a more holistic understanding of MCA that includes the user's perspective on MCA.

2   General Overview: Context and Mobile HCI

2.1   Context in HCI

Context either simplifies or enriches human-human interaction in different situations. Humans could predict the intention or behavior of another human based on contextual information (i.e., gender, culture and interaction experience). However, harnessing contextual information to enhance human-computer interaction remains an elusive challenge. Indeed, smart phones yield a diversity of contextual information from multiple sources, including those captured by sensors (e.g., brightness, gravity and direction), generated by users (e.g., activity logs, interactive behavior, sign-up information, sign in/out status and tags), inferred by computers (activities, hobbies, preferences). Although capturing contextual information via sensors has made significant strides over the past decade, providing users with meaningful and valuable contextual information on the basis of fusion, interpretation and adaption of raw information is still an uphill task. A common barrier in the appropriation of contextual information stems from the fact that there is no common, reusable model for context across these environments [17].

In its formative years, the notion of context is either conceived with select elements (e.g., location, time, people and objects in environmental, physical or social states) or described in general terms like situational information [18]. A widely acknowledged definition of context was put forth by Abowd et al. [18], who asserted that context entails "any information that can be used to characterize the situation of an entity. An entity is a person, place, or object that is considered relevant to the interaction between a user and an application, including the user and applications themselves". This implies that any information that characterizes the situation of a human in an interaction can be regarded as context. A number of studies have investigated the concept of context and refer to it as comprising location, identities of neighboring objects and users, environment characteristics such as season and temperature, date and time, user's emotional state, focus of attention, objects and people in the user's environment [1, 19, 20].

Although contextual information is promising in enabling smart phones to communicate with humans in implicit and intuitive ways, context is an underutilized source of information in our computing environments. The interaction between smart phone and users is still below expectation due to the impoverished ability of users to provide contextual input to smart phones and the inability of smart phones to take full advantage of the interactive context. As a consequence, we have a limited understanding of what context is and how it can be employed in developing HCI systems.

To render contextual information more usable for developers of mobile applications and services, they are organized into various categories and levels. From our review of extant literature, we realize two predominant trends governing past conceptions of context. One is that the definition of concept varies considerably depending on the types of applications and/or services. Another is that most definitions tend to categorize context according to the entity that is relevant to the interaction between an application and a user, be it human factors, location (or place), application (or object) and physical environment [21].

The inclusion of communal activity, social context and user tasks in the definition of context [22] indicates that contextual information can also be produced through interactions between humans and computers (Fig. 1). Compared with the three well-recognized categories of context, interactive contexts are either created by users as inputs to HCI systems or need to be reasoned by computers as output of HCI systems. Given that the context associated with the utilization of smart devices fluctuates over time, we hence subscribe to an *interactional* view by treating the scope of contextual features to be dynamic so much so that the relationship between activity and context becomes cyclical in nature. In this sense, we depart from the *representational* view that assumes context to be a form of static information, which is independent from the underlying activities [10].

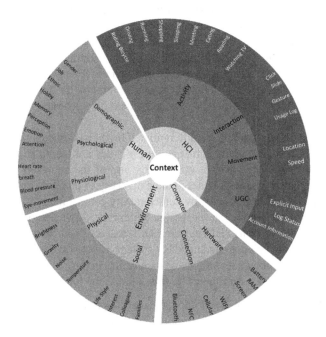

Fig. 1. The contextual information from HCI perspective

2.2   Level of Context

In addition to efforts in categorizing context by entity, context can also be categorized according to hierarchical levels in HCI. [23] defined contextual information with three levels, namely low-level context (sensed), high-level (inferred) and situational relationships (presumed). Contextual information captured by sensor are considered as low-level context that is directly referred to a raw data. A sensor in context-aware applications is described not only a physical device, but also a data source that could be useful for context representation. Furthermore, sensed context can be split into three types, that is physical, virtual and logical sensors [23]. Higher level of context are abstract and usually inferred by fusing multiple lower level contexts [6–10].

According to predominant viewpoint of depicting HCI as a closed 'information processing loop', an appropriate conceptual basis for studies of HCI at different levels of context (cultural, organizational and social context) is absent for modelling the contextual information in HCI systems [24]. Alternative theoretical models are required to interpret, design and develop HCI systems by deploying contextual information in an effective and efficient manner (this issue will be discussed in greater detail later in the paper).

2.3   Model of Context

Due to difficulties in theorizing the dynamism of context, researchers have turned their attention to the construction of context meta-models. A context meta-model is a generic description of the contextual environment on a meta-level that is not targeted towards a particular system [21]. Context-meta models thus serve as the theoretical foundation for deriving context-specific models for adaptive systems, guiding system developers in determining what contextual variables to take into account for a given context-adaptive system. While context-specific models denote relevant context for a given context-adaptive system, context meta-models express context on a generic meta-level and are not bound to any particular system.

Existing context meta-models are differentiated by their degree of abstraction from the real world context [21]. Although seven meta-codes are identified, there are still approximately 20% of variables not covered by any of the analyzed context meta-models. With the boom in smart phones and the diversity of mobile scenarios, contexts might emerge that cannot be covered by contemporary context meta-models.

From the perspective of HCI, a successful context meta-model should interpret the role of contextual information in HCI systems. Different levels and categories of contextual information should be integrated into HCI systems to support developers in making decisions about what contextual variables to include in a given context-adaptive system [21]. Specifically, context meta-models have to address the following issues:

- Contextual information consists of inputs that are captured by sensors and/or generated by users, thereby giving rise to issues of fusing different types of contextual information as input to make it meaningful for users as output.
- Contextual information as computer outputs involving both low-level (battery life, data connection and CPU speed) and high-level (activities such as running, sleeping and shopping, demographics such as gender, age and occupation and psychological status such as fatigue, happiness and depression) contexts, thereby giving rise to issues of inferring and gauging high level of contextual information based on their low level counterparts.
- Diverse modalities and types of contextual information are acquired through interactions between humans and computers (e.g., haptic, speech and vision), thereby giving rise to issues of integrating multiple modalities of contextual information in the design of HCI systems.

2.4 Active and Passive Roles of Human and Computer in Interaction

The MCA systems can be categorized into two types depending on whether computers play an active or passive role in executing inferred actions [13, 15]. For active MCA systems, computers execute inferred actions automatically and implicitly on the basis of contextual information. Conversely, for passive MCA systems, the sensed information and inferred actions will be presented to users explicitly, giving the latter an opportunity to decide on whether to execute the actions or not.

From the perspective of HCI, a core discrepancy between active and passive CA systems resides in the mode of interaction. Active CA systems adapt implicitly to users' activities by altering system behavior whereas passive CA systems explicitly presents novel or updated contextual information to users, allowing the latter to make decision on whether the system should continue or abandon the execution. In this sense, active CA systems are characterized by the implicit input and output of computers whereas passive CA systems are characterized by the explicit output of computers. While explicit interaction contradicts the idea of invisible computing, implicit interaction might be helpful in realizing the vision of ubiquitous computing in delivering intuitive interaction [13]. For example, implicit interaction happens when a smart phone activates mute mode automatically for a meeting event in the calendar. Conversely, an example of an explicit presentation may take the form of a smart phone prompting a user with information about the calendar event, thereby enabling the user to decide whether to mute the phone or not.

Although implicit and explicit interaction are well recognized as a method for categorizing CA systems from the perspective of HCI, attitudes towards them tend to diverge [12]. Active CA systems are deemed to be much more interesting as a sign of computing capability while passive CA systems permit users to control the interaction with computers.

3 Computing Centric View of MCA

As a defining characteristic of ubiquitous (ambient, pervasive) computing, context-awareness is developed to acquire, decipher, fuse, infer and utilize the contextual information of a device in order to provide services that are appropriate (how) to select people (who), place (where), time (when), event (what) and intention (why) [15]. Consequently, much scholarly attention was paid to dealing with computing issues about concept and research, network, middleware and application of MCA [25, 26].

3.1 Value of Context-Aware for Computing

When humans interact with humans, contextual information is usually deployed to help us effectively and efficiently convey thoughts and emotions to one another and react appropriately. Contextual information plays a pivotal role in helping humans to sense, decipher, reason, infer and predict one another in social networking [18, 19]. This ability of humans to acquire situational awareness was introduced into the field of computing to allow computers to easily sense and decipher the world of ubiquitous computing.

Supposedly, context-awareness enables computing devices to interact with humans in natural, implicit, intelligent, automatic and sophisticated ways like human-human interaction [18]. Context-aware computing promises a smooth and intuitive interaction between humans and computing systems. However, interaction between humans and computers fails to achieve that goal until the last ten years with the widespread penetration of smart devices.

3.2 Context-Awareness Application Development for Mobile HCI

"One of the most ubiquitous tools in the progress of context awareness has been the mobile device. Its enormous popularity and permeation into daily life—coupled with increasingly sophisticated hardware—has greatly increased the potential for context awareness in the world." [18]

Over the past decade, mobile devices, especially smart phones, have been widely adopted by a vast user population across the world. In many countries, more than 50% of population are mobile phone users. Nowadays, mobile phones are equipped with miniaturized sensors and enhanced computing capability, enabling smart phones to interact with humans in implicit, intelligent and human-like ways.

Technological advancements have transformed smart phones into a powerful tool with tremendous capacity for context-awareness. Firstly, human perceptual ability is extended with a variety of sensors like brightness, proximity, infrared and gravity, to name a few. Secondly, the diversity of smart phone usage generated dynamic, rich and complicated contextual information that is valuable for context-awareness [27]. Context-awareness is reflective of the 'smart' side of mobile phone and adopted commonly in mobile services and applications to enhance the user experience. To help developers harness contextual information, Google even released express API for context-awareness to facilitate the development of mobile applications and services based on Android platform.

3.3 Issues for MCA Computing

The major objective of technical efforts of MCA is to make sure that mobile devices could be aware of their contexts and automatically adapt to the changing contexts [15]. Technical efforts made to realize that vision include modeling, monitoring, capturing, filtering, processing and reasoning context, together with detecting inconsistency and resolution [25, 27].

A variety of context models are proposed to represent patterns representing the object of context, such as key-value, markup, graphical, object-oriented, logic-based, domain-focused and ontology-based context model. New solutions about multi-sensor data fusion is employed extensively to merge data collected by heterogeneous sensors to improve the accuracy of probabilistic inference systems by including context information. Event-driven and query-based paradigms of context-awareness were proposed to depict different kinds of context-aware. Usually sensors are employed to capture the physical contexts (e.g., light and vision, audio, movement and acceleration, location and position) while image recognition, machine learning and data mining are utilized to capture the virtual contexts (e.g., user preferences, emotions and satisfactions) [25, 28]. To preprocess and filter out the noise intrinsic to the original contextual information, centralized, distributed and hybrid paradigms are formulated [25].

Despite extensive scrutiny of the technical issues of MCA computing, there are still many issues worthy of further exploration, such as how to acquire novel types of contexts that may enable applications to be more adaptive to changeable contexts, eliciting contexts from user behavior and communities as well as incorporating schemas for detecting and resolving contextual inconsistencies [25].

4   User Centric View of MCA

A computing-centric view of MCA focuses on how to capture contextual information efficiently, decipher context accurately and adapt to the context automatically. To this end, mobile devices tend to play a more proactive and intelligent role in the interaction with users. Nevertheless, concerns over the role of humans in HCI, as characterized by MCA and relevant user experience issues, have also been raised [29].

4.1   Implicit and Explicit Interaction

An abundance of intricate contextual information are exploited in human-to-human communication, such as eye contact, facial expression, hand gestures, body language and even more profound social attributes like culture and religions. Implicit interaction helps humans to understand situations of different human beings in an efficient and effective way. Unlike human-to-human communication, the traditional human computer system lacks the ability to detect implicit information as humans normally do in face-to-face interaction [30, 31]. Consequently, conventional interactions between humans and computers are constrained by the latter's computing power and number of embedded sensors in harvesting and harnessing contextual information.

Context-aware systems are able to adapt their behaviors to given contexts without explicit user intervention, thereby leading to increased efficiency and effectiveness by taking environmental context into account [4]. Thus, context-awareness systems also modified traditional modes of HCI through the introduction of implicit interaction. Implicit human computer interaction (iHCI) is originally defined by Schmidt [31] as *"the interaction of a human with the environment and with artefacts which is aimed to accomplish a goal. Within this process the system acquires implicit input from the user and may present implicit output to the user."*

Capturing and making sense of contextual information is essential for the success of designing interactive systems that run on MCA devices [18]. Contextual information is captured implicitly, intention of user is reasoned and potential options are presented to users subsequently. Mobile context-awareness is changing the interaction between humans and computers in several aspects. Firstly, the interaction is shifting from *explicit* to implicit ways. Secondly, information sources are much more diverse, comprising both human and computer inputs [15]. Thirdly, computers (or smart phones) are shifting from a *passive* role of accepting, processing and displaying information to a more *active* role of acquiring, deciphering, inferring, recommending information and at times, executing action automatically. Fourthly, context-aware systems can sense other computers and users in surrounding situation that enables smart phones to facilitate cross-device and social interaction.

Changes brought by mobile context-awareness to HCI might lead to the following challenges: How can users be aware of the implicit contextual information inputted and captured by smart phones? How to exploit and integrate contextual information in multiple models? Should smart phones be more active in executing actions that are undertaken by human traditionally? How should human beings deal with an intelligent and emotional device with social networking ability?

4.2   Active and Passive Roles of Human and Computer in Interaction

The MCA systems can be categorized into two types by the passive/active role of computer in executing the inferring actions [30, 31]. In passive MCA system, the sensed information and inferring actions will be presented to user explicitly and user make decision on whether to take execution or not. In active MCA, computer execute inferring actions automatically and implicitly on the basis of contextual information and inference of potential actions of user.

From the perspective of human-computer interaction, one of the key differences between passive and active CA system exist in the way of interaction. Active CA implicitly adapts to a user's activity by changing the system's behavior, where passive CA explicitly presents the new or updated context to the user and let the user make the decision whether the system should continue or stop the execution. Passive CA system is characterized by explicit output of computer and active CA system is characterized by implicit input and output of computer. While explicit interaction contradicts the idea of invisible computing, disappearing interfaces and natural interaction, implicit interaction might be helpful in realizing the vision of a Ubiquitous Computing which can offer natural interaction [30]. A simple example of implicit interaction is the mobile phone that changes its profile to mute mode automatically in a meeting event of calendar. In the corresponding explicit context-aware application, the mobile phone prompts the user with information about the calendar event and lets the user decide whether the phone should be muted or not.

4.3   MCA and Intelligent/Adaptive User Interface

Context-awareness is also widely deployed in designing intelligent/adaptive user interface in order to circumvent problems caused by the increasing complexity of mobile human-computer interaction [32, 33]. Contextual information and inferred intentions of user are utilized to adapt user interface to users' behavior and actions. The screen of mobile phone might switch between landscape and portrait mode as user rotate the mobile phone, the layout of interface might also change accordingly. In this case, the gesture of mobile phone is sensed by gravity sensor and gyroscope and then utilized to adapt the user interface to the gesture.

5   Dominant Theories of User-Centric MCA

Theory is critical to HCI as a research field [34]. It is generally accepted that the lack of an adequate theory of HCI is one of the most important reasons why progress in the field of HCI is relatively modest [24]. In contrast to the general agreement that current attempts to apply cognitive psychology to HCI are not very successful, there is little agreement on the most promising theoretical alternative.

Although the "information processing loop" proposed by the dominant theory of cognitive point of view provides a coherent description of the whole system of human computer interaction within the information processing framework and structures the problem space of HCI in a helpful way, its ecological validity is questionable for its inability to take into consideration the context that exist outside this loop [24]. Human computer interaction can only be understood within a wider context and any HCI model needs to provide an appropriate conceptual basis for studies of computer use in its cultural, organizational and social context.

Therefore, efforts in developing a solid and widely accepted theoretical foundation for HCI are related to context more or less [35, 36]. These approaches model use-context as yet another source of information that can be formalized and transmitted to computers [36]. As alleged by Clemmensen [34], "HCI researchers need to know more about the sociocultural contexts of other researchers' use of theory, in the same way that designers need to know users' context of use in order to design systems and products for them".

5.1   Situated Action and CA

Situated action places emphasis on environmental context and stresses how the environment provides context for actions [37]. According to situated action theory, the goal for interaction is to support situated action and meaning making in specific con-texts, and the questions that arise revolve around how to complement formalized, computational representations and actions with the rich, complex, and messy situations at hand.

Situated action analogize interaction as phenomenological situated and accentuate the significance of constructing meaning on the fly and in specific contexts and situations, designing interaction moves from attempting to establish one correct understanding and set of metrics of interaction to studying the local, situated practices of users. Interaction is seen as an element of situated action in the world, the deciphering or construction of the situation is the core of the design [36].

MCA can help address some of the challenges by capturing, understanding, structuring and modeling the specific contexts and then provide individualized and customized interactions. MAC is especially valuable in providing local, situated and context-dependent interactions by adapting the mobile phone actions to the specific contexts.

5.2   Activity Theory and CA

Activity theory is originally proposed by the Russian psychologist Alexey Leontiev [34], it argues that human mind emerges, exists, and develops within the context of human activity as a whole, and therefore analysis of object-oriented activities should be considered as a necessary prerequisite for comprehending the human mind. Activity theory was introduced to HCI in the late 1980s-early 1990s and has established itself as one of the most influential theories in HCI [34].

Activity theory proposes that the activity itself is the context. What takes place in an activity system composed of object, actions, and operation, is the context. Con-text is constituted through the enactment of an activity involving people and artifacts.

Activity-awareness means that the HCI system can actively construct and update a model of the ongoing activity by sensing, communicating, and interpreting changing conditions, resources and processes [32].

5.3 Distributed Cognition and CA

Distributed cognition intends to introduce computer technology into the workplace by remedying the shortcomings of the information-processing model in that it lacks cosid-erations for real-life action, work environment and user interaction [37]. It is a branch of cognitive science and considered as complementary to the information processing model that is devoted to the investigation of: (1) knowledge representation both inside the heads of individuals and in the world; (2) knowledge propagation between distinct individuals and artifacts, and; (3) transformations which external structures undergo when operated on by individuals and artifacts [35]. Distributed cognition emphasizes interaction over individual in HCI systems by construing the latter as a distributed collection of interacting people and artifacts.

In the vision of ubiquitous computing, context is spatially and temporally distributed in a ubiquitous computing environment. Distribution has a significant role and is central to the realization of context-awareness system in Ubiquitous Computing [31]. In a Distributed HCI system, MCA are capable of easing the sharing of contextual informa-tion, seeing and having access to context information that is around an application and distributing the contextual information within the HCI system spatially and temporally.

6   Challenges and Future Research Directions of User-Centric MCA

6.1 MCA and HCI

One of the significant changes that CA brought to the field of HCI is the roles of users and computers in interacting with each other. In traditional HCI systems, users are active and computers are passive when interacting with each other. In most cases, computers are simply waiting for user input and then executing the computing tasks as required. By contrast, computers tend to play a more active and even proactive role in context-aware HCI systems. Computer can sense, capture, decipher and reason about the contex-tual information of HCI and then execute certain actions based on the computing results of context-awareness. Despite progress in relevant technology and applications, atti-tudes towards active and passive context-awareness are divided by emphasis on CA computing capability of computers or users control over computers [7]. Although automatic execution of CA action and adaptation to con-textual information are critical metrics of MCA systems, the implicit interaction might lead to non-awareness of users over what's happening and unable to know what is required for users to do before s/he is required to do it [38]. High quality of MCA systems need to improve both the capability of computers and users at the same time by providing information to users at the right time and letting users control the interaction.

Furthermore, a novel theoretical framework of HCI is required to explain and structure the interaction characterized by context-awareness. We proposed a preliminary model named Context-Computer Interaction (CCI, Fig. 2.) to embody the above mentioned changes that context-awareness brought to HCI. CCI differs from traditional HCI as below:

• Human is not the only source of input any more but creates a context pool together with computing devices and environmental factors. This implies that computers are not interacting solely with humans, but as a whole contextual system in which humans are but one form of constituents and the three units interact with each other dynamically.
• Computer approaches the contextual system, captures the contextual information, deciphers the meaning behind, predicts plausible actions and executes actions proactively rather than waiting for the explicit input and command from users.
• Computers might predict and execute actions implicitly to improve the efficiency and unfetter human from selecting, judging and executing some apparent and predictable actions. The computer itself has a closed loop of information (context) processing characterized by executing behaviors implicitly.

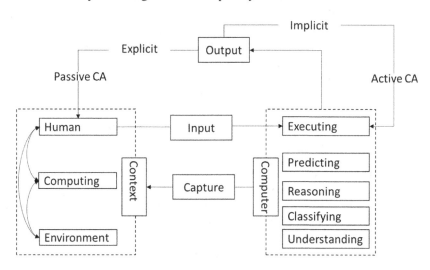

Fig. 2. Context Computer Interaction (CCI)

6.2 Non-instrumental User Experience and MCA

Much of the ongoing efforts to apply context-awareness to the interaction and inter-face design of mobile applications or services focus on improving the efficiency of HCI systems [3, 4, 16]. Context-awareness is valuable in improving the instrumental or pragmatic user experience of mobile application and services by sensing, deciphering, interpreting and adapting to the contextual information automatically. However, users of mobile applications might expect more from interacting with mobile phone than improvements to efficiency.

Past studies have shown that users are aware of hedonic and non-instrumental qualities such as interactive aesthetics, privacy, stimulation and social status in long-term UX of mobile phones [39], although some of them (e.g., privacy) are already addressed [14]. Social, emotional or informational state were considered as parts of contextual information that should be employed in context-aware systems at the early era of relevant areas [20]. Mobile context-awareness is also widely adopted in developing and designing applications dedicated for social-networking, shopping, sharing and well-being as well. Any efforts of MCA UX should address both instrumental and non-instrumental issues instead of focusing on productivity.

6.3 Research, Evaluation and Design of HCI System in Context

Research and evaluation is considered as one of the major cornerstones of HCI. During the last decade, attention was paid to the pros and cons of lab and field evaluations in the wild, as well as how to balance research methods in natural, artificial, and environment independent settings [37, 40, 41].

Traditional laboratory-based usability testing methods are questioned as they are often expensive, time consuming and fail to reflect real use cases [30]. It tends to measure the efficiency, effectiveness and satisfaction of products or services by constraining users in artificial usability test settings and getting them to complete predefined 'typical' tasks. Users' interactions with computers in this situation is distinct from the real scenarios given that the interactions is interfered by moderators and fragmented by discrete tasks. By contrast, there is a growing tendency to infer and extract user experience information implicitly from user interface events and behaviors in the field of HCI in order to fully experience and explore real world usage [41].

Exploring usage of mobile applications and devices is still challenging despite much attention being paid to this issue. Traditional issues associated with conducting HCI studies (e.g., incentives and recruiting) are confounded with the highly mobile, dynamic and complicated context that makes explorations in this area creepy [42].

Over the past decade, a range of methodologies have been adopted to evaluate mobile services and conducing HCI studies in non-intrusive and ecologically valid ways [42]. Amongst them, experience sampling is proposed as an ideal alternative of traditional research method. Conventional long-term ethnographic observation is too intrusive in certain domains, such as sleeping habits or bathing rituals [43]. Collecting data in the wild through sensor-equipped prototypes is considered as one of the optional approaches of conducting user studies in evaluating product or services. This form of data collection also allows researchers and developers of HCI systems to glean insight into activities and contexts where an observer might be an undesirable presence.

Involving users in the context of use in the design of mobile systems was proposed as "The Final Frontier in the Practice of User-Centered Design" [44]. New design methods were also proposed by utilizing an open contextual and experiential design approach that makes extensive use of varying kinds of knowledge [43]. These sort of methods try to explore how mobile context-aware technologies and applications can effectively support contextualized learning and the relationships among different aspects of context. Amongst them, Experiential Design Landscapes and Living Labs allow in-context experimentation and data collection "that put all stakeholders (e.g., designers, users, researchers, developers, officials, producers…) in context of using products and services".

7   Conclusion

Context-awareness is playing an increasingly vital role in developing mobile HCI systems. Little attention was paid to the user-centric view of MCA in comparison to the extensive studies from the computing-centric point of view. Attitudes towards implicit/explicit interactions and active/passive roles of humans and computers are divided, influence of MCA on user experience and related measures are not clear enough in which both instrumental and non-instrumental user experience might be considered. Dedicated theoretical framework is required to structure and illustrate the interactions characterized by context-awareness in mobile HCI.

Acknowledgements.   This study is part of the project *Mobile context-aware cross-cultural applications (MOCCA)* funded by Marie Skłodowska-Curie Action. The grant number is 708122.

References

1. Schilit, B.N., Theimer, M.M.: Disseminating active map information to mobile hosts. IEEE Netw. **8**(5), 22–32 (1994)
2. Kiseleva, J., Williams, K., Jiang, J., et al.: Understanding user satisfaction with intelligent assistants. In: Proceedings of the 2016 ACM on Conference on Human Information Interaction and Retrieval, pp. 121–130 ACM (2016)
3. Feng, J., Liu, Y.: Intelligent context-aware and adaptive interface for mobile LBS. Comput. Intell. Neurosci. **5**, 1–10 (2015)
4. Zheng, M., Cheng, S., Xu, Q.: Context-based mobile user interface. J. Comput. Commun. **4**(09), 1–9 (2016)
5. Forkan, A., Khalil, I., Tari, Z.: CoCaMAAL: a cloud-oriented context-aware middleware in ambient assisted living. Future Gener. Comput. Syst. **35**, 114–127 (2014)
6. Lin, C.H., Ho, P.H., Lin, H.C.: Framework for NFC-based intelligent agents: a context-awareness enabler for social internet of things. Int. J. Distrib. Sens. Netw. **2014**(7), 1–16 (2014)
7. Perera, C., Zaslavsky, A., Christen, P., Georgakopoulos, D.: Context aware computing for the internet of things: a survey. IEEE Commun. Surv. Tutorials **16**(1), 414–454 (2014)

8. Ogata, H., Yano, Y.: Context-aware support for computer-supported ubiquitous learning. In: Proceedings of the 2nd IEEE International Workshop on Wireless and Mobile Technologies in Education, pp. 27–34. IEEE (2004)

9. Emmanouilidis, C., Koutsiamanis, R.A., Tasidou, A.: Mobile guides: taxonomy of architectures, context awareness, technologies and applications. J. Netw. Comput. Appl. **36**(1), 103–125 (2013)

10. Adomavicius, G., Tuzhilin, A.: Context-aware recommender systems. In: Ricci, F., Rokach, L., Shapira, B. (eds.) Recommender Systems Handbook, pp. 191–226. Springer, USA (2015)

11. Canny, J.: The future of human-computer interaction. Acm. Queue. **4**(6), 24–32 (2006)

12. Barkhuus, L., Dey, A.: Is context-aware computing taking control away from the user? three levels of interactivity examined. In: Dey, Anind K., Schmidt, A., McCarthy, Joseph F. (eds.) UbiComp 2003. LNCS, vol. 2864, pp. 149–156. Springer, Heidelberg (2003). doi: 10.1007/978-3-540-39653-6_12

13. Schmidt, A.: Implicit human computer interaction through context. Pers. Ubiquit. Comput. **4**(2), 191–199 (2000)

14. Dey, A.K., Häkkilä, J.: Context-awareness and mobile devices. User Interface Des. Eval. Mob. Technol. **1**, 205–217 (2008)

15. Hong, J., Suh, E., Kim, S.J.: Context-aware systems: a literature review and classification. Expert Syst. Appl. **36**(4), 8509–8522 (2009)

16. Vetek, A., Flanagan, John A., Colley, A., Keränen, T.: SmartActions: context-aware mobile phone shortcuts. In: Gross, T., Gulliksen, J., Kotzé, P., Oestreicher, L., Palanque, P., Prates, R.O., Winckler, M. (eds.) INTERACT 2009. LNCS, vol. 5726, pp. 796–799. Springer, Heidelberg (2009). doi:10.1007/978-3-642-03655-2_86

17. Ranganathan, A., Campbell, R.H.: An infrastructure for context-awareness based on first order logic. Pers. Ubiquit. Comput. **7**(6), 353–364 (2003)

18. Abowd, G.D., Dey, A.K., Brown, P.J., et al.: Towards a better understanding of context and context-awareness. In: Gellersen, H.W. (ed.) HUC 1999. LNCS, vol. 1707, pp. 304–307. Springer, Heidelberg (1999)

19. Dey, A.K.: Understanding and using context. Pers. Ubiquit. Comput. **5**(1), 4–7 (2001)

20. Abowd, D., Dey, A.K., Orr, R., et al.: Context-awareness in wearable and ubiquitous computing. Virtual Reality **3**(3), 200–211 (1998)

21. Bauer, C.: A comparison and validation of 13 context meta-models. In: European Conference on Information Systems (2012)

22. Schmidt, A., Beigl, M., Gellersen, H.W.: There is more to context than location. Comput. Graph. **23**(6), 893–901 (1999)

23. Yürür, Ö., Liu, C.H., Sheng, Z., et al.: Context-awareness for mobile sensing: a survey and future directions. IEEE Commun. Surv. Tutorials **18**(1), 68–93 (2013)

24. Kaptelinin, V.: Activity theory: Implications for human-computer interaction. In: Context and Consciousness: Activity Theory and Human-Computer Interaction, vol. 1, pp. 103–116 (1996)

25. Zhang, D., Huang, H., Lai, C.F., Liang, X., Zou, Q., Guo, M.: Survey on context-awareness in ubiquitous media. Multimedia Tools Appl. **67**(1), 179–211 (2013)

26. Makris, P., Skoutas, D.N., Skianis, C.: A survey on context-aware mobile and wireless networking: On networking and computing environments' integration. IEEE Commun. Surv. Tutorials **15**(1), 362–386 (2013)

27. Pather, D., Wesson, J., Cowley, L.: A Model for Context Awareness for Mobile Applications Using Multiple-input Sources (Doctoral dissertation, Nelson Mandela Metropolitan University) (2015)

28. Hibbeln, M., Jenkins, J.L., Schneider, C., Valacich, J.S., Weinmann, M.: How is your user feeling? Inferring emotion through human-computer interaction devices. Manage. Inform. Syst. Q. **41**(1), 1–21 (2017)
29. Gallego, D., Woerndl, W., Huecas, G.: Evaluating the impact of proactivity in the user experience of a context-aware restaurant recommender for Android smartphones. J. Syst. Architect. **59**(9), 748–758 (2013)
30. Rötting, M., Zander, T., Trösterer, S., et al.: Implicit interaction in multimodal human-machine systems. In: Schlick C. (ed.) Industrial Engineering and Ergonomics, pp. 523–536. Springer, Heidelberg (2009)
31. Schmidt A.: Ubiquitous computing-computing in context. Lancaster University. Ph.D Thesis (2003)
32. Cai, G., Xue, Y.: Activity-oriented context-aware adaptation assisting mobile geo-spatial activities. In: Proceedings of the 11th International Conference on Intelligent User Interfaces, pp. 354–356. ACM (2006)
33. Baldauf, M., Dustdar, S., Rosenberg, F.: A survey on context-aware systems. Int. J. Ad Hoc Ubiquitous Comput. **2**(4), 263–277 (2007)
34. Clemmensen, T., Kaptelinin, V., Nardi, B.: Making HCI theory work: an analysis of the use of activity theory in HCI research. Behav. Inform. Technol. **35**(8), 608–627 (2016)
35. Nardi, B.A.: Studying context: A comparison of activity theory, situated action models, and distributed cognition. In: Nardi, B.A. (ed.) Context and consciousness: Activity theory and human-computer interaction, pp. 69–102. MIT Press, Cambridge (1996)
36. Harrison, S., Tatar, D., Sengers, P.: The three paradigms of HCI. In: Alt. Chi. Session at the SIGCHI Conference on Human Factors in Computing Systems San Jose, California, USA, pp. 1–18 (2007)
37. Proctor, R.W., Vu, K.P.L.: The cognitive revolution at age 50: has the promise of the human information-processing approach been fulfilled? Int. J. Hum. Comput. Inter. **21**(3), 253–284 (2006)
38. López, G., Guerrero, L.A.: Ubiquitous notification mechanism to provide user awareness. In: Rebelo, F., Soares, M. (eds.) Advances in Ergonomics in Design. AISC, vol. 485, pp. 689–700. Springer, Cham (2016)
39. Kujala, S., Roto, V., Väänänen-Vainio-Mattila, K.: Identifying hedonic factors in long-term user experience. In: Proceedings of the 2011 Conference on Designing Pleasurable Products and Interfaces, p. 17. ACM (2011)
40. Kjeldskov, J., Paay, J.: A longitudinal review of Mobile HCI research methods. In: Proceedings of the 14th International Conference on Human-Computer Interaction with Mobile Devices and Services, pp. 69–78. ACM (2012)
41. Menezes, C., Nonnecke, B.: UX-Log: understanding website usability through recreating users' experiences in logfiles. Int. J. Virtual Worlds Hum. Comput. Interact. **2**, 47–55 (2014)
42. Church, K., Ferreira, D., Banovic, N., et al.: Understanding the challenges of mobile phone usage data. In: Proceedings of the 17th International Conference on Human-Computer Interaction with Mobile Devices and Services, pp. 504–514. ACM (2015)
43. Gardien, P., Djajadiningrat, T., Hummels, C., et al.: Changing your hammer: the implications of paradigmatic innovation for design practice. Int. J. Des. **8**(2), 119–139 (2014)
44. Eshet, E., Bouwman, H.: Context of Use: The Final Frontier in the Practice of User-Centered Design?. Interact Comput. **29**(3), 368–390 (2017)

Consumer Involvement in NPD Different Stages

Yanmin Xue[✉] and Menghui Huang

School of Art and Design, Xi'an University of Technology,
Xi'an, Shaanxi, People's Republic of China
xueym@xaut.edu.cn

Abstract. The positive significance of consumers involving in enterprise NPD has been generally realized. But the involvement condition in each stage of the NPD and involving modes remain to be further research. This paper USES field experience and questionnaire survey to research consumers involving in Chinese SMEs NPD. Main content includes typical stages of NPD, which NPD stages consumers are involved in and should be involved in, and involving mode in each NPD stage, etc. Based on the investigation results, a case study of integrated consumers into wardrobe, umbrella stand and clothes rack design is carried out on a Chinese furniture enterprise. Customer is involved in multiple stages of NPD, in which crowd- sourcing model based on web2.0 has been applied. The application introducing customer in stages of NPD has been achieved good results.

Keywords: Customer involving · NPD · Stages · Case study · Crowdsourcing

1 Introduction

Consumer involving in NPD has a positive significance. Good cooperation with customer can reduce developing cost to achieve a certain innovation, bring higher creative efficiency (Juho Ylimäki 2014), reduce the number of faulty prototypes until attaining the desired product (Gloria 2014), reduce manufacturer's planning time and inventory obsolescence, allowing it to be more responsive to customer needs. (Yuanqiong He 2014). Some literature researched stages in which consumers involved. Klaus Brockhoff (2003) mentioned some stages in NPD: Idea Generation, Concept Development, Product Design, Prototyping/Testing, pre-announcement and market launch. The research needs more about the customer involving degree and modes study. Customer Involving mode in NPD stages is mentioned in some literature, but there is no specialized research. In recent years, research on crowdsourcing began to rise. Souad Djelassi (2013) concluded that crowdsourcing generates a win-win relationship, creating value for both firms and customers, he also analyzed on the Negatives of Crowdsourcing: time consuming, uncertainty, employee morale. This paper will do some preliminary survey on crowdsourcing in Chinese SMEs.

Based on the above literature review result, this paper did further survey on consumers involving condition of Chinese SMEs. The survey content includes: NPD typical stages, consumers involving condition in NPD, the stages suitable for customers

© Springer International Publishing AG 2017
F.F.-H. Nah and C.-H. Tan (Eds.): HCIBGO 2017, Part I, LNCS 10293, pp. 128–136, 2017.
DOI: 10.1007/978-3-319-58481-2_11

to involve in, customer involving mode, the view on crowdsourcing and its application, etc. Research includes field survey in plant and questionnaire. Finally, the paper applied research results in one China enterprise NPD. Some online sections corresponding to the typical NPD stages are integrated into the enterprise website. Through the consumers' online crowdsourcing, the NPD received a better effect.

2 Methodology

2.1 Enterprise Investigation

To have a preliminary understanding on consumer involvement in NPD, the authors interned in one Chinese furniture enterprise for three months. The NPD process is observed and summarized. In general, the NPD process is as follows: The designers get the sales condition, the need of customer and dealer from trade ministry. Then they start to do brainstorm to get concepts expressed through 2D sketch and the final 3D rendering. In this period, they constantly communicate with the director of the technique department. The selected product concept is made into prototype for testing. After testing qualified, it will be produced for a small amount of trial production. Use internet platform such as Tmall shop or Taobao website to market a small scale. The product with good market feedback will be formally mass-produced. At this point, departments including design, internet marketer, marketing, trade will actively cooperate with each other to put this product to the market. The authors also made some research on several other enterprises' NPD process. They are similar with above. Analysis of this kind of NPD process, some certain problems exist in it.

1. Lack of product planning, new product market positioning is not accurate. NPD is generally based on information from sales report, dealer's demand and manager's decision, etc. The study of consumer demand is lacking. Once lack of dealer orders, enterprises will fall into a passive situation and finally be eliminated by the market.
2. Consumer participation in NPD process is less. At the beginning of the NPD process, sales can reflect consumer attitude towards products. The later trial sale also can get consumer preferences for this product. Besides the above two stages, there is almost no consumers participation.

Companies hope to be able to accurately grasp the market demand and attract a wider range of consumer involvement. What suffer them are lack of management and financial support.

2.2 Questionnaire

On the basis of investigation in enterprise, the authors designed a questionnaire to investigate consumer involving stage and mode in NPD. Respondents mainly are managers, designers and users. There are three parts in it. The first is background questions. The second is the main part including 30 titles about the main stages in NPD. Depending on the different types of the respondents, they need to answer different questions. Managers and designers need to answer enterprise background, typical stages of NPD, the NPD stages in which consumer involved in, consumer involving condition in each stage, etc. Consumers are to answer which stages once involved in and the involving mode. The questionnaire also wanted to know which stages the consumers are expected to participate in. Likert five-point rating scale method is used to explore the involving degree in each stage. At the end of questionnaire, crowdsourcing is asked for reviews. Research mainly takes the following two ways. First is the network mode: send questionnaire to employees and consumers through network means, such as QQ, MSN and Email. Followed by is the field investigation, carry the printed questionnaire to the enterprise, and communicate with employees. Personnel filled in it after understanding or interviewer filled in it.

There are 136 electronic questionnaires, 50 printed (field research) and 15 interview notes. The involved companies come from Zhejiang, Guangdong, Jiangsu, Shaanxi Province in China. Invalid 20 are excluded. The valid copy is 181.

3 Survey Result

3.1 Customer Involving Rate in NPD Stages

Products of enterprises in this survey are household appliances, furniture, toys, daily necessities, etc. Majority is SMEs. Survey shows that the NPD process can be divided into three main phases, which is early phase, middle phase and later phase.

Typical NPD stages in these three phases includes: in the early phase of NPD, there are many stages, including market research (customer needs), concept generation, concept selection, concept test. In middle phase, system design and refinement design and improvement are included. In the later phase, trial production stage and market promotion.

The customer can be divided into three categories according to the involving degree, which are lead users, common users and potential users. The involving mode can be online and offline, which presents many modes.

Through overall analysis of questionnaires data, the results show that consumers involving rate in each stage is as shown in Table 1.

There are some difference between the real and hope condition. The actual involving condition is not hopeful. Only trial production seems getting some emphasis, with 81% for the involving rate. Other four stages shows small rate. So enterprises are

Table 1. Customer involvement rate in each NPD stage

Questions	Respondents	Need Identification	Concept generation	Concept selection	Concept test	Trial production
Customer Involving condition	Employee	13%	21%	16.67%	23.6%	66.67%
	Customer	33%	15%	16.1%	41%	81%
Which stage suitable to involve in	Employee	83.33%	50%	86%	83.33%	100%
	Customer	78%	33%	83%	85.2%	90.2%

short of guidance and organization for customer involvement in some important stages. This is disadvantageous to catch consumption psychology and trends. While the role of the stages has been recognized. We can see that both employee and customer think most stages are suitable to involve in, especially in need identification, concept selection, concept test and trial production. This reflects some urgent desire to exactly hold the customer need and market need. But the ability to collect customer need for NPD is still short and need to be improved.

For the question of main problems SMEs facing to consumer cooperation, lack of management ability, human resource shortage is major concern.

3.2   The Cooperation Source in Each NPD Stage

In different stages of NPD, acquiring phase achievements needs the help of some external force. The channels to get the design ideas are collected as Table 2. Customer, product expos, dealers, suppliers, expert, patent, manager, inner team, technique test, all devote their own strength to the NPD. However, the result shows that companies mainly depend on the internal staff, managers and clients.

That customer involve in the early and late stage is usual, they are supposed to be in part of many stages, such as Concept Generation, Concept Selection and Concept Test. While the enterprise meets with some trouble to get enough consumers to join the actions. Organizing focus group, running expert seminar need time, money and personnel. They also lack of the ability to change and innovate the original process.

The last two questions of the investigation try to explore some ways to solve the problem. Firstly, we want to know about perceptions on new media application under Web2.0. The results show that the respondents hold hopes on consumers involvement in NPD based on new Media. They hope that inter- active communication with customers through various media platforms could improve the efficiency of cooperation so as to improve enterprise innovation ability, to solve this money, personnel problem. New ways based on internet should help a lot. This research is also to explore the possible modes for each stage for the enterprise to guide and attract the customers involve in their NPD, most modes based on new media, such as some APPs on smart phone, competitions around the nation, some actions on the portal website. Through these newborn modes, the crowdsourcing width and depth is increased with better effect.

Table 2. The main channels for each NPD stage to cooperate

Stages	Channels			
Customer need identification	Customer	Product expo	Dealer	Supplier
Concept generation	Customer	Inner team	Expert	Patent
Concept selection	Customer	Inner team	Manager	Dealer
Concept test	Customer	Technique test		
Trial production	Customer	Dealer		

3.3   Customer Involving Mode in Each NPD Stage

Research also explores on consumer involving modes at every stage of the enterprise NPD. The involving channels can be divided into online and offline. Table 3 is the summary of consumer involving mode in every stage, combining with the research results.

In the customer need identification stage of the early phase, the suggestions from the costumer are important source for innovation and the modes for enterprises to guide the customer involve includes electrical questionnaire, printed questionnaire, interviews. And in web2.0 era, online need collection is another very useful way to get more voice. These modes are proper for lead users, common users and potential users.

In concept generation, select and test stages, observation (common users), focus group (lead users) and prototype (lead users and common users) are to assure the coincidence with the customer need.

While there are new modes emerging in this web2.0 era. Online idea submission is good for lead users too. And design competitions are adopted by many enterprises in recent years. For example, the China Hardware Product Design Awards has been held for 11 sessions and has obtained sustainable awareness and success. In each session, there should be 4 or 5 enterprises sponsored for it. And the design objectives are mainly oriented to the main products of these sponsored enterprises. The competition attract dozens of national universities, design companies as well as many independent designer's participation and support. The quantity and quality of the submitted design is in constant progress. The competition give a good propaganda for the enterprise, sometimes with a better role than advertisement. And the thousands of submitted designs provide wonderful design innovation ideas for the product improvement and new generation product. The enterprises benefit a lot from the competitions. It is good for product planning, product production and design.

It is important to note that in Concept Selection stage, the present condition is that the decision right is often in the hands of managers and suppliers. They choose their own admired design, not considering the customers' comment. Actually, the managers have a lot of experience based on good understanding of their own products. And suppliers can choose the proper design based on the materials and manufacturing process. Also the clients have their opinion on the design according to their requirement. Only the customers' comment is omitted, which has a big role on the right design selection. In the past, maybe it is not convenient to gather a certain amount of customers to do the selection job. While in this web 2.0 time, it is easier to get the customer comment. Online selection can be run. The design pictures with high resolution, online interaction can make customers preliminary understand of the design. The customers can vote for the many pictures and the winning designs will come out of them. Combing the customers' comment will give the managers some rational voice.

In Concept Test stage, besides the traditional way of providing prototype to some lead users and get their feedback, some new and effective modes based on internet are popular in recent years. The user interaction design, virtual reality technique give more presenting forms and make them easy to understand. The users also can interact with the product by moving, rotating, operating it through the computer mouse. Product simulation, multimedia interaction, online display are some useful ways for user interaction.

Table 3. The involving modes in each NPD stage

Stages	Modes			
Customer need identification	Electronic questionnaire	Printed questionnaire	Interview	Online need collection
Concept generation	Observation	Focus group	Online idea submission	Design competitions
Concept selection	Inviting customers	Online selection	Expert, client, managers, suppliers selection	
Concept test	Product simulation	Multimedia interaction	Prototype	Online display
Trial production	Questionnaire	Sampling survey		

In trial production stage, questionnaire, sampling survey can be online and offline forms too.

4   Application

The authors provided the investigate report to one medium-sized enterprise in Zhejiang province. It integrates development, manufacturing and market. The main products are furniture and daily family products. The company adopts some of the suggestions for its NPD.

Consumers are involved in some critical stages to refine NPD design. The involving detail modes is shown in Table 4. Traditional offline involving mode is interview, focus group in customer need identification stage and prototype using in concept test stage. In addition, the company integrates consumer participating section in its portal web, through the crowdsourcing to expand the involving scope. Some interesting section are designed to fully collect customer need, to inspire their concept generation, to get their comment, which include "Fancier", "communication Bar", "creativity", "I choose", etc. These online sections are good-designed with nice visual images and easy usability, thus attracting many lead users, common users to join them and give out their comment.

The related products are wardrobe (Fig. 1), umbrella stand (Fig. 2) and clothes rack (Fig. 3). These three designs undergo online and offline segments. The young designers explore more physiology feeling and use need through these channels than traditional ways. And they get clear design directions and feel confidential.

In customer need identification stage, designers invite common customers and dealers to visit the product pavilion, one-on-one interview and focus group are both used. Some suggestions are given for the product improving. By "Fancier", "Communication Bar" on the portal website, there are also some other detail showing. Combining the two folio, urgent shortages or need come out. For the wardrobe, the prominent problem is assemble hard, single internal display mode. For the umbrella stand, taking big space is a main concern. And customers hope the clothes rack be folded, adjusted the length, and be easy to carry.

Facing the analyzed customers' interest and need list, combining the production condition and future plan of the company, more than 20 design are generated and submitted on the portal web. Among the submitted designs there are also some from customers by "creativity". Dealers, suppliers are invited to do "I choose", while the main vote are from customers. Finally, these 3 designs come out with high votes.

Prototypes are made to further test the products by manufacturing process and cost calculation. Some customers including lead users, common users and potential users sign and are chosen to trial use the products. Also the user evaluation about the usability is important for next refinement.

The 3 designs are described simply as follows. They have been granted utility model patent. Because they fully consider the opinions of suppliers, dealers and customers, they fit to the manufacturing process without material refinement. So far they have been produced and marketed in a good condition.

The wardrobe can be easily changed into a bookstore by pushing the two sides to the middle. When it is used in a small room, the bookstore form is good. When a big room is available, the bookstore can be changed into wardrobe. It provides the different application and convenience.

Table 4. The involving modes in case application

Stages	Modes		
Customer need identification	Interview Focus group	"Fancier" section	"Communication Bar" section
Concept generation	"Creativity" section	Online idea submission	
Concept selection	"I choose" section	Online selection	
Concept test	Online register	Prototype	

Fig. 1. The wardrobe design

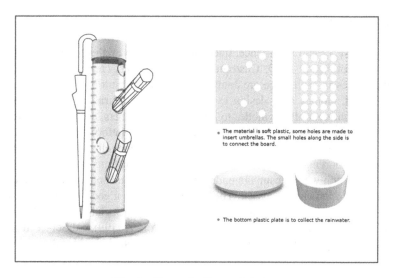

Fig. 2. The umbrella stand design

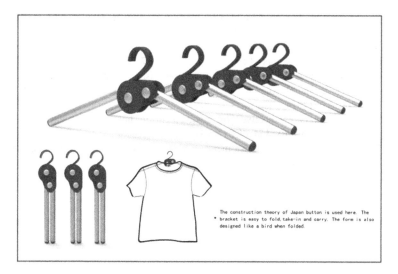

Fig. 3. The clothes rack design

The material of the umbrella stand is soft plastic, some holes are made to insert umbrellas. The small holes along the side is to connect the board. The bottom plastic plate is to collect the rainwater. The design considers the package problem, cost problem. The stand assembles easily. When it is not used, it is easy to discompose and store, saving the indoor space.

The clothes rack design uses the construction theory of Japanese button. It is easy to fold, take-in and carry. The form is also designed like a bird when folded.

5 Conclusion

This article USES Field experience, questionnaire to survey the condition of Chinese consumers involving in NPD. Customer involving stages, creative idea sources and involving modes in each stage are analyzed. The study result is applied in wardrobe, umbrella stand, clothes rack design cycle in one China furniture design enterprise. Besides the traditional offline modes to involve the customers, each stage is integrated consumer's participation by online consumer innovation platform based on enterprise's portal website. The NPD process is modified and get a better effect. The paper proposes that the crowdsourcing models based on new Media platforms will be advantageous way of cooperation with consumers under Web2.0 age. And some effective and useful modes are suggested and discussed. The research result is a good reference to NPD in China SMEs. (Thank for the support by Humanity and Social Science Youth foundation of Chinese Education Ministry (Grant No.14YJCZH199) and Sci-Tech research plan project of Xi'an University of Technology (Grant No.117-211408))

References

Ylimäki, J.: A dynamic model of supplier - customer product development collaboration strategies. Ind. Mark. Manage. **43**, 996–1004 (2014)

Sánchez-González, G., Herrera, L.: Effects of customer cooperation on knowledge generation activities and innovation results of firms. Bus. Res. Q. **17**, 292–302 (2014)

He, Y., Lai, K.: The impact of supplier integration on customer integration and new product performance: the mediating role of manufacturing flexibility under trust theory. Int. J. Prod. Econ. **147**, 260–270 (2014)

Brockhoff, K.: Customers perspectives of involvement in new product development. Int. J. Technol. Manage. **26**(5/6), 464–481 (2003)

Djelassi, S.: Isabelle Decoopman, Customers' participation in product development through crowdsourcing. Ind. Mark. Manage. **42**, 683–692 (2013)

Information Systems in Healthcare, Learning, Cultural Heritage and Government

Communication in Co-innovation Networks

A Moderated Mediation Model of Social Affordances, Social Experience, and Desire for Learning

Kaveh Abhari[✉], Bo Xiao, and Elizabeth Davidson

University of Hawaii at Manoa, Honolulu, USA
{abhari,boxiao,edavidso}@hawaii.edu

Abstract. The aim of this study is to develop an integrative understanding of the factors fostering communication activities in co-innovation networks. Participants in these social networks must communicate actively to foster collaboration and idea generation, but communication may not develop naturally, even if the platform provides the software features to do so. This study clarifies the mechanism underlying the relationship between co-innovation platform affordances and communication. We explored the role of sociotechnical affordances, social experience, and desire for learning that are believed to influence individuals' continuous communication intentions. We outline how social technology affordances that enable socialization may affect actors experience and behavior and ultimately the co-innovation outcomes. We conclude with a discussion of future explorations of this perspective.

Keywords: Co-innovation · Socialization · Communication · Social affordances · Experience · Desire for learning

1 Introduction

Communication and information technologies (ICTs) have created new opportunities for firms to innovate, by engaging external actors in innovation processes (Gassmann et al. 2010). A recent and notable development involves the application of social technologies to extends opportunities for collaboration across the spectrum of innovation activities to individuals who are socially-engaged in the co-innovation process (Wu et al. 2016). These co-innovation actors – independent members of a co-innovation community – are the key source of intellectual and social capital in co-innovation projects. Social technologies afford massive multi-agent socio-professional interactions among social actors, which transform innovation from a firm-based R&D process to a collective social experience (Martini 2012). In this setting, communication activities play a key role in driving and supporting co-innovation outcomes by increasing participation, egalitarian engagement, and ideation.

Recently we have seen a shift in Information System (IS) and Human-computer interaction (HCI) research from a predominant focus on the features and potential impact of digital innovation platforms to the exploration of how actors experience and co-create

© Springer International Publishing AG 2017
F.F.-H. Nah and C.-H. Tan (Eds.): HCIBGO 2017, Part I, LNCS 10293, pp. 139–153, 2017.
DOI: 10.1007/978-3-319-58481-2_12

value in these sociotechnical environments (Lusch and Nambisan 2015; Yoo 2010). In a co-innovation network, actors' socio-professional experience has been found to be crucial to network productivity and efficiency (Nambisan and Nambisan 2008). We define socio-professional experience as the socialization experience gained in a professional community or triggered by professional interactions. It is a form of actor experience gained at the intersection of social and professional interactions. Co-innovation networks are professional communities enabled by social mechanisms and socialization is the main aspect of co-innovation processes. Therefore, in a co-innovation network, actor experience is neither purely social (because of professional goals) nor merely professional (because of social triggers).

An actor's socio-professional experience is associated with the interactions between the actor and the social features of the platform that connect the actor to the other members of the network. The social features of the technology platform enable the possibilities of socio-professional interactions that, if actualized, will form the actor's socio-professional experience. We conceptualize these possibilities as sociotechnical affordances (social affordances in short) (Zhao and Rosson 2009). Social affordances, therefore, refer to the properties of a social technology — co-innovation platform in our case — that permit socio-professional actions. Social affordances are potentials (action possibilities) that enable social exchange and may lead to experience formation.

Recent research suggests that social affordances may increase social experience formation due to the possibilities the former offer for interaction and exchange between social actors in a professional setting (Treem and Leonardi 2012). However, more possibilities are not necessarily associated with positive experience and even the higher intention to socialize. This uncertainty about the associations between affordances, experience, and intention has not been properly addressed yet. To this end, this study represents an early effort toward explaining how affordances-driven co-innovation experience influences an important aspect of co-innovation, that is, actors' continuous intention to communicate (or socialize) with others in the co-innovation network. Modeling and measuring this effect can provide new insights to understand, explain, and predict the consequence of technology affordances (Leonardi 2013; Volkoff and Strong 2013). The findings enhance our understanding of the effect of platform social affordances on actors' continuous intention to communicate by investigating the mediating role of actors' socio-professional experience. The study also reveals how the intervening effect of socio-professional experience is moderated by the actors' desire for learning.

The remainder of this paper is organized as follows. In the next section, we review relevant prior research on social affordances, actor experience, and socialization. We then present our research model and develop the hypotheses. Next, we report our research method and the results of hypothesis testing. We conclude the paper with a discussion of the results, contributions, and future study avenues.

2   Background

Social technologies provide functionalities to support the process of human social interaction. However, social technologies go beyond computer-mediated communication as simple realizations of communication media by enabling social relationships and affording new ways of social value co-creation (Sutcliffe et al. 2011). The benefits of engaging social actors by using social technologies have been argued persuasively (e.g. Parameswaran and Whinston 2007; Sutcliffe et al. 2011; Zhou 2011). However, basic research is as yet needed to understand the underlying mechanisms fostering or hindering social engagement and participation in technology-mediated social networks (Curley et al. 2013; Gassmann et al. 2010).

Actor socialization mediated by a social platform is the initial and essential phase of co-innovation (Abhari et al. 2016b). Platform technologies connect social actors who are often physically dispersed to establish virtual innovation communities and facilitate cooperative telework. Social actors who use the platform develop their own social norms and experience, as the nature of the platform affordances both constrains and facilitates social participation (Wellman et al. 2003). While there appears to be overall agreement on the effect of platform technology on actor experience (Martini et al. 2013), the effect of technology affordances on actors' socialization experience and intention is yet the subject of debate. We argue that understanding the underlying mechanism with respect to the human factors affecting this relationship is a critical step to inform the design of co-innovation platform technology.

2.1   Communication in Co-innovation Networks

Co-innovation networks engage individual actors in reciprocal value exchanges to build a knowledge-driven socially-enabled enterprise and co-create new organizational, individual, and shared values (Lee et al. 2012). Communication between actors such as networking and sharing knowledge is an inherent aspect of co-innovation processes (Paulini et al. 2013). Due to the distributed nature of the co-innovation process, actor communication is also a key to the success of innovation process (Gressgård 2012). Connecting actors and facilitating collaboration are the two primary goals that co-innovation networks can achieve through communication functions. For example, these networks rely on actors' continuous communication to build co-innovation team and develop shared interests, professional relationships, and trust among the members. Continuous communication helps actors establish and enhance their socio-professional image and identity. Furthermore, maintaining effective communication among actors facilitates and supports inter- and intra-project collaboration (Nambisan 2013; Paulini et al. 2013; Wu et al. 2015). Communication activities familiarize actors with one another thereby facilitating collaboration activities. With limited communication between actors, and between actors and the innovation sponsor, establishing such working relationships is impossible. Likewise, collaboration activities involve actors discussing opinions, sharing knowledge, asking for help or votes, or participating in general discussions. Although communication may lead to collaboration, they are different processes in terms of actor goals and expected outcomes. Actors communicate to learn, network, self-promote or share their understanding without necessarily teaming up with other actors to improve a specific new product or solution.

Communication is a goal-directed behavior and therefore, human factors such as motivation, goals and personalities can maintain or discourage communication (Füller 2010; Füller et al. 2014). For example, the actors with a higher desire for developing their creative skills are more likely to participate in communication activities because of the of ample learning opportunities (Lakhani and Wolf 2006). Co-innovation environments facilitate actors' interactions with other professionals who openly share their expertise and thus help actors acquire new knowledge, enhance competencies, and gain first-hand experience (Füller et al. 2014; Weber 2004).

2.2 Sociotechnical Platform Affordances

There have been several attempts to model the relationship between IT artifacts and actor behavior using an affordance lens (Majchrzak et al. 2013; Strong et al. 2014; Treem and Leonardi 2012; Volkoff and Strong 2013). Affordance refers to the possibilities of actions afforded by the designed features of an IT artifact (e.g. Grgecic et al. 2015). Co-innovation platforms have a variety of social technology features and functions that enable ideation, collaboration, and communication (Gloor 2006). The affordances of a co-innovation platform depend on the interactions between actors' perception of the technology and their context-specific goals (Leonardi 2013; Majchrzak and Markus, 2013; Strong et al. 2014; Volkoff and Strong 2013). For socialization goals, affordances are associated with communication and networking possibilities that different socio-technical features of co-innovation platforms offer to its users (Treem and Leonardi 2012). Therefore, we can define platform social affordance —or sociotechnical affordances — as the perceived opportunities that the social space provides for the emergence of social actions (Kreijns 2004).

Whether social affordances triggers and forms socialization depends not only on the technological properties but also on the actor's ability to perceive the possibilities (Gaver 1991; Norman 1999). From the perspective of a social actor, social affordances are potentials and opportunities to perform goal-oriented communications. Social affordances can be purposefully designed in the co-innovation platform to enable socialization, although the actors may not choose to act on the affordance.

Previous studies have associated social affordances with tasks such as messaging, chatting, developing and sharing personal profiles, and networking (Sutcliffe et al. 2011). These interactional properties facilitate co-innovation tasks through communal or social interactions in a relatively complex co-innovation network (Mathiesen et al. 2013; Mesgari and Faraj 2012; Olapiriyakul and Widmeyer 2009).

2.3 Socio-professional Experience

The social context of co-innovation communities offers interactivity and socialization opportunities (Dingler and Enkel 2016). These networks constitute a socio-professional space wherein goal-oriented social relationships are formed among the actors and a common set of professional values are established and co-created

(Nambisan and Watt 2011). When actors relate to other like-minded professionals, they experience value co-creation in different forms and capacities (e.g. pragmatic, social, cognitive and hedonic values) (Kohler et al. 2011; Nambisan and Nambisan 2008). Socio-professional experience is one of the key values co-created within co-innovation spaces (Lusch and Nambisan 2015) and it can affect actors' attitude toward (P. Nambisan and Watt 2011) and participation in the co-innovation process (Kohler et al. 2011).

Socio-professional experience is formed through the actor-to-actor interactions such as discussions, knowledge sharing, and social networking. It is neither fully social nor fully professional; rather, it is socio-professional because it depends on social norms and mechanisms while being initiated by professionals with professional goals in a professional space. This form of experience is enabled or facilitated by affordances such as social connectivity, social interactivity, and profile management (O'Riordan et al. 2012). For example, a visible list of connections and a profile page in a co-innovation social space enable actors to present themselves and find other actors to collaborate with Kietzmann et al. (2011). Social affordances that enable these possibilities contribute to the formation of experience that ranges from socio-professional presence to self-actualization.

3   Research Model

Design features that provide actors with better social cues offer richer socio-professional experience and enhanced communication in co-innovation networks, thereby generating greater opportunities for value co-creation (Lusch and Nambisan 2015). These opportunities do not reflect solely the technological features of the online environment; instead, they reflect how well the actors and their activities or interactions can shape the sociability potential of the online environment for other members (Kreijns et al. 2004; Nie 2001). These opportunities are actualized in the form of socio-professional experience as a result of the interaction between the 'social space' enabled by social affordances, the 'social mechanisms' defined by the social context of the network, and the 'social intention' motivated by actors' goals. Therefore, when goal-directed actors perceive the sociotechnical potentials of a co-innovation network (as a socio-professional space), they may utilize the social technology features and social mechanisms to enhance their socio-professional experience. Integrating research on platform affordances with the actor social experience literature, we expect that in co-innovation networks, *actors' perception of Platform Social Affordances positively influences their Socio-professional Experience (H1)*.

The positive socio-professional experience offered by the various activities and social media channels may motivate communication activities among actors to acquire new knowledge, enhance competencies, and expand their professional network (Füller et al. 2014; Weber 2004). Additionally, socio-professional experience often enhances actors' self-perception as members of the co-innovation community, and thus increases their continued intention to engage in community dialogues and social interaction (Lusch and Nambisan 2015; Näkki and Koskela-Huotari 2012). The higher the intention, the higher the actual participation in communication activities. Therefore, we expect that *actors' Socio-professional Experience positively influences their Continuous Intention to Communicate (H2), which in turn leads to Actual Communication (H3).*

We argue that actors' socio-professional experience mediates the relationship between their perception of platform social affordances and their continued intention to communicate with others in the co-innovation networks. While an IT artifact cannot directly drive actors' activities, the consciousness constructed through actors' experience of the space can (Yoo 2010). Accordingly, we expect that the continuity of actors' intentional activities such as communication is the result of their personal experience shaped by the possibilities offered by the space (Yoo 2010). In other words, actors' continuous intention may be negatively affected if actors cannot experience the possibilities afforded by the platform. Therefore, we expect *that the effect of Social Affordances on Continuous Intention to Communicate is mediated by Socio-professional Experience (H4).*

Prior research has validated the significant relationship between the desire for learning new skills and participation in value co-creation (Lakhani and Wolf 2006). Actors with positive socio-professional experience are more likely to participate in co-innovation networks if they are motivated to learn or develop their innovation skills (Füller 2010). For example, positive socio-professional experience with a Q&A system would lead to a higher intention to ask questions only if the actor is motivated to learn more by using the Q&A system. Therefore, considering the literature on actor differences in co-innovation motivations (e.g. Gemser and Perks 2015) and the previously discussed direct effect of socio-professional experience on continuous intention to communicate, we expect that *the higher the level of Desire for Learning, the greater the indirect effect of perceived Platform Social Affordances on Continuous Intention to Communicate via Socio-professional Experience (H5)* (Fig. 1).

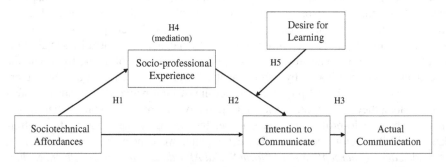

Fig. 1. Conceptual model

4   Method

To test our research model, a field survey was conducted to gather data on actors' socio-professional experience, desire for learning, their perception of platform social affordances, continuous intention to communicate, and actual communication in a co-innovation network (Quirky.com). Quirky is a social product development network with diverse co-innovation tools and processes as well as learning opportunities that make it an appropriate setting for this study. Quirky solicits new product ideas for broad categories of consumer products and shares up to 10% of revenue with the actors who contribute to product ideation, selection, design, development, and promotion. As part of the ideation process, prospective inventors can submit their ideas for social evaluation. The submitted ideas, if selected by the community, are collaboratively designed, developed, and commercialized by network members. The developed product ideas are then put to production by Quirky and finally distributed via the Quirky website and its retail partners. At the time of our study, this network of 1,500,000 members had collaboratively developed and launched more than 150 consumer products.

The measurement items for continuous intention to communicate (reflective), socio-professional experience (reflective), social platform affordances (formative), and desire for learning (reflective) were respectively adapted from Chen (2007) ($\alpha = 0.84$), Nambisan and Baron (2009) ($\alpha = 0.86$), Abhari et al. (2016a, b) ($\alpha = 0.90$), and Oreg and Nov (2008) ($\alpha = 0.82$) – see, Appendix A. The actual communication activities were measured by four proxies, namely number of messages actors sent and received as well as the number of followers and followees they had.

Partial Least Squares (PLS-SEM) using SmartPLS 3.0 (Ringle et al. 2015) was employed to test both the measurement and structural properties of our research model. PLS analysis is preferred over other analytical techniques because (a) it simultaneously assesses the psychometric properties of the measurement items (i.e., the measurement model) and analyzes the direction and strength of the hypothesized relationships (i.e., the structural model), and (b) it facilitates the modeling of formative constructs (Hair et al. 2013). Covariance-based SEM was not recommended for this study because the goal of the study was theory development (not theory testing) and sample size for each group was smaller than 200 (Hair et al. 2011).

To test the moderating effect of desire for learning on the relationship between social experience and continuous intention to communicate, we categorized responses into two groups with high and low desire for learning respectively. The discretizing was limited to only two groups to satisfy the minimum sample size required for each group. To compare the group-specific effects (Baron and Kenny 1986; Sarstedt et al. 2011), we used nonparametric Henseler's MGA method built on PLS-SEM bootstrapping procedure (Sarstedt et al. 2011). This new approach combines the advantages of previous methods because (a) it relies only on bootstrap outputs; (b) it does not affect the estimate of the group difference; and (c) it does not require distributional assumptions (Sarstedt et al. 2011). The new approach uses the empirical cumulative distribution provided by bootstrap re-sampling as the basis for calculating the probability of differences in subgroup parameters (Henseler et al. 2009).

5   Results

5.1   Descriptive Statistics and Respondents' Profiles

Participants were 229 Quirky's members who completed a web-based survey. Most of the respondents were females (52%), between 26 and 65, and over 70% received at least some college education. Close to 60% of the respondents were employed full time or part time. More than 60% of the respondents had more than six months' experience with Quirky and more than 70% visited Quirky at least once a week. Over 80% of the respondents had also received monetary credits for their contribution, an indicator of co-innovation success.

5.2 Evaluation of Reflective Measurements

The evaluation of reflective measurement items involves the test of construct reliability (item reliability and internal consistency) and construct validity (convergent validity and discrimination validity). Construct reliability indicates how well the items correlate with their corresponding construct. All the loadings of the measurement items on their latent constructs exceed 0.7, indicating acceptable item reliability (Hair et al. 2013). In addition, Cronbach's alpha and composite reliability of all the constructs are higher than 0.7, indicating good internal consistency among the items measuring each construct (Hair et al. 2013). Three criteria were adopted to assess convergent validity and discriminant validity: (a) all Average Variance Extracted (AVE) are higher than 0.50 (Hair et al. 2013); (b) the square root of the AVE of each constructs is larger than the correlations of this construct with the other constructs (Fornell and Larcker 1981); and (c) an indicator's loadings should be higher than all of its cross-loadings (Hair et al. 2013). As summarized in Table 1, the results of these tests suggest adequate convergent and discriminant validity.

Table 1. Psychometric properties of first-order constructs

Construct	Items	Loading	α	CR	AVE	LAD	SPX	CICM
Desire for learning	LAD1	0.86	0.85	0.90	0.69	0.83		
	LAD2	0.83						
	LAD3	0.80						
	LAD4	0.83						
Socio-professional experience	SPX1	0.92	0.93	0.95	0.84	0.37	0.91	
	SPX2	0.91						
	SPX3	0.92						
	SPX4	0.91						
Continuous intention to communicate	CICM1	0.91	0.89	0.95	0.70	0.36	0.69	0.84
	CICM2	0.90						
	CICM3	Removed[a]						
	CICM4	0.87						

[a]Removed due to its low loading (0.64)

5.3 Evaluation of Formative Measurements

The evaluation of formative measurements involves an assessment of the formative indicators' (predictive) validity and multicollinearity. Indicator validity, which gauges the strength and significance of the path from the indicator to the construct, was estimated using the PLS algorithm method with a bootstrapping of samples to calculate the weight (relative importance) and loading (absolute importance) of each indicator on its corresponding construct. As Table 2 shows, the weights and loadings of all the indicators (except PCMA4) are significant, suggesting satisfactory indicator validity (Hair et al. 2013). We decided to retain PSA4 because of its significant loading (Hair et al. 2011). Multicollinearity among indicators was the next concern for formative constructs (Diamantopoulos and Winklhofer 2001). In this study, multicollinearity was tested by computing the Variance Inflation Factor (VIF) of each indicator. All computed VIF values are below the threshold of 5.0 (Hair et al. 2013), suggesting that multicollinearity is not a threat to the validity of the study's findings.

Table 2. Weights and loadings of the formative indicators

Construct	Formative indicator	Loadings		Weights	
		Loadings	t-value	Weights	t-value
Platform social affordances	PSA1	0.88	29.16**	0.33	3.69**
	PSA2	0.87	31.29**	0.23	2.93*
	PSA3	0.92	43.07**	0.43	4.58**
	PSA4	0.85	22.49**	0.12	1.34 ns

$*p < 0.01$, $**p < 0.00$

5.4   Assessment of the Structural Model

The results of data analysis show that platform social affordances positively affect actor social experience in co-innovation networks (H1: $b = 0.57$, $p < 0.01$), which in turn increases actors' intention to communicate (H2: $b = 0.48$, $p < 0.01$). Higher intention to communicate is also associated with the higher rate of actual communication (H3: $b = 0.30$, $p < 0.01$). As none of the control variables (i.e., age, employment, education, gender, co-innovation experience) showed significant effects on continuous intention to communicate, they were excluded in further data analysis.

We followed established guidelines (Baron and Kenny 1986) to test the proposed role of socio-professional experience in mediating the influence of social affordances on continuous intentions to communicate. In Step 1, we examined the effects of affordances on the continuous intention to communicate ($b = 0.65$, $p < 0.00$). In Step 2, we analyzed the impact of the social affordances on socio-professional experience and found the effects to be significant ($b = 0.57$, $p < 0.01$). In Step 3, we assessed the relationships between socio-professional experience and continuous intention to communicate ($b = 0.48$, $p < 0.01$). In Step 4, we built a model with both the direct effect and indirect effect (via socio-professional experience) of social affordances on continuous intention to communicate ($b = 0.38$, $p < 0.01$). The results suggest that socio-professional experience partially mediates the impact of social affordances on intention to communicate. We also conducted a Sobel test to further assess the significance of the mediation effect. The results demonstrate that perceived socio-professional experience significantly carries the influence of the independent variable on the dependent variable (H4: Sobel $z = 5.5$, $p < .01$).

Lastly, we tested for multi-group moderated mediation using Henseler's multi-group analysis (MGA) approach and confidence set method based on established guidelines for PLS-MGA (Sarstedt et al. 2011). The confidence set method is nonparametric, can handle relatively small sizes, and is more conservative than the other approaches and thus is less prone to Type-II errors (Henseler et al. 2009). Group 1 (105 members) and 2 (124 members) were respectively defined as groups of actors with high and low desire for learning. We limited the discretization to two levels (Low and High) and used the mean as the midpoint to have enough sample in each group. The path coefficient estimates of multi-group comparison revealed the significance difference between actors with high and low desire for learning (H5: b |diff| = 0.31, $p_{Henseler} < 0.05$) suggesting the moderation effect of desire for learning. Confirming the significance differences, the bias-corrected 95% confidence intervals did not fall within the corresponding confidence interval of the other group (0.36 – 0.79 vs. 0.1 – 0.48). Therefore, positive socio-professional experience does not always lead to higher continuous intention to communicate; rather, socio-professional affordances relates to greater intention to communicate through social experience when actors have a high desire for learning. We observed the same difference affecting the relationship between social affordances and socio-professional experience (b |diff| = 0.22, $p_{Henseler} < 0.05$). This finding suggests that social affordances may have a higher impact on actor socio-professional experience when actors have a higher desire for learning.

6   Discussion

In this study, we conceptualized social affordances of co-innovation platforms and examined their effects on socio-professional experience and the behavioral intention to communicate. We also explained this relationship by examining actors' socio-professional experience as an underlying mechanism. Further, we explored how actors' desire for learning moderates the experience-intention relationship. The results reveal that compelling socio-affordances leads to higher continuous intention to communicate when the actors have a high desire for learning. In other words, social affordances do not guarantee future communication among actors unless actors have a high desire for learning.

6.1   Theoretical Contributions

Our empirical findings lay a solid foundation for future inquiry that could advance our understanding of the relationship between platform affordances and behavioral intention. First, this study shows that actors' socio-professional experience can drive communication efforts such as knowledge sharing and social exchange in the network. Second, this study demonstrates that actors' socio-professional experience as an underlying mechanism drives the influence of platform social affordances on actors' intention to communicate in co-innovation networks. Third, confirming the relationship between social affordances and socio-professional experience, our results suggest that platform affordances play a significant role in the formation of actor's co-innovation experience.

Lastly, results of our moderated-mediation model reveal that social affordances are less influential for actors with low desire for learning. This finding highlights the need to account for individual differences, specifically actors' goals and desires, in investigating affordance-driven actor experience and behavior. Further research, however, would need to address the ways in which affordances develop other types of experience (e.g. pragmatic, usability, and hedonic experience) and how other motivations influence the impact of positive experience on actor behavioral intention.

6.2 Practical Implications

Several managerial implications of the present research are worth noting. The effect of affordances on socio-professional experience and continuous intention suggests that co-innovation network designers should pay more attention to social affordances as a driver of co-innovation. This study also recommends maintaining actors' participation by enhancing their socio-professional experiences such as successful networking and meaningful learning. Thus, our findings encourage monitoring actors' experience as one practical way to manage the sustainability and productivity of the co-innovation networks. Of further importance to managing relationships between actors and technology is the finding that the effects of social affordances vary in accordance with actors' desires for learning. Therefore, the right combination of learning opportunities with positive social experience can be planned by co-innovation communities to enhance the effect of social technologies on actor communication activities. Co-innovation sponsors should consider that the platform social affordances are most likely to produce a lasting effect on communication activities when the co-innovation platform engage the actors who are highly motivated to learn from other members. This study thus recommends considering the desire for learning in both designing co-innovation platforms and governing co-innovation processes. Identifying the actors who may respond more favorably to platform affordances can assist co-innovation networks in more thoughtfully engaging potential actors.

7 Conclusion and Future Research

Effective communication in co-innovation networks cannot be forced or mandated. Networks desiring to enhance and improve communication among actors must foster socialization opportunities. By supporting the view that social affordances augment the intention to communicate, and providing empirical evidence regarding the underlying mechanism, we have contributed to the understanding of socialization in co-innovation communities. Given the importance of sustainable communication and exchange among co-innovation actors, we hope that our findings will be useful to scholars and practitioners aimed at enhancing co-innovation efforts and outcomes.

We strongly encourage further examination of our findings through different research designs and across different co-innovation contexts. We also recognize the value, in future studies, of extending our research model to (a) include actors' actual communication behaviors; (b) examine specific types of communication activities, (c) examine communication beyond the boundaries of a single co-innovation community; and (d) evaluate the effects of specific IT artifacts used by actors in communication or socialization with others actors.

Appendix A – Questionnaire Items

Construct	Item	Survey questions[a]
Platform social affordances		*The platform enables me to...*
	PSA 1	*... share my knowledge*
	PSA 2	*... solicit votes/support*
	PSA 3	*... discuss new ideas with community*
	PSA 4	*... network with community*
Socio-professional experience		*My experience with this network has...*
	SPX1	*...expanded my personal/social network*
	SPX2	*...enhanced the strength of my affiliation with online communities*
	SPX3	*...enhanced my sense of belongingness to inventor communities*
	SPX4	*...helped me socialize with other inventors*
Continuous intention to communicate[b]	CICM1	*I intend to continue communicating with the members of this network*
	CICM2	*Even if I use alternative platforms, I will continue communicating with the members of this network*
	CICM4	*I plan to communicate with a greater number of members in future*
Desire for learning		*I contribute to the network because*
	LAD1	*... it provides me with a means of developing my creative skills*
	LAD2	*... it gives me an opportunity to learn new things about inventions*
	LAD3	*... it helps me become better in product development*
	LAD4	*... it helps me test my creativity*

[a]All measures employ a seven-point Likert scale from "strongly disagree" to "strongly agree."
[b]CICM3 was removed due to low loading.

References

Abhari, K., Davidson, E. J., Xiao, B.: Measuring the perceived functional affordances of collaborative innovation networks in social product development. In: Hawaii International Conference on System Sciences, pp. 929–938. IEEE Computer Society (2016a)

Abhari, K., Davidson, E., Xiao, B.: Taking open innovation to the next level: a conceptual model of social product development (SPD). In: AMCIS 2016 Proceedings (2016b)

Baron, R.M., Kenny, D.A.: The moderator-mediator variable distinction in social psychological research: conceptual, strategic, and statistical considerations. J. Pers. Soc. Psychol. **51**(6), 1173–1182 (1986)

Chen, I.Y.L.: The factors influencing members' continuance intentions in professional virtual communities a longitudinal study. J. Inf. Sci. **33**(4), 451–467 (2007)

Curley, M., Donnellan, B., Costello, G.J.: Innovation ecosystems: a conceptual framework. In: Open Innovation 2.0, pp. 18–29. European Commission, Luxembourg (2013)

Diamantopoulos, A., Winklhofer, H.M.: Index construction with formative indicators: an alternative to scale development. J. Mark. Res. **38**(2), 269–277 (2001)

Dingler, A., Enkel, E.: Socialization and innovation: insights from collaboration across industry boundaries. Technol. Forecast. Soc. Chang. **109**, 50–60 (2016)

Fornell, C., Larcker, D.F.: Structural equation models with unobservable variables and measurement error: algebra and statistics. J. Mark. Res. **18**, 382–388 (1981)

Füller, J.: Refining virtual co-creation from a consumer perspective. Calif. Manag. Rev. **52**(2), 98–122 (2010)

Füller, J., Hutter, K., Hautz, J., Matzler, K.: User roles and contributions in innovation-contest communities. J. Manag. Inf. Syst. **31**(1), 273–308 (2014)

Gassmann, O., Enkel, E., Chesbrough, H.: The future of open innovation. R&D Manag. **40**(3), 213–221 (2010)

Gaver, W.W.: Technology Affordances. In: Proceedings of the SIGCHI Conference on Human Factors in Computing Systems Reaching Through Technology CHI 1991, vol. 51, pp. 79–84 (1991)

Gemser, G., Perks, H.: Co-creation with customers: an evolving innovation research field. J. Prod. Innov. Manag. **32**(5), 660–665 (2015)

Gloor, P.A.: Swarm Creativity: Competitive Advantage Through Collaborative Innovation Networks. Oxford University Press, New York (2006)

Gressgård, L.J.L.: Text-based collaborative work and innovation: effects of communication media affordances on divergent and convergent thinking in group-based problem-solving. J. Inf. Knowl. Manag. **7**, 151–176 (2012)

Grgecic, D., Holten, R., Rosenkranz, C.: The impact of functional affordances and symbolic expressions on the formation of beliefs. J. Assoc. Inf. Syst. **16**(7), 580–607 (2015)

Hair, J.F., Hult, G.T.M., Ringle, C., Sarstedt, M.: A Primer on Partial Least Squares Structural Equation Modeling (PLS-SEM). SAGE Publications, Thousand Oaks (2013)

Hair, J.F., Ringle, C.M., Sarstedt, M.: PLS-SEM: indeed a silver bullet. J. Mark. Theor. Pract. **19**(2), 139–152 (2011)

Henseler, J., Ringle, C.M., Sinkovics, R.: The use of partial least squares path modeling in international marketing. Adv. Int. Mark. **20**(2009), 277–319 (2009)

Kietzmann, J.H., Hermkens, K., McCarthy, I.P., Silvestre, B.S.: Social media? Get serious! Understanding the functional building blocks of social media. Bus. Horiz. **54**(3), 241–251 (2011)

Kohler, T., Fueller, J., Matzler, K., Stieger, D.: Co-creation in virtual world: the design of the user experience. MIS Q. **35**(3), 773–788 (2011)

Kreijns, K.: Sociable CSCL Environments: Social Affordances, Sociability, and Social Presence. Datawyse Boek-Grafische producties, Maastricht (2004)

Kreijns, K., Kirschner, P.A., Jochems, W., van Buuren, H.: Determining sociability, social space, and social presence in (a)synchronous collaborative groups. CyberPsychol. Behav. **7**(2), 155–172 (2004)

Lakhani, K.R., Wolf, R.G.: Why hackers do what they do: understanding motivation and effort in free/open source software projects. In: Feller, J., Fitzgerald, B., Hissam, S., Lakhani, K.R. (eds.) Perspectives on Free and Open Source Software, pp. 1–27. MIT Press, Cambridge (2006)

Lee, S.M., Olson, D.L., Trimi, S.: Co-innovation: convergenomics, collaboration, and co-creation for organizational values. Manag. Decis. **50**(5), 817–831 (2012)

Leonardi, P.M.: When does technology use enable network change in organizations? A comparative study of feature use and shared affordances. MIS Q. **37**(3), 749–776 (2013)

Lusch, R.F., Nambisan, S.: Service innovation: a service-dominant logic perspective service. MIS Q. **39**(1), 155–175 (2015)

Majchrzak, A., Faraj, S., Kane, G.C., Azad, B.: The contradictory influence of social media affordances on online communal knowledge sharing. J. Comput. Mediat. Commun. **19**(1), 38–55 (2013)

Majchrzak, A., Markus, M.L.: Technology affordances and constraint theory of MIS. In: Kessler, E. (ed.) Encyclopedia of Management Theory. Sage, Thousand Oaks (2013)

Martini, A.: The role of social software for customer co-creation: does it change the practice for innovation. Int. J. Eng. Bus. Manag. **4**, 1–10 (2012)

Martini, A., Massa, S., Testa, S.: The firm, the platform and the customer: a "double mangle" interpretation of social media for innovation. Inf. Organ. **23**(3), 198–213 (2013)

Mathiesen, P., Bandara, W., Watson, J.: The affordances of social technology: a BPM perspective. In: International Conference on Information Systems (ICIS 2013), pp. 3709–3719 (2013)

Mesgari, M., Faraj, S.: Technology affordances: the case of Wikipedia. In: 18th Americas Conference on Information Systems (AMCIS 2012), vol. 5, pp. 3833–3841 (2012)

Näkki, P., Koskela-Huotari, K.: User participation in software design via social media: experiences from a case study with consumers. AIS Trans. Hum. Comput. Interact. **4**(2), 129–152 (2012)

Nambisan, P., Watt, J.H.: Managing customer experiences in online product communities. J. Bus. Res. **64**(8), 889–895 (2011)

Nambisan, S.: Information technology and product/service innovation: a brief assessment and some suggestions for future research. J. Assoc. Inf. Syst. **14**(4), 215–226 (2013)

Nambisan, S., Baron, R.A.: Virtual customer environments: testing a model of voluntary participation in value co-creation activities. J. Prod. Innov. Manag. **26**(4), 388–406 (2009)

Nambisan, S., Nambisan, P.: How to profit from a better "Virtual Customer Environment". MIT Sloan Manag. Rev. **49**(3), 53–61 (2008)

Nie, N.H.: Sociability, interpersonal relations, and the internet: reconciling conflicting findings. Am. Behav. Sci. **45**(3), 420–435 (2001)

Norman, D.: Affordance, conventions, and design. Interactions **6**(3), 38–43 (1999)

O'Riordan, S., Feller, J., Nagle, T.: Exploring the affordances of social network sites: an analysis of three networks. In: European Conference on Information Systems (ECIS 2012) (2012)

Olapiriyakul, K., Widmeyer, G.R.: Affordance of virtual world commerce: instrument development and validation. In: Americas Conference on Information Systems (AMCIS 2009) (2009)

Oreg, S., Nov, O.: Exploring motivations for contributing to open source initiatives: the roles of contribution context and personal values. Comput. Hum. Behav. **24**(5), 2055–2073 (2008)

Parameswaran, M., Whinston, A.B.: Research issues in social computing. J. Assoc. Inf. Syst. **8**(6), 336–350 (2007)

Paulini, M., Murty, P., Maher, M.L.M.: Design processes in collective innovation communities: a study of communication. CoDesign **9**(2), 90–112 (2013)

Ringle, C., Wende, S., Becker, J.: SmartPLS 3. SmartPLS GmbH, Boenningstedt (2015)

Sarstedt, M., Henseler, J., Ringle, C.M.: Multigroup analysis in Partial Least Squares (PLS) path modeling: alternative methods and empirical results. Adv. Int. Mark. **22**, 195–218 (2011)

Strong, D.M., Johnson, S.A., Tulu, B., Trudel, J., Volkoff, O., Pelletier, L.R., Bar-On, I., Garber, L.: A theory of organization-EHR affordance actualization. J. Assoc. Inf. Syst. **15**(2), 53–85 (2014)

Sutcliffe, A.G., Gonzalez, V., Binder, J., Nevarez, G.: Social mediating technologies: social affordances and functionalities. Int. J. Hum. Comput. Interact. **27**(11), 1037–1065 (2011)

Treem, J.W., Leonardi, P.M.: Social media use in organizations: exploring the affordances of visibility, editability, persistence, and association. Commun. Yearbook **36**(1), 143–189 (2012)

Volkoff, O., Strong, D.: Critical realism and affordances: theorizing IT-associated organizational change processes. MIS Q. **37**(3), 819–834 (2013)

Weber, S.: The Success of Open Source. Harvard University Press, Cambridge (2004)

Wellman, B., Quan-Haase, A., Boase, J., Chen, W., Hampton, K., De Diaz, I.I., Miyata, K.: The social affordances of the internet for networked individualism. J. Comput. Med. Commun. **8**(3) (2003)

Wu, D., Rosen, D.W., Panchal, J.H., Schaefer, D.: Understanding communication and collaboration in social product development through social network analysis. J. Comput. Inf. Sci. Eng. **16**(1), 11001 (2015)

Wu, D., Rosen, D.W., Panchal, J.H., Schaefer, D.: Understanding communication and collaboration in social product development through social network analysis. J. Comput. Inf. Sci. Eng. **16**(3), 1–10 (2016)

Yoo, Y.: Computing in everyday life: a call for research on experiential computing. MIS Q. **34**(2), 213–231 (2010)

Zhao, D., Rosson, M.B.: How and why people twitter: the role that micro-blogging plays in informal communication at work. In: The ACM 2009 International Conference on Supporting Group Work, New York, pp. 243–252 (2009)

Zhou, T.: Understanding online community user participation: a social influence perspective. Internet Res. **21**(1), 67–81 (2011)

Implementing Digital Parliament Innovative Concepts for Citizens and Policy Makers

Fotios Fitsilis[1]([✉]), Dimitris Koryzis[2], Vasilios Svolopoulos[2],
and Dimitris Spiliotopoulos[3]

[1] Scientific Service, Hellenic Parliament, Athens, Greece
`fitsilisf@parliament.gr`
[2] European Programs Implementation Service (EPIS), Hellenic Parliament, Athens, Greece
`{dkoryzis,v.svolopoulos}@parliament.gr`
[3] Institute of Computer Science (FORTH), Heraklion, Greece
`dspiliot@ics.forth.gr`

Abstract. The organizational stability of Parliaments comes in direct contradiction with rapid progress in digital technology in recent decades, particularly in the ICT domain. By participating in a series of networking activities through European funded research programs, the Hellenic Parliament and the Austrian Parliament have placed themselves in the forefront of parliamentary innovation. This paper will focus on these activities and relevant findings on their impact, citizen adoption and application-to-end-user acceptance, where end users are parliaments and citizens alike. A range of technological challenges that modern Parliaments face and discrete actions of parliamentary innovation will also be shown. Finally, the paper will present the prospects that arise from the use of the latest ICT technologies in Parliaments. We shall also examine limitations in the use of such tools and shall propose potential areas of technological research and innovation for parliamentary application.

Keywords: Europe · Parliaments · Project · User adoption · User interaction · Policy making · Policy adoption · LEX-IS · Spaces+ · NOMAD · ARCOMEM · METALOGUE

1 Digital Democracy Trends

What is evident, nowadays, is that on the one hand Governmental Institutions and Public Authorities are trying to understand the upcoming complex world and its needs. Citizens on the other hand demand more openness, transparency and commitment to results. Other institutions such as Parliaments struggle to understand, enhance and transform their institutional role within the new digital society, so they tend to apply new digital technologies and tools with a characteristic lag due to their role and in a rather unstructured way. In the Digital Democracy era, these institutions seem not to have a clear communication, dissemination and exploitation plan for the role of social media in the policy making process, as in the Hellenic Parliament case. At the same time, other European Parliaments, such as the Austrian Parliament, have clearly identified the

© Springer International Publishing AG 2017
F.F.-H. Nah and C.-H. Tan (Eds.): HCIBGO 2017, Part I, LNCS 10293, pp. 154–170, 2017.
DOI: 10.1007/978-3-319-58481-2_13

possibilities that emerge through applications of new technologies in the legal informatics, digital democracy with public participation, digital transformation and parliamentary communication domain.

The latest trends in social networking analytics closely related to policy making cycles and legislative procedures could be found in a series of recent EU funded projects in digital democracy, e-participation and civic engagement addressing mostly citizen's enhancement in the policy making process. According to latest digital market trends, people engagement in politics and policy-making makes the whole decision-making process easier to understand, thanks to Information and Communication Technologies (ICTs) [1]. Additionally, collective social awareness projects cover many issues, from open democracy to collaborative consumption and internet science [2].

A lot of sibling research EU-funded projects in the field have been conducted the last 7 years, thanks to the latest evolution of the Social Web [3]. The list of demonstration use cases (among them pilot actions for the Hellenic and Austrian Parliaments) is not exhaustive, as the digital democracy trends and society's digital transformation is proceeding faster than in the last decade. Policy makers like Members of Parliament (MPs), who participated in these projects mainly as users, face a task of unprecedented complexity and difficulty to fully understand the pilot applications and demonstration use cases. Trying to adopt or to assess their innovative outputs, results and primary outcomes, they tend to compare them with the traditional policy making approaches used so far, they still seem to find difficulties in capturing the society's complex and interconnected nature [4].

Moreover, governments may have neither the resources nor the necessary know-how to deal with countless innovative challenges that have arisen the past decade, by horizontally sharing and analyzing each and every involved citizens' status, opinion, preferences, reviews, ratings and needs around specific issues in the various social media, respecting their privacy at the same time which is crucial, especially for data protection authorities, brings to the table the need for a global expertise that reduces the information asymmetry between governments and citizens. As presented in [5, 6], the aforementioned approach so far did not successfully involve in the overall process all significant stakeholders, whose interests are affected by decisions and relevant policy outputs, as well as individuals, although their working environment, financial conditions, social presence and consequently their well-being is tightly dependent on the formulated policies.

2   ICT in the Parliamentary Context

Parliaments, as institutional foundations of democracy, are traditional organizations in the sense that they heavily rely on tradition. As a direct consequence, parliaments are inert to changes. Their institutional identity, their organizational structure, their Rules of Procedure often remain stable over longer periods of time. The recognition that new means of political communication from the bottom-up, or from the top-down, are critical to parliamentary life and that political parties can no longer be the most effective channels for this communication has convinced political leaders, parliamentarians and parliamentary staff of the need for alternative means of interaction through ICT [7].

For this reason, parliaments struggle to maintain and advance their institutional role within the new digital society, as they tend to apply new technologies with significant time lag and in a rather unstructured and often reluctant way. For this reason, over recent years, the intensive use of ICT in parliaments has formed a new concept and role for parliaments, that of an electronic parliament or e-parliament [8].

On top of that, a few European parliaments have clearly identified the possibilities that emerge through applications of new technologies in the legal, public participation and parliamentary communication domain, through participation in EU-funded research activities in the ICT domain, within the context of the 7th Framework Programme (FP7). Both the Hellenic Parliament and the Austrian Parliament have been active in such research consortia that can be also described as European research networks. The nature of these networks, which also include a variety of non-parliamentary actors (universities, research institutes, civil society organizations, small and medium sized enterprises etc.), is going to be examined. In particular, data from the EU funded projects LEX-IS, +Spaces, NOMAD, ARCOMEM, METALOGUE are going to be analyzed and presented in a structured way.

As reported before, mainly due to the capabilities offered by Web 2.0 tools and channels, an array of new techniques and opportunities are emerging through the massive use of the social web, both into the policy-making process and the legislative procedures. The implications due to the use of social media go well beyond the simple advancements in traditional interaction between audiences and stakeholders, e.g. dialogue, collaboration, exchange of ideas etc. These new media have the potential to radically change politics for good, on all levels and in every sector; a true paradigm shift in the policy development.

Based on the above projects' results there are many novel ideas, cases, tools and techniques to exploit the recent market trends for identifying the best exploitable policy implications or models with advanced linguistic analysis on the social Web, giving an emphasis on policies implementation and civic engagement on them. However, the use of ICT poses significant challenges to parliaments, many of which do not readily adopt new technology with exceptions of the Scottish, Austrian, Portuguese and UK Parliament. As a result, most parliaments have acquired some of the forms and elements of ICT and the new social media, but most have not yet been able to use them in a highly successful manner or incorporate them effectively into their work procedures. Adequate staff and funding are clearly important. However, cultural and institutional factors, along with how a parliament uses technology, can have as significant an effect as management procedures and financial resources [9]. Although the methodologies used may extend to other areas like brand monitoring and reputation, the ICT techniques used basically rely on data and opinion mining and on the conceptual representation of policies and argumentation theories.

The abovementioned facts show that parliaments could promote citizen participation, either in formal or informal context, is able to promote both representative and participatory democracy. Unfortunately the lack of comprehensible visualizations, useful to citizens and policy makers for easing out the complexity in policy decisions, the under-performance of existing policy models in conjunction with real life simulation mechanisms, and the insufficient use of the huge amounts of data that are available on the web, are among the important issues that need to be tackled in order to take the leap forward in policy making. Therefore, ICT tools still have untapped potential and remain a "novelty" for the majority of government systems, despite their already acknowledged benefits in their application by governments related to the quality and speed of policy making, as well as to evidence-based policy decision making.

Last, but not least, citizen participation can establish at the end of the day a two-way collaboration and a long-term cooperation between parliamentarians and citizens with the use of these ICT tools. The 3Cs' scheme "coordination, collaboration and cooperation" corresponds to the components of inclusion, awareness, engagement and participation [10].

3 Parliamentary Participation in EU Programmes

3.1 LEX-IS

The LEX-IS project is aimed at improving the legislative process in National Parliaments. By using of state-of-the-art ICT-tools and methodologies LEX-IS strengthened public participation within the legislative process, e.g. during drafting and public debate of draft law. With the introduction of a web-based platform, a set of specialized services was made available to the project stakeholders: Parliaments, businesses, citizens and, especially, youngsters.

In particular, stakeholders had the ability to query and view the legal structures and elements, such as draft laws, legal components, legal documents and supportive information, in multiple levels of abstraction and decomposition, using content management engines and legal metadata schemas. Moreover, the argumentation structure of a law under formation could be made visible, using semantic annotation and argument visualization techniques. Finally, stakeholders had the opportunity to express opinions around legal components, arguments that are presented by the participating organizations, or opinions of other parties, in a structured way that promotes participative decision-making.

Figure 1 presents the operation principle of the LEX-IS platform. The system provided adequate argumentation support to every category of users. To achieve this, it implemented a specific methodology that determined the best course of action at a user's request based on the nature of the user and the current state of the legislative process.

The LEX-IS platform, as presented in [11], may contribute in improving political accountability and in enhancing trust into democratic institutions and their representatives. It also became possible to attract citizens who were not willing to participate in face-to-face events or were generally reluctant to openly express their opinion.

In order to bridge the growing gap between citizens and the state, parliamentary institutions were included to the implementation team. The LEX-IS project was implemented by 7 partners from 4 EU Member States. The majority of the partners (4) was Greek, with 3 partners coming from Germany, Austria and Lithuania. As for the nature of partners, most of them (4) were universities, 2 were Parliaments and 1 a private company. One has to take into account that Kauno Technologijos Universitetas, the Lithuanian University, has been providing data and insights of the Lithuanian Parliament. Hence, in total,

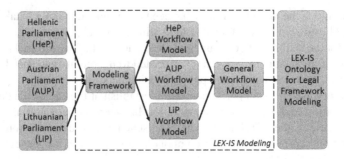

Fig. 1. LEX-IS operation principle

legislative procedures and case studies from 3 Parliaments have been examined: Hellenic Parliament, Austrian Parliament, and Lithuanian Parliament.

The LEX-IS project demonstrated that it is possible to use state-of-the-art ICT tools and methodologies to attract public attention and participation in the preparatory stages of the legislative process, that is during the (a) preparation phase, (b) policy debate, and (c) draft legislation formation. Such tools can be applied to model e.g. through legal role-activity-document ontologies and workflow management technologies, and, consequently, manage complex legislative frameworks and legal structures, e.g. draft legislation, existing legislation, amendments and changes, effectively. The semantic annotation of legal elements, as well as the development of internet-based tools for information retrieval and argument visualization is of key significance in the evolutionary process of such endeavors.

3.2   +Spaces

The project +Spaces (Policy Simulation in Virtual Spaces) uses existing social media spaces to model real world behavior [5]. The goal was to bring together citizens from different online communities into a common virtual framework. Analysis of these virtual spaces has the potential to provide insight to policy makers and assist them in forming and presenting their arguments to the ever growing on-line community, thus increasing potential acceptance of new policies.

The +Spaces platform creates and deploys applications in virtual spaces (Facebook, Blogger, Twitter, Open Wonderland), which provide information about the policy with a clear description of the policy topic, pre-defined roles, selected keywords, standard questions and moderated statements, guiding the public to react to it in various ways. Feedback from the civil society is obtained through well-defined and structured polls and debates, as well as through role playing simulation, in which the citizens are invited to take a certain role, in favor or against a certain policy, and express thoughts and opinions from the respective point of view. This novel approach, the details of which may be found in [12], provides users with new insights and a better understanding of various aspects of the discussed policy.

+Spaces provides governments with an integrated environment where policy makers can propose regulations, run simulations and then study the real users' reactions on a large, and a mere focus group, real-world scale. Simulation evaluation is performed by utilizing the +Spaces tools, which also include several data visualization schemes. Hence, policy makers are able to draw immediate conclusions on the impact of their policy to the virtual communities, and even fine tune different aspects of the policy to match its expected outcome.

In order to achieve the desired functionality, several technologies for the aggregation, filtering and analysis of the textual data contained in the virtual spaces were developed. Particular care was placed in the development of recommender and reputation systems, as one needs to ensure that only reliable sources of data are taken into account. Figure 2 presents a schematic diagram of the +Spaces project. Its vital modules include functionality for Reputation & Recommendations (R&R), Identity Management & Authorization (IM&A), Data & Statistical Analysis (D&SA) and Data Management & Baseline Security (DM&BS).

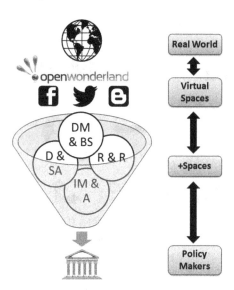

Fig. 2. +Spaces schematic diagram

The +Spaces project was implemented by 8 partners from 6 countries. There was a large geographical distribution of the partners that also included one non-EU actor from Israel. From the EU partners, 3 were Greek, and each one from Belgium, Germany, Spain and the United Kingdom. This project was heavily based on private company participation (3 partners), with equal participation of universities and research institutes (each represented with 2 entities) and one Parliament (Hellenic Parliament).

As a benefit for government agencies, the use of virtual spaces supports efficient collection of citizens' feedback and enables governments to extrapolate conclusions for real societies. This improves the prediction of how planned policy measures impact people. Through the +Spaces platform the Hellenic Parliament was possible to address several public groups on different stages of the policy making process. In addition, +Spaces was able to support policy makers' presence in social networks. Moreover, the advanced 3D & 2D role-playing simulations and the 3D debates created fresh ideas for policy makers, that could make the +Spaces platform useful as a policy marketing tool.

3.3 NOMAD

The core of the NOMAD projects lies in the interpretation of citizens' discussions available on the web and using them as the basis for end-to-end policy development, from the setting of the political agenda towards definition, implementation and monitoring of single policies [6]. The project improves the monitoring of policy-delivery in the face of citizens' rising expectations and enhances the citizens' active participation in the decision-making process. NOMAD provides fully automated solutions for content search, acquisition, categorization and visualization that work in a collaborative form in the policy-making arena. A basic sketch of the NOMAD policy modeling environment functionalities includes: data acquisition via web and social media crawling, opinion mining, argument extraction and advanced visualization, as summarized in Fig. 3.

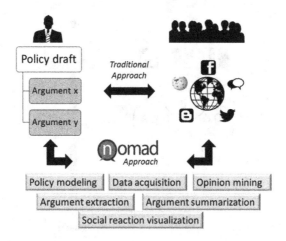

Fig. 3. NOMAD policy modeling environment

The project reported on the study on need finding and usability testing of a user interface for collaborative policy formulation. The task complexity required extensive need finding procedures and more than two iterations of design prototyping in order to ensure the high usability of the proposed visually driven policy modeling authoring process. The hardest challenge was to derive interaction scenarios from users that lacked the expertise and scientific background to utilize the deeper linguistic concepts of the content. This was a first try on creating a policy-modeling environment for users who traditionally use other means for collecting information.

All project modules have been available to the decision-makers via a web plat-form containing an integrated Tool-Suite, which enabled users to easily switch between them.

The Suite was used to scan both the formal and informal web, such as forums, social networks, blogs, newsgroups and wikis etc., in order to gather feedback on the level of acceptance of policy proposals, thus creating a stable feedback loop between policy formation and public opinion.

The NOMAD project has been being implemented by 9 partners from 6 EU Member States. It has been a Greek-centered project, with 4 of its partners being Greek. There are also partners from Austria, Belgium, Germany, Ireland and the United Kingdom. Regarding the partner mix, it relies mostly to the private sector (4 companies). The consortium also includes 1 university, 2 research institutes and 2 Parliaments (Hellenic Parliament and Austrian Parliament).

The Hellenic Parliament's pilot of the NOMAD program was conducted in the frame of the country's policy making process. Aiming to promote NOMAD's use as a policy making tool, the parliament aspired to create a policy model that would simplify the work of the policy maker by providing the people's opinion on each relevant subject.

3.4 ARCOMEM

Social media are becoming more and more pervasive in all areas of life. This kind of digital material is both ephemeral and highly contextualized, making it increasingly difficult for a political archivist to decide what to preserve. These new world challenges the relevance and power of our memory institutions. ARCOMEM's aim is to help transform archives into collective memories that are more tightly integrated with their community of users, and exploit Social Web and the wisdom of crowds to make Web archiving a more selective and meaning-based process. For this purpose, in order to help exploit the new media and make our organizational memories richer and more relevant, an innovative socially-aware and socially-driven preservation model was developed and investigated.

In Fig. 4 we depict the overall ARCOMEM system architecture [12]. The ARCOMEM system comprises of the following basic structural components:

1. The intelligent crawler. This module is responsible for retrieving the appropriate web content as initially defined by the archivist. Moreover, based on the feedback from both the analysis module and the archivist it refines its strategy in order to harvest only the most relevant parts of the web.
2. Detection of Entities, Topics, Opinions and Events (ETOE). ETOEs are informational elements, i.e. advanced data structures. This component comprises a collection of modules that are responsible for detecting different entities, topics, opinions and events on a given object or sets of objects.
3. Social Web analysis. This module builds upon the detected ETOEs and performs social analysis for extraction of more high-level information on the harvested data (group relations, trust, reputation, etc.). This analysis includes linguistic, machine learning and NLP methods in order to provide a rich set of metadata annotations that are interlinked with the original data.
4. Dynamics analysis. These modules are responsible for analyzing the evolution of terms, opinions, topics, etc. across several crawls and therefore over time through

advanced processing methods. The Social Web Analysis modules especially benefit from the term and entity evolution detection.

5. Database. This is the storage module of the ARCOMEM system. It features a distributed storage engine that stores raw web objects as well as annotations and information from ETOE – Social – Dynamics.

6. Applications. The ARCOMEM applications interact with the system in two ways. First, they can influence the direction of the crawling that they have initiated. Results from the various analysis modules are taken into account in order to amend the crawling strategy and harvest only the most interesting/important content. Second, they can retrieve data from the ARCOMEM database to provide an information-rich, multidimensional means of searching through a vast archive.

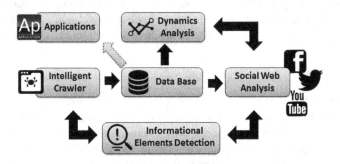

Fig. 4. ARCOMEM system architecture

The ARCOMEM project was implemented by 12 partners from 7 countries. Each 3 of its partners were from Greece and Germany, 2 from the UK and each one from France, Netherlands, Spain and Austria. There was also a broad and nearly even distribution of partner types: Media, research institutes, companies and Parliaments were each represented with 2 partners. In addition, there were 3 university partners and 1 foundation. Preservation of digital information is thought to be a very useful tool to researchers and politicians of the future. In addition, synergies with other research projects for crawling services (e.g. NOMAD) were identified. Also recognized was ARCOMEM's potential of moderating political discussions in the Parliamentary context. Hence, there is potential necessity for ARCOMEM functions as part of parliamentary service, e.g. the library.

3.5 METALOGUE

Natural dialogue systems have shaped a significant and fast-growing market segment, which is widely used in public services. At the same time, state-of-the-art dialogue systems do not fully support flawless machine-human interaction. The goal of METALOGUE is the development of a multimodal dialogue system with the ability to display seamless interactive behavior. In order to achieve this, both the system's own and the users' cognitive processes need to be understood, controlled and manipulated. Dialogue strategies are planned and deployed be a dialogue manager, which incorporates a cognitive model based on meta-cognitive skills. The system constantly monitors both its own and the users' interactive performance in order to evaluate the users' intentions and adapt its dialogue behavior.

As negotiation skills play a key role in the decision-making processes, research in the framework of the METALOGUE project focuses mainly on educational and coaching applications [13]. The developed components and algorithm comprise a prototype platform, which provides an adaptive environment that helps learners to develop their metacognitive skills, increase motivation, and stimulate creativity in the course of a given decision making and argumentation process.

The METALOGUE system is able to generate virtual dialogue agents for natural interaction using speech (in English, German and Greek), gesture, mimicry and body language. Hence, it allows learners, and particularly the young ones, to train and further develop their train presentational, interactional, semantic, pragmatic and meta-cognitive skills within a scalable and controlled learning environment.

The overall project architecture is presented in Fig. 5. The system was deployed and tested in two use-case scenarios: in social educational contexts for training young entrepreneurs and active citizens in the framework of educational activities of the Hellenic Youth Parliament, and in a business education context for training call center employees to successfully handle their customers. Therefore, METALOGUE may have a strong impact on both the economic and social level.

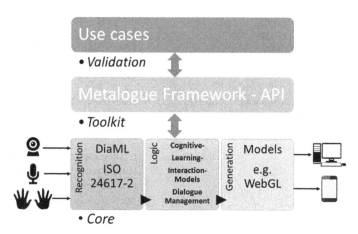

Fig. 5. Overall METALOGUE architecture

The METALOGUE project was implemented by 10 partners from 4 countries. 3 of the partners were German, each 2 were from Greece, Netherlands and the UK, and 1 originated from Ireland. It was heavily University-centered (6 partners). Moreover, 2 companies, 1 research center and 1 Parliament (Hellenic Parliament) were represented in the partner-mix.

4   Structure Analysis of Parliamentary Networks

The five aforementioned FP7 research programmes started to be implemented in the year 2007 and resulted in the creation of large partner networks across the European Union and Israel. In general, particular care has been taken in building most capable consortia specialized to each of the relevant FP7 calls, so that the proposed research could be conducted on-time and efficiently, in order produce sustainable results. Table 1 presents the partners and the duration for each of the discussed projects.

Table 1. Project partners per FP7 project

LEX-IS	+Spaces	NOMAD	ARCOMEM	METALOGUE
2007–2009	2009–2012	2011–2014	2010–2014	2013–2016
Athens Technology Center SA	IBM Research	University of the Aegean	University of Sheffield	German Research Centre for Artificial Intelligence
National Technical University of Athens	Institute of Communication and Computer Systems	Google Ireland	Internet Memory Foundation	Universität des Saarlandes
University of the Aegean	SCAI Fraunhofer	Athens Technology Center	University of Southampton	Rijksuniversiteit Groningen
Kauno Technologijos Universitetas	University of Essex	NCSR'D'	Athena Research and Innovation Center in ICKT	Trinity College Dublin University Dublin
University of Koblenz	ATOS Origin	CP	Télécom ParisTech	Charamel GmbH
Austrian Parliament	K.U. Leuven	Fraunhofer IGD	Deutsche Welle	University of Peloponnese
Hellenic Parliament	Athens Technology Center	Kantor Qwentes	Südwestrundfunk	Hellenic Parliament
	Hellenic Parliament	Austrian Parliament	Yahoo! Iberia	Open University of the Netherlands
		Hellenic Parliament	L3S Research Center	DialogConnection
			Hellenic Parliament	University of Essex
			Austrian Parliament	
			Athens Technology Center SA	

The number of partners varies from 7 (LEX-IS) to 12 (ARCOMEM) with an average partner number per project of 10. Further statistical analysis of partner participation in the mentioned FP7 projects is presented in Fig. 6. The analysis reveals that 36 unique partners from 11 countries participated in these 5 programmes (out of a total of 47 partners). The Hellenic Parliament and the Austrian Parliament have 5 and 3 appearances as projects partners, respectively.

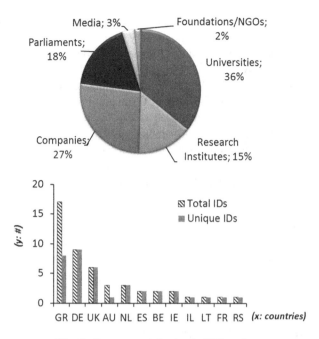

Fig. 6. Partner participation in FP7 projects

Similarly, a broad distribution of the partners' working sectors can be observed. On average, Universities comprise the largest share of partners with 36%, followed by private companies (26%, both Small and Medium sized Enterprises -SMEs- and large corporations) and Parliaments (18%). Two parliaments are represented here, the Hellenic Parliament and the Austrian Parliament. It has to be noted that the LEX-IS programme also used data from the Lithuanian Parliament that was provided by the Kauno Technologijos Universitetas.

The most significant research topics tackled by the individual projects are depicted in Table 2 below. What is of interest is that there are several common research topics

Table 2. Research topics in FP7 programmes

	LEX-IS	+Spaces	NOMAD	ARCOMEM	METALOGUE
Policy discourse	●	●	●	●	●
eParticipation	●	●	●		
Policy modeling	●		●		
Social Network Analysis		●	●	●	
Visualization		●	●	●	
3D role playing		●			●
Crowdsourcing			●	●	
Multimodal dialogue					●

between these projects, but also a clear evolution and expansion of research over time towards more complex topics in the parliamentary context.

With the know-how collected by the participation in the FP7 research projects the Hellenic Parliament was awarded in 2011 the EU funded IPA (Instrument for Pre-Accession Assistance) Twinning Project "Strengthening the Capacities of National Assembly of the Republic of Serbia towards EU Integration". This complex project of inter-institutional cooperation was managed solely by the Hellenic Parliament and covered five (5) distinct sectors of parliamentary operation: "law-making process", "transposition of EU Acquis Communautaire", "organizational structure and procedures", "oversight" and "parliamentary communication".

More than 100 short term experts (STEs) on parliamentary affairs from 10 countries (Greece, Austria, France, Germany, UK, Belgium, Slovakia, Poland, Hungary and Montenegro) facilitated the necessary know-how transfer to their Serbian counterparts from the National Assembly, the Government, Independent State Bodies and Civil Society Organizations. The project was successfully completed in early 2015 and made use of the networking capabilities developed through the aforementioned FP7 projects, as well as of specific know-how in the areas of eParticipation, Policy Modeling and Social Network Analysis.

5   Assessment and Outlook Research

Over the last 10 years, the Hellenic Parliament and its research partners have utilized the opportunities of the EU framework programmes for research to understand evolution and transformation of the digital society and the potential impact on political institutions.

All these interesting innovations, the approaches and the models presented above, the evolution of the digital market, the efforts of the Governmental Institutions and especially the commitments of the legislative branch, reveal that there is a need for immediate feedback to the discourses in the policy making arena, in real time, based on citizens' reactions in the social media. The abovementioned research projects from the previous framework period (2006–2013) could partially identify the users' needs, described thoroughly in the previous paragraphs.

On top of that, the political communication has been transferred in Web 2.0 or Web 3.0 that radically transforms the policy discourse, and strategic planning of election campaigns, political debates and dialogue with well-grounded transparency in political activities, diffusing messages and information. It is evident that the policy makers need to assess the interests and requirements of their voters/citizens, upgrade the role of political marketing and web communication, and create supportive networks with the interaction of citizens through social media.

However, real-life experience has proved that there are still many unsolved challenges in policy making ICT techniques, which restrain policy makers from providing sustainable and inclusive decisions and citizens from getting engaged in policy discussions. Public policy issues are not generally appealing and interesting, as citizens fail to understand the relevance of the issues and to see "what's in it for me" as the decline in voters' turnout and the lack of trust in politicians. Citizens demand more openness, transparency and commitment to results and increasingly seek to express their views or opinions and influence policy decisions through the new media.

While the Web has long promised an opportunity for widespread involvement, e-participation initiatives often struggle to generate participation and there is a huge gap between the technological advancements and the active participation of citizens and other stakeholders in the policy-making processes with sustainable policy modelling interactive tools. As a direct result, ICT tools still have untapped potential and remain a "novelty" for the majority of governments, parliaments, policy makers despite the already acknowledged benefits for their use by all of them related to the quality and speed of policy making, as well as to evidence-based policy decision making [14].

These projects are closely related to the idea of monitory democracy, as defined in [15], so individual ICT tools extracted from them and could be used accordingly. On the other hand, "citizen participation in the political process is considered highly important to foster greater government accountability, transparency and responsiveness" and the ICT tools provided can foster participatory democracy (see also [16]). A new trend where these projects could potentially contribute in is the e-Parliament concept where citizens can, and in fact could, be included in decision-making processes, through projects and services that enable everyday life citizens to actively participate and engage in interaction with members of parliament and (just as, if not more, importantly) in peer-to-peer interaction with fellow citizens. Overall, based on the results of these 5 research projects, it seems that there is a need for user friendly integrated ICT tools that allows policy makers to have, among others [17]:

- an interpretation of citizens' discussions, for or against a policy agenda,
- a stable feedback loop between the vast amount of crowd opinion on the Web and the agenda of the decision-maker, for a given policy,
- a clear and complete plan on the understanding of how the citizens' opinion, arguments and needs can (or should) affect the policy-making agenda,
- a complete set of tools for the discovery, aggregation, analysis and visualization of arguments, expressed in the Web in support or against a given policy,
- a continuous usability testing bringing more closely the digital transformation and the digital society,
- full integration of multimedia archives (video, image, text) with customized services addressed to citizens' needs,
- access to interconnectivity, open prototypes, open source tools, open data and open architecture.

Taking into account all the above, the EU Digital Agenda 2020 prospects and goals addressed to National Parliaments could be summarized to the tackling of the following issues:

- Availability of e-Government digital tools and systems
- Language Technologies online content available in every European language
- Transforming Digital Science open, global, collaborative and closer to society
- Cultural Heritage available online
- Making Big Data work
- Tackling societal challenges

– Use of ICT for governmental accountability

The successful results of the described use cases could also be used as a potential marketing tool for the promotion of policy discourse in the digital Parliament context. Hence, they could be further distributed through the main dissemination channels available: the research & scientific community, the industrial community, the public sector and the public community. Real world applications could be created for several potential customers like political institutions, mass media organisations, individual politicians and policy makers. The promotion and distribution of an integrated tool for brand monitoring as a package is the preferred strategy in the beginning and, as the product gains more market share, its modules could also be advertised and sold individually, especially in the more competitive market of Big Data and Content Analysis.

6 Summary

It is evident that the digital environment creates new opportunities for policy discourse and public participation, and the EU is heavily investing in relevant research areas. This paper presents the outcome of a series of 5 research projects, with the particularity of the participation of National Parliaments in the partner-mix. Careful assessment and evaluation of these projects leads to interesting results relating to the evolution of contemporary Parliaments.

By using the described set of tools modern politicians may test, detect and understand how citizens perceive their own political agendas, and also stimulate the emergence of discussions and contributions on the formal and informal web (e.g. forums, social networks, blogs, newsgroups and wikis), so as to gather useful feedback for immediate (re)action. In this way, politicians can create a stable feedback loop between information gathered on the Web and the definition of their political agendas based on this contribution. Vice versa, digital citizens may also employ such tools in order to discuss and evaluate a given policy within the respective community or directly with the policy makers. At the same time, one will be able to track the development of the political discourse, evaluate the consistency and clarity of the political arguments, and ultimately form an opinion or a political choice. However, it must be noted that the aforementioned approaches so far, failed to widely involve in the overall process important stakeholders, both on the policy and the society side.

This contemporary study and concluding evaluation shows that concepts like e-Parliament or Smart Parliament are still far away from the real digital democracy where citizens and policy-makers cooperate, collaborate, or, simply, interact, having a common platform of communication. Above all, this interaction has to take place in a seamless and transparent way, while respecting the users' privacy. The exploitation of this kind of research projects points towards a certain direction. The ultimate scope of such projects is to provide excellent science, facing the societal challenges and showing industrial leadership, in order to improve the research results by building connections between scientists and people, while involving real life institutions, such as Parliaments, and the related stakeholders in the process.

Acknowledgements. The authors would like to thank the associates of the European Programs Implementation Service (EPIS) of the Hellenic Parliament (HeP), a key stakeholder of the described FP7 European Commission projects. The present work would not be possible without their steady support and cooperation throughout the project cycle, and their commitment in parliamentary excellence.

References

1. European Commission: eParticipation. https://ec.europa.eu/digital-single-market/eparticipation
2. European Commission: CAPS projects. https://ec.europa.eu/digital-single-market/caps-projects
3. Crossover EU Programme: Links. http://crossover-project.eu/Project/Links.aspx
4. Charalabidis, Y., Lampathaki, F., Misuraca, G., Osimo, D.: ICT for governance and policy modelling: research challenges and future prospects in Europe. In: Proceedings of the 45th Hawaii International Conference on System Sciences (HICSS). IEEE Computer Society (2012)
5. Koryzis, D., Fitsilis, F., Schefbeck, G.: Moderated policy discourse vs. non-moderated crowdsourcing in social networks – a comparative approach. In: Proceedings of the 16th International Legal Informatics Symposium (IRIS), Jusletter IT (2013)
6. Spiliotopoulos, D., Koryzis, D., Schefbeck, G.: Crowdsourcing and transparency in the legislative process: the NOMAD approach. In: Proceedings of the 17th International Legal Informatics Symposium (IRIS), Jusletter IT (2014)
7. Kindra, G., Stapenhurst, F., Pellizo, R.: ICT and the transformation of political communication. Int. J. Adv. Manag. Sci. **2**(1), 32–42 (2013)
8. Papaloi, A., Gouscos, D.: E-parliaments and novel parliament-to-citizen services. eJournal eDemocracy Open Gov. **3**(1), 80–98 (2011)
9. Griffith, J., Leston-Bandeira, C.: How are parliaments using new media to engage with citizens? J. Legis. Stud. **18**(3–4), 496–513 (2012)
10. Papaloi, A., Gouscos, D.: Parliamentary information visualization as a means for legislative transparency and citizen empowerment? eJournal eDemocracy Open Gov. **5**(2), 174–186 (2013)
11. Scherer, S., Neuroth, C., Schefbeck, G., Wimmer, M.A.: Enabling eParticipation of the youth in the public debate on legislation in Austria: a critical reflection. In: Macintosh, A., Tambouris, E. (eds.) ePart 2009. LNCS, vol. 5694, pp. 151–162. Springer, Heidelberg (2009). doi:10.1007/978-3-642-03781-8_14
12. Spiliotopoulos, D., Schefbeck, G., Koryzis, D.: Obtaining societal feedback on legislative issues through content extraction from the social web. In: Proceedings of the 16th International Legal Informatics Symposium (IRIS), Jusletter IT (2013)
13. Alexandersson, J., Aretoulaki, M., Campbell, N., Gardner, M., Girenko, A., Klakow, D., Koryzis, D., Petukhova, V., Specht, M., Spiliotopoulos, D., Stricker, A: Metalogue: a multiperspective multimodal dialogue system with metacognitive abilities for highly adaptive and flexible dialogue management. In: 10th International Conference on Intelligent Environments (IE), pp. 365–368. IEEE (2014)
14. Lampathaki, F., Charalabidis, Y., Osimo, D., Koussouris, S., Armenia, S., Askounis, D.: Paving the way for future research in ICT for governance and policy modelling. In: Janssen, M., Scholl, H.J., Wimmer, M.A., Tan, Y. (eds.) EGOV 2011. LNCS, vol. 6846, pp. 50–61. Springer, Heidelberg (2011). doi:10.1007/978-3-642-22878-0_5
15. Keane, J.: The Life and Death of Democracy. Simon and Schuster, London (2009)

16. Milakovich, E.M.: The internet and increased citizen participation in government. eJournal eDemocracy Open Gov. **2**(1), 1–9 (2010)
17. Schefbeck, G.: Workshop «Elektronische Rechtsetzung». In: Proceedings of the 18th International Legal Informatics Symposium (IRIS), Jusletter IT (2015)

An Analysis for Difficult Tasks in e-Learning Course Design

Ling-Ling Lai$^{(\boxtimes)}$ and Shu-Ying Lin

Tamkang University, Tamsui, Taipei, Taiwan
llai@mail.tku.edu.tw, meiyin0705@gmail.com

Abstract. The goal of the study is to fulfill the gap and examine the usability of a well-known e-learning program, Moodle, from the perspective of course instructors. In particular, the study put emphasis on analyzing the difficult tasks for expert and novice users. A multiple data collection method was used to understand the difficult tasks and the possible reasons behind them. Participants were recruited from across disciplines in a university setting. Overall, 8 teaching assistants (TA) who have past Moodle teaching experience and 8 TAs with non-Moodle experience were recruited. A round of 18 usability tasks was carried out, post-task interviews were conducted, and finally a survey with 25 questions was administered to the participants. The research identified five main types of difficulties that experts and novices encountered. Essentially, failed connection between users' conceptual model and the structuring and labeling of the interface brings the greatest difficulty for both groups of users. Past experiences and knowledge that experts retrieved from pre-existing cognitive categories were found not applicable for problem solving. Experts were not able to recognize features and meaningful patterns on Moodle. Lastly, the complicated editing system embedding in the interface was difficult for novices to figure out ways to complete needed tasks. The findings of the study bring further understandings and implications for online platform designs as well as for advancing and supporting the development of intelligent interactive systems in future applications.

Keywords: Computer-supported collaboration · e-Learning · Usability

1 Introduction

In the digital age, technology has greatly improved and enhanced the e-learning experience. For instructors, it is becoming very common teaching online courses via an e-learning platform. Computer-supported collaboration has exemplified to a great extent in all possible types of e-learning activities designed and provided by instructors. For both learners as well as instructors, e-learning should provide both parties with positive user experience. In most human computer interface (HCI) research, the focus of studies as well as the "user" in many of the designers' minds are set on the needs and preferences of the learner as well as the student, very rarely the focus is on those of the instructor.

© Springer International Publishing AG 2017
F.F.-H. Nah and C.-H. Tan (Eds.): HCIBGO 2017, Part I, LNCS 10293, pp. 171–180, 2017.
DOI: 10.1007/978-3-319-58481-2_14

The goal of the study is to fulfill the gap and examine the usability of a well-known e-learning program, Moodle, from the perspective of course instructors. In particular, the study put emphasis on analyzing the difficult tasks for expert and novice users.

2   Related Literature

Recent HCI research has impacted many fields in terms of implications for user-centered and intuitive designs. From traditional web-based computer interface to the mobile interface, from personal information management gadgets to broad-scaled collaborative work tools, there are different challenges for the various types of tools for their intended audience. The following literature are centered on research studies on e-learning platform and the Moodle, which is the research target for this study.

2.1   e-Learning Platform and Moodle

E-learning is an efficient way of delivering training sessions and retaining materials. This is also the reason 77% of American corporations rely on e-learning programs [1]. E-learning is regarded as best practices in business in recent years. By definition, e-learning is a terms that covers a wide set of applications and processes, including web-based learning, computer-based learning, virtual classrooms, and digital collaboration. This method of teaching means the content is delivered via Internet, intranet/extranet, audio- and videotape, satellite broadcast, interactive TV, CD-ROM, and more [2]. In this mode of online learning, teaching materials, quizzes and exams are all uploaded and stored in a specific platform for learners to download and use. Take Moodle, a very popular e-learning platform for example, the file types that can be uploaded include .txt, .html, .doc, .pdf, .ppt, .zip, .jpeg, .gif, .mp3, .mov, .wmv, or any other file type that is readable by the audience's local software. Given that technology advances so quickly, the challenges for instructors and learners might not be what an e-learning platform can or cannot do, but how easy and intuitive the interface is for users, both instructors and learners, to accomplish their tasks and to finish the intended work efficiently and with delight.

Moodle is chosen for the current study, which is an e-learning program originally designed by the Australian designer, Martin Dougiamas, and later widely adopted in a number of learning environments, ranging from businesses and organizations, elementary schools, and many campuses of higher education systems. The online users of Moodle are over 90 millions globally, including Google, Shell, London School of Economics, State University of New York, Microsoft, etc. [3]. Moodle is used in over 220 countries worldwide and is available in more than 95 languages. In Taiwan, 48 colleges and universities choose to use Moodle as their e-learning platform. In the university setting where the researchers belong, there has been a dramatic increase of faculty users from 31 to 205; the number of courses offered increased from 39 to 507 in the past 7 years [4]. The usability issues from the perspective of course designs are critical for those who offer online courses and/or those who assist the faculty members.

2.2 Usability Testing

In the field of HCI, user-centered design is much valued and stressed. The essential goal of such concern is to deign any product with its intended audience in mind, so that users could accomplish their tasks in an efficient and effective manner. According to Eberts [5], four HCI design approaches that could be applied to user interface designs for achieving user-friendly, efficient, and intuitive user experiences for humans include the anthropomorphic approach, the cognitive approach, the predictive modeling approach, and the empirical approach. In these approaches, the anthropomorphic approach means that the interface possesses "human-like" qualities. The cognitive approach considers the abilities of the human brain and sensory-perception, so the design of the interface will support the user in accomplishing their tasks. The empirical approach is for examining and comparing with conceptual models that are most suitable for targeted users. In addition to qualitative assessments of user preferences, measuring users' task performance is crucial for determining how intuitive an interface is. The predictive modeling is essentially the GOMS model (Goals, Operators, Methods, and Selection Rules) that is based on human information processing theory. The model requires that certain measurements of human performance are used to calculate the time it takes to complete a goal [6].

Nielsen's [7] usability testing criteria are well known worldwide and are adopted commonly in HCI research. His criteria include learnability, efficiency, memorability, errors, and satisfaction. Furthermore, based on Nielsen, Quesenbery [8] developed 5Es, which are effective, efficient, engaging, error tolerant, easy to learn. Shneiderman and Plaisant [9] also proposed 5 criteria for usability evaluation, which include time to learn, speed of performance, rate of error by users, retention over time, and subjective satisfaction. Regardless of slightly different criteria proposed by HCI researchers and scholars, the essence of testing is to identify problem areas of an interface, to improve user experience, and to eliminate troubles users encounter in future designs.

2.3 Expert vs. Novice Users

In any online programs, it is nature that users carry past experiences to the new online environment. How efficient a user is in accomplishing the needed tasks in the new and unfamiliar realm depends on the level of expertise. According to Bransford et al. [10], accumulated research studies regarding how people learn showed that experts demonstrate a number of key principles. For instance, (1) experts notice features and meaningful patterns of information that are not noticed by novices; (2) experts are able to retrieve important knowledge with little effort and much flexibility; (3) experts have varying levels of flexibility in applying strategies to new situations (p. 31).

Research studies also showed that it is not the general abilities such as memory or intelligence, not the use of general strategies that differentiates experts from novices, as people assume. It is because experts have acquired extensive knowledge that affects the things they notice, they way they organize, represent, and interpret information in their environment. All these abilities are critical factors that affect their ability to remember, reason, and solve problems [10].

In HCI related studies that identified similarities and differences between expert users and novices users of an interface, researchers found that past knowledge, mental representation, cognitive categories, conceptual structural, and domain-specific knowledge played a role in differentiating expert and novice users [11, 12]. Expert users know how to retrieve and use past knowledge in dealing with new situations and solve their problems with ease.

3   Research Method

To focus on the teaching role of the instructors in e-learning programs, two groups of participants depending on the levels of expertise in Moodle as instructors was the main focus when designing the study. The methods of data collection included usability tests, post-task interviews, and questionnaires. First, the researchers recruited participants for usability tests with 10 categories of evaluations with 18 specific tasks, which are ranked the most-used functions and features in the process of course design. With two level of e-learning expertise, i.e., expert users and novice users, the researchers then conducted post-tasks interviews. Finally, a questionnaire was distributed to the participants for further analysis to elicit the overall perception of the interface. Details are given in the following sections.

3.1   Participants

The participants were recruited from Tamkang University (TKU) in Taiwan, which is a 4-year university with graduate programs in multiple fields. TKU has a long history of incorporating new technologies for facilitating teaching. The number of e-learning programs, including undergraduate and graduate programs using Moodle as the teaching platform has increased dramatically over the past years. Originally, WebCT was the platform being used in the university, yet since 2010, the university decided to move to Moodle as the school-wide e-learning platform. The version used at the time of the study was Moodle version 1.9. According to the user analytics provided by the university, the faculty members who use Moodle as the online teaching program was 69 in 2010; the number increased to 218 in 2016. Furthermore, the number of courses increased from 136 to 564 in the past 6 years [13].

At TKU, at least one e-Tutor is assigned to each e-learning course, sometimes two are provided, depending on the needs of the faculty and the nature of the course. The role of the e-Tutor is generally to manage the course setup on the Moodle platform and facilitate the faculty during the semester. More specifically, the e-Tutor needs to (1) provide help for both the faculty and the students with interface related questions as well as the course related questions in the asynchronous teaching sessions; (2) upload needed online course materials before and during each class sessions, including developing course needed materials and managing course related issues on Moodle; (3) troubleshoot technical problems encountered during asynchronous as well as synchronous teaching sessions. Essentially, e-Tutors are responsible of various aspects of the e-learning process, including being familiar with the interface of Moodle as well as carrying out the actual course related tasks, such as choosing the appropriate methods of giving tests among all the possible choices of exam features available on Moodle. Considering the heavy responsibilities of e-Tutors at TKU, the researchers believed e-Tutors are suitable participants for this study in identifying interface related issues from the perspective of course instructors.

The study also aims to know how expert e-Tutors and novice e-Tutors react to Moodle interface and the difficult tasks they encounter; therefore, 8 e-Tutors for each group were recruited. Expert e-Tutors in this study were the graduate teaching assistants who have teaching experience before participating in the study, while the novice e-Tutors were graduate teaching assistants who have no prior experience for e-learning courses. The methods of recruiting e-Tutors include three sources. First, through the assistance of the online teaching workshop provided by the university, email lists were obtained and invitations were sent to all graduate students. Secondly, an invitation of the study was posted on the Facebook page of the Association of Teaching Assistants at TKU. Lastly, snowballing method was used to invite interested teaching assistants with and without teaching experience on Moodle.

Regarding the demographics of the 16 e-Tutors, 7 (43.7%) of them were from the School of Business; 6 (37.5%) were from School of Liberal Arts; 2 (12.5%) were from the School of Engineering; and 1 (6.2%) was from the School of Science. Nine (56.2%) of the e-Tutors were male and seven (43.7%) were female.

3.2 Research Design

The research questions are targeted on the following areas: (1) What are the problematic usability issues by expert users and novice users? (2) What are the difficulties of the course design for expert users and novice users? (3) What are the differences expert users and novice users have in the process of course design? The criteria of the usability study included learnability, efficiency, effectiveness, errors, and satisfactions. Memorability is not included for the analysis, as it did not fit in the scope of the study.

A triangulation of data collection approach including usability tests, post-task interviews, and questionnaires was used. A pretest was carried out to ensure the feasibility of the research tools; modifications were made accordingly. To capture the overall on-screen process, EverCam7 was installed for the purpose of data analysis and the retrospective interviews. In order to design representative usability tasks, according to Nielsen's principle of "real tasks and real users", the research team obtained the use analytics of Moodle with the permission from the Distance Education Development at TKU, a university unit responsible for e-learning related matters. Based on the usage analysis of Moodle, the most popular and used functions/features are Online Resources, Discussion Board, Exams, Assignments, Tags, User Analytics, Files, Reflections and Sharing, Course Management, and Course Setting. Ten categories of tasks, including 18 specific tasks, were designed to test the usability.

For post-task interviews, the main focus was to collect the participants' thoughts on the tasks they think were difficult, had trouble completing, and the perceived reasons for encountering difficulties. Questions were also designed for the participants to express their ideas and suggestions for revision of the interface.

Based on Nielsen, Quesenbery, Shneiderman and Plaisant, Shackel and Richardson, Preece, Rogers and Sharp, Brooke, and Finstad [7–9, 14–17], a System Usability Scale (SUS), which is a 5-point Likert-scaled survey with 25 questions was designed, modified, and distributed to the participants. The survey asked questions regarding five aspects of usability testing: learnability, efficiency, effectiveness, error rate, and satisfaction.

4   Research Findings

The results of the study revealed a number of design issues for the e-learning platform. In this paper, the researchers report on the findings of the analysis of difficult tasks among expert and novice e-Tutors on areas of learnability, efficiency, effectiveness, and error rate. Three aspects are discussed in the following sections based on the findings, which are problematic usability issues, difficult tasks, and differences of experts versus novices.

4.1   Problematic Usability Issues

The usability data showed that there are a number of fine designs in Moodle platform that fit in Nielsen's criteria of good learnability, efficiency, and effectiveness, such as links of websites, submission of assignments, as well as areas for discussions. However, participants experienced a number of problematic usability issues.

The usability testing on learnability revealed that both experts and novices found the procedures of setting up exam questions to be very difficult. For novices, the most difficult task in terms of learnability was to upload needed files to a new folder in a designated place and make it public to students, which is a very critical function often required for online courses. The top two most difficult tasks were exam questions setup (56.2%) and new folder setup (37.5%).

In the area of efficiency, the researchers used the number of clicks as the criteria for the judgment of efficiency. One of the members in the research team was an e-Tutor at TKU for 8 courses, therefore, was equipped with sufficient knowledge regarding the most efficient way of accomplishing each task. For novices, the highest number of clicks (i.e., the least efficient task) was 94, on average, for the tasks of adding online resources. The second least efficient task was the 89 clicks for the tasks regarding setting up exam questions. The third was the 84 clicks for the tasks regarding adding new folders with needed files. For the experts, an average of 62 clicks was needed for the task of setting up exam questions; 58 clicks were needed for adding new folders with needed files; 46 clicks needed for adding online resources. Aside from the number of clicks, time spent on the tasks was also calculated and analyzed to identify the least efficient tasks. The results showed that the most time consuming task for novices was adding online resources (14:27), setting up exam questions being the second (13:37), and adding new folder(s) with needed materials being the third (7:16). For experts, the top three most time consuming tasks were exactly the same with the novices, with the time for adding online resources being the least efficient tasks. The average length of time spent on the three least efficient tasks was 10:31, 9:43, and 5:41, respectively.

In the area of effectiveness, overall speaking, for both groups of users the least effective task was adding online resources, with only one e-Tutor finishing the task successfully. The next two least effective tasks were adding new folders with needed materials and setting up exam questions. These appeared to be difficult tasks for both experts and novices.

For errors occurring in the usability testing, novice users and expert users both made the most errors when adding online resources, with an error rate of 93.75%. The next two tasks that received the highest error rate were adding new folders with needed materials, and setting up exam questions (75%). The interview data identified the reasons for making errors. According to Reason's [18] three categorizations for errors, which are skill-based errors, rule-based mistakes, and knowledge-based mistakes, 70% of the errors in this study were found to be rule-based mistakes, which means that the users followed the rules but made wrong decisions along the way when trying to accomplish the intended tasks. On the other hand, if we calculated the tasks that most users gave up, we found that adding new folders with needed materials ranked the highest for novices users, while setting up exam questions ranked the highest for expert users.

All these problematic areas reflected that the connection between the labels used for the intended functions, the conceptual model of the user, and the mapping of past knowledge and experience, if any, were mismatched. This made it fairly difficult for users to make proper connections conceptually and to figure out the intended functions of the labels.

4.2   Difficult Tasks

Analyzing the difficult tasks perceived by users, five types of difficulties are identified.

(1) **Unclear Organization of Functions.** Users revealed that the first and foremost difficulty found across tasks is to clearly understand the organization of the platform structure, which made remembering and memorizing corresponding functions/ features very difficult. Users were often confused by the seemingly unclear distinctions of similar functions seen in different categories. The most obvious behavior resulted by the problem was observing users lingered between two possible drop-down menus when trying to complete their tasks. For instance, they saw discussion boards in the tasks of adding new folders with needed materials, managing student learning activities, and adding the actual discussion board for class discussion. In all these tasks the participants were confused seeing "discussion board" in different places, which made it difficult remembering the structure of the platform.

(2) **Unclear Labeling of Functions.** In course setup related tasks, the labels and the corresponding functions/features are not clearly connected, thus, it became difficult for the user to choose correctly and intuitively. This happened repeatedly among users when adding online resources. In addition, in the task of adding new folders with needed materials, users were unaware of the correct order of how specific task should be done; they were also unable to figure out how to make new folders. The label of "folders" shown on the course interface and the steps of actually adding new folders with needed materials were mismatched. The unclear labeling of

functions and the users' perceived ideas of what the label meant caused great troubles for the user in this study.

(3) **Complicated Editing System.** The third difficulty is the complicated editing system, which could be seen when users tried to set up exam questions for teaching purposes. Interview data revealed that setting up exam questions to be a very complicated process. Participants shared that it was simply too complicated, thus, felt unsure of how to accomplish the task. The many steps and clicks required of going deep down a number of layers in the design structure brought frustrations to users, both experts and novices.

(4) **Exceeding Number of Menu Selection.** Participants shared that they felt overwhelmed when seeing the exceeding number of selections under the menu, which brings heavy cognitive burden for users. It is also in the process of setting up exam questions, users felt unsure of what to choose from. Also, in adding assignments, users noted that there were too many choices. the impression users have was messiness.

(5) **Inconsistency between Users' Experience and Platform Functions.** Users noted that many of the past experience in other platforms and software were different from what they saw in Moodle, which again caused confusion and frustration. This was especially obvious in the tasks of adding online resources and setting up exam questions.

4.3   Differences Between Expert Users vs. Novice Users

The usability tests showed that there were similarities and differences between expert users and novice users, in particular in the areas of course setting and course management. Also, it is worth mentioning that course planning related tasks were difficult for both exert users and novice users. Past experiences did not benefit the performance of expert users in the study. Furthermore, the error rates for expert users are even higher than novice users.

Examining all the areas of similarities in difficult tasks, including the analysis of learnability, efficiency, effectiveness, errors, and post-task interviews, the common problems lie in that the tasks themselves were to be completed in very complicated ways. In particular, past experience in other e-learning tools did not bring efficiency nor effectiveness to the tasks e-Tutors were required to accomplish. On the contrary, for the tasks that both groups performed well, the procedures were straightforward, the number of clicks was few, the labels of the functions were easy to understand and matched with users' past experience.

By looking at the comparisons for novices and experts, we are able to conclude that the learnability of Moodle is fine for expert users because of their familiarities with the platform, but low for novice users because novice users needed much time to figure out ways to complete the tasks. For efficiency, effectiveness and errors, it is all clearly noted by the participants that when the labels are clear and matched with their conceptual knowledge about what the labels are, tasks were completed in efficient and correct form, and less mistakes were made along the way.

5   Conclusion

Based on the results of the study, implications can be found for design principles. For the problem of misinterpreted labeling, this is a continual design problem that is extensively discussed in the field of HCI and information architecture (IA). Especially, for the professionals of library and information science who are concerned about how information is organized, categorized, and labeled in the digital realm, the design of a proper labeling system that follows solid logic and yet matches with common practices is a great concern.

Implications for the difficulties expert users encountered in this study is that connections with past user experience and conceptual models are critical in that they provide the needed bridge for experts to identify features and meaningful patterns to use in solving current problems. Easy recognition and retrieval from previous knowledge for expert users is an important factor for them to succeed. On the other hand, designs that are intuitive in naming, organizing, and require simple steps for all tasks will help ease the learning curve for novices users. E-learning platforms should provide instructors with completed course planning functions such as uploading teaching materials and setting up teaching activities, so to provide a well-designed learning environment. Therefore, the usability of the e-leaning platform becomes very important and affects many. By examining the usability of Moodle for its course planning related interface issues and the difficulties encountered by user groups with different expertise, the study showed how expert users and novice users were similar and different in the process of course design. The study concludes and contributes with suggestions for e-learning platform designers as well as business, organizations, and schools that design online courses.

References

1. eLeanring Brothers. 4 top elearning and development trends for 2016. https://elearningbrothers.com/4-top-elearning-training-development-trends-2016/
2. Glossary of E-learning. Association for Talent Development. https://www.td.org/Publications/Newsletters/Learning-Circuits/Glossary
3. Israel, J.: Moodle in business (2014). https://www.paradisosolutions.com/blog/moodle-in-business/
4. Moodle. https://moodle.org/
5. Eberts, R.E.: User Interface Design. Prentice Hall, Englewood Cliffs (1994)
6. Card, S., Moran, T., Newell, A.: The Psychology of Human-Computer Interaction. Lawrence Erlbaum Associates, Hillsdale (1983)
7. Nielen, J.: Usability Engineering. Academic Press, Boston (1993)
8. Quesenbery, W.: Balancing the 5Es of usability. Cutter IT J. **17**(2), 4–11 (2004)
9. Shneiderman, B., Plaisant, C.: Designing the User Interface: Strategies for Effective Human-Computer Interaction. Addison-Wesley, Boston (2010)
10. Bransford, J., Brown, A.L., Cocking, R.R.: How People Learn: Brain, Mind, Experience, and School: Expanded Edition. The National Academies Press, Washington D.C., pp. 31–32 (2000). doi:http://doi.org/10.17226/9853

11. Popovic, V.: Expert and novice user differences and implications for product design and useability. Hum. Factors Ergon. Soc. Ann. Meeting Proc. **44**(38), 933–936 (2000)

12. Cockburn, A., Gutwin, C., Scarr, J., Malacria, S.: Supporting novice to expert transitions in user interfaces. ACM Comput. Surv. **47**(2), 31–36 (2014). http://www.malacria.com/media/pdf/expertisejournal.pdf

13. Moodle analytics of Tamkang University (2016). https://moodle.tku.edu.tw/mod/page/view.php?id=97735

14. Shackel, B., Richardson, S.: Human Factors for Informatics Usability. Cambridge University Press, Cambridge (1991)

15. Preece, J., Rogers, Y., Sharp, H.: Interaction Design: Beyond Human-Computer Interaction. Wiley, New York (2002)

16. Brook, J.: Usability Evaluation in Industry. Taylor & Francis, London (1996)

17. Finstad, K.: The system usability scale and non-native speaker. J. Usability Stud. **1**(4), 185–188 (2006)

18. Reason, J.: Human Error. New York University Press, Cambridge (1990)

Explore the Business Model of MOOCs

Yuan Long[(✉)]

Colorado State University Pueblo, Pueblo, USA
yoanna.long@csupueblo.edu

Abstract. Massive Open Online Courses (MOOCs) as disruptive innovation attract attention from both researchers and practitioners. This research selected ten popular MOOCs websites and explored primary sponsors, customer segments, and revenue models of each case. The paper further discussed the impact of MOOCs on higher education.

Keywords: MOOCs · Open education · Higher education · Business models · Disruptive innovation

1 Introduction

Massive Open Online Courses (MOOCs) as disruptive innovations attract increasing attention from both researchers and practitioners in the past few years. This research aims to explore the business models of MOOCs and discuss its impact on traditional higher education.

The rest of the paper is organized as following: the research background including the key features, the brief history, and the motivations of MOOCs is discussed first. Research questions are raised right after that. Research methods and sample selection are then described and followed by analysis and results. In the end, the discussion and the conclusion summarize the entire paper.

2 Research Background

2.1 Key Features of MOOCs

Massive Open Online Courses (MOOCs) refer to online education that opens to public. Most of the MOOCs are free while some charge small fees. MOOCs have become widely accepted and been extremely popular in the past five years; the typical examples include Coursera, Khan Academy, Edx, and Udemy, etc.

Comparing to traditional face-to-face education, MOOCs are featured by:

- Scalability (*massive*): The number of students is unlimited and they are not restricted to certain locations. The participation is far beyond a physical classroom.
- Open access (*open*): The courses are open to the public without the restriction of registration requirements, tuition fees, and certain resources such as facilities.

© Springer International Publishing AG 2017
F.F.-H. Nah and C.-H. Tan (Eds.): HCIBGO 2017, Part I, LNCS 10293, pp. 181–193, 2017.
DOI: 10.1007/978-3-319-58481-2_15

- Technology enabled (*online*): Network and educational technology enable the platform through which instructors and students are able to teach, learn, and collaborate simultaneously.
- Educational oriented (*courses*): The courses are mainly for educational purpose, aiming to make the expensive education accessible to the public.

2.2 Brief History of MOOCs

Along the short history of MOOCs, the development of online courses has experienced multiple stages that stem from different philosophies. The first stage is called cMOOC (connectivist MOOC) or MOOC 1.0 [18, 19], which is motivated by collaborative learning pedagogy. The concept comes from an online course named Connectivism and Connective Knowledge in 2008 or CCK08 [16]. cMOOC creates an interactive and dynamic educational environment, emphasizing the collaboration between learners and the connectivity within a community [16]. cMOOC believes that learners are the center of education while instructors play an assistant role.

The second stage is called xMOOC (extended MOOC) or MOOC 2.0 [18, 19], which is considered as an extension of traditional instructional education. The content delivered through xMOOC is normally well structured using traditional instructional methods such as presentation, assignments, and tests. Instructors play a leading role similar to that of in the traditional classroom setting [20]. The typical example of xMOOC includes Coursera, EdX, and Udacity, etc. Table 1 summarizes the main difference between cMOOC and xMOOC [30].

Table 1. Typologies of MOOC [30]

xMOOCs		cMOOCs
Scalability of provision	Massive	Community and connections
Open access - Restricted license	Open	Open access & licence
Individual learning in single platform	Online	Networked learning across multiple platforms and services
Acquire a curriculum of knowledge & skills	Course	Develop shared practices, knowledge and understanding

The third stage of MOOC is called hMOOC (hybrid MOOC) or MOOC3.0 [19], which combines the ideas of cMOOC and xMOOC. hMOOC is normally offered by institutions or universities on a hybrid basis to balance between traditional instructional-based courses and online collective-based courses. For examples, some faculty uses MOOCs in a flipped class, meaning students learn the basic concepts online before class and only come to the class for discussion and activities. Other faculty refers students to MOOCs for tutorials or additional contents. Some universities also suggest students to finish entry-level classes through MOOCs and consider the completion of those MOOCs in the admission [18]. The institutions are now using hMOOC creatively to find a cost-effective way to benefit both students and institutions.

2.3   Motivations of MOOCs Providers

Filling the gap of current education motivates the innovators such as Salman Khan, the funder of Khan Academy, to develop an online platform that provides courses to fit people's diverse learning style. In the traditional classroom, teachers deliver course content in the same pace with the same format to the entire class with no customization to individual student. On Khan Academy, students in K12 are able to choose different levels of classes that meet their own learning goals with their comfortable pace. They become the owners of their education rather than the passive receivers.

Creating open and collaborative learning environment motivates innovators such as Luis von Ahn, one of the founders of Duolingo, a language learning and translation platform. People share their knowledge on various languages and help each other learn beyond classroom.

Providing affordable and easily accessible education has been the most important motivation for MOOC developers such as Shai Reshef, the founder of the University of the People [17]. The tuition of higher education is increasing every year therefore the cost becomes the main obstacle for the students who have financial difficulty. Additionally, life-long learning becomes reality in contemporary world however continuous education challenges the working class who is restricted to time and location. Moreover, in some countries certain race and gender are forbidden to receive higher education. MOOCs as open education provide the opportunities for people who have difficulty to step into a traditional classroom. Currently above two thousand students from about one hundred and seventy countries have enrolled into the University of the People [27].

3   Research Questions

Though cMOOC, xMOOC, and hMOOC stem from different learning philosophies, they share the same key features with which the size of the audience has no limits (i.e., massive), the content can be accessed by public (i.e., open), and the knowledge is delivered through the Internet (i.e. online). As MOOCs are new and developing constantly, not many literatures explored the business models and their impact on higher education. I attempt to fill in this gap and aim to answer the following four research questions in order to contribute to both academic research and MOOCs practice.

1. Who are the major sponsors and advocators of MOOCs?
2. What are the market segments of MOOCs?
3. What are the revenue models of different MOOCs?
4. How would MOOCs impact higher education?

4   Research Methods and Sample Selection

Case study has been used as the main research method. Two criteria have been applied to decide the sample cases. First the website has to sustain in the past three years, and second the website has to be relatively popular. A large percentage of MOOCs in the market only last a short lifetime; in order to study the business models of MOOCs it makes sense to focus on those that holds both sustainability and popularity.

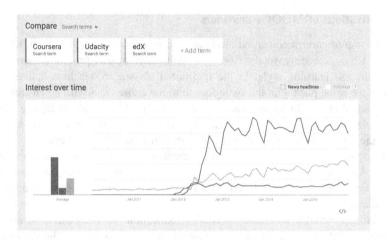

Fig. 1. Popularity trend of Coursera, Udacity, and edX using Google Trends analysis

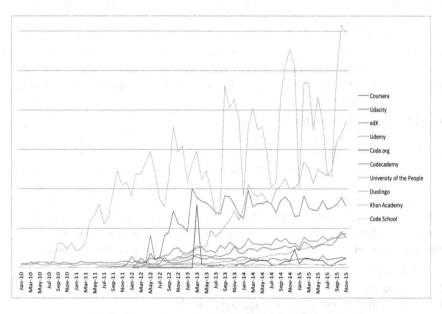

Fig. 2. Popularity trend of ten sample MOOCs websites

www.mooc-list.com provides a relatively complete list of MOOCs websites. The researcher first checked the existence of each individual website and deleted those that are not available. The researcher then collected the history data for the existing websites to exclude those that last less than three years. Finally the research used Google Trends to choose ten popular MOOCs from the rest websites.

Google Trends, an analytical tool, has been used to visualize the popularity. The researcher first studied the popularity trend of three widely accepted MOOCs websites:

Coursera, Udacity, and edX as shown in Fig. 1. Udacity shows the lowest trend among the three therefore has been used as the baseline. The researcher compared all the websites from step 2 to Udacity and found ten websites have higher popularity than it (Fig. 2).

These ten websites satisfy both criteria including sustainability and popularity are chosen for the further study. The brief description of these ten website including Coursera, Udacity, Udemy, edX, Khan Academy, University of the People, Code.org, Codecademy, Code School, and Duolingo, are shown on Table 2.

Table 2. Description of the sample MOOC websites

Name	Description	Founded
Coursera www.coursera.org	A platform that offers university-style courses provided by universities or organizations world-wise	April 2012 by Daphne Koller, Andrew Ng
Udacity www.udacity.com	A platform that mainly provides courses in the IT field by "Silicon Valley" to teach the skills industry employees need	June 2011 by Sebastian Thrun, David Stavens, Mike Sokolsky
Udemy www.udemy.com	An open marketplace through which anyone can create and take courses. It offers a large variety of topics from technology skills such as programming to hobby and entertainment such as yoga and photography	February 2010 by Eren Bali, Oktay Caglar, Gagan Biyani
edX www.edx.org	A MOOC platform that is similar to Coursera and provides traditional instructional education. The main difference from Coursera is edX is non-profit funded by Harvard and MIT	May 2012 by Anant Agarwal, Chris Terman, Piotr Mitros
Khan Academy www.khanacademy.org	Non-profit MOOC platform that mainly focuses on K-12 education with some extensions	September 2006 by Salman Khan
University of the People www.uopeople.edu	A tuition-free online university that provides degree program that mainly focuses on Business Administration and Computer Science currently	January 2009 by Shai Reshef
Code.org www.code.org	Website that offers the basic concept of programming to beginners	January 2013 by Hadi Partovi, Ali Partovi
Codecademy www.codecademy.com	An educational company that teaches coding in different programming languages such as Python, JavaScript, and Ruby	August 2011 by Zach Sims, Ryan Bubinski
Code School www.codeschool.com	A platform that teaches programming such as Ruby, JavaScript, HTML/CSS, iOS, Git, and databases via video, in-browser coding, and screencasts	February 2011 by Gregg Pollack
Duolingo www.duolingo.com	A language-learning website that teaches over 40 different languages	November 2011 by Luis von Ahn, Severin Hacker

5 Analysis and Results

5.1 Major Sponsors and Advocators of MOOC

Based on the analysis of the ten MOOCs cases, the researcher found that the sponsors and advocators of MOOCs are mainly from the following groups.

States:
Improving and supporting education is one of the major goals of State government. Some states have already taken the steps to subsidize MOOCs in order to extend educational horizon.

For example, San Jose State University in California received funds from the State government to transfer some traditional face-to-face courses to online on the platforms of edX and Udacity. The State planned to apply the experience to other state universities if it succeeds [12]. Another example is from Arizona State University (ASU). ASU is partnered with edX to create freshman classes that students can earn credits online. These courses do not have any admission requirements [24]. Moreover, Texas State system announced a partnership with edX to create 'Freshman Year for Free' program through which students can earn tuition-free college credits online in their freshman year. This program started in fall 2016 and required students to take Advanced Placement (AP) or College Level Examination Program (CLEP) before enrolling into the program [25].

Universities:
Universities including both public and private schools are the main sponsors and the participants of MOOCs. MIT and Harvard joined force to create edX in May 2012. The initial funding was about $60 million [6, 21]. University of Pennsylvania and the California Institute of Technology invested in $3.7 million to Coursera. "We look forward to working even more closely with Coursera and our university partners to continue to shape the future of online education", said by Penn State Provost Vincent Price [14].

Companies:
Companies sponsored MOOCs in different ways. Some companies pay MOOCs to develop online training courses for their employees. Some others sponsor MOOCs mainly for advertisement purpose for example having their brand or products introduced in the courses. Other companies sponsor MOOC to get exchange of students' data to find potential qualified employees.

Venture capitalists and non-profit organizations:
Venture capitalists have foreseen the potentials of MOOCs and become investors. Additionally, some non-profit organizations make donations to MOOCs expecting to contribute to the future of education.

Figure 3 illustrates the ten MOOCs websites, each linked to its major sponsors. The five major sources of the investment are from State government, universities, companies, venture capitalists, and non-profit organizations.

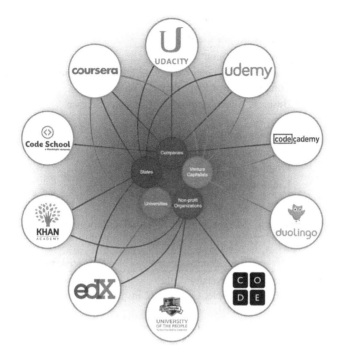

Fig. 3. MOOCs and their sponsors

5.2 Market Segments of MOOCs

Table 3 lists the primary fields offered by the ten MOOCs websites, each has its own emphasis and target customers. Some MOOCs websites such as Coursear and Udemy target on a horizontal market by offering courses across a large variety of topics, while others focus on a vertical market by offering courses in a specific field such as Code.org in coding and Duolingo in language.

Moreover, some websites stem from K-12 (e.g., Khan Academy) or higher education (e.g. edX) therefore are more academic-oriented, while others are supported by industry (e.g., Udacity) therefore are not restricted to academics.

Table 3. The teaching fields covered by the ten MOOCs websites

Name	Courses offered/specific field
Coursera	Arts and Humanities, Business, Computer Science, Data Science, Life Sciences, Math and Logic, Personal Development, Physical Science and Engineering, Social Sciences
Udacity	Data Science, Web Development, Software Engineering, Android, iOS, Computer Science, Non-Tech
Udemy	Development, Business, IT & Software, Office Productivity, Personal Development, Design, Marketing, Lifestyle, Photography, Health & Fitness, Teacher Training, Music, Academics, Language, Test Prep

(continued)

Table 3. (*continued*)

Name	Courses offered/specific field
edX	General Education
Khan Academy	Math, Science, Economics and Finance, Arts and Humanities, Computing, Test Prep, Partner Content
University of the people	Business Administration and Computer Science
Code.org	Programming Languages
Codecademy	Programming Languages
Code school	Programming Languages
Duolingo	Languages

Table 4. Market segment of ten MOOCs wesbites

		Market orientation	
		Academic-oriented	Non-academic oriented
Market type	Vertical market (specific field)	University of the People, Code.org (2 in total)	Udacity, CodeAcademy, Code School, Duolingo (4 in total)
	Horizontal market (Variety fields)	Coursera, edX, Khan Academy (3 in total)	Udemy (1 in total)

To compare the target market of MOOCs websites, Table 4 classifies the ten MOOCs into four blocks along two dimensions: horizontal vs. vertical market, academic vs. non-academic oriented. Please note the total number of MOOCs in each category does not indicate the percentage of MOOCs in the entire market; it only represents the statistics over ten sample MOOCs in this research.

5.3   Revenue Models of MOOCs

The revenue models of MOOCs are still under development and the new models are immerging every day. The researcher coded the revenue sources for the ten MOOCs websites (as show in Table 5) and then classified the sources into six major categories. The explanation of the numbers in Table 5 and the description of the revenue models are in appendix attached to the end of the paper.

- **Sales** of courses or other products. For example, the charges related to the courses such as tuition fees, program and specialization fees, and certificate. There are other sales through store shops and books or materials though not very common.
- **Service** to provide MOOCs as a platform for the organizations that either refer their employees to take training courses on MOOCs or develop their own training programs on MOOCs. MOOCs therefore charge course fees, platform usage fee, and customer support fees, etc.

Table 5. Revenue models of ten MOOCs websites

	1[a]	2	3	4	5	6	7	8	9	10	11	12	13	14	15	16	17	18
Coursera	■	■			■	■	■											
Udacity	■		■	■	■													
Udemy				■	■		■											
edX		■					■	■										
Khan Academy									■		■	■						
University of the People									■			■						■
Code.org										■		■	■				■	
Codecademy	■				■		■				■							
Code School							■					■	■			■		
Duolingo													■	■	■			
Total	3	2	1	2	4	1	5	1	2	1	2	4	3	1	1	1	1	1

[a]Note: the numbers and the corresponding revenue models are described in Appendix.

- **Advertising** fee (either direct or indirect) to charge organizations that want to put their names, brands, or products in the courses or capstone projects.
- **Subscription** fee to charge students who take unlimited courses in a period of time.
- **Special programs.** Examples in this category are diverse and creative. Some MOOCs charge for holding events and contests, some providing testing center, and some serving as career center and sharing students' data (with the approval and agreement of students) with potential employers.

6   Discussion

The discussion focuses on the impact of MOOCs on education in general, and higher education in particular. Would MOOCs be merely an online version of traditional face-to-face class? How to use technology to enable the innovation in pedagogy? Would MOOCs replace the traditional universities? These are the questions attract attention from both researchers and practitioners.

Higher education needs to change rapidly and dramatically to face the challenge of open education. Education is one of the basic human rights. However the increasing cost and the non-flexible schedule build a barrier preventing some students to enter the door of the universities. In order to face the challenge, the higher education may first develop a hybrid model combining online vs. face-to-face courses. For example, universities may consider offering entry level courses that need the least interaction online, while keeping those higher level courses that need more instruction and discussion face-to-face. This approach may lower the cost for both students and universities.

Second, universities need to encourage pedagogy innovation. The classroom becomes smaller and is facilitated by multimedia and modern technologies. The classroom teaching becomes more interactive and customized (e.g., adjusting teaching strategy based on individual student needs). The classroom learning is more of experience and an expensive investment to a student. A good analogy could be watching movie in movie theaters. People can watch movie steaming online at home (similar to take online courses), which costs less and is more convenient. However, a large number of people still like to watch movie at the movie theater (similar to take face-to-face classes) because they enjoy the experience and view movie-out with popcorn as a way of entertainment. Face-to-face teaching has to tailor to individual student needs and become an experience that students cannot get from online environment.

Third, universities may consider joining forces to teach common courses and focus their resources on featured fields. For example, almost every university offers general education courses that have similar curriculum. If universities collaborate in building a platform through MOOCs to offer general education courses online and accept those credits, this will greatly save teaching resources of individual universities and is more cost effective for higher education as a whole. The individual universities are then released from those repetitive efforts and able to focus more on featured fields and build their own brand.

Forth, some universities may consider to move the direction to become pure research institution. Certain teaching may be replaced by computers however comprehensive research questions needs human brain to solve it.

Last but not the least, current MOOCs are far from using the best of the technology. With the development of big data (e.g., individual student needs can be identified), machine learning (e.g., individual learning styles can be discovered), and virtual reality (e.g., learning environment becomes more real and interactive), MOOCs have great potentials and is capable to create more exciting experience for students.

7 Conclusion, Limitation, and Future Research

This paper explores the business models of MOOCs and discusses its impact on higher education. MOOCs have great potentials and higher education needs to be smart to face the challenge.

The research results are limited to the ten sample MOOCs websites. The future research may extend the sample size and explore the cost-efficient model to combine the benefits of both open education and current higher education. Additionally, the researcher is interested in exploring the application of certain technologies such as machine learning and virtual reality and how would this technology enable the innovation in education.

Appendix: Description of the Revenue Models

MOOCs revenue models:

1. Recruiting Program
2. Verified Certificate
3. Capstone Project
4. Specializations
5. Employee Training
6. Course Sponsorship
7. Tuition Fees
8. Credit-Eligible Courses
9. Platform usage fee
10. Platform service fee
11. Events/Contests/fundraising
12. Donation
13. Store Shop
14. Crowdsourced Translation
15. Test Center
16. Subscription
17. Cloud-funding
18. Other Fees (Application, Exam)

Below are some detailed descriptions:

Recruiting Program

The website generates profit by sharing students' data with the employees who search candidates to fill the job positions requiring certain skills.

Verified Certificate

Once students complete a class (or a program) that is normally free, they can decide if they want a certificate that normally charges a small fee.

Specializations

It is a strategy for the MOOCs to sell the courses in a bundle in one time. For example Coursera develops specialization by combines the relevant courses and the capstone project in a package and sell to students. If students want to achieve the certificate from the specialization, they have to pay every individual course in that bundle.

Employee Training

Companies and originations pay MOOC to conduct certain employee training.

Course Sponsorship

Companies and organizations pay MOOCs to mention their brand or product in classes, or simply a banner to advertise in lecture videos.

Tuition Fees

Though it's not common, some MOOCs charge students (normally a small fee comparing to college education) to take certain courses.

Credit-Eligible Courses

Some universities, being a partner with MOOC websites, can let students take their courses by paying cheaper tuitions. Students have to study by using the MOOC first. After passing the course with C or better, they can earn academic credits and transfer the credits to the actual university.

Platform usage fee

Companies and organizations can pay MOOCs to use the platform (i.e. website) to offer their own courses.

Platform service fee

Companies and organizations can pay MOOCs for the support and service when they use the MOOC platform to offer their own courses [11].

Events/Contests/fundraising

Some MOOCs hold events or contents to raise funding.

Subscription

The students can subscribe MOOCs and access all the courses during the subscribed time period.

References

1. Ahn, L.V.: Massive-scale online collaboration [Video file] (2011). https://www.ted.com/talks/luis_von_ahn_massive_scale_online_collaboration/
2. Cormier, D.: Dave's Educational Blog (2008). http://davecormier.com/edblog/2008/10/02/the-cck08-mooc-connectivism-course-14-way. Accessed 12 Nov 2015
3. Dellarocas, C., Van Alstyne, M.: Money models for MOOCs. Commun. ACM **56**(8), 25–28 (2013). doi:10.1145/2492007.2492017
4. Downes, S.: The rise of MOOCs: past successes, future challenges (2014). http://www.downes.ca/presentation/337. Accessed 22 Jan 2016
5. Duolingo (n.d.). Duolingo Test Center (2015). https://testcenter.duolingo.com/. Accessed 5 Dec 2015
6. EdX (n.d.). About Us (2015). https://www.edx.org/about-us. Accessed 2 Dec 2015
7. Google (n.d.). Trends graphs and forecasts (2015). https://support.google.com/trends/answer/4355164?hl=en. Accessed 28 Nov 2015
8. Hsu, J.: Professor leaving Stanford for online education startup (2012). http://www.nbcnews.com/id/46138856/ns/technology_and_science-innovation/. Accessed 20 Dec 2015
9. Kennedy, J.: Characteristics of massive open online courses (MOOCs): a research review, 2009–2012. J. Interact. Online Learn. **13**(1), 1–15 (2014)
10. Khan, S.: Let's use video to reinvent education [Video file] (2011). https://www.ted.com/talks/salman_khan_let_s_use_video_to_reinvent_education
11. Kolowich, S.: How edX plans to earn, and share, revenue from free online courses (2013). http://chronicle.com/article/How-EdX-Plans-to-Earn-and/137433/. Accessed 22 Feb 2016
12. Lewin, T., Markoff, J.: California to give web courses a big trial (2013). http://www.nytimes.com/2013/01/15/technology/california-to-give-web-courses-a-big-trial.html. Accessed 28 Nov 2015

13. Liqin, Z., Ning, W., Chunhui, W.: Construction of a MOOC based blend learning mode. In: 2015 10th International Conference on Computer Science & Education (ICCSE), p. 997 (2015). doi:10.1109/ICCSE.2015.7250397
14. Lerner, E., Sequeira, N.: Penn and caltech become equity investors in coursera as 12 new institutions come aboard (2012). http://www.upenn.edu/pennnews/news/penn-and-caltech-become-equity-investors-coursera-12-new-institutions-come-aboard. Accessed 3 Dec 2015
15. Meyer, S.J.: The world's best-known teacher is learning to lead (2014). http://www.forbes.com/sites/stevemeyer/2014/12/03/salman-khan-the-worlds-best-known-teacher-is-learning-to-lead/. Accessed 19 Dec 2015
16. Parr, C.: Mooc creators criticise courses' lack of creativity (2013). https://www.timeshighereducation.com/news/mooc-creators-criticise-courses-lack-of-creativity/2008180.article. Accessed 10 Nov 2015
17. Reshef, S.: An ultra-low-cost college degree [Video file] (2014). https://www.ted.com/talks/shai_reshef_a_tuition_free_college_degree/
18. Sandeen, C.: From Hype to Nuanced Promise: American Higher Education and the MOOC 3.0 Era (2013a). http://www.huffingtonpost.com/cathy-sandeen/from-hype-to-nuanced-prom_b_3618496.html. Accessed 12 Nov 2015
19. Sandeen, C.: Integrating MOOCS into traditional higher education: the emerging "MOOC 3.0" era. Change 45(6), 34–39 (2013b)
20. Schoenack, L.: A new framework for massive open online courses (MOOCs). MPAEA J. Adult Educ. 42(2), 98–103 (2013)
21. Shumski, D.: MOOCs by the numbers: How do EdX, Coursera and Udacity stack up? (2013). http://www.educationdive.com/news/moocs-by-the-numbers-how-do-edx-coursera-and-udacity-stack-up/161100/. Accessed 2 Dec 2015
22. Simonite, T.: Duolingo is a crowdsourced translation service that teaches French. MIT Technology Review (2012). http://www.technologyreview.com/news/506656/the-cleverest-business-model-in-online-education/. Accessed 7 Dec 2015
23. Stevenson, S.: Duolingo: The future of language learning that puts a personal tutor in everyone's pocket (2014). http://www.independent.co.uk/life-style/gadgets-and-tech/features/duolingo-the-future-of-language-learning-that-puts-a-tutor-in-your-pocket-9110192.html. Accessed 7 Dec 2015
24. Straumsheim, C.: Arizona State, edX team to offer freshman year online through MOOCs. Inside Higher Ed. (2015). https://www.insidehighered.com/news/2015/04/23/arizona-state-edx-team-offer-freshman-year-online-through-moocs. Accessed 30 Nov 2015
25. Texas State University System. TSUS Joins 'Freshman Year for Free' Program (2015). http://www.tsus.edu/news/news-releases/release-091015. Accessed 30 Nov 2015
26. Udemy (n.d.). About Us (2015). https://about.udemy.com/. Accessed 12 Nov 2015
27. University of the People. (n.d.). Meet Our Students (2015). http://uopeople.edu/groups/meet_our_students. Accessed 20 Dec 2015
28. Yuan, L.: MOOCs and Open Education Timeline (updated!) (2015). http://blogs.cetis.org.uk/cetisli/2015/05/11/moocs-and-open-education-timeline-updated/. Accessed 12 Nov 2015
29. Yuan, L., Powell, S.: MOOCs and open education: implications for higher education. JISC CETIS (2013). http://publications.cetis.org.uk/2013/667
30. Yuan, L., Powell, S., Olivier, B.: Beyond MOOCs: sustainable online learning in institutions. CETIS (2014). http://publications.cetis.org.uk/2014/898. Accessed 12 Nov 2015

Mobile Web Strategy for Cultural Heritage Tourism: A Study on Italian Opera Houses

Luisa Mich[1(✉)] and Roberto Peretta[2]

[1] Department of Industrial Engineering, University of Trento, Trento, Italy
luisa.mich@unitn.it
[2] Department of Foreign Languages, Literatures and Cultures,
University of Bergamo, Bergamo, Italy
roberto.peretta@unibg.it

Abstract. Italian Opera is renowned the world over. It has recently been proposed for nomination to the Representative List of the Intangible Cultural Heritage of Humanity and still, though confronted with sustainability issues, cooperates in typifying Italy as a cultural tourism destination. This paper focuses on Italian Opera Houses, comparing their mobile web strategies, in terms of the mobile friendliness of their websites and their m-commerce models, in the frame of a global and generational competition. Besides, availability of English content for an international audience is specifically considered. Results confirm some general trends in web communication and marketing – namely a predominance of responsiveness within technical solutions, and outsourcing among e-commerce policies – and highlight weak points. The study was based on a systematic process and free web tools, that can be used for other sorts of cultural heritage institutions, like theatres, museums, art collections, or historic sites.

Keywords: Intangible heritage · Cultural tourism · Opera · Italy · Mobile web strategy · Mobile-friendliness · m-commerce

1 Introduction

The importance of mobile web technology in cultural heritage tourism has been recognized since its very inception [1–5]. Mobile web technology opens unexplored scenarios by changing customers' behaviours as well as operators' business models and services [6–8].

Many Italian cities and places are known as cultural destinations and are visited for their cultural heritage and in particular for their "must see sites". Several studies have investigated the strategies for promoting tangible cultural resources [9, 10]. Less investigated is the role of attractions related to intangible cultural resources [11]. This paper focuses on the performing arts and in particular on Opera, also considering that four kinds of Operas (those of Peking, Tibet, Yueju and Kun Qu) have been included in the UNESCO Intangible Cultural Heritage Lists [12].

Italian Opera is renowned the world over, as Opera itself was born in Italy thanks to 16th- and 17th-century composers Peri, Caccini and Monteverdi. It contributes to

© Springer International Publishing AG 2017
F.F.-H. Nah and C.-H. Tan (Eds.): HCIBGO 2017, Part I, LNCS 10293, pp. 194–208, 2017.
DOI: 10.1007/978-3-319-58481-2_16

characterise Italy as a cultural tourism destination [13], and has been proposed for nomination for the UNESCO Intangible Cultural Heritage lists.

As part of a larger study, whose goal is to explore how Italian Opera Houses use the Internet and the Web or, in more technical words, their web presence strategy [14], this paper reports analyses of Italian Opera Houses' mobile web strategies, in terms of how they support mobile access to their websites, including e-commerce options [15–17].

The analyses start from the identification of the business challenges [18] facing the Italian Opera Houses. These challenges are related to three main issues: high production costs, elderly audience, and local market [19, 20]. Even if Opera is a sector characterised by the Baumol effect – i.e. the technological evolution has not improved productivity, nor reduced costs [21, 22] – the Web and the mobile Web offer new ways to address promotion and marketing problems [1–4]. In particular, the role of the mobile Web is more and more important, due the increasing number of accesses from mobile devices [8]. A crucial event marking the role of mobile technologies took place in 2014, when mobile exceeded PC Internet usage for the first time [23].

In our study, the Italian Opera Houses fully recognized as such, the so called "Fondazioni Lirico-Sinfoniche" were considered, including milestones in the world history of theatres like La Scala in Milano, La Fenice in Venice, and the Arena di Verona [24].

The paper is structured as follows. The next section illustrates the background of the study: intangible cultural tourism, Opera and mobile. Section 3 introduces the Opera Houses selected for the analysis of the mobile Web strategy, and the tools used in the study. Section 4 illustrates the results. Section 5 discusses the results, and concludes the paper.

2 Background

2.1 Intangible Cultural Tourism

The role and impact of cultural tourism has been investigated from many points of views, focusing on different kind of cultural and heritage attractions [25]. Italy is known as a cultural tourism destination for its art and heritage resources. As recent indicators of this perception we can cite the number of UNESCO World Heritage sites (47 inscribed on the World Heritage, and many more submitted on the Tentative list [26], and the results of the last survey run by FutureBrand. Italy was one of the 22 out of 75 countries recognized as owning a "Country Brand". Even if Italy only ranks 12th in the overall ranking of the European Countries and 18th in the world ranking, it gained the first position in two of the parameters investigated by FutureBrand, namely Tourism and Heritage and Culture [27].

To effectively promote cultural tourism in a destination it is necessary to exploit all its distinctive elements [15, 17]. That implies a shift from conventional models of cultural tourism to new models of tourism based also on intangible culture and creativity [16, 28–30]. In this paper we are focusing on Italian Opera. Italy was the birthplace of Opera in the 17th century [31]. Italian composers are renowned the world over and Italian is used for many musical terms. Italian Operas are among the most performed (see e.g. the statistics produced by Operabase [32]).

There is also a UNESCO nomination proposal for the inscription of Italian Opera on the Representative List of the Intangible Cultural Heritage of Humanity [33]. The potential tourism appeal for Italian Opera Houses has been thoroughly investigated by Fisichella [34]. The study describes the problems faced by Italian Opera Houses and their tourist attractiveness. Common problems are related to economic sustainability (that is reduction of public funding and difficulty to get private financing), the need of a generational change attracting young spectators and, in many cases, a local branding and promotion of the Opera seasons (see also [35, 36]). Italian Opera Houses have been transformed in private foundations, maintaining part of their public nature. Their funding are almost all public, and in the last years they have reduced to the 0.1% of the GDP [37]. Besides, private funding – private donations and business sponsorship – is not adequately supported by the Italian law.

Opera is "an art form in which singers and musicians perform a dramatic work combining text (libretto) and musical score, usually in a theatrical setting" [38]. As a result, it involves a large numbers of people, an average of two hundred for a single performance and high costs. From a tourist point of view, Opera is (mostly) an elitist cultural product. It represents a niche market, and art tourists spend more but are older than spectators of other performing arts, as Opera goers are over 60 years old on average. So that enlarging and renewing the audience are major concerns for the Opera Houses [39].

2.2   Opera and Mobile

Mobile accesses concern a variety of devices, from featured and smart phones to tablet and laptops. Recent surveys report that mobile has exceeded PC Internet usage worldwide and will account for 75% in 2017 [40]. Another reason why companies and organizations, including Opera Houses, have to adopt a mobile web strategy is related to the role of the so-called Generation Z teenagers, the actual and future customers, also named "smartphone generation", referring to their extensive use of mobile technologies [41–44]. It is comprised of young people aged 13–20 years (the age range varies in different countries and studies), a cohort that will soon outnumber the Millennials and that is crucial to support any initiative an Opera House plans to increase visitors of their websites and reduce the average age of Opera goers. Among the most recent we can cite those of La Scala [45], that had great success [46], and of the Teatro Massimo in Palermo [47].

From a technical point of view, eTourism scholars have analysed the gradual transition from the initial server-side approach to the responsive one [48, 49]. The responsive approach, which is client side, and aimed at allowing desktop webpages to be viewed in response to the size of the device, is currently predominant [50–52].

3   Methodology

The goal of the study has been to analyse the mobile web strategies of Italian official Opera Houses in the light of their business challenges [18], namely, high production costs, elderly audience, and local market, challenges that can be tackled reaching an economic sustainability, supporting on the Web a wider audience and the promotion of Opera as a tourism attraction. The mobile web strategy was analysed in terms of:

- the mobile-friendliness of the official B2C websites of the Italian Opera houses;
- their m-commerce models.

The availability of English editions of the websites, intended to promote the Opera Houses' seasons and performances outside the domestic market, was also verified.

3.1   Italian Opera Houses

As summarized by the MIBACT ministry (Ministero dei Beni e delle Attività Culturali e del Turismo, Ministry of Cultural Heritage and Activities and Tourism [24], the historical Enti lirici (literally, "Opera Institutions") have been clearly recognized as such and turned into private foundations, or "Fondazioni Lirico-Sinfoniche." The process started in 1996, was completed in 2010, and involved fourteen Opera Houses, including the Teatro alla Scala in Milano which was recently granted a legal status on its own, with no significant changes as far as this study has been concerned.

The list of the "Fondazioni Lirico-Sinfoniche" includes the Accademia di Santa Cecilia in Rome, which was not considered in this study due to its different mission: Santa Cecilia is mainly focused on concerts. Similarly skipped were the twenty-eight minor "Teatri di tradizione" ("traditional theatres"), which aim to promote, facilitate and coordinate musical activities – Opera among them – on a local scale. We therefore considered the thirteen Opera Houses in Table 1.

Table 1. Italian Opera Houses, their towns, and B2C websites, August 2016.

Fondazione Petruzzelli e Teatri di Bari	Bari	www.fondazionepetruzzelli.it
Teatro Comunale di Bologna	Bologna	www.tcbo.it
Teatro Lirico di Cagliari	Cagliari	www.teatroliricodicagliari.it
Maggio Musicale Fiorentino	Firenze	www.operadifirenze.it
Teatro Carlo Felice di Genova	Genova	www.carlofelicegenova.it
Teatro alla Scala di Milano	Milano	www.teatroallascala.org
Teatro San Carlo di Napoli	Napoli	www.teatrosancarlo.it
Teatro Massimo di Palermo	Palermo	www.teatromassimo.it
Teatro dell'Opera di Roma	Roma	www.operaroma.it
Teatro Regio di Torino	Torino	www.teatroregio.torino.it
Teatro Lirico Giuseppe Verdi di Trieste	Trieste	www.teatroverdi-trieste.com
Teatro La Fenice di Venezia	Venezia	www.teatrolafenice.it
Arena di Verona	Verona	www.arena.it

3.2   Testing Mobile-Friendliness

The concept of mobile-friendliness has been formally used by the World Wide Web Consortium (W3C) – whose mission is "to lead the Web to its full potential" – since 2005 [53]. The deliverables of the Mobile Web Best Practices Working Group (BPWG) of the W3C include the W3C Recommendation on "Mobile Web Application Best Practices" [54] released on December 14, 2010. They have come with the W3C mobileOK Checker, subtitled "Is your Web site mobile-friendly?" The debate on "Standards for Web Applications on Mobile" is still ongoing [55], but the Recommendation has not been updated after August 2015, and the W3C mobileOK Checker has been disabled [56].

To investigate the mobile-friendliness of the official B2C websites of Italian Opera Houses, or "Fondazioni Lirico-Sinfoniche", a more recent tool was used: the Google Mobile-Friendly Test (MFT) [57]. The MFT belongs to a group of Google webpages related to mobile-friendliness [58], which developers worldwide have been induced to consider as a de-facto standard since early 2015. Starting from April 21, 2015, Google has "expand[ed] its use of mobile-friendliness as a ranking signal, [...] affect[ing] mobile searches in all languages worldwide and hav[ing] a significant impact in Google Search results" [59]. The move had been announced two months before.

The MFT is basically a Boolean test, i.e. it states whether the relevant webpage "appears to be" – or not to be – "mobile-friendly". In case it does not, the MFT lists the problems it has identified (though limited to a checklist of potential "usability issues" acknowledged as such, see Table 2), and recommends visiting the "Make this page mobile-friendly" webpage, where Google advice is offered to that purpose.

One more factor, download time, has been considered, as it influences mobile experience [60, 61]. Consequently, this study has used another tool made available to web developers by Google: the Google PageSpeed Insights [62]. This tool provides percent evaluations of download speeds from mobile devices, presented as results of compliance assessments based on a checklist of 10 speed-related recommendations, as for example, optimise images, minify HTML and reduce server response time. Similar percentages are supplied for desktop navigation. The relevance of download time to mobile friendliness has been confirmed by a recent choice of Google: from June 2016 PageSpeed Insights has moved the User Experience test for mobile pages into the Mobile Friendly Test [62].

In order to gather more data, and compare them with those provided by Google, download times from the websites of the Opera Houses were also recorded through Pingdom [63], a free web tool which tracks the uptime, downtime, and performance of websites. Based in Sweden, Pingdom monitors websites from multiple locations globally so that it can distinguish actual downtime from routing and access problems [64]. For each of the Opera Houses' websites, data about download times were obtained through Pingdom from servers in Stockholm (Sweden), New York, NY (USA) and Melbourne (Australia).

Similar tools are currently available, like WebPageTest or VarVy. They add to the range of no-cost opportunities which website managers can use to gather dedicated and relevant data in terms of mobile-friendliness and page speed (Table 3). Website

Table 2. Mobile-friendliness usability issues acknowledged as such by Google and their meaning

Flash usage	Most mobile browsers do not render Flash-based content. Therefore, mobile visitors will not be able to use a page that relies on Flash in order to display content, animations, or navigation
Viewport not configured	This tag tells browsers how to adjust the page's dimension and scaling to suit the device
Fixed-width viewport	This report shows those pages with a viewport set to a fixed width
Content not sized to viewport	This report indicates pages where horizontal scrolling is necessary to see words and images on the page. This happens when pages use absolute values in CSS declarations, or use images designed to look best at a specific browser width (such as 980px)
Small font size	This report identifies pages where the font size for the page is too small to be legible and would require mobile visitors to "pinch to zoom" in order to read
Touch elements too close	This report shows the URLs for sites where touch elements, such as buttons and navigational links, are so close to each other that a mobile user cannot easily tap a desired element with their finger without also tapping a neighboring element
Interstitial usage	Many websites show interstitials or overlays that partially or completely cover the contents of the page the user is visiting. These interstitials, commonly seen on mobile devices promoting a website's native app, mailing list sign-up forms, or advertisements, can make for a bad user experience. In extreme cases, the interstitial is designed to make it very difficult for the user to dismiss it and view the real content of the page. Since screen real-estate on mobile devices is limited, any interstitial negatively impacts the user's experience

Table 3. Tools considered in this study, those used [*], and their URLs

W3C mobileOK Checker		validator.w3.org/mobile
Google Mobile-Friendly Test	[*]	www.google.com/webmasters/tools/mobile-friendly
Google PageSpeed Insights	[*]	developers.google.com/speed/pagespeed/insights
Pingdom	[*]	tools.pingdom.com
WebPageTest		www.webpagetest.org
VarVy		varvy.com

managers might also consider usability issues that were recently raised by mobile-first approaches [8, 65, 66].

3.3   E-commerce Models

As for e-commerce practices implemented by the identified Opera Houses, they have been assessed by visiting the B2C official websites, and taking into consideration whether

- e-commerce functions were available;
- e-commerce functions, if any, were purposefully developed, or outsourced;
- navigation along the e-commerce process, if any, kept the Opera's look-and-feel;
- e-commerce functions, if any, allowed to choose where to seat in the theatre room.

Lastly, the availability of English editions of the B2C official websites was checked, as it is important for promoting the Opera Houses' seasons and performances outside the domestic market and the e-commerce.

4 Results

The Google Mobile-Friendly Test established that three out of thirteen Italian Opera Houses websites were not mobile-friendly when checked in August 2016 (Table 4).

Though none of them used Flash or interstitials, the data collected showed that non-compliance – where this was the case – was total; in other words, the three non-compliant Opera Houses looked as they had not started the process to become mobile-friendly at all.

According to Google (Table 5), only two of the mobile-friendly websites – those by La Scala and Arena – were found to be 100% compliant in August 2016. The latter was positively ranked by Google also in terms of mobile download speed (74%), while La Scala performed considerably worse under this respect (49%). More analytical data collected through Pingdom substantially confirmed the overall results from Google. Download times tested from different continents, however – significantly worsening with physical distance – suggested that no specific policies were adopted by none of the identified Italian Opera Houses as far as Content Delivery Networks (CDN) were concerned. Among the non-compliant and less proficient Italian Opera Houses websites, the Teatro Regio's (Turin) was at least relatively fast, while the Carlo Felice's (Genoa) apparently added time-consuming download to non-compliance.

All the mobile-friendly websites by the identified Opera Houses appeared to have adopted a responsive approach.

As for e-commerce, ten out of the thirteen Opera Houses identified had implemented e-commerce functions by August 2016 (Table 6). The shopping carts' webpages invariably sported brands of their outsourced developers or shared platforms, indicating that none of the e-commerce functions had been built in-house. Differences were instead found in graphic environments, depending on whether the Opera Houses' online customers were directed to:

1. the home page of a ticket-selling platform, with no further indications;
2. a specific page of a ticket-selling platform, with the platform's look-and-feel;
3. a specific page of a ticket-selling platform, with the Opera House's look-and-feel.

The last case – i.e. where the customer is not abruptly carried somewhere else – was clearly the best, though only the websites of Maggio Musicale (Florence), La Fenice (Venice) and La Scala (Milano) kept the Opera House's look-and-feel along the purchase process. La Scala, actually, took customers to a different browser's window,

Table 4. Italian Opera Houses, mobile-friendliness usability issues identified by Google, and Google-evaluated mobile user experience percentages, August 2016 (~ partially mobile-friendly)

Opera House	Flash usage	Viewport issues	Content not sized	Fonts too small	Touch elements too close	Interstitial	User Experience, as quantifed by Google	Mobile-friendliness
Fondazione Petruzzelli e Teatri di Bari							98%	~
Teatro Comunale di Bologna	x			x	x		65%	
Teatro Lirico di Cagliari							99%	~
Maggio Musicale Fiorentino							97%	~
Teatro Carlo Felice di Genova	x	x		x	x		58%	
Teatro alla Scala di Milano							100%	x
Teatro San Carlo di Napoli							91%	~
Teatro Massimo di Palermo							96%	~
Teatro dell'Opera di Roma							92%	~
Teatro Regio di Torino	x	x		x	x		68%	
Teatro Lirico Giuseppe Verdi di Trieste							90%	~
Teatro La Fenice di Venezia							99%	~
Arena di Verona							100%	x

Table 5. Italian Opera Houses, download performances according to Google (Mobile and Desktop, percentages resulting from compliance assessments) and download times according to Pingdom (seconds), August 2016

Opera House	Mobile	Desktop	Stockholm	New York	Melbourne
Fondazione Petruzzelli e Teatri di Bari	14%	18%	3.36	4.27	12.14
Teatro Comunale di Bologna	56%	68%	1.64	2.55	6.18
Teatro Lirico di Cagliari	35%	14%	2.45	4.14	9.29
Maggio Musicale Fiorentino	56%	69%	1.87	3.81	10.44
Teatro Carlo Felice di Genova	31%	35%	6.53	8.55	17.88
Teatro alla Scala di Milano	49%	63%	3.23	5.32	8.97
Teatro San Carlo di Napoli	45%	32%	1.22	2.12	6.18
Teatro Massimo di Palermo	68%	87%	1.39	2.38	6.16
Teatro dell'Opera di Roma	72%	87%	1.41	3.22	4.40
Teatro Regio di Torino	67%	78%	1.11	2.73	6.84
Teatro Lirico Giuseppe Verdi di Trieste	34%	10%	1.88	3.39	7.81
Teatro La Fenice di Venezia	34%	40%	2.16	7.97	12.87
Arena di Verona	74%	90%	0.64	1.56	4.93

Table 6. Basic e-commerce strategies by Italian Opera Houses, August 2016 ($\sim$ look-and-feel of La Scala website only partially kept)

Opera House	e-commerce	Same look-and-feel	Interactive plan
Fondazione Petruzzelli e Teatri di Bari			
Teatro Comunale di Bologna	x		x
Teatro Lirico di Cagliari			
Maggio Musicale Fiorentino	x	x	x
Teatro Carlo Felice di Genova			
Teatro alla Scala di Milano	x	$\sim$	x
Teatro San Carlo di Napoli	x		x
Teatro Massimo di Palermo	x		x
Teatro dell'Opera di Roma	x		x
Teatro Regio di Torino	x		
Teatro Lirico Giuseppe Verdi di Trieste	x		
Teatro La Fenice di Venezia	x	x	x
Arena di Verona	x		x

where only details of La Scala graphic brand (the background color and the logo) were kept. The Opera Houses from Bari, Cagliari and Genoa did not provide e-commerce functions at all.

As for m-commerce, the difference between mouse-driven desktop design and gesture-driven touch-screen design is still a general theme, as is the interface size in e-commerce. Choosing a seat in an Opera theatre may be crucial for the purchase process, while interacting with the plan of an theatre through a smartphone is ergonomically unfriendly.

None of the visited e-commerce pages seemed to comply with mobile-friendliness needs, with the exceptions of instances of 1 (the home page of a ticket-selling platform with no further indications), where the relevant ticket-selling platform's website was itself mobile-friendly. Specifically, interactive plans of the theatre – which Opera websites frequently make available, allowing customers to choose where to sit – showed usability issues when navigated through mobile devices: content was not sized to viewport.

With regard to the languages used, eight out of the thirteen Opera Houses websites were found to provide English editions by August 2016 (Table 7) besides Italian. The Italian content was not always entirely translated, or translated in due time.

Table 7. English editions of Italian Opera Houses websites, August 2016

Opera House	English edition	Mobile-friendly English edition
Fondazione Petruzzelli e Teatri di Bari		
Teatro Comunale di Bologna		
Teatro Lirico di Cagliari	x	x
Maggio Musicale Fiorentino	x	x
Teatro Carlo Felice di Genova		
Teatro alla Scala di Milano	x	x
Teatro San Carlo di Napoli		
Teatro Massimo di Palermo	x	x
Teatro dell'Opera di Roma	x	x
Teatro Regio di Torino	x	
Teatro Lirico Giuseppe Verdi di Trieste	x	x
Teatro La Fenice di Venezia	x	x
Arena di Verona		

With the exception of the Teatro Regio (Turin), the Italian Opera Houses which run English editions of their websites also grant those pages' mobile-friendliness. Peculiarly, the most mobile-friendly of all the identified websites – the Arena di Verona's – only provides an Italian edition.

5 Discussion, Conclusions and Future Research

In our study, the thirteen Italian Opera Houses fully recognized as such were considered, including milestones in the world history of theatres like La Scala in Milano, La Fenice in Venice, and the Arena di Verona [24].

The goal of the study was to investigate the mobile web strategies of Italian Opera Houses focusing on the mobile-friendliness of the official B2C websites and on their m-commerce models.

The analysis of the mobile web strategies of the Opera Houses was based on a systematic process and free web tools.

First, the websites of the Opera Houses were tested against Google MFT [57], PageSpeed Insights [62] and Pingdom [63], in order to state their mobile-friendliness. These tools were chosen because of their consistency, reliability, ease of use and constant updating.

Second, the availability of e-commerce options was checked, as were their possible outsourcing – considering whether brand awareness and perception were preserved – and usability through mobile devices [65].

Finally, due to the need of targeting a wider international audience, and of a wider marketing effort to promote Opera as a tourist attraction, the availability of English-language versions was considered.

The results of our study reflect an unsatisfactory situation. None of the thirteen Opera Houses fully embraced a mobile web strategy. Three out of the thirteen Italian Opera Houses websites were not mobile-friendly at all, while only two of the mobile-friendly websites – those by La Scala and Arena di Verona – were found to be 100% compliant. Even cases where Google tests assess a 100%-good mobile experience fall under the usability problems raised by mobile-first approaches [8, 65, 66] (e.g., the horizontal navigation adopted by La Scala website in its home page).

From a technical point of view, the results highlight the predominance of responsiveness, adopted by all the ten mobile-friendly websites.

With regard to e-commerce policies, ten out of the thirteen Opera Houses allow to buy tickets online, and an outsourcing model is adopted – that is the transaction is supported by an external platform – but only three of the e-commerce carts found keep their Opera website's look-and-feel.

Concerning the languages used, eight out of the thirteen Opera Houses provide an English version. The Italian content was not always entirely translated, or translated in due time.

Italian Opera houses could use the results of our study to improve their mobile web strategies. In particular, results suggest that Opera Houses should revise their e- (and in turn) their m-commerce functions – supplying specific webpages from a ticket-selling platform, where the Opera House's look-and-feel is kept and the zooming feature of the theatre's plan is implemented to help the purchase process – and provide or improve their English content.

The process to analyse mobile web strategies that our study adopted – checking mobile friendliness, e-commerce and the availability of English-language versions – can be used for other sorts of cultural heritage institutions, like theatres, museums, art collections, or historic sites.

Future research is related to three areas: (a) analyze dedicated apps produced by Italian Opera Houses, in relationship with their web presence strategies; (b) extend the study to the "Teatri di tradizione"; (c) identify best practices to promote Opera as a tourist attraction through mobile devices.

A preliminary scouting of apps highlighted that only two of the Opera Houses considered in this study had produced a dedicated app by May 2016, while similar projects for kids were started but came to a halt. On the other hand, almost all the Opera Houses identified had lively social profiles on Facebook, Twitter and YouTube [67].

The second area of future research, concerning the "Teatri di tradizione", aims to cover all the Italian theatres where Opera is performed, even if not on a regular basis, taking into account their different missions and funding mechanisms.

Finally, the third area moves from the critical issues identified when assessing the websites of the Opera Houses: only a couple of them provide information on how to plan a trip that includes attending one or more performances, and even basic information on how to get to the theatre, or on the building as a place to visit, is missing. This area should also survey the websites and the apps of the tourist destinations where the theatre is located, to check if and how it is listed. [68]

References

1. Rasinger, J., Fuchs, M., Höpken, W., Tuta, M.: A customer based approach to discover accepted mobile information services in tourism. In: Research@EyeforTravel, London, 5–6 June, pp 31–46 (2006)
2. Buhalis, D., Law, R.: Progress in information technology and tourism management: 20 years on and 10 years after the internet - the state of eTourism research. Tour. Manage. 29(4) 609–623 (2008). doi:10.1016/j.tourman.2008.01.005
3. Lee, J.K., Mills, J.E.: Exploring tourist satisfaction with mobile experience technology. Int. Manage. Rev. 6(1) 92–102 (2010). doi:10.1007/978-3-211-69566-1_14
4. Schneider, S., Ricci, F., Venturini, A., Nota, E.: Usability guidelines for WAP-based travel planning. In: Gretzel, U., Law, R., Fuchs, M., (eds.) Information and Communication Technologies in Tourism 2010, pp. 125–136. Springer, Vienna (2010). doi:10.1007/978-3-211-99407-8_11
5. Wang, D., Park, S., Fesenmaier, D.R.: The role of smartphones in mediating the touristic experience. J. Travel Res. 51(4), 371–387 (2012). doi:10.1177/0047287511426341
6. Peltier, D.: 6 charts that show mobile booking's gain on desktop around the world. Skift (2015). http://skift.com/2015/09/19/6-charts-that-show-mobile-bookings-gains-on-desktop-around-the-world
7. Abramovich, G.: July fourth online travel spend to top cyber Monday (2016). http://www.cmo.com/adobe-digital-insights/articles/2016/4/21/adi-us-travel-report-2016.html#gs.lygRu2M
8. Chaffey, D.: Mobile marketing statistics compilation (2016). http://www.smartinsights.com/mobile-marketing/mobile-marketing-analytics/mobile-marketing-statistics
9. Prentice, R.: Tourism and Heritage Attractions. Routledge, London (1993)
10. Borowiecki, K.J., Castiglione, C.: Cultural participation and tourism flows: an empirical investigation of Italian provinces. Tour. Econ. 20(2), 241–262 (2014). doi:10.5367/te.2013.0278
11. Hughes, H.: Arts, Entertainment and Tourism. Butterworth Heinemann, Oxford (2000). doi:10.1002/jtr.394
12. UNESCO lists of intangible cultural heritage and register of best safeguarding practices. http://www.unesco.org/culture/ich/en/lists

13. Timothy, D.J., Boyd, S.W.: Heritage Tourism. Pearson Education, London (2003)
14. Mich, L., Kiyavitskaya, N.: Mapping the web presences of tourism destinations: an analysis of the European countries. In: Law, R., Fuchs, M., Ricci, F., (eds.) Information and Communication Technologies in Tourism 2011, pp. 379–390. Springer, Vienna (2011). doi:10.1007/978-3-7091-0503-0_31
15. Colbert, F., et al.: Marketing Culture and the Arts, 4th Edn. Hec, Montréal (2012)
16. Vasile, V., Surugiu, M.-R., Login, I.-O., Cristea, A.: Changes in cultural heritage consumption model: challenges and limits. Procedia Soc. Behav. Sci. **188**, 42–52 (2015). Elsevier Ltd. doi:10.1016/j.sbspro.2015.03.337
17. WTO - World Tourism Organization. Handbook on Tourism Destination Branding (2009). doi:10.18111/9789284413119
18. Laudon, K.C., Laudon, J.P.: Management Information Systems: Organizational and Technology in the Networked Enterprise. Prentice Hall, New Jersey (1999)
19. Feroni, G.C.: Organization, management and funding of opera houses, Florence. In: International Week for Cultural and Environmental Heritage - Florens 2012. Quaderno Cesifin 61 (2012). (in Italian)
20. Leon, A.F., Ruggeri, M.: Il costo del melodramma. Il Mulino, Bologna (2004). (in Italian)
21. Baumol, J.W., Bowen, G.W.: Performing Arts: The Economic Dilemma: A Study of Problems Common to Theater, Opera, Music and Dance. MIT press, Cambridge (1968). doi:10.1017/S0770451800055287
22. Heilbrun, J.: Baumol's cost disease. In: Towse, R., (ed.) A Handbook of Cultural Economics. Edward Elgar Publishing, Cheltenham (2013). doi:10.4337/9780857930576. 00016
23. Mobile internet usage skyrockets in past 4 years to overtake desktop as most used digital platform, 13 April 2015. https://www.comscore.com/Insights/Blog/Mobile-Internet-Usage-Skyrockets-in-Past-4-Years-to-Overtake-Desktop-as-Most-Used-Digital-Platform
24. Ministero dei beni e delle attività culturali e del turismo. Fondazioni Lirico-Sinfoniche. http://www.spettacolodalvivo.beniculturali.it/index.php/fondazioni-liriche. (in Italian)
25. OECD. The Impact of Culture on Tourism. OECD Publishing, Paris (2009). doi:10.1787/9789264040731-en
26. UNESCO World Heritage, States Parties, Italy. http://whc.unesco.org/en/statesparties/it
27. FutureBrand. Country Brand Index 2014–15 (2014). http://www.futurebrand.com/uploads/CBI-14_15-LR.pdf
28. OECD. Tourism and the Creative Economy. OECD Publishing, Paris (2014). doi:10.1787/9789264207875-en
29. Richards, G.: Cultural tourism 3.0: the future of urban tourism in Europe? In: Garibaldi, R., (ed.) Il turismo Culturale Europeo. Città ri-visitate. FrancoAngeli, Milano (2014)
30. Salazar, N.B., Zhu, Y.: Heritage and tourism. In: Meskell, L. (ed.) Global Heritage: A Reader. Blackwells, Oxford (2015)
31. Kimbell, D.R.B.: Italian Opera. Cambridge University Press, Cambridge (1991)
32. Operabase. http://www.operabase.com/
33. Candidatura UNESCO Opera Lirica Italiana (2016). https://youtu.be/iNoTywhuI8U (in Italian)
34. Fisichella, C., Milito, A.M.: Indicators of Tourist Market Appeal and Sustainability: An Analysis of Italian Opera Houses, pp. 1–4. Bulletin of the International Statistical Institute (2007)
35. SL&A-Turismo e territorio. Osservatorio nazionale "Cultura e turismo: impresa e lavoro" (2015). http://www.ebnt.it/documenti/osservatori/Dati_Osservatorio_H_II_Edizione_2015.pdf. (in Italian)

36. Morelli, G., Fisichella, C.: Il turismo culturale nell'esperienza delle Fondazioni Liriche italiane (Cultural tourism in the italian opera houses' experience). Economia dei Servizi **1**, 85–106 (2014). (in Italian)
37. Ministero dei beni e delle attività culturali e del turismo. Opera lirica: Un patrimonio culturale italiano da valorizzare. http://www.beniculturali.it/mibac/export/MiBAC/sito-MiBAC/Contenuti/Ministero/UfficioStampa/News/visualizza_asset.html_84569120.html. (in Italian)
38. Wikipedia. Opera. https://en.wikipedia.org/wiki/Opera
39. Agid, P., Tarondeau, J.C.: The Management of Opera: An International Comparative Study. Palgrave Macmillan, London (2010). doi:10.1057/9780230299276
40. StatCounter. Mobile and tablet internet usage exceeds desktop for first time worldwide (2016). http://gs.statcounter.com/press/mobile-and-tablet-internet-usage-exceeds-desktop-for-first-time-worldwide. Accessed 1 Nov 2016
41. Nielsen, J.: Mobile Millennials: Over 85% of Generation Y Owns Smartphones. Newswire (2014). http://www.nielsen.com/us/en/insights/news/2014/mobile-millennials-over-85-percent-of-generation-y-owns-smartphones.html
42. Euromonitor. The New Online Travel Consumer (2014). http://www.etoa.org/docs/default-source/presentations/2014-the-new-online-travel-consumer.pdf
43. Amadeus. Future Traveller Tribes 2030. Amadeus, Madrid (2015). http://www.amadeus.com/documents/future-traveller-tribes-2030/travel-report-future-traveller-tribes-2030.pdf
44. WTM - Travel Market. World Travel Market Global Trends Report (2015). http://news.wtmlondon.com/wp-content/uploads/2015/11/Global-Trends-Report-2015.pdf
45. Teatro alla Scala. Box Office. Tickets and prices (Official Ticket Office). Concessions. Young People and Promotions. http://www.teatroallascala.org/en/box-office/tickets-prices/concessions/young-people-and-promotion/young-people-and-promotions.html
46. Corriere della Sera. Giovani in coda di notte per la Scala (2016). http://milano.corriere.it/foto-gallery/cronaca/16_novembre_05/giovani-coda-notte-la-scala-bd9f7d74-a33e-11e6-b242-6c6c02e892ab.shtml. (in Italian)
47. Giovani per il Teatro Massimo. http://www.teatromassimo.it/eng/education-and-young-audiences/giovani-per-il-teatro-massimo.html
48. Gibbs, C., Gretzel, U.: Drivers of responsive website design innovation by destination marketing organizations. In: Tussyadiah, I., Inversini, A. (eds.) Information and Communication Technologies in Tourism 2015, pp. 581–592. Springer, Cham (2015). doi:10.1007/978-3-319-14343-9_42
49. Groth, A., Haslwanter, D.: Perceived usability, attractiveness and intuitiveness of responsive mobile tourism websites: a user experience study. In: Tussyadiah, I., Inversini, A. (eds.) Information and Communication Technologies in Tourism 2015, pp. 593–606. Springer, Cham (2015). doi:10.1007/978-3-319-14343-9_43
50. Marcotte, E.: Responsive Web Design (2010). alistapart.com/article/responsive-web-design
51. Budiu, R.: The State of Mobile User Experience. Nielsen Norman Group (2015). www.nngroup.com/articles/mobile-usability-update
52. Mich, L., Peretta, R.: Italian flagship museums: web presence and mobile-friendliness (2016). http://ertr.tamu.edu/files/2016/01/ENTER2016_submission_119.pdf
53. W3C. Scope of mobile web best practices. https://www.w3.org/TR/mobile-bp-scope/
54. W3C. Mobile web application best practices. https://www.w3.org/TR/mwabp/
55. W3C. Standards for web applications on mobile: current state and roadmap. https://www.w3.org/Mobile/mobile-web-app-state/
56. W3C. The W3C mobile checker. https://www.w3.org/2016/11/mobile-checker-disabled/
57. Google. Mobile-friendly test. www.google.com/webmasters/tools/mobile-friendly
58. Google. Mobile-friendly websites. https://developers.google.com/webmasters/mobile-sites/

59. Google. Make sure your site's ready for mobile-friendly Google search results. https://support.google.com/adsense/answer/6196932
60. Kaikkonen, A., Kekäläinen, A., Cankar, M., Kallio, T., Kankainen, A.: Usability testing of mobile applications: a comparison between laboratory and field testing. J. Usability Stud. **1** (1), 4–16 (2005)
61. Wroblewski, L.: Mobile First. A Book Apart, New York, NY (2011)
62. Google. PageSpeed Insights. https://developers.google.com/speed/pagespeed/insights/
63. Pingdom website speed test. https://tools.pingdom.com
64. Wikipedia. Pingdom. https://en.wikipedia.org/wiki/Pingdom
65. Nielsen, J.: Mobile Usability 2nd Research Study. Nielsen Norman Group (2011). www.nngroup.com/articles/mobile-usability-2nd-study
66. Budiu, R., Pernice, K.: Mobile First is not Mobile Only. Nielsen Norman Group (2016). www.nngroup.com/articles/mobile-first-not-mobile-only
67. Mich, L., Peretta, R., (eds): The Web Presence of Opera Houses, Working paper. University of Trento, Trento (2016a)
68. WTO - World Tourism Organization. Conceptual Framework. Destination Management & Quality Programme (2016). http://destination.unwto.org/content/conceptual-framework-0

Improving Healthcare with Wearables: Overcoming the Barriers to Adoption

Ksenia Sergueeva$^{(\boxtimes)}$ and Norman Shaw

Ryerson University, Toronto, Canada
{sergueeva.ksenia,norman.shaw}@ryerson.ca

Abstract. Wearable technology devices (WTDs) record exercise activity and capture vital health statistics. These details can be shared with healthcare providers to monitor patients, manage chronic illness and save lives. The adoption of these devices continues to grow, but so does their abandonment. Within the context of healthcare, protection motivation theory (PMT) explains that individuals seek to protect themselves from health threats that they perceive to be severe. We combine this theory with the unified theory of adoption in order to investigate the factors that motivate individuals to adopt WTD to manage their health. The results of the quantitative study show that consumers need to be convinced that the data collected from these devices can lead to improved health outcomes.

Keywords: Wearables · PMT · UTAUT · Personalization · PLS

1 Introduction

Wearable technology devices (WTDs), such as smartwatches, FitBits, Nike, Jawbone, and others, are becoming increasingly popular. WTDs are small electronic devices that consist of one or more sensors with computational capabilities that provide information and entertainment for the wearer. These sensors are embedded into the WTDs which are attached to the body, for example, to the wrist or to the head. WTDs capture health data such as the number of steps taken in a day, duration of physical activity, calories burned, stress level, body temperature, number of hours that the individual sleeps, location, and even ECG measurements. For output, WTDs can showcase information through the flashing of LED lights on a wrist device to a complex display of data on a mobile app.

It is expected that WTDs will play a transformative role in fitness, health, and other medical applications [1]. Individuals are more inclined to self-monitor their health with this technology. There is a growing population of WTD users who are interested in personal analytics as a concept of self-discovery, a movement called the Quantified – Self (QS) [2]. As WTDs motivate people to exercise and walk, they are considered to be a preventative tool for chronic disease [3]. WTDs are often used to improve sleep, to increase productivity and to lose weight [1]. To increase user engagement, WTD manufacturers utilize different techniques such as the gamification of physical activity with competitions and challenges, while publishing the feedback of their performance on social media. WTDs such as FitBit, allow individuals to compete against their friends

© Springer International Publishing AG 2017
F.F.-H. Nah and C.-H. Tan (Eds.): HCIBGO 2017, Part I, LNCS 10293, pp. 209–223, 2017.
DOI: 10.1007/978-3-319-58481-2_17

or strangers [4]. Social influence is used to alter beliefs, attitudes, motivations and intentions [5]. The prediction is that wearable computing market will reach more than $171.2 billion in 2021, with a compound annual growth rate (CAGR) of 50% [6].

WTDs collect health and fitness data. Up until recently, there was little value in sharing this information with the healthcare industry. Today, Google and Apple are linking the two with bridging applications. Apple recently launched ResearchKit, which is an open-software platform to create health apps and uses WTDs for medical research. They also launched CareKit, which is an open-software platform to create health apps that help people manage various medical conditions and share that information with their physicians [7]. Among the first four apps that were released by Apple were those that help manage diabetes, and track symptoms of depression [8]. This is Apple's step to accelerate integration of WTDs into healthcare. It is also predicted that other wearable manufactures will follow this approach, therefore making it easier for medical researchers and doctors to collect data and resolve issues regarding reliability and safety of WTDs. Another issue is that consumer surveys showed that more than 50% of WTD owners abandon their devices after only one year or less of using the technology [3]. Furthermore, according to research conducted by PwC (2014) [9] only half of those who own the technology wear them on a daily basis (n = 1000). Previous research has identified that most WTDs do not provide additional functionality other than the basic functions such as recording steps or heart rate [5]. Most consumers are unaware that WTDs can share their data with a health care provider, or that they can save their lives by sending data to their physician's office. While the adoption rate has increased, the abandonment rate is still high. Researchers also found that the technology might require too much effort in order to use it, which makes the experience unpleasant for the users [10].

Consumers fail to recognize the potential health benefits of WTDs beyond the counting of steps and the calories burned [11]. However, there are new improvements in WTDs such as the hands-free data collection of measurements of heart rate, blood flow and blood oxygen, which allow for a real-time view of personalized data by the healthcare provider [1]. These devices may also improve disease control and survival rates. For example, Apple watch was able to save a person who suffered a heart attack because the watch showed an abnormal heart rate. The patient was able to call an ambulance and the paramedics determined that he was having a heart attack. The doctors cleared the blockage prevented other occurrences and were able to save a life [12]. WTDs are an example of a protection technology whose efficiency is improved when they provide personalized feedback in order to protect users from unforeseen health conditions, such as heart attacks. As of today, they have not been widely adopted. This leads to our research question: *what motivates individuals to use wearable technology devices in order to protect themselves against unforeseen health related threats?*

Practitioners need to not only attract, but also to motivate users to continue using their WTDs. In order to provide customized feedback, WTDs collect health data by implicitly monitoring individuals' behaviours and vital signs. According to Park [13], personalization increases adoption and continued use of an IT innovation. Extant studies of WTDs have determined that feedback, information display, and specific design principles all play a role in keeping the user engaged with the technology [11]. This suggests that personalization could have an impact on behavioural intention to use WTDs. Studies of user adoption of WTDs have combined theories of acceptance and use of technology with Protection Motivation Theory (PMT) [14]. WTDs can be considered as protective technology, as they have been designed to protect users against health fears and concerns. None of the studies have been conducted in North America. We address this gap in the literature by proposing the theoretical foundation of Protection Motivation Theory (PMT) and extending it with the construct of personalization together with behavioural antecedents from the unified theory of acceptance and use of technology (UTAUT) [15].

The remainder of this paper is organized as follows. The next section is the review of the literature, which includes our development of the hypotheses and concludes with the research model. The third section of this paper describes the methodology. The results are then discussed, followed by conclusion that includes implications for the practitioners, limitations and suggestions for future studies.

2 Literature Review

WTDs can be considered a protective technology. Features such as the measurement of blood glucose level and heart rate can protect users from potential unforeseen health risks, such as heart attacks, and help to recognize disease symptoms. Because our investigation is in the context of healthcare, we develop a theoretical framework which includes health information technology (HIT) [16].

We chose Protection Motivation Theory (PMT) as our theoretical foundation as WTDs have the potential to protect individuals against a threat (such as managing a disease) or a fear (such as a heart attack) by providing personalized feedback. Our model of PMT resembles that of the Fear Appeals Model (FAM) from the study by Johnston and Warkentin (2010) [17] where researchers applied the theory to the adoption of spyware. In this section, we provide a background on PMT and its constructs [17, 18]. We also describe personalization which is added to the model and we add further information on UTAUT [15], which was included in our theoretical framework.

2.1 Protection Motivation Theory (PMT)

PMT is one of the leading theories of health behaviour [19, 20]. Researchers have used PMT to predict behaviours that promote health as well as those which compromise health [21]. PMT was developed by Rogers [18] in 1975 to identify the key factors in fear appeals and their cognitive mediation [21]. In other words, Rogers [18] theorized that motivation to protect oneself from potential harm is influenced by fear appeals. These fear appeals are composed of three components: 1. The magnitude of noxiousness of a depicted event; 2. The probability of that event's occurrence; and 3. The efficacy of protective response [22]. Protection motivation arises through this cognitive process, which produces an appropriate behavioural intention [23]. Since its inception in 1975, the theory has undergone a number of revisions and extensions.

PMT involves the appraisals of two components: threat and coping [24]. Health behaviour is induced by the threat appraisals and by the coping appraisals [18]. Threat appraisals include two constructs: perceived vulnerability and perceived severity. Coping appraisals focus on the coping responses that are available to the individual to deal with the threat: response efficacy, self-efficacy and response cost. An individual's cognitive processes evaluate the threat appraisals depending on the expectancy and the severity of exposure, and the actions that they take will depend upon their beliefs in the efficacy of the coping response. The PMT model used by Johnston and Warkentin [17] is shown in Fig. 1. Our research model (Fig. 2) is an adaptation of Johnston and Warkentin's model. Arrows in the model indicate directional associations and influences between variables, with positive (+) and negative (−) associations.

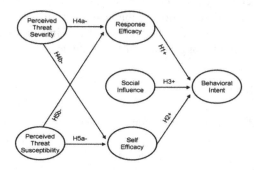

Fig. 1. Adapted PMT (Johnston and Warkentin 2010 [17])

2.1.1   Response Efficacy (RE)

Response efficacy refers to the beliefs that a recommended response will effectively protect a user from a threat [17, 18]. This is a measure of the individual's confidence in the effectiveness of the WTD in preventing a risk to health. In the context of our research, when individuals believe that using WTDs can enable them to reduce threats to their health because of the personalized feedback, they are more likely to adopt and use the technology. The effectiveness of the technology can be regarded as the degree to which the device can help them monitor their daily physical conditions, make personal healthcare plans, and reduce health related threats. For example, a user may decide to monitor their heart rate because of a previous heart attack, or a family history of heart attacks. To reduce the risks of having a heart attack (the threat), the user may monitor the data collection and later review the results with their health care provider (the response). PMT predicts that RE would have a positive relationship with behaviour intention and this positive relationship is widely supported in PMT [18]. Therefore, we hypothesize:

H1: Response Efficacy is positively associated with intention to use wearable device

2.1.2   Self-Efficacy (SE)

Self-efficacy is defined as the level of confidence of individual in their ability to perform the coping behavior. In the case of WTDs, they must be confident that they are able to monitor their health correctly. When individuals are confident of their competency to use the technology, they are more likely to use the technology. According to Bandura (1977) [25], self-efficacy is a strong predictor of behaviour intention.

However, previous PMT research found that self-efficacy does not significantly influence user intention to adopt technology, but it has been suggested that self-efficacy would have a greater importance in intention to use technology in health-related fields [14, 26]. For example, WTD users can use technology to self-monitor their physical conditions with personalized feedback, but the determinant factor is their belief that they are competent to deploy the functionality of the WTDs. This positive relationship between self-efficacy and intention behaviour to adopt technology has been well established in previous technology acceptance studies as verified by Venkatesh et al. (2003) [15] and other extant studies [14, 17, 26]. Hence, we hypothesize:

H2: Self-Efficacy is positively associated with intention to use wearable devices

2.1.3 Perceived Vulnerability (PV)

Perceived vulnerability refers to the assessment of the likelihood that individuals will encounter a threat to their health [18]. Perceived vulnerability is an important element that impacts one's reaction to a threat appeal [17]. According to the theory, when the probability of encountering a threat is high, an individual adopts new health information technology (HIT) in order to reduce or avoid health threats [19]. Previous PMT research found that individuals appear to make decisions that are predictable based on the assessment of their perceived health risks [17, 26]. Researchers identified that in instances where perceived vulnerability was high, users' become increasingly concerned with their knowledge and ability to respond to the threat [19]. For example, a person who has a history of heart attacks in the family, feels that they will increase the probability of a heart attack is high if they live an unhealthy life style (eg. smoking, lack of exercise). Hence, they consider themselves to be highly vulnerable to the threat. As the fear of a heart attack rises, they feel more vulnerable and their self-confidence to use the technology correctly decreases. Therefore, we hypothesize:

H3a: Perceived vulnerability will negatively influence perceptions of response efficacy.
H3b: Perceived vulnerability will negatively influence perceptions of self-efficacy

2.1.4 Perceived Severity (PS)

Perceived Severity refers to the degree of physical harm that may arise from unhealthy behaviour [18]. Several studies showed that users are more likely to adopt health technology when the threat to their health is severe [14, 26]. However, PMT also defines the threat severity perception as the ability to influence the strength of the response to the health threat. For example, in medical practice, if someone suffers a heart attack, they are aware of the probability of it being followed by another. When the patient goes home and understands the possible consequence, their fear of a severity of the threat increases. This causes an emotional response to the threat. In the context of our study, when the perception of the severity of suffering another heart attack is high, it decreases their confidence in the WTD and their own ability to use the WTD successfully to address the threat [17]. Accordingly, we hypothesize:

214 K. Sergueeva and N. Shaw

H4a: Perceived severity will negatively influence perception of response efficacy.
H4b: Perceived severity will negatively influence perception of self- efficacy

2.1.5 Response Cost (RC)

Response cost refers to the extent to which individuals have adequate resources to perform a behaviour. Within the context of our research, response cost is associated with external resources such as money, time and effort, that are required in order to use WTDs. If a significant amount of money must be spent or it takes a large effort to learn to use the technology (these are examples of high response costs), individuals might be reluctant to use the technology, indicating a negative relationship between response cost and behavioural intention [18]. Hence, we hypothesize:

H5: Response Cost is negatively associated with intention to use wearable devices

2.2 Unified Theory of Acceptance and Use of Technology (UTAUT)

Previous studies of technology acceptance in healthcare have built upon technology acceptance theories, such as the Unified Theory of Acceptance and Use of Technology (UTAUT) [26–29]. Studies in the past have investigated the professionals' technology acceptance rather than the patients' technology acceptance [14]. One of the interesting findings of these studies is that while they did find performance expectancy and facilitating conditions to have significant impact on IT use, effort expectancy and social influence were not significant [26, 30]. Therefore, further investigation is needed in the context of technology acceptance in healthcare.

In addition to using PMT to understand user behavioural intention of a health technology, we have also included constructs from UTAUT [15]. UTAUT is a widely used theory to explain technology acceptance [15, 26, 31]. In UTAUT, Venkatesh et al. (2003) [15] evaluated the most common adoption technology theories and proposed the Unified Theory of Acceptance and Use of Technology (UTAUT) by integrating elements from eight major user acceptance models. UTAUT has four key constructs that determine technology intention and behaviour usage. These are: performance expectancy, effort expectancy, social influence and facilitating conditions. From a number of empirical tests of UTAUT, the theory explained approximately 70% of the variance in behavioural intention and 50% in actual use of the technology [16].

We have extended our theoretical foundation of PMT with UTAUT because the model is easily extended, scales are readily available from extant literature and its core constructs have been validated across different disciplines, including HIT.

2.2.1 Performance Expectancy (PE)

Performance expectancy is defined as the degree to which an individual believes that using the system will help him or her attain gains in job performance" [15]. In the context of our research, where wearable technology is the technology of interest, its effectiveness is captured by the extent to which it can help users reduce the health-related threat, and hence Response Efficacy in PMT is s a proxy for PE [14, 26]. Therefore, we exclude the

Performance Expectancy construct from our model and substitute it with Response Efficacy from PMT.

2.2.2 Effort Expectancy (EE)

Venkatesh et al., (2003) [15] described effort expectancy as users' opinions of the level of ease related to the use of technology. Previous studies indicated a small significance of EE on intention to use [32]. WTD do not come with clear instructions on how to use the technology, and therefore their design should be easy to use. Hence, we hypothesize:

H6: Effort expectancy is positively associated with intention to use wearable devices.

2.2.3 Social Influence (SI)

Social influence is defined as "the degree to which an individual perceives that important others believe he or she should use the new system" p. 451 [15]. Previous studies on professionals' health technology acceptance behaviour found that social influence is not significant in intended behaviour of users [33]. However, other studies of technology adoption in healthcare using UTAUT demonstrated that social influence is a significant factor to adoption intention [14, 26]. In the context of WTDs, individuals tend to make their decision based on the opinion and suggestions of others, since this is still a fairly new technology. We therefore hypothesize:

H7: Social influence is positively associated with intention to use a wearable device

2.2.4 Facilitating Conditions (FC)

According to UTAUT, facilitating conditions are derived from two sources: external and internal [15]. External control refers to the extent to which individuals believe that necessary resources are in place to perform an action, while internal control refers to their assessment of their own abilities to perform the action [26, 34].

In the context of this study, response cost (a construct previously described in PMT) is associated with external control because it describes the resources (such as monetary and effort) that are require in order to learn to use WTDs. Self-efficacy (another construct from PMT previously described) is associated with internal control because it refers to an individual's ability to learn to use WTDs.

Following the framework of UTAUT [15], facilitating conditions can be interpreted with self-efficacy and response cost [26]. Hence, we drop FC from our model and replace it with response cost and self-efficacy. This elimination and replacement of constructs have been confirmed in several HIT adoption studies [14, 26].

2.3 Personalization

New personalization technologies and applications are becoming increasingly popular [35]. Personalization involves customizing the feedback context to each of the user's needs. Personalization exists in many fields and has been previously defined in the literature [36]. Sun et al. (2015) [26] has defined personalization as delivering "the right content to the right person in the right format at the right time". In the context of WTDs, personalization is the delivery of appropriate health services for specific health conditions and preferences via a WTD. Park [13] identified that personalization increases adoption and continued use of IT. WTD's personalized services can efficiently increase effectiveness of the interaction of WTD provider, and hence could lead to higher satisfaction among users, and have a positive relationship with intention to use. We therefore hypothesize:

   H8: Personalization positively affects intention to use a wearable device

3   Research Model

The research model is shown in Fig. 2.

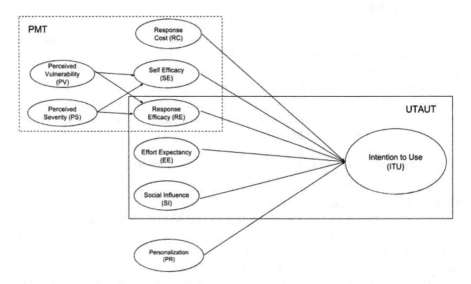

Fig. 2. Research model

4   Methodology

An online survey of the general public in United States of America was used as an instrument to gather the data. Items were measured on seven-point Likert scales with 1 being "strongly agree" and 7 being "strongly disagree". Initial consultation was done with survey experts to examine the logical consistency, contextual relevance, and question clarity of the measurements. The suggestions were incorporated into the next version of the questionnaire. In addition, a pilot study with 20 participants was conducted to collect more feedback to further improve the questionnaire. The comments and suggestions from participants were incorporated via minor modifications of the measurements, such as formatting of the questionnaire and clarity of the items. The main study was then launched after finalizing the questionnaire. The survey was sent to 239 participants, utilizing the service of an organization that offers an incentive to individuals who are willing to respond to questionnaires.

The statistical tool was PLS, which was selected for the development of a new theory. PLS is a suitable software for prediction and building theory [37]. PLS is used widely in the MIS field. SmartPLS was selected to analyze the data and provide various reports that tests the measurements of the model and the structural model in this study.

The structural model was tested via PLS algorithm that calculated the path coefficients and R^2 for the endogenous variables. The bootstrapping was used to calculate the t-values for this research by setting it to sample 5000.

5   Results

5.1   Descriptive Statistics

The survey was sent to 239 participants. Analysis was conducted on 141 responses (59.0%) that were completed. 49.6% were male and 50.3% were female. Average age was 48, oldest 77, while youngest was 18.

5.2   The Measurement Model

The outer loading for each construct was calculated through the SmartPLS algorithm. All indicators were convergent, as their correlation coefficients were greater than 0.708 [38].

The internal consistency of the model was confirmed by SmartPLS where Cronbach's alpha was greater than 0.8 [39]. Average Variance Extracted (AVE) was greater than 0.5 and Composite Reliability was greater than 0.6 [38].

Fornell Larckler scores [40] were also prepared by SmartPLS and the resulting table showed that the square root of AVE was greater than the correlation coefficient.

5.3   The Structural Model

The coefficient of determination, R^2 is the portion of the variance of the dependent variable that is explained by the independent variables. The intention to use, $R^2 = 0.784$, which is considered moderate [41].

For each path in the model, the t-values were calculated by bootstrapping with 5000 samples. A number of independent variables did not have a significant influence on intention to use: Perceived Severity, Response Cost, and Self Efficacy. All other hypotheses were supported with $p < 0.05$, and $p < 0.01$.

The effect size of each variable is measured by f-squared. Each construct is removed from the model and the change in R^2 is calculated. The value of f^2 is:

$$F^2 = (R^2 \text{ included} - R^2 \text{ excluded})/R^2 \text{ included}$$

where R^2 included is all constructs and R^2 excluded is when the selected construct is removed from the model.

The effect size is considered small if it is between 0.02 and 0.14, medium if it is between 0.15 and 0.34 and large if it is 0.35 and over [42]. Table 1 shows the effect size.

Table 1. Effect size.

Construct	Dependent variable	f^2	Effect size
Effort expectancy	Intention to use	0.038	Small
Perceived vulnerability	Response efficacy	0.100	Small
Perceived vulnerability	Self-efficacy	0.091	Small
Personalization	Intention to use	0.027	Small
Response efficacy	Intention to use	0.237	Medium
Social influence	Intention to use	0.391	Large

5.4   Wearable Technology Device Functions

The survey also provided a list of functions that could be useful for wearable technology devices. The most popular function was to record number of steps, track fitness activities, and recording of calorie burn. See Table 2.

Table 2. Wearable technology device functions ranked.

Function	Rank
Record number of steps	1
Track fitness activities	2
Record calorie burn	3
Monitor my heart rate	4
Track sleeping pattern/quality of sleep	5
Record change in behaviour/movement to monitor disease	6
Record my moods	7

5.5   Summary of Results

Six of the 10 hypotheses were supported. Table 3 shows the results.

Table 3. Summary of results

No.	Construct	Path coeff.	t-statistic	P value	Supported
1.	RE → ITU	0.370	4.982	0.000	p < 0.01
2.	SE → ITU	−0.010	0.117	0.907	
3a.	PV → RE	0.411	3.536	0.000	p < 0.01
3b.	PV → SE	0.418	3.067	0.002	p < 0.05
4a.	PS → RE	0.126	0.999	0.318	
4b.	PS → SE	−0.023	0.159	0.876	
5.	RC → ITU	−0.062	1.225	0.221	
6.	EE → ITU	0.135	1.895	0.047	p < 0.05
7.	SI → ITU	0.455	6.567	0.000	p < 0.01
8.	PR → ITU	0.117	1.955	0.051	p = 0.051

6   Discussion

Social influence was one of the main factors that influenced individual's intention to use WTDs to monitor their health. Individual's value the opinion of others in adoption of health information technology. In addition effort expectancy was significant. These results suggest that social influence and effort expectancy should be considered when investigating health technology acceptance. PMT assumes that people base their decision on their own evaluations, but the theory does not take into account that people might be influenced by others in their social circle, such as family members and friends. For example, Fitbit is successful partly because they encourage their users to compete against each other and share their fitness results online [4], hence influencing others to purchase the technology in order to participate with friends.

Because this technology is a protective technology, family members might influence those that are vulnerable to health threats, because of their unhealthy lifestyle (e.g. smoking). Since social influence can positively affect user behavior, companies should carry out certain promotion strategies to obtain more users through social influence (for example, through word of mouth). Another way to attract new users is through healthcare providers, as they have direct access to patients and can recommend WTDs and specific apps.

Response efficacy is a significant factor (P < 0.01). This is one of the important factors when deciding to use the technology, as users must feel confident in the effectiveness of the WTDs in preventing risks to their health. They must be confident that the technology is reliable and will function as designed.

In our study, self-efficacy was not significant, but effort expectancy was. WTDs are designed to be easy to use, and can be learned quickly. Perhaps because of the wide availability of apps in general, users are confident of their ability to use them and hence self-efficacy is a non-significant factor. However, given the significance of ease of use, companies should reinforce the simplicity of the apps. Simple instructions and online tutorials could make users aware of all the extra functions that WTDs offer. If the app has shortcuts and has valuable functionality, users will engage with the technology for a longer period of time.

The results of the structural model analysis confirm the negative relationships between perceived vulnerability on response efficacy ($p < 0.01$) and self-efficacy ($p < 0.05$). H3a and H3b are supported as perceived vulnerability has a significant effect on both perceptions of response efficacy and self-efficacy. These results are consistent with the Fear Appeals Model (FAM) [17]. In the context of health care, when users perceive that the probability of a threat (eg. suffering a heart attack) is high, their fear also increases. They might have experienced similar threats (eg. a previous heart attack) or they are might have knowledge of these threats (eg. family history of heart attacks). They are then influenced by their perceived probability of the outcome (eg. death or paralysis). Therefore, the perception of the WDTs to function effectively decreases. The perception of using the technology correctly also decreases. Users might experience fear or panic and loss of confidence that they can correctly use the technology and they may perceive that the technology has lost the potential to protect them from threats or their fears. Understanding this, practitioners need to emphasize that WTDs have the potential to save lives by identifying the symptoms early enough through data collection.

The results also indicate that the relationships between perceived severity and response efficacy and that of self-efficacy are not significant, thereby confirming that H4a and H4b are unsupported ($p > 0.05$). These results are inconsistent with FAM [17], but are consistent with previous PMT studies. FAM predicts that when individual's perceived severity is high, their confidence in using the technology decreases. However, this prediction is unsupported. An individual suffering from a preexisting health condition, such as heart condition, if they perceive that the threat to their health is severe (eg. previous heart attack), they are more likely to use WTDs to protect their health from malicious consequences. In order to keep consumers using WTDs providers should emphasize that the technology has capabilities to manage their disease or condition long term.

Personalization was also a significant influencing factor ($p = 0.05$). WTD users receive personalized feedback based on the data that they collect. This personalization might be related to response efficacy of the technology as individuals expect the technology to function effectively. For example, individuals that previously suffered a heart attack or those that use WTDs to record their vital signs to manage their disease expect reliable information based on their personal data. Personalization might be a factor for consumers who identify themselves as the qualified-self (QS) and use personalized feedback to better monitor their health. Healthcare providers might be successful in identifying these individuals and could recommend health apps based on their health needs.

Response Cost had no significance on intention to use ($p > 0.05$). Price, time and effort spent on using WTDs were not an issue for the participants. We predicted that if individuals must spend significant amount of money for the service or effort to learn to use the technology or the app, they might be reluctant to use WTDs. However, neither money nor effort were significant factors in decision making among consumers. Perhaps people believe if it is more expensive, then it must be better. Companies such as Apple and Fitbit, who sell WTDs in the higher price bracket, are still growing in the wearable sector.

7   Limitations and Future Research

We used the services of a professional research organization that recruits individuals who like to respond to survey questionnaires in return for a monetary reward. This does not represent a general population. Since WTD adoption is still in the early stage, the survey respondents are likely to be early adopters who are more self-motivated to purchase and experiment with this technology than are mainstream consumers. A further limitation is that the survey was only sent to United States consumers and therefore reflects their experience with the technology and excludes opinions of Canadian and Mexican markets, which would be a greater representation of North American markets. This research did not consider the potential influence of technology adoption among different cultures. Hence, testing whether the provided relationships are still held in other countries is necessary. Future researchers could extend this study by conducting a comparison of consumer acceptance between different cultures of different countries.

8   Conclusion

As the adoption of wearable technology devices is increasing, so does the abandonment of these devices. More people are monitoring their health with the use of technology in order to stay healthy or to manage disease. Today, software platforms, such as Apple's CareKit, are trying to close the gap between everyday wearables and the use of wearables in healthcare. This study provides an understanding of users' intentions to use of wearable technology in a healthcare setting.

Our study has contributed to the evaluation of PMT and UTAUT within a specific context, namely the use of WTDs. From a survey of 142 participants, our results indicate that in the current wearable device market, users are more affected by social influence and response efficacy when they decide to use a WTD to manage their health. It is also noted that in threat appraisals, perceived vulnerability has an effect on response efficacy and self-efficacy, while perceived severity showed to be not significant. The approach is applicable to adoption and intent to use of other health information technologies and we suggest that future researchers do a culture comparative study on adoption of WTDs.

For researchers, our study provides evidence that PMT as a foundation theory may be a valuable tool for understanding and explaining why individuals do or do not use protective technologies such as WTDs in the context of healthcare.

Practitioners should ensure that WTDs have useful functions to protect vulnerable users against health threats. Consumers also highly value the opinion of others, and perhaps look to their loved ones or their healthcare providers for advice.

References

1. Salah, H., MacIntosh, E., Rajakulendran, N.: Wearable tech: leveraging canadian innovation to improve health. MaRS (2014). http://www.marsdd.com/news-insights/mars-reports/

2. Swan, M.: Emerging patient-driven health care models: an examination of health social networks, consumer personalized medicine and quantified self-tracking. Int. J. Environ. Res. Public Health **6**(2), 492–525 (2009)
3. Ledger, D., McCaffrey, D.: Inside wearables: how the science of human behaviour change. Endeavour Partners (2014)
4. FitBit: What should I know about challenges? (2017). https://help.fitbit.com/articles/en_US/Help_article/1531
5. Piwek, L., Ellis, D., Andrews, S., Joinson, A.: The rise of consumer health wearables: promises and barriers. PLoS Med. **13**(2), e1001953 (2016)
6. BBC Research: Wearable Computing: Technologies, Applications and Global Markets (2016). http://www.reportlinker.com/p02042684-summary/Wearable-Computing-Technologies-Applications-and-Global-Markets.html
7. Apple: ResearchKit & CareKit (2016). http://www.apple.com/ca/researchkit/, Accessed 24 Apr 2016
8. CBCnews: New Apple CareKit health apps help users manage medical conditions, 28 April 2016. http://www.cbc.ca/news/technology/apple-carekit-1.3557633
9. PwC: The wearable future. Consumer Intelligence Series (2014). https://www.pwc.se/sv/media/assets/consumer-intelligence-series-the-wearable-future.pdf
10. Fogg, B.J.: Persuasive technologies. Commun. ACM **42**(5), 27–29 (1999)
11. Wu, Q., Sum, K., Dan, N.R. (2016). How fitness trackers facilitate health behavior change. In: Proceedings of the Human Factors and Ergonomics Society Annual Meeting. SAGE Publications, Los Angeles (2016)
12. Nazarian, R.: This man suffered a serious heart attack, and his Apple Watch saved his life. Digital Trends (2016). http://www.digitaltrends.com/wearables/apple-watch-saves-man-heart-attack/
13. Park, J.H.: The effects of personalization on user continuance in social networking sites. Inf. Process. Manage. **50**(3), 462–475 (2014)
14. Gao, Y., Li, H., Luo, Y.: An empirical study of wearable technology acceptance in healthcare. Ind. Manage. Data Syst. **115**(9), 1704–1723 (2015)
15. Venkatesh, V., Morris, G., Davis, G., Davis, F.D.: User acceptance of information technology: toward a unified view. MIS Q. **27**(3), 425–478 (2003)
16. Holden, R.J., Karsh, B.T.: The technology acceptance model: its past and its future in health care. J. Biomed. Inf. **43**(1), 159–172 (2010)
17. Johnston, A.C., Warkentin, M.: Fear appeals and information security behaviors: an empirical study. MIS Quarterly, pp. 549–566 (2010)
18. Rogers, R.W.: A protection motivation theory of fear appeals and attitude change. J. Psychol. **91**(1), 93 (1975)
19. Prentice-Dunn, S., Rogers, R.W.: Protection Motivation Theory and preventive health: beyond the Health Belief Model. Health Educ. Res. **1**(3), 153–161 (1986)
20. Siponen, M., Mahmood, M.A., Pahnila, S.: Employees' adherence to information security policies: an exploratory field study. Inf. Manage. **51**(2), 217–224 (2014)
21. Norman, P., Boer, H., Seydel, E.R.: Protection motivation theory (2005)
22. Rogers, R.W.: A protection motivation theory of fear appeals and attitude change. J. Psychol. **91**(1), 93–114 (1975)
23. Chenoweth, T., Minch, R., Gattiker, T.: Application of protection motivation theory to adoption of protective technologies. In: Proceedings of the 42nd Hawaii Conference on System Sciences (2009)
24. Floyd, D.L., Prentice-Dunn, S., Rogers, R.W.: A meta-analysis of research on protection motivation theory. J. Appl. Soc. Psychol. **30**(2), 407–429 (2000)

25. Bandura, A.: Self-efficacy - toward a unifying theory of behavioral change. Psychol. Rev. **84**(2), 191–215 (1977)
26. Sun, Y., Wang, N., Guo, X., Peng, Z.: Understanding the acceptance of mobile health services: a comparison and integration of alternative models. J. Electron. Commer. Res. **14**(2), 183–200 (2013)
27. Alaiad, A., Zhou, L., Koru, G.: An exploratory study of home healthcare robots adoption applying the UTAUT model. Int. J. Healthcare Inf. Syst. Inf. **9**(4), 44–59 (2014)
28. Kohnke, A., Cole, M.L., Bush, R.G.: Incorporating UTAUT predictors for understanding home care patients' and clinician's acceptance of healthcare telemedicine equipment. J. Technol. Manage. Innov. **9**(2), 29–41 (2014)
29. Trimmer, K., Leigh, W.C., Wiggins, C., Woodhouse, W.: Electronic medical records: TAM, UTAUT, and culture. Int. J. Healthcare Inf. Syst. Inf. (IJHISI) **4**(3), 55–68 (2009)
30. Liang, H., Xue, Y., Ke, W., Wie, K.K.: Understanding the influence of team climate on IT use. J. Assoc. Inf. Syst. **11**(8), 414 (2010)
31. Yu, C.S.: Factors affecting individuals to adopt mobile banking: empirical evidence from the UTAUT model. J. Electron. Commer. Res. **13**(2), 104–121 (2012)
32. Dwivedi, Y.K., Rana, N.P., Chen, H., Williams, Michael D.: A meta-analysis of the Unified Theory of Acceptance and Use of Technology (UTAUT). In: Nüttgens, M., Gadatsch, A., Kautz, K., Schirmer, I., Blinn, N. (eds.) TDIT 2011. IAICT, vol. 366, pp. 155–170. Springer, Heidelberg (2011). doi:10.1007/978-3-642-24148-2_10
33. Chau, P.Y.K., Hu, P.J.H.: Information technology acceptance by individual professionals: a model comparison approach. Decis. Sci. **32**(4), 699–719 (2001)
34. Yang, S., Lu, Y., Gupta, S., Cao, Y., Zhang, R.: Mobile payment services adoption across time: an empirical study of the effects of behavioral beliefs, social influences, and personal traits. Comput. Hum. Behav. **28**, 129–142 (2012)
35. Toch, E., Wang, Y., Cranor, L.F.: Personalization and privacy: a survey of privacy risks and remedies in personalization-based systems. User Model. User-Adap. Inter. **22**(1–2), 203–220 (2012)
36. Akter, S., Ray, P., D'Ambra, J.: Continuance of mHealth services at the bottom of the pyramid: the roles of service quality and trust. Electron. Markets **23**(1), 29–47 (2013)
37. Gefen, D., Straub, D.W., Boudreau, M.C.: Structural equation modeling and regression: guidelines for research practice. Commun. AIS **4**(7), 1–77 (2000)
38. Henseler, J., Ringle, C.M., Sinkovics, R.R.: The use of partial least squares path modeling in international marketing. Adv. Int. Market., 277–319 (2009)
39. Cronbach, L.J., Meehl, P.E.: Construct validity in psychological tests. Psychol. Bull. **52**(4), 281–302 (1955)
40. Fornell, C., Larcker, D.F.: Evaluating structural equation models with unobservable variables and measurement error. J. Mark. Res. **18**(1), 39–50 (1981)
41. Hair, J.F., Ringle, C.M., Sarstedt, M.: PLS-SEM: indeed a silver bullet. J. Mark. Theor. Pract. **19**(2), 139–152 (2011)
42. Hair, J.F., Hult, G.T., Ringle, C.M., Sarstedt, M.: A Primer on Partial Least Squares Structural Equations Modeling (PLS-SEM). SAGE Publications, Thousand Oaks (2014)

Are you Willing to see Doctors on Mobile Devices? A Content Analysis of User Reviews of Virtual Consultation Apps

Vania Yuxi Shi, Sherrie Komiak(✉), and Paul Komiak

Memorial University of Newfoundland, St. John's, NL, Canada
{Ys8378, skomiak, pkomiak}@mun.ca

Abstract. Virtual doctor visiting technology has expanded dramatically around the world, which has the potential to alter the delivery of healthcare, the quality of patient experiences, and the cost of healthcare. In this study, we conducted a content analysis of the online reviews of five popular mobile healthcare systems. 257 patients' reviews of virtual consultation experience were collected and analyzed by two coders independently. This study aims at exploring why people are willing to see doctors online, examining different dimensions of healthcare quality, and recommending design features of virtual consultation systems. The results of the research show that there are different dimensions of healthcare quality in the context of virtual consultation as compared to traditional doctor visits. We generated nine factors of healthcare quality based on the content analysis, of which two factors related to convenience and consultation time (e.g., the time spent for registration, time spent for making an appointment, etc.) are most important in influencing people's satisfaction towards using virtual consultation systems. In addition, we found three critical limitations of current virtual consultation systems, which include insurance, customer service and follow-up service. The results shed light on how to improve patients' satisfaction with virtual consultation systems that would be of interest to healthcare providers. This study also broadens the academic body of healthcare quality in the context of virtual consultation that can contribute as the basis for future research.

Keywords: Virtual consultation · Content analysis · Face-to-face consultation · Healthcare quality · Patient satisfaction

1 Introduction

Online healthcare offers customers panoply of benefits such as convenience, ease of use, portability, and reduced operation cost [1–5]. Consequently, online healthcare has been growing dramatically around the world and has emerged as the leading edge of the healthcare research area. As one of the emergent research and implementation topics in the online healthcare area, seeing doctors online (hereinafter seeing doctors virtually, virtual consultation) has drawn much attention both in academia and practice [5–7].

F.F.-H. Nah and C.-H. Tan (Eds.): HCIBGO 2017, Part I, LNCS 10293, pp. 224–238, 2017.
DOI: 10.1007/978-3-319-58481-2_18

Traditionally, the patient may make a phone call to book an appointment, and then visit the doctor or specialist to discusses the patient's medical problem and begin the process of finding a treatment or solution. The entire appointment is done through face-to-face communications. But this scenario is looking more and more obsolete, making the traditional doctor visits yet another procedure transformed by the online healthcare rage [6]. The rapid proliferation of virtual consultations is challenging the norm, with the benefit of not having the need for patients to leave the comfort of their office or home, accessibility of the same good healthcare services as big cities for rural areas, and reduced charges for both patients and care givers. Some researchers attest that up to 70% of all patients who seek care do not even need face-to-face interaction [8]. Despite strong overall growth of virtual consultation services, however, not many people trust and use them [6, 9]. Evidence has shown that the healthcare service quality, cost and benefits have been consumers' serious concerns [10, 11]. People may be skeptical about the diagnosis accuracy through online consultation, and they also consider the cost including financial and time cost, and all the benefits online consultation brings compared with traditional face-to-face doctor visiting. Consequently, virtual consultation providers face a critical challenge in capturing and keeping users: what determines, and how to facilitate, users' positive attitudes towards virtual consultation?

As a viable way of promoting patient trust, user reviews have become an important venue for virtual consultation providers. Users can evaluate a virtual consultation system after use; other people can also check reviews before actually using the system. The reviews have different formats ranging from score scale to text comment. As viewed by researchers, more detailed information in user feedback is particularly valuable [12]. Users' text reviews may convey rich information about their attitudes towards the system and why, which cannot be wholly captured with other review formats including star/score scale and so on. This research applies content analysis to the text reviews on mobile virtual consultation systems. We seek to answer the following research questions: Why are patients willing to see doctors online, comparing with traditional face-to-face doctor-patient interaction? What are the most important factors affecting patients' attitudes towards virtual consultation systems? How can virtual consultation systems be better designed to improve patients' satisfaction?

This study could contribute both for implementation and academic research. From a practical perspective, many patients have difficulties accessing doctors traditionally, especially in Canada, where there is a vast territory with a sparse population. Our research reveals the feasibility and necessity of virtual consultation services. This study also identifies the factors that constitute virtual consultation system's reputation by studying real users' reviews. The results can shed light on what operational components virtual consultation providers should concentrate on to effectively improve patient's attitudes. For virtual consultation system developers, this research can help them to better design systems to improve care quality and gain competitive advantages in the virtual consultation market. Second, from a research perspective, this is a new effort to explore virtual consultation systems. better knowledge about the criteria patients use to evaluate online doctor visiting systems and the weight patients put on different factors can help us better understand the differences between face-to-face and online communications, and better design virtual consultation systems in the future.

The paper is organized as follows: Section 2 reviews the related literature and develops a conceptual framework for healthcare service quality in the context of virtual consultation. Section 3 discusses the data collection method, the categorization scheme of care quality and the detailed content analysis methodology we use in this research. Section 4 discusses the main findings based on the content analysis, and Sect. 5 concludes the paper with discussion of the research implication.

2 Conceptual Development

2.1 Literature Review

Traditionally, patients go to see doctors and receive healthcare primarily by face-to-face encounters. With healthcare changing at a rapid pace, nowadays patients will have a significant amount of their medical care delivered using the technology of the internet and not the traditional in-office visit where the doctor and patient are face-to-face [6]. In the past years, we have witnessed a proliferation of studies focusing on seeing doctors online and traditional consultation. According to Rosenzweig and Baum [6], virtual consultations are electronic discussions that are traditionally face-to-face encounters. That is, rather than meeting in person, both the medical expert and patients can interact and communicate online. Virtual consultation is convenient, economical, innovative and beneficial for both patients and healthcare provider [6]. A 2012 study by BioMed Central, an online publisher of free peer-reviewed scientific articles, administered a survey centered on the virtual consultation versus the traditional clinical encounter, and charted the follow-up care related to the original consultation [8]. The result shows that patients of virtual consults reported to be almost equally satisfied as patients of traditional consults.

Many factors will affect people's attitudes and intention to see doctors online. Wu et al. [13] develop a revised technology acceptance model to examine what determines mobile healthcare systems (MHS) acceptance by healthcare professionals. The results indicate that compatibility, MHS self-efficacy, and technical support and training significantly affect patients' attitudes towards mobile healthcare, including perceived usefulness and perceived ease of use. Yu et al. [14] conduct a survey to examine the factors determining the acceptance of health IT applications by caregivers in long-term care facilities. The antecedent variables in the paper include social influence factors such as subjective norm and image, and demographic variables including job title, age, work experience and computer skills. The results show that computer skills have significant positive impact, whereas image has significant negative impact on caregivers' intention to use health IT applications.

Of all the factors affecting people's adoption of healthcare systems, healthcare quality and patient satisfaction are key metrics used by healthcare providers in their continuous process improvement efforts [15]. Studies have shown that patients who are satisfied with their care are more likely to follow prescribed treatments [16]. Johnson et al. [15] models the impact of patient perceptions of care quality on overall patient satisfaction in a rural healthcare organization over a three-year time period, and find out dimensions and constructs of service quality significantly predict patient satisfaction.

Choi et al. [17] investigate the relationships between service quality and satisfaction under a South Korea healthcare system. The results indicate that the general causal relationship between service quality and patient satisfaction was well supported in the South Korean healthcare delivery system.

It is important to point out that most prior literature generally dwells on care quality and patient satisfaction in the context of common healthcare, which includes tele-medicine, tele-monitoring, personal health record and so on (e.g., [18, 19]). However, as one emergent and special format of healthcare, not many researchers study patient attitudes and care quality in the context of virtual consultation specifically [20, 21].

Table 1 lists patients' attitudes towards using virtual consultation, factors affecting patients' attitudes, and research methodology used in some previous studies, as well as patients' concerns about virtual consultation compared with traditional doctor visits. In the following section, we will develop a virtual consultation framework based on prior literature.

Table 1. Selected virtual consultation literature relevant to people's attitudes and concerns

Research paper	Concerns	Factors	Attitudes	Research methodology
Rosenzweig and Baum (2013)	Accuracy of virtual consult, regulations, privacy	For patients: cheaper, quicker For healthcare providers: revenue increased, can track appointments or follow-ups, web presence enhanced	Patient satisfaction and physician satisfaction	Prior study review
Zilliacus et al. (2010)	Rapport building inhibited, reduced emotional exploration	Convenience, efficiency	Practitioners' satisfaction	Semi-structured interviews with 15 practitioners. Interviews are audiotaped, transcribed, and thematically ananyzed
Palen et al. (2012)	N/A	Consultation requesting process, timeliness, utility	Patient satisfaction	Observational case-control survey study within Kaiser Permanente, Colorado

2.2 Framework of Patients' Attitudes Towards Traditional and Virtual Consultation

It is worth noting that patient perceptions/attitudes have become key inputs for the assessment of healthcare quality, as well as incentives of healthcare system adoption [15, 22]. Concentrating on the healthcare quality, we conduct content analysis based on the framework presented in Fig. 1.

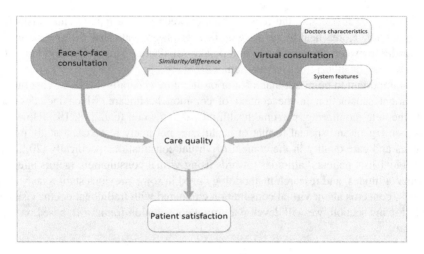

Fig. 1. Healthcare quality framework in virtual and face-to-face consultation.

Typically, both the format and quality of interaction between patients and doctors influence healthcare quality, consequently affect patients' satisfaction. In the context of face-to-face consultations, patients and healthcare providers interact with each other in a straightforward and natural way. The format and quality of interactions are determined by the characteristics of patients and doctors. In the context of virtual consultations, all interactions between patients and doctors are mediated by the virtual consultation systems, thus the virtual consultation systems' design, implementation, and usage will also affect the format and quality of interactions between patients and doctors.

Though some processes in virtual consultation are the same as in face-to-face consultation, for example, patients need to describe symptoms to the doctor, doctors need to diagnose and prescribe in both contexts, these processes may still influence healthcare quality differently. Healthcare system mediation changes the way patients interact with doctors by allowing them communicate in different locations [23, 24]. This change improves efficiency and convenience of doctor visiting, while also brings challenges on how to keep communication effect as good as face-to-face consultation, to improve healthcare quality. The current research uses content analysis of users reviews to explore the advantages and disadvantages of virtual consultation to investigate what aspects of healthcare quality influence people's attitudes towards the virtual consultation system.

3   Data Collection

To investigate patients' attitudes towards virtual consultation, we collected data with real users' text reviews from different sources. To reduce the workload of reading the unbelievably large amount of users' comments, we picked five virtual consultation systems. All these systems can be used on mobile devices. The basic information of these APPs, and our methods to collect data are described below.

3.1   Five Mobile Virtual Consultation APPs

There are many mobile apps/systems that can provide virtual doctor visit all over the world, among which, several are well known including MDLive, Zipnosis, Doctor on Demand, Teladoc, HealthTap and American Well and more. We choose five APPs to collect reviews of them. All the five APPs can be used on mobile devices, and have a certain quantity of users.

MDLive. Founded in 2009, MDLive is a "leading telehealth provider of online and on-demand healthcare delivery services and software that benefit patients, hospitals, employers, payers, physician practice groups and accountable care organizations" (https://welcome.mdlive.com/company/who-we-are/). Patients can see a doctor anytime, anywhere via smartphone with MDLive Telehealth.

MDLive has the largest network of online doctors for telehealth services in US. It's claimed that in the app description in Apple store, on average, their doctors have 15 years of experience practicing medicine and are licensed in the state where patients are located. Their online doctors are available in almost every state in the US.

Via MDLive, people can input symptoms and get information regarding their health and medical needs, schedule appointments, see a doctor online, and get prescription. The symptoms commonly treated are non-emergency issues, which include allergies, asthma, cold & flu, ear infection, headache, joint aches, insect bites and more.

Doctor on Demand. Dr. Phil, whose actual name is Phillip McGraw, is an adviser to the company, Doctor on Demand. As stated by its website, Doctor on Demand is the fastest, easiest way to see an urgent care doctor or psychologist on computer, tablet, or phone – from the comfort of home (http://www.doctorondemand.com/). Patients can do live video doctor visits including assessment, diagnosis and prescriptions when necessary via the app.

Doctor on Demand doctors and psychologists are rigorously screened, and board certified. The app is free to sign up – with no subscription fees. It costs $40 for each 15-minute visit without insurance. Users can rate each visit.

The top conditions treated by Doctor on Demand include cold & flu, sore throat, UTIs, skin issues & rashes, eye issues, travel illness, and more.

Teladoc. Teladoc is developed by Teladoc, Inc., which is a telehealth company that uses telephone and videoconferencing technology to provide on-demand remote medical care via mobile devices, the internet, video and phone. Patients can talk to a doctor anytime anywhere via Teladoc.

Doctors on Teladoc is board-certified and state licensed. They can diagnose, recommend treatment and prescribe medication via the APP. The fee is $35 for each visit plus annual fee.

Many medical issues can be treated via the APP, including sore throat and stuffy nose, allergies, cold and flu symptoms, pink eye, ear infection, urinary tract infection and more.

HealthTap. HealthTap is founded in 2010 and provide users secure video or text chat with a doctor anywhere, anytime. Patients can get instant free answers and help from more than 100000 top U.S. doctors right from mobile phone or tablet.

American Well. American well company provides telehealth services to hospitals, clinics and other organizations. In 2013, American Well announced that it would make their telehealth service available to the general public, and released Amwell mobile applications for both Android and IOS operating systems [25]. Patients can see a doctor on their mobile devices anytime, with no appointment needed.

As stated by Amwell app (https://itunes.apple.com/us/app/amwell-live-doctor-visit-now/id655783752?mt=8), it's the first telehealth service awarded accreditation by the American Telemedicine Association, and it's the first telehealth platform to integrate with Apple's Health App in America.

The issues can be treated via the APP include Brounchitis, cough, sore throat, fever, flu, headache, depression, anxiety, vomiting and more.

3.2   Accumulation and Tailoring of Reviews

We use Google to search for reviews on these systems/apps. The search parameters are constrained based on (a) a list of e-commerce stores and websites, such as Amazon, Apple store, iTunes, Google play and so on. (b) key search terms. Our scope focuses narrowly on seeing doctors via mobile healthcare systems, instead of general or other perspectives (e.g., search information, store personal medical record etc.).

Phase 1 Primary Accumulation. For each system/app, we apply the following three steps to collect reviews.

First, we choose to use the reviews for the five systems from websites including Amazon.ca, Amazon.com, and others including official websites.

Second, we choose to use the reviews for the selected systems from mobile App stores including iTunes and Google play.

The final constraint is based on key search terms "review" and system name, e.g., "Doctor on Demand/DoD"

We choose this way to collect the data we need because the websites and app stores normally enable users to review the app after their purchase. And most users are willing and tend to leave reviews on these websites and app stores instead of other places. Thus, these websites and app stores where people can download/purchase the systems provide many valuable reviews of the app. With Google as a supplementary tool to search, we believe we can accumulate most of the reviews of the app.

Phase 2 Tailoring of Data. To improve validity of our data, we apply the following rules to tailor the initially collected reviews:

- Irrelevant reviews
- Meaningless reviews, i.e., "I didn't use this app"

The final data set contains 257 reviews, of which 185 are positive reviews while the other 72 are negative.

Phase 3 Classification by Research Strategy. Once the researchers identified the reviews for the final data pool, each review is examined and categorized according to its research strategy. We draw on the literature and identify several aspects involved in human-computer interaction, including characteristics of human and computer, and interaction. The details of research strategy are presented in Table 2. Each review may be classified into multi-categories. For example, if one user reviews both doctor and system features, this review should be in both doctor and system features categories instead of just in one category. Number of reviews represents how many reviews are about each category. Number of mentions represents how many times all the reviews mention about each category. One review may mention one category many times, in this condition, the number of mentions is more than one while number of reviews is one.

For the first category, in the interaction between patients and doctors through virtual consultation systems, doctors play a very important role on improving healthcare quality and facilitating people's attitudes. A certified, professional doctor makes it easier to build patients' trust, because they have a tendency to feel more like visiting an actual doctor face-to-face as in traditional way. 126 reviews are about this category, while it has 205 mentions in the 126 reviews. That makes average 1.62 mentions throughout the 126 reviews.

For the second category, which is very important part of our study, it's about the characteristics of mobile healthcare systems. We are studying how to better design

Table 2. Research strategies and numbers for each categories

Research strategy	Description	Number of reviews	Number of mentions
Doctor	Reviews about professionalism of doctors	126	205
Features of system	Reviews about features and characteristics of virtual consultation systems, such as videoconferencing, easy to use etc	190	367
Similarity/difference	Reviews about the similarity/difference between virtual consultation and traditional doctor visiting	179	455
Healthcare service quality	Reviews about efficiency and effectiveness of healthcare, including and not limit to benefits, accuracy of diagnosis etc	257	482
Users' attitudes	Expression of people's attitudes and experiences, such as satisfaction, trust, enjoyment or so. Users' profile such as age, location, sex and so on	257	693
Others (insurance etc.)	Reviews about other issues including network, insurance and so on	41	57

healthcare system to improve healthcare quality in the context of virtual consultation. Different system features influence care quality differently. For example, some systems provide doctor recommendation, which reduce users' effort to pick one from numerous online doctors. Therefore, in practice, recommendation feature may be designed to improve healthcare quality.

The third category compares face-to-face doctor visiting with virtual consultation. Due to the nature of digitalized systems, seeing doctors online somehow changed traditional doctor visiting to a large extent, with less limitation of location, time and control. These changes may bring benefits as well as challenges, including cost, privacy, trust problems etc. Therefore, the similarity or differences between virtual and traditional consultation affect healthcare service, and consequently influence people's attitudes. The fourth category is the core concept of this paper which is introduced in detail in the following sections. The fifth category is the patients' attitudes towards the virtual consultation system, which is a critical consideration of intention to use. As can be seen, all the 257 reviews mention people's attitudes and healthcare quality, which means the data set after tailoring is valid to be used to analyze people's perceptions towards virtual consultation systems. The last category is about other issues, including insurance, internet connection, technical problem etc.

3.3 Categorization Scheme for Strategy Categories

Based on the above strategy, we develop our own healthcare service quality by examining the patients' reviews collected from above sources in Sect. 3.2 and by following the literature on healthcare quality. We review the literature and identify several dimensions and constructs measuring healthcare quality. These dimensions and constructs include issues related to cost (e.g., waiting time [26], cognitive effort [27] etc.), healthcare outcome (e.g., diagnosis [28, 29], effectiveness [30] etc.), and healthcare interaction [31, 32]. These dimensions and constructs provide us with the basic understanding about measuring healthcare service quality in the context of virtual consultation. We then applied the content analysis approach to the user reviews we collected and generated a list of 15 healthcare categories that had been mentioned in the users' reviews. Finally, we examined the occurring frequency of those categories and removed some with very low occurring frequency in the data. Therefore, our final number of categories is 9, which are listed below (category with the highest frequency is listed first). The definition of each category can be found in the appendix.

Categorization of healthcare quality in the context of virtual consultation:

1. Convenience
2. Consultation time
3. Prescription quality
4. Ease of interaction
5. Diagnosis quality
6. Usefulness of the system
7. Insurance availability
8. Usefulness of customer service
9. Follow-up service

Simply coding each review into different categories is not enough as that doesn't capture the rich information in the review [12]. We further assigned an ordinal measure to each review for each nominal category. We used number −1, 0 and 1 for the ordinal coding: −1 means the review is negative on the category while 1 means it's positive. Zero means the category is not mentioned in a review for that observation. If a user doesn't mention the category, we believe there is no discrepancy between the user's perception of healthcare service in this category for both face-to-face and virtual consultation, and people don't view it as an important factor. To summarize, the categorization scheme we developed is nominal (the 9 categories) but also ordinal (the coding scheme is ordinal from −1 to 1 within each of the 9 nominal categories).

4 Data Analysis

Content analysis has been extensively used in social sciences, information systems and healthcare area [12, 33–35]. Following content analysis procedure, two coders including the first and second author worked on the coding in this study.

First, we went through an initial training process. After categorization scheme and a description of each of the nominal and ordinal categories are provided, a sample of 20 reviews (not overlapping with the 257 reviews in the formal analysis) was used as training data set to ensure consistent understanding of the categories between the two coders. Then, following the coding instruction, each coder processes all the 257 reviews independently and two data sets are expected to be generated. Then we plan to compare the two interpretations and mediate any discrepancies. Following standard content analysis procedure [36, 37], a final data set is expected to be obtained to do analysis. Unfortunately, due to time restriction, only one coder finishes coding by the time this manuscript is submitted. Therefore, only one coder's data is presented in this paper. The descriptive statistics can be found in Table 3.

Among the nine categories, three have negative mean values, which represent the negative healthcare service components. Users seem to be mostly unsatisfied with the follow-up service, followed by customer service usefulness and insurance availability. Convenience and consultation time receive the highest level of satisfaction on average, which have the highest mean values. People seems to think convenience and saving

Table 3. Descriptive statistics for the nine categories (N = 257)

	Mean	Min	Max	S.D.
Convenience	1.694	−1	1	1.245
Consultation time	1.189	−1	1	1.021
Prescription quality	1.045	−1	1	0.908
Ease of interaction	0.647	−1	1	1.055
Diagnosis quality	0.582	−1	1	1.277
Usefulness of the system	0.089	−1	1	0.932
Insurance availability	−0.055	−1	1	1.030
Usefulness of customer service	−0.221	−1	1	0.863
Follow-up service	−0.550	−1	1	0.742

Table 4. Virtual consultation versus face-to-face doctor visiting

	Virtual consultation	Face-to-face
Convenience	√	
Consultation time	√	
Prescription quality	√	
Ease of interaction	–	–
Diagnosis quality		√
Usefulness of system	N/A	N/A
Insurance availability		√
Usefulness of customer service		√
Follow up service		√

('√' represents the consultation has advantage on that category than the other one; '–' represents people have almost equal perception on the category; 'N/A' represents the category only applies for one consultation.)

time are most important for virtual consultation. As can be seen, comparing with face-to-face consultation, virtual consultation benefits patients with convenience and less time cost, while still need to improve insurance, customer service and follow up services. We also coded how patients compare virtual consultation and face-to-face consultation on the nine categories. The comparison between virtual and face-to-face consultation is present in Table 4.

In Table 5, we present the correlation matrix for the nine categories we identified for capturing a patient's virtual consultation system usage experience. From the results, it

Table 5. Correlation matrix of the nine variables

	CVE	CT	PQ	EI	DQ	US	IA	UCS	FUS
CVE	1								
CT	.44	1							
PQ	.06	−.18	1						
EI	.14	−.20	.97	1					
DQ	.63	.72	.21	.27	1				
US	.53	−.34	.01	.07	−.25	1			
IA	.49	.10	.50	.54	.37	.29	1		
UCS	.64	.73	.01	.08	.96	−.15	.35	1	
FUS	.20	.14	.75	.71	.27	−.05	.76	.11	1

Note:

CVE	Convenience	US	Usefulness of the system
CT	Consultation time	IA	Insurance availability
PQ	Prescription quality	UCS	Usefulness of customer service
EI	Ease of interaction	FUS	Follow-up service
DQ	Diagnosis quality		

can be seen that our categorization did capture different aspects of users' concerns about virtual consultation systems, since most of the correlation coefficients are less than 0.5. Most of the values are positive, indicating a user's perception for each category are positively correlated.

5   Discussions and Conclusions

Virtual consultation versus face-to-face consultation is a critical issue in online healthcare area. Healthcare providers have to decide where to invest to improve healthcare service quality, to improve patients' satisfaction, and thus to promote their intention to use virtual consultation systems. In this study, we apply a content analysis approach to identify nine categories and to examine what categories are the most important determinants of people's attitudes towards using virtual consultation systems. Specifically, we identified the most important factors impacting patients' satisfaction about virtual consultation are convenience, consultation time followed by prescription quality, ease of interaction and diagnosis quality.

Our study can provide insight into healthcare providers' practices in virtual consultation area. Two factors including convenience and consultation time are found to be critical to determine patients' attitudes towards virtual consultation. Most patients who use virtual consultation think it is more convenient and faster than face-to-face consultation. Though these factors are not actually design features of virtual consultation systems, they are causal connected with system features. Therefore, we recommend virtual consultation system developers focus on how to design the system to improve the two factors. For example, to reduce consultation time further, the system can ask fewer questions to make the registration quicker. To enhance convenience, the platforms on which systems operate should be in multi-formats, including computer, mobile phone, wearable devices and so on. In this way, patients can access virtual consultation almost anytime at anyplace.

In addition, our study can also shed light on how to improve current virtual consultation systems. We find three significant limitations of current virtual consultation systems including insurance, customer service, and follow up service issues. All the three factors are related to the healthcare providers' operational strategies to do expansion, and make profit. Healthcare providers may seek the cooperation with insurance companies to provide more insurance options to patients. They can also recruit good customer service team to reduce the risk of mistakes, do follow-up services and maintain companies' reputation.

Our results are mainly limited to users for the five popular mobile virtual consultation systems (people may be more negative on virtual consultation if they use other not-so-popular systems). Future research can extend the analysis to more systems. The second direction can be analyzing categories beyond the nine constructs generated in this study. Although we rule out the categories which are barely mentioned in our data set, for example, privacy and security, consultation delays etc., these factors may still somehow impact patients' attitudes. In addition, the current nine categories can be further sub-categorized into some detailed indicators, which are more explicit and more feasible to be implemented. Finally, the future direction can be exploring actual design features for virtual consultation systems including doctor characteristics. Our framework indicates that the features of virtual consultation influence healthcare service quality. Current study compares virtual and face-to-face consultation on healthcare service quality, nevertheless, it doesn't involve much on actual design features. The next step will be retrieving actual system characteristics from different dimensions of healthcare service quality.

Appendix

Category definition

(1) Consultation time: The time cost to register/make an appointment/do payment.
(2) Diagnosis quality: The accuracy and speed of getting diagnosis.
(3) Prescription quality: the quality and speed of getting prescription/treatment.
(4) Usefulness of the system: The extent to fulfil people's expectation to be cured.
(5) Usefulness of customer service: Helpfulness of customer service to solve problems including refund, call delays and so on.
(6) Follow-up service: Whether doctor or the system will make follow-up calls/services or not.
(7) Convenience: Whether the system can be used conveniently both on computer and mobile devices anytime anywhere.
(8) Ease of interaction: The extent to easily use the system to do registration, payment, video chatting.
(9) Insurance availability: Whether users can use insurance or not.

References

1. Hillestad, R., Bigelow, J., Bower, A., Girosi, F., Meili, R., Scoville, R., Taylor, R.: Can electronic medical record systems transform health care? Potential health benefits, savings, and costs. Health Aff. **24**(5), 1103–1117 (2005)
2. Hailey, D., Roine, R., Ohinmaa, A.: Systematic review of evidence for the benefits of telemedicine. J. Telemedicine Telecare **8**(1-suppl.), 1–7 (2002)
3. Barlow, J., Singh, D., Bayer, S., Curry, R.: A systematic review of the benefits of home telecare for frail elderly people and those with long-term conditions. J. Telemedicine Telecare **13**(4), 172–179 (2007)
4. Ekeland, A.G., Bowes, A., Flottorp, S.: Effectiveness of telemedicine: a systematic review of reviews. Int. J. Med. Inf. **79**(11), 736–771 (2010)
5. McLean, S., Sheikh, A., Cresswell, K., Nurmatov, U., Mukherjee, M., Hemmi, A., Pagliari, C.: The impact of telehealthcare on the quality and safety of care: a systematic overview. PLoS ONE **8**(8), e71238 (2013)
6. Rosenzweig, R., Baum, N.: The virtual doctor visit. J. Med. Pract. Manage. MPM **29**(3), 195 (2013)

7. Waegemann, C.P.: mHealth: the next generation of telemedicine. Telemed JE Health **16**(1), 23–25 (2010)
8. Palen, T.E., Price, D., Shetterly, S., Wallace, K.B.: Comparing virtual consults to traditional consults using an electronic health record: an observational case–control study. BMC Med. Inform. Decis. Mak. **12**(1), 65 (2012)
9. Zilliacus, E., Meiser, B., Lobb, E., Dudding, T.E., Barlow-Stewart, K., Tucker, K.: The virtual consultation: practitioners' experiences of genetic counseling by videoconferencing in Australia. Telemedicine e-Health **16**(3), 350–357 (2010)
10. Santana, S., Lausen, B., Bujnowska-Fedak, M., Chronaki, C., Kummervold, P.E., Rasmussen, J., Sorensen, T.: Online communication between doctors and patients in Europe: status and perspectives. J. Med. Internet Res. **12**(2), e20 (2010)
11. Greenhalgh, T., Vijayaraghavan, S., Wherton, J., Shaw, S., Byrne, E., Campbell-Richards, D., Bhattacharya, S., Hanson, P., Ramoutar, S., Gutteridge, C., Hodkinson, I.: Virtual online consultations: advantages and limitations (VOCAL) study. BMJ Open **6**(1), e009388 (2016)
12. Qu, Z., Zhang, H., Li, H.: Determinants of online merchant rating: content analysis of consumer comments about Yahoo merchants. Decis. Support Syst. **46**(1), 440–449 (2008)
13. Wu, J.H., Wang, S.C., Lin, L.M.: Mobile computing acceptance factors in the healthcare industry: a structural equation model. Int. J. Med. Inf. **76**(1), 66–77 (2007)
14. Yu, P., Li, H., Gagnon, M.P.: Health IT acceptance factors in long-term care facilities: a cross-sectional survey. Int. J. Med. Inf. **78**(4), 219–229 (2009)
15. Johnson, D.M., Russell, R.S., Russell, R.S., White, S.W., White, S.W.: Perceptions of care quality and the effect on patient satisfaction. Int. J. Qual. Reliab. Manage. **33**(8), 1202–1229 (2016)
16. Manary, M.P., Boulding, W., Staelin, R., Glickman, S.W.: The patient experience and health outcomes. N. Engl. J. Med. **368**(3), 201–203 (2013)
17. Choi, K.S., Lee, H., Kim, C., Lee, S.: The service quality dimensions and patient satisfaction relationships in South Korea: comparisons across gender, age and types of service. J. Serv. Mark. **19**(3), 140–149 (2005)
18. Howard, M., Goertzen, J., Hutchison, B., Kaczorowski, J., Morris, K.: Patient satisfaction with care for urgent health problems: a survey of family practice patients. Ann. Family Med. **5**(5), 419–424 (2007)
19. Larsson, G., Wilde-Larsson, B.: Quality of care and patient satisfaction: a new theoretical and methodological approach. Int. J. Health Care Qual. Assur. **23**(2), 228–247 (2010)
20. Fatehi, F., Martin-Khan, M., Smith, A.C., Russell, A.W., Gray, L.C.: Patient satisfaction with video teleconsultation in a virtual diabetes outreach clinic. Diabetes Technol. Ther. **17**(1), 43–48 (2015)
21. Segura, B.T., Bustabad, S.: A new form of communication between rheumatology and primary care: the virtual consultation. Reumatología Clínica (English Edition) **12**(1), 11–14 (2016)
22. Naidu, A.: Factors affecting patient satisfaction and healthcare quality. Int. J. Health Care Qual. Assur. **22**(4), 366–381 (2009)
23. Krishna, S., Boren, S.A., Balas, E.A.: Healthcare via cell phones: a systematic review. Telemedicine e-Health **15**(3), 231–240 (2009)
24. Mosa, A.S.M., Yoo, I., Sheets, L.: A systematic review of healthcare applications for smartphones. BMC Med. Inform. Decis. Mak. **12**(1), 1 (2012)
25. Brink, S.: Telehealth: The Ultimate in Convenience Care. US News & World Report (2013)
26. Teng, C.I., Ing, C.K., Chang, H.Y., Chung, K.P.: Development of service quality scale for surgical hospitalization. J. Formos. Med. Assoc. **106**(6), 475–484 (2007)
27. Jabnoun, N., Chaker, M.: Comparing the quality of private and public hospitals. Managing Serv. Qual. Int. J. **13**(4), 290–299 (2003)

28. Narang, R.: Determining quality of public health care services in rural India. Clin. Gov. Int. J. **16**(1), 35–49 (2011)
29. Karassavidou, E., Glaveli, N., Papadopoulos, C.T.: Quality in NHS hospitals: no one knows better than patients. Measuring Bus. Excellence **13**(1), 34–46 (2009)
30. Sumaedi, S., Yarmen, M., Yarmen, M., Yuda Bakti, I.G.M., Yuda Bakti, I.G.M.: Healthcare service quality model: A multi-level approach with empirical evidence from a developing country. Int. J. Prod. Perform. Manage. **65**(8), 1007–1024 (2016)
31. Akter, S., D'Ambra, J., Ray, P.: Service quality of mHealth platforms: development and validation of a hierarchical model using PLS. Electron. Markets **20**(3–4), 209–227 (2010)
32. Dagger, T.S., Sweeney, J.C., Johnson, L.W.: A hierarchical model of health service quality: scale development and investigation of an integrated model. J. Serv. Res. **10**(2), 123–142 (2007)
33. De Figueiredo, J.M.: Finding sustainable profitability in electronic commerce. Sloan Manage. Rev. **41**(4), 41 (2000)
34. Vaismoradi, M., Turunen, H., Bondas, T.: Content analysis and thematic analysis: Implications for conducting a qualitative descriptive study. Nursing Health Sci. **15**(3), 398–405 (2013)
35. Corley II, J.K., Jourdan, Z., Ingram, W.R.: Internet marketing: a content analysis of the research. Electron. Markets **23**(3), 177–204 (2013)
36. Holsti, O.R.: Content analysis for the social sciences and humanities (1969)
37. Weber, R.P.: Basic content analysis (No. 49). Sage (1990)

Factors Influencing Acceptance and Continued Use of mHealth Apps

Hanna O. Woldeyohannes[1(✉)] and Ojelanki K. Ngwenyama[1,2]

[1] Institute for Innovation and Technology Management,
Ryerson University, Toronto, Canada
{hwoldeyo,ojelanki}@ryerson.ca
[2] Department of Information Systems,
University of Cape Town, Cape Town, South Africa

Abstract. By 2018, mHealth apps would have been downloaded by 50% of the more than 3.4 billion global smartphone and tablet users. As existing challenges to adoption are allayed, empirical evidence for factors that most predict successful adoption of mHealth apps will be useful to inform and guide the trajectory of mHealth development. To date, most research has looked into clinician perception of mHealth apps. However, only 2% of mHealth apps target healthcare providers/insurance, while the remainder target patients and other consumers [1]. This study was conducted to examine the following: What factors predict adoption of mHealth apps? Participants (n = 11) between ages of 18 to 65 were recruited. A cross-sectional, qualitative interview methodology was used to investigate the research question. The UTAUT2 model for technology adoption and continued use was used to inform the interview guide. Closed coding, thematic analysis and co-occurrence analysis were performed to identify factors. Performance expectancy, effort expectancy and habit were the most relevant constructs that predict adoption of mHealth apps. Flexibility of app to personal preferences positively contributes to performance expectancy. Usage of a specific feature is influenced by user's assessment of relevance to subjective overall health, or interest. Perception of limited features/value may lead to user boredom and use discontinuation. Social influence and hedonic motivation were the least directly implicated factors. Most participants were unwilling to purchase apps before a trial period. Emergent factors include trust for technology/information, required time for interaction with app, privacy of personal information/data, and app-generated feedback.

Keywords: mHealth · mHealth app · UTAUT2 · Technology adoption

1 Introduction

Widespread global adoption and use of mobile communication technology has led to a new phenomenon: mobile health (mHealth). mHealth has a unique potential to "transform the face of health service delivery across the globe" and enhance health outcomes, health quality, and health equity [2]. Telemedicine is an example of successful mHealth implementation that has extended the reach of healthcare specialists to geographically restricted patients who would otherwise not receive adequate care.

© Springer International Publishing AG 2017
F.F.-H. Nah and C.-H. Tan (Eds.): HCIBGO 2017, Part I, LNCS 10293, pp. 239–256, 2017.
DOI: 10.1007/978-3-319-58481-2_19

Earlier roles for mobile phones in healthcare include use of text messaging to promote healthy behaviours and to bring awareness to disease outbreaks using mass alerts [3]. Owing to expanded functions compared to former mobile phone generations, smartphones provide a platform for mHealth software (mHealth apps). mHealth apps are software that are designed to encourage illness self-management, to promote wellness and health education as well as to assist health care professionals in making diagnostic and treatment decisions [4, 5].

The current volume of mHealth apps exceeds 100,000 and continues to grow (6). It is estimated that, by 2018, mHealth apps will be downloaded by 50% of the more than 3.4 billion global smartphone and tablet users [6]. Notwithstanding the impressive growth trends, evidence for subsequent healthcare gains remain scarce. mHealth apps spur several concerns including quality and validity of content, medicolegal ramifications and risks to privacy and security [7, 8]. High turnover rates will likely add challenge to the assessment of effectiveness and clinical utility of mHealth apps. A recent US national survey of mobile phone use showed that approximately 58% of respondents used mHealth apps and, of those, 45.7% reported past discontinuation of mHealth apps use for reasons including "high data entry burden, loss of interest, and hidden costs" [9]. As regulatory frameworks become more established and existing concerns are allayed, factors that most predict successful adoption of mHealth apps will be useful to inform and guide the trajectory of mHealth app development.

To date, most research has looked into clinician perception of mHealth apps. However, only 2% of mHealth apps target healthcare providers/insurance, while the remainder target patients and other consumers [1]. Using the UTAUT2 model for consumer technology adoption studies, this qualitative study examined the following question: What factors determine the adoption and use of mHealth apps for personal use by healthcare consumers?

2 Literature Review

mHealth apps have the capacity to alter the scale and scope of healthcare services. Considering the ubiquity and portability of smartphones, the ease of access to the primary distribution channels of mHealth apps, i.e., app stores, and the low levels of technology literacy required for their use, mHealth apps are uniquely positioned to improve the quality and cost effectiveness of preventative care as well as treatment and management of medical conditions [10]. mHealth apps are also uniquely positioned to address issues of health inequities [11].

2.1 Filling Gaps in Healthcare

Illness Detection: Benefits of Healthcare any Time, any Place: mHealth apps can play an important role in early detection of medical conditions, reduction of illness burden as well as healthcare spending. Some medical conditions can be difficult to detect early at a doctor's office due to the unpredictability of the timing of symptom occurrence. For example, symptoms of atrial fibrillation, a heart condition marked by heart arrhythmia, may not occur during traditional ECG procedures. mHealth apps can lead to early treatment and better health outcome by allowing for detection of the condition in a non-clinical setting by virtue of ease of access to medical device, i.e., smartphone, and low cost barrier to app use [10].

Prevention of Illness Exacerbation: mHealth apps can assist in the prevention of illness exacerbation. For example, lack of time and financial constraints have been identified as reasons for individuals with chronic obstructive pulmonary disease (COPD) to delay seeking healthcare services [12]. A study reported that "the hospitalization costs for the treatment of acute COPD exacerbations represented about 45% of total costs" [12]. mHealth apps designed to support self-management of illness symptoms may help improve quality of life, reduce the frequency of hospitalization, and improve financial efficiency [12, 13].

Management of Chronic Conditions: Chronic conditions are often complex, require ongoing clinical care, and may also require self-management by ways of lifestyle changes, treatment adherence. mHealth apps can be useful in the management of chronic conditions. For example, decision support apps for diabetes can be designed to provide just-in-time guidance according to blood glucose levels, to calculate insulin bolus doses, as well as to track diet, physical exercise, and medication regimens [14, 15]. mHealth apps could be particularly useful in times when a healthcare provider cannot be reached or when the nature of their queries do not justify reaching out to a healthcare provider [15].

2.2 Cross-Generational Reach: From Pediatric to Geriatric Healthcare Consumers

Pediatric Population: Twelve percent of children between the ages of 8 to 12 and 37% of adolescents between the ages of 12 to 18 own smartphones [16]. In 2014, a minimum of 60% of children used apps by age 8 [16]. mHealth apps can, therefore, be a viable route to overcoming the challenge of engaging the pediatric population outside the healthcare setting and encouraging self-management. For example, children and adolescents in therapy for pain management can get easy access to reinforcement of pain management skills even when not in a therapist's office, thereby leading to improved health outcomes and quality of life [16]. A separate pilot study was able to show that a gamified diabetes app increased the frequency of blood glucose level assessment among adolescents with type I diabetes [17].

Elderly Population: Given the high prevalence of chronic illness in the elderly population, and the complexities often associated with their conditions, mHealth apps can assist the elderly population in self-management. Use of smartphones among individuals over the age of 65 is low. In 2013, only 18% owned a smartphone and over 25% of those who have smartphones never downloaded an app [11]. However, once familiarized with a new technology, individuals in this age group are reported to be frequent users of technology compared to younger individuals [11].

2.3 Technology Adoption and Use

Empirical evidence for the "real world" effectiveness of mHealth apps in healthcare is scarce. Various technology adoption models have been used to guide research design, data collection, as well as explanation of findings in studies of mHealth adoption.

A survey of 343 Korean adults based on the Post-Acceptance Model (PAM) and Technology Acceptance Model (TAM) showed that confirmation of a consumer's initial expectations of an mHealth app was a positive and significant predictor of perceived usefulness (PU), perceived ease of use (PEOU) and intention-to-use the app [18]. Furthermore, while both PU and PEOU predicted intention-to-use, only PEOU had significant influence on Satisfaction with the mHealth app [18]. A separate survey study based on the TAM framework conducted across universities in Bangladesh (n = 144) found different results where PU, and not PEOU, predicted intention-to-use [19]. Interestingly, the study found that PEOU was significantly associated with PU. The study also showed that intention-to-use was significantly and positively associated with actual use of mHealth.

A survey of 1,132 US consumers using a combination of theoretical constructs on "technology adoption, technology assimilation, consumer behaviour, and health informatics literature" showed that perceived innovativeness toward mobile services (PIMS) and perceived health conditions had a direct impact on intention-to-use [20]. Co-presentation of high PIMS with high perceptions of healthiness or high perceptions of vulnerability to chronic disease was significantly associated with increased levels of mHealth "assimilation and substitutive use" wherein substitutive use is defined as preference for mHealth use as compared to doctor visits. Co-presentation of high PIMS with high perception of healthiness was also significantly associated with adjunctive use of mHealth in addition to visits to the doctor [20].

A separate study used the value-attitude-behaviour model, theory of planned behaviour and aging characteristic factors to survey 424 Chinese adults over 40 years of age [21]. The results showed that subjective norm, i.e., a "person's perception that most people who are important to him think he should or should not perform the behaviour in question", and perceived physical condition did not influence intention-to-use mHealth apps. However, the predictive factors of intention-to-use differed between middle-aged and older users. Attitude (strongest), perceived value, perceived behaviour control and resistance to change (weakest) were positive predictors of intention-to-use among the middle-aged group. However, perceived value, attitude, perceived behavior control, technology anxiety, and self-actualization need were significant predictors of intention-to-use among the older group. Results also showed positive relationship between perceived value and attitude in both groups.

Using the UTAUT2 model, a survey of 317 college-aged users showed that performance expectancy, hedonic motivation, and habit positively predicted user's intention-to-use of a health and fitness app, whereas effort expectancy, social influence, facilitating conditions, and price value were positively, but not significantly, associated to intention-to-use [22]. The authors argued that the insignificant effect of effort expectancy may be due to a ceiling effect resulting from the study population's high comfort-level with the technology and the high level of usability of device interfaces [22]. While price value did influence intention-to-use, the authors suggested that participants would discontinue use of free apps that add no subjective value, whereas they would be willing to pay for apps that they find valuable [22].

A systematic literature review revealed that the main recognized factors that influence mHealth adoption are: 'perceived usefulness and ease of use, design and technical concerns, cost, time, privacy and security issues, familiarity with the technology, risk-benefit assessment, and interaction with others' [23].

3 Methods

3.1 Research Model

The UTAUT2 was selected as the model of choice in this study for the following reasons: (1) It has comparatively better explanatory power; (2) It is best positioned to explore use behaviour from consumer context rather than an organizational context. Table 1 lists UTAUT2 constructs and their definitions.

The UTAUT model explains 69% of technology acceptance, i.e., intention-to-use, when compared to prior models that explained approximately 40% of the phenomenon [24]. However, since its publication, only 16 studies used the full theory in its original form which is suggestive of the non-suitability of the theory across all contexts [25]. The UTAUT was developed for the organizational context where users may be required to use technology. An extended version of this model, the UTAUT2, includes additional core constructs to emphasize the consumer context where technology adoption is voluntary.

Table 1. UTAUT2 Constructs and their definition

Construct	Definition
Performance expectancy [24]	"The degree to which an individual believes that using the system will help him or her to attain gains in job performance"
Effort expectancy [24]	"The degree of ease associated with the use of the system"
Social influence [24]	"The degree to which an individual perceives that important others believe he or she should use the new system"
Facilitating conditions [24]	"The degree to which an individual believes that an organizational and technical infrastructure exists to support use of the system"
Hedonic motivation [26]	"The fun or pleasure derived from using a technology"
Price value [26]	"The cost and pricing structure"
Habit [26]	"The extent to which people tend to perform behaviours automatically because of learning"

3.2   Research Propositions

The following propositions were evaluated as part of this research study:

P1: Performance Expectancy influences Behavioural Intention and Use Behaviour.
P2: Effort Expectancy influences Behavioural Intention and Use Behaviour.
P3: Social Influence influences Behavioural Intention and Use Behaviour.
P4: Facilitating Conditions influences Behavioural Intention and Use Behaviour.
P5: Hedonic motivation influences Behavioural Intention and Use Behaviour.
P6: Price Value influences Behavioural Intention and Use Behaviour.
P7: Habit influences Behavioural Intention and Use Behaviour.

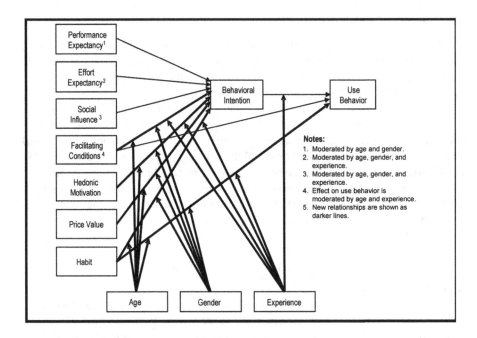

Retrieved from: Venkatesh, V., Thong, J.Y.L., Xu, X. (2012). Consumer acceptance and use of information technology: Extending the Unified Theory of Acceptance and Use of Technology. Vol. 36 No. 1 pp. 157–178..

3.3   Research Design, Data Collection and Analysis

This exploratory qualitative research study employed semi-structured interviews to obtain in-depth information from individuals who have adopted mHealth apps for personal use. An interview guide was developed by adapting previously validated questions from the UTAUT2 framework for consumer technology acceptance. Socio-demographic characteristics collected include age, sex, education, marital status, and household income. The interviewer obtained informed consent from all participants prior to conducting the interview. Ethics approval for the study was obtained from the Ryerson University Research Ethics Board.

Participants were recruited through face-to-face invitation at a doctor's office in the community. One-time semi-structured interviews were conducted using an interview guide. Interviews were digitally audio-recorded and transcribed verbatim. Data immersion, coding and content analysis was conducted to identify themes. The NVivo software supported the data analysis which included: (1) a closed coding deductive method using UTAUT2 concepts; (2) thematic analysis and open coding, an inductive method to identify factors not considered in UTAUT2; and (3) co-occurrence analysis.

4   Findings and Discussion

Individuals (n = 11; 3 males, 8 females) between the ages of 18 and 65 were interviewed as part of this study. Fitness and women's mHealth apps were the most prevalent mHealth apps, followed by general health apps. (see Tables 2 and 3).

Most participants (n = 8) had a single mHealth app installed on their mobile device at the time of interview. A possible explanation is that mHealth apps compete between themselves and other non-health apps for user's time. The Nielsen company, a consumer trends research company, reported that while the average smartphone user had 42 apps installed on their devices, 87% of those users declared that they use less than 10 apps in any given day [27]. Another possible explanation is that users conduct targeted search for apps that they predetermine as relevant to their specific interests or health needs.

Table 2. Demographic characteristics of participants.

Variable	Categories	n	%
Age	18–24	2	18.2
	25–29	3	27.3
	30–39	3	27.3
	40–49	1	9.1
	50–59	1	9.1
	60–65	1	9.1
Sex	Female	8	72.7
	Male	3	27.3
Marital status	Single	8	72.7
	Married	3	27.3
Education	High school	3	27.3
	Some college	2	18.2
	Undergraduate	5	45.5
	Some post-graduate	1	9.1
Household income	Under 35, 000	1	9.1
	35,000–50,000	3	27.3
	50,000–75,000	6	54.5
	75,000–100,000	1	9.1

Table 3. Description of device and mHealth apps

Variable	Categories	n	%
Device type	iPhone	6	54.5
	Android	5	45.5
No. of mHealth apps	1	8	72.7
	2	1	9.1
	3	1	9.1
	5	1	9.1
Types of mHealth apps	Healthy diet (incl. Weight loss)	2	18.2
	Fitness	5	45.5
	Women's health	5	45.5
	General health	4	36.4
	Rest & Relaxation (incl. Mental health)	1	9.1

4.1 Performance Expectancy

Generally, participants agreed that mHealth apps served their desired purposes. The following sub-themes emerged in relation to the concept of performance expectancy.

Time-Demand

Most users interacted with their mHealth apps for up to 15 min per day during days of use. Where apps are intructional/educational or where they support activities like meal-planning and diet tracking, participants interacted with apps for 30 min or more. Most participants (n = 10) reported that they had no desire to spend more time on mHealth apps than they already did. Only one person reported a desire for increased and regularized usage and identified low user-friendliness of the app as a deterrent.

Scope of Content

mHealth apps with limited, easily exhaustible scope of content may cease to be of value to the user after a certain period of time, particularly when they are designed for instructional purposes. One participant described an instructional fitness app, a cost-saving substitute for a personal trainer, that lost its usefulness once the full content was covered.

> *[Interviewee #04] ... I just deleted it because I'm like, I know what I'm doing now, there's nothing more.*

App Accuracy

Two multiple app users expressed disappointment with the performance of women's health apps. Both expressed a misguided expectation of predictive accuracy which highlights the importance of incorporating guiding material where necessary. Both reported deleting the apps and re-installing them at a later time. The implication is that perceived value impacts effort to learn. In contradistinction, three other users felt that the apps performed well for the task. Another participant continued use of the app after finding discrepancies in app-generated measurements.

Scope of Flexibility

One multiple app user reported that while a diet app performed as expected, i.e., provided information on healthy dietary options, the app lacked the flexibility to adjust to ethnic preferences. Nonetheless, she reported continued use to promote her weight loss and to guide healthy meal preparations for her family.

> *[Interviewee #06] ...It wasn't to my liking...for ethnic reasons, there're cenrtain things we don't really eat or never eaten before.*

Another user expressed satisfaction with the large database supported by her diet app of choice and its flexibility, i.e., ability to recognize her entries.

> *[Interviewee #07] ...it has a huge database. So anything, I can even put the most obscure thing, if I'm making my own spinach egg-drop soup, someone somewhere in the world seems to have entered it...*

App-Generated Feedback

Perceived quality of app-generated feedback was a common factor among three participants who reported that app performance exceeded expectations. App-generated feedbacks increased user awareness of existing behavioural patterns and encouraged behaviour modification for better personal health outcomes.

> *[Interviewee #05] ...fell in love with it. Cause it basically, if for whatever day I'm kinda feeling like a bit drowsy or down or you know like a bit tired then I know exactly why, cause I haven't really gotten enough sleep. I can actually see that on like a chart in front of me so it kinda measures it, right.*

> *[Interviewee #07] ...you track your weight daily and it does statistics, like it does like charts and it sends you daily little reports that you can print out, like actual reports well it will do everything for you including, weekly, how much, in a pie graph, you've been consuming in terms of carbs, fats and things like that and even your habits...*

> *[Interviewee #11] I just always assumed that when I was sleeping, it was solid. It's not. So sometimes, you're like, oh I got 6 h last night, and then you sync your [device/app] and like no you got like 4 cause you were tossing and turning or you woke up multiple times...*

Potential for Harm

Most users did not see harm in using mHealth apps. However, two potential harmful effects of mHealth apps were identified: anxiety in response to app-generated information, and propagation of clinically unsupported behaviours that may jeopardize users' health.

One participant recounted a time of significant concern over 'inaccurate' predictions of a women's mHealth app. She added that her friend had gone through a similar situation.

> *[Interviewee #04] "...when I got really scared, I just deleted the app..."*

One individual highlighted the potential harm of mHealth apps that promote extreme calorie restriction diet programs that would normally be monitored by a health care provider.

> *[Interviewee #07] "...it's a controversial diet..."*

Other Detractors of Performance Expectancy
Dependency on WiFi and functional errors were also reported to negatively affect performance expectancy.

4.2   Effort Expectancy

In general, participants were able to use mHealth apps with ease. One out of five users of womens health apps reported deleting an app after difficulty with data entry. The participant reinstalled the app at a later time and sought assistance from friends. The participant indicated that low perceived ease of use is a significant motivator for searching for alternative mHealth apps. Another participant expressed intention to reinstall a fitness app she had previously deleted after finding it comparatively more user-friendly than an alternative app.

> *[Interviewee #06] "I didn't know how to change the [date] so I deleted the app and I downloaded it again."*

> *[Interviewee #06] "If I can't use one I just delete it. Find one that's much easier."*

> *[Interviewee #08] "...there was another one that I had....I think I like that one a little bit more because it was a little bit more user-friendly."*

Most users do not use all the features of mHealth apps. Their usage is influenced by their assessment of relevance to their overall health, their interest, or the effort required to use the features. However, most expressed desire to further explore the apps in the future.

> *[Interviewee #01] "There is an option to check how much water do you drink, your calorie tracker. I don't use those. I only check the...more related to my....heart rate...and my steps to check my body condition."*

> *[Interviewee #06] "There is more stuff there. Yet to discover when I have the time."*

> *[Interviewee #11] "Predominantly laziness, I think what it comes down to. Just because it's a lot of work for some things."*

Presence of more features did not detract from effort expectancy. On the contrary, the availability of more features in mHealth apps may serve to maintain the user's interest in the app. As previously mentioned, limited number of app features risk user boredom and disengagement.

> *[Interviewee #07] "There is something about having so much variety offered to you. You know. It makes it somehow more enjoyable."*

4.3   Social Influence

Most participants learned of mHealth apps through browsing app stores and through YouTube advertisements/reviews. One user indicated that a TED Talk presentation may have been her introduction to a mHealth app. Two users reported that casual conversations sparked initial curiosity for specific types of mHealth apps that they later downloaded.

Approximately half of the participants had friends and family who use the same or closely similar apps. However, most users did not receive encouragement to use mHealth apps.

[Interviewee #06] "through my girlfriends. One of them was my sister-in-law, the other one was my soccer partner and the other one is my friend."

Only one of 11 participants reported mHealth app adoption as a consequence of direct social influence, that is, she expressed being embarrassed for being the last among her friends to adopt a women's health app.

[Interviewee #06] "I didn't know, I was laughed at because they knew about it, and I didn't know about it."

Only one participant reported use of mHealth app to track information in anticipation of questions from her healthcare provider.

4.4   Facilitating Conditions

Most users (n = 7) would turn to the internet, i.e., Google, YouTube, and online forums, as the primary tool for troubleshooting issues related to mHealth apps. Three participants indicated that they would seek help from friends and family. One participant indicated that in-app instructions were sufficient. Three partipants revealed app deletion and replacement with a more user-friendly app as a method of problem resolution.

[Interviewee #04] "There was one time I [tried to figure it out] but then it ws so confusing."

[Interviewee #04] "If I can't use one I just delete it. Find one that's much easier."

A limitation in interpreting this observation is that all, with the exception of two users, had never paid for mHealth apps and, therefore, were not faced with switching costs. A study found that the role of switching costs are significant in cases of above average customer satisfaction or perceived value [28]. It may, therefore, be conjectured that, where users are otherwise satisfied with an app, as the price for apps increase, the availability of facilitating conditions becomes increasingly relevant to switching costs.

4.5   Hedonic Motivation

Six out of 11 participants reported that there was nothing they didn't like about the mHealth apps they use. Nonetheless, only three participants brought up enjoyment in the context of in-app community competitions that promoted weight loss or physical fitness.

[Interviewee #05] "...they have like a bunch of different competitions that you can participate in with your friends, with your buddies, right and you can create that crew."

It is important to note that, by and large, participants commented on the app's performance and effort expectancy when asked about the likeability and enjoyability of an mHealth app. Participants associated absence of hedonic motivation with app dysfuntion (i.e., glitches), absence of variety in app features (i.e., boredom), absence of specific useful features (i.e., reminder notifications), insufficient ease of use, and app-dependence on internet. One participant quipped, "You won't use an app for fun." It, therefore, appears that user's perception of hedonic motivation overlaps with performance expectancy in the context of mHealth apps. This is not to mean that mHealth app appeal is not relevant in the selection of one app over another with similar function. When asked what pushed her to download a particular app, one participant replied:

[Interviewee #11] "Probably because I like the little logo."

4.6   Price Value

All participants used free apps and only 3 had purchased apps in the past. It was, therefore, not possible to assess users' attitude towards price value. However, two main sub-themes surfaced.

Willingness to buy
Most users (n = 8) were willing to pay for apps that they have tried and know work well for them. In some cases, users would prefer to compare apps against familiar, previously established tools before making a purchase.

[Interviewee #06] "I would pay for it because I am satisfied with it...I would prefer that applications have a trial period ...to see that it would fit your needs."

[Interviewee #03] "...I didn't trust it. When I come now to the doctor, when I checked the app and the [results] she gave me [after] she check it, they are equal. I like it. After this, I am going to use it."

Two participants who used mHealth apps in conjunction with an activity tracking device expressed that, in spite of the presence of additional features, the apps' value would be lost to them in the absence of the device. The convenience of low level interaction and continuous tracking of measures of physical activity and sleep quality was one of the main appeals of using the mHealth device/app combination. The added features in the apps, including tracking of diet and hydration, were of less appeal due to the level of engagement required for regular data entry.

It is unsurprising that the willingness to pay for an app also depends on the availability of a free alternative.

[Interviewee #11] "...but if there are free ones, I'm not going to pay for this one."

Three participants reported unwillingness to purchase apps; one of them stressed that she would not pay for an app but would search for a free alternative, highlighting the low switching cost for many mHealth apps. Another admitted her overall low interest in technology and therefore, low likelihood to pay for mHealth apps, the third expressed high doubts on reliability of app as deterrent to making a purchase.

Role of Trial Periods

Upfront fees for access may hamper app sales. All 3 participants who had bought apps in the past expressed post-purchase regrets. One participant pointed out her preference for lite versions of apps that offer a time-locked trial period for full access rather than those that require upfront payment for premium access. She contrasted her decision to purchase a "gimmicky" app after an effective trial period against a separate decision to not pay for premium access to an app with free lite version due to uncertainty of additional value.

> *[Interviewee #11] "I honestly don't like the idea of a membership where you have access to everything for this amount of money. Give me something where I can say look I want this one, this one, and this one. I will pay, you know, maybe pick 3 programs or something and then say ok you have a 3 month subscription for these 3 programs for like what $10. I can do something like that. I just don't like paying such a big chunk of money for a bunch of stuff I in there that I am probably never going to use."*

Another participant reported that she was satisfied with the free lite version of the app and was not convinced of the added value of the premium version of the app. Her position was also influenced by past dissatisfation with purchased premium access to an app.

> *[Interviewee #07] "I don't know if it actually is worth it. I don't understand what the benefits are...I found what I have is great so I don't know what they're really offering me that would step it up."*

> *[Interviewee #07] "...you get it and it's not that much, there is no difference between this and the lite version"*

mHealth apps are a relatively new phenomena and, therefore, trial periods may play an important role in dynamic pricing [29]. The valuations of mHealth apps by all but one participant ranged from $2–$15. However, two of those individuals use their apps in conjunction with an activity tracking device which is relatively costly. One person was an outlier in his willingness to pay as much as $50 for a general health app that makes accurate measurements and reasoned by saying that it was for his health, after all. Some app developers are likely using this pricing strategy. One participant was fairly certain that the price of an app that she purchased after a successful trial period, cost more at time of interview than when she bought it.

4.7   Habit

All but one participant were content with the frequency with which they use mHealth apps. The exception attributed inconsistency of use to dissatisfaction with user-friendliness of the app.

About half of the participants found reminder push notifications useful. One participant expressed disappointment that an app did not have reminders. Two participants indicated that too many reminders may alienate rather than retain them as users of mHealth apps. One of the two appreciated that the app gives her a nudge when she does not use the app for some length of time. The other opined that the usefulness of push notification reminders would be dependent on the type of mHealth app and the ability to customize over time.

[Interviewee #07] "If it did bother me every day, I'd feel hounded...[when there's a time gap] it's like when you want someone to notice you or something. Like a friend."

[Interviewee #11] "In reality, probably, I'd just get frustrated and be like leave me alone."

4.8   Behavioural Intention

All but one participant expressed their intention to continue use of their mHealth apps. The one exception intended to find a more user-friendly replacement for an app. Some participants added conditions such as:

[Interviewee #01] "as long as I need it"

[Interviewee #09] "Yes, for now yes. Unless, I find something else."

[Interviewee #11] "Till the new thing comes around"

These conditional statements may, in part, be a reflection of the novelty and fast-paced, changing nature of the mHealth app market, the voluntary nature of mHealth app adoption, the current state of low switching costs and the absence of a central guiding authority on the subject of mHealth apps.

4.9   Emergent Findings

Trust

Three out of four participants who used general health apps that measure medical parameters, i.e., heart rate and blood pressure, brought up trust as a factor for technology acceptance. One participant reported that his confidence in the reliability of the heart rate monitor that came pre-installed in his phone stemmed from the device manufacturer's assurance that the sensor on the specific type of smartphone functions in the same way as the sensor used in emergency rooms. A second participant expressed his former skepticism was supplanted by confidence after comparing pulse rate measured through his app with readings at his doctor's office.

[Interviewee #01] This one is really nice. It is integrated with the phone so. This program you cannot use in a different phone. You have to have this one actually has a special sensor that reads your blood heart rate. Exact same thing that they use in the ERs, similar kind of sensor.

[Interviewee #03] I was, you know, I didn't trust it. When I come now to the doctor, when I checked the app and the one she gave me, she check it, they are equal. I like it.

The third participant, a nurse by training, voiced her preference for a personal mobile medical device rather than her mHealth app to measure her blood pressure.

She believed the app to be inconsistent in its accuracy, perhaps due to its dependence on WiFi. She had noticed discrepancy between readings from the medical device and those from the app. Her suspicion is supported by a recent study that provided evidence for the inaccuracy of a popular blood pressure app [30].

[Interviewee #10] This is not accurate, no?

[Interviewee #10] Something it's same but sometimes there is a difference 5 points like that.

Privacy

Two participants reported privacy concerns due to the nature of information requested by the app such as a picture of the participant. Connectivity of mHealth apps with social media accounts can also be perceived as a threat to user's privacy, and therefore hinder app adoption.

[Interviewee #07] I didn't trust it. That's the thing. I felt like, even when they wanted a before and after picture, why do you need this? Who's gonna take this information? I just didn't trust the developers at all...like this big eye watching me.

[Interviewee #11] ...I got frustrated with it is because it links to your Facebook and I don't like linking things to my Facebook.

5   Limitations and Future Research

mHealth apps are a relatively new phenomena and therefore, significant factors not included in the UTAUT2 model may not have been captured. From among the UTAUT2 concepts, price value and facilitating conditions could not be sufficiently assessed using data from this study. Individuals were required to be over the age of 18 to participate in the study; data for hedonic motivation may differ in the pediatric population. Furthermore, the types of mHealth apps were unrestricted and it may be argued that a more targeted evaluation of mHealth app adoption by category may yield a different set of observations. Although the flexibility of semi-structured interviews allowed for additional insights, the small sample size constrained information saturation. The results from this study, while not generalizable, may be transferable by informing future research in the area.

The following questions were generated from this study: Do users exhibit varying degrees of risk aversion depending on the type of mHealth app? Is higher education, particularly in the medical field, associated with greater hesitation to adopt mHealth apps? Is the demand for facilitating conditions subject to price of mHealth apps? Is hedonic motivation relevant to mHealth apps targeted towards pediatric populations? A multi-site, qualitative study with a larger sample size and a wider representation of the consumer population would likely result in improved information saturation which could be used to design a theoretical framework with significant explanatory power.

6 Conclusions

The results of this pilot study suggest that some UTAUT2 constructs may be more significant than others in the assessment of mHealth apps. Performance and effort expectancy were the most relevant concepts. mHealth apps that require longer inter-action time are likely to be perceived as time sink. mHealth app developers should aim for enhanced app efficiency to lower the required user interaction time. Developers should also carefully consider the quality of information provided and feedback gen-erated by mHealth apps. For example, managing performance expectation through in-app education/information may help prevent undue distress stemming from an app's feedback on health status. Visual, easily digestible feedback may also enhance user engagement and user empowerment.

Social influence and hedonic motivation were the least directly implicated concepts. Although social interactions may serve to introduce people to mHealth apps, the decision to promote ones personal health and wellness is primarily within ones personal domain and, therefore, social influence is less likely to impact change in mHealth app use. Bandura (1998) stated, "People do not behave like weathervanes, constantly shifting to whatever social influences happen to impinge on them at the moment. They adopt personal standards and regulate their behaviour by their self-sanctions. They do things that give them self-satisfaction and self-worth, and refrain from behaving in ways that breed self-dissatisfaction" [31]. It is also important to consider that hedonic motivation may be more relevant in the context of a sub-population of mHealth app users such as pediatric populations.

Other factors that may influence mHealth app adoption include trust and privacy. Evidence-based, guideline concordant and, where appropriate, regulated mHealth apps are best poised to address concerns of trust. Developers should also prioritize mini-mization of risks to users' privacy. Most users did not consider the integrity of the source of the mHealth apps making them vulnerable to potential harm. Evidence-based, guideline concordant mHealth apps would likely be better received for medical func-tions such as diagnostic, educational, or measurement apps (e.g. to measure heart rate), particularly among those individuals with higher education.

References

1. IMS Institute for Healthcare Informatics. Patient adoption of mHealth: use, evidence and remaining barriers to mainstream acceptance (2015)
2. World Health Organization. mHealth: new horizons for health through mobile technologies (2011)
3. Déglise, C., Suggs, L.S., Odermatt, P.: SMS for disease control in developing countries: a systematic review of mobile health applications. J. Telemedicine Telecare 18(5), 273–281 (2012)
4. Segal, J.B., et al.: Reducing dosing errors and increasing clinical efficiency in Guatemala: first report of a novel mHealth medicaiton dosing app in a developing country. British Med. J. 1(3), 111–116 (2015)

5. Centers for Disease Control and Prevention. Centers for Disease Control and Prevention. CDC Mobile Activities (2016). http://www.cdc.gov/mobile/healthcareproviderapps.html, Accessed 10 March 2016
6. research2guidance. http://www.research2guidance.com/r2g/research2guidance-mHealth-App-Developer-Economics-2014.pdf, http://www.research2guidance.com, Accessed 6 May 2014
7. Buijink, A.W., Visser, B.J., Marshall, L.: Medical apps for smartphone: lack of evidence undermines quality and safety. Evid. Based Med. **18**(3), 90–92 (2013)
8. Agarwal, S.: Guidelines for reporting of health interventions using mobile phones: mobile health (mHealth) evidence reporting and assessment (mERA) checklist. BMJ **352**, i1174 (2016)
9. Krebs, P., Duncan, D.T.: Health app use among US mobile phone owners: a national survey. JMIR mHealth uHealth **3**(4), e101 (2015)
10. Hermans, C., et al.: Studying the added value of remote monitoring in the setting for the management of atrial fibrillation. In: Biomedica 2015: The European Life Sciences Summit, Belgium (2015)
11. Gilbert, B.J., et al.: The role of mobile health in elderly populations. Curr. Geriatr. Rep. **4**, 347–352 (2015)
12. Bitsaki, M., Koutras, C., Koutras, G., Leymann, F., Mitschang, B., Nikolaou, C., Siafakas, N., Strauch, S., Tzanakis, N., Wieland, M.: An integrated mHealth solution for enhancing patients' health online. In: Lacković, I., Vasic, D. (eds.) MBEC 2014. IFMBE, vol. 45, pp. 695–698. Springer, Cham (2015). doi:10.1007/978-3-319-11128-5_173
13. Hardinge, M., et al.: Using a mobile health application to support self-management in chronic obstructive pulmonary disease: a six-month cohort study. BioMed Central Med. Inf. Decis. Making **15**, 46 (2015)
14. Quinn, C.C., et al.: WellDoc TM mobile diabetes management randomized controlled trial: change in clinical and behavioral outcomes and patient and physician satisfaction. Diabetes Technol. Ther. **10**(3), 160–168 (2008)
15. Klonoff, D.C.: The current status of mHealth for diabetes: will it be the next big thing? J. Diabetes Sci. Technol. **7**(3), 749–758 (2013)
16. Smith, K., et al.: Apple apps for the management of pediatric pain and pain-related stress. Clin. Pract. Pediatr. Psychol. **3**(2), 93–107 (2015)
17. Cafazzo, J.A., et al.: Design of an mHealth app for the self-management of adolescent type 1 diabetes: a pilot study. J. Med. Internet Res. **14**(3), e70 (2012)
18. Cho, J.: The impact of post-adoption beliefs on the continued use of health apps. Int. J. Med. Informatics **87**, 75–83 (2016)
19. Hoque, M.R., Karim, M.R., Amin, M.B.: Factors affecting the adiotion of mHealth services among young citizen: a structural equation modeling (SEM) approach. Asian Bus. Rev. **5**(11), 60–65 (2015)
20. Rai, A., et al.: Understanding determinants of consumer mobile health usage intentions, assimilation, and channel preferences. J. Med. Internet Res. **15**(8), e149 (2013)
21. Deng, Z., Mo, X., Liu, S.: Comparison of the middle-aged and older users' adoption of mobile health services in China. Int. J. Med. Informatics **83**(3), 210–224 (2014)
22. Yuan, S., et al.: Keep using my healt apps: Discover users' perception of health and fitness apps with the UTAUT2 model. Telemedicine e-health **21**(9), 735–741 (2015)
23. Gagnon, M.P., Ngangue, P., Payne-Gagnon, J., Desmartis, M.: m-Health adoption by healthcare professionals: a systematic review. J. Am. Med. Inform. Assoc. **23**(1), 212–220 (2015)
24. Venkatesh, V., et al.: User acceptance of information technology: toward a unified view. MIS Q. **27**, 425–478 (2003)

25. Williams, M.D., et al.: Is UTAUT really used or just cited for the sake of it? A systematic review of citations of UTAUT's originating article. In: European Conference on Information systems (2011)
26. Venkatesh, V., Thong, J.Y., Xu, X.: Consumer acceptance and use of information technology: extending the unified theory of acceptance and use of technology. MIS Q. **36**, 157–178 (2012)
27. The Neilsen Company. Comsumers are sweet on mobile apps. www.Nielsen.com, http://www.nielsen.com/us/en/insights/news/2014/tech-or-treat-consumers-are-sweet-on-mobile-apps.html, Accessed 30 Oct 2014
28. Yang, Z., Peterson, R.T.: Customer perceived value, satisfaction, and loyalty: the role of switching costs. Psychol. Mark. **21**(10), 799–822 (2004)
29. Gaudeul, A.: Software marketing on the Internet: the use of samples and repositories. Econ. Innov. New Technol. **19**(3), 259–281 (2010)
30. Plante, T.B., et al.: Validation of the instant blood pressure smartphone app. J. Am. Med. Assoc. Internal Med. **176**(5), 700–702 (2016)
31. Bandura, A.: Health promotion from the perspective of social cognitive theory. Psychol. Health **13**, 623–649 (1998)

Embedding the Social Features into E-learning System: A Review

Yingying Ying, Qiqi Jiang$^{(\boxtimes)}$, and Hongwei Wang

School of Economics and Management, Tongji University, Shanghai, China
{1250035yyy,jiangqq,hwwang}@tongji.edu.cn

Abstract. E-learning has received considerable attentions in both universities and enterprises. However, a few related studies have advocated the benefits of social features as an important factor of E-learning but have not explored much further. In this work, we utilize social support theory to argue that embedding the social features into e-learning system is necessary and appropriate. Collectively, potential direction of e-learning has been simple summarized from theoretical and practical prospect. We hope our reviews on current literatures can benefit both scholars and practitioners.

Keywords: E-learning · Collaborative learning · Social support

1 Introduction

With the emergence of internet and explosive growth of knowledge, more and more people would like to use online tools or resources for further learning and knowledge sharing, one of these areas is known as E-learning. E-learning system refers to a web-based system that users or learners can obtain information or knowledge through digital activities [1]. A good example of this is MOOC (massive open online courses). This new tool has changed the way people learn, work and live. In this regard, E-learning system has been widely adopted by both universities and enterprises. An E-learning Market Trends & Forecast report made by Docebo, predicted that worldwide E-learning market will reach 51.5 billion of dollars by 2016 [2]. In particular, the enterprises are found as the largest customers for the E-learning systems in order to train or continue educating their staff. According to the report published by ASTD on 2016, 95% U.S. enterprises with more than 500 employees use e-learning system for staff training, with the highest amount being spent on information technology (IT) training.

Differing from traditional face-to-face learning approach, E-learning is characterized by several advantages, such as convenience, efficiency, and site openness [3, 4]. For example, staff can seamlessly learn and receive education by using electronic systems. Nowadays, with the fast development of web 2.0, more and more social features, such as social bookmarking or feedback mechanism, are considered in designing an e-learning system. Such findings sufficiently indicate that e-learning system has been shifted from a conventional web-based system to an IT artifact featured with dynamic and interactive features, namely, a collaborative learning system.

F.F.-H. Nah and C.-H. Tan (Eds.): HCIBGO 2017, Part I, LNCS 10293, pp. 257–265, 2017.
DOI: 10.1007/978-3-319-58481-2_20

Collaborative learning denotes a learning approach that students and teachers collaborate to accomplish a specific learning goal in order to promote learning outcomes, which emphasizes the teamwork and more proactive participation. Considerable works have proved the significance of collaborative learning [5] from various perspectives. For instance, by employing cognitive psychology, cooperative learning and social practice theory, Stahl [6] conceptualized a collaborative learning model with the combination of personal knowledge and social knowledge construction. Besides, Coll [7] and his colleagues (2014) emphasized that teacher's participation could improve learning outcomes when students engaged in online collaborative learning. In summary, collaborative learning can be more benefit to construction of knowledge and more efficient for learning.

In the studies of collaborative learning, interaction has been widely proved as a positive factor, which can be understood by the social support theory. As we know, learning is a process with the involvement of human factors and personal interactions [8]. People need social interaction to satisfy their social needs for support, and this psychology need can be reflected in the E-learning activity. For instance, by investigating 200 students' Facebook profiles, Bosch [9] investigated the role of social factors in community-based learning, where the users are found to like sharing and discussing with their friends. Detailed argument will be introduced in Sect. 3 subsequently.

For the remainder of this study, a literature review on E-learning is given. Next, we introduce social support theory to argue that embedding social features into E-learning is necessary. Finally, the future prospect and conclusion are presented.

2 Literature Reviews

Rather than a simple combination of Internet and learning materials, E-learning denotes "an environment in which the learners' interaction with learning materials, and/or instructors are mediated through advanced information technology" ([10], p. 2). In the past decades, many scholars from psychology, computer science and information system disciplines have identified the factors relating to E-learning systems. Among them, evaluating E-learning is an essential work. In order to enable managers to achieve optimum investment and allow learners to learn efficiency [11], several approaches have been introduced to evaluate the effectiveness of E-learning. A typical method for evaluating the e-learning system is the AHP (Analytical Hierarchy Process) method. For example, by conducting AHP methods' basic theory, Chen and Yang [12] established a set of indexes used to evaluating the intelligence of online learning system. Then, they used AHP to determine the weight of each index. Similar method has been used in Colace [13] and Alice [14] work. In addition, Matsatsinis et al. [15] argued that the evaluation process completely depends on the users' judgment. Thus, they applied Linear Programming (LP) for measuring satisfaction indexes and determining the weights of criteria. Besides, other scholars utilized different methods [16–18] to present an evaluation framework with multi-criteria design. We summarized the most significant criteria used in the evaluation of E-learning performance in Table 1 below. As we can see, most indexes focus on the technology aspect. However, the

Table 1. Summary of the significant criteria in E-learning evaluation

Author	Main criteria	Focus
Zhang et al. (2010) [19]	Usability, Response time, Interactivity, Accessibility, Security	Establishing the hierarchical structural model in order to assess the affecting factors of e-learning adoption in China
Munkhtsetseg et al. (2014) [20]	Usability, Accessibility, Stability	Identifying 13 criteria which can be divided into 4 groups. Then, AHP, as a technique, was used to evaluate open-source e-learning systems and edunet system
Shee and Wang (2008) [21]	Usability, Web and course design, Accessibility, Stability	Comparing and evaluating the user behaviors between pre-adoption and post-adoption of e-learning systems
Bhuasiri et al. (2012) [22]	Usability, Response time, Interactivity, Accessibility, Reliability, Functionality	Utilizing the AHP method to explore the key affecting factors of e-learning system in developing countries, and comparing the crucial success factors between experts and faculty
Jie (2010) [23]	Response time, Interactivity, Web and course design, Accessibility, Reliability	Evaluating the online course quality and considering more about factors like course content and system design
Hwang (2004) [24]	Usability, Functionality, Web and course design, Reliability, Security, Functionality	Proposing a combined group-decision method which includes AHP, fuzzy theory, and group decision method for evaluating educational website
Lo et al. (2011) [25]	Usability, Response time, Interactivity, Functionality, Stability	Identifying the crucial factors regarding to the successful implementation of customized e-learning system
Wang and Lin (2012) [26]	Functionality, Stability	Examining the interactive learning process from an integrated approach composed of fuzzy AHP and AR (associate rule)
Cobo et al. (2014) [43]	Interactivity	Developing a new model combined the AHP and data mining to evaluate the students' interactivity on online learning systems
Büyüközkan et al. (2010) [44]	Security, Web & Course design, Interactivity	Proposing a fuzzy TOPSIS (Technique for Order of Preference by Similarity to Ideal Solution) methodology which based on the axiomatic design method, then it has been used to analyze the quality of e-learning systems

(*continued*)

Table 1. (*continued*)

Author	Main criteria	Focus
Alptekin and Karsak (2011) [46]	Usability, Cost-Effectiveness	Presenting an e-learning evaluation/selection framework which includes QFD (Quality Function Development), fuzzy linear regression and optimization
Jeong and Yeo (2014) [47]	Usability, response-time	Identifying nine major criteria and establishing a quality model in accordance with multimedia factors. After that, adopting pairwise comparison approach to evaluate the model

human factor is the key role in the whole learning process. Thus, researchers gradually reshaped the view from advanced technology to human behavior.

As opposed to understanding e-learning from technological perspective [27, 28], more and more researchers interest in investigating factors that drive a successful E-learning from behavior perspective. For instance, Selim [29] proved that teacher characteristics (attitude and control techniques, teaching style), student characteristics (computer skills, interactive cooperation, e-learning content and design), technology (Easy access and infrastructure) and support served as determinant variables influencing the effectiveness of E-learning system. Besides, the learner's loyalty was found as another determinant influencing users' behaviors in Chiu's work [30]. In addition, Rodriguez-Ardura et al. [31] constructed a comprehensive model to explore the role of interactional features impacting learning outcomes. The result showed that interactivity was positively related to learner's response, but such effect was mediated by imagery, spatial and co-presence, and flow. Moreover, in order to understand the human psychological factors in e-learning systems, Eligio et al. [32] argued that emotion understanding could facilitate the effectiveness of online learning. Except technology, the factors affecting e-learning satisfaction proposed by previous scholars can be concluded into the following five dimensions, including learner dimension, teacher dimension, course dimension, design dimension and environment dimension.

In summary, existing researches largely focus on e-learning system design from following perspectives: E-learning effectiveness evaluation, affecting factors, instructional programming and other technological issues, and course design etc. A few related studies have advocated the benefits of social features as an important factor of collaborative learning but have not explored much further. With this in mind, in order to increase the successful rate of online learning implementations, these social features deserved attention from management and system designers. This work can be replenishment for this.

3 Social Support

E-learning is an adaptive learning activity relates to the interaction between users, the user interactivity has been proved as one of the most essential features in previous studies [33, 34]. Traditional E-learning system essentially neglects these social factors, which can no longer satisfy the needs of learner. Interactive system, which is based on the collaborative learning, is the emergence pattern. Current E-learning systems provide basic collaborative learning, learner can discuss with other students or teachers when they have questions. However, this interaction is deficient, the complex interaction activity still can't be achieved. The existing problems are concluded as follow:

- Lack of participation.
- Lack of specificity.
- Inconvenient to Knowledge sharing.

With the rapid development of social media, aggregating several Web 2.0 tools (et al. wiki, blog, and media sharing tools) and integrating the social features into e-learning systems can solve the above problems, which can be supported by social support theory. Social support refers to a perception that people feel about being responded to friends in their supportive social network. It builds a well-established foundation for understanding the social behavior of individual. Currently, online community has been found as a powerful channel for users to enhance their well-being [38–40]. In other words, more and more people will hang out on online communities to search warmth or belonging in order to satisfy their social needs. Compared to face-to-face communication, online social activities are more conductive to individual's social support [42]. Generally, online social support is virtual and intangible [45], which can mainly divide into information support and emotional support [35]. Information support refers to providing useful messages and advice during the learning process. Emotional support refers to giving emotional concerns such as understanding, caring and stimulating.

Since social support on the online learning activity is intangible in nature and is often relied-on interaction between users, the role of social factor in the practical application of collaborative learning systems is gaining much interest from recent scholars. For instance, Chatti and his colleagues (2007) [51] argued that web 2.0 technologies can help contribute to knowledge sharing and learning performance, and presented a social software which can benefit to online knowledge/learning management. Besides, Johnson [48] added the factor "social presence" into e-learning environment and found that social presence relating to satisfaction and interaction had a positive impact on performance and satisfaction. In addition, Yujong Hwang [49] introduced "social influence" concept in exploring the shaping attitudes toward knowledge sharing through email in online learning context, and the result indicated that all social influence factors are found to positive influence users' sharing attitude.

The role of social support in collaborative learning system can be described as follow. Since social support could enable individual obtain warmth and care, as a feedback, it would be natural for learners to collaborate and share information. Knowledge sharing is an important construct in e-learning context, on which incorporating social features [10, p. 2], [36, 50]. E-learners are interested in interacting with their friends such as sharing learning experiences or consulting learning questions in their learning process, through which their relationship can be enhanced. Learners' intentions to share knowledge in the online community often influence the success of E-learning systems [37]. In brief, E-learners are more willing to use the system that with a well social support [41]. Thus, the frequency interactivity may further increase the motivation to continue online learning, which in turn decides the outcomes of E-learning system.

In line with the above understandings, we believed that social support could be treated as an important theory in understanding the collaborative learning in current information system (IS) research. Therefore, considering more social factors in designing and exploring E-learning system is in accord with social support theory.

4   Conclusion

Collectively, the topics of E-learning have been received considerable attentions. Given the importance of social factors in online collaborative learning, this work explained that the social support theory helps contribute to a better online learning outcome. We hope our reviews on current literatures can benefit both scholars and practitioners. From the theoretical perspective, the feature of interactivity should be conceptualized into the emerging model of e-learning research. Besides, some scholars proceed from a social theory perspective with a more cross-cultural, Interdisciplinary engaged look at E-learning. Moreover, other factors like cognitive psychology, personalization and intelligent features, would have potential contribution to further shape the design of e-learning artifact. From the practical perspective, emerging services that can integrate face-to-face learning and online learning will be adoptive to increasing the learning effectiveness. In addition, aggregating e-learning features into mobile devices will be a crucial application in future.

Acknowledgement. The work was fully supported by the following grants: the National Nature Science Foundation of China (NSFC 71532015 and NSFC 71371144), the Program for Youth Excellent Talents in Tongji University (2014KJ002), the Innovation Program of Shanghai Municipal Education Commission (15CG20), the Shanghai Pujiang Program (16PJC086), and the Education Reformation Project of Tongji University.

References

1. Sloman, M.: The e-learning revolution from propositions to action. 1st edn. Charted Institute of Personnel and Development (2001)
2. Docebo. E-learning Market Trends & Forecast 2014–2016 report (2014)
3. Katz, Y.J.: Attitudes affecting college students' preferences for distance learning. J. Comput. Assist. Learn. **18**(1), 2–9 (2002)
4. Huang, H.: E-learning leading to public, lifelong and international education. J. Suzhou Univ. (2008)

5. Rohrbeck, C.A., Ginsburg-Block, M.D., Fantuzzo, J.W., et al.: Peer-assisted learning interventions with elementary school students: a meta-analytic review. J. Educ. Psychol. **95** (2), 240 (2003)
6. Stahl, G.: Group cognition: computer support for building collaborative knowledge (acting with technology) (2006)
7. Coll, C., Rochera, M.J., Gispert, I.D.: Supporting online collaborative learning in small groups: teacher feedback on learning content, academic task and social participation. Comput. Educ. **75**, 53–64 (2014)
8. Wenger, E.: Communities of Practice: Learning, Meaning, and Identity. Cambridge university press (1999)
9. Bosch, T.E.: Using online social networking for teaching and learning: facebook use at the University of Cape Town. Communicatio: South African J. Commun. Theor. Res. **35**(2), 185–200 (2009)
10. Alavi, M., Leidner, D.E.: Review: Knowledge management and knowledge management systems: conceptual foundations and research issues. MIS Q. **25**(1), 107–136 (2001)
11. Roffe, I.: E-learning: engagement, enhancement and execution. Qual. Assur. Educ. **10**(1), 40–50 (2002)
12. Chen, Y., Yang, M.: Study and construct online self-learning evaluation system model based on AHP method. In: IEEE International Conference on Information and Financial Engineering, pp. 54–58. IEEE (2010)
13. Colace, F., De Santo, M., Pietrosanto, A.: Evaluation models for E-learning platform: an AHP approach. Frontiers in Education Conference, pp. 1–6. IEEE (2006)
14. Alice, P.S., Abirami, A.M., Askarunisa, A.: A semantic based approach to organize eLearning through efficient information retrieval for interview preparation. In: International Conference on Recent Trends in Information Technology, pp. 151–156. IEEE (2012)
15. Matsatsinis, N.F., Grigoroudis, E., Delias, P.: User satisfaction and e-learning systems: towards a multi-criteria evaluation methodology. Oper. Res. **3**(3), 249–259 (2003)
16. Tzeng, G.H., Chiang, C.H., Li, C.W.: Evaluating intertwined effects in E-learning programs: a novel hybrid MCDM model based on factor analysis and DEMATEL. Expert Syst. Appl. Int. J. **32**(4), 1028–1044 (2007)
17. Kurilovas, E., Serikoviene, S.: New MCEQLS TFN method for evaluating quality and reusability of learning objects. Technol. Econ. Dev. Econ. **19**(4), 706–723 (2013)
18. Yuen, K.K.F.: A multiple criteria decision making approach for E-learning platform selection: the Primitive Cognitive Network Process. In: Computing, Communications and Applications Conference, pp. 294–298. IEEE (2012)
19. Zhang, L., Wen, H., Li, D., et al.: E-learning adoption intention and its key influence factors based on innovation adoption theory. Math. Comput. Modell. Int. J. **51**(11–12), 1428–1432 (2010)
20. Munkhtsetseg, N., Garmaa, D., Uyanga, S.: Multi-criteria comparative evaluation of the E-learning systems: a case study. In: International Conference on Ubi-Media Computing and Workshops, pp. 190–195. IEEE (2014)
21. Shee, D.Y., Wang, Y.S.: Multi-criteria evaluation of the web-based E-learning system: a methodology based on learner satisfaction and its applications. Comput. Educ. **50**(3), 894–905 (2008)
22. Bhuasiri, W., Xaymoungkhoun, O., Zo, H., et al.: Critical success factors for E-learning in developing countries: a comparative analysis between ICT experts and faculty. Comput. Educ. **58**(2), 843–855 (2012)
23. Jie, C.: Evaluation and modeling of online course using fuzzy AHP. In: International Conference on Computer and Information Application, pp. 232–235. IEEE (2010)

24. Hwang, G.J., Huang, T.C.K., Tseng, J.C.R.: A group-decision approach for evaluating educational web sites. Comput. Educ. **42**(1), 65–86 (2004)
25. Ta-Sheng, L.O., Chang, T.H., Shieh, L.F., et al.: Key factors for efficiently implementing customized E-learning system in the service industry. Syst. Sci. Syst. Eng. **20**(3), 346–364 (2011)
26. Wang, C.S., Lin, S.L.: Combining Fuzzy AHP and Association Rule to Evaluate the Activity Processes of E-learning System (2012)
27. Carr, N.G.: IT doesn't matter. Harvard Bus. Rev., 41–49 (2003)
28. Piccoli, G., Ahmad, R., Ives, B.: Web-based virtual learning environments: a research framework and a preliminary assessment of effectiveness in basic IT skills training. MIS Q. **25**(4), 401–426 (2001)
29. Selim, H.M.: Critical success factors for E-learning acceptance: confirmatory factor models. Comput. Educ. **49**(2), 396–413 (2007)
30. Chiu, C.M., Wang, E.T.G.: Understanding web-based learning continuance intention: the role of subjective task value. Inf. Manag. **45**(3), 194–201 (2008)
31. Rodríguez-Ardura, I., Meseguer-Artola, A.: E-learning continuance: the impact of interactivity and the mediating role of imagery, presence and flow. Inf. Manag. (2015)
32. Eligio, U.X., Ainsworth, S.E., Crook, C.K.: Emotion understanding and performance during computer-supported collaboration. Comput. Hum. Behav. **28**(6), 2046–2054 (2012)
33. Lee, S.H., Choi, J., Park, J.I.: Interactive E-learning system using pattern recognition and augmented reality. IEEE Trans. Consum. Electron. **55**(2), 883–890 (2009)
34. Liaw, S.S., Huang, H.M.: Perceived satisfaction, perceived usefulness and interactive learning environments as predictors to self-regulation in E-learning environments. Comput. Educ. **60**(1), 14–24 (2013)
35. Madjar, N.: Emotional and informational support from different sources and employee creativity. J. Occup. Organ. Psychol. **81**(1), 83–100 (2008)
36. Chiu, C.M., Hsu, M.H., Wang, E.T.G.: Understanding knowledge sharing in virtual communities: an integration of social capital and social cognitive theories. Decis. Support Syst. **42**(3), 1872–1888 (2006)
37. Malhotra, Y., Galletta, D.F.: Role of commitment and motivation in knowledge management systems implementation: theory, conceptualization, and measurement of antecedents of success. In: Hawaii International Conference on System Sciences, p. 10. IEEE (2003)
38. Obst, P., Stafurik, J.: Online we are all able bodied: Online psychological sense of community and social support found through membership of disability-specific websites promotes well-being for people living with a physical disability. J. Community Appl. Soc. Psychol. **20**(6), 525–531 (2010)
39. Shaw, L.H., Gant, L.M.: In defense of the internet: the relationship between Internet communication and depression, loneliness, self-esteem, and perceived social support. Cyberpsychology Behav. **5**(2), 157–171 (2002)
40. Xie, B.: Multimodal computer-mediated communication and social support among Older Chinese Internet Users. J. Comput.-Mediated Commun. **13**(3), 728–750 (2008)
41. Laurenceau, J.P., Barrett, L.F., Pietromonaco, P.R.: Intimacy as an interpersonal process: the importance of self-disclosure, partner disclosure, and perceived partner responsiveness in interpersonal exchanges. J. Pers. Soc. Psychol. **74**(5), 1238–1251 (1998)
42. Walther, J.B., Parks, M.R.: Cues filtered out, cues filtered In: Computer-Mediated Communication and Relationships. Handbook of Interpersonal Communication. Sage, Thousand Oaks (2002)
43. Cobo, A., Rocha, R., Rodríguezhoyos, C.: Evaluation of the interactivity of students in virtual learning environments using a multicriteria approach and data mining. Behav. Inf. Technol. **33**(10), 1000–1012 (2014)

44. Büyüközkan, G., Arsenyan, J., Ertek, G.: Evaluation of E-learning web sites using fuzzy axiomatic design based approach. Int. J. Comput. Intell. Syst. **34100**(1), 4–6 (2010)

45. Coulson, N.S., Buchanan, H., Aubeeluck, A.: Social support in cyberspace: a content analysis of communication within a Huntington's disease online support group. Patient Educ. Couns. **68**(2), 173–178 (2007)

46. Alptekin, S.E., Karsak, E.E.: An integrated decision framework for evaluating and selecting E-learning products. Appl. Soft Comput. **11**(3), 2990–2998 (2011)

47. Jeong, H.Y., Yeo, S.S.: The quality model for E-learning system with multimedia contents: a pairwise comparison approach. Multimedia Tools Appl. **73**(2), 887–900 (2014)

48. Johnson, R.D., Hornik, S., Salas, E.: An empirical examination of factors contributing to the creation of successful E-learning environments. Int. J. Hum. Comput. Stud. **66**(5), 356–369 (2008)

49. Hwang, Y.: Understanding social influence theory and personal goals in E-learning. Inf. Dev. **32**(3) (2016)

50. Powell, A., Galvin, J., Piccoli, G.: Antecedents to team member commitment from near and far: a comparison between collocated and virtual teams **19**(4), 299–322 (2006)

51. Chatti, M.A., Jarke, M., Froschwilke, D.: The future of E-learning: a shift to knowledge networking and social software. Int. J. Knowl. Learn. **3**(4), 404–420 (2007)

Learning as Adventure: An App Designed with Gamification Elements to Facilitate Language Learning

Leijing Zhou[1,2(✉)], Jie Yu[3], Chun'an Liao[2], and Yan Shi[4]

[1] International Doctoral Innovation Centre, University of Nottingham Ningbo China,
Ningbo 315100, China
leijing013@126.com
[2] Zhejiang University, Ningbo 315048, China
[3] University of Nottingham, Ningbo 315100, China
[4] School of Media and Design, Hangzhou Dianzi University, Hangzhou 310018, China

Abstract. The increasing spread of mobile technologies provides educators and developers with more opportunities for creating a wider range of education tools. In this paper we propose a game-based language learning system called ADVENTURE to improve the learners' skills for language learning and self-motivation to learn. Firstly we introduce a focus group conducted to understand learners' needs and language learning behavior, then we review some of the background research works in the field of gamification and language learning. Following the research finding and user study, the paper presents the design and development of ADVENTURE which creates immersive experience for language learners. The application adds not only the gamification elements included game mechanism and the aesthetics but also the elements in the process of learning. The final output reaches the target of improving the learning efficiency and interesting the progress of learning.

Keywords: Gamification elements · Language learning · Motivation · Mobile application design

1 Introduction

In the context of language learning learners tend to increasingly rely on independent, individual study—instead of taking conventional classes and have face to face oral practice. Learners do not have enough opportunities and appropriate situations to communicate in the second language. This paper introduces a gamified mobile learning tool in order to address this issue.

The development and usage of mobile apps for language learning has become increasingly popular in recent years [1]. Mobile apps have the advantages of providing new opportunities for visualizing learning material, allowing rapid feedback to learner's task, which enhance traditional teaching and learning process.

© Springer International Publishing AG 2017
F.F.-H. Nah and C.-H. Tan (Eds.): HCIBGO 2017, Part I, LNCS 10293, pp. 266–275, 2017.
DOI: 10.1007/978-3-319-58481-2_21

By reviewing research on gamification and learning strategy, we get design inspirations. The concepts explored from the game world is helpful for visualizing and distributing language learning materials and tasks in a motivational and effective manner. The aim is to increase motivation through the integration of gamification elements and learning.

Following this direction, we proposes ADVENTURE as a gamified learning application for second language acquisition. The application adds not only the gamification elements included game mechanism and the aesthetics but also the elements in the process of learning.

The main intension is to make independent learning more interesting, improve learning efficiency and effectiveness, and strengthen learning outcomes. In short, we seek to satisfy learners' language learning needs.

2   Identifying Learners' Needs

At the beginning of design process, we would like to have some general information about learners' needs and current products. A focus group was conducted with fifteen Chinese participants who were willing to self-learn English as a second language by using mobile learning tools. The participants were selected with both experience in using mobile English learning applications and playing various games. The aim of the focus group is to understand potential users' learning motivations, current products and in the consumer market and potential users' gaming behaviors. These are the set of subjective questions.

2.1   Learning Motivations

What's your aim and objective for learning English? Which language level are you at? How do you use the current mobile learning aid products? Are you satisfied with them?

The result shows more than half (60%) of the interviewees are learning English as a second language for specific time-limited goals, such as preparing for examinations or applying to study abroad. While 40% users left are learning second language just for personal interests. They have a long-term and on-going learning manner and believe mastering a second language will be beneficial in the future though there are no direct benefits for them right now. Their time schedule is quite flexible. For the users who have definite goals, the learning content is decided by the exact examination type e.g. TOEFL or IELTS. For the other users who have more flexible plan, they focus on strengthening practical language skills such as listening and speaking.

2.2   Market Landscape

What kind of apps have you used for language learning and why? Are they effective? If there is room for improvement, what features of products do you expect?

The language learning mobile applications on the current market can be divided into three categories: 1. Full-range app covers all dimensions of language learning aspects including listening, speaking, reading, writing and translating, e.g. VOA English; 2.

Particular-focus app concentrates on one specific aspect of language learning such as apps for vocabulary increase or grammar acquisition; 3. Play-and-learn app motivates users through singing songs or dubbing as native speakers for English movies. The examples in this category are Mofunshow, Sing English and etc.

2.3 Gaming Behaviors

What kind of games are you playing and why? Can you give an example? What are the elements in game attracting you?

Most of the respondents are keen on Role-playing games (RPG), online multiplayer games (MMO) and Adventure game (AVG), which are the main types of mobile games. People play games for various purposes, they seek for excitement, enjoy exploring in adventure, build social networking in virtual world and etc.

2.4 Summary

Regardless the growing trend of using apps for language learning, the great majority of learning tools still focus on individual vocabulary or grammar learning which do not enable learners to effectively communicate with others in the target language. Instead we should take advantage of the communication capabilities mobile devices provide its users with. The fragmented knowledge such as vocabulary and grammar need to be complemented by other skills such as interaction.

3 Gamification Theory

3.1 Gamification

Although games are originally designed to serve fun and entertainment, since they can motivate learners to engage with them with unparalleled intensity and duration, game elements have the capacity to make other non-game products and services more enjoyable and engaging [2]. Recent years have witness a fast expansion of consumer applications in various contexts that takes inspirations from games. This phenomena can be summarized as "gamification".

Industry has tried to describe "gamification" practically in terms of client benefits. Helgason, CEO of Unity Technologies (the company produces one of the most popular game engines Unity) described gamification as *"the adoption of game technology and game design methods outside of the games industry"* [3]. Zicherman presented in Gamification Summit about *"the process of using game thinking and game mechanics to solve problems and engage users"* [4]. Another famous game company Bunchball defines it as *"integrating game dynamics into your site, service, community, content or campaign, in order to drive participation"* [5]. In order to define the term for research use, Deterding examined the gamified applications and then described *"gamification"* as *"the use of game design elements in non-game contexts"* [6].

3.2 Gamification Elements

Deterding also suggests narrowing *"gamification"* to the description of *"gamification elements"* characteristic to games [6]. The elements should be found in most but not necessarily all games, and play a significant role in gameplay. This definition is quite blurred, which directly leads to the questions: what is *"characteristic"* for games? Which elements can be categorized into the list of *"gamification elements"*?

Obviously not only visible, easily distinguishable elements such as point and avatars are gamification elements, but also more fundamental game structure and mechanics. In the research field of game, there are already some similar, competing and overlapping definitions of gamification elements. MDA model is a formal game framework consisted with game mechanics, game dynamics and aesthetics [7]. The MDA model suggests that designers work with mechanics to create aesthetics, whereas players experience aesthetics, and in so doing, infer knowledge about mechanics [7]. It identifies mechanics as game elements on the technical level, dynamics as interaction with the player, and aesthetics as the desired player experience triggered by mechanics and dynamics. Based on MDA model, *"game design atoms"* was further identified by Brathwaite and Schreiber [8]: game state, game view, player representation, game rule system, game dynamics, goals, and game theme.

Haimari and Koivisto proposed nine dimensions of a gamified environment [9]: Challenge-skill balance, clear goals, control, feedback, experience, loss of self-consciousness, time transformation, concentration, and merging action awareness. These nine dimensions represent outcomes of gamification.

Reeves and Read listed the *"Ten Ingredients of Great Games"* as [10]: Self-representation with avatars; three-dimensional environments; narrative context; feedback and behavior reinforcement; reputations such as ranks and levels; marketplaces and economies; competition under rules; teams; parallel communication systems that can be easily configured; time pressure.

Some research looks at game structures. According to Prensky there are six elements of game structure [11]: Rules, Goals and Objectives, Outcomes and Feedback, Conflict/ Competition/Challenge/Opposition, Interaction, Representation or Story.

3.3 Gamification in Education

These definitions and lists above allows defining what specific elements that gamification cover and inspires us to make use of them for designing in education context. Garris believed that games have multiple advantages such as enabling knowledge acquisition, increasing learners' motivation, encouraging analysis, synthesis and evaluation of concepts [12]. Game-based learning refers to the process and practice of learning through games [13]. The use of gamification elements combines both fun and entertainment with educational purposes [14]. The integration of gamification elements can leverage people's natural desire for mastery, achievement, etc. Lawley values the complexity of a well-designed games, he argues that reducing the surface elements such as interface characteristics and game dynamics falls short of engaging students and can even damage users' emotions and engagement [15]. With so many research and literature at place, though few studies are conducted in the area of language learning to explore such new opportunities.

4 Learning Theory and Strategy

Although vocabulary input and grammar knowledge is a primary learning task during the early stages of language learning process, learners still require consistent, meaningful language interaction. The focus should be more on learning to use the language as a supporter for effective communication rather than the vocabulary or grammar alone [16]. Flipped Learning Approaches [17] place the emphasis on actively working through challenges, which is interacting and communicating with the second language in real situations instead of decontextualized learning. Some theories of language learning put emphasis mainly on enabling learners to communicate effectively in the second language [18]. Beth Kemp Benson describes Scaffolded learning [20] as framing, guiding, and supporting learners by organizing information into categories in order to focus attention. She believes it can eliminate the learning problem at the beginning and allow learners to restart whenever they gets stuck. It is noted that learners are not given enough opportunities to practice in the second language, which is essential to successful language acquisition [19].

5 App Design

Upon reviewing the available literature about gamification theory and learning strategies, we propose ADVENTURE as a gamified learning application for second language learning. The setting of the application take reference of AVG and RPG, which lets the learner play the main role in an adventure story. In order to support the learning process, this game based application creates an attractive storyline with mystery, user-friendly game environment and immersive and appropriate visual effects. Some featured dynamics and concepts found in game design are applied to this learning context, these are:

5.1 Storytelling by the Learner

Most games employ some type of story. Kapp notes that *"people learn facts better when the facts are embedded in a story rather than in a bulleted list"* [21]. Storytelling by the learner instead of by the system is featured in ADVENTURE. Once the game starts, the learner will play the main character in an adventure story and try to overcome the challenges step by step with the enhancement of language acquisition in order to complete and reveal the mysterious adventure story. The learner can get hints from the images and some random words generated by the application. A handy digital dictionary is always available (Fig. 1).

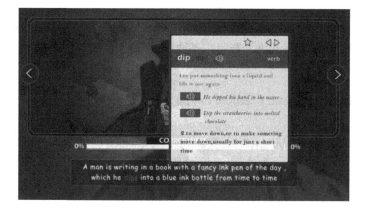

Fig. 1. The learner writes the narratives with a digital dictionary

It is the learner write and speak the narratives of the story himself. The experience created by the application is like acting in a movie and exploring in an adventure.

The gamification elements: challenge, curiosity and achievement are used to motivate learner to follow the storyline in ADVENTURE and gradually improve his or her language skills simultaneously. In this game-based learning tool, learners don't simply watch and memorize what the application has placed before them, they need to interact in second language to make things happen. Their learning effort decides how the story goes.

5.2 Progression

Progression is applied throughout ADVENTURE in the form of levels and missions. As shown below, the virtual credits are used as rewards for the learner to achieve each fragment of the adventure story. With more fragments unlocked, the result of the mysterious adventure story is being revealed (Fig. 2).

Fig. 2. Levels and missions in the app

Once all the levels are completed, a movie will be played as a final reward for the learner, in which the narratives are created by the learner. Here visualization is an effective way of sharing results as graphical representations, which create immersive experience for the learner.

5.3 Rapid Feedback and Freedom to Fail

In the adventure story set by this application, the learner has to interlink the images from the story with some meaningful words and phrases, which enhances his reading skills and broadens his vocabulary. A correctness bar is used to indicate whether the learner is using the appropriate words and correct grammar to describe a scene in the story (Fig. 3).

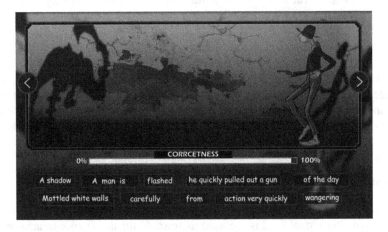

Fig. 3. The learner gets feedback from the correctness bar

In order to practice speaking skills, ADVENTURE requires learners to rehearse the narratives, which is like an actor read lines in a movie. The learner can also retry speaking the narratives as many times as he or she wants. The system examines learner's pronunciation and provide rapid feedback for correction afterwards (Fig. 4).

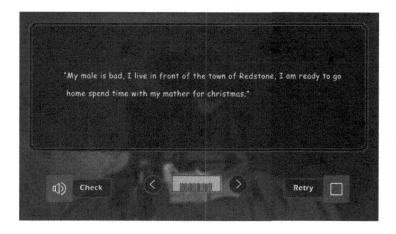

Fig. 4. The learner speaks the narratives

The rapid response and freedom to fail help learners to explore content, gain language skills through playing with the words.

5.4 Information Retrieve

According to the memory theory, people rehearsal the information in short term memory storage in order to transform it to long term memory, which is the knowledge and skills acquisition process. ADVENTURE provides learners with opportunities to retrieve the history data. The information including texts, images, audios and scenes are organized in timeline so that learners can always go back to revise and find the hints for exploration in this adventure story (Fig. 5).

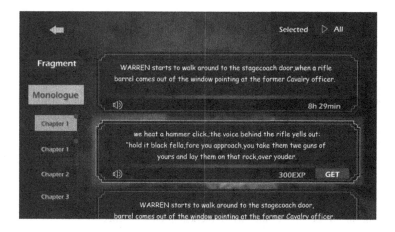

Fig. 5. The learner retrieves history data

By designing this application using gamification elements that not only delivers multimedia learning practice but also need learners to apply their language skills to contextual communication tasks.

6   Conclusions

In this paper, we present ADVENTURE as a gamified learning application for language learning. The application adds not only the gamification elements included game mechanism and the aesthetics but also the elements in the process of learning. The final output reaches the target of improving the learning efficiency and interesting the progress of learning. The results of the work contribute to evidence that gamification theory has the potential to engage users, and be useful in facilitating a language learning experience.

As future work we aim to make a user test to understand how the gamification elements facilitate the learning process for language learning. Some relevant data should be collected including pre-test and post-test results as well as learners' feedback on the learning experience. This way we will be able to draw stronger conclusions on how gamification used in mobile technologies may influence learners' behavior and learning outcomes when they are using ADVENTURE in the target language.

Acknowledgment. This work was carried out at the International Doctoral Innovation Centre (IDIC). The authors acknowledge the financial support from Ningbo Education Bureau, Ningbo Science and Technology Bureau, China's MOST and The University of Nottingham. The work is also partially supported by EPSRC grant no EP/L015463/1 and the Zhejiang Provincial Natural Science Foundation of China (Grant No. LQ14E050010), and the Social Science and Humanity on Young Fund of the Ministry of Education (Grant No. 16YJC760047).

References

1. Godwin-Jones, R.: Emerging technologies: mobile apps for language learning. Lang. Learn. Technol. **15**(2), 2–11 (2011)
2. Zichermann, G., Cunningham, C.: Gamification by Design: Implementing Game Mechanics in Web and Mobile Apps. O'Reilly, Sebastopol (2011)
3. Helgason, D.: 2010 Trends. Unity Technologies Blog (2010)
4. Zichermann, G.: A long engagement and a shotgun wedding: why engagement is the power metric of the decade. communication au Gamification Summit, San Francisco, en ligne (2011). http://goo.gl/jlaO0
5. Bunchball Company. http://www.bunchball.com/
6. Deterding, S., Dixon, D., Khaled, R., et al.: From game design elements to gamefulness: defining gamification. In: Proceedings of the 15th International Academic MindTrek Conference: Envisioning Future Media Environments, pp. 9–15. ACM (2011)
7. Hunicke, R., LeBlanc, M., Zubek, R.: MDA: a formal approach to game design and game research. In: Proceedings of the AAAI Workshop on Challenges in Game AI, vol. 4, p. 1 (2004)
8. Brathwaite, B., Schreiber, I.: Challenges for Game Designers. Nelson Education (2009)
9. Hamari, J., Koivisto, J.: Measuring flow in gamification: dispositional flow scale-2. Comput. Hum. Behav. **40**, 133–143 (2014)

10. Reeves, B., Read, J.L.: Total Engagement: Using Games and Virtual Worlds to Change the Way People Work and Businesses Compete. Harvard Business School Press, Boston (2009)
11. Prensky, M.: Fun, play and games: what makes games engaging. Digit. Game-Based Learn. **5**, 1–5 (2011)
12. Garris, R., Ahlers, R., Driskell, J.E.: Games, motivation, and learning: a research and practice model. Simul. Gaming **33**(4), 441–467 (2002)
13. Lilly, J., Warnes, M.: Designing mobile games for learning: the mGBL approach. Serious Games Move, 3–25 (2009)
14. Bellotti, F., Kapralos, B., Lee, K., et al.: Assessment in and of serious games: an overview. Adv. Hum. Comput. Interact. **2013**, 1 (2013)
15. Deterding, S.: Gamification: designing for motivation. Interactions **19**(4), 14–17 (2012)
16. Spada, N.: Form-focussed instruction and second language acquisition: a review of classroom and laboratory research. Lang. Teach. **30**(02), 73–87 (1997)
17. Bagby, M.: The flipped approach: past research, practical applications, and experiences in k-12 science and math classrooms. Practical Applications and Experiences in K-20 Blended Learning Environments, pp. 91–104. IGI Global (2014)
18. Sanders, D., Kenner, R.: Whither CAI? The need for communicative courseware. System **11**(1), 33–39 (1983)
19. Swain, M., Lapkin, S.: Problems in output and the cognitive processes they generate: a step towards second language learning. Appl. Linguist. **16**(3), 371–391 (1995)
20. Benson, B.K.: Coming to terms: scaffolding. Engl. J. **86**(7), 126–127 (1997)
21. Kapp, K.M.: Games, gamification, and the quest for learner engagement. T + D, **66**(6), 64–68 (2012)

Novel Interaction Devices and Techniques

Towards Accepted Smart Interactive Textiles

The Interdisciplinary Project INTUITEX

Philipp Brauner[1,2], Julia van Heek[1,2], Anne Kathrin Schaar[1,2], Martina Ziefle[1,2],
Nur Al-huda Hamdan[1,3], Lukas Ossmann[1,3], Florian Heller[1,3], Jan Borchers[1,3],
Klaus Scheulen[4], Thomas Gries[4], Hannah Kraft[5], Hannes Fromm[5], Marina Franke[5],
Christian Wentz[5], Manfred Wagner[5], Manuel Dicke[6], Christian Möllering[6(✉)],
and Franz Adenau[7]

[1] Human-Computer Interaction Center, RWTH Aachen University, Aachen, Germany
[2] Chair of Communication Science, RWTH Aachen University, Aachen, Germany
[3] Chair for Media Informatics, RWTH Aachen University, Aachen, Germany
[4] Institute for Textile Engineering, RWTH Aachen University, Aachen, Germany
[5] BraunWagner GmbH, Aachen, Germany
[6] Enervision GmbH, Aachen, Germany
christian.moellering@enervision.de
[7] AFP Textilveredelungs- und Vertriebs GmbH, Baesweiler, Germany

Abstract. Smart Interactive Textiles combine the warmth and omnipresence of textiles in our everyday lives with the benefits of modern information and communication technologies. The potential of innovation is not only based on technical ingenuity, but also on the consideration and embedding of peoples' fears, requirements, desires, and wishes regarding these innovative technologies. Thus, the development of smart interactive textiles requires the expertise of various disciplines. Foremost, appropriate conductive yarns must be selected and integrated into conventional fabrics. Sensors and actuators must be embedded in textiles in a way that they could be used as a user interface. The design of these textiles should meet human needs and should enable an intuitive, easy to learn, and effective interaction. To meet these requirements, potential users should be part of the development and evaluation processes of innovative smart textiles. In this article, we present a research framework that integrates several interdisciplinary perspectives (interface design, textile technology, integration and automation, communication and human factors). We realized three functional smart textile demonstrators (curtain, chair, jacket). We report on the results of this interdisciplinary research project as well as the research questions and key findings of the individual partners. In summary, this article demonstrates that interdisciplinary cooperation, user-centered and participatory design, and iterative product development are necessary for successful innovative technologies.

Keywords: Pervasive technology · Ubiquitous computing · Conductive yarn · Smart textiles · Smart interactive textiles · Design for all · Technology acceptance · Iterative product development

© Springer International Publishing AG 2017
F.F.-H. Nah and C.-H. Tan (Eds.): HCIBGO 2017, Part I, LNCS 10293, pp. 279–298, 2017.
DOI: 10.1007/978-3-319-58481-2_22

1 Introduction

Since the dawn of mankind, textiles have been an integral part of the human culture tracing back to 30.000 B.C. [1, 2]. Textiles are perceived to be warm, soft, and pleasurable; they come in large variety of different forms, sizes, textures, and colors; and they are used for clothes, furniture, and decoration. In contrast, integrated circuits, microprocessors, and the subsequent advances towards the Internet of Things are rather novel developments originating in the 1950s [3, 4]. The convergence of these two developments is highly promising. Novel input and output devices may profit from the ubiquity and qualities of textiles (e.g., flexibility, warmth, aesthetics) to integrate seamlessly into our environments.

Numerous technical innovations fail when they reach the market as they are not accepted by consumers. Reasons for this are manifold and include development processes that are solely product-oriented and feature-driven with the lack of focus on potential customers and their requirements [5, 6]. To ensure high acceptance, high suitability, and high usability of future smart interactive textiles, interdisciplinary perspectives should unite to an integrative and iterative product development process. These perspectives include expertise from textile engineering and textile industry, systems integration and embedded development, computer science and media informatics, product design and marketing, as well as communication science and user experience research.

This holistic unification of these diverse perspectives was carried out in the research project "INTUITEX – Intuitive Textiles". The goal of this project was to explore and develop novel interactive textile interfaces that are (1) intuitive (easy to use and learn), (2) consider the wants and needs of an increasingly diverse user population, (3) address age related changes, (4) have an attractive design and a familiar form, and (5) can be seamlessly integrated into the human habitat.

2 Related Work

This section provides an overview of the disciplinary state of the art regarding smart interactive textiles. The section starts with the technical perspectives, continues with related work from product design, and concludes by describing various models for assessing humans' perception and acceptance of technical innovations.

2.1 Smart Textiles in Engineering

In addition to the conventional input devices (e.g., mouse, touchpad, multi-button remote control), which are usually embedded in rigid housings, there are devices which are realized by functional textiles (a.k.a. smart textiles [7]). Many research projects deal with the question of how information technology can continue to gain a foothold in everyday life by integrating itself into clothing and other textiles. Examples of this are "intelligent" clothing, which capture vital parameters, such as the heart rate and perspiration, or a step counter that is integrated in shoes and not visible to the user. Often, in wearable computing, old interaction concepts and input techniques from the desktop computer are transferred without reflecting on the new requirements of the device or context. For example, integrating buttons or touchscreens in gloves and jackets for controlling an MP3 player demands the user's visual attention and input precision in contexts where the user is continuously moving or engaged in other primary tasks. Until now, smart interactive textiles have been mainly developed in research labs and design studios without considering the manufacturing and industrial aspects of these novel products, with one exception [10]. To realize smart textile interfaces, there are still some electrical components that need to be connected to the fabric. Using typical electrical connection methods, such as soldering, is often not suitable for or possible with conductive yarns, leading to handmade connections. The usability of textiles depends highly on the reliability of their functionality and lifetime. Recent developments in conductive yarns provide highly conductive and washable materials at an industrial level. This motivates investigating the holistic development process of creating smart textile interfaces for public consumption.

2.2 Smart Textiles in Human-Computer Interaction

In recent years, researchers have been investigating ways to augment and re-appropriate textiles as interactive media. Early work [8, 9] examined the benefits of integrating a capacitive touchpad into clothing. The result is a rich eyes-free input device to, e.g., write text notes on a phone that is in a pocket. Today, touch enabled textiles are produced commercially, e.g., Project Jacquard [10], and are ready to enter the market. These textiles detect touch input (taps and gestures) like touch screens [11–14]. But unlike touchscreens, they have similar properties as regular textiles–they are flexible, warm, and just as comfortable to wear.

Leveraging the textile nature of many of the objects that surround us enables natural interaction with and seamless integration into our environment [11]. Lee et al. [15] defined a gesture alphabet of possible fold, bend, and distort gestures for paper, plastic, and stretchable fabric. Natural interact with fabric (e.g., pinch, stretch, squeeze, drape, etc.) has been recently motivated as an interaction metaphor for deformable user interfaces [16–18].

Pinstripe [19] uses a parallel pattern of conductive stripes integrated into the sleeve of a t-shirt to detect the size and displacement of a fold in the cloth. This information is then mapped to a one-dimensional continuous value change. Gioberto et al. [20] use stretch sensors to detect fabric bends and folds around a single axis, such as the knee. However, integrating a stretch sensor for each possible axis would overload the fabric making in heavier and less flexible.

So far, most textile sensors have been designed to be integrated into garments as interfaces for wearable devices. In this project, we also look at textile interfaces in the home environment, more specifically, curtains and armchairs. So far, augmenting the large surface of a curtain as an interactive surface has been realized using image-based technologies. Funk et al. [21] present a shower curtain that senses touch input using a thermal camera. This allows to select between different applications, such as weather information or controlling a music player. A number of interactive chairs have been developed as input devices for navigation in computer games [22] and controlling the mouse cursor in the desktop environment [23]. Probst et al. [30] equipped a flexible office chair with motion sensing functionality. The chair becomes an input device that detects the user's movements over the chair (tilting, rotating, or bouncing) to control the computer. However, most of these systems use inertial measurement units for detecting movement and do not appropriate the fabric of the chair as an interactive surface.

2.3   Design Parameters of Smart Textile Interfaces

From the design perspective, there are various design heuristics, guidelines, and parameters that must be considered [24–26]. Established design parameters for textile interfaces are: ergonomic parameters (e.g., size and accessibility of the textile interfaces), functional parameters, easy handling, and a simple and self-explanatory usage of the textile interface.

The shape of the interface should blend well with the object's form. In this way, the interface becomes an integral part of the object. The interface should offer feedforward clues (haptic, tactile, or visual). For example, embroidered lines and ornaments should guide the interaction with the textile interface for easy learning and usage. The material of the interface owe to be as simple as possible and the design should be minimalistic due to an inconspicuous integration of the interface in the specific object.

Finally, design requirements and production requirements must be balanced. Here, a tradeoff between effort and costs of industrial production and the haptic, texture, and visual appearance of the textile interface must be considered in the concept phase.

2.4   Acceptance of Innovative, Interactive, and Textile Technologies

To understand which user and system factors influence the adoption of novel technologies, a systematic and model-based research approach is necessary. Key theories are Roger's Diffusion of Innovations [6], Davis's Technology Acceptance Model (TAM) [27], or Venkatesh's Unified Theory of Acceptance and Use of Technology 2 (UTAUT2) [28] serve as a foundation for the investigation of acceptance of smart interactive textiles. Still, to reflect the product characteristics of novel textile interfaces, these models and theories must be adapted, evolved, and refined.

In the first step, qualitative methods are necessary to identify new factors that are relevant for acceptance. For example, Kranz, Holleis, and Schmidt [29] conducted first qualitative usability studies on interactive textiles and identified preferred designs of interactive surfaces, as well as accepted body areas for the interaction gestures.

Results revealed that the context-of-use shapes the acceptance of wearable smart textiles [30]. Dependability, functionality, and data security were shown to be key determinants for the success of wearable smart textiles. As potential consumers are characterized by a high heterogeneity, it is important to consider that user diversity, especially age and technical expertise, turned out to be key predictors for acceptance. It should be evaluated if these results are transferable to non-wearable textile interfaces or if other factors will be relevant for acceptance.

3   Interdisciplinary Research Approach

As outlined in the previous section, the development of accepted novel smart textile interfaces requires the expertise of various disciplines. Therefore, partners from academia and industry, the domains of textile engineering, information technology, product design, marketing, psychology and communication science collaborated in the interdisciplinary research project INTUITEX founded by Germany's Federal Ministry of Education and Research.

The overarching goal is to design, realize, and evaluate functional demonstrators. The focus of this project are questions from psychology and communication science (acceptance, usability, design), engineering (producibility, software, and hardware), economic and marketing (feasibility, affordability). Each of the partners has individual perspectives, priorities, and concepts that are continuously related, weighted, and harmonized in all phases of the iterative development process. This model enables the development of novel, integrative, and extendable methodology that facilitates the design of smart textile interfaces and considers technical and textile requirements, users' wants and needs, as well as aesthetics.

The following section presents the individual perspectives of the research partners:

- Institute for Textile Engineering, RWTH Aachen University (perspective of textile engineering)
- AFP Textilveredelungs- und Vertriebs GmbH (perspective of textile finishing)
- Chair for Media Informatics, RWTH Aachen University (perspective of human-computer interaction)
- BraunWagner GmbH (perspective of (communication) design)
- Enervision GmbH (perspective of system integration)
- Chair for Communication Science, RWTH Aachen University (perspective of psychology and technology acceptance)

3.1   Integrating Different Perspectives on Smart Interactive Textiles

Textile Engineering and Finishing: The design of interactive textiles deals with the selection of suitable materials (e.g., fabrics, yarns, ...), the technical realization of the requested sensing (e.g., touch, folding,) and actuating functions (e.g., light, sound), and the manufacturing process. Smart textiles can be designed for various applications, yet the combination of the textile platform, i.e., the fabric, and the augmented and/or integrated electronics in the textile surface determines the overall suitability and producibility. The choice of material determines the properties of the textile platform, such as texture and deformability. The choice of functional material, such as the conductive yarn, determines the functional properties of the sensor, but also limits the design and producibility. This aspect of producibility is a very important factor, which is often insufficiently considered. Smart textile technology must be producible in a manufacturing process at scale or the industry would not adopt it because of the high manufacturing costs of single batch productions. Therefore, to increase the potential of the success, the aspect of producibility must be considered from the early stages of development. This also applies to contacting technologies, which are necessary to combine functional textile materials with electronic components [31, 32]. Furthermore, the user's requirements in smart textiles must be considered. For examples, smart textiles must be washable and should neither lose their electrical properties, nor their textile character.

The technology most often used to integrate conductive yarns into a fabric is embroidery [33]. Most embroidery companies are small and medium-sized enterprises (SMEs) and focus on products for a local market. Individualized products, up to small series are manufactured, using single or multiple head machines and given textile substrates. Fast processes are necessary, as it takes a few thousand stiches to embroider complex designs. For conductive yarns, this means to find process parameters that allow fast manufacturing and have the right friction and tension with the yarn (to avoid reduced conductivity due to mechanical abrasion or getting thread breaks). Using multifilament yarns cause too much friction resulting in lint formation or filament fraying leading to the failure of the process or short circuits later in the device.

Media Informatics: Fabric interfaces, especially in commercial products, often simply transfer known concepts to the textile domain, such as buttons [18] or touchpads [20, 21]. In this project, we as media computing experts focused on designing and developing textile sensors that enable natural user interaction borrowing metaphors from people's relations to surrounding fabric objects. Smart textiles, especially smart garments, share many of the challenges of wearable computing [34]. Textile sensors are expected to be visually unobtrusive [7] and socially acceptable in public contexts [35]. Holleis et al. [36] identified other factors such as the need for quick and easy eyes-free, one-handed interaction and methods to ensure that the sensor is robust against involuntary activation and garment shift. Existing systems, however, rarely address these issues, which are important for the general acceptance of such wearable controllers. This project proposes three textile user interfaces that build upon the natural affordances of fabric to address these challenges. We focus on the design of the smart textile layout, the input techniques, sensing technologies, and discuss some of the issues of textile integration into fabric.

System Integration: Smart home technologies still lack convenient human-machine-interfaces that keep pace with AI-driven innovations in mobile and connected applications. In project INTUITEX we look at how textile interfaces can become part of the smart home and wearables eco-systems. With a textile interface, one can seamlessly integrate system interfaces into readily available textile objects in order to enhance the user's comfort and preserve his sense of aesthetics and design in a given context.

Nowadays, there are dozens of different incompatible bus systems, many times, in a single building. In the future, integrating home, office, car, and personal devices will use protocols of the Internet of Things. But to verify the potential outcome of these trends, we must look at bridges between disparate technologies like LonWorks and Bluetooth.

Design: Smart textiles enable the seamless integration of interfaces as integral parts of objects. Consequently, the use of a conventional input device made of metal, glass, or plastics, such as mobile phones, tablets, or computers, becomes redundant. Entirely new haptic and visual user experiences can be implemented. The user is encouraged to interact with devices via individual shapes, graphics, and haptic elements.

Communication Science: Usability and studies on technology acceptance are often based on the evolution of fiction scenarios or of commercial products. By using the inherently interdisciplinary research approach, this discipline gains the potential to contribute towards the development of textile interfaces iteratively across all stages of the design process: From the design and evaluation of scenarios, over non-functional and then functional demonstrators. Along all these phases the user's requirements, acceptance, and diversity is integrated into the subsequent development steps, placing the human under the spotlight.

3.2 Disciplinary Research Challenges

To design textile interfaces, several aspects must be considered and solutions for research questions of different fields must be developed. First, the technical specifications must be known, such as the conductivity of the used yarn for signal transmission. It must be identified which fabrics can be used to integrate conductive yarns and electrical components while maintaining their original textile properties. Secondly, what processes are needed to enable the industrial manufacturing of reliable and economic textile interfaces. How to balance the design requirements with the constraints of manufacturing, e.g., cost, and technical implementation, e.g., electronics integration and conductive yarn. Finally, what aspects influence users decisions to purchase, use, and accept smart textile interfaces, e.g., the sensors' washability and durability, originality of the fabric (texture and deformability), and invisible integration.

Textile Engineering and Finishing: Weaving and embroidery are the most common textile integration technologies for conductive yarns. Processing parameters for the weaving technology are unknown yet. Here, the questions are, how close can the signal lines be laid out and how does the influence interaction design and product design. Regarding the embroidery, the friction behavior of the yarn during manufacture and post is essential because it determines the amount of mechanical stress onto the conductive material and how fast the yarns could loss of conductivity. To reduce yarn friction, production speed, e.g., the stitching speed of embroidery machines, must be controlled. Eventually, the technical specifications of conductive yarns and the production process could limit the creative freedom of both interaction and product designers.

Media Informatics: Working with smart textiles, we need to understand how the physical characteristic and the technical specifications of the yarn as well as the textile production process affect the design of textile sensors. We raise the following questions: How can the conductive thread be connected to the electronics in the PCB holding the sensing technology and intelligence that enable smart textiles? Can capacitive and/or resistive touch technologies with fabric be used? How can algorithms be developed to detect user input (e.g., touch, pinch) and to filter noise caused by fabric movements? How can we design textile sensors that are intuitive (easy to learn and use) and robust against accidental activation?

System Integration: One main obstacle in system integration is the automatic mapping between different technical systems. As the connection usually is of a more semantic nature, the improvements in the field of AI may help here to achieve better solutions. Furthermore, the overall performance of a solution is later relevant for acceptance in the market. As from the point of integration an entire integrated solution is seldom better than the weakest part. We look at the balanced quality and integrate-ability of solutions.

Design: From the design perspective, the following key research questions are of importance: First, what are some of the use cases of smart textile interfaces? Second, are shapes and graphics helpful to familiarize with the interface and ensure easy handling? Third, which ergonomic requirements need to be considered in the textile interface?

Communication Science: The role of user diversity in interaction and acceptance of textile surfaces is currently insufficiently understood. Although the body of technology-acceptance research models is constantly growing, there are currently no empirically validated models specifically tailored to textile input surfaces. Therefore, the new factors that might influence the projected and actual use of these interfaces must be identified, operationalized, and integrated into predictive research models. One key question is how the diversity of users, such as age, gender, affinity towards textiles, technical expertise, or mental models, shape the efficiency, effectivity, and satisfaction while using interactive textile surfaces. Based on these findings suitable interaction designs should be developed that facilitate a high usability and an overall acceptance of the proposed novel textile interfaces.

4   Key Findings

The following sections presents several engineering and research findings that have been generated during the project INTUITEX. Research and development started with experiments on interactive textile surfaces and eventually branched into three different application domains and an exemplary demonstrator for each domain.

4.1   Realized Demonstrators

Within this project we realized three different demonstrators to explore different levels of personal proximity to the interactive textile surface:

1. **Proximal textiles**, i.e. a wearable textile on or very near the body, such as a Smart T-Shirt or a Smart jacket.
2. **Extended surrounding area**, i.e., a textile that people frequently touch, use, or sit on, such as a Smart cushion, a sofa, or a bed.
3. **Surrounding space**, i.e., textiles that are present within the living or working environments that are usually not touched, used, or moved.

Demonstrator for Proximal Textiles: The Smart Jacket. This jacket can be used for sports and everyday situations. A stitching pattern (see Fig. 5, top row) is integrated into a jacket and offers two operation axles that can be grasped by hand. The two possible gestures are currently used for two different usage scenarios: (a) accepting or making a phone call; (b) stopping/playing the music or switching between songs. The interaction can be supported by an embroidered graphic as a haptic concretion on the fabric to enable the user to grope the handling area. Figure 1 illustrates the smart jacket in a user test.

Fig. 1. Proximal textiles demonstrator: smart jacket during user test: subject taking a phone call while riding a bike (left), focus group discussing the jacket's textile interface (right).

Demonstrator for the Extended Surrounding Area: Smart Armchair. An off-the-shelve armchair with motor-adjustable back- and footrest is augmented with an interactive textile interface. We realized different textile interfaces that are evaluated and compared to the conventional remote control. One of the interfaces is based on textile pleats that resemble the backrest and the footrest, respectively, integrated in the side of the chair. Either touching or bending (pushing) the pleat activates the motors and moves the rests upwards or downwards. Figure 2 presents the armchair with its smart pleats.

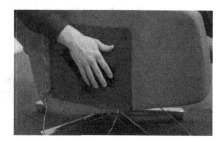

Fig. 2. Extended surrounding area demonstrator: motorized armchair with a textile interface.

Demonstrator for the Surrounding Space: Smart Curtain. As a demonstrator for the surrounding space we realized a smart curtain by integrating conductive yarns into a conventional curtain cloth (see Fig. 3). The yarn can be incorporated into textiles with different processes, such as embroidering and weaving. By touching and swiping across the respective areas, the curtain is opened or closed.

Fig. 3. Surrounding space demonstrator: Smart curtain.

4.2   Individual Research Contributions

Textile Engineering and Finishing: Within this project, the embroidery company AFP Textilveredelungs und –vertriebs GmbH, tested different conductive yarns on their multi-head embroidery machine from TAJIMA Type TFGN –910 (meaning 10 heads with 9 needles each) in cooperation with the Institute for Textile Engineering. Different conductive materials were tested and typical issues were yarn breaks, irregular appearance, slow running speed, lint formation or that the fabric is not processable. Tested yarns consist of copper multifilament wires, stainless steel yarn in different linear densities, silver coated yarns based on polyamide (PA) and twisted yarns made of polyester and silver coated PA-yarn and a spread between 100 and 560dtex. The best results were achieved with shieldex 117/17 dtex 2-ply HC+B from Statex and Silver-tech 120 from Amann. To get an impression of the different properties, some pictures of different conductive yarns can be seen in Fig. 4.

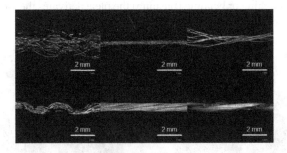

Fig. 4. Examples of different conductive fabrics, yarns, and process parameters.

Geometrical limitations regarding the distance between signal lines could reliably be decreased from 6 mm down to 2 mm. Due to the break of single filaments there were short circuits between several parallel lines. With better process parameters and a consideration during the punching in the embroidery software, the yarn could be processed without damaging it. This allows to create complex interface structures on a smaller area. Different kinds of stiches (flat stich, linear basting stitch, lock stitch or the use as lower thread) allow different haptic and electrical properties or protecting of signal lines. The back of embroidered devices is usually flamed, to avoid any lint and short circuits. Table 1 shows an excerpt of the design of experiments with different process parameters, stitching types, and yarns.

Table 1. Different conductive yarns with div. mechanical properties and stitching distances.

Stitch type	Variation parameter	Working limits	Samples pictures
Flat stitch	Stitch width: 1.2–1.6 mm	All working	
	Signal line distance: 1–3.5 mm		
Linear basting stitch	Stitch length: 2–3.6 mm	All working, best results with 2.6 mm	
	Signal line distance: 0.7–2.8 mm		
Offset	Stitch length: 2–3.6 mm	All working	
As lower thread (view from backside)	Stitch length: 2–3.6 mm	All length working, short circuits may occur below 1 mm	
	Signal line distance: 0.7–2.8 mm		
Linear basting stitch, isolated with non conductive yarn	2–3 lines isolated together with flat stitch (distance 2 mm); single isolation (distance 3.3 mm)	All working	

After figuring out which yarns and parameters work best, the realization of devices started. Different variations were produced to test functionality borders and behavior in user conditions. The functionality is achieved through resistive or capacitive sensing. For linear input devices, single signal lines can be used, e.g., for controlling the curtain (the lines detect the user hand and send the data to the microcontroller) (see Fig. 5, bottom row). Long linear signal lines can be produced by weaving as well, which allow higher length (up to "endless") and the use as platform material. Limitations are the unidirectional and parallel design; embroidery allows freedom in design but is much slower in production.

Stitched conductive bars are used as a haptic support for the user and to get wide signal detection areas. 2D-embroidered structures can be adapted to 3D-input-devices, similar to what we achieved with the Smart Armchair by folding the fabric and sewing pleats (see Fig. 5, middle row). A combination of different stitch types allows complex textile-based devices for detecting a 2D or 3D-folding and corresponding signals (see Fig. 5, top).

For more complex structures, one must consider that more signal transmission lines are necessary. However, as the required space on the substrate increases, the effort for designing the structure increases proportionally. For consumer products, textile manufacturing offers a lot of potential but must be inherently integrated into an iterative development cycle, as the technical realization is one critical factor for a product's commercial success.

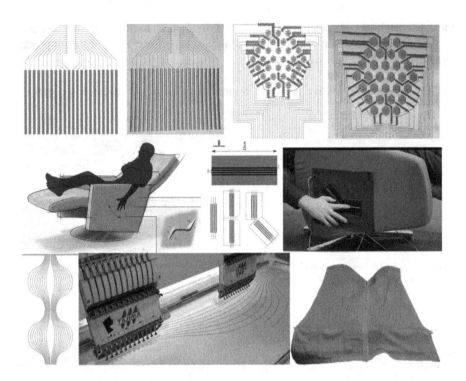

Fig. 5. Different stitch patterns for the three realized demonstrators (top: jacket, middle: armchair, bottom: curtain).

Media Informatics: The electrical connection between the conductive yarn and a PCB holding the electronics containing the intelligence of the smart textile is of great interest to research. Soldering conductive yarns onto a PCB is very challenging and error prone and for some yarns, e.g., silver-coated yarns, it is not possible. Linz et al. [38] suggested using flexible PCBs which can be stitched on fabric and connected directly with lines of conductive thread. This strong integration, however, requires the electronic components to be washable, which results in additional effort. In Project Jacquard [10], an industrial process is described to connect the conductive thread and completely seal the interconnections and electronic components.

We developed a clipping mechanism [39] to easily connect the ends of the conductive thread to a PCB. The clipping mechanism, depicted in Fig. 6, above and below the conductive lines are two horizontal holes to get the clip through the supporting fabric. The conductive thread is firmly pressed against the conductive plates on the bottom side of the PCB by a plastic clip. The plastic clips have raised edges between each connection point to prevent the threads from accidentally connecting with each other during, e.g., movement. This mechanism has the advantage that no sharp edges slowly cut into the yarn and thereby reduce its conductivity, and that the PCB can be removed before washing and clipped to another piece of fabric. One limitation is that the clip becomes bulky very quickly as we increase the number of connections.

Fig. 6. The orange clip provides bins for the endings of the conductive thread. The PCB just has simple contact areas on the bottom side and is pressed against the fabric by the orange plastic clip. The black part is the top case of the enclosure. (Color figure online)

Touch technologies, capacitive and resistive, enable a large input vocabulary that ranges from tapping, swiping, and gesturing on the fabric surface, to pinching and rolling the fabric between the fingers. We used capacitive touch technology to enable the curtain and the armchair. Both demonstrators have a 1D touch sensor that can detect swipes in two directions (curtain) or tap/touch (armchair). To detect these gestures, a microcontroller reads the difference in capacitance at each conductive thread and measures it against a threshold. The microcontroller filters noise by detecting permanent contacts, e.g., when the curtain folds touch, or when more than one touch area is activated on the armchair, e.g., when someone bumps into the side of the chair.

Capacitive sensing on clothing is very challenging. Searching for a capacitive touch-area cannot happen eyes-free since activation is triggered once the finger is near it. During movement the sensors deform and fold creating noise signal. Finally, the body capacitance makes it very difficult to place a sensor above the skin. The smart jacket uses resistive technology. The sensor consists of 30 pads of conductive yarn embroidered onto a piece of cloth (Fig. 7). When a user pinches a fold in the sensor, some of the pads come in contact with each other, which can easily be sensed by a microcontroller. Pinching is a natural gesture that is relevant to fabrics. It is an explicit gesture that activates the sensor and triggers an action at the same time, and it is robust against accidental activation. We used a machine learning algorithm, random forests, to classify

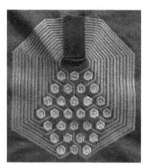

Fig. 7. The sensor consists of 30 pads of conductive thread embroidered onto a piece of cloth. When the user grabs a fold of the sensor, the interconnections are sensed by a microcontroller and mapped to relative 2D output.

at which angle the user is pinching the fabric relative to his body. We achieved 85% accuracy rate at 45° angle increments, and 90% accuracy at 90° angle increments [40].

Despite the limitations of the 2D embroidery structures, we could design visual and haptic affordances by manipulating the shape of embroidery and fabric. For example, in the armchair, we use fabric folds at two different angles to allow users to haptically determine, by swiping their hands across the side of the chair, which area controls the reclination of the back- or footrest of the seat. The direction of the touch is mapped naturally to the possible actions: pushing down on a fold brings the relevant part of the chair down, and the opposite applies. When designing the smart jacket, however, the minimum spacing recommended between any two parallel conductive threads (2–3 mm) became a major design and technical restriction limiting the number of touch points per inch fabric, thus the sensor's input resolution. Routing and insulating the extensions of the conductive pads also restricted the resolution and made the system bulkier. In the curtain, we took advantage of the naturally uninsulated conductive yarn to enable user interaction along the length of the fabric.

In summary, working with conductive threads requires a new design framework and guidelines for smart textile user interfaces and input techniques. Fabric characteristics, such as flexibility and movement, also influence how we design textile layouts and where we place them.

System Integration: We produced diverse technical bridges between the systems, with a focus on reliability and miniaturization. For example, we developed a LonWorks Bluetooth bridge and the possibility to connect this bridge also to one of the uprising Internet of Things platforms IzoT. In a further step, we compared different existing smart home and Internet of Things approaches for their semantic congruence. This is especially important, as seamless applicability will only be established if systems can integrate themselves automatically into peoples' habitat.

Design: From the design perspective, various evaluation parameters have been established during the project. Three levels of perception of personal smart interactive textiles were defined (proximal textiles, extended surrounding area textiles, surrounding space textiles). These levels guided the design and development of the three presented demonstrators (see Sect. 4.1 and Fig. 8). Accordingly, application scenarios were designed and visualized. For each demonstrator, the optimal position(s) for the textile interface was identified (see Fig. 8).

 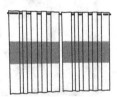

Fig. 8. Considered positions of the textile interfaces: proximal textiles (left), textiles in the extended surrounding area (middle), textiles in the surrounding space (right).

For all three demonstrators, the operating elements must be positioned ergonomically to ensure comfortable use while preventing unintentional activation. In cooperation with the research partners, we developed an optimal user-centered positioning of the interactive textile elements.

Concerning the smart jacket, it was most important that it could be operated eyes-free and while wearing gloves. Therefore, we investigated different sizes and positions of the textile interface and developed patterns and models of embroidered graphics that support the user haptically to be able to grab the handling area.

The textile interface of the armchair was integrated on the side to be operable blindly. We evaluated several designs to convey to the user how to control the different parts of the chair (footrest and back) without visual inspection (see Fig. 2). Prototypic users enjoyed the clear affordance and the direct mappings [37] between the folds and the movable parts of the armchair. We aimed for a comfortable operational experience by using a minimalistic design.

Relating to the curtain, it was our goal to insert the conductible yarn as a visual signifier and a design element: refined wavy lines, vertically processed, winging from left to right. Interaction with the curtain is realized by swiping both hands over the curtain's fabric to open or close it (see Fig. 3). The design needs to be subtle, as a decorative effect, in order to integrate well into the living. Until now, our goal has not been reached due to manufacturing problems. From the points of production technique and industrial realization, embroidery will be too extensive for large-scale production. By using current looms only dignified patterns can be reached and a conversion into large-area graphics will be limited. Therefore, the conductive paths must be weaved into the fabric and design elements transferred, e.g., via print, to the fabric.

Communication Science: Results were generated by studies on three different layers: first, scenario-based surveys that assessed the requirements, motives, and barriers for the acceptance of smart textile interfaces. Second, user-studies with non-functional demonstrators (i.e., interviews, focus groups, Wizard-Of-Oz experiments) that generated insights on intuitive interactions, applicable forms, and sizes for textile interfaces. Third, summative user studies with functional demonstrators that addressed the participant's evaluation of textile interfaces after a "hands-on experience".

Regarding the scenario-based approach, an Adaptive Conjoint Analysis was used to weight the most important dimensions that shape the acceptance of a textile product. The study revealed that the technical realization is the most decisive criteria for a products' success. Specifically, the prototypic users disliked visible electronics and asked for seamless integration of the required technology into the garments. Usage context, functionality, and haptics were found to be comparatively less-important [41]. In a second study, the motives, barriers, and conditions for using smart textiles were investigated [42]. The aesthetics and durability of the product were regarded as the most important criteria. The preferred locations for using smart interactive textiles in the home environment were the living room and office, whereas the bathroom or the bedroom were considered the least favored locations.

A scenario based survey with 136 participants identified the barriers and benefits for using smart interactive textiles in the home environment and derived a Smart Textile

Technology Acceptance Model that can predict over 86% in variance of the intention to use smart textiles at home [43].

Interviews and focus groups with non-functional demonstrators found that intuitive and preferred interaction styles differ with age. Using gesture elicitation method [44], subjects were asked to perform gestures to control a music player (change a song and control the volume) using a textile surface. Older people preferred interfaces with noticeable buttons, whereas younger generations imagined flat textile touchpads. Strikingly, other textile affordances, such as folding, wrinkling, or stretching were rarely used. Interestingly, textile interfaces were considered as valuable enablers for blind or visually impaired people to be able to interact with technology augmented environments.

In the evaluation of the three functional textile demonstrators the participants reported high usability of the smart curtain and the smart jacket but also a rather limited perceived usefulness. For the jacket, this might have been caused by the limited input spectrum in the current state of the development. Therefore, possible business cases should be carefully evaluated and suitable niches must be identified. In contrast, the smart armchair was found useful *and* easy to use by almost all our subjects. Furthermore, most participants preferred the textile interface over a conventional one in a randomized trial.

5   Discussion and Outlook

After nearly three years of work in project INTUITEX we concluded that an interdisciplinary consortium of textile and electronics engineers and designers is necessary to map the challenges and opportunities of smart interactive textiles. The following paragraphs discuss open research questions and the benefits of interdisciplinary cooperation.

From the perspective of textile engineering, there is still a lack of reliable technologies of conductive yarns which is needed for stitching, connecting with electronics, and using and washing these yarns. Current smart textile prototypes are specifically tailored for demonstration. Existing conductive yarn technologies can adapt for a small number of custom-made articles (scope), but producing larger quantities of interactive textiles (scale) is still difficult. Open questions include how conductive yarns can be connected to electrical components and how to integrate these components into the embroidery process. Interaction patterns may come in a variety of forms and sizes. In this case, a bridge between the production with scope and production at scale must be found (cf. [45]).

To date, the integration of novel sensors and actuators into our surroundings is mostly hand-crafted. In the near future, advancements towards the Internet of Things will provide better semantic and automatic integration of novel interfaces and devices into the home environment. In project INTUITEX, a series of new research questions emerged. From a technical perspective, two of the three presented demonstrators work very well. However, the smart jacket still has many problems, mainly due to constant fabric and body movements. Future research should focus on the integration and interconnection of textile devices in the home environment: this way, it would be possible to control typical smart home functions (such as the lighting, heating, and entertainment system) by using the textile interfaces of the armchair or curtain.

Regarding the design of textile interfaces, this project only explored flat textured surfaces. Textiles can also be manipulated into three-dimensional structures by using, e.g., 3D mashes or weaving in 3D. Thus, interactive interfaces may be realized as tangible objects with different design parameters.

Some of the presented studies investigated the suitability of smart interactive surfaces for aging users in the context of demographic change. In general, we found that adequately designed textile interaction surfaces are usable and useful independent of age and therefore, they can serve as additional and novel input devices to increase elderly's ICT participation. Still, there are open research questions and links to future research opportunities: How to design textile interfaces that can support and empower the elderly or chronically ill in their daily lives. Smart textile interfaces may potentially be used to prepare toddlers and children for the 21st century, as textiles and tangible surfaces may convey self-efficacy in digitalization [46].

From the perspective of technology acceptance research, we found that the established models are not able to capture the specific attributes of textile interfaces, nor the individual personality states and traits that are related to the acceptance of these interfaces. Therefore, further studies should identify, quantify, and weight the specific personality and system factors and their relationship to intended use and actual use of novel textile interfaces. A technology acceptance model specifically tailored to smart textiles with an increased overall predictive power might forecast and facilitate the success of textile products at the market.

The interdisciplinary cooperation in this project not only enabled the development of better products, but also facilitated a better understanding of the diverse wants and needs of the research partners from academia and industry. The project contributed to an enhanced interdisciplinary knowledge exchange and to a better understanding of the requirements, competencies, and methods of each partner. Retrospectively, we started as independent research partners, strengthened our ties as a team across the project period, and are now able to empower ourselves for a viable interdisciplinary collaboration beyond the project and the realized demonstrators.

Summarizing, the inherently interdisciplinary research methodology that included expertise from textile engineering, computer science, design, and psychology in combination with an early focus on users' requirements fostered the development of novel smart textile interaction surfaces and yielded increased usefulness, usability as well as high overall acceptance.

Acknowledgments. This project is funded by the German Ministry of Education and Research (BMBF) under project No. 16SV6270. We thank Hartmut Strese for valuable discussions during the progress of this project.

References

1. Robinson, S.: History of Dyed Textiles. MIT Press, Cambridge (1970)
2. Kvavadze, E., Bar-Yosef, O., Belfer-Cohen, A., Boaretto, E., Jakeli, N., Matskevich, Z., Meshveliani, T.: 30,000-Year-Old Wild Flax Fibers, vol. 325, p. 1359. Science, New York (2009)

296 P. Brauner et al.

3. Caceres, R., Friday, A.: Ubicomp systems at 20: progress, opportunities, and challenges. IEEE Pervasive Comput. **11**, 14–21 (2012)
4. Weiser, M.: The computer for the 21st century. Sci. Am. **265**, 94–104 (1991)
5. Bauer, R.: Gescheiterte Innovationen. Campus Verlag GmbH, Frankfurt (2006)
6. Rogers, E.M.: Diffusion of Innovations. Free Press, New York (2003)
7. Cherenack, K., van Pieterson, L.: Smart textiles: challenges and opportunities. J. Appl. Phys. **112**, 91301 (2012)
8. Rekimoto, J.: GestureWrist and GesturePad: unobtrusive wearable interaction devices. In: Proceedings Fifth International Symposium on Wearable Computers, pp. 21–27 (2001)
9. Saponas, T.S., Harrison, C., Benko, H.: Pocket touch: through-fabric capacitive touch input. In: Proceedings of the 24th Annual ACM Symposium on User Interface Software and Technology - UIST 2011, pp. 303–308 (2011)
10. Poupyrev, I., Gong, N.-W., Fukuhara, S., Karagozler, M.E., Schwesig, C., Robinson, K.E.: Project jacquard: interactive digital textiles at scale. In: Proceedings of the 2016 CHI Conference on Human Factors in Computing Systems, pp. 4216–4227 (2016)
11. Perner-Wilson, H., Buechley, L., Tech, H., Ave, M., Ma, C.: Handcrafting textile interfaces from a Kit-of-No-Parts. In: Proceedings of the 5th International Conference on Tangible, Embedded, and Embodied Interaction, pp. 61–68 (2011)
12. Heller, F., Ivanov, S., Wacharamanotham, C., Borchers, J.: FabriTouch: exploring flexible touch input on textiles. In: Proceedings of the 2014 ACM International Symposium on Wearable Computers, pp. 59–62 (2014)
13. Schneegass, S., Voit, A.: GestureSleeve: using touch sensitive fabrics for gestural input on the forearm for controlling smartwatches. In: Proceedings of the 2016 ACM International Symposium on Wearable Computers – ISWC 2016, pp. 108–115 (2016)
14. Schmeder, A., Freed, A.: Support vector machine learning for gesture signal estimation with a piezo-resistive fabric touch surface. In: Proceedings of the 2010 Conference on New Interfaces for Musical Expression (NIME 2010), pp. 244–249 (2010)
15. Lee, S.-S., Kim, S., Jin, B., Choi, E., Kim, B., Jia, X., Kim, D., Lee, K.: How users manipulate deformable displays as input devices. In: Proceedings of CHI, p. 1647 (2010)
16. Troiano, G.M., Pedersen, E.W., Hornbæk, K.: User-defined gestures for elastic, deformable displays. In: Proceedings of the 2014 International Working Conference on Advanced Visual Interfaces – AVI 2014, pp. 1–8 (2014)
17. Lepinski, J., Vertegaal, R.: Cloth displays: interacting with drapable textile screens. In: Proceedings of the Fifth International Conference on Tangible, Embedded, and Embodied Interaction, pp. 285–288 (2011)
18. Peschke, J., Göbel, F., Gründer, T., Keck, M., Kammer, D., Groh, R.: DepthTouch: an elastic surface for tangible computing. In: Proceedings of the International Working Conference on Advanced Visual Interfaces, pp. 770–771 (2012)
19. Karrer, T., Wittenhagen, M., Lichtschlag, L., Heller, F., Borchers, J.: Pinstripe: eyes-free continuous input on interactive clothing. In: Proceedings of the 2011 Annual Conference on Human Factors in Computing Systems – CHI 2011, pp. 1313–1322 (2011)
20. Gioberto, G., Coughlin, J., Bibeau, K., Dunne, L.E.: Detecting bends and fabric folds using stitched sensors. In: Proceedings of the 2013 International Symposium on Wearable Computers, pp. 53–56. ACM (2013)
21. Funk, M., Schneegaß, S., Behringer, M., Henze, N., Schmidt, A.: An interactive curtain for media usage in the shower. In: Proceedings of the 4th International Symposium on Pervasive Displays, pp. 225–231. ACM (2015)
22. Beckhaus, S., Blom, K., Haringer, M.: ChairIO – the chair-based interface. Concepts and technologies for pervasive games: a reader for pervasive gaming research, pp. 231–264 (2007)

23. Endert, A., Fiaux, P., Chung, H., Stewart, M., Andrews, C., North, C.: ChairMouse - leveraging natural chair rotation for cursor navigation on large, high-resolution displays. In: Extended Abstracts of the International Conference on Human Factors in Computing Systems, pp. 571–580. ACM (2011)
24. Ware, C.: Information Visualization: Perception for Design. Elsevier Academic Press, New York (2004)
25. Shneiderman, B., Plaisant, C.: Designing the User Interface: Strategies for Effective Human-Computer Interaction, 4th edn. Pearson Addison Wesley, Boston (2004)
26. Wertheimer, M.: Untersuchungen zur Lehre von der Gestalt II. Psychologische Forschung **4**, 301–350 (1923)
27. Davis, F.D.: Perceived usefulness, perceived ease of use, and user acceptance of information technology. MIS Q. **13**, 319–340 (1989)
28. Venkatesh, V., Thong, J.Y.L., Xu, X.: Consumer acceptance and use of information technology: extending the unified theory of acceptance and use of technology. MIS Q. **36**, 157–178 (2012)
29. Kranz, M., Holleis, P., Schmidt, A.: Embedded interaction: interacting with the internet of things. IEEE Internet Comput. **14**, 46–53 (2010)
30. Van Heek, J., Schaar, A.K., Trevisan, B., Bosowski, P., Ziefle, M.: User requirements for wearable smart textiles. Does the usage context matter (medical vs. sports)? In: Proceedings of the 8th International Conference on Pervasive Computing Technologies for Healthcare (2014)
31. Scheulen, K., Schwarz, A., Jockenhoevel, S.: Reversible contacting of smart textiles with adhesive bonded magnets. In: Proceedings of IEEE International Symposium on Wearable Computers (ISWC), pp. 131–132. ACM (2013)
32. Mecnika, V., Scheulen, K., Anderson, C.F., Hörr, M., Breckenfelder, C.: Joining technologies for electronic textiles. Electr. Text. Smart Fabr. Wearable Technol. 133–153. Elsevier (2015)
33. Mecnika, V., Hörr, M.: Embroidery for smart and intelligent textiles. In: 13th International Conference on Global Research and Education (2014)
34. Hurford, R., Martin, A., Larsen, P.: Designing wearables. In: Proceedings - International Symposium on Wearable Computers, pp. 133–134 (2007)
35. Profita, H.P., Clawson, J., Gilliland, S., Zeagler, C., Starner, T., Budd, J., Do, E.Y.-L.: Don't mind me touching my wrist. In: Proceedings of the 17th Annual International Symposium on Wearable Computers – ISWC 2013, p. 89. ACM (2013)
36. Holleis, P., Schmidt, A., Paasovaara, S., Puikkonen, A., Häkkilä, J.: Evaluating capacitive touch input on clothes. In: Proceedings of the 10th International Conference on Human-Computer Interaction with Mobile Devices and Services, p. 81 (2008)
37. Norman, D.A.: The Design of Everyday Things. Basic Books, New York (2002)
38. Linz, T., Vieroth, R., Dils, C., Koch, M., Braun, T., Becker, K.F., Kallmayer, C., Hong, S.M.: Embroidered interconnections and encapsulation for electronics in textiles for wearable electronics applications. Adv. Sci. Technol. **60**, 85–94 (2008)
39. Heller, F., Lee, H.-Y. (Kriz), Brauner, P., Gries, T., Ziefle, M., Borchers, J.: An intuitive textile input controller. In: MuC 2015: Mensch und Computer 2015 – Tagungsband, pp. 263–266. De Gruyter Oldenbourg Wissenschaftsverlag, Germany (2015)
40. Al-huda Hamdan, N., Heller, F., Wacharamanotham, C., Thar, J., Borchers, J.: Grabrics: a foldable two-dimensional textile input controller. In: CHI Extended Abstracts on Human Factors in Computing Systems, pp. 2497–2503 (2016)
41. Hildebrandt, J., Brauner, P., Ziefle, M.: Smart textiles as intuitive and ubiquitous user interfaces for smart homes. In: Zhou, J., Salvendy, G. (eds.) Human Computer Interaction International - Human Aspects of IT for the Aged Population, pp. 423–434. Springer, Switzerland (2015)

42. Ziefle, M., Brauner, P., Heidrich, F., Möllering, C., Lee, H.-Y., Armbrüster, C.: Understanding requirements for textile input devices: individually-tailored interfaces within home environments. In: Stephanidis, C., Antona, M. (eds.) Proceedings of Universal Access in Human-Computer Interaction HCII 2014, vol. 8515, pp. 589–600. Springer, Heidelberg (2014)

43. Brauner, P., Van Heek, J., Ziefle, M.: Age, gender, and technology attitude as factors for acceptance of smart interactive textiles in home environments. In: Proceedings of the 3rd International Conference on Information and Communication Technologies for Ageing Well and e-Health, ICT4AgingWell (in press)

44. Wobbrock, J.O., Morris, M.R., Wilson, A.D.: User-defined gestures for surface computing. In: Proceedings of the SIGCHI Conference on Human Factors in Computing Systems, pp. 1083–1092. ACM, New York (2009)

45. Schlick, C., Stich, V., Schmitt, R., Schuh, G., Ziefle, M., Brecher, C., Blum, M., Mertens, A., Faber, M., Kuz, S., Petruck, H., Fuhrmann, M., Luckert, M., Brambring, F., Reuter, C., Hering, N., Groten, M., Korall, S., Pause, D., Brauner, P., Herfs, W., Odenbusch, M., Wein, S., Stiller, S., Berthold, M.: Cognition-enhanced, self-optimizing production networks. In: Brecher, C., Özdemir, D. (eds.) Integrative Production Technology - Theory and Applications, pp. 645–743. Springer International Publishing, Heidelberg (2017)

46. Brauner, P., Leonhardt, T., Ziefle, M., Schroeder, U.: The effect of tangible artifacts, gender and subjective technical competence on teaching programming to seventh graders. In: Hromkovič, J., Královič, R., Vahrenhold, J. (eds.) ISSEP 2010. LNCS, vol. 5941, pp. 61–71. Springer, Heidelberg (2010). doi:10.1007/978-3-642-11376-5_7

Smartglasses Used by Forklift Operators: Digital Accident Hazard or Efficient Work Equipment? A Pilot Study

Michael Bretschneider-Hagemes[(✉)] and Benno Gross

IFA - Institute for Occupational Safety and Health, St. Augustin, Germany
michael.bretschneider007@gmail.com

Abstract. Smartglasses are in use at manifold workplace settings. A relatively new scenario is the usage of the glasses while driving forklift-trucks. The adaption of methodologies for a data-based risk assessment – in terms of distraction and line-of-sight obstructions – is the aim of the study. The prohibition of the specific use of the glasses is a possible result on one hand. On the other hand the development of recommendations for a safe adoption of the devices to the workplace, is a more likely consequence.

Keywords: Digitization of work · Safety · Healthy workplace · Smartglasses · HMD

1 Introduction

For a number of years, smart-glasses (e.g. Google Glass – see Fig. 1) have been used at so-called "picking workplaces" [1]. These are activities in warehouses, which cover warehousing, continuous warehousing and so-called picking (compilation of goods for shipping/sales). What is new, however, is the use of these digital tools by the drivers of forklift-trucks. In this work scenario the smart-glasses replace conventional monitor systems which are usually mounted on the upper bodywork of forklift-trucks for route guidance and information transfer. In rare cases analog clamping brackets are also still in use.

Through the Employer's Liability Insurance Association the Institute for Occupational Safety and Health (IFA) of the German Social Accident Insurance (DGUV) was made aware of the change in working scenarios and commissioned to investigate possible new hazards.

In the following summary, the research-questions, the methodology and the expected results of the study are outlined. The conference contribution will also present concrete interim results of the study and examples from the company's practice.

© Springer International Publishing AG 2017
F.F.-H. Nah and C.-H. Tan (Eds.): HCIBGO 2017, Part I, LNCS 10293, pp. 299–307, 2017.
DOI: 10.1007/978-3-319-58481-2_23

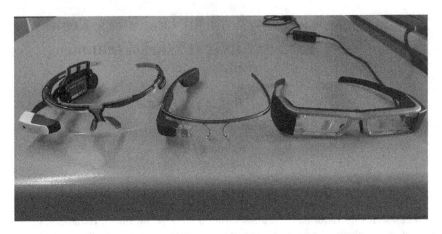

Fig. 1. Set of used smart glasses – Vuzix M100, Google Glass, Epson Moverio BT200

2 Question

The working scenarios can be differentiated by the aspects of...

- the used types of forklift-trucks and
- smart-glasses vs. conventional indicating systems (monitor – see Reference [2]).

There are a number of possible variations which may have an effect on the level of *distraction* and visual impairment. The key questions are therefore:

- Is the task load (in this case with the effect of distraction), caused by smart-glasses (HMD) less or possibly larger than caused by conventional monitor systems?
- Does the vehicle type have a significant influence for the interaction with the smart-glasses (*mast-to-pallet trucks* vs. *tugs*)?
- Is there a significant difference between the use of monocular (see trough/look around) vs. binocular smart-glasses?

3 Methodology

For safety and procedural reasons the study was conducted in a computer-based simulation environment. A high-quality simulator (see Figs. 2, 3, 4 and 5) of a typical forklift-truck was build, the simulation itself is based on Unity.

Fig. 2. Setup of the study (picture source: Bestsim - by kind permission)

Fig. 3. Indicated storage location – view through HMD

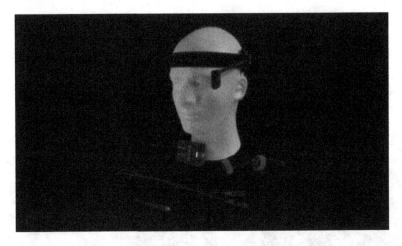

Fig. 4. Setup of the DRT (picture source: Red Scientific - by kind permission)

Fig. 5. Final lab setup

Only experienced professional practitioners who are in possession of a driving license for forklift-trucks have been admitted as participants for the study. At least 26 subjects are trained uniformly and considered for the study. Each participant performs the simulated runs with all relevant vehicle types and all variations of the secondary task whereby the order of use is crossed (leveling of training effects).

The primary task for the test subjects is:

Driving of the forklift-truck in a simulated environment (according to the instructions – see secondary task).

The secondary task (picking task – storage location is indicated each time) is:
Reading of the instructions which are presented by the 'indicating system' while driving and taking goods with the vehicle (+upstream task see below).

The secondary task is initially presented *conventionally* via a monitor system and is then differentiated by the different types of smart-glasses ("monocular" – google glass "see through" vs. vuzix "look around" vs. "binocular"). Both are described as 'indicating systems'. The task design is a detailed copy of a typical situation as observed in original companies usecases.

The interaction time with the original task was about 2 seconds/task-fulfillment. While the stimulus is presented every 3–5 s, the short interaction time retrieved the risk of not getting a stimulus at the period of the relevant task fulfillment. Therefore it was enriched by an *upstream task* – in this case a simple calculation task. The interaction time was raised to circa 6 s this way.

As far as the statement for practitioners is concerned after this variation, it has to be kept in mind, that the laboratory setting is always intended to push the burden to an extreme limit. We do not make final statements about what is better or worse under real conditions in this first step of the study, but rather that the cognitive-workload is relatively higher or lower. Given the case of the original setup without an upstream calculation task, the workload may be so low-threshold that it can be easily compensated in any case, so the relative difference will not become apparent unless we drive it to the top in the experiment. The final practical implications have to be found by the combination of this quantitative approach with qualitative contemplations.

For the assessment of the task fulfillment and the interpretation of the task loads (distraction by secondary task) different *'performance parameters'* were defined:

- Sum of the 'storage rack collisions' (usual problem in companies): Smaller collisions unfortunately happen everyday when handling forklift-trucks. Usually only special guide rails are touched on the storage racks. Nevertheless this is a quantifiable driving fault which is not unlikely to be caused by distractions.

The simulation platform was set up in such a way that every collision can be logged and transferred to a statistics program.

- Detection Response Task (DRT) according to ISO/DIS 17488 (visual): The *"Detection Response Task mainly intended for assessing the attentional effects of cognitive load on attention for secondary tasks involving interaction with visual-manual, voice-based, or haptic interfaces. Although the standard focuses on the assessment of attentional effects of cognitive load (…), other effects of secondary task load may be captured by specific versions of the DRT (…). Secondary tasks are those that may be performed while driving but are not concerned with the momentary real-time control of the vehicle"* [3].

Practically the response (Hitrate) and the reaction time (ms) on a visually presented stimulus will be measured. This stimulus is performed by an LED. The LED is in most cases brought to the participant by a headband to the edge of his field of vision (see Fig. 4 – alternatively a remote LED or a tactile vibration motor can be used – in our case a product of Red Scientific is in use). Every participant is instructed to react immediately to the periodic stimulus – every 3–5 s (see Sect. 4 for a critical discussion of the stimulus presentation in our specific case).

- Subjective assessment of the participants/survey (via Lime Survey): The *objective data* will be compared with a *subjective assessments* of the manifold indicating systems, and in particular with the various vehicle types. In this way, finer differences in terms of usability and risk assessment are to be identified.

It is self-evident to carry out a survey after each run to produce definable data. In addition to personal assessments, the NASA-TLX will be used for the *measurement* of the workload [4].

The detailed test procedure in collaboration with the mentioned professional participants is organized in 5 runs per participants. Every run is followed by the NASA-TLX survey:

- Training
  - Show the subject how the experiment looks like from outside (full task fulfillment by researcher)
  - Participant can familiarize himself with the secondary task
    On monitor: Display of the storage location + the following calculation tasks
    On HMD 1 (Vuzix/Google) – see above
    On HMD 2 (Epson) – see above
  - Participant can familiarize himself with the DRT
  - Participant can familiarize himself with the primary task - 5 min run
    Request whether operation is now possible without problems
  - After exercising, the participant can familiarize himself with the combined task set during the run
- Baseline Run
  - Proband should drive into the *test-hall*, as long as DRT is not active
  - Proband gets the first storage location verbally announced (!) – starts driving
    DRT stimuli start here
  - After a successful fulfillment of the driving task, another announcement of a storage location follows at a standstill. This procedure continues until 2 min (about 30 DRT-stimuli) passed
  - Survey NASA TLX
- Monitor Run
  - Start Secondary Task App – Participant gets first storage position on monitor still in standby – starts driving
    DRT stimuli start here
  - After starting the drive, the App will consistently display calculation tasks (in the cycle of 5 s) – to complete the tasks, the solution has to be pronounced loudly
  - After arrival at the storage location, the participants confirms via touchscreen/ HMD-Interface
  - Another storage location will be displayed, calculation tasks follow (see above).
  - Stop after 2 min (approx. 30 DRT stimuli)
  - Survey NASA TLX
- HMD 1 Run

- See above
- HMD 2 Run
  - See above
- Overlapping Survey of *comfort parameters* regarding the interaction:
  - Which indicating system did you like best?
    "Monocular" smart glasses
    "Binocular" smart glasses
    Monitor system
  - Which display system caused less distraction from driving?
    "Monocular" smart glasses
    "Binocular" smart glasses
    Monitor system
  - Did you experience any of the display systems as a visual handicap?
    "Monocular" smart glasses
    "Binocular" smart glasses
    Monitor system
    No
  - Other notes that you would like to inform us about?

The envisaged result matrix (summarized in Table 1) results from the consideration of the different vehicle types and indicating systems. The influence of the secondary tasks, in each case represented by different indicating systems, can thus be quantified and assessed in various typical application contexts (vehicle types). The performance parameters of each indicating system will be compared with the parameter of the baseline runs. As far as statistically significant deterioration results against the established monitoring system, the use of the devices at workplaces can not be tolerated without adaptation. The responsible employers' liability insurance association is strongly committed to this position.

Table 1. Proven result matrix: Type of forklift-truck/indicating system/performance parameter

	See through (Google Glass)	Look around (Vuzix)	Binocular (Epson)	Monitor	Baseline
Truck 1	• DRT visual • Driving fault • Survey	• DRT visual • Driving fault • Survey	• DRT visual • Driving fault • Survey	• DRT visual • Driving fault • Survey	• DRT visual • Driving fault • Survey
Truck 2	• DRT visual • Driving fault • Survey	• DRT visual • Driving fault • Survey	• DRT visual • Driving fault • Survey	• DRT visual • Driving fault • Survey	• DRT visual • Driving fault • Survey

Furthermore, an exemplary statement *"comparable secondary tasks on monocular systems can be tolerated on forklift-truck type x, binocular systems on forklift-truck type y not"* is possible for the very first time through this basic investigation. Workplace designs are thus made safer through the study. Risk assessments may be based on the results.

4   Critical Discussion – DRT Stimulus Presentation

The ISO 17488 discusses various variants of the presentation of the stimuli.

As mentioned, *"This includes two methods where the stimulus is presented visually and one method where the stimulus is provided by means of tactile stimulation. In the head-mounted DRT (HDRT), a visual stimulus (an LED) is presented through a fixture attached to the head of the participant at a specified visual angle. In the remote DRT (RDRT), a visual stimulus (e.g. an LED or embedded graphic in simulator scenario) is presented in the forward view of the participant. Finally, in the tactile DRT (TDRT), a tactile vibrator is placed on the participant's body"* [5].

In our specific case, we compare the indicating systems Monitor vs. smart glasses (HMD). The mentioned parameters are derived from the experiment. The critical discussion of the presentation of the stimuli is about the following aspect:

Do we possibly buy in an unreal disadvantage of the monitor system/preference of the smart glasses (HMD), if we work with a continuous HCI while driving and thereby performing the remote visual DRT?

That is why the monitor system always requires a head rotation that interferes with the perception of the stimuli in our specific scenario. The monitor would surely be worse in this extreme scenario, but under real conditions maybe even better. Where is the threshold, at which we adjust the setting so that it fits methodically and produces stable data, but the meaningfulness for the real work scenarios sinks?

This would be a clear argument for the tactile presentation of the stimulus (for HMD vs. monitor at first no disadvantage). Unfortunately there are strong arguments against the tactile presentation, from a quantitative/statistical point of view in terms of validity and discrimination of the data sets (see ISO 17488 - E.4.1.5 Poor absolute validity).

The final setup of the laboratory anticipates the ongoing discussion. The remote DRT is in use now (preference in statistical terms) and is positioned in a way, that no disadvantage for one of the indicating systems is given by the setup (remote DRT still in field of vision after head rotation).

5   Outlook

The adaptation of a relatively new method (DRT) into a context which is different from the context of the validation presented itself as a big challenge. First of all the difference is, that the application is not taken place in an *on the road traffic scenario* and the used task sets were not designed for an *in car use*. In addition, the relevant secondary tasks (picking task via indicating system) were structured by the practitioners very differently from the typical task sets that are used in cars (infotainment systems, for example). Nevertheless, the potential of the DRT appeared huge for our project.

The intensive discussion on the nature of the setup and the presentation of the stimuli is an expression of the adaption of the method into a new context. Also the question which stimuli presentation method is most beneficial for data processing and whether this is still suitable for the practice transfer, had to be answered anew in our field of research.

At the time of the presentation at the conference, first data will be available. The presentation will be enriched by specific case studies from the companies/practitioners.

Towards the end of 2017, the first series of experiments (N = 26) will be completed and will be submitted to the statistical evaluation. Further series of experiments are to be followed to include other forms of stimulus presentation. These data should be compared among each other.

References

1. Bretschneider-Hagemes, M., Ellegast, R., Friemert, D., Nickel, P.: Forschungsprojekte zum Einsatz von Datenbrillen in der Arbeitswelt, DGUV Forum - Ausgabe 11/2016, Arbeiten 4.0 (2016)
2. Bretschneider-Hagemes, M.: Mobile Informations- und Kommunikationstechnologie (IKT) am Fahrerarbeitsplatz - Beurteilung von Aufgabenlasten zur optimierten Arbeitsplatzgestaltung, sicher ist sicher - Arbeitsschutz aktuell, vol. 65 (2014)
3. ISO: ISO/DIS 17488 - Road vehicles — Transport information and control systems — Detection-Response Task (DRT) for assessing attentional effects of cognitive load in driving, p. 1. International Organization for Standardization (2015)
4. NASA: NASA Task Load Index (TLX) v. 1.0 Manual (1986)
5. ISO: ISO 17488 Road vehicles — Transport information and control systems — Detection-response task (DRT) for assessing attentional effects of cognitive load in driving. International Organization for Standardization (2016)

Finger Extension and Flexion: How Does the Trackpad Orientation Influence Product Evaluation in Social Media?

Wei Cui[1,2(✉)] and Deliang Wang[3]

[1] SAP Asia Pte Ltd., 30 Pasir Panjang Road #03-32,
Mapletree Business City 117440, Singapore
wei.cui01@sap.com
[2] National University of Singapore, 15 Computing Drive,
Singapore 117418, Singapore
cuiw07@u.nus.edu
[3] Institute of High Performance Computing, Agency for Science,
Technology and Research (A*STAR),
1 Fusionopolis Way, #16-16 Connexis, Singapore 138632, Singapore
wangdl@ihpc.a-star.edu.sg

Abstract. With the increasing prevalence of recommendation engine in social media, more research attention have been shifted towards understanding how can we influence better product evaluation from social media users. Multiple aspects of the design of the social media website have been extensively examined. However, in this study, we take a novel perspective by looking at the influence of users' actual physical behavior (bodily movement) during a viewing session. Three experiments are designed to examine how different trackpad orientations (natural vs. reversed) of laptop influence consumers' evaluation and memory of the recommended product displayed in social media. We predict that natural trackpad orientation will cause distinct perceptions of information processing fluency, resulting in differences in their evaluations and memories of the products online. The results are expected to show that when using natural scrolling, the high level of processing fluency are more likely to induce more positive evaluations but worse memory. In addition, we will demonstrate that shopping motivation will moderate the relationship. When consumers are conducting goal-oriented online shopping, the superior (inferior) effect of fluency on evaluation (memory) for natural orientation over reversed orientation will be weakened.

Keywords: Human-computer interaction · Finger movement · Social media · Information processing

1 Introduction

The past decade has witnessed a remarkable and unprecedented increase in e-commerce marketplace. This increase is represented by not only the skyrocketing sales numbers but also the surge in feature/function innovation and format/channel richness that are

© Springer International Publishing AG 2017
F.F.-H. Nah and C.-H. Tan (Eds.): HCIBGO 2017, Part I, LNCS 10293, pp. 308–321, 2017.
DOI: 10.1007/978-3-319-58481-2_24

driven by the constant advancement in technology. It gives consumers more choice, freedom, and better experience. And it also opens more research opportunities for us to better understand consumer behaviors. As such, multiple aspects of the design of the online shopping environment have been extensively examined. They predominantly focus on the interaction between consumers and the online content. Motivated by the recent trending imagination of the near-future virtual reality shopping design, this study takes a rather novel perspective by looking at the influence of users' actual physical behavior (bodily movement) during online shopping. We focus on the interaction between consumers and the technical devices. We believe that it is an easily-ignored but rather important aspect of online consumer behaviors.

It has been widely acknowledged that human bodily movement can reflect what people think as well as how they feel [1]. For example, a relaxed and open gesture delivers the signal of liking others [2], yet a stance of leaning backward indicates a negative feeling towards the object [3]. There also exists a stream of research describing attitude as a collection of motor activities [4]. Most researchers believe that postures capture human subjective evaluations of objects, and there exists a strong linkage between bodily movement and evaluation.

Further researches have also revealed that not only does this linkage exist but also that it is bi-directional, which means bodily movement can also in return influence the formation of evaluation and attitude. For instance, Casasanto [5] has found that right-handed individuals are more likely to associate rightward space with positivity but leftward space with negativity and vice versa for left-handed individuals. Such finding contains useful implications for marketers, with the intensive exposure to performing bodily movement using the dominant hand, right-handed (left-handed) consumers will be more likely to render a more positive evaluation when the product is placed in the rightward (leftward) space than leftward (rightward).

Following this branch of research, this study aims to investigate how bodily movement influences consumers' behaviors. Most existing literatures address the relationship between bodily movement and consumer behaviors in offline settings. For instance, arm flexion and extension have differential effects on attitude as arm flexion is more closely coupled with acquisition or consumption of the desired stimuli, leading to the association between arm flexion and positive attitude [6]. However, understanding how the influence of bodily movement transfer to the online context could also generate rich theoretical and practical implications. Without the real touch feelings and detailed assessment of product quality, how to let consumers have positive evaluation and deep impression is crucial. Despite product presentation formats, content details, reviews, and recommendations online, the interaction between consumers and the technological device that presents the production may also play an important role. Thus, the scope of this study is narrowed down to only investigating how the bodily movement in IT devices will influence consumers' behaviors.

More specifically, in this study, we are interested in how does finger movement influence online consumer behaviors when browsing shopping website using a touch device. According to Pew Research Center [7], a fact bank that provides information on social issues, computer ownership percentage among younger adults below 30-year-old has reached 78%. And for more convenient carry and use, consumers begin to abandon the habit of using mouse and turn to use trackpad embedded in the laptop. There are two types of trackpad orientation: natural and reversed. The natural scrolling orientation is that the website content flows in the same way as the movement direction of fingers, while the reversed scrolling orientation is inverted. Therefore, when the consumer scrolls the website from top to bottom to view the product information online, the conditions of figures are different. In the natural orientation, scrolling down the website makes the figures in the states of extension, yet flexion for reversed orientation.

Hence, this study aims to specifically investigate the impacts of the two trackpad orientations on consumers' evaluation and memory towards recommended products in social media. This study sheds lights into the interaction between physical movement and product evaluation, and fills in the research gap of lacking attention on the interaction between online consumers and technical devices. In order to establish the relationship between trackpad orientation and product evaluation as well as memory, information processing fluency is introduced as a mediator. We argue that natural orientation will produce a higher level of fluency, as a result of the fit between cognition and motor activity. Then the higher level of fluency will lead to a more positive evaluation but worse memory towards the product. Moreover, this study examines the role of shopping motivation, i.e. browsing-oriented shopping and goal-oriented shopping in moderating the effect of trackpad orientations. Thus, we further hypothesize that the superior (inferior) effect of fluency on evaluation (memory) for natural orientation over reversed orientation will be weakened in the condition of goal-oriented shopping.

The remainder of this study is organized as following. The next section reviews prior literature and provides theoretical foundations. The research model as well as hypotheses are developed, followed by experimental design procedures. Last but not least, conclusions including contributions and future work will be provided.

2   Theoretical Development

2.1   Embodied Cognition

When mind meets body, evaluations and judgments are subjected to be changed. For example, physical needs such as hunger can influence the person and transfer the person's attention to food; a smile may trigger the mental image of happiness and make the person to feel delightful when upset. Mind and body are tightly connected, in which way that cognition influences body movement, and body movement influences cognition [8]. Thus, instead of only assuming that perception leads to motor priming, researchers in embodied cognition (EC) argue a reversed causal chain – motor simulation actives and influences the perception [9]. In EC literature, there are two streams of research: mild embodiment and radical embodiment, which we will only focus on the former one.

One representative theory proposed in mild embodiment is perceptual symbols theory (PST) [10]. PST states that knowledge and perceptions are not developed from vacuum. Rather, they are originated from sensory and motor contexts of their occurrences. It is the sensorimotor information that helps to establish the conceptual representations. Thus, during the formation of conceptual representations, multimodal sensing including perceptual, motor and introspective states are recorded. Later when similar sensing is processed, the conceptual representations are reactivated.

2.2   Embodied Cognition and Processing Fluency

Researchers have demonstrated that actions are builders of how knowledge is represented, thus the motor cues will facilitate or inhibit decision making during information processing [11, 12]. The processing of information can be affected by many factors such as processing speed, accuracy and consistency [13]. All these factors combined lead to an experience of processing ease, which is defined as fluency [14].

When viewing social media websites, the multimode of sensing inputs are finger and the visual input from computer screen. In embodied research, a typical study is about how visual up and down affects the emotional valence. Implicit learning from daily associations between physical experiences and emotional states co-occurred, such as people are more likely to stand straight and tall when feeling proud but slouch when feeling depressed, it is easily to conclude that positive is up and negative is down [5]. Applying this metaphor to social media context, when consumers view the website from top to bottom, they will scroll the screen to let the screen move upwards. The upward motion may induce positivity for all consumers. However, different types of finger movements may cause distinct emotional valence, which will be congruent (incongruent) with the feelings caused by visual inputs, resulting in different processing fluencies. There is a lack of research in embodied cognition of finger, but we can refer to the arm motions to have a similar inference. When the fingers are in the state of extension, the state is more associated with daily experiences of approaching objects. On the contrary, when the fingers are in the state of flexion, it may remind consumers of being afraid of losing something. Thus, the finger extension may induce positivity, while negativity for finger flexion.

In the natural orientation, on the one hand, visual upward movement of website produces positivity; on the other hand, finger extension produces the positive feeling as well. Whereas, in the reversed orientation, finger flexion causes negative feeling, which is contracted with the positivity of visual sensing. The processing of information is considered as more fluent if two cognitions are congruent. In addition, natural orientation enables the movement directions of finger and visual input to be consistent, which may also enhance the feeling of fluency. Hence, we propose the following hypothesis:

Hypothesis 1. Compared to reversed orientation, natural orientation will produce a higher level of processing fluency.

2.3   Processing Fluency, Attitude and Memory

Multiple theoretical notions review that high fluency is reliably associated with more positive evaluations [13]. Regardless of the exposure repetition number, other variables that facilitate fluent processing also tend to increase liking. When the trackpad orientation is natural, processing fluency is expected to be higher, which will generate a more positive evaluation towards the product displayed online. Thus, we hypothesize as the following:

Hypothesis 2.1. The natural trackpad orientation will lead to a more positive evaluation towards the product via a higher level of processing fluency.

A more interesting relationship happens between processing fluency and memory. We argue that there is a twist here: though natural orientation gives rise to a positive attitude, it leaves a worse memory. Traditionally, researchers believe that a higher level of fluency will yield a better memory. However, in the social media context, this may not always apply. Usually the presentation content of product is not difficult to understand, i.e., it does not require a high cognitive load to fully digest the information, a relative lower fluency will not induce problems with understanding and memorizing the product. Instead, a lower level of processing fluency is possible to result in a better memory. Dual-process theories [15, 16] describe that there are two reasoning systems: system one is quick, effortless, and intuitive, yet system two is slow, effortful and analytical. The two systems are all related to human judgments, but which system dominates the process largely depends on the ease of difficult with which information comes to mind [17]. Alter et al. [18] verified that when the processing fluency was higher, system one would guide judgment; System two was operated to guide judgment when participants were experiencing disfluency. Therefore, the feeling of disfluency will activate analytical reasoning, pushing consumers to focus on the details of product and put more cognitive efforts to evaluate. When consumers viewing website using natural scrolling trackpad, the fluency may activate system one in a way that consumers tend to adopt holistic and quick viewing of the product information. As for reversed trackpad, the disfluency will trigger analytical viewing, which will leave a deeper impression of the product to consumers. Hence, we hypothesize the following:

Hypothesis 2.2. The reversed trackpad orientation will lead to a better memory towards the product via a higher level of processing fluency.

2.4   The Moderating Role of Shopping Motivation

Shopping motivations are categorized as two types: goal-oriented and browsing-oriented. Goal-oriented consumers have a targeted object in mind, and are more likely to process information of product in details in order to match their goal. Therefore, systematic processing is activated. Contrarily, browsing-oriented consumers have no specific goals in their minds. For example, large group of people in weibo like viewing products recommended by stars in their spare time. The main goal of browsing websites is to pursuit enjoyment [19]. Hence, they view product information more quickly and pay less attention to the details of product, employing heuristic processing strategy. In the previous section, we hypothesized that natural orientation will lead to a positive evaluation but worse memory due to fluency. But when consumers are goal-oriented, the systematic processing will neutralize the tendency of holistic viewing caused by fluency.

Essentially, even with natural trackpad orientation, consumers will still activate systematic information processing to evaluate product. In such case, evaluations towards the product will more depend on the assessment of the product itself, rather than the feeling of fluency. Hence, the positive attitude may be attenuated if the product viewed does not match consumer's goal. In terms of memory, since consumers will analyze the information of product naturally when they are using systematic processing strategy, so they will have a deeper impression regardless of the orientation of trackpad. In short, when consumers are goal-oriented when shopping online, systematic processing will dominate and moderate the effect of fluency. Stated formally, we propose the following hypotheses:

Hypothesis 3.1. The superior effect of fluency on product evaluation for natural orientation over reserved orientation will be weakened in the condition of goal oriented shopping motivation.

Hypothesis 3.2. The inferior effect of fluency on memory for natural orientation over reserved orientation will be weakened in the condition of goal oriented shopping motivation.

In summary, we argue that there is a fit between the emotion induced by finger motion and visual information, which helps to form a sense of processing fluency when the trackpad orientation is natural. Consequently, the processing fluency leads to a more positive product evaluation but worse memory towards the product. Finally, the shopping motivation is expected to moderate the effects between fluency and evaluation as well as memory. The theoretical framework is shown in Fig. 1.

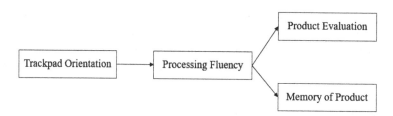

Fig. 1. Theoretical framework

3 Research Methodology

The relationship between trackpad orientation and product evaluation as well as memory is designed to be tested in three laboratory experiments. Study 1 tests the main effect of trackpad orientation on evaluation and memory. Study 2 tests the underlying processes and is expected to reveal that it is processing fluency that mediates the effect between trackpad orientation and attitude and memory. Combining the results of study 1 and 2, it should be possible to give some insights to the chain from trackpad orientation to fluency, and then to attitude and memory. Finally, study 3 examines the moderating effect of shopping motivation. Across the experiments, various products were used to generalize the results, ruling out the possibility of results validity being affected by product types.

The goal of study 1 is to test the main idea that different trackpad orientations have differential influences on product evaluation and memory towards the product viewed in social media. It is expected that natural orientation, compared to reversed orientation, participants will have a better evaluation towards the product, but a worse memory. When being recruited, participants are required to complete a short survey with demographic information, the laptop brand and experiences with using trackpad. Only participants using Apple laptops will be accepted. The laptop from Apple is chosen because most students who are using this device prefer to use trackpad than mouse. In addition, the design of trackpad of Apple laptops is more sensitive and comfortable. Also, the orientation of trackpad can be freely set as natural or reversed based on users' own preferences. Upon arriving at the lab, participants are randomly assigned to two groups and instructed to perform two tasks. All participants are provided with MacBook. In the natural condition, the trackpad orientation is set as natural, and similarly in the reversed group, the trackpad orientation is set as reversed. As participants may have their own habits of using trackpad, obvious sense of disfluency will occur if the trackpad orientation in experiment is contradicted with their habits, which will contaminate the interval validity of this study. In order to rule out this possibility, the first task aims to let participants get used to trackpad orientation in experiments. Basically the first task is to keep participants viewing website, using trackpad as much as possible. For example, the task can be viewing news website and providing feedbacks on the content or design. After an hour usage of trackpad, participants are given five minutes to relax. After finishing the first task, participants are required to proceed to the second task. A simple social media website with product recommendation is shown and there are five products with detailed information shown for each participant (Appendix 1). All five products are selected from various categories, and the sequences for five products displaying on the screen are counter balanced. The format of Amazon is chosen, and the product pages are usually in the waterfall format, meaning that the page lasts long, which guarantees that consumers will scroll down several times in order to see all the information listed. After this, participants are instructed to complete a post-experiment survey (Appendix 2). The dependent variable product evaluation is measured by a six-item and nine-point scale [20]. The participants will be presented with the image of the first product, and then rate from six aspects on nine-point scales (1 = bad/dislike/unfavorable/not useful/ undesirable/low-quality, 9 = good/like/favorable/useful/desirable/high-quality). Then participants will be presented the second product image and rated again, until the last one. The sequences of products presented will be counter balanced as well. For memory test, we have six memory questions for each product, asking its detailed information presented in the websites but not revealed in the images shown to participants.

Study 1 has several limitations that should be addressed by study 2. First, study 1 does not reveal the underlying mechanism between trackpad orientation and attitude and memory. Thus, study 2 is carried out to confirm the mediating effect of processing fluency. Second, mood will also influence the evaluation towards product, and the earlier exposure of certain product will affect the accuracy of memory results. Thus in study 2, we will measure the general mood state to ensure the validity of product, and ask participants whether they have seen same or similar product information before. After the first two tasks, participants are instructed to fill in a survey. Apart from the original questions in the survey, participants are asked to rate how fluent they perceived the website viewing procedure with the use of trackpad. Moreover, it is better to capture a more objective measure of processing fluency – the amount of time each participant takes to finish the website viewing for three products. Thus, another question is added to know whether there is a product that participants are particular interested in, which may interfere with the total duration on websites (Appendix 3). Besides the exact same two tasks (we choose different products displayed to prevent same participant memory or information contamination from Study 1), participants have two additional seemingly independent tasks after two weeks. The aim of the third and fourth tasks is to capture the emotion valance induced by finger movement and website movement as the processing fluency is predicted to be caused by emotion congruence. Two weeks later in the third task, participants are asked to rate their emotion valance after doing figure flexion and extension respectively. Similarly, in the fourth task, participants rate after seeing website moving up and down. The temporal separation is to prevent participants linking figure movements to the processing fluency questions in the survey, and then give fake answers due to demanding effect. They will be asked whether they have linked the two experiments together and guessed the true aim, and data will be removed if the answer is yes.

Study 3 is a 2 (trackpad orientation: natural vs. reversed) * 2 (shopping motivation: goal-oriented vs. browsing-oriented) experiment design. Same as in Study 1 and 2, participants are randomly distributed into one of the four conditions. The shopping motivation is manipulated by giving participants different tasks. For goal-oriented groups, participants are given a task of finding a birthday gift for friend, by knowing some function requirements from friend; in browsing-oriented groups, participants are told to browse websites naturally as usual to spend their leisure time. The experiment procedures are same as study 1: participants have same two tasks and fill in similar post-experiment surveys.

4   Conclusion

The study makes several theoretical contributions to different streams of research. First, it contributes to the knowledge body of embodied cognition literature. Prior research mainly focuses on the embodied cognition in offline setting. For example, researcher has studied how gestures changed thought [21]. However, few literatures really give insights into how gestures change behavior in online context. This study extends understanding of the relationship between motor activity and cognition by demonstrating how trackpad orientation and finger movement influence consumers' product evaluation and memory when browsing social media websites. It is shown that different finger movement can lead to different levels of processing fluency, which will affect evaluations of the product.

The study also contributes to the research stream of e-commerce. With most research stressing on online reviews, presentation formats and marketing strategies, this proposal creates a new angle of improving consumers' attitude towards the products. The research also examines the moderating effect of shopping motivation on attitude and memory. Thus, under the e-commerce context, although finger movement will influence consumers' evaluations, how much the evaluations and memory will be influences depends on shopping motivations. It is argued here that when consumers are browsing-oriented, natural trackpad orientation will result in positive attitude but reversed trackpad orientation will lead to a better memory. When consumers are goal-oriented, the differences will be weakened.

This research idea also has practical implications. It suggests that when designing the future highly interactive user viewing experience, social media networks should not only focus on designing the content but also designing how consumer physically interact with the content. With the current trend, future technologies and innovations should only make the physical device more and more interactive.

To point some future work directions for this research idea, first, one limitation of this study is that the emotions or feelings of fluency are measured by self-report surveys. Although viewing duration is added in order to support the fluency results, there is still a possibility that the results are biased. Hence fMRI is suggested to detect the differences between finger extension and flexion, as the brain activity level should be different for the two movement. Second, a more popular way to do online shopping now is to shop on mobile devices such as phones and pads. The most common interface of phones and pads are touchscreens, and there are different finger movements or gestures that can be recognized on the touchscreens. Thus, one possible future direction is to study how finger movements on touchscreen will change consumers' evaluations.

Acknowledgments. This research is supported by the National Research Foundation of Singapore and SAP Asia Pte Ltd. In addition, the authors would like to thank the editor and reviewers for expert comments and helpful advices.

Appendix 1 Website Format

Recommended products will be shown in the website with pictures and detailed product descriptions. An example of wallet is shown as below[1]. The descriptions of the product are long enough to ensure that participants scroll down the website several times and generate the feeling of fluency/disfluency.

---

[1] The source of the example is from https://www.amazon.com/Coffee-Thermal-Insulated-Tumbler-CF085Z/dp/B0160R1LEK/ref=gbps_img_s-3_bb19_5b4de19d?smid=ATVPDKIKX0DER&pf_rd_p=41fd713f-6bfe-4299-a021-d2b94872bb19&pf_rd_s=slot-3&pf_rd_t=701&pf_rd_i=gb_main&pf_rd_m=ATVPDKIKX0DER&pf_rd_r=CZJYASAZJZ9P83E06VJ4.

Appendix 2 Measurements of Variables in Experiment 1

Section A: Product Evaluation
Given the product above, please try to indicate the degree to which you agree with each of the following statements:

1. I think this product is good.

Strongly   o   o   o   o   o   o   o   o   o   Strongly
Agree   Disagree

2. I like this product.

Strongly   o   o   o   o   o   o   o   o   o   Strongly
Agree   Disagree

3. I have a favorable attitude towards this product.

Strongly   o   o   o   o   o   o   o   o   o   Strongly
Agree   Disagree

4. I think this product is useful to me.

Strongly   o   o   o   o   o   o   o   o   o   Strongly
Agree   Disagree

5. I want to buy this product.

Strongly   o   o   o   o   o   o   o   o   o   Strongly
Agree   Disagree

6. I think the quality of this product is high.

Strongly   o   o   o   o   o   o   o   o   o   Strongly
Agree   Disagree

Section B: Memory

Given the product above, please try to recall what you have viewed in the website and choose the most appropriate answer:

1. What is the capacity of the hot and cold tumbler?
   A. 16 oz.   B. 18 oz.
   C. 20 oz.   D. 22 oz.

2. Without a warming plate, how long does this machine keep your coffee hot?
   A. one hour   B. one and a half hours
   C. two hours   D. three hours

3. Which of the following serving sizes is not provided by this product?
   A. Travel mug   B. XL cup
   C. Half carafe   D. Full carafe

4. Which of the following functions is not available?
   A. Removable water reservoir   B. Integrated scoop
   C. Delay brew   D. Double-walled vacuum

5. How many paper filters does this product have?
   A. 3   B. 4
   C. 5   D. 6

6. What is the type of carafe of this product?
   A. Carafe with warming plate   B. Thermal carafe
   C. Table carafe   D. None of the above

Appendix 3 Additional Measurements in Experiment 2

Given the website viewing experience you just had, please try to indicate the degree to which you agree with each of the following statements:

1. The website viewing process was fluent.

   Strongly   o   o   o   o   o   o   o   o   o   Strongly
   Agree   Disagree

2. I could quickly understand the information in the website.

   Strongly   o   o   o   o   o   o   o   o   o   Strongly
   Agree   Disagree

3. I easily processed the information in the website.

Strongly
Agree   o   o   o   o   o   o   o   o   o   Strongly
Disagree

4. Is there any product that you are particularly interested in? Please indicate the product name if your answer is yes, or "N.A." if your answer is no.

References

1. Schneider, I.K., et al.: One way and the other: the bidirectional relationship between ambivalence and body movement. Psychol. Sci. **24**(3), 319–325 (2013)
2. Mehrabian, A.: Inference of attitudes from the posture, orientation, and distance of a communicator. J. Consult. Clin. Psychol. **32**(3), 296 (1968)
3. Eerland, A., et al.: Posture as index for approach-avoidance behavior. PLoS ONE **7**(2), e31291 (2012)
4. Darwin, C.: The Expression of the Emotions in Man and Animals, vol. 526. University of Chicago Press, Chicago (1872)
5. Casasanto, D.: Different Bodies, Different Minds: The Body Specificity of Language and Thought. Curr. Dir. Psychol. Sci. **20**(6), 378–383 (2011)
6. Burnstein, E., Crandall, C., Kitayama, S.: Some neo-Darwinian decision rules for altruism - weighing cues for inclusive fitness as a function of the biological importance of the decision. J. Pers. Soc. Psychol. **67**(5), 773–789 (1994)
7. Anderson, M.: Technology device ownership (2015). http://www.pewinternet.org/2015/10/29/technology-device-ownership-2015/
8. Weidler, B.J., Abrams, R.A.: Enhanced cognitive control near the hands. Psychon. Bull. Rev. **21**(2), 462–469 (2014)
9. Hauk, O., Johnsrude, I., Pulvermüller, F.: Somatotopic representation of action words in human motor and premotor cortex. Neuron **41**(2), 301–307 (2004)
10. Barsalou, L.W.: Grounded cognition. Annu. Rev. Psychol. **59**, 617–645 (2008)
11. Dijkstra, K., Kaschak, M.P., Zwaan, R.A.: Body posture facilitates retrieval of autobiographical memories. Cognition **102**(1), 139–149 (2007)
12. Niedenthal, P.M., et al.: When did her smile drop? Facial mimicry and the influences of emotional state on the detection of change in emotional expression. Cogn. Emot. **15**(6), 853–864 (2001)
13. Reber, R., Schwarz, N., Winkielman, P.: Processing fluency and aesthetic pleasure: is beauty in the perceiver's processing experience? Pers. Soc. Psychol. Rev. **8**(4), 364–382 (2004)
14. Reber, R., Winkielman, P., Schwarz, N.: Effects of perceptual fluency on affective judgments. Psychol. Sci. **9**(1), 45–48 (1998)
15. Kruglanski, A.W., Thompson, E.P.: Persuasion by a single route: a view from the unimodel. Psychol. Inq. **10**(2), 83–109 (1999)
16. Osman, M.: An evaluation of dual-process theories of reasoning. Psychon. Bull. Rev. **11**(6), 988–1010 (2004)

17. Kelley, C.M., Lindsay, D.S.: Remembering mistaken for knowing: ease of retrieval as a basis for confidence in answers to general knowledge questions. J. Mem. Lang. **32**(1), 1 (1993)
18. Alter, A.L., et al.: Overcoming intuition: metacognitive difficulty activates analytic reasoning. J. Exp. Psychol. Gen. **136**(4), 569 (2007)
19. Jiang, Z., Benbasat, I.: The effects of presentation formats and task complexity on online consumers' product understanding. MIS Q. **31**, 475–500 (2007)
20. Mukherjee, A., Hoyer, W.D.: The effect of novel attributes on product evaluation. J. Consum. Res. **28**(3), 462–472 (2001)
21. Beilock, S.L., Goldin-Meadow, S.: Gesture changes thought by grounding it in action. Psychol. Sci. **21**(11), 1605–1610 (2010)

Evaluation of the Usage of Support Vector Machines for People Detection for a Collision Warning System on a Forklift

Armin Lang$^{(\boxtimes)}$ and Willibald A. Günthner

Chair of Materials Handling, Material Flow, Logistics,
Technical University of Munich, Munich, Germany
{lang,guenthner}@fml.mw.tum.de

Abstract. Forklift drivers are required to work as quickly as possible while simultaneously being aware of humans crossing in front of the forklift. Many accidents in warehouses occur due to driver stress or negligence, some of which result in human injury. To reduce or prevent these accidents, solutions have been proposed to attempt to predict upcoming collisions. Since they are configured too sensitively, they display too many warnings, which causes them to be turned off by drivers. The research reported in this paper aims to reduce those accidents by using the latest camera technologies in combination with computer vision methods. A time-of-flight camera is used, which provides 2D as well as 3D data. The 2D data is used to detect humans in the driving path by using a support vector machine. Distinguishing between humans and other factors such as the storage facility allows a two-level warning system to be realized. The aim of this system is to allow warnings to be configured more sensitively when persons are in sight. The 3D data is used to calculate possible collisions and to segment the 2D image. The results presented in this paper focus on how the person detection with a support vector machine can be realized and optimized.

Keywords: Forklift safety · Warning system · Computer vision · People detection

1 Introduction

In 2015, about 11,687 reportable accidents with human involvement were caused by forklifts in Germany. In 38.6% of these cases, the injured persons were passive actors in the collisions, five of which ended mortally [1].

Commercially available products for accident prevention mostly use radar, radio, infrared or ultrasonic sensors and warn the driver acoustically [2–5]. One common property of all such available system is that they evaluate the distance between the forklift and an object. Thus, when the maximum allowed distance is exceeded, the driver is warned. But in practice, forklifts turn in very tight areas, which produces high numbers of warnings due to the violation of maximum distance. Consequently, forklift drivers often turn the warning system off. This problem is a result of the static distance threshold. Neither the driving path nor the speed of the forklift is considered, nor the movement of detected objects.

© Springer International Publishing AG 2017
F.F.-H. Nah and C.-H. Tan (Eds.): HCIBGO 2017, Part I, LNCS 10293, pp. 322–337, 2017.
DOI: 10.1007/978-3-319-58481-2_25

Recent developments in sensors, computer vision and in computer hardware have made it possible to calculate the trajectories of objects in real time by using 2D and 3D image data. As for sensors, in the last few years, a new sensor technology called time-of-flight has been established, mainly with the release of the first Microsoft "Kinect". Since the "Kinect" is only designed for gaming, there is also a development of 3D camera technologies in industrial sectors; this requires adaption of this technology to robust industrial standards like 24/7 use, e.g. SICK camera Visionary-T. Those cameras provide 2D and 3D data that can be used to capture the environment, e.g. of a forklift truck. The environment is ultimately not captured by the camera itself, but by methods of computer vision. These have made enormous progress in the last years. That is because the computing performance has also increased equivalently, especially graphics processing units (GPUs).

Combining this improved hardware (computers, sensors) with software led to the "PräVISION" project. The aim of this research project is to develop a two-level collision warning system. The main objectives are to develop a system that is:

- able to reliably detect up to 100%[1] of upcoming collisions
- able to distinguish between collisions with humans and those with other objects
- reliable, in the sense that all human-recognizable collisions are detected
- cheap
- robust with respect to industrial demands
- easy adaptable to every kind of forklift

2 Image Processing and Computer Vision Methods

The term image processing includes all actions that applied to images using a computer. Computer vision is one field of image processing and covers a wide field of applications. Most of these applications are in robotics and, more recently, in the automotive sector due to the development of autonomous cars [7]. One framework that supplies a large number of image processing methods is the "Open Source Computer Vision Library" (OpenCV) originally developed by Intel [8]. All the following methods can be found in this library.

2.1 People Detection

The algorithms used for people detection belong to the topic of machine learning. Few algorithms are specifically designed for people detection only; most methods implemented for this use case were actually intended for object detection in general. In order to detect specific objects, a classifier is needed. Classification means that data is allocated to a predefined category. The data can take various types. In the case of

---

[1] Obviously, a collision can only be avoided if it is possible for a human to avoid it. The time between the warning and the reaction of the driver and the braking time of the forklift cannot be influenced by the system.

people detection, the data is provided in the form of images. In this context, classification consists in allocating each whole image to a specific object category. Classifiers have to be trained with both data including the desired objects (positives) and data excluding them (negatives). One possibility approach is to train the classifier with raw images, i.e. with the color values. Another is to extract features from the image. One example of a well-established feature for person detection with a *support vector machine (SVM)* is the *histogram of oriented gradients* (hog). This approach mainly focuses on the extraction of contours [9]. *Cascade classifiers* typically use *(extended) haar-like features*, which represent a kind of standard lines e.g. horizontal lines [10, 11]. Another feature used for people detection with *cascade classifiers* is the *Multiscale Block Local Binary Patterns* [12]. This feature is designed for high performance, because only integer values are processed.

The above-mentioned classifiers *support vector machines* and *decision trees* (which also include *cascade classifiers*) are common choices of algorithms for people classification [13, 14].

The general operating principle of an *SVM* is to define vectors based on predefined features and training data. These vectors point toward the different kind of classes to be detected. Those vectors create regions in an n-dimensional space divided by a hyperplane. The vectors near to the hyperplane (i.e. within a certain margin) are most relevant and are called support vectors. The margin is specified during training in such a way that, during classification, samples will only be rated as positive if their vectors are in range [13].

Decision trees are the oldest type of classifier used for machine learning. These classifiers also have to be trained with predefined features before they are used. During training, the classifier adjusts the probability distribution of each object to be detected. The result of classification is binary, so it is not possible to define a threshold for object classification [14]. One special type of decision trees is given by *cascade classifiers* [10]. As the name suggests, multiple decision trees are arranged in cascaded loops. The deeper the stage of the loop, the smaller the analyzed features. Consequently, at the first stage, the input image can for example be analyzed by extracting four features, 20 features at the second stage, and so on. Each input image is only processed at deeper stages if it passes each of the previous stages. If the input image passes every stage, it is classified as positive; otherwise, it is classified as negative.

The term classification is often conflated with detection in the topic of image processing. In fact, detectors provide a classification and the position of the classified object. All classifiers can be converted to detectors by means of the so-called sliding-window method. The approach consists in running a window, smaller than the input image, over the whole image. At each step, the content of the sliding window is classified. In order to be able to detect differently sized objects, the size of the sliding-window is increased once the whole image has been processed [14].

2.2 Tracking

The aim of tracking is to improve the results of people detection, since it is not possible to detect every person in every frame. When an object is detected, distinctive pixels (often edges or corners) known as key points are extracted. These key points are subsequently located in the next frame. Another possible approach is to calculate some average value associated with the object, e.g. the average color value, and retrieve this value in the next frames.

3   Concept

The design of the collision warning system is essentially determined by defining the methodology, i.e. the sequence of applied methods (see Fig. 1). Firstly, the input data is preprocessed. Then the collision detection predicts upcoming collisions. The subsequent people detection differentiates between humans and facility storage. For each detected person, an object is created containing its history (recent positions, extracted key points). When a person is detected, he/she is allocated to an existing object, or a new object is created. Finally, in the output section, the driver is warned or some evaluation methods are processed. If a person is detected, the images also pass through the stages of 'prediction' and 'tracking'. In the 'prediction' stage, the new estimated position is calculated based on its previous positions. Tracking searches for the person near this estimated position.

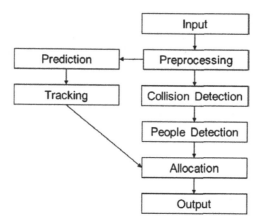

Fig. 1. Design of the methodology.

4   Implementation

Input. The collision warning system requires a greyscale (or color) image with a corresponding depth image as input. The greyscale (or color) image is used to detect people, and the depth image is necessary to calculate object movements. Time-of-flight cameras produce an infrared image that is more robust against environmental lightning as well as a corresponding depth image. With this type of camera, the depth data does not need to be calculated, unlike for stereo cameras. The Microsoft Kinect also produces a high-resolution color image. The color image cannot be used directly, because the scale and ratio values differ from the values of the depth data. It must first be mapped to the depth map. Pixels that cannot be found in both image types are removed during this process. This kind of image is called a registered color image in the following.

Preprocessing. The input of a people detector needs to be in a similar form to its training data. Since generating training data is very time-consuming, existing data is used (see Sect. 5.1), hence the input must be adapted to the training data. The existing training data typically consists of pictures taken by a stationary color camera pointed straight at a person with respect to the background. Since the databases contain colored images, there are no databases of infrared pictures. Moreover, the value of an infrared picture has 16 bits, with values ranging from 0 to 65536, hence more nuances are possible compared to an ordinary color frame, which has 8 bits and therefore values ranging from 0 to 255. In conclusion, the infrared image must be converted to 8 bits, and the color histogram must also be adapted.

People Detection. People detection is realized by implementing an *SVM* at this stage. The corresponding class in OpenCV provides a version that already implements the sliding-window method in order to extend the classification to a detection. The *histogram of oriented gradients* is used to classify the features, since it is commonly used for people detection (see Sect. 2.1). This implementation supports both CPU-based and GPU-based calculations.

Allocation. After a person has been detected, he/she must be allocated to an already found object, or a new object must be created. This decision is made by comparing the bounding boxes of the detected and saved objects. The equation describing this comparison is

$$r(i) = \frac{BB_e^i \cap BB_d}{BB_e^i} \geq c \ \forall \, i \tag{1}$$

$r(i)$:   resulting ratio of object
BB_e^i: bounding box of the last estimated area of the object i
BB_d: bounding box of the detected person

If the ratio $r(i)$ is greater than or equal to c, the new detected person is allocated to object i. A manual evaluation showed that the value of 0.6 for c works best. If it is not possible to calculate an estimate of the position because there has been only been one detection so far, the value of the last bounding box $BB_{t_1}^i$ plus a time-based factor is used for BB_e^i.

Prediction. Once a person has been detected at least twice, the estimated position can be calculated as follows:

$$BB_e^i = BB_{t_n}^i + \{[(1-\alpha)$$
$$* \frac{(BB_{t_n}^i - BB_{t_{n-1}}^i)}{(t_n - t_{n-1})} + \alpha^* \sum_1^{n-1} \frac{(BB_{t_{n-1}}^i - BB_{t_{n-2}}^i)}{(t_{n-1} - t_{n-2})}] + \beta\} * (t_n - t_{n-1}) \qquad (2)$$

Firstly, the latest movement change $(BB_{t_n}^i - BB_{t_{n-1}}^i)$ is normalized by the time between measurements $t_n - t_{n-1}$, followed by the past movements. The last movement is weighted by a factor of $(1 - \alpha)$, and the later movements are weighted by α. Secondly, a constant factor β representing the possible variation is added. Thirdly, the time-normalized change is multiplied with the timestamp of the last and the second-to-last detection. Fourthly, the new position is predicted by adding the average movement to the latest position. Finally, the rectangle is processed with a plausibility check whose aim is to check whether the borders of the picture are exceeded.

Tacking. Tracking is applied over the predicted area, so a person must be detected at least twice in order to be tracked. Several texture-based methods have been implemented: BOOSTING [16], MIL [17], TLD [18], MEDIANFLOW [19]. The classes used by these methods only support CPU-based calculation. The most relevant disadvantage of texture tracking methods is that they search for key points extracted from the first occurrence of the detected object. Because of the rectangular bounding boxes, key points are also extracted from the background. Consequently, in some cases the background is tracked as well as the person. In order to prevent this, the texture is only tracked for seven frames and then the tracked person is verified by the person detection algorithm. Furthermore, so-called retrieval detection is implemented. This approach consists in applying people detection to the predicted area, but with a lower acceptance threshold for detecting humans.

5   Evaluation

The methods used by the collision warning system depend on many parameters. The aim of the evaluation is to figure out which parameters are best in the given use case. The method of evaluation is based on Dollar et al. [15]. The first step was to generate the data used by all parts of the evaluation. The second step was to evaluate the training of the *SVM*. In the third step, the configuration of the people detector is considered.

5.1   Used Data

As described in Sect. 2.2, object detectors need training data to be able to distinguish between different kind of objects. In our use case, persons need to be detected, so the positive training images should contain people. As positive images, we used the pre-existing databases 'Daimler Monocular Pedestrian Detection Benchmark Dataset' [20] and 'INRIA Person Dataset' [9]. The images in these datasets simply show people in the middle of each picture. As negative images, pictures from a video taken at the experimental hall of our chair were used, because the negatives of pedestrian databases include streets, houses, etc. and do not represent the background of warehouses. Videos from Youtube showing the inside of warehouses were also used. Those videos were mostly advertising videos uploaded by intralogistical manufacturers. Parts that did not show facility storage were removed, as well as company logos, text, etc.

To test the algorithms, additional videos were taken with the Kinect mounted on the forklift truck, since the test data from the previously mentioned databases were taken by a stationary camera, but data from a moving camera was needed in order to guarantee representative comparison. This allowed all kind of streams (color, infrared, depth) to be saved. Those videos, designed to test the people detection, represented ordinary warehouse situations like people walking around or workers carrying a box.

5.2   People Detection

The efficiency of people detection depends on the training of the person detection algorithm and how the detector is configured during detection. The tracking of detected people also has an impact on the detection rate. In the following, the results of the training and configuration of support vector machines are described, as well as the effect of adding several tracking methods.

Training of Support Vector Machines. Firstly, the kind of data used for training was considered. We used different combinations of the image data described in Sect. 4.1. In the first run, pictures from the Daimler or the INRIA datasets were used as positive images. In both cases, the picture set showing the chair's experimental hall was used as negatives. The ratio of negative-to-positive training images was two-to-one.

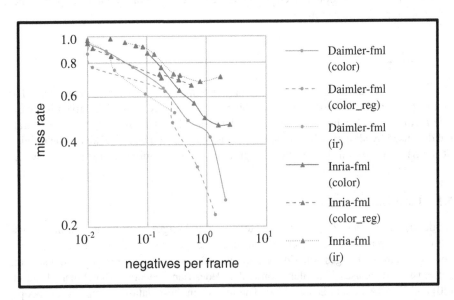

Fig. 2. Comparison of the different positive image sets used for training (database: Daimler and INRIA, input: all)

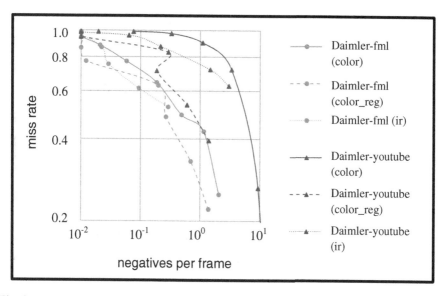

Fig. 3. Comparison of the different negative image sets used for training: experimental hall and experimental hall + youtube (database: Daimler, input: all).

Overall, the best results were obtained with the Daimler database (see Fig. 2). Out of the different input streams, the infrared ('ir') channel achieved the best results in terms of the ratio between the miss rate and negatives per frame. But even in the best case, 53% of the persons that needed to be detected were missed. The lowest miss rate of 22% was achieved when the registered color image ('color_reg') was chosen as input. The ordinary color ('color') input was consistently worse than the other inputs. But it cannot be assumed that the results of each input stream are directly transferrable to the other datasets. As shown in Fig. 2, with the INRIA database, the infrared input does not produce the best results, unlike with the Daimler database, in which case it does.

As well as varying the positive training data, alternative negative data was also used. The previously used negative data was extended by videos from Youtube. Adding this Youtube data led to a clear decrease in the detection quality (see Fig. 3).

One point mentioned in the description of the first test run was the ratio of negative-to-positive training images. In the third run, this parameter was investigated with both databases. It turned out that there is no universal value for the best ratio. In the case of the Daimler dataset, the detection worked best with a ratio of two-to-one (see Fig. 3). Consequently, there need to be twice as many negative training images. With the INRIA dataset, the best ratio was 1.8-to-one (not shown). The type of input stream did not make a difference in this case (Fig. 4).

The image provided by the camera is susceptible to motion blurring when the forklift truck is driving. Because of this, we also investigated the influence of softened training data. It became apparent that the softened training data does not make a noticeable difference, and detection even performs slightly worse for all input streams (see Fig. 5).

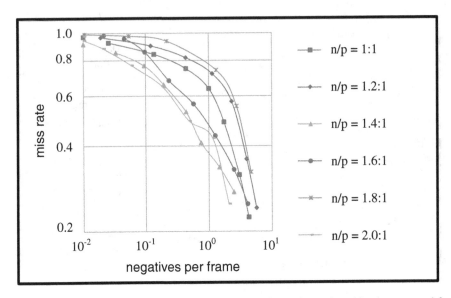

Fig. 4. Comparison of different ratios for the number of negative and positive images used for training (database: Daimler, input: color).

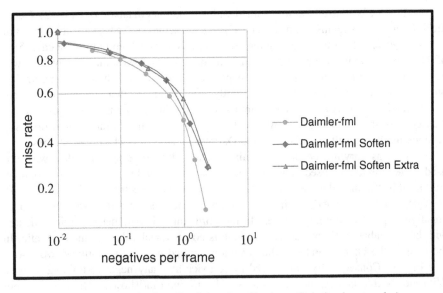

Fig. 5. Influence of softened training data (database: Daimler, input: color).

Application of Support Vector Machines. Once an *SVM* has been trained, it can be used to detect the objects for which it was trained. The detection then only depends on the given input and the configuration of the parameters of the *support vector machine*.

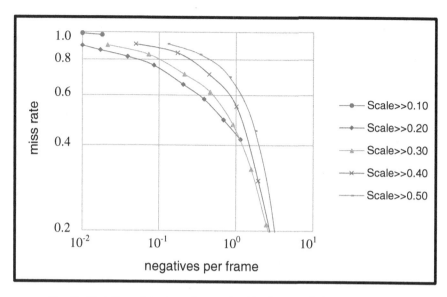

Fig. 6. Variation of the input image size (database: Daimler, input: color).

Some preprocessing steps can be applied to the input, as mentioned in Sect. 2.1. The colors are converted to greyscales and equalized anyway when the hog features are generated, and so these steps do not influence the detection. Softening and sharpening the input image as well as applying noise reduction did not make any difference at all. The only preprocessing method that affected the detection was changing the size of the input image. Scaling factors of 0.1 to 0.5 were tested on the color image, as well as scaling factors of 0.5 to 1.0 on the registered color and infrared image. The different scaling factors were chosen based on the different sizes of the streams of the Kinect. The ordinary color image has a resolution of 1980 × 1080 pixels, compared to 512 × 424 pixels for the registered color and infrared image.

In general, the smaller the input image, the fewer faraway persons are detected. This is also shown by the evaluation depicted in Fig. 6. The scaling factor of 0.10 led to almost no detection (color image). The best scaling factor was 0.20, corresponding to a resolution of 396 × 216 pixels. Like the color image, the best results for the registered color and infrared image were obtained using a resolution of 256 × 212 pixels (not illustrated).[2]

After having found the best resolution, some of the parameters of the *SVM* were varied. Specifically, there are two configurable parameters for the sliding window: *nlevels* and *h_scale*. The first defines how often the sliding window is enlarged, the second defines how much the window's size is increased at each level in percent.

---

[2] Note that the sensors of each stream have different opening angles, so the resolution cannot be transferred directly. Even though the registered color images are based on data from the color sensor, their opening angle differs because of the mapping onto the depth image.

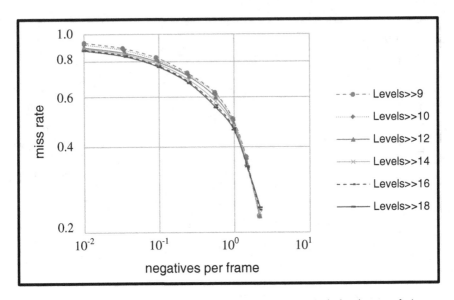

Fig. 7. Influence of the *nlevels* svm parameter (database: Daimler, input: color).

The influence of the *nlevels* parameter on the detection quality is very small (see Fig. 7). The miss rate can be decreased by at most 7.4% (comparison of *nlevels* = 9 and 18 at *negatives per frame* = 0.1) and the framerate drops by 14.3%. This result can be transferred to each type of stream. Basically, the test proved the obvious fact that the detection improves as more levels are used, while simultaneously causing the calculation time to increase. Saturation starts at the value of 16.

Varying the *h_scale* parameter (see Fig. 8) generates similar results. The worst detection was found for *h_scale* = 1.01, and the best was found for *h_scale* = 1.07.[3] The detection improved as the value increased for each kind of stream up to the value of 1.07. Values higher than 1.07 led to degradation. The difference between the highest and lowest miss rate was about 12.0% (*negatives per frame* = 0.1). Unlike the *nlevels* parameter, the framerate increased at higher values in addition to improving the results. This is because, at higher values, fewer sliding windows fit into the whole image, since each window is bigger. The increase of framerate thus obtained was about 11.5% (*h_value* = 1.01 → 1.07).

Improvement of Detection with Tracking. The previous section described the last optimization of the support vector machine itself. The following test run focused on the usage of tracking. The usage of tracking has two effects on the detection. On the one hand, true positives objects are tracked in consecutive frames, on the other hand false positives are also tracked. The last described behavior is not as strong when retrieval detection (*SVM*) was used as tracking method, because person detection is repeated in

---

[3] The value of 1.01 for 'h_scale' means that the size of the sliding window increases by one percent at each level.

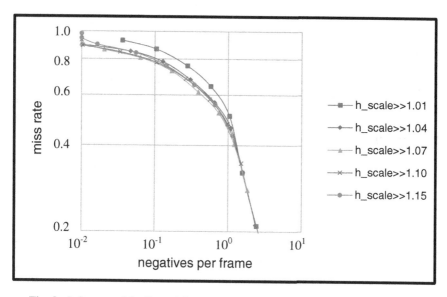

Fig. 8. Influence of the 'h_scale' svm parameter (database: Daimler, input: color).

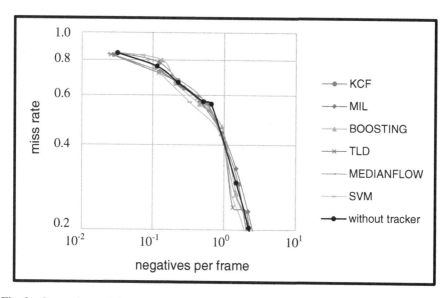

Fig. 9. Comparison of the detection of different tracking methods (database: Daimler, input: color).

the predicted area. *SVM* tracking performed best in the trial, followed by the *BOOSTING* texture tracking method (see Fig. 9).

The frames per second decreased when the texture-based tracking algorithms (*KCF*, *MIL*, *BOOSTING*, *TLD*, *MEDIANFLOW*) were used (see Fig. 10). The *MIL*, *BOOSTING*, *TLD* methods in particular radically reduced the framerate, by as much as

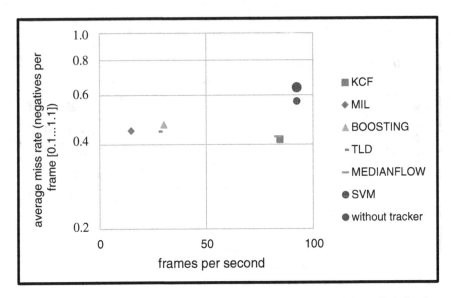

Fig. 10. Comparison of the framerate for different tracking methods (database: Daimler, input: color).

84% (*MIL*). Retrieval detection had no influence on the frame rate at all, because the algorithm runs anyway for ordinary people detection. Therefore, only the tracking methods *KCF*, *MEDIANFLOW* and *SVM* are viable because they do not need as much computing power, while simultaneously providing good results.

Optimized Algorithms. Finally, we applied all optimizations from the previous investigations. The parameters can be obtained from Table 1:

Table 1. Default and optimized settings for people detection.

	Default value	Optimized color value	Optimized color_reg value	Optimized infrared value
Training				
Positives	Daimler	Daimler	Daimler	Daimler
Negatives	fml	fml	fml	fml
Ratio (n/p)	1.5	2	2	2
Preprocessing				
Scale	0.5	0.2	0.6	0.6
SVM parameters				
h_scale	1.05	1.07	1.07	1.07
nlevels	13	16	16	16
Tracking				
Method	w/o	SVM	SVM	SVM

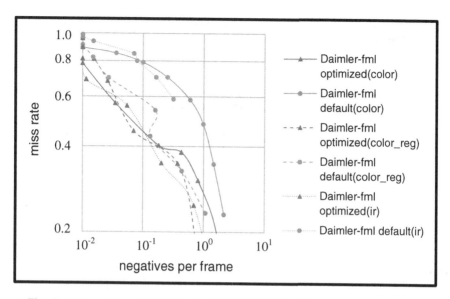

Fig. 11. Comparison of default and optimized *SVM* (Database: Daimler, input: all).

The detection of color images improved significantly. The miss rate could be reduced by 41% at *negatives per frame* = 0.1 relative to the default configuration (see Fig. 11). In the case of a registered color input, the *miss rate* was 25% lower at *negatives per frame* = 0.1. But the most important achievement was for infrared input. In this case, the *miss rate* dropped by 41% (*negatives per frame* = 0.1).

6 Conclusion and Outlook

The "PräVISION" project is currently researching a collision warning system for forklift drivers. Time-of-flight cameras are used to generate the input data, since they are independent of the environmental lightning and do not require calibration. The methodology of collision warning can be divided into input preprocessing, collision detection, people detection, and postprocessing or output. The algorithm used for people detection is the *support vector machine* algorithm. Several training and application parameters were tested to determine their influence on the detection quality. Different tracking methods were also implemented. Tracking algorithms based on texture matching in particular suffered from the fact that they required too much computational power. The best tracking method was to apply the people detector to a predicted area but with a lower threshold.

There are several upcoming tasks that we wish to complete before the end of the project:

- Addition of other features than *hog* to the *SVM*
- Implementation of the cascade classifier for people detection
- Implementation of a depth data-based tracker

- Segmentation of the 2D picture by using 3D data for clustering into objects
- Consolidation of all algorithms into one system
- Trials in an industrial environment

Acknowledgment. The research project "PräVISION" with proposal number FP 379 is funded by "Deutsche Gesetzliche Unfallversicherung". The following project partners are involved:

- Chair of Materials Handling, Material Flow, Logistics at the Technical University of Munich (TUM)
- Bremer Institut für Produktion und Logistik GmbH
- SICK AG
- STILL GmbH
- Berufsgenossenschaft für Handel und Warenlogistik.

References

1. Standtke, W.: Arbeitsunfallgeschehen, Deutsche Gesetzliche Unfallversicherung, München, p. 70f (2014)
2. tbm hightech control GmbH: RRW-207/3D; RAM-107; RRW-107plus. http://www.tbm.biz
3. ELOKON GmbH: ELOprotect; ELOshield; ELOback^2. http://www.elokon.com
4. U-Tech GmbH: http://www.u-tech-gmbh.de
5. ARCURE: Blaxtair®. http://www.arcure.net
6. SICK: Visionary-T. http://www.sick.com
7. Winner, H., Hakuli, S., Wolf, G.: Handbuch Fahrerassistenzsysteme – Grundlagen, Komponenten und Systeme für aktive Sicherheit und Kom-fort, p. 422ff. Vieweg+Teubner Verlag/Springer Fachmedien Wiesbaden GmbH, Wiesbaden (2015)
8. Open Source Computer Vision Library: http://www.opencv.org
9. Dalal, N., Triggs, B.: Histograms of oriented gradients for human detection. In: CVPR, pp. 886–893 (2005)
10. Viola, P., Jones, M.: Rapid object detection using a boosted cascade of simple features. In: CVPR (2001)
11. Liao, S., Zhu, X., Lei, Z., Zhang, L., Li, S.Z.: Learning multi-scale block local binary patterns for face recognition. In: Lee, S.-W., Li, S.Z. (eds.) ICB 2007. LNCS, vol. 4642, pp. 828–837. Springer, Heidelberg (2007). doi:10.1007/978-3-540-74549-5_87
12. Lienhart, R., Kuranov, A., Pisarevsky, V.: Empirical analysis of detection cascades of boosted classifiers for rapid object detection. In: Michaelis, B., Krell, G. (eds.) DAGM 2003. LNCS, vol. 2781, pp. 297–304. Springer, Heidelberg (2003). doi:10.1007/978-3-540-45243-0_39
13. Vapnik, V.: Estimation of dependences based on empirical data (1979). (in Russian)
14. Süße, H., Rodner, E.: Bildverarbeitung und Objekterkennung – Computer Vision in Industrie und Medizin, pp. 473ff–598ff. Springer Vieweg, Wiesbaden (2014)
15. Dollar, P., Wojek, C., Schiele, B., Perona, P.: Pedestrian detection: an evaluation of the state of the art. IEEE Trans. Pattern Anal. Mach. Intell. **34**(4), 743–761 (2012)
16. Grabner, H., Grabner, M., Bischof, H.: Real-time tracking via on-line boosting. BMVC **1**, 6 (2006)

17. Babenko, B., Yang, M.-H., Belongie, S.: Visual tracking with online multiple instance learning. In: IEEE Conference on Computer Vision and Pattern Recognition, 2009. CVPR 2009, pp. 983–990 (2009)
18. Kalal, Z., Mikolajczyk, K., Matas, J.: Tracking-learning-detection. IEEE Trans. Pattern Anal. Mach. Intell. **34**(7), 1409–1422 (2012)
19. Kalal, Z., Mikolajczyk, K., Matas, J.: Forward-backward error: automatic detection of tracking failures. In: International Conference on Pattern Recognition, pp. 23–26 (2010)
20. Enzweiler, M., Gavrila, D.M.: Monocular pedestrian detection: survey and experiments. IEEE Trans. Pattern Anal. Mach. Intell. **31**(12), 2179–2195 (2009)

A Comparison of Attention Estimation Techniques in a Public Display Scenario

Wolfgang Narzt[✉]

Johannes Kepler University, Linz, Austria
`wolfgang.narzt@jku.at`

Abstract. Human interaction with a public display presupposes a person's attention. An Interactive display, hence, aims at attracting attention by e.g. emitting a strong signal that makes the inattentive visitor turn towards it. The challenge in this regard is to reliably determine the attention of passers-by. In this article, we investigate different technical methods for estimating attention in a public display scenario by measuring physical expressive features, from which attention can be derived. In the course of an experimental setup we compare a Support Vector Machine, a neural network using a Multilayer Perceptron and a Finite State Machine and compare the results to a manual reference classification. We carve out strengths and weaknesses and identify the most feasible measuring method with regard to precision of recognition and practical application.

Keywords: Attention estimation · Support Vector Machines · Neural networks · Multilayer Perceptron · Finite state machines

1   Introduction

Public displays have evolved to an acknowledged enabling technology for shopping scenarios [9]. Retail traders recently aim at displaying interactive content and offer innovative (e.g., gesture-based [8, 10]) interaction in order to attract by-passers and to potentially increase sales. However, interaction with a public display presupposes a user stopping in front of the display and focusing to its content. Thus, enticing passers-by to a focused interaction (depending on how much attention they are already paying) has been recognized as a recent challenge in attention estimation research [3, 7]. An attention-aware display might want to present content in a way that indicates that a head-on looking visitor has been registered and is addressed individually.

Within advertising and marketing, such attentive user interfaces [1, 11, 16] are applied to raise attention of an already interested person, which is referred to as the AIDA principle (i.e. attract Attention, maintain Interest, create Desire, and lead customers to Action [12]). It either draws a user's attention or motivates interactions [19] and has led to a series of recent research projects (see e.g. [16, 20]), additionally stimulated by affordable and miniaturized sensing technology capable of measuring inadvertent cues from human subjects indicating their current state of attention.

Measuring attention is a means to the end of improving reaction of an interactive system to its users' attention. Attention-aware displays therefore need to continuously

© Springer International Publishing AG 2017
F.F.-H. Nah and C.-H. Tan (Eds.): HCIBGO 2017, Part I, LNCS 10293, pp. 338–353, 2017.
DOI: 10.1007/978-3-319-58481-2_26

estimate the attention of persons they can perceive and need to have internal models for what types of signals may be appropriate to reach the goal of raising or lowering the attention a person is devoting to the display.

Most of suchlike attention-aware systems are closed and only locally react to estimated states of their viewers, whereas networked solutions aim at interacting with viewers across larger spaces with multiple displays and sensors. This, however, is a highly interesting scenario, especially for the e-commerce sector, where visitors are not only addressed differently depending on their state of attention, but also depending on the history of interaction.

Networked systems also deliver the background for our research: In the course of a federal initiative for building a smart city in a suburban area near Vienna ("Seestadt Aspern"), Siemens intends to install City Hubs at public places around the city, i.e. interactive networked displays providing tailored information or services for passers-by. A City Hub is supposed to automatically and context-sensitively draw a visitor's attention to its screen and to simultaneously address an already interacting person as well as a glimpsing by-passer in its peripheral field of view. Due to NDAs, we are not permitted to give any example of a City Hub application, nor can we provide further insights regarding location or number of installation sites. However, we may mention that City Hubs will be used for e-commerce services, as well, (amongst other application domains) and act as connected network nodes across a city area that "globally" capture contextualized information for individual human-machine interaction.

In this paper, we aim at evaluating different attention estimation methods in the context of public displays and assess our results in terms of effectiveness, accuracy, configuration costs and practical application. We therefore present an appropriate tailored attention model for public displays (derived from well-known and established models [3]) and experimentally (i.e. in a public scenario with arbitrary visitors in front of a display) oppose performance, accuracy and error rates to a manual reference classification. A critical assessment of our research and the examined measuring methods and considerations for further research, conclude our work.

2   State-of-the-Art

Human attention has primarily been investigated from a psychological point of view. It has been characterized by relations between attention allocation, attention capacity and task effort [6]. Attention, in very general terms, is the *"process by which organisms select a subset of available information upon which to focus for enhanced processing and integration"* [17]. The link to the computer vision domain arose in the 1980s and is based on a seminal psychological contribution by Treisman and Gelade [13], who proposed an attention model explaining the transition from the pre-attentive processing of pure features to the identification of objects characterized by a conjunction of features (Feature Integration Theory). It proved highly influential in many attention models developed in the context of computer vision applications.

Wickens and McCarley [18] derived a formula that yields an attention estimate for particular objects from quantifiable factors called Saliency, Effort, Expectancy and

Value (SEEV). This approach has proven popular as a simple base model that helps to structure the parameterization of attention factors without specifying a concrete attention formation process. Most of the proposed models either satisfy pure computer vision goals without describing biological and neurophysiological processes, or manage to straddle both the computer vision and biological requirements [14].

Research that is in the line of automatic detection of attention of human subjects is less interested in the internal attention processes, and more in external indicators of the results of those processes, in the extent to which they can be analyzed for the purpose of estimating a subject's attentional status. Such cues are called overt attention and comprise body, head and eye movement, whereas mental shifts of focus are called covert attention and can, if they occur without any overt components, generally not easily be measured without interrogating the subject [17].

Meanwhile, inadvertent overt cues can be measured using affordable sensing technology, which has recently stimulated research on attention-based interactive systems. Gollan et al. [5] e.g. employed a consumer-grade and accordingly low-cost Microsoft Kinect depth camera for measuring attention. A suchlike system is affordable and, most of all, unobtrusive, i.e. people need not be aware that they are being tracked. The authors aimed at clustering by-passers in an uncontrolled public display scenario into one of several distinct categories using Support Vector Machines and referring to Wickens' SEEV model in their reasoning. A "short time frame" (STF, spanning the past three frames only) comprised categories such as "Peripheral Visual Range" and "Concentrated Gaze", whereas the "long time frame" (LTF, beginning with the first in which a subject appeared, up to the current one), contained categories such as "Glimpser" and "Stopper" (see Fig. 1).

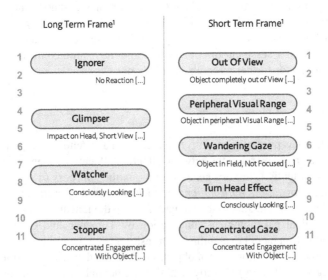

Fig. 1. Attention concept (Gollan et al.)

Validation of results was conducted against the results of manual tagging of the recorded material and showed an accuracy of 92.3% for LTF and 85.5% for STF. In general, the research done by Gollan et al. seems most promising of the minimally obtrusive approaches (also see [3]).

More recently, the authors also approached the same experimental context (using the same data) from a different perspective: They showed that using the aforementioned SEEV-Model, the factor of Effort exerted by a subject to change his/her movement, position or head pose is correlated to various degrees with the probability of increasing his/her level of attention [4]. An important difference to the method before is that relative changes in attention could be estimated without supervised machine learning methods.

3 Approach

The attention model proposed by Gollan et al. has been selected as the basis for our investigations as it is promising threefold:

1. It is derived from the proven SEEV model and therefore claims to build upon mature attention estimation structures.
2. Its accuracy is compelling in terms of correct estimation of attention states even when using low-cost sensors or cameras.
3. It is not necessarily dependent on the use of machine learning methods in order to estimate attention states. Also, other approaches apply (see [4]).

Particularly, point 3 is of major interest, as machine learning approaches require preceding training phases and appear to be inflexible regarding e.g. changes of camera position or untrained events. Our intention is to investigate different estimation techniques (whereby the SVM approach has turned out to be the most common in this domain – with the drawback of lengthy initialization) pursuing two objectives:

1. Identification of the most accurate and performant method in terms of detecting the correct attention state (disregarding complexity, effort or costs)
2. Identification of the most practical method in terms of simplicity, operational readiness and flexibility regarding changes in the setup (e.g. camera shifts)

For these comparisons, we opposed a classical SVM, a second automatic learning technique with neural networks using a Multilayer Perceptron (MLP) and a straight approach performed by a Finite State Machine (FSM). First, though, we have to discuss a few adaptations we did on the Gollan model in order to customize it to the requirements of our aforementioned City Hub scenario: The original model proposes 11 distinct attention states both for STF and LTF (see Fig. 1), but aggregates them to 4 (for LTF), respectively 5 (for STF) labeled states for better human comprehensibility. The remaining subparts (secondary states) primarily divide their higher-ranking labeled states by means of time (for LTF, e.g. how long is a person glimpsing? Short-medium-long) or distance (for STF, how distant is the stimulus? Far-medium-close).

For our requirements, we on the one hand suggest to reduce the number of attention states (both labeled and secondary states) and on the other try to merge STF and LTF classifications in a way that we always use current snap-shot data contextually considering the historic progress. This simplification is done in respect to practical applicability and is backed on the following arguments:

1. In the original model, it is difficult to distinguish between a "Glimpser" and a "Watcher" in the LTF showing a blurred borderline in the model definition when considering secondary states: How can we differentiate between a "long glimpse" and a "short conscious look"?
2. The "Concentrated Gaze" in the STF is characterized by a "concentrated engagement with an object" and distinguishes two secondary states with "medium stay" and "long stay" (again amongst other attributes). However, as the STF aggregates measurements from only 3 frames, we are not sure how to measure a medium or long stay in this context without a history of data.
3. Is an application using this attention model supposed to react on all attention states in each of the timeframes STF and LTF? As there is no justified answer to this question (it always depends on the application domain), it is up to the reader to subjectively rate on the quantity of states and on how he/she would react on a "long glimpse" in contrast to a "short conscious look".

The reduction process finally reveals three remaining (labeled) attention states "ignoring", "watching" and "ready to interact", which we use to estimate the degree of attention of passers-by (see Fig. 2).

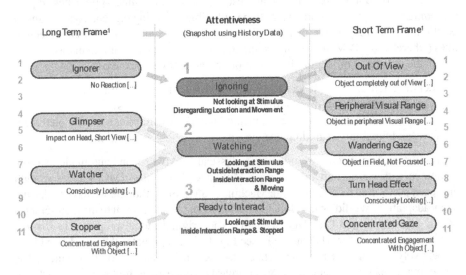

Fig. 2. Attention model deduction

These states are defined as follows:

1. The attention state A of a person p is "*ignoring*" when the person is not looking at a stimulus (display) regardless whether the person is moving or standing still at any location.

2. The attention state *A* of a person *p* is "***watching***" when the person is facing a stimulus, being too far away for interaction (outside an interaction zone). *p* remains "*watching*" inside the interaction zone while moving.
3. The attention state *A* of a person *p* is "***ready to interact***" when the person is facing a stimulus and has stopped inside the interaction zone (i.e., the person is close enough for interaction).

Following the example of the attention model of Gollan et al., our conceived labeled attention states are subdivided into secondary states offering a more focused distinction of what a person is actually doing. In our model, we introduce these secondary states using another layer of detail (see Fig. 3): Given that the three labeled attention states are settled on the highest layer representing the highest degree of abstraction (i.e. we put them on layer 3), the secondary attention states are on layer 2, including information on a person's focus, moving direction and distance, from which the layer 3 classifications can be inferred. Still, those states are abstract with features like "*moving away*" or "*moving perpendicular*", yet, they add information to the higher-ranking states on layer 3. The base layer 1 finally represents the technical basis and provides input data that can be measured by all kinds of sensors.

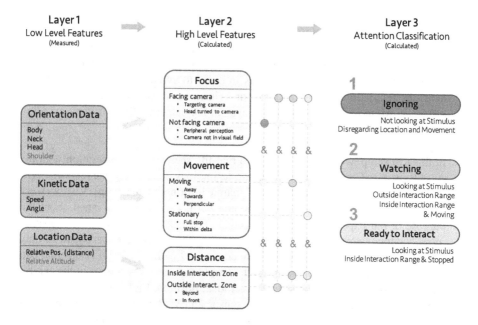

Fig. 3. 3-Layer attention model

Taking a closer look onto the model, we recognize that the attention states on layer 3 can be calculated by a logical combination of features from layer 2. While the attention state "*ignoring*" just utilizes the "*not facing stimulus*" feature of layer 2 (disregarding any movement or the location of a person), "*ready to interact*" combines focus, movement and distance in a way that a person must "*face the stimulus*" while "*stationary*" and "*inside the interaction zone*". Thus, we conclude that the attention states on layer 3 can be calculated using a rule-based system (i.e. a Finite State Machine, FSM). These findings are the basis for our investigations on different attention estimation methods. As the FSM seems to consist of a simple rule-set (although the actual implementation is more complex than depicted in Fig. 3, using e.g. grading at the transition between states) it potentially represents a manageable alternative for estimating attention compared to established but complex machine learning methods.

4   Experiments

For comparison of different attention estimation methods, we created an experimental setup in the context of a museum scenario using a Microsoft Kinect v2 depth camera. The camera delivers position data, orientation and, as much as possible, gaze of the visitors, from which attention parameters can be estimated. As the museum scenario is uncontrolled we also wanted to have a guided setup enabling us to compare results disregarding environmental factors, thus, resulting in the following two setups:

1. Laboratory setup
   In the laboratory setup, we ensured optimal camera angles, good contrast and light conditions in order to minimize measurement errors. All participating persons were aware of the experiment, and we created a rough screenplay ensuring a balanced output of all three labeled attention states. We limited the distance between stimulus and person to a maximum of 4 meters in order to avoid measuring errors due to hardware restrictions as the depth sensor's (infrared) reliability decreases at larger distances. Moreover, only one person was in the camera's field of view avoiding occlusions and feature data loss.

2. Museum setup
   In this test setup, we collected data in a real-life scenario. In cooperation with the Ars Electronica Center, a museum for art, technology and society, we recorded visitors near an exhibit (a screen showing dynamic information in a loop). Visitors were aware about video surveillance in this area but had not been informed about the purpose of our experiment. And, as manual classification took place in a separate room, visitors were unaware that their attention was part of an experiment, so they acted naturally. Unfortunately, we were confronted with a series of issues that had to be considered when comparing results: Due to technical restrictions of the exhibit we were unable to place the sensor in an ideal position. Lighting conditions were suboptimal, and the distance between sensor and visitors was often >4 m. As a consequence, we were expecting measuring errors, particularly at larger distances.

Right after capturing the test persons on video, we classified the attention levels manually in order to create a ground truth for all further evaluation. To do so we developed a classification tool capable of synchronously playing the recorded video and feature data files generated by the Microsoft Kinect v2 with options to classify every single video frame in arbitrary replays. The person operating the tool was able to stop the video at any time and move through the video frame by frame. This process was conducted by two persons independently in order to minimize subjective misinterpretations. In total, we classified about 23000 frames for all tests (with varying framerates between 15 and 30 fps – dynamically managed by the Kinect), i.e. we rely on video material of approx. 20 min net, where persons were classifiable (more than 2 h gross). We achieved accordance of 92.34% between the two classifiers. For differently rated frames we set the attention state by bilateral negotiations afterwards.

This ground truth was then used for further training and evaluation. As machine learning methods require training phases we provided 50% of the manually classified data as training data and performed 5-fold cross validation, i.e. we split the training set into 5 subparts, 4 of which contained training data, and used them to predict the attention levels in the remaining subpart. This procedure was repeated 5 times for every permutation for both SVM and MLP.

5   Results

We have evaluated three techniques for determining the attention. Due to its predominance in literature we trained a Support Vector Machine (SVM) on our datasets which proved to work reasonably well. However, the simplicity of our attention model and the low number of features used to estimate the three labeled attention states *ignoring*, *watching* and *ready to interact* (see Fig. 3) convinced us to implement a state machine for classification as this has several advantages over a machine learning approach:

- A state machine as a rule based system requires no training with a labeled data set, which in our scenario of public displays is a definite advantage.
- The state machine allows for easier adaption of sensor placement in relation to the stimulus via parameters.

While our implementation of a state machine doesn't achieve the same accuracy as an SVM it does work reasonably well to justify such an approach, especially considering the advantages it has over methods of machine learning in our scenario. In contrast, we compared the SVM with a neural network, in this case a Multilayer Perceptron (MLP), to see if results can be improved when pure accuracy is of utmost priority. Both SVM and MLP had problems with the quality of our recordings, as the dataset from the museum scenario turned out to be unbalanced regarding the three labeled attention states as predictably the majority of visitors captured by the sensor were ignoring the surveyed exhibit. This imbalance is expected in a public display setting; however, it does constitute a problem for training an SVM or MLP as this imbalance is likely to skew their respective predictions.

The dataset consists of 68678 frames recorded over two days. We then filtered this data, thus only frames containing valid values for head rotation remained. We also removed a small window of 10 frames directly around attention state changes to reduce the impact of sensor noise, which left us with 14177 frames. The skewed nature of the museum dataset has prompted the generation of a more uniformly distributed dataset; thus, this second dataset was recorded in our lab and contains 8591 usable frames with a roughly equal distribution in our defined attention states.

5.1 Support Vector Machine

A Support Vector Machine is a method of supervised machine learning introduced in [15]. The idea is to map input vectors to a high-dimensional feature space and then try to construct a decision surface to separate two given classes. Depending on the kernel used this surface can be linear, polynomial or with specialized kernels of arbitrary shape. As this method is only able to separate two classes there are tricks to generalize for multiclass problems. The predominant strategy is one-against-one where an SVM is trained for every pair of classes and the decision is made on which SVM gets the most votes. This is also the strategy employed by the implementation we use.

We trained several SVMs using 5-fold cross-validation with linear and Gaussian radial basis (RBF) kernels. Linear kernels proved to be unable to separate our classes satisfactorily but the RBF produced good results. The final parameters were selected by performing a grid search in a manageable parameter space. To satisfy the necessary condition for an SVM of samples being independent, they are randomized prior to training with values between 1 and 10 for costs C and 0.1 to 1 for *gamma*. The parameters for our final model were $C = 5$ and $gamma = 0.75$ as this parameter setting worked equally well for both our datasets.

As has already been stated, the dataset from our real-world scenario is heavily skewed towards one class. Therefore, we introduced class weights to the SVM algorithm to account for this imbalance. In the end, we achieved an overall accuracy of 97.83%. Table 1 shows the results of the SVM classifier detailed by class and distinguished by sensitivity (true positive rate, TPR) and specificity (true negative rate, TNR). The table reads as follows: We had 6424 matches for the attention state ignoring. 74 were estimated to be watching while their manual reference classification was ignoring, etc. The skew towards the ignoring state is immediately obvious.

Table 1. SVM results on the museum dataset.

		Predicted			Sensitivity (TPR)	Specificity (TNR)
		Ignoring	Watching	Ready to interact		
Actual	Ignoring	6424	74	6	98.77%	87.52%
	Watching	73	296	1	80.00%	98.90%
	Ready to interact	0	0	215	100.00%	99.90%
	Sum (frames)	7089			**Accuracy**	**97.83%**

Results of our second dataset from lab recordings are shown in Table 2. While overall classification accuracy for this dataset is slightly lower at 96.35% than for our museum dataset the accuracy per class is more balanced. Overall, the SVM classifier performs well both in real-world testing and on simulated data.

Table 2. SVM results on the lab dataset.

		Predicted			Sensitivity (TPR)	Specificity (TNR)
		Ignoring	Watching	Ready to interact		
Actual	Ignoring	2204	65	43	95.33%	98.08%
	Watching	41	1975	15	97.24%	97.43%
	Ready to interact	3	1	256	98.46%	98.66%
	Sum (frames)	4603			**Accuracy**	**96.35%**

5.2 Artificial Neural Network

In recent years, neural networks emerged as state-of-the-art for machine learning tasks due to the advances in GPU processing and now generally outperform SVMs. Therefore, we decided to compare results of our SVM classifier with an artificial neural network, specifically a Multilayer Perceptron (MLP). We used the implementation provided by the KNIME Analytics Platform. A Multilayer Perceptron is a feed-forward artificial neural network with a certain number of hidden layers. Each layer consists of perceptrons, which are simple linear classifiers. The input is fed into the network and passed from layer to layer where on each layer the perceptrons learn the appropriate threshold for the given classification problem. In contrast to a Support Vector Machine classifier tuning a neural network is more complex and generally requires more insight into the data at hand.

For our datasets, a shallow network with 3 layers and 50 neurons per hidden layer delivers good results but is not on par with the SVM classifier. Table 3 shows the results of the MLP classifier on the museum dataset. It reveals that the MLP also has problems with the imbalanced nature of the data but while the SVM classifier can take class weights into account this option does not exist for the MLP classifier we used. The MLP classifier achieves an overall accuracy of 97.97% on the museum dataset and therefore slightly beats the SVM classifier. However, this is mainly achieved by increasing accuracy of the over-represented ignoring samples.

Table 3. MLP results on the museum dataset.

		Predicted			Sensitivity (TPR)	Specificity (TNR)
		Ignoring	Watching	Ready to interact		
Actual	Ignoring	6465	54	3	99.13%	86.42%
	Watching	77	268	1	77.46%	99.07%
	Ready to interact	0	9	212	95.93%	99.94%
	Sum (frames)	7089			**Accuracy**	**97.97%**

On our lab dataset, the MLP classifier again achieves slightly higher overall accuracy at 97.41% when compared to the SVM classifier. However, when looking at the results in detail it can be observed that MLP still has slight problems with class imbalance (see Table 4).

Table 4. MLP results on the lab dataset.

		Predicted			Sensitivity (TPR)	Specificity (TNR)
		Ignoring	Watching	Ready to interact		
Actual	Ignoring	2204	26	2	98.75%	96.75%
	Watching	52	2054	4	97.35%	98.56%
	Ready to interact	25	10	226	86.59%	99.86%
	Sum (frames)	4603			**Accuracy**	**97.41%**

While we expect that it is possible to increase the accuracy of the MLP classifier for our task, this would require vastly more effort and more processing power. Therefore, we see little benefit to using a neural network instead of a SVM for our task.

5.3 Finite State Machine

The attention model as presented in Fig. 3 suggested the implementation of a state machine. This is a similar approach to Gollan and Ferscha [4]. While methods of machine learning generally have higher accuracy for such tasks this comes with certain drawbacks when compared to a rule-based system as discussed earlier. However, while the advantage of a state machine, namely easy configurability, is useful when setting up the system in different locations it also introduces a new problem: For each feature one or multiple thresholds have to be determined to optimize accuracy and specificity. Furthermore, implementations using methods of machine learning are able to handle noise better than simple linear thresholds. Therefore, we did expect a rule-based classifier to achieve the same accuracy as our SVM implementation, but, given the advantages, we would also be ready to accept a slightly worse accuracy.

To simplify parameterization of our state machine we use slightly different features than for the machine learning classifiers. Specifically, we calculate a single measure for gaze distance as the distance from the center of the focus object whereas the SVM and neural network classifiers are given the distances on the horizontal and vertical axis separately. Another difference is the use of a simple smoothing algorithm which suppresses state changes as a result of sensor noise. This is achieved by allowing a state change only after the majority of a certain number of consecutive frames (which is a parameter for our classifier) show a consistent changed state. This means that samples are no longer independent from each other as a previous sample has an effect on the prediction of the current frame, which is not the case for the other classifiers. However, in contrast to the other methods independent samples are no requirement for a state machine. Therefore, this doesn't pose a problem, but increases classification performance.

Table 5 shows the results of our state machine implementation on the museum dataset. As there is no need to hold back part of the dataset for verification, we used all 14177 frames. The offsets on the sensor plane to the center of the focus object is set to 25 cm to the left and 45 cm below the sensor. The smoothing algorithm was configured to consider the majority of the last 10 frames and the interaction range was set to 1.4 m as a simple threshold for gaze distance.

Table 5. FSM results on the museum dataset.

		Predicted			Sensitivity (TPR)	Specificity (TNR)
		Ignoring	Watching	Ready to interact		
Actual	Ignoring	11469	1238	292	88.23%	85.48%
	Watching	107	508	96	71.45%	90.72%
	Ready to interact	64	11	392	83.94%	97.17%
	Sum (frames)	14177			**Accuracy**	**87.25%**

Overall accuracy is 87.25% and therefore slightly short of our target of at least expected 90%. Threshold selection in this scenario is quite difficult and probably also inappropriate as thresholds tend to either under- or overestimate a subjects' attention state. Additionally, while we built in mechanisms to reduce the impact of sensor noise in the museum setting and also for the lab setting, our implementation is unable to compete with the SVM in this regard.

Again, in the more balanced and less noisy lab setting the results are quite a bit better and comparable to the results of the SVM implementation on the same dataset with an overall accuracy of 93.84% (see Table 6).

Table 6. FSM results on the lab dataset.

		Predicted			Sensitivity (TPR)	Specificity (TNR)
		Ignoring	Watching	Ready to interact		
Actual	Ignoring	4005	380	7	91.19%	96.67%
	Watching	122	3742	0	96.84%	91.92%
	Ready to interact	18	2	315	94.03%	99.92%
	Sum (frames)	8591			**Accuracy**	**93.84%**

6 Discussion

When looking at the results of our measurements by comparing prediction accuracy values for samples in different distance ranges it can be seen that the rule-based classifier FSM has difficulties predicting the class of samples in close proximity to the sensor. On the museum dataset, for instance, samples in close proximity to the sensor were especially problematic for the state machine to predict correctly, as can be seen in Table 7.

Table 7. Performance of the FSM classifier on the museum dataset on samples between 0 and 2 m distance to the sensor.

		Predicted			Sensitivity (TPR)	Specificity (TNR)
		Ignoring	Watching	Ready to interact		
Actual	Ignoring	642	570	288	42.80%	91.12%
	Watching	26	424	96	77.66%	70.46%
	Ready to interact	64	11	392	83.94%	81.23%
	Sum (frames)	2513			**Accuracy**	**58.02%**

The machine learning based classifiers could handle these samples significantly better, indicating that a simple threshold is ill-suited to separate these samples. Results of the SVM classifier are shown in Table 8.

Table 8. Performance of the SVM classifier on the museum dataset on samples between 0 and 2 m distance to the sensor.

		Predicted			Sensitivity (TPR)	Specificity (TNR)
		Ignoring	Watching	Ready to interact		
Actual	Ignoring	716	54	6	92.27%	92.03%
	Watching	40	246	1	85.71%	94.55%
	Ready to interact	0	0	215	100.00%	99.34%
	Sum (frames)	1278			**Accuracy**	**92.10%**

Table 9. Performance of the MLP classifier on the museum dataset on samples between 0 and 2 m distance to the sensor.

		Predicted			Sensitivity (TPR)	Specificity (TNR)
		Ignoring	Watching	Ready to interact		
Actual	Ignoring	688	40	3	94.12%	91.79%
	Watching	40	225	1	84.59%	94.85%
	Ready to interact	0	9	212	95.93%	99.60%
	Sum (frames)	1218			**Accuracy**	**92.36%**

Performance of the MLP is similar to the SVM classifier, as can be seen in Table 9. This is true for all distance classes within the lab dataset.

On the lab dataset, this discrepancy in accuracy between 0 and 2 m vanishes and the FSM, SVM and MLP classifiers perform equally well (exact figures not shown here). This indicates that the FSM classifier in its current state has problems with the noisy environment of the museum setting. In the lab setting no clear advantage for either the FSM, SVM or MLP classifier emerges.

At medium distances (between 2 and 4 m) all three classifiers perform at equal accuracy levels, on the museum dataset with 92.32% accuracy for FSM, 97.56% for SVM and 98.38% for MLP, and on the lab dataset with 93.16% for FSM, 99.02% for SVM, and 99.06% for MLP. However, the samples in this distance class within the museum dataset are heavily skewed towards the *ignoring* class due to the experiment setup, distorting statements on the quality of our results. The samples within the lab dataset are more uniformly distributed across distance classes and therefore accuracy of the classifiers is evaluated on this dataset.

At far distances (>4 m) results are washed out. While we cannot provide accuracy values for the lab setup for this distance class (note that the experiment had been restricted to distances <4 m) figures for the museum setup range above 99% for all classifiers, which we believe is due to the unequal distribution of the state *ignoring* in this area (i.e. people were distantly passing the stimulus without recognizing it).

As a summary, our results show that the rule-based classifier, while delivering solid accuracy on our lab dataset, performs below expectations in the museum setting. As the features are the same for both our settings, we believe this to be a result of sub-optimal sensor placement. Additionally, the sensor we used had problems when groups gathered in front of the exhibit it was installed on. In our lab setting the sensor performed best with up to 4 subjects simultaneously, but deteriorated after that. This indicates that a better sensor would highly benefit our rule-based classifier. With several subjects in front of the exhibit the sensor was unable to track multiple targets reliably and would often lose track of subjects. This inhibited the smoothing algorithm of our rule based classifier and therefore introduced more noise to the results, which the SVM and MLP are obviously better at dealing with.

7   Conclusion

Estimating attention in public scenarios is growing more important as pervasive information systems become prevalent and previously manually controlled machinery becomes semi-automatic, deferring to human judgment only when necessary. Research initiatives in human-computer interaction such as *Raising Attention* [2] work towards establishing attention estimation as a tool in user experience design, in particular where information overload needs to be addressed.

Besides predominating machine-learning estimation techniques for determining human attention, we feel that the attempt of modeling a lightweight classifier immune to location changes of sensor or stimulus and without the necessity of training phases turned out to be a feasible alternative to ponderous machine learning approaches and merits further research, especially comparing different sensors and techniques for extracting low level features (e.g. thresholds step functions). Particularly, in public display scenarios, training constitutes a significant effort, which could be avoided using FSMs.

At once, our "reduced" model of attention states is meant to provide a balance for practical application requirements: *"ignoring"*, *"watching"* and *"ready to interact"* should already cover a wide range of scenarios, but an API designed around the model could also provide access to details of lower layers where necessary. The experimental results have shown that the three principal states are consistently separable.

References

1. Bulling, A.: Pervasive Attentive user interfaces. Computer **49**(1), 94–98 (2016)
2. Ferscha, A.: Raising attention. http://www.pervasive.jku.at/raisingattention/index.php/ra
3. Ferscha, A., Zia, K., Gollan, B.: Collective attention through public displays. In: International Conference on Self-Adaptive and Self-Organizing Systems, SASO, pp. 211–216. IEEE (2012). http://dx.doi.org/10.1109/SASO.2012.35
4. Gollan, B., Ferscha, A.: SEEV-effort - is it enough to model human attentional behavior in public display settings. In: Future Computing 2016, the Eighth International Conference on Future Computational Technologies and Applications (2016)
5. Gollan, B., Wally, B., Ferscha, A.: Automatic human attention estimation in an interactive system based on behavior analysis. In: Proceedings of the 15th Portuguese Conference on Artificial Intelligence (EPIA2011), pp. 978–989 (2011)
6. Kahneman, D.: Attention and effort. Am. J. Psychol. **88**(2), 339–340 (1973)
7. Kukka, H., Oja, H., Kostakos, V.: What makes you click: exploring visual signals to entice interaction on public displays. In: Proceedings of the SIGCHI Conference on Human Factors in Computing Systems (CHI 2013), pp. 1699–1708. ACM (2013)
8. Mubin, O., Lashina, T., Loenen, E.: How not to become a buffoon in front of a shop window: a solution allowing natural head movement for interaction with a public display. In: Gross, T., Gulliksen, J., Kotzé, P., Oestreicher, L., Palanque, P., Prates, R.O., Winckler, M. (eds.) INTERACT 2009. LNCS, vol. 5727, pp. 250–263. Springer, Heidelberg (2009). doi: 10.1007/978-3-642-03658-3_32
9. Muta, M., Masuko, S., Shinzato, K., Mujibiya, A.: Interactive study of WallSHOP: multiuser connectivity between public digital advertising and private devices for personalized shopping. In: Proceedings of the 4th International Symposium on Pervasive Displays (PerDis 2015), pp. 187–193. ACM, New York (2015)
10. Perry, M., Beckett, S., O'Hara, K., Subramanian, S.: WaveWindow: public, performative gestural interaction. In: ACM International Conference on Interactive Tabletops and Surfaces (ITS 2010), pp. 109–112. ACM, New York (2010)
11. Selker, T.: Visual attentive interfaces. BT Technol. J. **22**(4), 146–150 (2004)
12. Strong, E.K.: The Psychology of Selling and Advertising. McGraw-Hill, New York (1925)
13. Treisman, A.M., Gelade, G.: A feature-integration theory of attention. Cogn. Psychol. **12**(1), 97–136 (1980)
14. Tsotsos, J., Rothenstein, A.: Computational models of visual attention. Scholarpedia **6**(1), 6201 (2011). http://dx.doi.org/10.4249/scholarpedia.6201
15. Vapnik, V.N.: The Nature of Statistical Learning Theory. Springer Science & Business Media, Heidelberg (1998)

16. Wang, M., Boring, S., Greenberg, S.: Proxemic peddler: a public advertising display that captures and preserves the attention of a passerby. In: Proceedings of the 2012 International Symposium on Pervasive Displays (PerDis 2012), 6 p. ACM, New York (2012). Article 3

17. Ward, L.: Attention. Scholarpedia 3(10) (2008). http://dx.doi.org/10.4249/scholarpedia

18. Wickens, C., McCarley, J.: Applied Attention Theory. CRC Press, Boca Raton (2007)

19. Wolfe, J.M., Horowitz, T.S.: What attributes guide the deployment of visual attention and how do they do it. Nat. Rev. Neurosci. 5(6), 495–501 (2005)

20. Zhang, Y., Bulling, A., Gellersen, H.: SideWays: a gaze interface for spontaneous interaction with situated displays. In: Proceedings of the SIGCHI Conference on Human Factors in Computing Systems (CHI 2013), pp. 851–860. ACM, New York (2013). https://doi.org/10.1145/2470654.2470775

Is Augmented Reality Leading to More Risky Behaviors? An Experiment with Pokémon Go

Romain Pourchon[✉], Pierre-Majorique Léger[✉], Élise Labonté-LeMoyne[✉],
Sylvain Sénécal[✉], François Bellavance[✉], Marc Fredette[✉],
and François Courtemanche[✉]

HEC Montréal Tech3lab, Montréal, Canada
{romain.pourchon,pml,
elise.labonte-lemoyne,ss,francois.bellavance,marc.fredette,
francois.courtemanche}@hec.ca

Abstract. Released in the summer of 2016, Pokémon Go is one of the world's most downloaded applications. Using augmented reality technology, this game has become the latest craze among young people and adults. However, it has also caused several accidents because of players getting distracted while walking. Following the research that has been conducted on texting while walking, it would be interesting to compare the risks arising from gaming while walking. This research therefore compares dangerous behaviors exhibited in three conditions using a smartphone while walking, Pokémon Go with augmented reality, Pokémon Go without, and texting while walking. We can conclude that playing Pokémon Go, with and without augmented reality, leads to more dangerous behaviors overall than texting. We also observe the appearance of a new risky behavior when playing Pokémon Go that is unseen in texting while walking, abrupt stops.

Keywords: Mobile multitasking · Augmented Reality · Attention · Real context study

1 Introduction

In this paper, we investigate the effect of Augmented Reality (AR) on the behavioral risk associated with playing on a smartphone while walking. Previous studies have demonstrated that multitasking on a smartphone while walking is a risky behavior. An observation study found that more than 7% of pedestrians engage in mobile multitasking [1], which we define here as the behavior of individuals who change their attention quickly between different activities on a technology while walking. Some studies report that mobile multitaskers took longer to cross the street and to initiate crossing when they saw an available safe gap, looked left and right less often, and were more likely to be hit or almost hit by an oncoming vehicle [2, 3]. Researchers found that texting causes more cognitive distractions and decision-making mistakes compared to talking on a cell phone because attention is divided between more than one stimulus and this negatively impacts the performance of these tasks. When subjects change from task A to task B,

© Springer International Publishing AG 2017
F.F.-H. Nah and C.-H. Tan (Eds.): HCIBGO 2017, Part I, LNCS 10293, pp. 354–361, 2017.
DOI: 10.1007/978-3-319-58481-2_27

their mental resources need to be reconfigured to accommodate the upcoming task and thus take more time, this is called a "switch cost" [4]. To our knowledge, no studies have yet been conducted on the mobile multitasking risks associated with AR games.

During the summer of 2016, Pokémon Go (Niantic Company, Tokyo, Japan), an AR-based entertainment application inspired from the Pokémon anime TV series became the most rapidly downloaded application in history. Breaking all records, it was downloaded by more than 30 million people [5]. The objective of the game is to walk around until you find a Pokémon monster, select the monster (an action which opens a secondary game window), and throw a ball at the monster to capture it. There are two modes of play in the secondary window: with or without AR. Unlike virtual environments, in which a virtual world replaces the real world, AR involves the addition of extra information to the real world. Turning on the AR mode switches on the camera and the animated Pokémon appears on the screen along with the real-life background, as is illustrated in Fig. 1. Turning off the AR mode switches off the camera and the animated Pokémon appears on the screen along with the still background world of Pokémon.

Fig. 1. Use of AR in Pokémon Go

Such a gaming technology holds promise, however, there is also some obvious potential for further distraction-related risks. Many warnings have been issued in the media by physicians and police as to the risks of playing this game [6]. For example, a 15-year-old girl was struck by a car, when crossing a busy road while playing Pokémon Go [7]. In another instance, a Frenchman traveling to Indonesia was arrested for entering a military base, as he wanted to catch a Pokémon [8]. In France, a young man was hit by a train while crossing a railroad to catch a Pokémon [9]. Finally, in San Diego County, California, two 20-year-old men nearly died after falling off a 30-m cliff, because they had crossed a security barrier while trying to capture a Pokémon [10].

In addition to incidents related to burglars and racketeers using Pokémon Go or motorists playing the game while driving, the application is now a public danger for phone enthusiasts while walking. Notwithstanding its increasing popularity, as evidenced by the application's record-breaking downloads on all platforms combined [11], it is undeniable that such accidents will continue to occur if the population is not aware of the risks it takes.

Notably, the media does not mention which mode, AR or not, was activated when accidents occurred, leading to the question: was AR really the cause of this distraction? This study investigated the increasing existence of dangerous behaviors when using AR as opposed to the more commonly accepted texting while walking behavior. We also contrasted the two modes of gameplay as the incident reports blaming AR never seem to mention whether the AR mode was, in fact, activated at the time.

Participants in our study were engaged in multitasking episodes of texting while walking and playing while walking. We used a neurophysiological approach to fully capture both the explicit (self-reported) and implicit (unconscious and automatic) measures of mobile multitasking. The experiment took place in a real context environment in which subjects had to walk while wearing SMI Eye Tracking Glasses 2 (SensoMotoric Instruments, Berlin, Germany), their electroencephalographic (EEG) activity being recorded with a wireless headset (Cognionics HD-72, San Diego, USA) (Fig. 2). We present the different behaviors observed and discuss our preliminary results in the rest of this paper.

Fig. 2. Experimental set-up

2 Method

We conducted an experiment with 18 Pokémon Go players. This project was approved by the Institutional Review Board of our institution. This study took place in a risk-free public place in a major North American city. The recruitment was done via an online platform and the participants were given a compensation of C$20 (about US$15).

2.1 Experimental Design and Protocol

In a within-subject experimental design, participants had to perform three different tasks while walking: Texting, Gaming with AR and Gaming without AR. These tasks were distributed in random order between the participants. Overall, the experiment lasted one hour. The participants were instructed to walk in the public area as they would normally do in real-life. In order to provide a higher degree of ecological validity, no path was predefined. Nevertheless, an exact meeting point was given to the participants. They could walk in the park or on the sidewalk but they had to stay in the pedestrian area for safety reasons. In the texting condition, they had to chat with a research assistant via SMS. In the gaming condition, they were instructed to catch the maximum number of Pokémon possible. During the tasks, the participants were followed by 3 assistants who had to ensure their safety and film the tasks.

We used several measurement tools. Firstly, the participants had to play on a given iPhone 6 (Apple, Cupertino) with an already created account, they all played the game at the same difficulty level (level 21). The application contained measures such as miles traveled and number of Pokémon caught. Secondly, we used Eye Tracking Glasses 2 (SMI, SensoMotoric Instruments, Berlin, Germany) to track visual attention. Thirdly, body cameras (GoPro, San Mateo, USA) attached to the research assistants were used to film the participants during the tasks. Finally, electroencephalographic measures (Cognionics, San Diego, USA) were acquired during the tasks. EEG and others measures (miles traveled, number of Pokémon caught) are currently being analyzed and are not reported in this article.

2.2 Operationalization of Behavioral Measures

Table 1 presents the age of our participants as well as the player's Pokémon Go level, which represents the experience of the participant. We only selected those who had played ample Pokémon Go and had already reached level 5.

Table 1. Age, Pokémon Go experience

Average age	Standard age deviation	Average Pokémon Go level of the player based on his personal account (experience)	Standard deviation of the Pokémon Go level of the player based on his personal account (experience)
21.89 years	2.63	16.17	8.06

Table 2 presents the playing mode used by the players, i.e., with or without AR. The majority of our participants usually play without AR. We believe the two main reasons for this are that the phone's battery drains faster when AR is activated and that the participants feel that the challenge of catching a Pokémon is more difficult when AR is activated.

Table 2. Usability of the participants

% of participants who usually play with activated AR	% of participants who usually play with inactivated AR
33%	67%

The GoPro camera recordings revealed different risky behaviors by our participants. We used these videos to identify the five most common risky behaviors that participants displayed during the experience. They are described as follows:

- **Collision avoidance by a stranger**: The participant looks at his phone while crossing a passer-by who must shift course to avoid a collision.
- **Crossing a street while looking at his/her phone**: The participant looks at his phone while he crosses the street.
- **Crossing a street without checking the road:** The participant doesn't look left or right before he/she crosses the street.
- **Avoiding an obstacle**: The participant narrowly avoids an obstacle in his path (post, bench, trash can, miniature train).
- **Stop walking abruptly**: The participant stops abruptly on the sidewalk.

3   Preliminary Results and Analysis

The sample included 18 participants who completed the texting condition as well as the Pokémon Go without AR condition while 17 of them also completed the Pokémon Go with AR condition. This represents a total of 18 participants and 53 observations overall. We used the SAS statistical program (SAS Institute Inc, Cary, USA) to determine if there was any significant difference between the three conditions associated with each risky behavior, so as to determine if these risky behaviors were more frequently linked to any one particular condition than to another.

First, we determined each time the participant exhibited a risky behavior per minute. We coded "0" if the participant had no risky behavior during a task and "1" if the participant had one or more risky behavior during a task. We observed that there were many "0s" for our 18 participants. The risky behaviors were also very rare. Our tasks were relatively long and there were only a few instances when our participants displayed dangerous behaviors. This was also an important criterion to be taken into account when analyzing our results.

Since the numbers of risky behaviors exhibited by participants are being collected, the negative binomial model would appear to be the most fitting statistical model. However, as few events for each type of risky behavior are observed, the logistic regression model is used to model the risky behaviors individually. Logistic regression allows us to model the probability of occurrence of an event without taking into account the number of observed events, which is less precise but can be seen as more robust than a negative binomial model in our experiment given that many participants did not exhibit a risky behavior while doing the task.

For the overall risks, which correspond to the sum of the 5 types of risky behaviors, we used a negative binomial model as more events were observed. In our analyses, each participant was tested in all three conditions (Texting, Pokémon, Pokémon AR). Therefore, a random effect for intercept was added to the regression models to take into consideration the repeated measurements on the participants. SAS' GLIMMIX procedure for generalized linear mixed models was used for the regression models.

This explicative model allows us to conclude that three of our risky behaviors occur significantly more often in one condition than in another. First, we found that people cross the street while looking at their phone more often when they are playing Pokémon with AR than when they are texting. Second, we found that people cross the street while looking at their phone more often when they are playing Pokémon without AR than when they are texting. Third, we found that people cross the street without checking the road more often when they are playing Pokémon with AR than when they are texting. Fourth, we found that people cross the street without checking the road more often when they are playing Pokémon without AR than when they are texting. Fifth, we observed a new risky behavior with the arrival of Pokémon Go. We noted that our participants abruptly stop walking on the sidewalk without checking around them. This risky behavior doesn't occur when participants are texting on their phones. We found that people stop abruptly more often when they are playing Pokémon Go with activated AR than when they are playing without AR. Finally, we analyzed the overall danger by taking into account the five risky behaviors in all conditions. The Poisson regression model led us to observe that Pokémon AR generally induces significantly more frequent

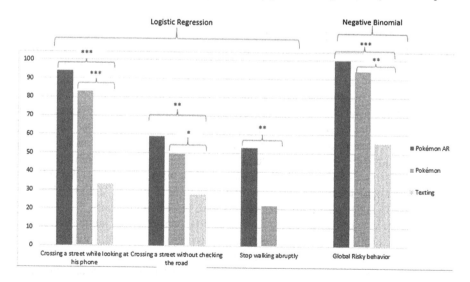

Fig. 3. % of participants who have exhibited one or more of each risky behavior *p < 0.1 **p < 0.05 ***p < 0.01

risky behaviors than Pokémon and texting. We can also observe that, while there isn't a significant difference, it appears to be more dangerous to play Pokémon Go with activated AR than without.

These five significant conclusions are presented in Fig. 3. We used the sample means of each incidence rate per hour of our experience to show these results on a graph and to clarify these comparisons.

4   Discussions and Concluding Comments

This paper presents the rate of dangerous behaviors displayed by pedestrians engaging in mobile multitasking while texting and while playing Pokémon Go, with and without the AR function activated. Preliminary results suggest that this game has introduced a new dangerous behavior that is not present when texting while walking: "Stop walking abruptly". Moreover, pedestrians playing Pokémon Go with AR or without AR mode exhibit a higher incidence of dangerous behavior than pedestrians texting while walking. Overall, we find evidence that using an application with augmented reality is more dangerous than using one without augmented reality and that the former scenario is even more dangerous than texting while walking.

It is important to point out that these results do not, under any circumstances, advocate texting while walking. Almost all participants exhibited dangerous behaviors during both the playing and texting sessions. These results only suggest that texting might be less risky than Pokémon Go.

These results are preliminary and further analysis is required to understand their cognitive underpinnings. The next question we need to explore is why multitasking in a gaming context induces more dangerous behavior than texting does. One explanation could be linked to the difficulty of catching the Pokémon and the time required, which might be a greater source of distraction than simply a social act, i.e. texting.

Our next step is to analyze the electroencephalographic data to obtain a richer understanding of the phenomenon. The brain activity will be analyzed in the frequency domain with a fast Fourier transform (FFT) and compared between the three conditions to assess the general state of the participant during each condition.

After that, we would also like to analyze the attentional perspective. We could suppose that augmented reality causes more risky behaviors because participants look at their phone more often than at their external environment. Moreover, during the experiment, we presented a few posters with a letter and a color during each task. The participants had to memorize these letters and colors thus we can evaluate if the participants indeed paid less attention to these posters when playing Pokémon. We will also compare each participant's results according to their level of play and experience in Pokémon Go to understand if amateur players have more memory bias.

Finally, we would like to evaluate the perceptual perspective of augmented reality in a mobile multitasking context. Despite the known risks of using texting while walking, many people behave overconfidently and underestimate the dangers associated with such an activity. It would be interesting to see if people perceive the game as being more or less dangerous than texting while walking. It would also be interesting to see if people perceive augmented reality as being a greater challenge and if people think augmented reality allows them to avoid obstacles and be more aware of their environment.

In conclusion, these and other forthcoming results could lead to recommendations for developers of AR games that require players to be on the move. They could also help develop safety advice for current players and policy makers. An interesting result here is that the game leads to abrupt stops, a dangerous new behavior that was almost non-existent in texting while walking. Future game developers could perhaps introduce pop-up warnings such as "GAME PAUSED TILL YOU STOP AT A SAFE LOCATION, PRESS HERE TO RESTART", at specific moments in the game that might lead to such stops. Developers of Pokémon Go could perhaps add the following warning message at the exact moment a Pokémon is about to be caught: "LOOK AROUND BEFORE YOU STOP TO CATCH THIS POKÉMON".

References

1. Thompson, L.L., et al.: Impact of social and technological distraction on pedestrian crossing behaviour: an observational study. Inj. Prev. **19**(4), 232–237 (2013)
2. Schwebel, D.C., et al.: Distraction and pedestrian safety: how talking on the phone, texting, and listening to music impact crossing the street. Accid. Anal. Prev. **45**, 266–271 (2012)
3. Byington, K.W., Schwebel, D.C.: Effects of mobile Internet use on college student pedestrian injury risk. Accid. Anal. Prev. **51**, 78–83 (2013)
4. Wylie, G., Allport, A.: Task switching and the measurement of "switch costs". Psychol. Res. **63**(3–4), 212–233 (2000). Works Cited
5. Apoorva, A., Rao, A.: A human computer interface-augmented reality. IJESC **6**(8), 2 (2016)
6. Stevenson, V.: Injuries related to Pokemon Go on the rise. https://www.thestar.com/news/gta/2016/08/18/injuries-related-to-pokemon-go-on-the-rise.html. Accessed 18 Aug 2017
7. Reilly, K.: Pennsylvania teenager hit by car while playing Pokémon Go. http://time.com/4405221/pokemon-go-teen-hit-by-car/. Accessed 13 July 2017
8. Le Point: Indonésie: un Français dans une base militaire à cause de Pokémon Go. http://www.lepoint.fr/high-tech-internet/indonesie-un-francais-dans-une-base-militaire-a-cause-of-pokemon-go-19-07-2016-2055508_47.php. Accessed 19 July 2017
9. Gaetan, H.: Pokémon Go: Un jeune fauché par un train alors qu'il essayait d'attraper un carapuce. http://nordpresse.be/pokemon-go-jeune-belge-fauche-train-quil-essayait-dattraper-carapuce/. Accessed 9 Feb 2017
10. Hazard, C.: "Pokémon Go": 5 histoires déjà incontournables qui vont se répéter. www.parismatch.com/Vivre/High-Tech/Pokemon-Go-5-histoires-deja-incourtournables-qui-vont-se-repeter-1020316. Accessed 19 July 2017
11. Froment, E.: Pokémon Go dépasse la barre des 100 millions de téléchargements. http://geeko.lesoir.be/2016/08/02/pokemon-go-depasse-la-barre-des-100-millions-de-telechargements/. Accessed 2 Aug 2016

Usage and Physiological Effects of Dynamic Office Workstations - A Field Pilot Study

Vera Schellewald[1][✉], Jens Kleinert[2], and Rolf Ellegast[1]

[1] Institute for Occupational Safety and Health, Sankt Augustin, Germany
vera.schellewald@dguv.de
[2] German Sports University, Cologne, Germany

Abstract. Prolonged sedentary work is increasingly discussed as a health risk factor for developing musculoskeletal disorders and cardiovascular diseases. Dynamic workstations are a modern concept to combine light physical activity and desk-based office work. Their effects are evaluated under laboratory conditions but research in occupational settings is limited. This pilot study examined the effects of two dynamic workstations, the Deskbike and the activeLife Trainer regarding aspects of lending and usage and physiological effects. Preliminary results for 8 male subjects show general interest in using these stations and an increased heart rate and energy expenditure compared to working while seated.

Keywords: Dynamic workstations · Usage · Physiological effects · Heart rate · Energy expenditure · Deskbike · activeLife Trainer

1 Introduction

Prolonged bouts of sitting are increasingly discussed as an independent health risk factor for the development of chronic complaints and diseases. Observational studies pointed on a negative correlation between physical inactivity and musculo-skeletal disease, adipositas, cardio-vascular diseases, Type-II-Diabetes and premature mortality [1–3]. Additionally to these long-term effects short-term effects like the loss of endurance and performance ability can occur.

According to the EuroBarometer study the average self-reported sitting time in northern European countries was 5–6 h daily [4], mostly spend at the office desk. In Germany today there are about 18 million employees working on office and monitor-based desks which partly require prolonged seated postures and therefore negatively support a lack of physical activity. Regarding the digitalization of future work environment it can be expected that the number of seated workplaces will increase steadily. As engaging in moderate to vigorous activity during leisure time seems not to be sufficient enough to adequately address the negative consequences [5], the development of workplace health interventions is required.

Besides behaviour-oriented prevention approaches like taking walks or exercising at the lunch break [6], new concepts for work tasks and work stations evolve rapidly in the last years. The promotion of possible ways to facilitate an increase of physical activity for desk-bound office workers includes sit-to-stand desks and so called

© Springer International Publishing AG 2017
F.F.-H. Nah and C.-H. Tan (Eds.): HCIBGO 2017, Part I, LNCS 10293, pp. 362–373, 2017.
DOI: 10.1007/978-3-319-58481-2_28

"dynamic workstations" like adapted computer desks with integrated treadmills or seated elliptical machines. These stations offer a way to engage in light physical activity like walking or pedaling without leaving the desk. To examine the ability to consider these stations as feasible alternatives to conventional work stations scientific research on the effects on physiological parameters as well as the acceptance of the users and feasibility in the work environment had been conducted.

Beneath the effect on sitting time throughout working hours several studies assessed parameters like heart rate (HR) and energy expenditure (EE) while using dynamic workstations to analyze the impact on energy metabolism. The results of Carr et al. [7] and Straker and Levine [8] showed significant effects on these parameters by using an under-desk pedaling machine and an upright exercise cycle. A lab study by the Institute of Occupational Safety and Health (IFA) in cooperation with TNO was conducted in 2013 to investigate the contribution of a treadmill desk and a seated dynamic workstation to physical activity, the effect on posture and muscular activity and the subjective perception of the users. Main results showed that these stations may lead to an increase of physical activity but user acceptance and ergonomic design still had to be improved [9].

Current refinements in the development of dynamic workstations are portable devices which are commercially available, lightweight and can be fitted under standard or height-adjustable desks. According to their novelty on the market scientific research on health benefits and limitations in comparison to other dynamic workstations is limited. As knowledge about these parameters and users acceptance as well as examinations of feasibility is essential to implement these stations in real life working environments the conduction of field studies is required. Thus, the present paper aims to describe the acceptance of portable dynamic workstations by the employees and physiological loads associated with the use in real life office settings. Moreover, different types of dynamic workstations are compared in this regards.

Therefore the present study aims to answer three research questions:

1. Are dynamic workstations used as alternative workplaces in an occupational field setting?
2. Which physiological activation appears while using a dynamic workstation in an occupational field setting?
3. Does physiological activation while using a dynamic workstation differ between different types of work stations?

2   Methods

This study was conducted as a pilot study to generate preliminary findings about multiple effects of dynamic workstations being implemented in real-life occupation settings. It was conducted in a large telecommunication company in Germany with a modern approach to future office environments.

2.1 Participants

The departments of the Company were informed about the intention to conduct the study and could declare their interest to participate. Randomly one of these departments was chosen and an information event was held for all employees. After the participation to this event a total sample of 38 employees decided voluntarily to take part in the study, 29 of them agreed to complete all measurements required. As the pilot study is ongoing, here the results for 8 male participants are presented.

The participants were offered two different dynamic workstations for their voluntarily use. The sample for the statistical comparison of the physiological effects of the stations was limited to 8 participants who used both types of workstations. The anthropometric data of the whole sample and the sample of participants using both types of workstations is shown in Table 1.

Table 1. Data of 8 male participants using both types of workstations; BMI: Body Mass Index

	User of both workstations
Number	8
Age in years	42,88 (±10,43)
Height in m	1,82 (±0,72)
Weight in kg	84,88 (±13,29)
BMI in kg/m2	25,81 (±4,87)

2.2 Dynamic Workstations

The conventional workplaces of the participants and two commercial available dynamic workstations were chosen to be evaluated in the field. The first dynamic workstation was a portable ergometer called Deskbike, which can be placed under height-adjustable desks (following: DB), manufactured by the company "Worktrainer". The second one was a portable pedaling machine manufactured by CCLab, which can be fitted under standard desks as well (following aLT). Both types of workstations can be moved from one desk to another by using integrated rolls. The workstations can be seen in Fig. 1. When using the Deskbike the upper body of the participant is in an upright position and the legs are moving in a cycling motion. The saddle is adjustable to fit the height of the user. The resistance can be infinitely adjusted by using a rotary knob. The activeLife Trainer can be used with a standard office chair and the use will lead to an elliptical foot motion. The user can choose between 8 levels of resistance by using a rotary knob as well.

Fig. 1. Dynamic workstations; left: Worktrainer Deskbike (source: Deutsche Telekom AG, Thomas Ollendorf), right: activeLife Trainer (source: IFA)

2.3 Treatment

Participants were provided free access to 8 dynamic workstations in total. The 4 Deskbikes and 4 activeLife Trainer were located in the office for a period of 30 working days in total. They were stored at two separated niches called lending stations. The dynamic workstations could be picked up there and had to be brought back after use. All participants were given an introduction on how to use the dynamic workstations and recommendations for the frequency and duration of use. The actual duration of lending and use as well as the intensity of use could be chosen voluntarily.

2.4 Measures

All data was assessed pseudonymized using participant codes, serial numbers and by coding the technical measurement systems. Anthropometric data was self-reported.

Lending and Usage of Dynamic Workstations. In cooperation with employees of the Hochschule Koblenz a system to register the duration of lending of each dynamic workstation was developed. Each participant received a Chipcard with a RFID (radio-frequency identification) system. Each workstation was numbered and assigned to a stationary device being located at the tables at the lending stations. These devices included a card reader and a computer system. By placing the RFID-card data on the device the record of the lending duration started and stopped when the card was being removed. The actual use of the station was measured as cadence of the movement of pedals and being registered and recorded with Sigma Rox 5.0 bike sensors (Sigma). All data was synchronized and saved once a week by a member of the study.

Recording and Valuation of Physiological Activation. The parameters heart rate (HR) and energy expenditure (EE) served as an indicator for individual cardiovascular load. Each participant was given an activity tracker "Fitbit Charge HR" (Fitbit) to assess these parameters. With the use of optical heart rate sensors (called PurePulse technology by Fitbit [10]) Heart Rate can be assessed every 3 s and is summarized as beats per minute (bpm). Resting heart rate was calculated as the average of the five lowest heart rate values recorded with the Fitbit tracker. Heart rate measurements for sitting and while using dynamic workstations were calculated as the average of all values recorded during these periods.

The calculation of the metabolic rate by the Fitbit Charge HR is based on typed-in information on the user's profile about age, height and weight and expressed as kilocalories per minute (kcal). According to the number of steps taken and the current heart rate the caloric expense when being active is calculated using standardized logarithms [10]. Energy consumption while working seated and using a workstation was calculated as the average of all values recorded during these periods.

2.5 Procedure

All participants were informed about aims of the study and the study design before the intervention period started an introduction to the concept of dynamic workstations including recommendations for use. Afterwards they filled in the baseline questionnaires containing anthropometric data. Then they were shown the location of the lending station and were instructed on how to use the lending system correctly. Afterwards all participants received their individual RFID-Cards and Fitbit activity trackers. They were instructed to wear them every day spent at the office from entering their desks up to leaving them. The displays of the trackers were blinded and the trackers were set to just show the number of steps taken if the blinding tape was removed. All data assessed by technical measurement systems (lending, use and physiological measurements) was recorded constantly throughout the intervention period. As the employees have flexible working hours the period from 6 am to 8 pm on every workday was included in the analysis. It was synchronized and saved once a week by a member of the study.

2.6 Processing of Data and Statistical Analysis

The combination of data being recorded by the lending system, the bike sensors and the Fitbit activity tracker illustrates the individual behaviour of each participant regarding physical activity at the workplace. The comparison of duration of lending, cadence of the pedals and steps recorded by the Fitbit tracker lead to the identification of intervals for working while seated, lending a dynamic workstation but not using it, working while using a dynamic workstation or moving in any other way (walking) for every participant individually. For each of these intervals individual average heart rate and energy expenditure values were calculated and summarized as an overall average value per person. For statistical comparison the average values of this data were calculated for the sample of 8 male participants using Microsoft Excel (version 2010).

For statistical analysis ANOVA repeated measures (general linear model) were used to examine differences between the main effect of the inner subject factor dynamic workstation on physiological activation (HR, EE) with a level of significance of $p \leq 0.05$. With the help of post hoc analysis possible differences between the mean values of working while seated and working while using dynamic workstations were examined. Because of the cumulative probability of errors occurring for multiple comparisons the significance level was adjusted according to Bonferroni. Working while seated was used as a reference and compared to the two different types of dynamic workstations regarding significant effects.

3 Results

3.1 Lending and Actual Use of Dynamic Workstations

Descriptive results for the lending and the usage of the dynamic workstations can be seen in Table 2. The results show very intra-individual variances between the subjects and strong differences between the two types of workstations. The total values of lending time in minutes and time of usage in minutes show a minimum of 34 min and a maximum of 4067 min, for the activeLife Trainer values vary between 63 min and 766 min. Therefore average values show very high standard deviations equally for the lending of the dynamic workstation and the time of usage.

Table 2. Descriptive results for the time of lending periods and usage periods for both dynamic workstations and 8 male subjects; SD: standard deviation

	Deskbike	activeLife Trainer
Lending periods in minutes		
Sum	8129	2668
Mean (SD)	1016,1 ($\pm$1341,1)	333,5 ($\pm$250,2)
Minimum	34	63
Maximum	4067	766
Sum	8129	2668
Usage periods in min		
Sum	3965	1161
Mean (SD)	495,6 ($\pm$479,5)	145,1 ($\pm$150,2)
Minimum	29	4
Maximum	1411	466

The analysis of minutes in sum shows that both workstations were actually used nearly one fourth of the lending period. The comparison of the total lending period between the Deskbike and the activeLife Trainer illustrates a nearly three times as long lending period for the Deskbike as for the activeLife Trainer. For the total time of usage the comparison shows that the Deskbike was even 3,5 times longer used than the activeLife Trainer. These results are illustrated in Fig. 2.

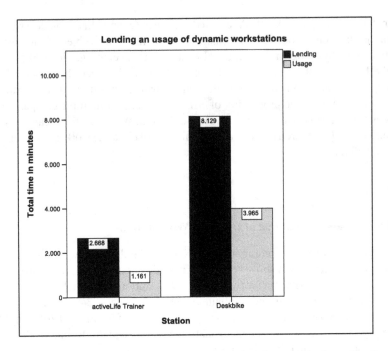

Fig. 2. Summarized time periods of lending and usage in minutes of both workstations for a sample of 8 male subjects

3.2   Results of Heart Rate Measurements

The average individual heart rate for each subject while using the Deskbike and the activeLife Trainer is displayed in Fig. 3. For the Deskbike average heart rate values vary between 62,4 bpm and 79,1 bpm, for the activeLife Trainer average heart rate values vary between 59 bpm and 80,7 bpm. The group mean value of heart rate while using the Deskbike is 69,5 (±6,2) bpm and 70,3 (±6,6) bpm while using the active-Life Trainer.

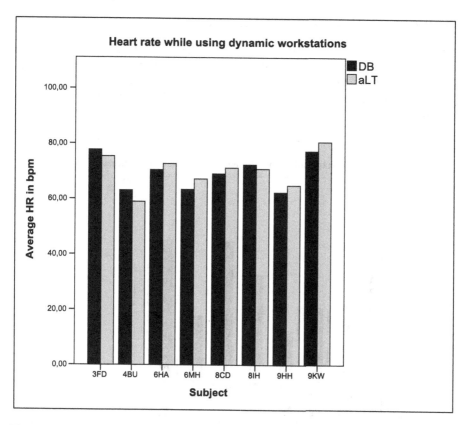

Fig. 3. Average heart rate (HR) measurements of each subject of the sample while using the Deskbike and activeLife Trainer

The results of the statistical analysis for the average heart rate calculated in beats per minute (bpm) are displayed in Table 3.

Table 3. Mean values and statistical results of 8 male subjects for heart rate (HR) for working while seated and the dynamic workstations, significant effect $p \leq 0.05$

	Conventional	Dynamic workstation		Factor workstation	Seated versus	
	Seated	Deskbike	activeLife Trainer		Deskbike	activeLife Trainer
Average HR in bpm (SD)	62,6 (5,6)	69,5 (6,2)	70,3 (6,6)	*	*	*

The average heart rate shows significant effects for the factor dynamic workstation. The use of both of the dynamic workstations results in a significant increase in average heart rate in comparison to working while seated.

3.3 Results of Energy Expenditure Measurements

For the Deskbike average individual energy expenditure values range from 1,3 kcal/min to 2,2 kcal/min. For the activeLife Trainer average individual energy expenditure values range from 1,2 kcal/min to 1,9 kcal/min. The results for each subject can be seen in Fig. 4. The group mean value of energy expenditure is 1,8 (±0,4) kcal/min while using the Deskbike and 1,6 (±0,2) kcal while using the activeLife Trainer.

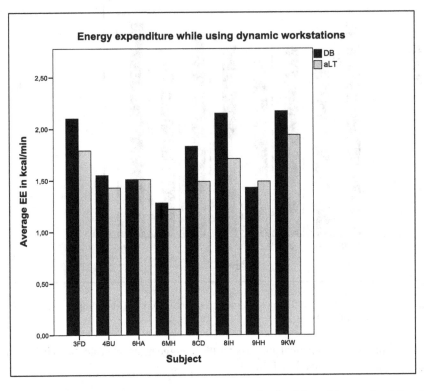

Fig. 4. Average energy expenditure (EE) measurements of each subject of the sample while using the Deskbike and activeLife Trainer

Table 4 includes all group values for the average energy expenditure calculated in kcal/min and the results of statistical analysis. The average energy expenditure in kcal/min shows significant effects for the factor dynamic workstation. And using the dynamic workstations while working in comparison to working seated causes a significant increase of average energy consumption for both types of stations.

Table 4. Mean values and statistical results of 8 male subjects for energy expenditure (EE) for working while seated and the dynamic workstations, significant effect $p \leq 0.05$

	Conventional	Dynamic workstation		Factor workstation	Seated versus	
	Seated	Deskbike	activeLife Trainer		Deskbike	activeLife Trainer
Average EE in kcal/min (SD)	1,4(0,2)	1,8 (0,4)	1,6(0,2)	*	*	*

4 Discussion

The present study examined two different dynamic workstations and their suitability as alternative workplaces based on the assessment of lending periods and the actual use of the stations and parameters of cardio-vascular load and metabolic effects. Moreover, two types for workstations which can be applied in different working environments were compared to each other regarding the assessed parameters.

The initial results show that the concept of both workstations caught the attention of the participants and were frequently used within the working hours. Regarding the physiological effects the usage of both types of workstations leads to a significant increase of heart rate and energy expenditure.

The results of the values recorded by the lending station and the comparison to the behaviour of the individual subjects of the study shows that both types of workstations have been lent and used at least once by all subjects, the other subjects used one of the different types. Therefore it can be concluded that the upright cycle Deskbikes and the under-desk pedaling machine activeLife Trainers demanding character is strong enough to result in testing and frequently using. However, the Deskbike seemed to be more attractive to the subjects than the activeLife Trainer being lent three times as much as the activeLife Trainer. One factor could be the change of the body position when using the Deskbike compared to using the activeLife Trainer which doesn't require getting up from the standard office chair. Another difference is the direction of movement of the legs. The Deskbike can be characterized as an upright ergometer where the legs move in a more vertical way. The body position when sitting in a standard office chair and using the activeLife Trainer can be compared to a semi recumbent ergometer which is characterized by a more horizontal movement of the legs [11]. According to personal preferences and the body physique one or the other type of movement alignment and therefore type of workstation will be chosen.

Another reason could be that the construction of the Deskbike enhances the impression and sense of the user to "do sports" a little more than the activeLife Trainer because of its' similarity to a real bicycle. Although the workstations were lent frequently the actual time periods of usage differ quite clearly. One possible explanation that the lending periods were three times longer than the actual usage could be the novelty of the concept combining physical activity with working at the desk for the subjects of the study. Although the level of physical activity might be not quite demanding it is likely that the subjects needed an initial phase of adaptation to moving while working. Another aspect to consider might be the different types of performed tasks while using the dynamic workstations. Although results of the IFA lab study showed no negative effects on work performance it was subjectively percieved as worse by the participants of the study while using y dynamic workstation compared to working while seated [9].

The results of assessing the cardiovascular load and metabolic effects are comparable to other studies examining these parameters. While using the dynamic workstations the heart rate increases compared to the conventional workplace. Results show that the average heart rate value is slightly higher for the time periods of using the activeLife Trainer than for the Deskbike. This seems to be a surprising effect regarding the comparatively smaller movement amplitude of the legs. On the one hand the individual values for average heart rate in between the subjects of the study sample show a greater range for the activeLife Trainer than for the Deskbike. On the other hand heart rate can be influenced by other factors than physical activity causing increased activity of the sympathetic nervous system like the emotional state, stress or excitement and caffeine [12]. Alternative methods to assess and compare individual heart rate values are calculating the individual heart rate reserve (HRR) [13] as an indicator for cardio-vascular load. The analysis of metabolic effects with the interpretation of energy expenditure showed that energy consumption in kcal per min increased while using both workstations compared to working while seated. As this is an important factor to consider the implementation of dynamic workstations as a preventive health measure at office environments they should be interpreted with particular care. The assessment of energy expenditure was made with the help of the activity tracker Fitbit Charge HR. Like the multitude of wearable activity tracker on the commercial market caloric consumption is estimated by combining self-reported anthropometric data, accelerometer data and heart rate measurements using standardized algorithms [10]. This method is prone to errors because of possible movement artefacts registered by the activity tracker. Furthermore the estimation of metabolic rates while being physically active is based on the assumption of standardized values of calorie consumption for specific movements. In comparison to more specific methods to assess energy expenditure like a breathing gas analysis [14] these devices are just able to display these parameters roughly.

5   Conclusion

The results for this sample of male participants show that the modern concepts of dynamic workstations like the Deskbike and the activeLife Trainer can be considered as alternatives to conventional seated workplaces. Both types of workstations generated interest and their practicability allowed them to be implemented in an occupational setting. Because of the relatively small sample size the interpretation of the effects on physiological parameters should be made with the high influence of individual measurements in mind. Future studies should investigate these effects with larger samples and both gender to generate more complex and reliable findings about the effect of dynamic workstations in occupational settings.

References

1. van Uffelen, J.G., Wang Chau, J.Y., van der Ploeg, H.P., Riphagen, I., Gilson, N.D., Burton, N.W., Healy, G.N., Thorp, A.A., Clark, B.K., Gardiner, P.A., Dunstan, D.W., Bauman, A., Owen, N., Brown, W.J.: Occupational sitting and health risks: a systematic review. Am. J. Prev. Med. **39**(4), 379–388 (2010). doi:10.1016/j.amepre.2010.05.024
2. Thorp, A.A., Healy, G.N., Owen, N., Salmon, J., Ball, K., Shaw, J.E., Zimmet, P.Z., Dunstan, D.W.: Deleterious associations of sitting time and television viewing time with cardiometabolic risk biomarkers: Australian diabetes, obesity and lifestyle (AusDiab) study 2004–2005. Diabetes Care **33**(2), 327–334 (2010). doi:10.2337/dc09-0493
3. Sjøgaard, G., Jensen, B.R.: Low-level static exertions. In: Marras, W.S., Karwowski, W. (eds.) Fundamentals and Assessment Tools for Occupational Ergonomics. Occupational Ergonomics Handbook, vol. 1, pp. 14.1–14.13. CRC Press LLC, Florida (2006)
4. Bennie, J.A., Chau, J.Y., van der Ploeg, H.P., Stamatakis, E., Do, A., Bauman, A.: The prevalence and correlates of sitting in European adults - a comparison of 32 Eurobarometer-participating countries. Int. J. Behav. Nutr. Phys. Act. **10**, 107 (2013). doi: 10.1186/1479-5868-10-107
5. Ekblom-Bak, E., Hellénius, M.L., Ekblom, B.: Are we facing a new paradigm of inactivity physiology? Br. J. Sports Med. **44**(12), 834–835 (2010). doi:10.1136/bjsm.2009.067702. Epub 4 February 2010
6. Commissaris DACM, Douwes, M., Schoenmaker, N., de Korte, E.M.: Recommendations for sufficient physical activity at work. In: Pikaar, R.N., Koningsveld, E.A.P., Settels, P.J.M. (eds.) Meeting Diversity in Ergonomics. Proceedings IEA 2006 Congress. Elsevier, Oxford (2006)
7. Carr, L.J., Maeda, H., Luther, B., Rider, P., Tucker, S., Leonhard, C.: Acceptability and effects of a seated active workstation during sedentary work: a proof of concept study. Int. J. Workplace Health Manag. **7**, 2–15 (2014). doi:10.1108/IJWHM-03-2013-0008
8. Straker, L., Levine, J., Campbell, A.: The effects of walking and cycling computer workstations on keyboard and mouse performance. Hum. Factors **51**(6), 831–844 (2009)
9. Botter, J., Burford, E.M., Commissaris, D., Könemann, R., Hiemstra-van Mastrigt, S., Douwes, M., Weber, B., Ellegast, R.: Comparison of the postural and physiological effects of two dynamic workstations to conventional sitting and standing workstations. Ergonomics **59**(3), 449–463 (2015). doi:10.1080/00140139.2015.1080861. Epub 21 September 2015
10. Fitbit Inc. www.help.fitbit.com
11. Lopes, A.D., Alouche, S.R., Hakansson, N., Cohen, M.: Electromyography during pedaling on upright and recumbent ergometer. Int. J. Sports Phys. Ther. **9**(1), 76–81 (2014)
12. Strath, S.J., Swartz, A.M., Bassett Jr., D.R., O'Brien, W.L., King, G.A., Ainsworth, B.E.: Evaluation of heart rate as a method for assessing moderate intensity physical activity. Med. Sci. Sports Exerc. **32**, 465–470 (2000)
13. Karvonen, M.J., Kentala, E., Mustala, O.: The effects of training on heart rate: a longitudinal study. Ann. Med. Exper. Fenn. **35**(3), 307–315 (1957)
14. Wanger, J.S., Culver, B.H.: Quality standards in pulmonary function testing: past, present, future. Ann. Am. Thorac. Soc. **13**, 1435–1436 (2016). doi:10.1513/AnnalsATS.201604-300ED

Driving Under Voluntary and Involuntary Distraction: An Empirical Study of Compensatory Behaviors

Yuhan Shi and Ronggang Zhou[✉]

School of Economics and Management, Beihang University,
Beijing 100191, People's Republic of China
zhrg@buaa.edu.cn

Abstract. To minimize the risk of distracted driving, drivers will take compensatory behaviors, such as deceleration and raising mental efforts. Moreover, it has been proved to be significantly different between voluntary and involuntary distractions which worth further exploration. Therefore, this study carried out an experiment of mobile communication distracted behaviors in simulated driving environment among 34 nonprofessional drivers. Independent variables include two triggers of driving distraction and two communication ways of mobile phone with complete within-subjects design. Dependent variables contain four dimensions, including driving behaviors, physiological indexes, mobile phone usage and NASA task load index (NASA-TLX). The results of vehicle driving simulator experiment reveal that drivers will take compensatory behaviors when taking driving distraction tasks, and the degree of compensatory behaviors is significantly different between voluntary and involuntary driving distraction. Generally, drivers would like to compensate more under involuntary driving distraction than voluntary driving distraction. The results of this paper give a new way to improve driving safety.

Keywords: Compensatory behaviors · Voluntary and involuntary driving distraction · Mobile phone communication · Simulation driving

1 Introduction

With the rapid popularization and development of driving technology, people are less satisfied with monotonous driving process. To enrich the monotonous driving process, driving distraction happens frequently nowadays. Driving distraction refers to a phenomenon that drivers' controllability of vehicle decline as the result of distraction by unrelated activities (Pettitt et al. 2005). According to the long-term observation of driving behaviors, 80% car crashes were related to driving distraction (NHTSA 2006). Using mobile phone while driving will improve the driving risk to 23.2-fold than that of normal driving (Olson et al. 2009) and bring 16,414 more deaths each year (Wilson and Stimpson 2010). In accordance with the investigation report by Chinese transportation network, the number of traffic accidents caused by driving distraction occupied a large proportion of all traffic accidents. In 2015, the number of traffic offense caused by

© Springer International Publishing AG 2017
F.F.-H. Nah and C.-H. Tan (Eds.): HCIBGO 2017, Part I, LNCS 10293, pp. 374–386, 2017.
DOI: 10.1007/978-3-319-58481-2_29

driving distraction reached 403,000, with a year-on-year growth of 11.1% (122 Transportation Network (2015)).

Overall, driving distraction is widespread and hazardous. The reason why drivers take the risk of distracted driving lies in the effects of compensatory behaviors. They may believe compensatory behaviors can neutralize the passive impacts of distracted driving. Decelerating is the most common compensatory behavior as we have known. The extant literatures only concentrate on the actual behaviors of driving distraction and the differences between different kinds of driving distraction separately, but do not study them together.

Narrowing the scope of research, we focus on the mobile phone usage while driving, which threatens driving safety seriously. Using mobile phone to keep communication is a typical kind of driving distraction, such as making phone calls and sending WeChat message. To our knowledge, WeChat is the most popular mobile messenger application in China. Sending text message through WeChat is similar to sending traditional text message. People need to type characters through input method with mobile phones holding in their hands all the time while sending WeChat messages, which requires more mental and physical efforts than making phone calls, and may deviate driver's attention from the road. Therefore, making phone calls and WeChat message can be distinguished as two tasks. In both situations, drivers may take compensatory behaviors, for instance, decelerating and increasing mental efforts, to compensate for the risk of using mobile phone while driving.

On the other hand, based on the extant literatures, there are two forms of triggers that give rise to mobile phone usage while driving. The two forms can be defined as voluntary and involuntary distraction. Considering of a combination of mobile phone usage and their triggers, we categorized four tasks, namely sending WeChat message, replying WeChat message, making a phone call and answering a phone call. The purpose of our study is to check whether there is a significant difference between compensatory behaviors among the four tasks.

2 Literature Review

2.1 Voluntary and Involuntary Distraction

The triggers of driving distraction can be defined as voluntary and involuntary distraction (Feng et al. 2014), but there are few study that focus on the differences between voluntary and involuntary distraction. Feng et al. (2014) only used susceptibility to driver distraction questionnaire (SDDQ) to check the differences between voluntary and involuntary distraction, but did not further test the results of the questionnaire by simulation driving experiments. The results showed that voluntary distraction is related to personality traits, and that involuntary distraction is related to cognitive mechanism, thus recognizing the difference between voluntary and involuntary distraction. Hoekstra (2015) drew on the achievement of SDDQ to conduct a simulation driving experiment to find the difference between voluntary and involuntary distraction. The task of the experiment was to pick statements and pictures on Surface Pro2 while driving. The results revealed that driver may press on the brake when taking the voluntary distraction task, which did not happen during the involuntary distraction task. However, the differences between voluntary and involuntary driving distractions towards mobile phone communication have not been proved through simulation driving experiment.

2.2 Compensatory Behaviors Towards Driving Distraction

Previous literature only used the concept of adjusted behaviors in distracted driving rather than compensatory behaviors. For an example, drivers will decelerate to adjust the balance between normal driving and driving distractions (e.g., making phone calls) and to minimize the frequency of traffic collision and lane departure (Haigney et al. 2000; Tornros et al. 2005). With more details, Zhou et al. (2012) indicate that 95% drivers may control the time of holding mobile phones while driving, and the drivers who hold the mobile phone by one hand believe the holding time should be controlled within 60 s. The result is similar to the research of Young et al. (2010), which shows that 61% drivers deem it necessary to control the holding time within 60 s while driving. At present, extant literatures gradually focus on using compensatory behaviors to explain the driving distractions. On the basis of the research of Zhou (2014) on mobile phone usage while driving, researchers should not only pay attention to whether drivers take compensatory behaviors (e.g., decelerating) or not, but also to the compensatory degree of compensatory behaviors (e.g., deceleration).

2.3 The Application of Physiological Indexes in Simulation Driving Experiment

Compensatory behaviors include external and internal behaviors. External behaviors like decelerating have been listed before. Internal behaviors, however, can be seen as mental efforts. Therefore, we need to use physiological indexes to quantify the mental efforts.

Oxygen is taken through breath, the amount of oxygen needed is decided by metabolic rate of body and the activities of the various tissues and organs. Breathing extent and respiratory rate are the most common respiration parameters, data acquisition of which need the help of bandage wrapped around the thoracic. On the ground of the simulation driving experiment of Duan (2013) and Mehler et al. (2009), respiratory rate will increase as the mental load in driving task increases, so we can take respiratory rate as an effective index for the mental load evaluation of driver. At the same time, Duan points out that respiration parameters may be affected by other factors besides mental load, such as talking and physical activity. As a consequence, the result of respiration parameters may not reach a significant level. These results confirm the previous study that energy expenditure reflected by breathing extent and respiratory rate may be induced by mental load increase (Waard 1996).

2.4 The Aims of the Current Study

As expounded above, there have been literatures respectively concerning compensatory behaviors (e.g., driving behaviors, mobile phone usage, physiological indexes) during driving distraction and the differences between voluntary and involuntary distractions.

As far as we know, no literature has integrated these aspects with each other, which is what we try to accomplish in our study.

Considering of a combination of mobile phone usage and their triggers, we categorized four tasks, namely sending WeChat message, replying WeChat message, making a phone call and answering a phone call. We devised a simulation driving experiment, and collected data of four dimensions. The four dimensions can be described as driving behavior indexes (e.g., speed, lateral displacement and crash times), physiological indexes (e.g., breathing extent, respiratory rate), mobile phone usages (e.g., usages of phone call, input methods, correct rate of delivering a fixed information) and NASA-TLX mental load evaluation. All drivers were asked to finish the four tasks on the same simple road. The purpose of our study is to check whether there is a significant difference between voluntary and involuntary compensatory behaviors (e.g., decelerating, increasing mental load).

3 Methods

3.1 Questionnaire Measures

After the simulation driving experiment, we asked each driver to finish two questionnaires in self-report form.

Basic Information of Individuals. The first questionnaire gathered the basic information of individuals, which contained seven items, including gender, age, educational qualifications, driving experience, driving frequency per week, annual mileage, and traffic accidents times per year caused by driving distraction.

NASA-TLX. The second questionnaire was NASA-TLX, which was the most general scale in driving safety field, exploited by NASA. NASA-TLX contains six dimensions of mental load, including mental demand, physical demand, temporal demand, performance, effort and frustration. Grade of each dimension ranges from 0 to 20 (Hart and Staveland 1988).

3.2 Experimental Design

Independent variables. This experiment took a two-factor experimental design that is 2 (triggers of driving distraction: voluntary and involuntary)* 2 (communication ways of mobile phone: phone calls and WeChat message). Therefore, we divided four tasks as sending WeChat message, replying WeChat message, making a phone call and answering a phone call.

Dependent variables. We designed four dependent variables, which could be described as driving behavior indexes (e.g., speed, lateral displacement, crash times), physiological indexes (e.g., breathing extent, respiratory rate), and mobile phone usages (e.g., usages of phone call, input methods, correct rate of delivering a fixed information) and NASA-TLX mental load evaluation. Analyzing driving behaviors was to explore the external compensatory behaviors and the effects of driving distraction towards secondary task performance. Analyzing physiological indexes was to explore the internal compensatory behaviors. NASA-TLX was intended to reflect the allocation of mental efforts during the four tasks.

Control Variables. All participants drove the car by automatic mode under the same experimental scene. In addition, the whole experiment were launched under the same experiment environment with the same experimental equipment, and the interface of the call records and WeChat was the same as well. Each participant needed to finish the tasks alone, without any disturbance of irrelevant personnel except two experimenters.

Experimental Equipment. A Logitech G27 peripheral, including a steering wheel, an accelerator pedal and a brake pedal, was used to collect the data of driving behaviors. A portable physical multi-conductor NeXus-10 Mark II was used to collect breathing extent and respiratory rate. A DELL T desktop was used to run the simulation driving software UC-win/Road10, and present the experiment environment. A ThinkPad X1 laptop was used to run Biotrace + which was mating with NeXus-10 Mark II. Mobile phone participants used was IPhone6s with a matching earphone and a vehicle mount.

Experimental Scenes. We programmed the driving environment in UC-win/Road10. Each participant needed to drive on a 14 km dual three-lane carriageway. They were required to keep vehicle on the center lane within 80 km per hour. The situation of the road was simple, which meant the rate of the homodromous and counter flow was low, and the road was clear. Buildings and trees on both sides of the road were the same as those in the real world.

Experimental Tasks. Each participant needed to drive two loops of the 14 km road. In the first loop, participants were asked to finished two tasks (e.g., making a phone call and replying WeChat message), while participants were asked to finished the others two tasks (e.g., answering a phone call and sending WeChat message) in the second loop. In the four tasks, they must try to convey a fixed information accurately. The information included capital English words, lowercase English words, Chinese words, figure and punctuation, which might be difficult for typing WeChat message. Translating the fixed information into English, it equals with "Hi, I have already set out, 10 min to Chaoyang Joy City. See you then!"

3.3 Participants

We recruited 34 nonprofessional drivers (including 23 male and 11 female) through WeChat Moments. All participants had already got Motor Vehicles driving license of the People's Republic of China and had a certain experience.

Each participant voluntarily participated in the experiment and they would be remunerated for their anonymous responses. Specific statistical data of participants' basic information is shown in Table 1. Age of participants ranged from 20 to 26, and the average age was 22.29 (SD = 1.34). As for educational qualifications, 2.94% were college degree or below, 79.41% were bachelor degree and 17.65% were master degree or above. Average driving experience was 2.66 year (SD = 1.43). Average driving frequency per week was 1.71 days (SD = 1.71), while the average annual mileage was 5550 km. 17.65% drivers had traffic accidents caused by driving distraction.

Table 1. Statistical data of participants' basic information

Indexes	Frequency	Percentage(%)
Age		
20–26	34	100.00
Gender		
Male	23	67.65
Female	11	32.35
Educational qualifications		
College degree or below	1	2.94
Bachelor degree	27	79.41
Master degree or above	6	17.65
Driving experience		
1 year	8	23.53
2–5 years	24	70.59
6 years	2	5.88
Driving frequency per week		
1 day	20	58.82
2 days	9	26.47
3 days	3	8.83
4 days	1	2.94
5 days	0	0
6 days	0	0
7 days	1	2.94
Annual mileage (km)	5550	–
Person-time that bring traffic accidents caused by driving distraction	6	17.65

4 Differences Between Compensatory Behaviors of Voluntary and Involuntary Distraction

4.1 Driving Behaviors

Average Driving Speed. Average driving speed is a most common and effective reflection of driving situation. To contrast the average driving speed under voluntary and involuntary distraction, or to compare the degree of compensatory behaviors under the two triggers, we also list the average driving speed under normal driving. Average driving speed under five driving behaviors and deceleration relative to normal driving are listed in Table 2.

Table 2. Descriptive statistics of average driving speed under different behaviors

Driving behaviors		Average driving speed (km/h)		Deceleration relative to normal driving
		Mean	SD	
Normal driving		73.11	4.65	–
Phone call	Voluntary	68.64	5.29	4.47
	Involuntary	65.13	7.24	7.98
WeChat	Voluntary	55.91	12.32	9.22
	Involuntary	53.30	11.28	11.83

As can be seen in Table 2, there are three obvious laws. Basically, the average driving speed under four driving distraction tasks are lower than the average driving speed under normal driving. Moreover, the average driving speed under involuntary phone call and WeChat usage are respectively lower than the average driving speed under voluntary phone call and WeChat usage. More importantly, the average driving speed under voluntary and involuntary WeChat usage are respectively lower than the average driving speed under voluntary and involuntary phone call usage.

We verify the significant differences of these laws through pared-samples T test, and find that the five driving behaviors are totally different from the others. Except that the significance level between voluntary and involuntary WeChat usage reaches 0.004, the significance level of the other 7 pairs are all about 0.000.

Therefore, deceleration relative to normal driving can be regarded as the degree of compensatory behaviors. We compare the degrees of compensatory behaviors, and list that of four driving distractions from high to low: replying WeChat message> sending WeChat message> answering a phone call> making a phone call. It's confirmable that the degree of compensatory behaviors under involuntary distractions is higher than that under voluntary distractions. There is a probable cause that voluntary distraction is a more controllable behavior than involuntary distraction. Drivers can choose the occurrence time of voluntary distraction, and make some adjustment voluntarily before or after the occurrence time. On the opposite, involuntary distraction is a kind of stress reaction, which demands quicker reaction and shorter adjustment time. As a result, drivers decelerate more under involuntary distractions to compensate more. On the other hand, we can find that the degree of compensatory behaviors under WeChat usage is higher than that under phone call usage. It is reasonable in that typing WeChat message needs more cognitive resources and brings much more disturbance to drivers than talking in a phone call.

Vehicle Lateral Displacement. We asked participants to keep the vehicle on the center lane, so the vehicle lateral displacement may reflect their controllability of the vehicle. Using this index helped us realize driving distractions' impact on primary task performance of driving and compare the impact of the four driving distraction tasks. Through the original data, it is easy to get the vehicle's distance to the left edge and the right edge, which shows the location of the vehicle. Therefore, we used the location of distracted driving separately minus the location of normal driving, and got eight different values shown in Table 3. Take voluntary phone call usage as an example, the left-lateral displacement was −0.25 while the right-lateral displacement was 1.85. Comparing to the location under normal driving, it meant the distance to the left edge shrunk, and vehicle moved leftwards. As shown in Table 3, except that involuntary phone call usage moved rightwards, the others all moved leftwards. In general, drivers' controllability of the vehicle decline when they are driving distractedly, which is detrimental to road safety and primary task performance of driving.

Table 3. Descriptive statistics of vehicle lateral displacement under different driving distractions

Driving behaviors		Left-lateral displacement (metre)		Right-lateral displacement (metre)	
		Mean	SD	Mean	SD
Phone call	Voluntary	−0.25	2.47	1.85	4.63
	Involuntary	0.78	1.99	−2.21	9.62
WeChat	Voluntary	−0.15	1.34	1.81	3.34
	Involuntary	−0.47	3.37	1.36	7.56

Only vehicle lateral displacement of voluntary and involuntary phone call usage had significant differences through the pared-samples T test ($p = 0.011 < 0.05$), while the others had not. Totally, the lateral displacement had no significant differences between voluntary and involuntary, phone call and WeChat. However, vehicle may move leftwards if the driver is using mobile phone to keep communication. This can be a possible law that the descriptive statistics present.

Crash and Speeding. Crash and speeding are the most dangerous driving behaviors, and speeding is forbidden by the traffic law. Crashes include rear-end, rear-ended and guardrail impact. In addition, speeding is likely to cause crashes. As the simulation driving software could not record the crash times, the experimenter recorded the data by observation. In the experiment, 15 participants crashed because of driving distraction, and the proportion reached 44.11%. Some participants complained that controllability of steering wheel and pedals decline while using the mobile phone. As well, we observed the data of speed, and found that 13 participants oversped for a little while after they hung up the phone or sent WeChat message successfully, and this proportion reached 38.24%. Some participants indicated that phone call or WeChat competed the cognitive resources with driving. As a consequence, they could not help speeding after finishing the driving distraction tasks.

Through the analysis of the three indexes above, it is explicit that mobile phone usage will lead to more lateral displacements, crashes and unconscious speeding, which have passive impact on primary task performance of driving. To compensate the risk of these driving distractions, drivers will take compensatory behavior as decelerating. Furthermore, they will compensate more for involuntary distractions.

4.2 Physiological Indexes

We chose breathing extent and respiratory rate as physiological indexes. Breathing extent refers to deformation quantity of the bandage wrapped around the thoracic with every breath. Respiratory rate refers to breath times per minute. According to medical experience, normal adults' respiratory rate range from 16 to 20. The purpose is to discover the differences between voluntary and involuntary distractions.

As is shown in Table 4, breathing extent of four distraction tasks was lower than that of normal driving. Moreover, breathing extent of involuntary phone call and WeChat usage were respectively higher than that of voluntary situation. In terms of respiratory rate, we list the value from high to low: four distraction tasks> normal driving>idle state. According to Mehler's study (2009), this rank equals the rank of mental load. In other words, the distraction tasks increase drivers' mental load. Drivers pay out more mental load when taking the distraction tasks, which can be seen as a kind of compensatory behavior. To compensate the distraction tasks, breathing extent will decrease, while respiratory rate will increase. The result of respiratory rate was the same as Duan's (2013) and Mehler et al.'s (2009) studies.

Table 4. Descriptive statistics of breathing extent and respiratory rate under different driving distractions

Driving behaviors		Breathing extent		Respiratory rate	
		Mean	SD	Mean	SD
Normal driving		767.37	120.56	23.66	4.14
Phone call	Voluntary	764.64	117.45	25.51	6.70
	Involuntary	766.14	113.55	26.48	5.16
WeChat	Voluntary	763.95	116.04	24.14	3.61
	Involuntary	766.25	118.37	23.93	4.05

By means of pared-samples T test, we tested the significant differences among five driving behaviors, but only three pairs passed the test. Normal driving and voluntary phone call usage had significant differences on breathing extent ($p = 0.019 < 0.05$). Normal driving and involuntary phone call usage had significant differences on respiratory rate ($p = 0.020 < 0.05$). Involuntary phone call usage and involuntary WeChat usage had significant differences on respiratory rate ($p = 0.037 < 0.05$). The reason why we got the non-significant results was partly due to the high susceptibility of NeXus-10 Mark II. Although all participants were asked to keep upper body erect, they could not avoid turning the steering wheel or taking mobile phone that might cause small movement of upper body. The small movement might induce remarkable error in the record. Another possible reason was the unavoidably manual errors in processing mass of raw data. Overall, respiratory rate behaves better in distinguishing differences which is worth further study.

4.3 Mobile Phone Usage

Experimental tasks included sending WeChat message, replying WeChat message, making a phone call and answering a phone call. In the four tasks, participants must try to convey a fixed information accurately. Especially, participants must input text message through WeChat. All participants were given enough time to memorize this information before the formal experiment. Usages of phone call, input methods and correct rate of delivering a fixed information were recorded by experimenters. Part of the results are represented in Table 5.

Table 5. Descriptive statistics of compensatory behaviors under different driving distractions

Driving behaviors	Compensatory behaviors	Voluntary		Involuntary	
		Frequency	Percentage (%)	Frequency	Percentage (%)
Phone call	Shorten words	9	26.47	8	23.53
	Control holding time	22	64.70	23	67.65
WeChat	Shorten words	18	52.94	22	64.70
	Text instead of numbers	11	32.35	11	32.35
	Didn't capitalize the "H"	26	76.47	25	73.53
	Ignore some punctuation	23	67.65	22	64.71

In the phone call task, 28 participants (82.36%) chose to hold the mobile phone by one hand, three participants (8.82%) chose to use earphone, and three participants (8.82%) chose the hands-free mode. All participants delivered the correct message on the premise of compensatory behaviors, including shortening words and controlling holding time. Shortening words means that participants change the original words into their own words. Controlling holding time means that participants speed up speech rate with the original words. Both of the essence of shortening words and controlling holding time are shortening the distracted driving time. Over 90% participants took compensatory behaviors as shown in Table 5. What's more, there was no significant differences between voluntary and involuntary distraction under phone call usages.

In the WeChat task, all participants chose the traditional input method rather than IPhone enable dictation. Take involuntary WeChat usage as an example, 64.70% participants shortened words, 32.35% participants used text instead of numbers, 75.53% participants did not capitalize the "H", while 64.71% participants ignored some punctuation. The four behaviors can be seen as compensatory behaviors, while the latter three are helpful with reducing cognitive load of switch input methods. Total compensatory times of involuntary distraction was 80, which was higher than 78 times for voluntary distraction. It gave a possible law that drivers might compensate more under involuntary distractions.

As previously stated, mobile phone usage will lead to more lateral displacements, crashes and unconscious speeding, which have passive impact on primary task performance of driving. The same thing happens in return. Using mobile phone while driving also has negative impact on the accuracy of expression, especially towards correct rate of expression of WeChat. Both voluntary and involuntary distraction had five participants (14.71%) who expressed the wrong message, such as wrong time and wrong destination. It is apparent that driving distraction is bad to both primary and secondary task performance of driving, which confirms the results in Gao et al.'s study (2005). Mobile phone usage brings more mental load to drivers, which leads to worse performance. Therefore, it is necessary to further analyze the metal load.

4.4   Mental Efforts

Driving behaviors, physiological indexes and mobile phone usage can be regarded as observable compensatory behaviors, while mental efforts is a kind of invisible psychological activity. Analyzing the mental load may help enrich the analysis of compensatory behaviors. The tool we chose was NASA-TLX scale, which had been used for decades in driving safety field. NASA-TLX scale contains six dimensions of mental load, including mental demand, physical demand, temporal demand, performance, effort and frustration. Grade of each dimension ranges from 0 to 20. Since the reliability and validity of NASA-TLX have been checked many times, we used it directly.

To examine the effectiveness of our data, we carried out exploratory factor analysis, which extracted two principal components. Explain variance rate reached 77.592%, while KMO coefficient reached 0.788. Communality of each variance was greater than 0.40, which meant good construct validity. Furthermore, Cronbach's Alpha reached 0.773, which meant great reliability. Being consistent with Yang and Deng's (2010) and Xiao et al.'s studies (2005), principal component 1 concludes mental demand, physical demand, temporal demand, effort and frustration, while principal component 2 only concludes performance. Principal component 1 can be named as efforts to finish the task, while principal component 2 can be named as satisfaction after achievement.

Through correlation test, we found each dimension of principal component 1 and total points of principal component 1 both had negative correlation with principal component 2. Nonetheless, performance only had significant correlation with mental demand frustration, while the others had not. Non-significant correlation might be explained by small sample size and random errors. On the other hand, each dimension of principal component 1 had significantly positive correlation with each other. The same law happened among each dimension of principal component 1 with total points of principal component 1. Statistics is presented in Table 6.

Table 6. Correlation coefficient matrix of NASA-TLX dimensions

Dimensions	1	2	3	4	5	6	Total points of principal component 1
1 mental demand	1	.413[b]	.652[a]	−.340[b]	.744[a]	.569[a]	.826[a]
2 physical demand	–	1	.615[a]	.120	.582[a]	.360[b]	.707[a]
3 temporal demand	–	–	1	−.159	.801[a]	.636[a]	.908[a]
4 performance	–	–	–	1	−.235	−.360[b]	−.246
5 effort	–	–	–	–	1	.527[a]	.901[a]
6 frustration	–	–	–	–	–	1	.755[a]

Note. [a] $p < 0.01$.
[b] $p < 0.05$.

Summarizing the correlation coefficient results, we found the following inferences. Firstly, drivers need multi-dimension efforts to finish the voluntary and involuntary distraction tasks. Secondly, the more mental efforts drivers pay out, the lower satisfaction they get, the significance of which need to be checked further.

5   Conclusion and Limitations

Overall, we can conclude the findings in the current study. (1) Mobile phone usage has passive impacts on performance of driving and message passing. On one hand, mobile phone usage will lead to more lateral displacements, crashes and unconscious speeding, which have passive impacts on primary task performance of driving. On the other hand, driving distraction may reduce the accuracy of expression, especially the accuracy of expression in WeChat. (2) Drivers will take compensatory behaviors to neutralize the passive effects, such as decelerating, speeding up respiratory rate and shortening words in phone calls and WeChat, etc. The degree of compensatory behaviors under WeChat usage is higher than that under phone call usage. It is reasonable because typing WeChat message demands more cognitive resources and brings much more disturbance to drivers than talking in phone call. (3) Generally, drivers compensate more mental and physical efforts under involuntary distractions than voluntary distractions. To improve the road safety, we wonder whether it is possible to shield mobile signals from the time drivers start driving to the time they pull the hand brake up. In this situation, only emergency call can be dialed out. To be more practical, family numbers can be set as emergency contacts, but the quantity of numbers must be limited. (4) One more interesting finding in this study is that the vehicle moves leftwards during distracted driving. We guess whether it is possible to connect the mobile phone with the vehicle by USB or Bluetooth, and install an alarm and a small extent leftwards detector on the vehicle. If the detector finds the small extent leftwards, the alarm on the vehicle will ring to warn the driver. However, the sensitivity of the detector will be a problem in the future.

What's more, several limitations do exist in this study. (1) In order to guarantee the success of the experiment, the order of the four driving distraction tasks is fixed rather than random. Learning effect might occur to the memory of the fixed message, which might cause some unavoidable errors. (2) Simulation driving software and physical multi-conductor software were installed in two computers, and every time nodes would be connected by manual work. Sample frequency of two software was 32 Hz, which might bring avoidable errors as well. (3) NeXus-10 Mark II collected data from the bandage wrapped around the thoracic, therefore a small movement of upper body might cause larger errors of data with the higher sensitiveness of device. (4) We only asked participants to finish NASA-TLX scale for one time, which made it difficult to compare the differences of mental efforts between voluntary and involuntary distractions. The future study will focus on these limitations and meliorate them.

Acknowledgements. This research was supported by the National Natural Science Foundation of China (NSFC, 31271100 and 73050901).

References

Pettitt, M., Burnett, G.E., Stevens, A.: Defining driver distraction. In: 12th World Congress on Intelligent Transport Systems. ITSA, Francisco (2005)

Klauer, S.G., Dingus, T.S., Neale, V.L., et al.: The impact of driver inattention on near-crash/crash risk: an analysis using the 100-car naturalistic driving study data. NHTSA, Washington, DC (2006)

Olson, R.L., Hanowski, R.J., Hickman, J.S., Bocanegra, J.L.: Driver distraction in commercial vehicle operations. Virginia Tech Transportation Institute, Blacksburg, Virginia (2009)

Wilson, F.A., Stimpson, J.P.: Trends in fatalities from distracted driving in the United States: 1999–2008. Public Health **100**(11), 2213–2219 (2010)

122   Transportation   Network.   http://auto.sina.com.cn/service/j/2015-12-03/detail-ifxmifze7542695.shtml

Feng, J., Marulanda, S., Donmez, B.: Susceptibility to driver distraction questionnaire (SDDQ): Development and relation to relevant self-reported measures. TRR: Transportation Research Record: Journal of the Transportation Research Board (TRR Journal) (2014)

Hoekstra, L.: Driving under Involuntary and Voluntary Distraction: Individual Differences and Effects on Driving Performance. University of Toronto Press, Toronto (2015)

Haigney, D.E., Taylor, R.G., Westerman, S.J.: Concurrent mobile (cellular) phone use and driving performance: task demand characteristics and compensatory process. Transp. Res. Part F **3**, 113–121 (2000)

Tornros, J.E.B., Bolling, A.K.: Mobile phone use-Effects of handheld and handsfree phones on driving performance. Accid. Anal. Prev. **37**, 902–909 (2005)

Zhou, R., Rau, P., Zhang, W., Zhuang, D.: Mobile phone use while driving: predicting drivers' answering intentions and compensatory decisions. Saf. Sci. **50**, 138–149 (2012)

Young, K.L., Lenne, M.G.: Driver engagement in distracting activities and the strategies used to minimize risk. Saf. Sci. **48**(3), 326–332 (2010)

Zhou, R.: Mobile phone use while driving: self-regulatory behavior based on compensatory beliefs. Adv. Psychol. Sci. **22**(8), 1328–1337 (2014)

Duan, L.: Driver Mental Workload Evaluation and Application in Driver Assistance System. Jilin University, Jilin (2013)

Mehler, B., Reimer, B., Coughlin, J.F., et al.: Impact of incremental increases in cognitive workload on physiological arousal and performance in young adult drivers. Transp. Res. Rec. J. Transp. Res. Board **2138**(1), 6–12 (2009)

Waard, D.D.: The measurement of drivers' mental workload. Groningen University, Traffic Research Center (1996)

Hart, S.G., Staveland, L.E.: Development of NASA-TLX (Task Load Index): results of empirical and theoretical research. Hum. Mental Workload, **1**(3), 139–183 (1988)

Gao, Z., Duan, L., Zhao, H., Rui, H.: Assessment of driver's cognitive workload under multitask based on physiological signals. Automot. Eng. **37**(1), 33–37 (2005)

Yang, Y., Deng, C.: A study on the reliability and validity of NASA-TLX as a measurement of subjective fatigue after computer operation. Psychol. Res. **3**(3), 36–41 (2010)

Xiao, Y., Wang, Z., Wang, M., Lan, Y.: The appraisal of reliability and validity of subjective workload assessment techique and NASA-task load index. Chin. J. Ind. Hyg. Occup. Dis. **6**(3), 178–181 (2005)

Cognitive Load by Context-Sensitive Information Provision Using Binocular Smart Glasses in an Industrial Setting

Jan Terhoeven[✉] and Sascha Wischniewski

Federal Institute for Occupational Safety and Health, Dortmund, Germany
{terhoeven.janniklas,wischniewski.sascha}@baua.bund.de

Abstract. New forms of technological work assistance can help to handle the increasing amount and availability of information and support the decision-making processes of employees by providing context-sensitive information. When looking at the vision of Augmented Reality especially binocular see-through smart glasses can be useful for this purpose. Therefore, a strong focus should be put on the analysis of information and interaction design as well as its influence on cognitive load and visual comfort when using it in the working environment. Consequently, two systematic reviews are implemented to examine how to ensure the usability of smart devices and which influence factors on human strain exist due to the information and interaction design of smart glasses. The aim of the reviews is to identify the need of further research in the mentioned topics and derive an experimental setup for investigations on binocular see-through smart glasses. Results indicate that the established usability methods and criteria of conventional screen work are still adequate, but they have to be adjusted to the rapid development of new technologies. As potential influence factors on human strain the accommodation-convergence conflict and the positioning of information for primary as well as secondary task instructions are identified. Furthermore, the question arises, if the possibility to individualize the information provision based on users' needs is helpful to support learning effects and optimize mental strain. Therefore a laboratory study will be carried out, which investigate the described effects. The experimental setup of the study is presented in this paper.

Keywords: See-through smart glasses · Cognitive load · Context-sensitive information · Suitability for learning

1 Introduction

The increasing amount of customized solutions of products and services and the resulting variety lead to a rising complexity in industrial production systems [1]. In order to keep up competitiveness, various activities to control this complexity were launched in research and development in Germany. Based on the rapid progress in information and communication technologies the connection of autonomous objects, machinery and equipment as well as whole production systems in a so called smart factory move into

© Springer International Publishing AG 2017
F.F.-H. Nah and C.-H. Tan (Eds.): HCIBGO 2017, Part I, LNCS 10293, pp. 387–399, 2017.
DOI: 10.1007/978-3-319-58481-2_30

focus [2]. In a pilot study concerning the future of production work [3] experts gave the opinion that human work still will remain a key factor for flexibility and productivity in the industrial environment. Humans possess abilities which cannot be replaced by artificial intelligence in the near future. In addition to flexibility and adaptability, this also includes human creativity, sensorimotor skills and association abilities. Together these give humans a clear advantage over technological solutions, particularly in decision-making processes in the production [4]. However, due to the increasing amount and availability of information, new forms of technological work assistance are required to support the decision-making processes. As a result of the decentralized organization, these assistance systems act as a mobile human-machine interface and should be able to provide people with context-sensitive information [5]. Thereby it is important to ensure suitability for learning in the working environment so that the risk of deskilling will be avoided and the practical knowledge of employees will be considered and supported [6].

Based on the described requirements for technological work assistance, new concepts for the decentralized representation of task-relevant information by means of different smart devices are being discussed and developed, especially with binocular see-through smart glasses due to the concept of Augmented Reality [7, 8]. The goal is to reduce the mental strain for employees in complex work systems, to achieve a high level of technology acceptance and, in addition, to increase their efficiency [9, 10]. However, taking into account the emerging amount of data in production, the question arises as to how information provided using binocular see-through smart glasses and especially the manner of media presentation affect the cognitive load of the employees [9, 11]. Furthermore, it is to analyze if different types of information provision can support the suitability for learning.

This paper will give an insight into actual research investigations about the correlation between the manner of media presentation on binocular see-through smart glasses as work assistance and the cognitive load of employees. For this purpose, the results of two reviews are presented to derive a need of further research, which results in a prepared study design.

2   Systematic Literature Reviews on Smart Glasses

The research of the Federal Institute for Occupational Safety and Health (BAuA) aims at assessing the impacts of innovative technologies at work. The analyzes shall identify chances and potential risks of the use of adaptive work assistance with regards to humane work design, deskilling, loss of competence, mental overload and other safety-related risks [12]. The present systematic literature review focused on studies addressing different topics in the subject area of smart devices, especially smart glasses.

2.1   Methodical Approach

The surveys were conducted following Arksey and O'Malley [13] and Mattioli et al. [14], who describe a systematic review procedure based on appropriate search strings.

For the literature search the five big and established databases EBSCOhost, PubMed, ScienceDirect, Scopus and Web of Science as well as their embedded smaller databases were used. For the subject orientation different superordinate search categories (e.g. usability, smart glasses, cognitive load) were chosen to classify each search term.

After defining and classifying each search term, a scheme for an iterative identification was set up. As relevant search fields the title (T) as well as abstract or keywords (A) were selected. Consequently search classes for clustering the results were defined depending on whether the particular search term category was located in the title or abstract/keywords. For an amount of three categories the search groups TTT, TTA, TAT etc. resulted and it was possible to prepare search strings for each of the five databases in order to collect the population of relevant publications [15].

Exemplary, the search string for the database Scopus in the group TTA with the individual terms 1 to n was as follows:

```
TITLE((term X1 OR term X2 ... OR term Xn) AND(term Y1 OR
term Y2 ... OR term Yn) AND NOT(term Z1 OR term Z2 ... OR
term Zn)) AND(ABS (term Z1 OR term Z2 ... OR term Zn) OR
KEY(term Z1 OR term Z2 ... OR term Zn))
```

The review was divided into the four stages identification, initial screening, in-depth screening and full text analysis. After each of the first three stages several publications were excluded [15].

The results of two reviews will be presented below, which build the basis for further research at the Federal Institute for Occupational Safety and Health in the topic of information provision in the work context by using binocular see-through smart glasses. The first review investigated to what extend established methods of usability engineering including criteria for conventional screen work can be adopted for smart devices. The second review analyzed studies, addressing the influence of different parameters of the information provision by smart glasses on cognitive load.

2.2 Usability and Smart Devices

The requirements related to the usability of an interactive system and the resulting evaluation criteria are clearly defined by the DIN EN ISO 9241-11 [16]. Thereby, the design of the interaction and the presentation of information have the strongest impact on the usability. Common methods exist for these influence factors with different criteria in the usability or software engineering. In case of the interaction design the DIN EN ISO 9241-110 [17], the usability heuristics of Jakob Nielsen [18] or the eight golden rules by Shneiderman and Plaisant [19] have to be pointed out. For the presentation of information the DIN EN ISO 9241-12 [20] and the requirements concerning information design by Wickens & Hollands [21] are given as an example. However, all these toolkits were developed for conventional screen work instead of smart devices with significant smaller screens and different control systems like a touch-screen. The review analyzed how existing criteria and procedures in the area of usability design of interactive systems can be applied for smart devices or whether they have to be adapted for the new technologies [15].

In the first systematic review, out of a population of n = 3523 publications a basis of effective n = 766 matches remained, which could be thematically classified as publications dealing with the evaluation of usability in respect of smart devices. This amount of publications already pointed out some potential trends considering the topic usability and smart devices. Table 1 shows the distribution of the publications with regard to the different smart devices across the individual years [15].

Table 1. Distribution of the search results by the different technologies [15]

Year	2007	2008	2009	2010	2011	2012	2013	2014	2015
Overall	40	50	63	62	101	77	109	134	130
Smartphone	17	17	25	28	48	46	63	90	91
tablet-pc	6	4	6	3	10	15	31	26	28
Smartwatch	0	0	0	0	0	0	0	0	2
Smart glasses	1	2	2	2	2	0	1	2	4

As Table 1 illustrates, the number of studies, which deal with smartphones, is still well above those exploring tablet-PCs. Studies concerning smart watches or smart glasses are limited to a minimum.

A small number of studies (<25), which dealt with or used different (heuristic) methods or criteria for the usability evaluation of mobile devices, were found. A high correlation was identified between the criteria of usability for mobile devices and conventional screen work. In particular the usability heuristics of Jakob Nielsen [18] are mostly applied. The following criteria, which have to be regarded in the information provision by smart devices, were identified [15]:

- Match between system and real world
- Aesthetic and minimalistic design
- Visibility of system status
- User control and freedom
- Recognition rather than recall
- Flexibility and efficiency of use
- Help users recognize, diagnose and recover from errors
- Help and documentation
- Error prevention
- Consistency and standards

Overall the established methods in information and interaction design from the area of conventional screen work are still adequate, even for mobile devices. But the rapid development of new technologies, innovative interaction concepts like gesture control and the possibility of Augmented Reality are not represented in conventional criteria. So there is the need of further research about the influence of such parameters on acceptance, usability and strain.

2.3 Potential Stress Factors in the Use of Smart Glasses

According to Shiffrin and Schneider [22], errors in human information processing can be explained by too much information or too little individual processing speed mainly. This is also reflected in the cognitive load theory of Chandler and Sweller [23], in which the cognitive load is divided into an extrinsic, an intrinsic and a germane cognitive load. The extrinsic cognitive load is dependent of the amount and medial presentation of the information, the intrinsic load of the inter-individual processing capacities. The smaller these two are, the more information processing capacity remains for learning. Taking this into account and due to the previously described aims of supporting the suitability of learning as well as avoiding deskilling, loss of competence or mental overload, the second review was carried out to point out, which influence factors in information provision by smart glasses has to be considered.

For the review process 74 individual search terms were chosen and assigned to one of the three search categories "smart glasses", "mental strain" and "research studies". Using the developed search strings for each search class a cumulative population of $n = 522$ publications were identified. After excluding duplicates and hits due to dual word meanings an amount of $n = 303$ remained. This amount was thematically analyzed on title and abstract level. As a result another $n = 96$ publications were excluded and the remaining hits were inspected on abstract and full text level. In total there were $n = 44$ studies identified, which investigated influences of different parameters in the information provision by smart glasses on performance, mental or physical stress against the background of a possible use in the working environment.

Figure 1 shows the review process including the search hits and exclusions of the individual review phases. The results of the review illustrate two main research topics in connection with information provision by smart glasses, especially for Augmented Reality applications. First the system response time or rather latency seems to be an influence factor on human performance and mental strain [24, 25]. Second the accommodation-convergence conflict, known from the topic of three-dimensional stereoscopic television, may function as a physical as well as psychological stressor [26, 27]. Concerning the response time previous research recommend a preferably short [24] and constant or predictively varying system delay [25]. The second point is especially important for binocular optical see-through smart glasses aiming Augmented Reality. The main problem of this type of smart glasses with AR is the fact that the source of information usually is a two-dimensional even surface at a fixed distance in front of the human eye, which simultaneously looks at a three-dimensional real or virtual object. Because the human eye has to change the lens focus between the fixed surface by accommodation and the three-dimensional object by convergence, a mismatch leads to visual discomfort and fatigue. Therefore, in designing application for binocular optical see-through smart glasses it is important to minimize the gap between displayed information and real world object as well as avoid distance variation [27, 28].

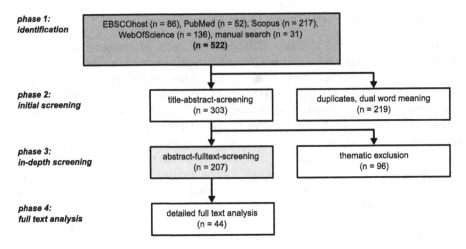

Fig. 1. Review process and results of the individual phases

Furthermore, some further research topics should be taken into account. For example the following topics were mentioned:

- Field of View [29]
- Font size for smart glasses [30]
- Physical ergonomic factors, e.g. weight [31]

Another interesting influence factor extracted was the position where information is displayed on smart glasses. Surprisingly there only a small amount of studies dealing with this topic could be found. Especially Chua et al. [32] investigated the influence of different display positions on human performance and visual comfort using monocular see-through smart glasses while performing a visually intensive primary task. As a result they found, notifications, which were positioned in the central field of vision, leading to a quicker performance. But the positioning of the notifications in the peripheral field of vision were more comfortable and preferred. In a survey of Wille [33] subjects got building instructions on smart glasses for a primary assembling task while they had an additional monitoring task in the peripheral field of vision. In this case the subjects felt less comfortable with the information in the peripheral field of vision. An assumption was that the visual discomfort could be traced to the continuous information provision at the secondary-task. Overall the questions remains, where to place information on the display of binocular see-through smart glasses for primary-task instructions as well as for secondary-tasks and which influence it has, whether the information is continuous or only a notification.

Before the review it was expected, that the possibility to adapt the information provision to the users need and its influence on acceptance and motivation could be investigated previously. Unfortunately none of the studies identified dealt with this question.

3 Experimental Setup

As a result of the previously described reviews different potential influence factors in the topic of binocular see-through smart glasses were identified. Against the background of supporting industrial work by providing context-sensitive information on binocular see-through smart glasses, the influence of different design parameters on visual comfort and human strain shall be investigated in representative tasks.

Based on previous research activities in the field of physical and mental strain as well as user acceptance during the use of smart glasses [10, 11, 15, 33], a laboratory study on the effects of context-sensitive information provision by binocular see-through smart glasses on humans working in networked production systems will be carried out. With regards to the suitability for learning in the working environment the study is inspired by the Cognitive Load Theory [23] and examines the effects of the variation of different parameters concerning the information provision.

3.1 Determination of a Representative Task

By taking into account the increasingly complex industrial tasks due to customize ordered products, it is important to choose a representative task for the experimental setup. Based on the previously described changes in the context of Industrie 4.0 employees will maybe not only perform assembly tasks but also quality inspection, order picking, monitoring and further more. In case of assembly tasks Funk et al. [34] made a benchmark for Augmented Reality instructions and set up the following requirements on standardized tasks for the purpose of scientific investigations:

- Cheap to setup: the tasks has to consist of affordable off-the-shell components
- Easy to replicate: the tasks have to be easily replicable
- Representative: the tasks have to cover three main actions (pick, place, assemble)
- Easy to scale up: the amount of working steps have to be easily changeable

Regarding these requirements and an affiliated evaluation Funk et al. [34] suggest the use of small toy bricks for pick-and place or rather assembly tasks.

In a study of Büttner et al. [35] a comparison between projection-based, paper-based and HMD[1]-based task instructions is presented. The results showed that projection-based and paper-based instructions were ranked significantly higher in the ease of use and helpfulness compared to HMD-based instructions. They result in significantly shorter assembly time as well. The weak results of the smart glasses may be explained due to the isolated work task. To begin with the subjects in this study performed an assembly task, where each instruction method was used one time only, so no habituation to a new technology like smart glasses could be derived. Secondly the workstation in the study was fixed due to the projection-based instructions. The biggest advantage of smart glasses, the freedom of movement while using these, was not exploited. However, the need of mobility, tasks with variation instead of highly repetitive tasks and mixed primary and secondary tasks are important usage criteria of smart glasses [11].

---

[1] HMD = Head-Mounted Display.

Based on the previously described studies an experimental setup was chosen, which investigates the effects of binocular see-through smart glasses as technological work assistance by using tasks with small toy bricks for a representative industrial setting. For this purpose the visual provision of instructions will be realized with the Epson Moverio BT-300 binocular see-through smart glasses. The investigation will be divided into three preliminary smaller studies and one main study. The three preliminary studies will analyze the identified effects, which were described in Sect. 2.3 to define information and interaction design conditions for the main study. The main study will investigate the effects of the possibility to adapt the information provision to the users need on acceptance, stress and learning. Contrary to the studies of Funk et al. [36] concerning an isolated assembly task as well as Iben et al. [37] concerning an isolated picking task, the participants have to execute three different production related tasks, order picking, quality inspection and assembling with variants, randomly.

3.2 Variation of Information Distance

The first preliminary study aims to analyze the effects of the precision of overlaying objects with information. In particular the gap between the accommodation distance to the real object and the perceived depth of the visualized information will be varied and the influence on mental strain and visual comfort will be analyzed. Therefore, a within-subject design is chosen, in which the participants have to perform one of the previously mentioned tasks with the small toy bricks. The task will take place on a workplace with a fixed location for the participants, individually adjusted by parameters like body height, arm-length etc. Each participant will perform the task in three conditions regarding the information provision. In the first condition the perceived depth distance between the visualized work instruction and the real task location will be significant negative, in the second condition significant positive and in the third condition approximately nil. The conditions will be arranged randomly, so that no learning effects will influence the results. As dependent variables the performance time and the number of errors are suggested to measure as objective parameters on the one hand. Furthermore the perceived cognitive load, e.g. by using the NASA-TLX [38], the visual fatigue and the participant's preferences will be examined as subjective parameters. The sample size of the study will be determined by common methods depending on the considered population and the expected effect size.

3.3 Position of Information in the Field of Vision

The question of the second preliminary study is in which position of the field of vision instructions for a primary-task have to be placed on the display of binocular see-through smart glasses. Chua et al. [32] did a quiet similar investigation, but he implemented instructions for a primary-task with notifications, which are ordinarily used for secondary-task information. The experimental setup will be the same as in the first preliminary study with the difference, that the position of the instruction will be varied on the x-axis and y-axis of the display instead of varying the depth. As fixed location for the z-axis the results of the first preliminary study will be used as reference. The tasks, randomization of conditions and the dependent variables will be similar to the previous study. The sample size of the study will be determined by common methods depending on the considered population and the expected effect size.

3.4 Location and Design of Notifications

In the third and last preliminary study the location and design as well as the effects of notifications for a secondary-task will be analyzed. Following the results of Cidota et al. [38] visual notifications will be used for this purpose. In this study the participants will perform the three work tasks order picking, assembly and quality inspection randomly at workplaces with different locations. The instructions for each task will be visualized in accordance to the results of the first and second study. The insertion of notifications during the primary-task will be used to inform the participant, which task is to perform next. Thereby the following conditions are varying:

- Temporary notification, overlaying the instruction for a short term
- Temporary notification in the periphery of the instruction for a short term
- Permanent notification, overlaying the instruction until users confirmation
- Permanent notification in the periphery of the instruction until users confirmation

The experimental setup will be a within-subject design. The randomization of conditions and the dependent variables will be similar to the previous study. The sample size of the study will be determined by common methods depending on the considered population and the expected effect size.

3.5 Individualization of Information Provision

Based on the huge amount of data in the context of future production work innovative technologies like smart glasses have to be used to support in decision making and learning processes. Furthermore, the practical knowledge of employees should be involved [39]. For this purpose the possibility of individualization and the suitability of learning as criteria of the usability of interactive human-machine interfaces will be more and more important. For this purpose the influence of the possibility to adapt instructions to the own needs on psychological comfort, acceptance as well as performance and learning effects are supposed to be tested.

In this main study the chosen participants have to perform the three different tasks order picking, assembly and quality inspection using small toy bricks instructed by binocular see-through smart glasses. The results of the three preliminary studies will be integrated in the instruction design to exclude unintentional disturbance variables.

For the experimental setup a between-group design is chosen. Both groups are planned to perform about 20 task sets. Every task set contains each of the three work tasks one time. The work tasks are designed in a way, that there is fixed contingent of repetitive standard work steps and a subsequent variant, which is unknown to the partic-ipants. The instructions display all work steps from beginning with the standard compo-nents up to the variants. Both groups will perform about 5 tasks sets with the whole instruction. After this initial runs the condition is split up between the groups. For the first group the procedure stays unchanged. The participants have to go through every step of the instruction, standard component and variant, which will be time-consuming. The second group gets to exclude single work steps of the instruction for the standard component, if they feel confident in their standard component performance. This way the participants can start with the variant earlier. After twelve task sets there will be three additional sets for both groups, where the participants will unexpectedly not get any instructions about the standard component but only about the variant. In doing so, it will be investigated, if the individualization of instructions has a positive influence on learning effects.

In this study again the performance time, number of errors, cognitive load and visual fatigue will be measured as dependent variable. The sample size of the study will be determined by common methods depending on the considered population and the expected effect size.

4   Conclusion

In this paper two systematic literature reviews about different influence factors in the topic of information provision by smart glasses were presented. It was determined, that for the usability of the information provision by smart glasses common methods and criteria of conventional screen work can be applied for smart glasses as well. But the rapid development of new technologies, innovative interaction concepts like gesture control and the possibility of Augmented Reality are not represented in conventional criteria and lead to a need of adapt the common toolkits. In the area of information and interaction design of smart glasses there are additional influence factors like the over-laying real objects with information (depth distance) and the positioning of information and notifications in different areas of the field of vision, which have to be taken into account. Furthermore, regarding future production work the suitability of learning gets more important to support employees and avoid deskilling. As a result of the reviews the experimental setup of a study is presented, in which these influence factors will be investigated against the background of a humane work design. Therefore, a set of three preliminary studies is supposed to be the basis for a main study, in which the influence of the possibility to adapt the information provided to the users' skills will be tested especially. It is assumed, that this possibility has a positive influence on learning effects and motivation.

Acknowledgement. The research and development project Glass@Service that forms the basis for this report is funded under project No. 01MD16008B within the scope of the Smart Services World technology program run by the Federal Ministry for Economic Affairs and Energy and is managed by the project management agency at the German Aerospace Center (DLR-PT). The author is responsible for the contents of this publication.

References

1. Borcherding, H.: Der mittelständische Maschinenbau – flexibel und höchst innovativ auch in der Systementwicklung. In: Sendler, U. (ed.) Industrie 4.0. Beherrschung der industriellen Komplexität mit SysLM, pp. 55–72. Springer, Heidelberg (2013)
2. Ittermann, P., Niehaus, J.: Industrie 4.0 und Wandel von Industriearbeit. In: Hirsch-Kreinsen, H., Ittermann, P., Niehaus, J. (eds.) Digitalisierung industrieller Arbeit, pp. 32–53. Baden-Baden, Nomos (2015)
3. Spath, D., Ganschar, O., Gerlach, S., Hämmerle, M., Krause, T., Schlund, S.: Produktionsarbeit der Zukunft - Industrie 4.0. Fraunhofer Verlag, Stuttgart (2013)
4. Lüder, A.: Integration des Menschen in Szenarien der Industrie 4.0. In: Bauernhansl, T., Ten Hompel, M., Vogel-Heuser, B. (eds.) Industrie 4.0 in Produktion, Automatisierung und Logistik, pp. 493–507. Springer, Heidelberg (2014)
5. Deuse, J., Busch, F., Weisner, K., Steffen, M.: Gestaltung sozio-technischer Arbeitssysteme für Industrie 4.0. In: Hirsch-Kreinsen, H., Ittermann, P., Niehaus, J. (eds.) Digitalisierung industrieller Arbeit, pp. 148–165. Nomos, Baden-Baden (2015)
6. Hirsch-Kreinsen, H.: Entwicklungsperspektiven von Produktionsarbeit. In: Botthoff, A., Hartmann, E.A. (eds) Zukunft der Arbeit in Industrie 4.0, pp. 89–98. Springer, Heidelberg (2015)
7. Jost, J., Kirks, T., Mättig, B., Sinsel, A., Trapp, T.U.: Der Mensch in der Industrie – Innovative Unterstützung durch Augmented Reality. In: Vogel-Heuser, B., Bauernhansl, T., Ten Hompel, M. (eds.) Handbuch Industrie 4.0 Bd. 1, pp. 153–174. Springer, Heidelberg (2015)
8. Tegtmeier, A.: Augmented Reality als Anwendungstechnologie in der Automobilindustrie. Dissertation, Otto-von-Guericke-Universität Magdeburg (2006)
9. Mayer, F., Pantförder, D.: Unterstützung des Menschen in Cyber-Physical-Production-Systems. In: Bauernhansl. T,, Ten Hompel, M., Vogel-Heuser B. (eds.) Industrie 4.0 in Produktion, Automatisierung und Logistik, pp. 481–491. Springer, Heidelberg (2014)
10. Grauel, B.M., Terhoeven, J.N., Wischniewski, S., Kluge, A.: Erfassung akzeptanzrelevanter Merkmale von Datenbrillen mittels Repertory Grid Technik. Zeitschrift für Arbeitswissenschaft **68**, 250–256 (2014)
11. Terhoeven, J., Grauel, B., Wille, M., Wischniewski, S.: Head Mounted Displays als Arbeitshilfen der Zukunft – Gestaltung eines beanspruchungsoptimalen Einsatzes. In: Schenk, M. (ed.) Digitales Engineering zum Planen, Testen und Betreiben technischer Systeme, 18. IFF-Wissenschaftstage, 24–25 Juni 2015. Fraunhofer IFF, Magdeburg, pp 125–129 (2015)
12. Federal Institute for Occupational Safety and Health (2014) Research and Development Programme 2014–2017. BAuA, Dortmund
13. Arksey, H., O'Malley, L.: Scoping studies: towards a methodological framework. Int. J. Soc. Res. Methodol. **8**, 19–32 (2005)
14. Mattioli, S., Zanardi, F., Baldasseroni, A., Schaafsma, F., Cooke, R.M.T., Mancini, G., Fierro, M., Santangelo, C., Farioli, A., Fucksia, S., Curti, S., Violante, F.S., Verbeek, J.: Search strings for study of putative occupational determinants of disease. Occup. Environ. Med. **67**, 436–443 (2010)
15. Terhoeven, J., Wischniewski, S.: How to evaluate the usability of smart devices as conceivable work assistance: a systematic review. In: Schlick, C.M., Duckwitz, S., Flemisch, F., Frenz, M., Kuz, S., Mertens, A., Mütze-Niewöhner, S. (eds.) Advances in Ergonomic Design of Systems, Products and Processes, pp. 261–274. Springer, Heidelberg (2017)
16. DIN, Deutsches Institut für Normung. Ergonomische Anforderungen für Bürotätigkeiten mit Bildschirmgeräten. Teil 11: Anforderungen an die Gebrauchstauglichkeit. EN ISO 9241 11 (1998)

17. DIN, Deutsches Institut für Normung. Ergonomie der Mensch-System-Interaktion. Teil 110: Grundsätze der Dialoggestaltung. EN ISO 9241 110 (2008)
18. Nielsen, J.: Usability Engineering. Morgan Kaufmann, San Francisco (1993)
19. Shneiderman, B., Plaisant, C.: Designing the User Interface: Strategies for Effective Human Computer Interaction. Addison Wesley, Boston (2005)
20. DIN, Deutsches Institut für Normung Ergonomische Anforderungen für Bürotätigkeiten mit Bildschirmgeräten. Teil 12: Informationsdarstellung. EN ISO 9241 12 (2000)
21. Wickens, C.D., Hollands, J.G.: Engineering Psychology and Human Performance. Prentice Hall, New Jersey (2000)
22. Shiffrin, R.M., Schneider, W.: Controlled and automatic human information processing II: perceptual learning, automatic attending, and a general theory. Psychol. Rev. **84**, 127–190 (1977)
23. Chandler, P., Sweller, J.: Cognitive load theory and the format of instruction. Cogn. Instruction **8**(4), 293–332 (1991)
24. Kohlisch, O., Kuhmann, W.: System response time and readiness for task execution the optimum duration of inter-task delays. Ergonomics **40**(3), 265–280 (1997)
25. Thomaschke, R., Haering, C.: Predictivity of system delays shortens human response time. Int. J. Hum. Comput. Stud. **72**(3), 358–365 (2014)
26. Hua, H., Javidi, B.: A 3D integral imaging optical see-through head-mounted display. Opt. Express **22**(11), 13484–13491 (2014)
27. Kimura, R., et al.: Measurement of lens focus adjustment while wearing a see-through head-mounted display. In: Antona, M., Stephanidis, C. (eds.) UAHCI 2016. LNCS, vol. 9738, pp. 271–278. Springer, Cham (2016). doi:10.1007/978-3-319-40244-4_26
28. Kramida, G.: Resolving the vergence-accommodation conflict in head-mounted displays. IEEE Trans. Vis. Comput. Graph. **22**(7), 1912–1931 (2016)
29. Kishishita, N., Kiyokawa, K., Orlosky, J., Mashita, T., Takemura, H., Kruijff, E.: Analysing the effects of a wide field of view augmented reality display on search performance in divided attention tasks. In: Proceedings of the 2014 IEEE International Symposium on Mixed and Augmented Reality, Munich, Germany, pp. 177–186 (2014)
30. Renkewitz, H., Kinder, V., Brandt, M., Alexander, T.: Optimal font size for Head-Mounted-Displays in outdoor applications. In: Proceedings of the 2008 IEEE International Conference on Information Visualisation, London, UK, pp. 503–508 (2008)
31. Theis, S., Alexander, T., Mayer, Marcel ph., Wille, M.: Considering ergonomic aspects of head-mounted displays for applications in industrial manufacturing. In: Duffy, Vincent G. (ed.) DHM 2013. LNCS, vol. 8026, pp. 282–291. Springer, Heidelberg (2013). doi: 10.1007/978-3-642-39182-8_34
32. Chua, S.H., Perrault, S.T., Matthies, D.J.C., Zhao, S.: Positioning glass: investigating display positions of monocular optical see-through head-mounted display. In: Proceedings of the Fourth International Symposium on Chinese CHI. ACM, New York (2016)
33. Wille, M.: Head-Mounted Displays - Bedingungen des sicheren und beanspruchungsoptimalen Einsatzes: Psychische Beanspruchung beim Einsatz von HMDs. Final report. BAuA, Dortmund (2016)
34. Funk, M., Kosch, T., Greenwald, S.W., Schmidt, A.: A benchmark for interactive augmented reality instructions for assembly tasks. In: Proceedings of the 14th International Conference on Mobile and Ubiquitous Multimedia, pp. 253–257. ACM, New York (2015)
35. Büttner, S., Funk, M., Sand, O., Röcker, C.: Using head-mounted displays and in-situ projection for assistive systems - a comparison. In: Proceedings of the 9th ACM International Conference on Pervasive Technologies, pp. 1–8. ACM, New York (2016)

36. Funk, M., Kosch, T., Schmidt, A.: Interactive worker assistance: Comparing the effects of in-situ projection, head-mounted displays, tablet, and paper instructions. In: Proceedings of the 2016 ACM International Joint Conference on Pervasive and Ubiquitous Computing, pp. 934–939. ACM, New York (2016)

37. Iben, H., Baumann, H., Ruthenbeck, C., Klug, T.: Visual based picking supported by context awareness: comparing picking performance using paper-based lists versus lists presented on a head mounted display with contextual support. In: Proceedings of the International Conference on Multimodal Interfaces, pp. 281–288. ACM, New York (2009)

38. Cidota, M., Lukosch, S., Datcu, D., Lukosch, H.: Comparing the effect of audio and visual notifications on workspace awareness using head-mounted displays for remote collaboration in augmented reality. Augmented Hum. Res. **1**(1), 1–15 (2016)

39. Hart, S.G., Staveland, L.E.: Development of NASA-TLX (Task Load Index): Results of empirical and theoretical research. Adv. Psychol. **52**, 139–183 (1988)

40. Stich, V., Gudergan, G., Senderek, R.: Arbeiten und Lernen in der digitalisierten Welt. In: Hirsch-Kreinsen, H., Ittermann, P., Niehaus, J. (eds.) Digitalisierung industrieller Arbeit, pp. 109–130. Nomos, Baden-Baden (2015)

Modifications of Driver Attention Post-distraction: A Detection Response Task Study

Oliver M. Winzer[1]([✉]), Antonia S. Conti[1], Cristina Olaverri-Monreal[2], and Klaus Bengler[1]

[1] Institute of Ergonomics, Technische Universität München, Garching, Germany
{o.winzer,antonia.conti,bengler}@tum.de
[2] University of Applied Sciences Technikum Wien, Vienna, Austria
olaverri@technikum-wien.at

Abstract. Previous research showed that reaction time (RT) on driving related stimuli did not return to its performance level as per baseline immediately after periods of distraction. In this paper, a Detection Response Task (DRT) experiment is reported, implemented to investigate performance differences across different phases of driver distraction: before, during and post-distraction. Different task types were implemented (cognitive and primarily visual-manual) to venture whether these types were associated with differences in the speed at which drivers were able to respond to visual stimuli during the aforementioned phases.

Keywords: Post-distraction · Driver attention · Cognitive distraction · Head-mounted Detection Response Task · Secondary task · Dual-task

1 Introduction

Previous research has contributed to the standardization of different DRT variants (e.g., tactile, head-mounted, remote) [1]. The DRT is sensitive to online changes of attention resulting from additional task performance and measures these changes through a reaction time (RT) to a signal and a respective hit rate (HR). Prior research has used this method to detect the cognitive distraction from DRT RT and HR (e.g., [2–5]). Typically, the DRT is performed together with another task (or multiple tasks) and, therefore, previous research investigated the DRT performance while performing such tasks (e.g., [6–8]). This research is very important for designing human machine interactions. The known examples are the designing of In-Vehicle-Infotainment-Systems (IVISs) or creating standards and driving safety guidelines (e.g., Alliance of Automobile Manufacturers AAM, National Highway Traffic Safety Administration NHTSA).

However, one of the first research works that investigated the long term effect of tasks was presented in Strayer et al. [9]. They showed that RT during driving related stimuli did not return to its performance level as per baseline immediately after periods of distraction. They investigated different phone and car voice-command systems and concluded that drivers can be distracted up to 27 s after finishing a highly distracting task and up to 15 s after interacting with a moderately distracting system [9]. The

© Springer International Publishing AG 2017
F.F.-H. Nah and C.-H. Tan (Eds.): HCIBGO 2017, Part I, LNCS 10293, pp. 400–410, 2017.
DOI: 10.1007/978-3-319-58481-2_31

classification of highly and moderate distracting was self-definite with a model presented in Strayer et al. [10].

Although previous DRT research concentrated on RTs and HRs during the performance of some other task, DRT performance prior to and after these tasks were performed has not yet been documented. The aim of this study was to holistically observe DRT performance prior to, during and post additional tasks performance to assess how driver attention changed across these phases. Figure 1 shows the qualitative outcomes of the DRT RT over the different phases of the experiments preformed. The behavior before and during the distraction phases can be very well estimated, because of the many previous studies (e.g., [6–8]). The phase after distraction, however, has not been yet investigated with the DRT and is of interest here. In terms of expectations, Fig. 1 shows a few possible outcomes in terms of RT prior to, during and after a phase of distraction.

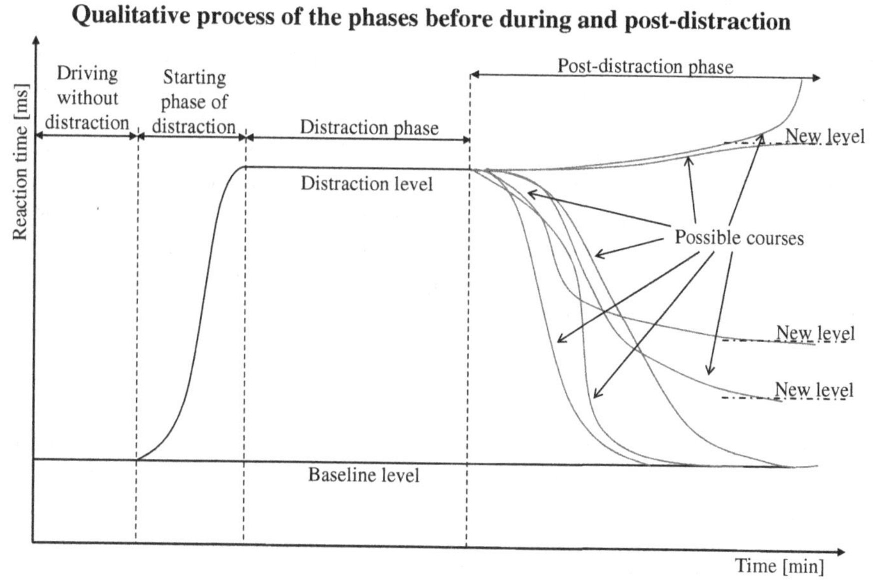

Qualitative process of the phases before during and post-distraction

Fig. 1. Possible courses of DRT RT after finishing a secondary task

Additionally, driving performance was also measured during these phases to identify if the participants tried to compensate for the level of workload [11, 12]. According to Wickens [13], tasks that stimulate different modalities or use human resources other than that used by the main task (driving), can be combined and performed well together. If the driving task and secondary task have to share the modalities or human resources, the performance of one of these tasks will suffer. This means that the participants can neglect the driving task for a better performance in the other tasks (DRT or secondary task). Therefore, in order to check this performance tradeoff, the driving performance should be measured. To this end, an experiment was implemented where participants performed different (3) tasks (hereafter referred to as secondary tasks) while driving in a simulated environment and at the same time responding to a visual signal (the head-mounted DRT; HDRT). To investigate performance differences across different phases of driver distraction, each task consisted of five performance phases: baseline, before, during, post and post-baseline. In the current paper, the phases with HDRT (before, during and post) are analyzed. Two cognitive tasks with a different level of load and one visual-manual task were selected. The spelling task was used as the cognitive task with a lower level of cognitive distraction. For the higher cognitive distraction, the n-back task (with the level of two) was carried out. The visual-manual task was the sorting for colored candies, designed after Bengler et al. [14].

2   Methods

2.1   Participants

Thirty-one participants (9 females, 22 males) between the ages of 22 and 56 years (M = 28.16, SD = 7.29), were involved in this study and each of them had a valid driver's license. Slightly more than half of the participants (17 of 31) reported that they had performed at least "sometimes" a secondary task while driving. One person reported to have color vision related deficiencies (red-green color blindness), but this participant was able to distinguish the different colors of candy wrappers and was retained for the analysis. All participants possessed a valid driver license. Seven of the 31 persons reported to drive less than 5,000 km (nearly 3,107 miles) per year and the other 24 participants reported driving more.

2.2   Apparatus

The experiment was conducted in the static driving simulator of the Chair of Ergonomics, Technical University of Munich (Fig. 2). Three of the six visual projectors displayed a 180°-degree view in the front of the BMW E64 mockup and the other three displayed the back view. Furthermore, six sound channel complete the experimental environment (Software: SILAB from WIVW GmbH, Würzburg, Germany).

Fig. 2. Setup of the static driving simulator of the Institute of Ergonomics, TUM

2.3   Tasks

Primary task: simulated driving. The primary task was a simulated driving task where participants drove on a highway with two lanes in each direction. The participants were instructed to follow a leading car on the right-hand lane with a speed of approximately 80 km/h and a distance of 50 meters. For a more approximate estimation of the instructed distance, the participants were able to orient themselves to street posts positioned at the side of the motorway, located 50 meters away from each other.

Secondary Task: Head-mounted Detection Response Task (HDRT). To measure the cognitive distraction of drivers the HDRT method was used. In the current experiment, a red LED was attached to participants' head at a distance of 12–13 cm from the left eye. The LED turned on every 3000–5000 ms and remained on for a duration of 1000 ms or until a response button was pressed. For responses to the presented signals the participants wore a button attached on their left index finger. Participants were instructed to respond as quickly and accurately as possible to the DRT. During distraction phases, participants performed all three tasks together: driving, DRT and one secondary task. The participants were instructed to drive safely at all times and to perform the other tasks (HDRT and secondary tasks) to the best of their ability.

Secondary Task: n-back, spelling and candy sorting task. Two different types of task were tested: two cognitive (with a variable level of cognitive load) and one visual-manual task. The two-cognitive tasks were the n-back [15] and a spelling task. The spelling task was intended to approximate a normal conversation, for example with someone on a hands-free cell phone, which according to Conti et al. [2] has a lower level of cognitive distraction potential than the 2-back task. The visual-manual type candy sorting task (modeled after a task reported in Bengler et al. [14]) was additionally performed.

The n-back task is a system-paced task. In the current experiment, a recorded audio file dictated four sequences of each 10 randomized numbers to the participants. The participants were instructed to repeat the numbers with a delay of two steps (n = 2). This means for the current experiment that per sequence a maximum of 8 numbers can repeated (in total 32 numbers). The duration for this task was approximately 2:14 min.

The spelling task was a self-paced task where participants were presented with up to 20 different words to be spelled aloud. The selected words were every day words (e.g., "Flugzeug" [German for "aircraft"]). All the participants were German native speakers. The duration for this task was 2:30 min. or until the last word was completed.

The candy sorting task was also self-paced. For this task, two containers were positioned on the front passenger seat. One of the containers was filled with four different colored candy (green, red, yellow and orange) and the other was empty. For this task, participants had to search for and move all candies of an instructed color into the empty container. After finishing the first color (red) they received a further color. Similar to the spelling task, this task was terminated after 2:30 min or until only one type of color was left.

2.4 Procedure

The session began with a demographic questionnaire and a multimedia presentation introducing and explaining the tasks to be performed in the experiment. A written handout with the instructions was also offered to each of the participants. Following this, participants acquainted themselves with the simulator and practiced all tasks. At this point they also had the chance to ask questions if anything was not clear. When participants were comfortable with the tasks and the experimenter deemed their performance acceptable, the experiment began. Throughout the experiment, each secondary task (3) was performed separately, one time each. DRT performance was measured before, during and after the secondary task was activated and driving performance was continuously recorded.

Except for the sections of the secondary tasks, all other tasks had the performance time of 1 min. As previously mentioned, the performance time of the secondary tasks are: 2-back task 2:14 min and spelling/candy sorting task 2:30 min.

2.5 Statistics and Dependent Variables

For calculating the average data (see Table 1) of the current experiment the range of data were adapted. Extreme values per participant per variable were excluded (top and bottom 2.5%) as suggested by Eckey, Kosfeld and Dreger [16]. As the same subjects were tested in the performed experiment, a 3 × 3 repeated measures ANOVA statistical approach was run to assess the effects of task and phase on mean DRT RTs.

The driving performance was assessed though longitudinal and lateral vehicle control. The longitudinal vehicle control was measured as the "following distance" (FD). This was rectified by the instructed safety parameter of 50 m. The standard deviation of lane position (SDLP) was used to measure the lateral vehicle control.

The quality of how the participants had performed the secondary task while driving was measured as presented in formula 1 [17]. Specifically, the quality (Q) of the 2-back task was measured as the quotient of the sum correctly responses to events (event) as a ratio to all possible numbers (task).

$$quality = event/task \qquad (1)$$

3 Results

The Mauchly's test to verify the equality of the variances of the differences indicated that the assumption of sphericity for the HDRT RT had been violated, $\chi^2 (2) = 21.413$, $p < .001$. Hence the Greenhouse-Geisser correction ($\varepsilon = .657$) was applied to reduce the error rate for the effect on RT. A significant effect of phases was found: $F (1.314, 39.419) = 144.518, p < .001$. The Bonferroni post hoc test was significant ($p < .001$) between all phases. For the other main effect of task type, was no significant effect identified.

Table 1. Average and standard deviation for measured data (N = 31)

Tasks	Phases		RT	HR	SDLP	FD*	Q
			[ms]	[%]	[m]	[m]	[%]
2-Back	Driving (D)	M	–	–	0.260	7.221	–
		SD	–	–	0.079	14.397	–
	D + HDRT	M	330.487	98.491	0.253	7.575	–
		SD	70.660	3.604	0.098	13.605	–
	D + HDRT + Task	M	600.074	84.381	0.224	3.732	91.810
		SD	161.635	12.364	0.070	13.705	8.855
	D + HDRT	M	362.473	98.338	0.235	1.143	–
		SD	70.390	3.163	0.101	12.923	–
	Driving	M	–	–	0.270	4.415	–
		SD	–	–	0.103	13.235	–
Spelling	Driving	M	–	–	0.264	5.384	–
		SD	–	–	0.098	12.348	–
	D + HDRT	M	319.097	99.109	0.252	7.695	–
		SD	66.0768	2.268	0.105	11.802	–
	D + HDRT + Task	M	537.162	92.545	0.222	4.741	89.739
		SD	144.328	7.830	0.095	13.765	9.307
	D + HDRT	M	344.011	99.379	0.250	3.676	–
		SD	70.536	1.862	0.092	11.648	–
	D	M	–	–	0.253	2.148	–
		SD	–	–	0.112	11.763	–
Sorting Candy	Driving	M	–	–	0.234	3.204	–
		SD	–	–	0.088	9.953	-
	D + HDRT	M	321.120	99.109	0.239	7.988	–
		SD	62.120	2.268	0.080	11.683	-
	D + HDRT + Task	M	559.7116	90.118	0.566	5.795	84.858
		SD	136.062	10.991	0.200	18.823	10.466
	D + HDRT	M	390.398	97.057	0.275	11.260	–
		SD	104.015	4.526	0.114	15.663	–
	Driving	M	–	–	0.236	6.926	–
		SD	–-	–	0.097	13.651	–

HDRT = Head-mounted Detection Response.
HR = Hit rate.
SDLP = Standard Deviation Lane Position.
Following Distance: $FD* = FD–50$ m.
Q = Quality of secondary tasks.

Table 1 shows the means and standard deviations of the five measured performance phases for 31 participants. To comply with the recommendation of the ISO 17488:2016 [1] valid RTs are only possible within the range between 100–2500 ms. Outside of this range they were declared as a cheat (between 0 and 100 ms) or a miss (over 2500 ms) [1]. The raw data show no cheats. Another indicator for cheating is the button-down rate, which shows how often the response button has been pressed in relation to the number of stimuli presented. For example, it is possible that a participant pushed the button constantly. The analysis of this measurement indicates that there was no observable attempt to cheat. The highest button down rate of one participant was 137% the average was between 100% and 108% depending on the phases, which is acceptable. The ISO 17488:2016 [1] includes an another condition for valid RTs: the average of HR must be over the level of 80% per phases to measure a valid RT. This requirement was met in all phases.

No participant had a lower average safety distance (longitudinal vehicle control) then 50 meters in average. The highest corrected average distance was measured in the post-distraction phases of the sorting candy task. The phases of during the sorting candy task had the greatest standard deviation. While the phases of post-distraction of the 2-back task the lowest FD* was measured. During the visual-manual task the worst mean value of SDLP was recorded. The quality of the three secondary tasks were measured: sorting candy task 85%, spelling task 87,9% and 2-back task 92%.

The following three Figs. (3, 4 and 5) show the detailed performed RT of each presented signal on average. Each chart also presents the mean RT of the three phases (before, during and post-distraction) per secondary task. In the diagrams, it can be seen that during secondary task performance, the mean RT of the counters varies more than before and post-distraction. Furthermore, for the candy sorting and spelling task the first three signals are clearly over the average of the respective part.

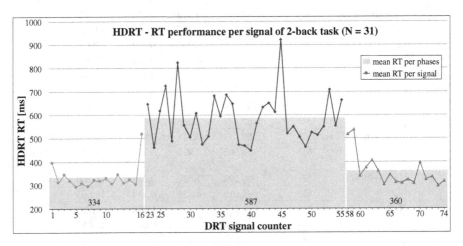

Fig. 3. Reaction time performance of HDRT per signal and phases (before [left], during [middle] and post [right]) 2-back task (N = 31). Number of signals per person varied slightly due to the signal being presented at a random interval between 3000–5000 ms.

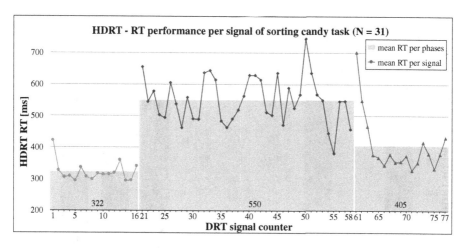

Fig. 4. Reaction time performance of HDRT per signal and phases (before [left], during [middle] and post [right]) sorting candy task (N = 31). Number of signals per person varied slightly due to the signal being presented at a random interval between 3000–5000 ms.

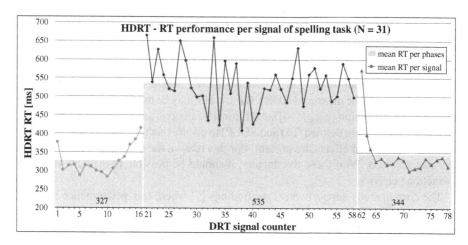

Fig. 5. Reaction time performance of HDRT per signal and phases (before [left], during [middle] and post [right]) spelling task (N = 31). Number of signals per person varied slightly due to the signal being presented at a random interval between 3000–5000 ms.

Figure 6 shows the total HDRT performance evaluation of the current investigation. Both the mean HDRT RT and HR are depicted. Independently of the distractions tasks, all averages RTs of post-distraction phases are higher than their associated baseline. It can also be seen, that during the distraction phases the mean RT is higher and the HR is lower than before.

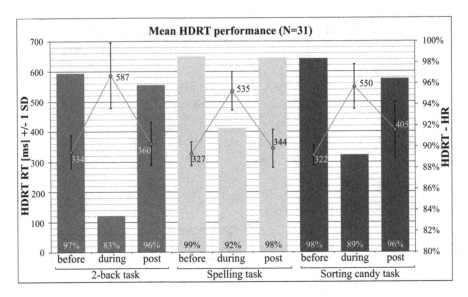

Fig. 6. Mean HDRT RT (±1 SD) and HR Performance overview (N = 31)

4   Discussion

The aim of the current investigation was to measure changes in driver attention post-distraction. Mainly the measured HDRT RT and HR may be used for a conclusion about the cognitive distraction (e.g., [1–4]). Additionally, a lateral and longitudinal parameter of vehicle control were defined (FD and SDLP) to ensure that the participants drove safe and no compensation effects are present. For this reason, the quality of secondary task was also assessed. With these five factors, it should be possible to estimate the post-distraction behavior.

The current study supports previous findings [9] where task performance required additional time to return to its baseline level after a period of distraction. In line with previous research, the findings of mean HDRT RTs and standard deviations before and during the distraction phases are similar to Conti et al. [2]. Comparing the measured mean RTs before the 2-back task there was a difference between 20 up to 30 ms; during the 2-back task there was a difference of nearly 40 ms to Conti et al. [2]. Therefore, it can be assumed that the presented results of during distraction phases are comparable to previous findings. The analysis of the quality of secondary task performance indicated that all participants performed the secondary tasks well and no participant tried to neglect in one of the tasks. This means that no participant tried to cheat by neglecting the secondary task for a better performance in DRT or driving.

The total overview of HDRT mean performance (see Fig. 6) shows that there are differences in RTs and HRs both before and after distractions. The Bonferroni post hoc test identified that there are significant differences of the RTs between all phases, but especially the difference between before and post-distraction are interesting. This means that the participants did not have the same average RT in a period of 1 min after a distraction than before. Furthermore, this performance difference is independent of the kind of secondary task. The lateral vehicle control is thus recognizable that during the visual-manual task the SDLP is almost twice as high like the other phases (see Table 1). For the FD, it is striking that highest average value is achieved in the phase post-distraction of sorting candy. Regarding the high FD at the post-distraction phases of sorting candy (see Table 1) is no clear reason indicated. Perhaps the participants used this phases to improve their decremented lateral control during the task. Another possibility could be that the participants started to relax after the task and so they neglect longitudinal control.

Looking at the three detailed Figs. (3, 4 and 5) shows a similar image. In all three cases the best mean performance was recorded in the phases before the distraction. During each distraction, the mean RTs between the signal counters strongly fluctuated. Perhaps this indicates a higher level of cognitive distraction comparable to the higher standard deviation in phases during secondary task performance. The parts of the Figs. (3, 4 and 5) regarding the post-distraction phases show that over the time of 60 s the mean reaction time is higher than before. Especially, the visual-manual task (see Fig. 4) is critical. In this case, we can see that the RT of all signal counter (nr. 61 to 77) are higher than the mean of the phases before distraction (322 ms). Furthermore, the first RT of post-distraction (nr. 61) is over and the second one (nr. 62) is on the average level of during distraction (550 ms). This results suggest that visual-manual tasks have a longer influence on the RT and thus also on the distraction like the cognitive tasks. In comparison to the two cognitive tasks, the mean RTs per signal in the post-distraction phase for the visual-manual task do not return to the overall mean RT level recorded in the pre-distraction phase. The 2-back task has a higher fluctuation in the post-distraction phase than the spelling task. Hence, from the higher overall mean HDRT RTs on post-distraction phases comparing to phases before, can be deduced that a modification of driver attention post-distraction has occurred.

5   Conclusion

The current study used the HDRT method static driving simulator to investigate the effect of task and phase on DRT performance. Thirty-one participants performed three different secondary tasks (two cognitive [n-back and spelling] and one visual-manual [candy sorting]) while also performing a simulated driving task and the HDRT. HDRT performance was measured during three phases: prior, during and after distraction. The results show that mean HDRT RTs were significantly affected by task phase. This indicates that the participants did not have the same mean RT before and after a period of distraction despite which secondary task was performed. In terms of real-world relevance, the reported data suggests that secondary tasks may affect the driver even after a task/distraction phase has been completed.

References

1. ISO 17488, Road vehicles – Transport information and control systems – Detection-Response Task (DRT) for assessing selective attention in driving (2016)
2. Conti, A.S., Dlugosch, C., Schwarz, F., Bengler, K.: Driving and speaking: revelations by the haed-mounted detection response task. In: Proceedings of the Seventh International Driving Symposium on Human Factors in Driver Assessment Training, and Vehicle Design, pp. S. 362-S.368 (2013)
3. Young, R.A., Hsieh, L., Seaman, S.: The Tactile Detection Response Task: Preliminary validation for measuring the attentional effects of cognitive load. In: Proceedings of the 7th International Driving Symposium on Human Factors in Driver Assessment, Training, and Vehicle Design, Iowa City and Iowa: The University of Iowa, Public Policy Center, pp. 71–77 (2013)
4. Engström, J., Larsson, P., Larsson, C.: Comparison of static and driving simulator venues for the tactile detection response task. In: Proceedings of the Seventh International Driving Symposium on Human Factors in Driver Assessment Training, and Vehicle Design, pp. 369–375 (2013)
5. Dlugosch, C., Conti, A.S., Bengler, K.: Driver distraction through conversation measured with pupillometry. In: Proceedings of the Seventh International Driving Symposium on Human Factors in Driver Assessment Training, and Vehicle Design, pp. 198–204 (2013)
6. Bengler, K.: Driver distraction. In: Crolla, D., Foster, D.E., Kobayashi, T., Vaughan, N. (eds.) Encyclopedia of Automotive Engineering. Wiley-Blackwell (2014)
7. Stephens, A.N., Lansdown, T.C.: Couples arguing when driving, findings from local and remote conversations. Cork and Republic of Irel and Edinburgh and United Kingdom (2012)
8. Conti, A.S., Bengler, K.: Measuing driver distraction in dual-task settings, GfA - Frühjahrskongress (2014)
9. Strayer, D., Cooper, J., Siegel, L.: Up to 27 seconds of inattention after talking to your car or smartphone: Distraction rated 'high' for most devices while driving (2015)
10. Strayer, D.L., Cooper, J.M., Turrill, J., Coleman, J., Medeiros-Ward, N., Biondi, F.: Measuring cognitive distraction in the Automobile. AAA Found. Traffic Saf. (2013)
11. Engström, J., Victor, T., Markkula, G.: Attention selection and multitasking in everyday driving: A conceptual model. In: Regan, M.A., Lee, J.D., Victor T.W., (eds.) Driver Distraction and Inattention: Advances in Research and Countermeasures, 1st ed., pp. 27–54. Ashgate Publishing (2013)
12. Platten, F., Schwalm, M., Hülsmann, J., Krems, J.: Analysis of compensative behavior in demanding driving situations. Transp. Res. Part F Traffic Psychol. Behav. 26(Pt. A), 38–48 (2014)
13. Wickens, C.D.: Processing resources in attention. In: Parasuraman, R., Davies, D.R. (eds.) Varieties of attention, pp. S.63–S.102. Academic Press, Orlando (1984)
14. Bengler, K., Praxenthaler, M., Theofanou, D., Eckstein, L.: Investigation of Visual Demand in Different Driving Simulators within the ADAM Project, pp. 91–104 (2004)
15. Mehler, B., Reimer, B., Coughlin, J.F., Dusek, J.A.: Impact of incremental increases in cognitive workload on physiological arousal and performance in young adult drivers. Transp. Res. Rec. J. Transp. Res. Board 2138, 6–12 (2009)
16. Eckey, H.-F., Kosfeld, R., and Dreger, C.: Statistik: Grundlagen — Methoden — Beispiele. Gabler, pp. 455–476 (2000)
17. Schmidtke, H., Jastrzebska-Fraczek, I.: Ergonomie. München: Carl Hanser Verlag GmbH & Co. KG (2013)

Author Index

Printed in the United States
By Bookmasters